THE

AMERICAN ADMIRALTY

ITS

JURISDICTION AND PRACTICE

WITH

PRACTICAL FORMS AND DIRECTIONS.

By ERASTUS C. BENEDICT.

"The worst Civil Code would be one which should be intended for all nations indiscriminately.—
The worst Maritime Code, one which should be dictated by the separate interests
and influenced by the peculiar manners of only one people."—PARDESSUS.

THE LAWBOOK EXCHANGE, LTD.
Clark, New Jersey

ISBN-13: 978-1-58477-191-3 (cloth)
ISBN-10: 1-58477-191-7 (cloth)
ISBN-13: 978-1-61619-019-4 (paperback)
ISBN-10: 1-61619-019-1 (paperback)

Lawbook Exchange edition 2002, 2009

Printed in the United States of America on Acid-Free Paper

The Lawbook Exchange, Ltd.
33 Terminal Avenue
Clark, New Jersey 07066-1321

*Please see our website for a selection of our other publications
and fine facsimile reprints of classic works of legal history:*
www.lawbookexchange.com

Library of Congress Cataloging-in-Publication Data

Benedict, Erastus Cornelius, 1800-1880.
    The American admiralty, its jurisdiction and practice with practical forms
and directions / by Erastus C. Benedict.
        p. cm.
        Originally published: New York: Banks, Gould & Co., 1850.
        Includes bibliographical references and index.
        ISBN 1-58477-191-7 (cloth: alk. paper)
        1. Admiralty—United States. I. Title.

    KF1112 .B38 2001
    343.7309'6—dc21   2001041402

THE

AMERICAN ADMIRALTY

ITS

JURISDICTION AND PRACTICE

WITH

PRACTICAL FORMS AND DIRECTIONS.

By ERASTUS C. BENEDICT.

"The worst Civil Code would be one which should be intended for all nations indiscriminately.—
The worst Maritime Code, one which should be dictated by the separate interests
and influenced by the peculiar manners of only one people."—PARDESSUS.

NEW YORK:

BANKS, GOULD & CO. LAW BOOKSELLERS.

ALBANY:

GOULD, BANKS & GOULD, 104 STATE STREET.

1850.

PRINTED BY A. S. GOULD, 144 Nassau Street, N. Y.

TO THE

HON. SAMUEL R. BETTS LL. D.

JUDGE OF THE UNITED STATES

FOR THE SOUTHERN DISTRICT OF

NEW YORK

WHO AS AN ADMIRALTY JUDGE

FOR NEARLY A QUARTER OF A CENTURY

WITH SO MUCH HONOR TO HIMSELF

HAS ADMINISTERED THE MARITIME LAW

IN ITS SIMPLE AND EQUITABLE SPIRIT

THIS WORK IS BY PERMISSION INSCRIBED

IN TESTIMONY OF

RESPECT FOR HIS LEARNING AND ABILITY

AND WITH A GRATEFUL SENSE OF HIS KINDNESS AND COURTESY.

PREFACE.

THE Practice of the Admiralty Courts of this country, notwithstanding the very considerable attention which has been sometimes given to it, has been so generally neglected, that, with the exception of a few lawyers in the larger commercial cities, the whole bar make no secret of their ignorance of this branch of legal learning. Having imbibed the English notions on the subject, they have supposed the jurisdiction to be confined to a small class of cases, not worth the labor of learning a new course of proceeding. They do not seem to have adverted to that American view of the subject, which, springing out of the peculiar character of our institutions, considers the jurisdiction of that class of cases, as a most important branch of the national sovereignty, given to the General Government for the wisest purposes.

Every day gives new cause to admire the profound sagacity, the practical wisdom and forecast of our fathers, in providing for an unknown future, and a territory to be extended indefinitely, under the forms of our double government. In the judicial and commercial grants in the Constitution, that wisdom is especially apparent, at this time, when the Commercial Era, with its new means and its new discoveries, is opening before us a most conspicuous and responsible career among the nations. To me, it is quite clear, that those grants, in all the plenitude of their simple and comprehensive phraseology, convey to the General Government, only what is necessary to secure the equality and fraternity of the States, and the strength and respectability of the Union. With fifty thousand miles of coast and shore of navigable waters, no one can estimate the extent of our future commerce, or the value to us, of a system of commercial law, with its course of procedure, uniform throughout the nation, and harmonious with that of the rest of the world.

The following work, is but an attempt to present the American view of the subject, in such a light as to exhibit its proper importance and to make it practically useful. If it comes up to the intention of the author, it will take a place left unoccupied by the highly useful works on Admiralty Practice, which have previously appeared. His purpose was, so to exhibit the subject, that the most inexperienced learner, as well as the riper professional student, could not fail, in reading it, to have his mind interested in the subject, and be directed to the means of settling, to his satisfaction, its general principles as well as its practical details.

He has endeavored to avoid a common error in elementary books of practice, of writing for those only who already understand the subject—leaving the beginner, to pick up by experience and observation, those rudimental principles and directions, which to him, are of the first necessity. This has led to the insertion in each portion of the work—the Jurisdiction—the Practice—and the Forms—of many things which to some may seem unimportant.

In a practical matter, nothing can well supply the place of that emphasis and distinctness which come from visible illustrations. The practical forms, are for that reason, very full and various—they commence with the entire proceedings in an admiralty suit, consecutively arranged, and embrace numerous and important classes of maritime cases, presented under various aspects. As precedents from actual practice, they are intended to inculcate and illustrate principles, as well as to serve for practical forms—and, it is believed, they may be read with profit, if not with interest.

In offering the work to the profession, the author makes no

apology for some obvious departures from the common standard of excellence, which professional, as well as literary criticism, may find occasion to censure. They were adopted as a part of his plan, and, in general manner and substance, the book is what he intended to make it. If it fails to give to the reader, a theoretical and practical view of " *Cases of Admiralty and Maritime Jurisdiction*," and of the Practice of " *Courts of Admiralty, as contradistinguished from Courts of Common Law*," the author has not accomplished his purpose.

In printing a new work from manuscript, verbal and typographical errors seem to be unavoidable—a few of them are noticed in the *Errata*, and the reader is requested to make the corrections with a pen.

E. C. B.

New York, 1850.

TABLE OF CONTENTS.

B

APPENDIX.

ERRATA.

The reader is requested to correct with a pen, the following errors:

Page 10, line 18, for "*Power*" read "*Persons*"

Page 16, line 5, after "necessary" insert a comma.

Page 17, note, for "4 Wend." read "4 Cond."

Page 92, for "§ 159" read "§ 169."

Page 107, line 2, for "their" read "these."

Section 199, line 2, for "form" read "power."

Page 144, at the end of note (*b*), add "vid. 11 Pet. 175."

Page 167, line 14, for "receive" read "recover."

Section 321, line 4, for "1807" read "1809."

Section 350, line 1, for "1772" read "1792."

Section 431, line 13, for "Scotland" read "scattered."

Page 250, line 16, after libellant, insert "to appear," and for "notice" read "motion."

Page 266, line 2, dele "to."

Page 274, line 11, dele "to."

Section 575, line 14, for "but" read "best."

Page 481, line 9, from the bottom, for "and" read "or."

Page 558, form No. 145, the words "as within commanded," in the title are a part of the return. Read "as within commanded, I attached," &c.

Page 571, at the end of form No. 172, insert "Sworn, &c."

THE AMERICAN ADMIRALTY.

CHAPTER I.

General View.

§ 1. As the commerce of the world has increased, so have the laws regulating its transactions, and prescribing the rights and duties of its agents, and the proper jurisdiction of the tribunals authorized to hear and decide causes arising out of those transactions, increased in importance. Not the least important of these, are causes connected with maritime commerce, which so often brings together in interest and in conflict, the people of different nations, speaking different languages, and familiar with different codes and usages. Most especially is this true in our country, where from the peculiar form of our institutions, there are two governments, with separate and independent judicial establishments, extending over the same territory and the same individuals, that territory acquired from other nations and originally subject to their laws ; and those individuals consisting, in large part, of the citizens and subjects of the other great commercial nations of the world, domiciled among us.

§ 2. The character and pursuits of sea-faring life, and of maritime commerce, have in all countries been considered as of a peculiar nature. Their agents and instruments, animate and inanimate, have rights, privileges and liabilities which do not belong to those of the land, and there are rules of conduct and intercourse, and courts of justice, and codes of law, and modes of administering them, which are especially devoted to the relations of maritime affairs : and the encouragement of navigation, and the proper regulation and employment of ships have always been favorite objects of the laws of all commercial nations.(*a*)

§ 3. In the earlier history of nations, when absolute rule and stong executive powers have exercised most of the functions of government, the affairs of the sea and of the navigable waters of the nation, have been usually administered by a naval officer of the highest dignity and station, holding his authority directly from the sovereign power, subordinate to the monarch alone, and clothed with many of the prerogatives of royalty.   Almost all nations possessed of any maritime commerce, have thus had an officer, known sometimes by one name and sometimes by another in a greater or less degree similar to the English word admiral, and, originally, admiralty jurisdiction was but another phrase for the power of the Admiral.   The mild and equitable system of admiralty law, thus derives its descent through a long line of modifications and meliorations from the absolute and irresponsible rule of naval command, as the peaceful law of real estate, and the common law generally, have descended from the iron despotism of military conquest and dominion carried to its perfection in the feudal system.(*b*)

§ 4. The declaration of the great Roman orator, *cedant arma togæ*, uttered when Rome was the military mistress of the world, was then true only in the forum ; the lapse of eighteen centuries has made it the law of society, and the truth of history, wherever civilization has shed its light on organized government.   The administration of the law of the sea has passed into the hands of properly constituted courts of justice, while the admiral has been left in possession of the power and prerogatives of naval command alone, and has become judicially

---

(*a*) Zouch's Jurisdiction of the Admiralty, Ass. 1.   Ibid. Ass. 9.   2 Brow. Civ. and Ad. Law, chap. 2.   3 Kent's Com. 1 to 21.   Edw. Ad. Jur. 33.   Abbott Ship. 98.

(*b*) Hall's Ad. intro. 7, 8.   Godolphin's View of the Admiral Jurisdiction, chap. 1, 2.   Zouch, Ass. 2, 3.

subject to the courts which exercise, with less show, more quiet-
ly and usefully, the functions which he considered his most
homely attributes, and the system of law which is thus administered in maritime transactions, retains the name of admiralty
law, after the name and power of the admiral have ceased to be
known in its execution. As maritime commerce came to be
extended, and international commerce and intercourse became
more frequent, the sea was considered the common highway of
nations, where, for the purposes of business, all nations must be
equal in right, and the common convenience, as well as the
common right, rendered necessary, and ultimately established general rules, as the law of the sea, to which all submitted
as to a sort of maritime law of nations, and the courts of each
nation enforced it. This is now called the general maritime
law, and sometimes the general admiralty law.

§ 5. The admiralty law is indebted for many of its characteristics to the circumstances of the countries in which it was first administered. The countries that earliest reduced the law of the sea
to a system, and adopted codes of maritime regulations, having
been countries in which the Roman or civil law prevailed, the
principles of that great system of jurisprudence, were incorporated
with, and gave character to the maritime law, and so much
were pure reason, abstract right and practical justice mingled
in that system, and so important was it that the general maritime law should be uniform and universal, that in England,
where the common law was the law of the land, the civil law
was held to be the law of the admiralty, and the course of proceedings in admiralty, closely resembled the civil law practice.(a)

§ 6. A court thus proceeding according to the course of the civil
law, and without a jury, in England, was looked upon with jealousy by the judges of the courts of common law, who considered
themselves the proper judicial guardians of English subjects.
They professed to look upon the admiralty as an intruder, administering a foreign code, and under a pretence of justice, seek-

---

(a) 2 Bro. Civ. and Ad. Law, 34.

ing to steal away the hearts of the people from the trial by jury, and the sterner proceedings of the common law, and a con-certed and vigorous effort was made to deprive the Court of Admiralty of a large portion of the jurisdiction, which it exercised ; and the jurisdiction of that court was for a long time a vexed question. The bench and the bar, on both sides, were characterized by great learning and talent, and the contest was managed with much ability. It is not easy, now, to see how a candid mind could fail to yield to the argument of the admiralty judges. The numerical strength, however, of the party of the common law, was vastly superior to the other, and was led by Lord Coke, then chief justice of the King's Bench, as unscrupulous and tyranical, as he was learned, and as that court was superior to the court of admiralty, having the power to control its proceedings by the writ of prohibition, it is easy to see that what the common law lacked in right, was more than made up in might, and the result could not long be doubtful. The jurisdiction of the Admiralty was contracted to the narrowest limits in that country, and with some fluctuation has remained so till recent statutes have again extended it in a most beneficial manner.(a)

§ 7. The contest between the two jurisdictions in England, and the triumph of the common law, came over to us in the English books, and did much to create in the minds of American lawyers, before, and even since the revolution, a prepossession in favor of a narrower jurisdiction of the English Admiralty, and occasionally, up to the present time, lawyers and judges of the most distinguished ability, have sought to transfer the English argument and authority to our country, and have insisted that the American Admiralty has not the liberal and beneficial jurisdiction which the English Admiralty anciently possessed, and which the continental courts still enjoy, but is confined to the exercise of those powers, which the sternest necessity had compelled the king's bench, in the days of its most arrogant triumph, to tolerate in England. This has not

---

(a) Zouch, *passim.* Godolphin, *passim.* Prynne's Animadversions, *passim.* 5 How. 453. 2 Gal. 348. 3 and 4 Vict. c. 65. 9 and 10 Vict. c. 99.

failed to keep unsettled the law of admiralty jurisdiction in this country, although in the clearest language, the constitution of the United States gives to the federal judiciary, cognizance of "*all* cases of admiralty and maritime jurisdiction," and the act of congress in the same language, bestowed upon the District Courts original jurisdiction of all civil cases of admiralty and maritime jurisdiction.(*a*)

§ 8. Among the distinguished jurists who have insisted that the grant in the constitution, embraces only those few cases of admiralty and maritime jurisdiction, which were admitted by the English common lawyers at the time of our Revolution, to be within the jurisdiction of the English Admiralty, is Chancellor Kent, who after the elaborate investigation which the subject had received in the courts of the United States, still says, "the argument for the extention of the civil jurisdiction of the admiralty beyond the limits known and established in the English law, at the time of the formation of the constitution, is not free from great difficulty." And it is not to be denied, that decisions, arguments and judicial dicta, abound in our reports, on both sides of the general question and of many of its subordinate points, and have served to keep the whole question open, so far as the decisions of the highest tribunal are concerned. But few cases, comparatively, involve a sufficient amount to give the Supreme Court jurisdiction, on appeal, and in the cases which have been before that court, although it has been clearly and repeatedly, indeed uniformly, decided that the English rule of jurisdiction does not prevail here, still many cases seem to have been decided, even in that court, on purely English authority. It can hardly be doubted that at some future time, when the same questions shall be again presented in a different form, and discussed with a wider range, rules will be established entirely consistent with the early elementary cases, and with the fundamental principles of maritime law.(*b*)

(*a*) 1 Kent's Com. 371, 377. 12 Wheaton's Rep. 614. Baldwin's Rep. 544. 5 Howard, 441. 6 Howard, 385. Const. Art. 3, § 2. Jud. Act of 1789, § 3.

(*b*) 1 Kent's Com. 371, 377. Conk. Treat. 2 Edit. 137. Ibid. 145. 1 Pet. Ad. 104, 113. 4 Gal. 426, 429. 1 Paine, 111, 117. 2 Gal. 398. 5 How. 473. 5

§ 9. Till that is done, however, the whole question is in many minds involved in so much uncertainty, that any part of it, even what is now considered as settled, may be expected to come up again for review and settlement. This uncertainty is, in part, to be attributed to the fact that a portion of the more ancient evidence of the admiralty law is not easily accessible. The commendable caution of the members of the Supreme Court in confining their written opinions to the points necessary to be decided, and the impracticability of giving, in the reports, the arguments of counsel at length, have deprived the profession of the benefit of the great learning and research, as well as of the broad and generous commentaries of the distinguished lawyers who have discussed this subject before the courts. The interests of the community will therefore, be promoted by bringing together, in convenient form, documents connected with the subject, which have either not been before published, or can only be found in an authentic form, in books which are procured with some difficulty, and by accompanying them with such suggestions, principles and authorities, as a somewhat extended and various practice in admiralty cases, and a careful examination of the subject have shown to be important. In doing this, no apology will be considered necessary, for giving to the whole, the form of a brief, historical and elementary treatise on the admiralty jurisdiction of the United States, from which the simplest rudiments and the most familiar common places, will not be excluded, and where sometimes arguments and speculations will be mingled with decided cases, and with the dicta of judges and elementary writers.

§ 10. The admiralty and maritime law consists of the principles and rules which regulate the conduct the business, and the property of the citizen in matters of admiralty and maritime character.

It is no part of the object of this work to treat of the elements of that system of law. They are to be found in the numerous

---

Howard, 441. 6 How. 385. 5 How. 473. 7 Howard, 733. Opinion of Judge Wayne.

elementary works and books of decided cases to which reference will be made in the following pages.

It is after the law of the case is ascertained that the question of great practical importance arises, what is the remedy, and where and how can it be obtained? To this the answer is found in that system of courts and officers, and of professional art and technical forms and proceedings, by and according to which justice is administered. This is Practice, in that sense which distinguishes it from Law, and it is in this sense that the practice of the American Admiralty is the subject of this work. This embraces the jurisdiction and organization of the Admiralty Courts, as well their forms, modes, and rules of procedure, and the rights, duties and responsibilities of their various functionaries.

§ 11. The Practice of admiralty courts in that narrower sense, which embraces only the course of procedure in courts, is established with more certainty and uniformity, but is even less understood, than the jurisdiction of the courts and the system of law, which is administered in them. That course of procedure was intended to be uniform throughout the nation, and in general harmony with the practice in the maritime courts of other nations, and the congress by an early statute prescribed such general uniformity, and in 1842, authorized the Supreme Court of the United States, still further to perfect a general and uniform course of procedure in admiralty and maritime cases, and in 1845, that court adopted rules, regulating the practice in civil causes. There have been several American works on the admiralty practice, of great merit and usefulness to the few lawyers who have hitherto cultivated this field of professional activity. Hall's Admiralty Practice; Dunlap's Admiralty Practice; Betts' Admiralty Practice; and Conkling's Admiralty Practice. Had either of those works been intended by their authors to meet what has long seemed to me the greatest want in this department of law, this treatise, probably would not have been written. They are well known and valuable auxiliaries to the well versed and experienced practiser in the admiralty courts, but those who were entering for the first time upon this unknown region of inquiry, have too often complained of the want of rudimental simplicity and clearness of instruction and direction, which in subjects of this sort, are as convenient, if not as necessary to ripe and cultivated men, as they are to children in the elements of general education. The promulgation of those rules of the Supreme Court, seems to be a fit occasion for an attempt to exhibit the practice, in that simplicity and intelligibility which characterize it, and which, if properly exhibited, cannot fail greatly to facilitate and extend a knowledge of the subject.

§ 12. The whole subject is invested with a new importance, by the recent act of congress extending the admiralty jurisdiction of the courts to the great lakes, the inland seas of this continent, and the rivers connecting them—already the theatre of a maritime commerce, far outvaluing that of all antiquity; and by the still more recent extension of our territory and settlements, embracing nearly twenty degrees on the Pacific ocean, thus adding to our coasting trade immense voyages of four to six months, constant sailing, and making us the nearest maritime neighbors of the oriental world, and of most of the islands of the sea. If my labors shall help to establish that uniformity of principle and decision which are necessary to the system, and which alone can give to this branch of the national judiciary, its greatest usefulness, I shall enjoy the highest reward of professional industry.

The first question which presents itself in this inquiry, is what court has jurisdiction of the controversy.

CHAPTER II.

Jurisdiction.

§ 13. Jurisdiction, as applied to courts, is the power to hear and determine judicially the subject matter in controversy between parties to a suit or legal proceeding. The action of a court is either judicial or extra-judicial. If the law confers the power to render a judgment or decree in a case, then the court has jurisdiction, and its action is judicial. If the law does not confer such power, then the action of the court therein is extra-judicial. It has not jurisdiction.(*a*)

§ 14. The jurisdiction of courts, is a branch of that which is possessed by the nation as an independent power. The jurisdiction of the nation within its own sphere is necessarily exclusive and absolute. It is susceptible of no limitation not conferred by itself; any restriction upon it, deriving validity from an external source, would imply a diminution of its sovereignty to the extent of the restriction, and an investment of that sovereignty, to the same extent in that power which would impose such restriction. All exceptions, therefore, to the full and complete power of a nation within its own territory, must be traced up to the consent of the nation itself. They can flow from no other legitimate source.(*b*)

§ 15. The judicial power of the United States is limited, and of course, all the courts of the United States are of limited jurisdiction. Limited by the grant of judicial power in the constitution, and limited by the acts of congress distributing that jurisdiction to the courts, their action extends and must be confined to the cases, controversies and parties over which both the constitution and the laws have authorized them to act. As any proceeding is within or without the limits thus prescribed,

---

(*a*) 12 Pet. 718. Dupon. on Jurisdiction, 21.

(*b*) 7 Cranch, 116.

it is or is not judicial, valid and effectual. The constitution and the law must both concur in conferring jurisdiction. The judicial power of the government is derived from the Constitution. The disposal of it belongs to the Congress. Many subjects of jurisdiction which are clearly embraced in the constitution, lie actually dormant, because the Congress has never authorized their exercise by any of the courts.(*a*)

§ 16. This power may be limited to *places*, to *persons* or to *subjects* of a particular kind or character.

Place.—There are a variety of cases, offences and controversies, which are within the jurisdiction of certain courts, simply, because they happen or are committed in particular places. If an offence be committed in a fort, arsenal, or dock-yard of the United States, or on the high seas, no matter what the offence may be, nor by whom committed, it is, by reason of the place alone, subject to the jurisdiction of the courts of the United States. In such cases, jurisdiction depends on *place* alone.

Power.—The judicial power of the United States extends to all cases affecting ambassadors and other public ministers and consuls, and in other nations wherever there are privileged orders in the state, there will usually be found tribunals specially devoted to controversies, to which ecclesiastics, or nobles, or other privileged persons are parties. In such cases, the jurisdiction depends solely upon the *person*.

Subject Matter.—Other courts are confined in their jurisdiction to subjects of a particular character. Subject matter is as various as the law itself, embracing any thing which properly comes within the sphere of legislation ; crimes and punishments, natural and social relations, contracts, obligations, duties, rights and wrongs ; these are distributed among different tribunals, as the convenient administration of justice may require. Hence there are civil courts, and criminal courts, ecclesiastical, military and testamentary courts, courts of equity, of revenue of international law, and courts of admiralty and maritime jurisdic-

---

(*a*) 12 Pet. Rep. 720 10 ibid. 474. 1 Kent Comm. 314. 4 Dal. 8. 7 Cranch, 504. 1 Paine, 453.

tion. Such courts have jurisdiction of their respective classes of cases, not by reason of the place where they arise, nor of the persons who may be parties to them, but by reason of the subject matter of the controversy.(a)

§ 17. Whenever a court has jurisdiction of a controversy, whether it depend on place, person or subject matter, it has the power, according to its own course of procedure, to administer justice between the parties, so far as that controversy extends. If it be a court, and have jurisdiction, then from the very force of these terms, it has the power necessary to enable it fully to adjudicate between the parties, and to enforce its decree. If it have power over the principal matter, it has it also over the incidents. If it have power to begin, it has power to finish, although in its course it may be called upon to consider and decide matters, which, as original causes of action, would not be within its cognizance, and the duty of a court is commensurate with its power. It is as much the duty of a court to exercise jurisdiction where it is conferred, as not to usurp it where it is not conferred.(b)

§ 18. A peculiarity of our form of government, compels us to look at the question of jurisdiction of the courts of the United States, in two points of view, the political and the judicial. The political view of the question, involves the inquiry as to what is the extent of the constitutional grant to the Government of the United States, as a political sovereignty, seperate and distinct from the State Governments. This question arises before and independently of all courts and their organization, and depends upon the Constitution alone. It was the question which was presented to the first congress, that met under the constitution, when they came to provide for the judicial wants of the New Government, by organizing courts to exercise the judicial power conferred on that government. The judicial view involves only the question as to the extent of the legal jurisdiction of the tribunals created by the Congress,

(a) Dupon. on Juris. 21 to 27. 5 Cranch, 61.
(b) 5 Cranch, 61.

and upon which it bestowed the power to exercise certain judicial powers of the National Government. The constitutional grant to the nation was fixed and inflexible the moment the constitution was adopted. On the other hand, the organization and jurisdiction of the courts, and the distribution of judicial powers was left to the Congress, and has been always subject to such changes as the wants or the wisdom of successive, periods, may from year to year suggest. Thus the question of the American admiralty jurisdiction is not a question, as in England, between a Court of Admiralty, and a Court of Common Law, (for there is no court of admiralty proper in this country, nor is there any common law of the United States,) nor between trial by jury and trial by a judge, but it is only a question between the General Government and the State Governments. If it had always been considered in this light, the argument would have been found to turn upon consid erations widely different from many of those which have been presented, and much of the difficulty which has been encountered on the subject, would have vanished away. It is in this point of view that I shall first consider it, inasmuch as upon this, every thing else depends. There is indeed a question as to what may be the proper court, but there lies behind it the more difficult and important question to what government or sovereignty we must resort. If any controversy belongs to the judicial cognizance of the United States Government, there can be no doubt or difficulty in ascertaining the proper tribunal which must decide it.(a)

§ 19. The constitution of the United States grants to the Federal Government, judicial power over * * " *all cases of admiralty and maritime jurisdiction.*" This is the whole of the grant of that branch of judicial power, and brief and simple as it is, upon its true construction depends the whole of the American admiralty jurisdiction. It has received five different constructions. It has been contended,

1. That this constitutional grant embraces only those few

(a) Const. Act. 3, § 2.   8 Pet. 658.   12 Pet. 781.   12 Pet. 721.   8 Pet. 658. 7 Cranch, 32.

cases of which the English High Court of Admiralty, was permitted to take cognizance at the tine of the American Revolution.

2. That it embraces all cases of which the English Admiralty anciently had jurisdiction, before the common law courts had by prohibition prevented the exercise of most of its powers.

3. That it embraces only the cases which were within the acknowledged competency of the British colonial courts of Vice-Admiralty, as they existed at the time of the American Revolution.

4. That the actual jurisdiction of the State Courts of Admiralty, which were in existence at the adoption of the constitution of the United States, was alone embraced in the grant.

5. That the words admiralty and maritime, relate simply to subject matter, and were used in that general sense which embraces all those cases relating to ships and shipping, which arise under the municipal maritime regulations of each nation, and those which arise under the general maritime law.(a)

In endeavoring to ascertain which of these constructions ought to prevail, I shall in the first place recur to some general principles and well known facts connected with the constitution, which although their relation to this subject may not at first be apparent, cannot fail to aid us in our inquiry.

(a) 5 How. 473.

CHAPTER III.

Constitutional Construction.

§ 20. The Constitution is to be construed according to the obvious import of its own phraseology. We cannot by evidence from other sources of the views or intentions of individuals, in framing or adopting that instrument divert the language from its plain import. The intention of a people, or of a popular body, can be known only from their corporate acts, or from the results in which the whole, by the legal majority, concur.

The Constitution was fully discussed in the convention, and before the people, and there is no evidence that the people or their representatives, did not understand the constitution as it is written. Emanating from the people, its powers are granted by them, and it is the highest evidence of their will and intention. Most especially is this so, since the constitution, in the whole and in its parts, was the result of compromises. The views of no party were there embodied, nor were the intentions of any set of men, there carried out ; but after full discussion and long deliberation, from patriotic motives, all yielded to it, and it was adopted as it was written.(*a*)

§ 21. Its grants of judicial power, as well as of political sovereignty, are brief, sententious and comprehensive. None of its words are to be disregarded, as without meaning, nor to be considered as used to round a period, or to give fulness and euphony to a sentence. Its phraseology was most carefully chosen, and all its words are significant, and introduced for the purpose of conveying their appropriate shades of meaning.(*b*)

§ 22. It is a constitution, not a code. It has indeed the force of law, but it is also still higher than a law, in the usual

---

(*a*) 1 Wheat. 326, 341.   9 id. 187, 196.   Mad. Pap. 1593 to 1604.   5 How. 441.
(*b*) 12 Pet. Rep. 723, and cases cited.

sense of that word. It is an organic law, made by the people, and not by the legislature, and in a few brief sections establishes the frame of government, and fixes the general relations and inflexible guards of political society for a great nation, for successive ages. It is necessarily brief in its language, but far reaching and comprehensive in all its provisions. It was not intended to settle details, enumerate instances, or explain by illustration ; but to establish principles, describe outlines, and fix the landmarks of political power, in such general manner as to provide for an unknown future, and the circumstances of a territory indefinitely to be extended.(a)

§ 23. It is a constitution of grants, and not of restrictions ; grants made under peculiar circumstances, and for characteristic purposes. In this it differs from other constitutions. Those of other constitutional governments, are limitations or restrictions of that universal sovereignty or governmental omnipotence, which belongs to an independent state, and which makes the state, however organized, the irresponsible master of the life, liberty, property and conduct of the individual, except so far as the state has voluntarily limited its power.(b)

§ 24. Of this latter class, were the Constitutions of the Individual States, before the Federal Constitution was formed. The American Revolution commenced in rebellions of separate colonies bounded on the great common highways of national intercourse. For a common purpose, they consulted together, and in 1776, declared themselves " free and independent states," not a free and independent nation. They then separately, each in its own manner, adopted forms of government, under which as independent nations, they had all the functions of good government. The prerogatives of the Crown, and the transcendent power of Parliament, all elemental and ultimate national supremacy, devolved upon the states and the people thereof, in a plenitude unimpaired by any act, and controllable by no authority. Each State was in itself an Independent Nation, and

---

(a) 4 Wheat. 316.   Const. Preamble.   ibid art. 4, § 3.
(b) 12 Pet. Rep. 720.   7 Cranch, 33.

foreign to the other states of the Union, as well as to other nations. It was competent for the people of the states, although thus foreign to each other and independent, to create by common consent, a General Government, and to invest it with all the powers which they might deem proper and necessary, to extend or restrain these powers according to their own good pleasure, and to give them a permanent and supreme authority.(*a*)

§ 25. For mutual aid, these states, in 1777, formed a league or articles of perpetual union of feeble character, known as the Articles of Confederation, creating a sort of general government ; and finally, in 1789, to form a more perfect union, and especially to establish justice, the present General Government was formed by the Constitution of the United States, and to it was granted by that instrument a portion only of the powers previously existing in the states, and the people thereof. It was a government made by taking from the states, and the people thereof, and transferring to the United States, and the people thereof, certain portions of sovereignty ; so that while under most other constitutional governments, including those of the States of this Union, the legislature or supreme power may lawfully do any thing which is not forbidden in their constitutions, the government of the United States, having no powers except such as are granted to it directly or indirectly in its constitution, can do nothing except those things for which it can show a constitutional authority.(*b*)

§ 26. Some of these grants convey elemental powers of government in all their fulness and force, while others are conveyed in a modified and restricted form. They were grants by governments already organized, and possessing and actually exercising, with few restrictions, unlimited sovereignty. They were made by the " People of the United States," but not by the people as a primary and unorganized mass solely, but by the people already formed into regular communities, and acting through or under their established constitutions ; they were thus, direct grants by the people, of these primitive powers, which, on the

---

(*a*) 1 Wheat. 324, 325. 8 Pet. 658.
(*b*) 12 Pet. Rep. 720. 7 Cranch, 33.

theory of our governments, are supposed to emanate from the People, and they were also grants, by established popular governments, of powers constituting a part of their own acknowledged functions; and while they were the act of the constituted authorities, in the name of the People, they were also ratified by the People as the ultimate source of political power. They are therefore, all of them, to their proper extent, and for the accomplishment of their proper purpose, of the most uncontrollable and irresistible character, and they are without any limit, except such as is prescribed by the constitution itself. Thus the power of peace and war, of international negotiation, of coinage, the judicial power over all cases affecting ambassadors, and over all cases of admiralty and maritime jurisdiction, and others are transferred to the general government, free from all restriction and limitation.(*a*)

§ 27. All the powers in the constitution were conferred upon the general government for purposes expressed in the constitution, in view of which purposes they are respectively to be construed. The constitution was made "to form a more perfect union, establish justice, ensure domestic tranquillity, provide for the common defence, promote the general welfare, and secure the blessings of liberty," to all the people of all the states. Its grand purpose was to *unify* the whole in the relations of internationality, and all its minor purposes were subordinate and ancillary to this. Its grants therefore consist of great classes of powers. Those which should especially regulate our intercourse with foreign nations and their subjects, and with the sister states and their citizens, and those in the exercise of which we were ourselves to be emphatically one people, and to be clothed with equal rights, although in other respects we were to remain members of different communities, were granted to the General Government, that our intercourse with foreign powers, might be so regulated as to make us one of the great family of nations, acknowledging the laws and respecting and adopting the usages which constitute the rule of international intercourse, and that

---

(*a*) 4 Wend. 472. 4 Wheat. 316. Const. Art. 1, § 8, 10. Ibid. Art. 3, § 2.

the separate States might not by jarring, inconstant and antago-
nizing laws, destroy the harmony which could alone make
us, and keep us the United States.(*a*)

§ 28. This is especially evident in the constitutional grants
of judicial power. They are not grants to this or that court of the
United States. The Constitution does nothing but draw the
line between the cases which belong to the United States Government and those which belong to the State Governments. It
transfers from the States and the people of the states to the
General Government, the judicial sovereignty in great national
classes of cases to be exercised, not necessarily by courts constituted like the British Admiralty, or the British courts of common law or equity, but by such courts, and in such manner as
the congress of the newly created Government should provide.
When the Constitution was made, there were no courts of the
United States of any sort, nor was it certain that there would
be here, (as there never has been,) a purely Admiralty Court,
but it was certain that in the multifarious transactions on the
ocean, seas, lakes and rivers, which were to be the highways of
our intercourse and commerce, between the several states and
the various nations of the world, a thousand questions might
continually arise, when the law of nations and the law of maritime commerce—the maritime law of the world—ought to take
the place of the numerous conflicting and changing rules which
could not fail to result from the various legislation and adjudication of the states, and in no manner could a uniform administration of that great branch of the law of nations, known as
the general maritime law, be secured, except by the transfer of
all cases of admiralty and maritime jurisdiction, to the cognizance of the National Judiciary.(*b*)

§ 29. A fruitful source of error in relation to the Government
of the United States, is its supposed relation to the British Government. The United States is sometimes said to be, and in

---

(*a*) Const. Preamble.   Art. 1, § 8, 9, 10.   Ibid. Art. 3,   § 2, Art. 4.   1 Wheat.
334, 335, 347, 348.
   (*b*) Const. Art. 3, § 2.   5 Howard, 451 to 457.

a limited historical sense, is an offset from Great Britain, and most of the people of the colonies at the time of the Revolution, were the descendants of British subjects. And many of the states are really shoots from the Government of Great Britain, and as such were subject to the common law. It was therefore quite natural, that in matters relating to the foundation and powers of our Government, many would first look to the nation from which we had just been severed by a revolution, and whose language and literature were our own. Still, it is not to be forgotten, that our people were not homogeneous, but consisted of persons from all civilized nations, and the English, Scotch, Irish, Welsh, Dutch, Swedes and French, some by conquest, and some by emigration, were mixed and united to make the American Nation, and had all brought with them to some extent, a knowledge of and an attachment to, the institutions of their parent countries, and the creation or incorporation of other states from other conquered or revolted colonies, with other laws and usages, was also contemplated.(a)

And in all these nations having ships and commerce as well as in England, causes of admiralty and maritime jurisdiction, had always arisen and such cases had been decided in different nations by courts of different names. In some nations courts were expressly devoted to such cases under the name of Consular Courts, Tribunals of Commerce, Maritime Courts and Courts of Admiralty. In other nations, as in England, cases of maritime jurisdiction were in one form or another, entertained by all the courts of law and equity in the kingdom, and decided according to that system of maritime law, which derives its force from the universal consent of commercial nations.

§ 30. These circumstances may not have been without their influence to induce the framers of our Constitution to make as they did, a new and original government. They did not in any manner address themselves to national prejudices or predilections, nor adopt or even allude to any previously existing government, as a pattern or standard, nor re-enact any known code of laws, in whole or in part, but they passed by in silence,

---

(a) Holmes Annals, *passim.* Art. of Conf. Art. 11. Const. Art. 4, § 3.

the institutions of the whole world, and invented a constitution and laws which had neither pattern nor prototype, in the actual and present state, or past history of the human race. When, therefore, they created or granted a power, it was a grant of that power, not as it existed in one government or another, but a grant of the power in the abstract. It was a creation of the mere governmental function, to be exercised by the new Government in its own prescribed manner, without any regard to the manner in which it had been exercised before or elsewhere.(a)

§ 31. The Government and Laws of the United States as established by and under the Constitution, cannot in any proper sense be called an offset from those of Great Britain, nor have they any relation or similarity to them. Our Constitution was a new creation made after the Revolution—after twelve years of actual independence under the Confederation, and made, not from any parent state, but from ourselves, and nothing else. The existence of such a state as Great Britain, (to say nothing of her peculiar laws, courts or institutions,) is not even remotely hinted at in the Constitution or in the Articles of Confederation, and her institutions cannot, justly, be considered, as in any manner, the exponents of our own. Indeed, in the convention that formed the Constitution, the institutions and example of Great Britain were, with singular consistency, referred to only that they might be avoided ; and in the Constitution itself every thing is studiously omitted which might even recall to mind those institutions. The common law of England has never been by adoption, by inheritance, or by re-enactment, the law of the United States, although it has been of some of the states.(b)

§ 32. Our Constitution and laws are written in the English language, and of course to that language we must look for the proper meaning and force of their terms, and this is the only link that connects the laws and institutions of the General Government with those of any other nation. When, therefore,

---

(a) Mad. Pap *passim.* 1 Wheat. 331, 2. 12 Pet. 729, 730.
(b) 1 Pain. Rep. 117. Mad. Pap. *passim.* *Supra,* § 36. 8 Pet. 591. 7 Cranch, 32.

the constitution or laws uses the words equity—common law—admiralty—maritime law—civil law—trial by jury—felony, &c., it is to the English law and to English dictionaries that we must resort for the meaning of those terms, but it by no means follows, that we must look to the same source for the structure and jurisdiction of our national courts, or for the rules of decision which they are to follow. The force of a common language even added to that of our historical connection, was altogether too feeble, properly, to give to our new made and original political institutions any transatlantic odor, much less to characterize them by strong English analogies.

§ 33. In view of these considerations, it may be further observed that the grant in the Constitution of admiralty and maritime jurisdiction is confined solely to the judicial power properly so called—"The judicial power of the United States shall be vested in one Supreme Court, and in such inferior courts as the Congress may from time to time establish."—" The judicial power shall extend * * to all cases of admiralty and maritime jurisdiction."—The Admiral, in many countries, had numerous powers, duties and rights which sprang from and related to his military or naval character, and to his dignity and station as a high executive officer, clothed with many of the prerogatives of royalty, rather than to his judicial character. He was a high naval commander and nothing else, a commander-in-chief, subordinate only to the king, and some of his mere perquisites and privileges have been subjects of the jurisdiction of the admiralty court. All those portions of the power of the Admiral which may be properly called executive or administrative are unknown to the American Admiralty. The trappings, perquisites, prerogatives and droits of the admiralty are left to governments with which they are in harmony and a purely judicial function, to be exercised only in cases of maritime character, between party and party, by judges and courts, and not by the admiral nor his deputies, was thus granted to the United States in the simplest and most comprehensive language. It provides for nothing but " *cases* " in *courts.(a)*

(a) § 34, 21, 38, 39. 6 Wheat. 264.

§ 34. As it embraces nothing but cases, so it embraces *all* cases of admiralty and maritime jurisdiction, nothing can be more full, simple, clear and unquestionable than the words of the grant, " *all cases.*"   It is subject to neither condition, exception nor limitation.(*a*)

§ 35. There are two classes of cases granted to the Federal Judiciary.   In one the nature of the case is every thing, and the character of the parties nothing—in the other the character of the parties is every thing, and the nature of the case nothing— a distinction springing naturally out of the purpose and character of the constitution, to which allusion has already been made.   " All cases affecting ambassadors and other public ministers and consuls," " Controversies between citizens of different states," &c. ; in these, every thing depends upon the character of the parties.
" All cases in law and equity arising under this constitution." " All cases of admiralty and maritime jurisdiction ;" in these every thing depends upon the nature of the case, the subject matter of the suit, and nothing upon the character of the party.(*b*)

§ 36. In none of these cases does the jurisdiction depend upon the question what British court, or what court of any other country, had jurisdiction of the case—and as jurisdiction in cases in law and equity, depends simply on the question whether they arise under the constitution and laws of the United States, so jurisdiction in cases of admiralty and maritime jurisdiction, depends upon the admiralty or maritime nature of the case, and in no manner upon the question whether in England the cause would be heard in the High Court of Admiralty, the Court of King's Bench, the Court of Exchequer, or the Court of Chancery, with or without a jury.

§ 37. We are not at liberty to say that in an instrument so well considered and so carefully drawn, any words are not signi-

---

(*a*) Ante, § 21.
(*b*) Ante, § 26, 27, 28.   6 Wheat. 264.

ficant, much less can we reject such a word as *all*, or deprive it of its proper significance. It cannot be construed to mean a small, unspecified and debateable portion. Nor can we add a condition or limitation to it. All cases of law and equity *arising under this constitution*, &c., all cases *between citizens*, &c., all cases *affecting ambassadors*, &c. In these clauses, limitations are carefully inserted and as cautiously they are omitted in the one under consideration. It would have been easy to say, " all cases of which the Court of King's Bench in England shall permit the English High Court of Admiralty, from time to time, to take jurisdiction," if it had been intended to leave a portion of our legislative and judicial power, to be exercised or regulated in Great Britain through all time.(*a*)

(*a*) Ante, § 21.   5 How. 457.

CHAPTER IV.

Admiralty and Maritime Law.

§ 38. The word *admiralty*, in the constitution, cannot be deprived of any of its proper force. The word is of frequent use in the maritime systems of many countries, and refers, especially, to that class of cases which originally came within the proper cognizance of the admiral. It is not necessary here to repeat the ingenious and fanciful etymologies of the word, nor even the more sound and rational ones. It is sufficient to say, that they are but so many modes of showing the relation between his title and his duties. Godolphin devotes the first chapter of his View of his Admiral Jurisdiction to " the etymon or true original of the word, with the various appellations thereof," in which, and the authorities there cited, the curious will find all they desire.(*a*)

§ 39. Every maritime nation has certain rules or laws in relation to ships, shipping and maritime matters, which are peculiar to itself—such as its navigation acts—its municipal regulations of its harbors, creeks, and bays, and navigable rivers, and of its own vessels—its rules in relation to drowned persons—wrecks—obstructions in rivers—prohibited nets—royal fisheries, and other *droits* of the admiralty, constituting its maritime police. These were originally enforced by the Admiral exercising in part a high executive and administrative function, which was a portion of the royal prerogative, and was in substance confined to the waters and the vessels of his own nation. The Admiralty Court was the forum through which, and by the aid of whose process, when necessary, these local municipal and administrative laws were enforced, and their violators punished. These are, properly, the admiralty law of any country. Cases arising under these laws, are cases of purely admiralty jurisdiction. Each

---

(*a*) Ante, § 21. Godolphin, chap. 1.

nation has its own system of admiralty law, which it changes and modifies at pleasure. It has been remarked, that the mere executive functions of the Admiral, his prerogatives and perquisites, have no existence here.(a)

§ 40. So the word *maritime* is also to have its appropriate meaning—relating to the sea. The words admiralty and maritime, as they are used in the Constitution and acts of the Congress, are by no means synonimous, although able lawyers, on the bench as well as at the bar, seem sometimes to have so considered them. The word admiralty and the word maritime, were evidently both inserted to preclude a narrower construction, which might be given to either word, had it been used alone.(b)

§ 41. Maritime cases are more properly those arising under the maritime law, which is not the law of a particular country, and does not rest for its character or authority, on the peculiar institutions and local customs of any particular country, but consists of certain principles of equity and usages of trade, which general convenience and a common sense of justice have established to regulate the dealings and intercourse of merchants and mariners, in matters relating to the sea, in all the commercial countries of the world.(c)

§ 42. This maritime law does not in the least depend upon the court in which it is to be administered, but furnishes the proper rule of decision in cases to which it applies, no matter in what courts they may be brought ; and it has in fact, been administered in different countries, in different courts, each con-

---

(a) Ante, § 3, 4. *Supra*, § 43. Laws of Oleron, 35 to 47. Laws of Hanse towns, Art. 1. Mar. Ord. Fran. Lib. 1, *passim*. Nav. & Rev. Laws, U. S. Pardessus Loix Mar., *passim*. Godolphin, 43. Zouch, 1 to 28. Sea Laws, 51, 54.

(b) Jud. Act, § 9. 1 Wheat. 335. 6, Id. 264. Gilp. 528. 12 Pet. 744. Ante, § 21 ; 1 Wheat. 304.

(c) 3 Kent Com. 3 edit. 1. Laws of Oleron, Art. 14, 15. Laws of Wisby, Art. 26, 27. Marine Ord. of France. Roccus, introd. Pardessus Loix Mar. 2 Valin. 177, 188. Rhod. Law, 36. Coumlat, 18. Godolp. 43, 155. Zouch, Ass. 9. Sea Laws, *passim*. Malynes, 110. Zouch, Ass. 6.

stituted in its own manner—some called Admiralty Courts—some Maritime Courts—some Consular Courts—some Tribunals of Commerce. In England, the Court of Admiralty, and the Court of Chancery, especially enforced it, while truth was required in pleading, but when by the use of a fictitious venue, the facts might be laid as occurring in London, the King's Bench took jurisdiction and prohibited the Admiralty, and thus, in the King's Bench more than in the Court of Admiralty, and especially under Lord Mansfield, the maritime law was built up and extended. In like manner, that large portion of the admiralty law which relates to the royal revenue, is in England administered in the Court of Exchequer, instead of the Court of Admiralty.(a)

§ 43. The jurisdiction of the Admiral and the administration of the admiralty law proper—the local maritime law—as it became a judicial function has thus passed into the hands of the courts, and they now administer the admiralty law and the maritime law—both of which are sometimes called the admiralty law, sometimes the Maritime Law, and sometimes the Admiralty and Maritime Law, and cases arising under them are cases of Admiralty and Maritime jurisdiction.(b)

§ 44. In the different maritime nations, these two, the local admiralty law and the general admiralty law, have been codified for convenience, and are found united in the maritime codes and ordinances which those nations have compiled or enacted, and which will be further noticed in future pages of this work, when the actual maritime law as administered in the civilized nations of the world, will be more particularly the subject of inquiry.

§ 45. In further endeavoring to ascertain what the framers of the constitution meant by the words " admiralty and maritime," it is important to inquire more especially into the admiralty and

---

(a) Spen. Eq. Juris. 1 Vern. 54. Gilb. Rep 227. 3 Myl. & Craig, 454. 2 Jur. 909. 3 Beav. 409.

(b) Ante, § 4. Hall Ad. intro. 11. Erskine's Laws of Scot. 32. 2 Gall. Rep. 398.

maritime systems of *England*—of *Scotland*—of the *British American Colonies*—of the *American States under the Confederation*, and of *France*. At the time when the Constitution was formed, English, Scotch, American and French commercial enterprize, composed most of the maritime commerce of the world, and such was our relation to them all, that the great men who were laying the foundations of our government, while they did not adopt in detail, the institutions of any other people, cannot be presumed, in so important a matter, to have been ignorant of, or to have overlooked the maritime courts of either of those jurisdictions, and they must have been, in some sort, historically acquainted with them all.

CHAPTER V.

The Ancient Jurisdiction of the English Admiralty.

§ 46. The jurisdiction of the English Admiralty, as actually exercised in its earliest days, and for centuries afterwards, was most extended, various and ample, embracing all maritime causes of action, civil and criminal, of contract and of tort, and all causes of action arising on sea or beyond sea in foreign countries.(*a*) In bringing together the proofs of this proposition, (which, perhaps, many will consider sufficiently evident without formal proof,)— the hazard of being considered prolix and common place, will not deter me from entering at length into the subject, and spreading before the reader the more important documents relating to it.

§ 47. There are no statutes granting jurisdiction to the English Admiralty and other superior courts in England. The chancery, king's bench, common pleas, exchequer and admiralty are all, in theory, branches of the royal prerogative. It is, therefore, in the acts and records of prerogative, in the commissions and ordinances of the monarch, that we are to look for the grants of jurisdiction, and the proper evidence of its legitimate extent, except when they are limited by statute.

§ 48. The commission of the Admiral of England, by the ancient and the later patents, conferred a most ample jurisdiction, in the most unequivocal terms. It was as follows:—" *Damus et concedimus, &c.* We give and grant to N. the office of our great Admiral of England, Ireland and Wales, and the dominions and islands belonging to the same, also of our town of Calais and our marches thereof, Normandie, Gascoigne, and

---

(*a*) 1 Gal. 574. 2 Gal. 398. Stewart's Ad. R. 396.

Aquitaine; and we make, appoint and ordain him our Admiral &c., with all privileges, jurisdictions, &c., and power in civil causes, *ad cognoscendum de placitu*, to hold conusance of *pleas, debts, bills of exchange, policies of insurance, accounts, charter parties, contractions, bills of lading, and all other contracts which any ways concern moneys due for freight of ships hired and let to hire, moneys lent to be paid beyond the seas at the hazard of the lender, and also of any cause, business, or injury whatsoever, had or done in or upon or through the seas or public rivers, or fresh waters, streams, and havens and places subject to overflowing, whatsoever, within the flowing and ebbing of the sea, upon the shores or banks whatsoever adjoining to them or either of them, from any the said first bridges whatsoever, towards the sea,* throughout our kingdom of England and Ireland, or our dominions aforesaid, or elsewhere beyond the seas, or in any parts beyond the seas whatsoever," &c.(*a*)

§ 49. All the patents of the office of Lord High Admiral, from the beginning of Queen Mary's time (1553) to the time of Charles the Second, are said by Zouch to have been conceived after one and the same form and tenor; and from his declaration and that of Selden, and from the commissions to the colonial vice-admirals and judges, hereafter set forth, which are said by Judge Story to be copied from them, I presume that, in the matter of judicial jurisdiction, the whole series of commissions, for many centuries, has conferred the same ample powers, and they will be found to be fully sustained by the other solemn royal acts relating to the same subject.(*b*)

§ 50. By the commission of Oyer and Terminer, also granted to the Admiral, according to stat. 28, Henry 8, cap. 15, power is granted to hear and determine " Of all and singular treasons, robberies, murders, &c., as well in and upon the sea, as any river, port, or fresh water creek, or place whatever within the flowing of the sea to the full, beneath the first bridges towards the sea, or upon the shore of the sea, or elsewhere within the King's maritime jurisdiction of the admiralty of the realm, &c.,

---

(*a*) Zouch Ass. 2. Stewart's Ad. R. 394.   (*b*) 5 How. 441.

as well against the peace and the laws of the land, as against
the King's laws, statutes and ordinances of the King's Court of
Admiralty ; and also touching *all and singular other matters
which concern merchants and proprietors of ships, masters,
shipmen, mariners, shipwrights, fishermen, workmen, laborers,
sailors, scavengers, or any others.*"(*a*)

§ 51. The judgments or laws of Oleron, made by King
Richard I., on his return from the Holy Land, in the latter part
of the twelfth century, (according to English judicial histories,)(*b*)
are among the earliest records of prerogative legislation on the
subject, of which we have any proper evidence. That monarch
is said to have remained some time in the Island of Oleron,
then a part of his dominions, and to have pronounced the judgments, as they are called, of Oleron ; and which seem to be of
the nature of the rescripts of the Roman Emperors, and being
collected together, have now existed as a code of maritime law
for nearly seven hundred years, as respectable for its universal
authority, justice and equity, as venerable for its high antiquity·
This code is accessible to all, and will only be referred to here
as embracing in the most obvious construction of its sententious
judgments, almost all the variety of maritime contracts, offences,
and liabilities, occurring as well in ports and harbors, and on
the coasts, as on the open sea.

In the time of Henry the 8th, they were published as " *The
judgment of the sea of Masters, of Mariners, and Merchants,
and all their doings ;*" which is but a literal translation of the
earlier French title of the same code. Later English publications entitle them " The Naval Laws of Oleron, instituted by
Richard I., King of England, on his return from the Holy Land
in the end of the eleventh century, for the better regulation of

---

(*a*) Zouch, Ass. 2.

(*b*) I am not ignorant that Pardessus has clearly shown, that the laws of Oleron
were not the production of Richard I. ; but as affecting the question under consideration, the English view of their origin is alone important ; and the ablest English
writers, including the learned Selden, have claimed them as the production of that
monarch.

merchants, owners and masters of ships, and mariners, and all seafaring persons, in maritime affairs."(a)

§ 52. Zouch thus classifies their provisions in a very general manner :

1. Touching ships hired for sea voyages, and their proceedings in the same.

2. Touching the safe keeping and delivery of goods received into ships.

3. Touching the engaging (selling or hypothecating) of ships or goods, in case of necessity.

4. Touching contributions to be made for loss, upon occasion of common danger.

5. Touching damages done by or betwixt several ships.

6. Touching the charge for hiring pilots, and their duty.

Under each of these classes, he gives several specifications, and there are many matters of which he makes no mention, including mariner's wages.

§ 53. The Black Book of the Admiralty, is an ancient book or register of admiralty laws, decisions, ordinances, and proceedings and acts of the King, the Admiral, and the Court of Admiralty of England, from the earliest periods. It is not known with certainty when, or by whom, it was collected or compiled. It is of an ancient hand apparently, not written all at once, nor by one person ; but the first part in the reign of Edward III., or Richard II., and the latter part in the reigns of Henry IV., Henry V., and Henry VI., long before the angry controversies between the common law courts and the court of Admiralty. It has been always considered, by all writers on maritime law, as a book of very great authority, containing the ancient rules or statutes of the English Admiralty.   Mr. Selden styles it, *Vetusti Tribunalis Maritimi Commentarii*—and *Codex Manuscriptus de Admiralitatu ;* and says, there are in it constitutions touching the Admiralty of Henry I., Richard I., King John, and Edward I.(b)

(a) Cleirac, 7. Pet. Ad. App. Zouch, Ass. 3. 1 Pardessus, 320. Prynne, 107. Miege's Sea Laws, 3. Godolph. 163. Sea Laws, 120.

(b) Zouch, Ass. 3. Prynne, 115. 2 Brow. Civ. and Ad. 42. Zouch, Ass. 1. Seld. Dom. Mar. b. 2, c. 28. 2 Gall. 398. Seld. Dom. Mar. b. 2, c. 28. Notes to Fortescue, cap. 32.

§ 54. The records of the Black Book of the Admiralty make frequent reference to the laws of Oleron in maritime matters, and show clearly that they were the rule of decision in these early days. At that time, however, judicial as well as executive jurisdiction was a source of power and profit from the numerous forfeitures and other perquisites, and all courts were ingenious and grasping in their efforts to extend their power. The lords, in their liberties and franchises, by their bailiffs and other officers, encroached upon the proper jurisdiction of the Admiral, and the subject was brought before the king and his council in the second year of Edw. I., and the following ordinances were the result of that resort to royal prerogative. They are taken from the learned Prynne who says he transcribed them from the Black Book of the Admiralty.(a)

§ 55. In the 2d year of Edward I. these two laws and ordinances were made and published by him and his lords at Hastings, registered in the Black Book of the Admiralty, page 29.

Item. It is agreed at Hastings by the King Edward the first and his lords, that as many lords had divers franchises to hold pleas in parts, their seneschals and bailiffs shall hold *no plea if it touch merchant or mariner*, as well by deeds as by obligations or other deeds, whether the same amount to 20 or 40 shillings, and if any one shall be indicted for doing the contrary and shall be convicted, he shall have the same judgment as below provided.

§ 56. *Item. Every contract made between merchant and merchant, or merchant and mariner beyond sea or within the flood mark, shall be tried before the Admiral and not elsewhere, by the ordinance of the said King Edward and his lords.*

To which this 3d was added,

§ 57. *Item.* Those who are indicted because they hold before them hue and cry, or blood shedding in salt water or within the flood marks, if they are of this convicted, shall be imprisoned for two years, and afterwards shall be fined at the pleasure of the king and the Admiral.(b)

(a) Prynne Animad. 116. Prynne Animad. 111.
(b) Prynne, 111. Anderson Rep. 89.

§ 58. The ordinances of Edw. I. were the foundation of a consistent usage for a long period of time. The entries in the Black Book of the Admiralty as quoted by Prynne, show clearly that the same usage prevailed in the time of Edward III. He quotes case of prizes—mariners wages—demurrage— freights from and to several ports, and marine torts, in which constant reference is made to the laws of Oleron, and the ordinances of Edward I. as the ancient law of the admiralty. He also quotes from the same book to the same effect, the inquisitions following : (a)

" Black Book of the Admiralty.

§ 59. *Item.* Let inquisition be made of all those who implead *any merchants, mariners* or other men at the common law of *any thing pertaining to the ancient marine law, and if any one is indicted* and convicted, he shall pay a fine to the King for his improper suit and vexation, and *shall besides withdraw his suit from the common law, and bring it before the Admiral's Court,* if he will further prosecute it." Page 36.

"*Item.* Let inquisition be made of those seneschals and bailiffs of lords having domains on the coasts of the sea, who hold a claim to hold any plea concerning *merchants or mariners* exceeding 40 shillings sterling. * * * *And this is the ordinance of Edward I. at Hastings in the* second year of his reign.

Et nota. That all contracts began and made inter merchant and merchant beyond sea or within the flow and reflow commonly called flood mark, shall *be tried and determined before the Admiral, and not elsewhere,* by the aforesaid ordinance."(b)

§ 60. And in the 49th year of Edward III. (A.D. 1376,) the inquisition at Quinborough, was taken by eighteen expert seamen, " men of knowledge and experience in maritime causes," before William Neville, Admiral of the North ; Philip Courtney, Admiral of the West ; and Lord Latimer, Lord of the Cinque

---

(a) Prynne Ad. 116, 119.
(b) Black B. Ad. 142, 147. And see pp. 38, 58 to 63, 66 to 73. *Vid.* Prynne, 114 to 117. 4 Inst. 144.

Ports.   The verdicts there given were desired to be established by the King's letters patent in the Cinque Ports and towns adjoining to the Thames to be observed by the owners, masters and mariners of ships under penalties.   They were enrolled amongst the records of the tower, for the government of the Admiralty.   They cover a very wide range of maritime causes of complaint and of actions.   The heads of them are given by Zouch and are as follows:(a)

§ 61. *Heads of the Articles of the Inquisition taken at Quin-borow in the year* 1376, *in the* 49th *of King Edward the Third, by eighteen expert seamen, before William Nevil, Admiral of the North, Philip Courteney, Admiral of the West, and the Lord Latimer, Warden of the Cinque Ports.*

I. OFFENCES AGAINST THE KING AND KINGDOM.

1. Of such as did furnish the enemy with victuals and ammunition, and of such as did traffic with the enemies without special licence.

2. Of Traytors goods detained in ships and concealed from the King.

3. Of Pirates, their receivers, maintainers and consorters.

4. Of murthers, manslaughters, maimes and petty felonies committed in ships.

5. Of ships arrested for king's service; breaking the arrest; and of sergeants of the admiralty, who for money discharge ships arrested for the king's service; and of mariners who having taken pay, run away from the king's service.

§ 62. II. OFFENCES AGAINST THE PUBLIC GOOD OF THE KINGDOM.

1. Of ships transporting gold and silver.

2. Of carrying corn over sea without special licence.

3. Of such as turn away merchandizes or victuals from the king's ports.

(a) Zouch Ass. 1, 90. Malyn, Cap. 17, 18. Hall Ad. Int. xix. Zouch, Ass. 3, 96.

4. Of forestallers, regrators, and of such as use false measures, balances, weights, within the jurisdiction of the admiralty.

5. Of such as make spoil of wrecks, so that the owners, coming within a year and a day cannot have their goods.

6. Of such as claim wrecks, having neither charter nor prescription.

7. Of wears, riddles, blindstakes, water mills, &c., whereby ships and men have been lost or endangered.

8. Of removing anchors, and cutting of buoy-ropes.

9. Of such as take salmons at unreasonable times.

10. Of such as spoil the breed of oysters or drag for oysters and muscles at unreasonable times.

11. Of such as fish with unlawful nets.

12. Of taking royal fishes, viz., whales, sturgeons, porpoises, &c., and detaining one half from the king.

§ 63. III. OFFENCES AGAINST THE ADMIRAL, THE NAVY, AND DISCIPLINE OF THE SEA.

1. Of judges entertaining pleas of causes belonging to the admiral, and of such as in admiralty causes sue in the courts of common law, and of such as hinder the execution of the admiral's process.

2. Of masters and mariners contemptuous to the admiral.

3. Of the admiral's shares of waifs or derelicts, and of deodands belonging to the admiral.

4. Of *Flotson*, *Jetson* and *Lagon*. belonging to the admiral.

5. Of such as freight strangers' bottoms, where ships of the land may be had at reasonable rates.

6. Of ship-wrights taking excessive wages.

7. Of masters and mariners taking excessive wages.

8. Of pilots, by whose ignorance ships have miscarried.

9. Of mariners forsaking their ships.

10. Of mariners rebellious and disobedient to their masters.

§ 64. Chief Justice Anderson also, in 1664, declares that according to these ordinances of Edward I., which he sets forth, the admirals have used their authorities, to his time, for things done beyond the sea and on the sea, and between high and low water mark, which proves that the space between high and low

water mark is to be taken as part of the sea, when the tide is
in.(a)

§ 65. These ordinances of Edward I. and Edward III, appear to have so strengthened the Admiralty, that in its turn it
encroached upon other jurisdictions, and usurped that which did
not belong to it ; and complaints were made to the King, not of
the Admirals exercising their ancient jurisdiction in all maritime
matters, but that within the bodies of the counties of the nation
they took jurisdiction of trespasses, house breaking, carrying
away goods on lands, of the King's deodands and wrecks, of
regulating the prices of provisions, the wages of labor, and
other things of this sort, interfering with the every-day business
of the common people on land. This produced the statute 13
Rich. II., cap. 5, re-enacting the proper maritime law, and the
usage of the time of Edward III.(b)

A. D. 1389—13 Rich. 2, cap. 5.

§ 66. " *Item*—Forasmuch as a great and common clamor and
complaint hath been oftentimes made before this time, and yet is,
for that the Admirals and their deputies hold their sessions within divers places of this realm, as well within franchise as without, accroaching to them greater authority than belongeth to their
office, in prejudice of our Lord the King, and the common law
of the realm, and in diminishing of divers franchises, and in
destruction and impoverishing of the common people, it is ac-
corded and assented, that the Admirals and their deputies shall
not meddle from henceforth of anything done within the realm,
but only of a thing done upon the sea, as it hath been used in
the time of the noble Prince, King Edward, grandfather of our
Lord the King that now is."(c)

§ 67. " *But only*," is but another phrase for *unless* or *except*,
and if either of those words had been used, (the realm of England including all the British seas), there would hardly have

---

(a) Aud. 89.   (b) Prynne, 83.
(c) 4 Evans' Stat. 271.

been any dispute about the meaning of this act. The Admiral "shall not meddle of any thing done within the realm, except of a thing done upon the sea, as it hath been and in the time of King Edward I.," was evidently intended only to enforce the ancient maritime jurisdiction, and to cut off the new usurpations of the Admirals on the land, and not on the water, to the prejudice of the King's perquisites, in diminishing the franchises of the lords, and impoverishing the common people, who were thus subject to double exactions.(a)

§ 68. Between high and low water was, on all hands, held to be the sea when the tide was in, and the Admiral, it seems, took occasion, from his admitted right over the sea and between high and low water mark, to extend it to the land when the tide was out, and to claim the valuable perquisites of wrecks, always a *droit* of the King and not of the Admiralty, which were often on the land and the water alternately as the tide ebbed and flowed, and to the dams and wears in the small rivers and streams, and to the ponds—and in the franchises, liberties, cities and boroughs within the bodies of the counties, as well on land as on water, they usurped the perquisites and privileges of the King and the Lords.(b)

§ 69. Another statute was accordingly passed two years after the last, evidently intended to remedy this abuse, and to protect the common law jurisdiction in the bodies of the counties, that is, on the land, when the tide was out and above high water mark, and in the tideless rivers and streams and ponds; as Chief Justice Anderson says, "the rivers which were in the counties," and to protect the King and the Lords in their perquisites. It was in these words:

A. D. 1391.—15 *Richard* 2, *cap.* 3.

§ 70. *Item.*—At the great and grievous complaint of all the commons, made to our lord the King in this present parlia-

---

(a) Prynne, 86.
(b) Aud. 89.   Ante, art. 64.   Coke Rep. part 5, 106.   Prynne, 116.

ment, for that the Admirals and their deputies do incroach to them divers jurisdictions, franchises, and many other profits, pertaining to our lord the King, and to other lords, cities and boroughs, other than they were wont, or ought to have of right, to the great oppression and impoverishment of all the commons of the land, and hindrance and loss of the King's profits, and of many other lords, cities and boroughs, through the realm : It is declared, ordained and established, that of all manner of contracts, pleas and quarrels, and all other things rising within the bodies of the counties, as well by land as by water, and also of wreck of the sea, the Admiral's Court shall have no manner of cognizance, power nor jurisdiction, but all such manner of contracts, pleas and quarrels, and all other things rising within the bodies of counties, as well by land as by water as afore, and also wreck of the sea, shall be tried, determined, discussed and remedied by the laws of the land, and not before nor by the admiral, nor his lieutenant in any wise ; nevertheless of the death of a man, and of a mayhem, done in great ships, being and hovering in the main stream of great rivers, only beneath the bridges of the same rivers, nigh to the sea, and in none other places of the same rivers, the admiral shall have cognizance, and also to arrest ships in the great flotes for the great voyages of the king and the realm, saving always to the king all manner of forfeitures and profits thereof coming, and he shall have also jurisdiction upon the said flotes during the said voyages, only saving always to the lords, cities and boroughs their liberties and franchises."(a)

§ 71. This statute is not perfectly clear, and the obscurity arises apparently from the use of the phrase, " within the *bodies of the counties*, as well by land as by water," which by the common law judges, in later times, has been considered as equivalent to " within the territorial limits of the counties." This can hardly be the proper force of the language, since all the counties of England bounded upon the seas or the navigable rivers, include a large portion of the water within their territorial limits even beyond low water mark, and it has never been doubted

---

(a) 4 Evan's Stat. 271.

that the counties extend at least to low water mark, no matter what may be the state of the tide; yet it seems to be equally well settled, that, at high water, the space between high water mark and low water mark, is not within the *body* of the county. That phrase, apparently, must be considered as applying only to the land and to such water, (probably not navigable waters,) as could not be considered as a part of the sea, or did not connect with it. Such seems to have been the opinion of Chief Justice Anderson, and of Lord Coke himself. The Admiral's jurisdiction extended only to what was done in the water, including the water between high water mark and low water mark, by the ordinary and natural course of the sea. "Where the sea ebbs and flows, every thing done on the land when the sea is ebbed, shall be tried at the common law, for it is *then* parcel of the county, *infra corpus comitatus.* Below the low water mark, the Admiral has the sole and absolute jurisdiction. Between the high water mark and the low water mark, the common law and the admiral have *divisum imperium*, interchangeably, as aforesaid, which seems to be proved by the statute 13 Ric. II., cap. 5, confirming the usage in Edward I.'s time—and 15 Ric. II., cap. 3, not mentioning this well known usage, does not take it away, but only new usurpations of things done in rivers which were in the counties." This is declared by the learned Prynne, to be a most clear resolution of the thing in question, both in point of right, law and usage, from 2 Edw. I., to his (Ch. Justice Anderson's,) time, with his genuine interpretation of the Statutes of 13 and 15 Ric. II. Indeed, by a familiar rule of construction, the Statute 13 Ric. II., recognizing and establishing as law, the usage of the time of Edw. I., could not be held to be repealed by the Statute 15 Ric. II., unless the act or the usage were expressly repealed or abrogated.(a)

§ 72. This statute, however, though plainly not intended to limit the ancient jurisdiction of the Admiralty, but simply to secure to the king and the lords their perquisites, was, nevertheless, the means of making the Admiralty subject to the same encroachments and usurpations as it had previously been, and

---

(a) Zouch, Ass. 5. Coke's Rep. part 5, 106. Aud. Rep. 89. Prynne, 111.

which the statute was intended to prevent, and in the year 1400, the Statute 2 Hen. IV., was passed.   It was in these words:

A. D. 1400.   2 *Henry* 4, *Cap.* 11.

§ 73. "*Item.*—Whereas in the statute made at Westminster, in the 13th year of the Second King Richard, amongst other things it is contained that the Admirals and their deputies shall not intermeddle from thenceforth, of any thing done within the realm, but only of a thing done upon the sea, according as it hath been duly used in the time of the noble King Edward, grandfather to the said King Richard, our Lord the King, willeth and granteth that the said statute be firmly holden and kept and put in execution."   This statute was obviously passed for the sole purpose of precluding the narrow construction which has sometimes been given to 13 Rich. II. in connection with 15 Rich. II.(*a*)

(*a*) § 65, 66.   4 Evan's Stat. 272.

CHAPTER VI.

The strife between the Common Law Courts, and the Admiralty, in the 16th and 17th Centuries.

§ 74. Up to this period the strife between the two jurisdictions was a less hostile rivalry than at a later period, when the Admiralty Court was the subject of much irrational jealousy and strong controversy; and in the 16th and 17th centuries suffered much from the violence of this jealousy. Jealousy, says Edwards, is perhaps a mild word to apply to the passion with which the Superior Courts took up this question, for there appears to have been more greediness than emulation at the bottom of it. It was, says Prynne, for more jurisdiction, for gain, not for the public good, but that one jurisdiction might swallow up the other. It is to be regretted that to no less illustrious a personage than Lord Coke, is to be ascribed the origin of this jealousy; and that being the case, it is not wonderful that others should, from subserviency to the opinion of so great a man, have followed in the same track, or even have gone beyond it. Matters raged so high, that a war was declared between the two courts. Prohibitions were hurled from Westminster Hall, and without much order; serving, therefore, more to irritate than to subdue the Admiralty Court, which, though powerless and without the means of attack, obstinately held out for its ancient and time honored privileges.(*a*)

§ 75. In 1575, in the reign of Elizabeth, the judges of the Admiralty and the Common Law judges, before the controversy had assumed that angry character which it afterwards exhibited, entered into an agreement on the subject of prohibitions. To this agreement, the Queen does not appear to have been in any manner a party, but it indirectly had the effect to keep the peace between the two jurisdictions; as, subsequently, during the reign of Elizabeth, no prohibition appears to have

---

(*a*) Edward's Ad. Juris. 17. 3 T. R. 348.

been issued against the Admiralty, except two or three, which are mentioned by Lord Coke in 4th Institutes. The agreement of 1575 is worthy of notice as an evidence that the Common Law Courts claimed a sort of legislative or prerogative power in matters of jurisdiction. They do not appear so much to be deciding principles and declaring the law, as granting requests, consenting to agreements, and making promises. It was indeed so—the law was on the side of the Admiralty—the power was in the hands of the Common Law judges.(a)

The agreement of 1575 was as follows :

The Request of the Judge of the Admiralty to the Lord Chief Justice of her Majesty's Bench and his Colleagues, and The Judges' Agreement, the 7th of May, 1575.

REQUEST.

§ 76. That after judgment or sentence definitive given in the Court of the Admiralty in any cause and appeal made from the same to the High Court of Chancery ; that it may please them to forbear granting of any writ of prohibition, either to the judge of the said court, or to Her Majesty's delegates, at the suit of him by whom such appeal shall be made, seeing by choice of remedy that way, in reason he ought to be contented therewith, and not to be relieved any other way.

AGREEMENT.

It is agreed by the Lord Chief Justice and his colleagues, that after sentence given by the delegates, no prohibition shall be granted ; and yet if there be no sentence, if a prohibition be not sued within the next term following sentence in the Admiral Court, or within two terms next after, at the farthest, no prohibition shall pass to the delegates.

REQUEST.

§ 77. Also, that prohibitions be not granted hereafter upon bare suggestions or surmises, without summary examination and proof made thereof, wherein it may be lawful to the Judge of the Admiralty and the party defendant, by the favor of the

---

(a) Hall's Ad. Intro. x. Prynne, 98. Edw. Ad. 21.

court, to have counsel, and to plead for the stay thereof, if there shall appear cause.

AGREEMENT.

They have agreed, that the Judge of the Admiralty and the party defendant shall have counsel in court, and plead the stay, if there may appear evident cause.

REQUEST.

§ 78. That the Judge of the Admiralty, according to such ancient order as hath been taken 2 Ed. I., by the king and his council, and according to the letters patents of the Lord Admiral for the time being, and allowed of by other kings of this land ever since, and by custom, time out of memory of man, may have and enjoy the cognition of all contracts, and other things arising as well beyond as upon the sea, without any let, or prohibition.

AGREEMENT.

This is agreed upon by the said Lord Chief Justice and his colleagues.

REQUEST.

§ 79. That the said Judge may have and enjoy the knowledge and breach of charter-parties made between masters of ships and merchants, for voyages to be made to the parts beyond the seas, and to be performed upon, and beyond the sea, according as it hath been accustomed, time out of mind, and according to the good meaning of the statute of 32 H. VIII. c. 14, though the same charter-parties happen to be made within the Realm.

AGREEMENT.

This is likewise agreed upon, for things to be performed either upon, or beyond the seas, though the charter-party be made upon the land, by the statute of 32 H. VIII. c. 14.

REQUEST.

§ 80. That writs of *corpus cum causa* be not directed to the said Judge in causes of the nature aforesaid ; and if any happen to be directed, that it may please them to accept the return thereof, with the cause, and not the body, as it hath always been accustomed.

AGREEMENT.

If any writ of this nature be directed in the causes before specified, they are content to return the bodies again to the Lord Admiral's goal, upon certificate made of the cause to be such, or if it be for contempt, or disobedience done to the court in any such cause.

---

§ 81. The Admiralty jurisdiction, at that time, appears to have extended to all cases of freight, charter parties, bottomry, mariners wages, debts due to material men for the building and repairing of ships, and generally to all maritime contracts. When, however, the Queen was dead, as well as most of those who were parties to the agreement, and reference was made to it, Lord Coke denied its authority, because, as he said, the paper from which it was read to him, was not subscribed with the hand of any judge, and, on his own responsibility, he declared that the judges of the King's Bench had never assented to it—and prohibitions were granted by him more than ever before. The learned doctors of the Admiralty, however, still endeavored to convince the higher powers, that their jurisdiction had no temptation to encroachment; and that, without wishing to enlarge the limits of their courts, they were only actuated by a love of justice and respect for their native dignities; but their outcries were little listened to by their rapacious invaders. The practisers in the Admiralty were not the only sufferers from this useless conflict. The merchants —the people—called loudly for a cessation of hostilities, and the Crown was appealed to in 1611, when the agreement of 1575 was read before the King, James I., as an agreement to which the judges of the common law and the Admiralty were parties. At that time a specification of grievances was submitted to the King by the Lord High Admiral, and the Judge of the Admiralty. His Majesty ordered Dr. Dunn, the Judge of the Admiralty, to arrange the matters of complaint in specific articles, and, it seems, to submit them to the common law judges, to be answered by them; and they are said, by Lord Coke, to have made the answers which he gives, and which breath his imperious spirit. The irresolute James does not appear to have made any order in the premises, but to have allowed the agreement of 1575 and the Court of Admiralty, to defend themselves as they best could, and Lord Coke triumphed.(a)

This list of grievances is known as *Articuli Admiralitatis.* They are as follows, with the caption of Lord Coke :

Articuli Admiralitatis.

§ 82. The complaint of the Lord Admiral of *England* to the Kings most Excellent Majesty against the Judges of the Realm, concerning Prohibitions granted to the Court of the Admiralty 11 *die Febr. ultimo die Termini Hillarii, Anno* 8 *Jac. Regis :* The effect of which complaint was after by his Majesties commandment set down in Articles by Doctor *Dun,* Judge of the Admiralty ; which are as followeth, with answers to the same by the Judges of the Realm : which they afterwards confirmed by three kinds of Authorities in Law. 1. By Acts of Parliament. 2. By Judgments and judicial proceedings : and lastly, by Book cases.(b)

Certain Grievances, whereof the Lord Admiral and his Officers of the Admiralty do especially complain, and desire redress.

§ 83. *1st Objection.* That whereas the conusance of all contracts and other things done upon the sea belongeth to the Admiral jurisdiction, the same are made triable at the common law, by supposing the same to have been done in Cheapside, or such places.

The Answer. By the laws of this realm the Court of the Admiral hath no conusance, power or jurisdiction of any manner of contract, plea or querele within any county of the realm, either upon the land or the water : but every such contract, plea or querele, and all other things rising within any county of the realm, either upon the land or the water, and also wreck of the sea ought to be tried, determined, discussed and remedied by the laws of the land, and not before, or by the Admiral nor his Lieutenant in any manner. So as it is not material whether

---

(a) Hall's Ad. Intro. x. Prynne, 99. Edward's Ad. 20. Hall's Ad. Intro. xxii
(b) Zouch Intro. 4 Inst. 134.

the place be upon the water *infra fluxum and refluxum aquæ :* but whether it be upon any water within any county. Wherefore we acknowledge that of contracts, pleas and querels made upon the sea, or any part thereof which is not within any county (from whence no trial can be had by twelve men) the Admiral hath, and ought to have jurisdiction. And no precedent can be showed that any prohibition hath been granted for any contract, plea or querele concerning any marine cause made or done upon the sea, taking that only to be the sea wherein the Admiral hath jurisdiction, which is before by law described to be out of any county. See more of this matter in the answer to the sixth article.

§ 84. *2d Objection.* When actions are brought in the Admiralty upon bargains and contracts made beyond the seas, wherein the common law cannot administer justice, yet in these cases prohibitions are awarded against the Admiral Court.

The Answer. Bargains or contracts made beyond the seas wherein the common law cannot administer justice (which is the effect of this article) do belong to the constable and marshal : for the jurisdiction of the Admiral is wholly confined to the sea, which is out of any county. But if any indenture, bond or other specialty, or any contract be made beyond sea for doing of any act or payment of any money within this realm, or otherwise, wherein the common law can administer justice, and give ordinary remedy ; in these cases neither the constable and marshal, nor the Court of the Admiralty hath any jurisdiction. And, therefore, when this Court of the Admiralty hath dealt therewith in derogation of the common law, we find that prohibitions have been granted, as by law they ought.

§ 85. *3d Objection.* Whereas time out of mind the Admiral Court hath used to take stipulations for appearance and performance of the acts and judgments of the same court : it is now affirmed by the judges of the common law that the Admiral Court is no Court of Record, and therefore not able to take such stipulations : and hereupon prohibitions are granted to the utter overthrow of that jurisdiction.

. *The Answer.* The Court of the Admiralty proceeding by the civil law is no Court of Record, and therefore cannot take any such recognizance as a Court of Record may do. And for taking of recognizances against the laws of the realm, we find that prohibitions have been granted, as by law they ought. And if an erroneous sentence be given in that court, no writ of error, but an appeal before certain delegates doth lie, as it appeareth by the statute of 8 Eliz. Reginæ, cap. 5, which proveth that it is no Court of Record.

§ 86. *4th Objection.* That charter-parties made only to be performed upon the seas, are daily withdrawn from that court by prohibitions.

The Answer. If the charter-party be made within any city, port, town or county of this realm, although it be to be performed either upon the seas or beyond the seas, yet is the same to be tried and determined by the ordinary course of the common law, and not in the Court of the Admiralty. And therefore when that court hath incroached upon the common law in that case, the Judge of the Admiralty and party suing there have been prohibited, and oftentimes the party condemned in great and grievous damages by the laws of the realm.

§ 87. *5th Objection.* That the clause of *Non obstante Statuto*, which hath foundation in his Majesty's Prerogative, and is current in all other grants, yet in the Lord Admiral's Patent is said to be of no force to warrant the determination of the causes committed to him in his Lordship's Patent, and so rejected by the judges of the common law.

The Answer. Without all question the statutes of 13 R. 2, cap. 3, 15 R. 2 cap. 5, and 2 H. 4, cap. 11, being statutes declaring the jurisdiction of the Court of the Admiral, and wherein all the subjects of the realm have interest, cannot be dispensed with by any non obstante, and therefore not worthy of any answer: but by colour thereof, the Court of the Admiralty hath contrary to those Acts of Parliament incroached upon the jurisdiction of the common law to the intolerable grievance of the subjects, which hath oftentimes urged them to complain in your Majesty's Courts of ordinary justice at Westminster for their relief in that behalf.

§ 88. *6th Objection.* To the end that the Admiral Jurisdiction may receive all manner of impeachment and interruption, the rivers beneath the first bridges,(*a*) where it ebbeth and floweth, and the ports and creeks are by the judges of the common law affirmed to be no part of the seas, nor within the Admiral Jurisdiction : and thereby prohibitions are usually awarded upon actions depending in that court, for contracts and other things done in those places; notwithstanding that by use and practice time out of mind, the Admiral Court have had jurisdiction within such ports, creek and rivers.

The Answer. The like answer as to the first. And it is further added, that for the death of a man, and of mayhem (in those two cases only) done in great ships, being and hovering in the main stream only beneath the points(*a*) of the same rivers nigh to the sea, and no other place of the same rivers, nor in other causes, but in those two only, the Admiral hath cognizance. But for all contracts, pleas and querels made or done upon a river, haven or creek within any county of this realm, the Admiral without question hath not any jurisdiction, for then he should hold plea of things done within the body of the county, which are triable by verdict of twelve men, and merely determinable by the common law, and not within the Court of the Admiralty according to the civil law. For that were to change and alter the laws of the realm in those cases, and make those contracts, pleas and querels triable by the common laws of the realm to be drawn *ad aliud examen,* and to be sentenced by the Judge of the Admiralty according to the civil laws. And how dangerous and penal it is for them to deal in these cases, it appeareth by judicial precedents of former ages. But see the answer to the first article.

§ 89. *7th Objection.* That the agreement made in Anno Domini, 1575, between the Judges of the Kings Bench and the Court of the Admiralty for the more quiet and certain exe cution of Admiral Jurisdiction, is not observed as it ought to be.

(*a*) *Pontes, pontibus,* bridges—it will be perceived, are translated by Lord Coke, points, meaning the head lands at the mouth of the rivers—a gross perversion of language.

The Answer. The supposed agreement mentioned in this article hath not as yet been delivered unto us, but having heard the same read over before his Majesty (out of a paper not subscribed with the hand of any judge) we answer, that for so much thereof as differeth from these answers, it is against the laws and statutes of this realm; and therefore the Judges of the King's Bench never assented thereunto, as is pretended, neither doth the phrase thereof agree with the terms of the laws of the realm.

§ 90. *8th Objection.* Many other grievances there are, which, in discussing of these former, will easily appear worthy also of reformation.

The Answer. This article is so general, as no particular answer can be made thereunto, only that it appeareth by that which hath been said, that the Lord Admiral, his Officers and Ministers principally by colour of the said void *non obstante* and for want of learned advice, have unjustly incroached upon the common laws of this realm, whereof the marvail is the less, for that the Lord Admiral, his Lieutenants, Officers and Ministers have without all colour, incroached and intruded upon a right and prerogative due to the crown, in that they have seized and converted to their own uses, goods and chattels of infinite value, taken by pirates at sea, and other goods and chattels which in no sort appertain unto his lordship by his letters patents, wherein the said *non obstante* is contained, and for the which he and his Officers remain accountable unto his Majesty. And they now wanting, in this blessed time of peace, causes appertaining to their natural jurisdiction, they now incroach upon the jurisdiction of the common law, lest they should sit idle and reap no profit. And if a greater number of prohibitions (as they affirm) hath been granted since the great benefit of this happy peace, than before in time of hostility, it moveth from their own incroachments upon the jurisdiction of the common law. So as they do not only unjustly incroach, but complain also of the Judges of the Realm for doing of justice in these cases."

§ 91. The common law judges seem to have met with no

further check during the residue of the reign of James I., and the first seven years of the reign of Charles I. In that year, the Lord High Admiral and Sir Henry Martyn, the Judge of the Admiralty, brought the matter again before the King and Lords of his Council, before whom the matters between the Admiralty and the Judges were several times heard and debated at large, and at last these ensuing articles were drawn up, read, agreed, and resolved at the Council board, by the King himself, and all the Lords of his Council, twenty-three in number, including Lord Keeper Coventry and Lord Privy Seal Montague, eminent lawyers, and signed by all the twelve judges of the common law courts, and by the " grand lawyer, Mr. William Noye, Attorney-General, a great professor and pillar of the common law," and by the Judge of the Admiralty, entered in the Council Table Register of Causes, and the original by his Majesty's command, kept in the Council chest.(*a*)

At Whitehall, 18th of February, 1632.

Present :

The King's Most Excellent Majesty.

Lord Keeper,	Lord V. Wimbleton,
Lord Archb. of York,	Lord Vis. Wentworth,
Lord Treasurer,	Lord V. Faukland,
Lord Privy Seal,	Lord Bishop of London,
Earl Marshall,	Lord Cottington,
Lord Chamberlain,	Lord Newburgh,
Earl of Dorset,	Mr. Treasurer,
Earl of Carlisle,	Mr. Comptroller,
Earl of Holland,	Mr. Vice-Chamberlain,
Earl of Darby,	Mr. Secretary Coke,
Lord Chancellor of Scotland,	Mr. Secretary Windebanke.
Earl Morton.	

§ 92. " This day his Majesty being present in Council, the articles and propositions following for the accommodating and settling of the differences concerning prohibitions arising between his Majesty's Courts of Westminster and his Court of

---

(*a*) Prynne Ad. 100.

Admiralty, were fully debated, and resolved by the Board. And were then likewise upon reading the same as well before the Judges of his Highnesse said Courts at Westminster, as before the Judge of his said Court of Admiralty, and his Attorney-General, agreed unto and subsigned by them all in his Majesty's presence, and the transcript thereof ordered to be entered into the register of Council Causes and the original to remain in the Council chest.

§ 93. " 1. If suit shall be commenced in the Court of Admiralty upon contracts made, or other things personally done beyond the seas, or upon the sea, no prohibition is to be awarded.

§ 94. " 2. If suit before the Admiral for freight or mariners' wages, or for the breach of charter-parties for voyages to be made beyond the sea, though the charter-parties happen to be made within the realm, and although the money be payable within the realm, so as the penalty be not demanded, a prohibition is not to be granted ; but if suits be for the penalty, or if question be made whether the charter-partie were made or not ; or whether the plaintiff did release or otherwise discharge the same within the realme, that is to be tried in the King's Courts at Westminster, and not in the King's Court of Admiralty, so that first it be denied upon oath, that a charter-partie was made, or a denial upon oath tendered.

§ 95. " 3. If suit shall be in the Court of Admiralty for building, amending, saving, or necessary victualling of a ship, against the ship itself, and not against any party by name, but such as for his interest makes himself a party, no prohibition is to be granted, though this be done within the realm.

§ 96. " 4. Likewise the Admiral may inquire of, and redresse all annoyances and obstructions in all navigable rivers, beneath the first bridges, that are any impediments to navigation, or passage to, and from the sea, and also try personal contracts and injuries done there, which concern navigation upon the sea, and no prohibition is to be granted in such cases.

§ 97. "5. If any be imprisoned, and upon *Habeas Corpus,* if any of these be the cause of imprisonment, and that be so certified, the partie shall be remanded.

(Signed,)

Thomas Richardson,	William Jones,	Robert Barkley,
Ro. Heath,	George Croke,	Fran. Crawley,
Humphry Davenport,	Tho. Trevor,	Henry Marten,
John Denham,	Geo. Vernon,	William Noye.
Rich. Hutton,	James Weston,	

Ex. T. Meautys."

§ 98. I take these from Prynne, who was keeper of the records, and had the means of securing the greatest accuracy, and who seems to have had them carefully examined and certified, and sets them out at length, in form, and with the signatures. They may be found in one form or another published in many other places, but no two copies that I have seen, agree in all the important particulars, especially in the second and fourth paragraphs ; and it is not a little remarkable that, having been preserved by Sir George Croke, (who himself signed them,) and published in two editions of his reports, without criticism or comment, as evidence of the law, and referred to in the index—word Admiralty—in the third edition of those reports, after the death of Sir George Croke, and of most, if not all, the Judges and Councillors who signed them, they should have been, without reason or apology, omitted, and their place left blank on the page, while the original reference to them was allowed to stand in the index, and so remains in all subsequent editions of Croke, to this day. This very extraordinary mutilation of a book, then of high authority in the courts, tends to show that the common law jurists, who did not themselves actually perpetrate, were still willing to connive at acts of falsification of documents and books, to accomplish a triumph originally attempted from unworthy motives, and pursued with persevering zeal, apparently, from pride of opinion or motives as discreditable as those in which the controversy had originated.(*a*)

(*a*) Dunlap's Ad. Prac, 13.   Zouch, Ass. 7.   Godolph. 158.   Cro. Car. Lond. 1657, first edit. and 1671, second edit. ; and subsequent editions.   Prynne, 100.

§ 99. These articles were not liable for the objection that they were not signed, and for a number of years they kept the peace between the courts. The troubles however between the King and the Parliament and his people soon commenced, and resulted in the overthrow of the royal authority and the establishment of the Protectorate. Little more is now known of the contest, except that it was probably renewed as soon as the check of royal authority was withdrawn. The Republican Parliament was then called upon by the friends of trade and commerce, to take sides with the Admiralty, and to secure to the people the benefits of its more enlarged jurisdiction, and the ordinance of 1648 was the consequence.(a)

It was as follows:

Extract from Scobell's Collection of the Acts and Ordinances of the Republican Government of England. Anno 1648—page 147.

CHAPTER 112.

The Jurisdiction of the Court af Admiralty settled.

§ 100. "The Lords and Commons assembled in Parliament, finding many inconveniences daily to arise, in relation both to the trade of this Kingdom, and the Commerce with foreign parts, through the uncertainty of jurisdiction in the trial of maritime causes, do ordain and be it ordained by the authority of Parliament. That the Court of Admiralty shall have cognizance and jurisdiction against the ship or vessel, with the tackle, apparel and furniture thereof; in all causes which concern the repairing, victualling and furnishing provisions for the setting of such ships or vessels to sea; and in all cases of bottomry, and likewise in contracts made beyond the seas concerning shipping or navigation or damages happening thereon, or arising at sea in any voyage; and likewise in all cases of charter parties or contracts for freight, bills of lading, mariners' wages, or damages in goods laden on board ships, or other damages done by one ship or vessel to another, or by anchors, or want lying of buoys, except always that the said Court of Admiralty shall not hold pleas or admit actions upon any bills of exchange or accounts betwixt merchant and merchant or their factors.

(a) Hall's Ad. intro. xxi.

§ 101. "And be it ordained, That in all and every the matters aforesaid, the said Admiralty Court shall and may proceed and take recognizances in due form, and hear, examine, and finally end, decree, sentence and determine the same according to the laws and customs of the sea, and put the same decrees and sentences in execution without any let, trouble or impeachment whatsoever, any law, statute or usage to the contrary heretofore made in any wise notwithstanding; saving always and reserving to all and every person and persons, that shall find or think themselves aggrieved by any sentence definitive, or decree having the force of a definitive sentence, or importing a damage not to be repaired by the definitive sentence given or interposed in the Court of Admiralty, in all or any of the cases aforesaid, their right of appeal in such form as hath heretofore been used from such decrees or sentences in the said Court of Admiralty.

§ 102. "Provided always, and be it further ordained by the authority aforesaid, that from henceforth there shall be three judges always appointed of the said court, to be nominated from time to time by both houses of Parliament or such as they shall appoint; and that every of the judges of the said court for the time being, that shall be present at the giving of any definite sentence in the said Court, shall at the same time, or before such sentence given openly in Court, deliver his reasons in law of such his sentence, or of his opinion concerning the same; and shall also openly in Court give answers and solutions (as far as he may) to such laws, customs or other matter as shall have been brought or alleged in Court, on that part against whom such sentence or opinion shall be given or declared respectively."

Provided also, That this Ordinance shall continue for three years and no longer.

Passed, the 12th April 1648.

Made perpetual by Ordinances of 2nd April, 1641. C. 3.—1654. C. 21. and 1645. C. 10.

Expired at the Restoration, anno 1660.(a)

§ 103. Under this Ordinance the Admiralty was administered

(a) Hall's Ad. intro. p. xxiv.

till the Restoration by Dr. Godolphin, who had been one of the Judges of the Admiralty under Cromwell, and had written his View of the Admiral Jurisdiction. So great was his reputation for integrity and knowledge, that at the Restoration he was made King's Advocate, and he immediately published his work in which the actual jurisdiction of the Court is thus set forth.(a)

§ 104. "Within the cognizance of this jurisdiction are all affairs that peculiarly concern the Lord high Admiral, or any of his officers *quatenus* such; all matters immediately relating to the navies of the kingdome, the vessels of trade, and the owners thereof, as such; all affairs relating to mariners, whether ship-officers or common mariners, their rights and privileges respectively; their office and duty; their wages; their offences, whether by wilfulness, casualty, ignorance, negligence, or insufficiency, with their punishments. Also all affairs of commanders at Sea, and their under-officers, with their respective duties, privileges, immunities, offences, and punishments.

§ 105. "In like manner all matters that concern owners and proprietors of ships, as such; and all Masters, Pilots, Steersmen, Boatswains, and other Ship-Officers; all Ship-wrights, Fishermen, Ferry-men, and the like; also all causes of seizures, and Captures made at Sea whether *jure Belli Publici*, or *jure Belli Privati* by way of Reprizals, or *jure nullo* by way of Piracy; Also all Charter-parties, Cocquets, Bills of Lading, Sea-Commissions, Letters of safe Conduct, Factories, Invoyces, Skippers Rolls, Inventories, and other Ship-papers; Also all causes of Fraight, Mariners wages, Load-manage, Port-charges, Pilotage, Anchorage, and the like.

§ 106. "Also all causes of Maritime Contracts *indeed*, or *as it were* Contracts, whether upon or beyond the Seas; all causes of mony lent to Sea or upon the Sea, called *Fænus Nauticum*, *Pecunia trajectitia, usura maritima, Bomarymony*, the Gross Adventure, and the like; all causes of pawning, hypothecating, or pledging of the ship it self, or any part thereof, or her Lading, or other things at Sea; all causes of *Jactus*, or casting goods over board; and Contributions either for Redemption of Ship

---

(a) Godolph. 43.

or Lading in case of seizure by Enemies or Pyrats, or in case of goods damnified, or disburdening of ships, or other chances, with Average; also all causes of spoil and depredations at Sea, Robberies and Pyracies; also all causes of Naval Consort-ships, whether in War or Peace; Ensurance, Mandates, Procurations, Payments, Acceptilations, Discharges, Loans or Oppignorations, Emptions, Venditions, Conventions, taking or letting to Fraight, Exchanges, Partnership, Factoridge, Passage-money, and whatever is of Maritime nature, either by way of *Navigation* upon the Sea, or of *Negotiation* at or beyond the Sea in the way of Marine Trade and Commerce; also the Nautical Right which Maritime persons have in ships, their Apparel, Tackle, Furniture, Lading, and all things pertaining to Navigation; also all causes of Out-readers, or Out-riggers, Furnishers, Hirers, Fraighters, Owners, Part-owners of ships, as such; also all causes of Priviledged ships, or Vessels in his Majesties Service or his Letters of *safe Conduct;* also all causes of shipwreck at Sea, Flotson, Jetson, Lagon, Waiffs, Deodands, Treasure-Trove, Fishes-Royal; with the Lord Admiral's shares, and the Finders respectively.

§ 107. "Also all causes touching Maritime offences or misdemeanours, such as cutting the Bouy-Rope or Cable, removal of an Anchor whereby any Vessel is moored, the breaking the Lord Admiral's Arrests made either upon person, ship, or goods; Breaking Arrests on ships for the King's Service, being punishable with Confiscation by the Ordinance made at *Grimsby* in the time of *Rich.* I. Mariners absenting themselves from the Kings Service after their being prest. Impleading upon a Maritime Contract or in a Maritime Cause elsewhere then in the Admiralty, contrary to the Ordinance made at *Hastings* by *Ed.* I. and contrary to the Laws and Customes of the Admiralty of *England;* Forestalling of Corn, Fish, &c. on ship-board, regrating and exaction of water-officers; the appropriating the benefit of Salt-waters to private use exclusively to others without his Majesties Licence; Kiddles, Wears, Blind stakes, Water, mills, and the like, to the obstruction of Navigation in great Rivers; False weights or measures on ship-board; Concealing of goods found about the dead within the Admiral Jurisdiction, or of Flotsons, Jetsons, Lagons, Waiffs, Deodands, *Fishes Royal*, or other things wherein the Kings Majesty or his Lord Admiral have interest; Excessive wages claimed by Ship-wrights, Mariners, &c. Maintainers, Abettors, Receivers, Concealers or Comforters of Pyrats; Transporting Prohibited goods without Licence; Draggers of Oysters and Muscles at unseasonable times, *viz.* between May-day, and Holy-rood-day; Destroyers of the brood or young Fry of Fish; such as claim Wreck to the prejudice of the King or Lord Admiral; such as unduly claim privileges in a Port; Disturbers of the Admiral Officers in execution of the Court-Decrees; Water-Bayliffs and Searchers, not doing their duty; Corruption in any of the Admiral-Court-Officers; Importers of unwholesome Victuals to the peoples prejudice; Fraighters of strangers Vessels contrary to the Law; Transporters of prisoners or other prohibited persons not having Letters of safe Conduct from the King or his Lord Admiral; Casters of Ballasts into Ports or Harbours, to the prejudice thereof; Unskilful Pilots, whereby ship or man perish; Unlawful Nets, or other prohibited Engines for Fish; Disobeying of Embargos, or going to Sea contrary to the Prince his command, or against the Law; Furnishing the ships of Enemies, or the Enemy with ships; All prejudice done to the Banks of ·Navigable Rivers, or to Docks, Wharffs, Keys, or any thing whereby Shipping may be endangered, Navigation obstructed, or Trade by Sea impeded; Also embezilments of ship-tackle or furniture; all substractions of Mariners wages; all defraudings of his Majesties Customes or other Duties at Sea; also all prejudices done to or by passengers a shipboard; and all damages done by one ship or Vessel to another; also to go to Sea in tempestuous weather, to sail in devious places, or among Enemies, Pyrats, Rocks, or other dangerous places, being not necessitated thereto; all clandestine attempts by making privy Cork-holes in the Vessels, or otherwise, with intent to destroy or endanger the ship; also the shewing of false Lights by Night either on shore or in Fishing Vessels, or the like, on purpose to intice Sailers, to the hazard of their Vessels; all wilful or purposed entertaining of unskilful Masters, Pilots or Mariners, or sailing without a Pilot, or in Leaky and insufficient Vessels; also the over-burdening the ship above her birth-mark, and all ill stowage of goods a shipboard; also all Importation of *Con-*

8

trabanda goods, or Exportation of goods to prohibited Ports, or
the places not designed; together with very many other things
relating either to the state or condition of persons Maritime,
their rights, their duties, or their defaults."(*a*)

§ 108. This ordinance ceased to be in force at the Restoration,
and the common law judges again prohibited the Admiralty.
The merchants petitioned for a re-observance of the rules of
1632; but neither their petitions, nor Judge Godolphin's arguments and learning, were regarded; and the civilians, tired of
the struggle, appear to have preferred a peace, however disad-
vantageous, to war, however justly it might be carried on.
The violent opinions, first expressed by Lord Coke, and afterwards supported by others with more subserviency than reason,
could not be resisted, and the Admiralty submitted.   It is well
remarked by Edwards—" Although so much of the ancient
authority of the Admiralty Court has been rendered nugatory
—in this nineteenth century that court may look back with
pride and observe how well it has survived the conflict—how
the arguments which were put forth with force, by those learned
civilians in the 16th and 17th centuries appear, at last, to be
listened to; for now the rule of *locality*, to which it was attempted to confine the jurisdiction of the Admiralty, has almost
entirely given way to the more rational one of the *subject
matter* to be adjudicated upon."   The wants of commerce, in
this commercial age, have become too imperious to be disregarded; and even in England, in the stat. 3 and 4 Vic. c. 65,
a great step has been taken towards restoring to the High Court
of Admiralty those cases of admiralty and maritime jurisdiction
of which the common law courts had deprived them.(*b*)

§ 109. The commissions to the vice-admirals, issued from the
Lord High Admiral, and to the vice-admiralty courts, issued from
the High Court of Admiralty, during the next hundred years,
while they furnish evidence of the extent of the jurisdiction of
the courts to which they were issued, and also evidence of the

---

(*a*) Godolph. Ad. Juris. 43 to 48.
(*b*) Hall Ad. Intro. xi. 2 Brown Civ. and Ad. Law, 78.

jurisdiction of the High Court of Admiralty from which they issued, showing that, wherever prohibitions could not reach the
Admiralty, there its ancient plenary and beneficial jurisdiction
was deputed and exercised, originally and on appeal, without
restraint.

§ 110. It cannot, therefore, rationally, be doubted by any one
that has examined the subject, that the ancient jurisdiction of
the English Admiralty was of a most extended and beneficial
character, embracing all maritime causes of action. It is equally
true, that by prohibitions, on most inconsistent and extraordinary grounds, "granted," as Prynne says, " on sudden motions
without solemn argument," the exercise of that jurisdiction had
been restrained within very narrow limits at the time our Constitution was formed. The mode and character of the opposition to that jurisdiction, I have not gone into in detail. The
curious inquirer will find all that he can desire on this subject
in the great case of De Lovio v. Boit, 2 Gallison, 398, and the
works and cases there quoted, and referred to and examined by
Judge Story with an affluence of learning and a wisdom and
acuteness of criticism which, in that early period in his judicial
career, promised for him that fame which, afterwards, equalled
his highest hopes, and shed a permanent lustre on the judicial
history of the nation.

CHAPTER VII.

The English Admiralty at the time of the American Revolution.

§ 111. It has been remarked, that our situation previous to the Revolution as British colonies, and the adoption of the English common law, as interpreted in the English books, did much to influence opinion in this country in favor of the narrow English rule of admiralty jurisdiction which prevailed at that time, and that that narrow platform of jurisdiction was only what was left after centuries of strife between the Courts of Common Law and the Court of Admiralty, which resulted in confining the Admiralty to the following very inconsiderable class of cases :—

To enforce judgments of foreign Courts of Admiralty, where the person or the goods are within the reach of the court—Mariner's Wages, where the contract is not under seal, and is made in the usual form—Bottomry, in certain cases and under many restrictions—Salvage, where the property was not cast on shore—Cases between part owners disputing about the employment of the ship—Collisions and injuries to property or persons on the high seas—and *droits* of the admiralty.

This was the whole of what was left of that large jurisdiction which it had before rightfully exercised for centuries.

It is not easy to perceive any satisfactory reason why those few causes of action alone (having no peculiar odor of nationality) should be deemed of so much importance as to be withdrawn from the judicial power of the States, and made the subject of a constitutional grant to the National Government. Indeed it would seem more like puerile caprice than that ripe wisdom which we habitually look for in the fathers of the republic.(*a*)

§ 112. The struggle between these courts originated in the

(*a*) 5 Howard, 452, 3. 3 Black. Com. 106.

same spirit that attempted to break down the whole system of Equity—and none can deny that the courts of common law manifested a great degree of jealousy and hostility, fostered by strong prejudice and a very imperfect knowledge of the subject. The English Admiralty has always rightfully had jurisdiction over all maritime contracts, and the decisions of the courts of common law, prohibiting its exercise, are neither consistent in themselves nor reconcilable with principle. Had the common law courts had the power to issue writs of prohibition to the Chancellor, and had that high officer been any thing less than the highest judicial functionary, and the first subject in the realm—in those days when might was right, in courts as well as camps, and jealousy, and prejudice, and arrogance, to say nothing of the love of gain, influenced judicial decisions of judges, the Court of Chancery would have met the fate of the Court of Admiralty, and have been stripped of the most useful portion of its jurisdiction.(a)

§ 113. The Court of King's Bench has power to issue prohibitions, but it has no power to extend or diminish the jurisdiction of the Admiralty. That jurisdiction is conferred by the King's prerogative and royal commission, or by statute or immemorial usage, and not otherwise, and can be limited only in the same manner. If the King's commission, or the proper exercise of the royal prerogative, or a statute, give the jurisdiction, the King's Bench cannot deprive the court of its jurisdiction—that is to say, of its right to take cognizance of causes—although by an improper exercise of irresponsible power, it can prevent the Admiralty from exercising the jurisdiction which properly belongs to it. The right of the Admiralty depends upon the construction of the grant of jurisdiction alone, no matter how often or for what causes, prohibitions may have been issued. The Court of King's Bench has neither legislative nor executive powers, which enable it rightfully to dispense with the law, whether the law be founded in parliamentary or prerogative legislation.

If at the time of the American Revolution, and before the

(a) 2 Gall. 348.

adoption of the Constitution of the United States, the King's Bench had determined to carry out, to their legitimate extent, the rules under which the Admiralty jurisdiction had been so much restricted, then prohibitions must have issued in all cases of mariner's wages—contracts under seal, (bottomry and respondentia bonds,)—contracts signed on shore, or within any county, including every port in the realm—the English Court of Admiralty would have been denied its entire jurisdiction. It will hardly be contended, that, in such cases, the English Court of King's Bench would have annihilated all cases of admiralty and maritime jurisdiction throughout the world, so that the words used in the Constitution would have no force or signification whatever. That court surely has not now, nor could it have then had, any such power to affect the legislation and institutions of other nations. It had no such power in the days of Lord Coke. If it could not have abolished all cases of admiralty and maritime jurisdiction, how could it abolish any of them?(a)

(a) § 14, 28, 37.　7 Cranch, 116.

CHAPTER VIII.

The Admiralty Jurisdiction of Scotland and Ireland.

§ 114. The admiralty and maritime jurisdiction of the other portions of the Empire of Great Britain, and even of that island, by no means harmonized with this narrow jurisdiction of the High Court of Admiralty of the kingdom of England. In the kingdom of Scotland, and in the American Colonies, the Admiralty jurisdiction was of the most extensive and beneficial character.(*a*)

§ 115. " It is true that in Scotland, before the creation of an Admiral, after the example of other nations, the Deans of the Gild were ordinarily judges in civil debates betwixt mariner and merchant, as the Water-Bailey betwixt mariner and mariner, like as the High Justice was judge in their criminals. Which actions, all were (A. D. 1682,) falling forth betwixt the persons aforesaid, of due, appertain to the jurisdiction of the Admiral, and therefore his Judge Depute or Commissar, called Judge Admiral, and none other, should sit, cognosce, determine and minister justice in the aforesaid causes. As likewise upon all complaints, contracts, offences, pleas, charges, assecurations, debts, counts, charter parties, covenants, and all other writings concerning lading and unlading of ships, fraughts, (freights), hires, money lent upon casualties and hazard at sea, and all other businesses whatsoever amongst seafarers, done on sea, this side sea or beyond sea, not forgetting the cognition of writs and appeals from other judges, and the causes and actions of reprisals or letters of mark," and also a most extended police and criminal jurisdiction.(*b*)

The Scotch Admiralty Court has always had jurisdiction also in cases arising on Bills of Exchange and other mercantile

---

(*a*) 2 Gal. Rep 468, 475.
(*b*) The Collection of Sea Laws, a Scotch tract, in Malynes, chap. 2, 47, 48.

causes not maritime, and also jurisdiction to arrest a debtor about to depart the country, and compel him to give security to pay the debt.(*a*)

§ 116. The High Admiral is His Majesty's Justice General upon the Seas, and in all ports, harbors, creeks, and upon the navigable rivers below the first bridges and within the flood mark, he hath jurisdiction in all maritime and seafaring causes, foreign and domestic, whether civil or criminal within the realm. The jurisdiction of the Court of Admiralty is both civil and criminal. In civil matters, the Judge Admiral is judge in the first instance, in all maritime causes as in questions on charter parties, freights, salvages, wrecks, bottomries, policies of insurance, and all questions relating to the lading and unlading of ships, or any act to be performed within the bounds of his jurisdiction. He has jurisdiction also in all actions for recovery of goods or their value, where the goods have been sent by sea from one port to another. In criminal matters, he has the exclusive cognizance in the crimes of mutiny and piracy on ship board.(*b*)

§ 117. There has also been in Ireland, from time immemorial, an Instance Court of Admiralty, and up to the year 1782, it also exercised the powers of a prize court. By the articles of Union, and by the act of 1782, its jurisdiction was confined to causes civil and maritime only.(*c*)

I have not thought it necessary to inquire into the details of the actual jurisdiction of the Irish Admiralty, and give it this passing notice only, further to illustrate the remark which has been made before that, in the different portions of the British Empire, Admiralty jurisdiction was exercised in a widely different extent, and that " all admiralty and maritime cases" was not necessarily confined to the small class permitted to the English Admiralty.

(*a*) Boyd's Proceedings of the Admiralty of Scotland, 67.   Ibid. 69.

(*b*) Dunlap's Prac. 35.   Boyd's Proceedings, 4, 5, 6.   2 Brown Civ. & Ad. 30. Bell's Dic. of the Laws of Scotland, 29—(words, Admiral and Court of Admiralty,) Erskine's Laws of Scotland, 32.

(*c*) 2 Brown Civ. & Ad. 32.

CHAPTER IX.

The Admiralty and Maritime Jurisdiction of the British Colonies.

§ 118. At the time of the American Revolution, in addition to the admiralty and maritime tribunals of England and Scotland, there existed the Admiralty Courts of the British Colonies.

Under the British Constitution, the Statutes of the Imperial Parliament do not bind the colonies, unless they are expressly named, while the King's commissions runs through his whole dominions. It is under the King's commissions, that the colonial Vice-Admiralty Courts were created, and their jurisdiction remained as it had been originally granted. Those commissions were issued from the High Court of Admiralty, and thus furnished, at their respective dates, evidence not only of the jurisdiction of the Colonial Courts to which they were issued, but also of the High Court of Admiralty at home, from which they emanated. They issued from time to time to the Governors, Vice-Admirals, and Judges of Vice-Admiralty in the colonies. They are of four kinds. 1st. The commission to the Governor as Governor, which issued from the office of the Secretary of State. 2nd. The commission to the Governor as Vice-Admiral, which issued from the High Court of Admiralty. 3rd. The general commission to the Governor, and all the principal officers of state, under the act for the more effectual suppression of piracy, which issued from the office of the Secretary of State. 4th. The commission to the Judges of the Vice-Admiralty Court, which issued from the High Court of Admiralty.(a)

§ 119. Many of these commissions may be found in the offices of the various Secretaries of State of the States ; but as they are not easily accessible, I shall insert one of each at full length, although some portion of their contents has no particular rela-

---

(a) 2 Gall. 470. 5 How. 461.

tion to the matter of the admiralty jurisdiction. They are inserted without regard to chronological order, because from the
imperfection of the records in the State of New York, they
are not preserved in that order. The commission of the Governor gave him power to create courts of admiralty according
to the commissions which he should receive from the High
Court of Admiralty at home.(a)

§ 120. A large portion of the commission of the governor, as the
political head of the colony, has no further relation to this question than as showing how completely the organization and power
of the courts was kept within the control of mere prerogative regulation. That portion of it will not be inserted here. The
clauses giving the power to create courts are inserted, to show
as well that the common law and admiralty jurisdiction were
created in the same manner, as that the admiralty jurisdiction
was granted in very general terms.

Commission of the Governor.

§ 121. "Willliam the Third, by the grace of God, of England,
Scotland, France and Ireland, King, defender of the faith, &c.
To our right trusty and well beloved Edward Hide, Esq., commonly called Lord Cornbury, greeting.   *   *   *   And we do
by these presents, give and grant unto you full power and
authority, with the advice and consent of our said council, to
erect, constitute and establish such and so many courts of judicature and public justice, within our said province and the territories under your government, as you and they shall think fit
and necessary for the hearing and determining of all causes, as
well criminal as civil, according to law and equity, and for
awarding of execution thereupon, with all reasonable and necessary powers, authorities, fees and privileges belonging unto
them, as also to appoint and commissionate fit persons, in the
several parts of your government, to administer the oaths appointed by act of parliament, to be taken instead of the oaths of
allegiance and supremacy and the test, unto such as shall be
obliged to take the same, and likewise to require them to sub-

(a) 5 How. 454.

scribe the forementioned association. And we do hereby authorize and empower you to constitute and appoint judges and justices of the peace and other necessary officers and ministers in our said province, for the better administration of justice and putting the laws in execution, and to administer or cause to be administered such oath or oaths as are usually given for the due execution and performance of offices and places, and for the clearing of truth in judicial causes."

*   *   *   *   *

§ 122. "And we do hereby give and grant unto you, the said Lord Cornbury, full power and authority to erect one or more Court or Courts Admiral within our said province and territories, for the hearing and determining of all marine and other causes and matters proper therein to be heard, with all reasonable and necessary powers and authorities, fees and privileges, as also to exercise all powers belonging to the place and office of Vice-Admiral of and in all the seas and coasts within your government, according to such commission, authorities and instructions as you shall receive from ourself, under the seal of our admiralty, or from our High Admiral, or commissioners for executing the office of High Admiral of our foreign plantations for the time being."

§ 123. The commission to the Governor as Vice-Admiral was very full, granting, in language so clear that it cannot be misunderstood, an admiralty jurisdiction as wide and beneficial as the most zealous supporters of the English Admiralty ever claimed for it.

The commission to Lord Cornbury as Vice-Admiral was as follows. The original commission is in Latin, and I have availed myself of the English translation of similar commissions given by Stokes and Du Ponceau.(a)

Commission of the Vice-Admiral.

§ 124. "Letters patent granted to the very noble and honorable, Edward, Lord Cornbury, Governor of the provinces and colonies of New York, Connecticut, and East and West New

---

(a) Dunlap's Ad. Prac. 35. Stokes' View of the Colonies, 166. Du Ponceau, 158.

Jersey, in America, and of the same Commander in Chief, for the time being, for the office of Vice-Admiral in the said provinces and colonies of New York, Connecticut, and East and West New Jersey.

"William the Third, by the grace of God, of England, Scotland, France and Ireland, King, and Defender of the Faith, to our well beloved, and liege Edward, Lord Cornbury, our Governor of our provinces and colonies of New York, Connecticut, and East and West New Jersey, in America, and Commander in Chief of the said provinces and colonies for the time being, greeting :

§ 125. " We confiding very much in your fidelity, care, and circumspection in this behalf, do, by these presents, which are to continue during our pleasure only, constitute and depute you the said A. B. Esq., our Captain General and Governor in Chief aforesaid, our Vice-Admiral, commissary, and deputy in the office of Vice-Admiralty in our provinces and colonies, aforesaid, and the territories depending thereon in America, and in the maritime parts of the same and thereto adjoining whatsoever ; with power of taking and receiving all and every the fees, profits, advantages, emoluments, commodities, and appurtenances whatsoever due, and belonging to the said office of Vice-Admiral, commissary, and deputy in our provinces and colonies, and the territories depending thereon, and maritime parts of the same and adjoining to them whatsoever, according to the ordinances and statutes of our High Court of Admiralty in England.

§ 126. "And we do hereby remit and grant unto you, the aforesaid A. B., our power and authority in and throughout our provinces and colonies, aforementioned, and the territories depending thereon, and maritime parts whatsoever of the same and thereto adjacent, and also throughout all and every the sea shores, public streams, ports, fresh water rivers, creeks, and arms, as well of the sea as of the rivers and coasts whatsoever of our said provinces and colonies, and the territories depending thereon, and maritime parts whatsoever of the same and thereto adjacent, as well within liberties and franchises as without.

"To take cognizance of, and proceed in, all civil and maritime causes, and in complaints, contracts, offences, or suspected offences, crimes, pleas, debts, exchanges, accounts, charter-parties, agreements, suits, trespasses, injuries, extortions, and demands, and business civil and maritime whatsoever, commenced or to be commenced between merchants, or between owners and proprietors of ships and other vessels, and merchants or others whomsoever, with such owners and proprietors of ships and all other vessels whatsoever, employed or used within the maritime jurisdiction of our vice-admiralty of our said provinces and colonies, and the territories depending thereon, or between any other persons whomsoever, had, made, begun, or contracted for any matter, thing, cause, or business whatsoever, done or to be done within our maritime jurisdiction aforesaid, together with all and singular their incidents, emergencies, dependencies, annexed or connexed causes whatsoever or howsoever, and such causes, complaints, contracts, and other the premises above said, or any of them, which may happen to arise, be contracted, had or done, to hear and determine according to the rights, statutes, laws, ordinances, and customs anciently observed.

§ 127. "And moreover, in all and singular complaints, contracts, agreements, causes, and businesses civil and maritime, to be performed beyond the sea, or contracted there, howsoever arising or happening : and also in all and singular other causes and matters, which in any manner whatsoever touch or any way concern, or anciently have and do, or ought to belong unto the maritime jurisdiction of our aforesaid Vice-Admiralty in our said provinces and colonies, and the territories depending thereon, and maritime parts thereof, and to the same adjoining whatsoever ; and generally, in all and singular all other causes, suits, crimes, offences, excesses, injuries, complaints, misdemeanors, or suspected misdemeanors, trespasses, regrating, forestalling, and maritime businesses whatsoever, throughout the places aforesaid, within the maritime jurisdiction of our Vice-Admiralty of our provinces and colonies aforesaid, and the territories depending thereon by sea or water, on the banks or shores of the same howsoever done, committed, perpretrated, or happening.

§ 128. "And also to inquire by the oaths of honest and lawful

men of our said provinces and colonies, and the territories depending thereon, and maritime parts of the same and adjoining
to them whatsoever, dwelling both within liberties and franchises and without, as well of all and singular such matters
and things, which of right, and by the statutes, laws, ordinances,
and the customs anciently observed were wont and ought to be
inquired after, as of wreck of the sea, and of all and singular
the goods and chattels of whatsoever traitors, pirates, manslayers, and felons, howsoever offending within the maritime jurisdiction of our Vice-Admiralty of our povinces and colonies aforementioned, and the territories depending thereon, and of the
goods, chattels, and debts of all and singular their maintainers,
accessaries, councillors, abettors, or assistants whomsoever.

"And also of the goods, debts, and chattels of whatsoever person or persons, felons of themselves, by what means, or
howsoever coming to their death within our aforesaid maritime
jurisdiction, wheresoever any such goods, debts, and chattels, or
any part thereof, by sea, water, or land in our said provinces
and colonies, and the territories depending thereon, and maritime parts of the same and thereto adjacent whatsoever, as well
within liberties and franchises as without, have been or shall
be found forfeited, or to be forfeited, or in being.

§ 129 "And moreover, as well of the goods, debts, and chattels, of whatsoever other traitors, felons, and manslayers wheresoever offending, and of the goods, debts, and chattels of their
maintainers, accessaries, counsellors, abettors, or assistants, as
of the goods, debts, or chattels of all fugitives, persons convicted,
attainted, condemned, outlawed, or howsoever put or to be put
in exigent for treason, felony, manslaughter, or murder, or any
other offence or crime whatsoever; and also concerning goods
waived, flotson, jetson, lagon, shares and treasure found or to be
found; deodands, and of the goods of all others whatsoever
taken or to be taken, as derelict, or by chance found, or howsoever due or to be due; and of all other casualties, as well in,
upon, or by the sea and shores, creeks or coasts of the sea, or
maritime parts, as in, upon, or by all fresh waters, ports, public
streams, rivers, or creeks, or places overflown whatsoever, within the ebbing and flowing of the sea or high water, or upon the

shores and banks of any of the same within our maritime jurisdiction aforesaid, howsoever, whensoever, or by what means soever arising, happening or proceeding, or wheresoever such goods, debts, and chattels, or other the premises, or any parcel thereof may or shall happen to be met with, or found within our maritime jurisdiction aforesaid.

"And also concerning anchorage, lastage, and ballast of ships, and of fishes royal, namely sturgeons, whales, porpoises, dolphins, kiggs, and grampusses, and general of all other fishes whatsoever, which are of a great or very large bulk or fatness, anciently by right or custom, or any way appertaining or belonging to us.

§ 130. "And to ask, require, levy, take, collect, receive, and obtain for the use of us, and to the office of our High Admiral of Great Britain aforesaid for the time being, to keep and preserve the said wreck of the sea, and the goods, debts, and chattels of all and singular other the premises.

"Together with all and all manner of fines, mulcts, issues, forfeitures, amerciaments, ransoms, and recognizances, whatsoever forfeited or to be forfeited, and pecuniary punishments for trespasses, crimes, injuries, extortions. contempts, and other misdemeanors whatsoever, howsoever imposed or inflicted, or to be imposed or inflicted for any matter, cause, or thing whatsoever in our said provinces and colonies, and the territories depending thereon, and maritime parts of the same and thereto adjoining, in any Court of our Admiralty there held or to be held, presented or to be presented, assessed, brought, forfeited, or adjudged ; and also all amerciaments, issues, fines, perquisites, mulcts, and pecuniary punishments whatsoever, and forfeitures of all manner of recognizances, before you or your lieutenant, deputy or deputies in our said provinces and colonies, and the territories depending thereon, and maritime parts of the same and thereto adjacent whatsoever, happening or imposed, or to be imposed or inflicted, or by any means assessed, presented, forfeited, or adjudged, or howsoever by reason of the premises, due or to be due in that behalf to us, or to our heirs and successors.

§ 131. "And further to take all manner of recognizances, cautions, obligations, and stipulations, as well to our use as at the instance of any parties, for agreements or debts, or other causes whatsoever, and to put the same into execution, and to cause and command them to be executed; and also to arrest, and cause and command to be arrested, according to the civil and maritime laws, and ancient customs of our said court, all ships, persons, things, goods, wares and merchandizes, for the premises and every of them, and for other causes whatsoever concerning the same, wheresoever they shall be met with, or found throughout our said provinces and colonies, and the territories depending thereon, and maritime parts thereof and thereto adjoining, as well within liberties and franchises as without; and likewise for all other agreements, causes or debts, howsoever contracted or arising, so that the goods or persons may be found within our jurisdiction aforesaid.

§ 132. "And to hear, examine, discuss, and finally determine the same, with their emergencies, dependencies, incidents, annexed and connexed causes and businesses whatsoever; together with all other causes, civil and maritime, and complaints, contracts, and all and every the respective premises whatsoever above expressed, according to the laws and customs aforesaid, and by all other lawful usage, means and methods, according to the best of your skill and knowledge.

"And to compel all manner of persons in that behalf, as the case shall require, to appear and to answer, with power of using any temporal correction, and of inflicting any other penalty or mulct, according to the laws and customs aforesaid.

"And to do and administer justice, according to the right order and cause of law, summarily and plainly, looking only into the truth of the facts.

§ 133. "And to fine, correct, punish, chastise, reform, and to imprison, and cause and command to be imprisoned in any gaols, being within our provinces and colonies, aforesaid, and the territories depending thereon, the parties guilty, and the contemners of the law and jurisdiction of our Admiralty aforesaid, and violators, usurpers, delinquents and contumacious absenters, masters of ships, mariners, rowers, fishermen, shipwrights, and other workmen and artificers whatsoever exercising any kind of maritime affairs, according to the rights, statutes, laws and ordinances, and customs anciently observed; and to deliver and absolutely discharge, and cause and command to be discharged, whatsoever persons imprisoned in such cases, who are to be delivered.

§ 134. "And to preserve, or cause to be preserved, the public streams, ports, rivers, fresh waters and creeks whatsoever within our maritime jurisdiction aforesaid, in what place soever they be in our provinces and colonies aforesaid, and the territories depending thereon, and maritime parts of the same and thereto adjacent whatsoever, as well for the preservation of our navy royal, and of the fleets and vessels of our kingdom and dominions aforesaid, as of whatsoever fishes increasing in the rivers and places aforesaid.

"And also to keep, and cause to be executed and kept, in our said provinces and colonies, and the territories depending thereon, and maritime parts thereof and thereto adjacent whatsoever, the rights, statutes, laws, ordinances and customs anciently observed.

"And to do, exercise, expedite, and execute all and singular other things in the premises, and every of them, as they by right, and according to the laws and statutes, ordinances and customs aforesaid should be done.

§ 135. "And moreover to reform nets too close, and other unlawful engines or instruments wheresoever for the catching of fishes whatsoever, by sea or public streams, ports, rivers, fresh waters or creeks whatsoever, throughout our provinces and colonies aforesaid, and the territories depending thereon, and maritime parts of the same and thereto adjacent, used or exercised, within our maritime jurisdiction aforesaid wheresoever.

"And to punish and correct the exercisers and occupiers thereof, according to the statutes, laws, ordinances and customs aforesaid.

§ 136. "And to pronounce, promulge and interpose all manner of sentences and decrees, and to put the same in execution;

10

with cognizance and jurisdiction of whatsoever other cause s, civil and maritime, which relate to the sea, or which any manner of ways respect or concern the sea, or passage over the same, or naval or maritime voyages, or our said maritime jurisdiction, or the places or limits of our said Admiralty and cognizance aforementioned, and all other things done or to be done.

"With power also to proceed in the same, according to the statutes, laws, ordinances and customs aforesaid, anciently used, as well of mere office mixed or promoted, as at the instance of any party, as the case shall require and seem convenient.

§ 137. "And likewise with cognizance and decision of wreck of the sea, and of the death, drowning, and view of dead bodies of all persons howsoever killed or drowned, or murdered, or which shall happen to be killed, drowned, or murdered, or by any other means come to their death, in the sea, or public streams, ports, fresh waters, or creeks whatsoever, within the flowing of the sea and high water mark, throughout our aforesaid provinces and colonies, and the territories depending thereon, and maritime parts of the same, and thereto adjacent, or elsewhere within our maritime jurisdiction aforesaid.

"Together with the cognizance of Mayhem in the aforesaid places, within our maritime jurisdiction aforesaid, and flowing of the sea and water there happening; with power also of punishing all delinquents in that kind, according to the exigencies of the law and customs aforesaid.

"And to do, exercise, expedite, and execute all and singular other things, which in and about the premises only shall be necessary or thought meet, according to the rights, statutes, laws, ordinances and customs aforesaid.

§ 138. "With power of deputing and surrogating in your place for the premises, one or more deputy, or deputies, as often as you shall think fit; and also with power from time to time of naming, appointing, ordaining, assigning, making, and constituting whatsoever other necessary, fit, and convenient officers and ministers under you, for the said office, and execution thereof in our said provinces and colonies, and the territories depending thereon, and maritime parts of the same, and thereto adjacent whatsoever.

§ 139. "Saving always the right of our High Court of Admiralty of England, and also of the Judge and Register of the said Court, from whom or either of them, it is not our intention in any thing to derogate by these presents ; and saving to every one who shall be wronged or grieved by any definitive sentence or interlocutory decree, which shall be given in the Vice-Admiralty Court of our provinces and colonies aforesaid, and the territories depending thereon, the right of appealing to our aforesaid High Court of Admiralty of England.

§ 140. "Provided nevertheless, and under this express condition, that if you, the aforesaid A. B. our Captain General and Governer in Chief, shall not yearly, to wit, at the end of every year, between the feast of Saint Michael the Archangel and All Saints duly certify, and cause to be effectually certified (if you shall be thereunto required) to us, and our Lieutenant Official, Principals, and Commissary-General and Special, and Judge and President of the High Court of our Admiralty of England aforesaid, all that which from time to time, by virtue of these presents, you shall do and execute, collect, or receive in the premises, or any of them, together with your full and faithful account thereupon, to be made in an authentic form, and sealed with the Seal of our Office, remaining in your custody, that from thence, and after default therein, these our Letters Patent of the Office of Vice-Admiralty aforesaid, as above granted, shall be null and void, and of no force or effect.

§ 141. "Further we do, in our name, command all and singular our Governors, Justices, Mayors, Sheriffs, Captains, Marshals, Bailiffs, Keepers of all our Gaols and Prisons, Constables, and all other our Officers and faithful liege subjects whatsoever, and every of them, as well within liberties, and franchises as without, that in and about the execution of the premises, and every of them, they be aiding, favouring, assisting, submissive, and yield obedience, in all things as is fitting to you, the aforesaid A. B. our Captain-General and Governor in Chief of our provinces and colonies aforesaid, and to your Deputy whomsoever, and to all other Officers by you appointed, and to be appointed, of our said Vice Admiralty aforesaid, and the territories depending thereon, and maritime parts of the same, and thereto adjoining, under pain of the law, and the peril which will fall thereon.

> " Given at London, in the High Court of our Admiralty,
> of England aforesaid, under the Great Seal there-
> of, this 3d day of October, 1701."

§ 142. There was, next, the commission or letters patent to the Governor and principal officers, under the act of 11th and 12th Wm. III., for the more effectual suppression of piracy.(a) This authorized the creating or assembling, whenever occasion might require, Admiralty Courts for the trial of piracies, felonies, and robberies committed on the sea, or within any harbor, river, creek or place, where the Admiral had power, authority, and jurisdiction, according to the civil law and the course of the Admiralty. The commission to Governor Bellamont was as follows :

General Admiralty Commission.

§ 143. " William the Third, by the grace of God of England, Scotland, France, and Ireland, King, Defender of the Faith, &c., To our Right trusty and right well beloved cousin Richard, Earle of Bellamont, our Capt. Genl. and Govr. in Chief of our province of New York, and Territories depending thereon, in America ; and to the Governor or Commander in Chief of the said province of New York for the time being : To our Trusty and well beloved John Nanfan, Esquire, our Lieut. Govr. of the said province of New Yorke, and to our Lieut. Govr. of the said province for the time being : To our Trusty and well beloved, the Govr. of our Collony of Connecticut for the time being : To our Vice Admirall or Vice Admiralls of our Province of New Yorke, East and West New Jersey, and Connecticut, now and for the time being : To our Trusty and

---

(a) 6 Evan's Stat. 126.   Stokes' Colonies, 231, 4.

well beloved Stephen Cortland, Wm. Smith, Peter Schuyler, John Young, James Graham, Abraham DePeyster, Robt. Livingston, Sam'l. Staats, John Carbell, and Robert Walters, Esqs., members of our council in the said province of New Yorke, during their continuance in our said council, and to the members of our council in the said Island for the time being : To our Chief Justice of our province of New York, now and for the time being : To our Judge or Judges of the Vice Admiralty in the said province of New Yorke, East and West New Jersey and Connecticut, now and for the time being : To our trusty and well beloved, the Captains and Commanders of our ships of Warr within the Admiralty Jurisdiction of the said provinces of New York, East and West New Jersey, and Connecticut, now and for the time being : To our Trusty and well beloved, our Secretary of the said province of New York, now and for the time being : To our Trusty and well beloved Thomas Weaver, Esquire, Receiver of our Revenue of our said province of New Yorke, and to the receiver of our revenue in the said province for the time being : To our Trusty and well beloved Patrick Mayne and Edward Randolph, Esqrs., Surveyors Genl. of our Customs in America, and to the Surveyors Genl. of our Customs in America for the time being : To our Trusty and well beloved, the Collectors of our plantation duties in the said provinces of New York, East and West New Jersey, and Connecticut, appointed in pursuance of an act made in the Twenty-fifth year of the reign of our Royal Uncle, King Charles the Second, for the better securing the plantation trade, now and for the time being : and to our trusty and well beloved George Larbin, Esquire, Greeting :

§ 144. " Whereas, by an act passed last session of parliament, entitled an act for the more effectual suppressing of pyracy, it is, amongst other things, enacted, that all piracies, fellonies and roberies, committed in or upon the sea, or in any haven, river, creek, or place where the Admiral or Admiralls have power, authority or jurisdiction, may be examined, enquired of, tryed, heard, and determined and adjudged, according to the directions of the said act, in any place at sea, or upon the land, in any of our Islands, plantations, Colonies, Dominions, forts or factories, to be appointed for that purpose by our Commission or Commissions, under the great seal of England, or the seal of the Admiralty of England, directed to all or any of the Admirals, Vice Admirals, Rear Admirals, Judges of Vice Admirals, or Commanders of any of our Ships of War; and also to all or any such person or persons, officer or officers, by name, or for the time being, as we should think fit to appoint, which said Commissioners shall have full power, jointly or severally, by warrant under the hand and seal of them, or any of them, to commit to safe custody any person or persons against whom Information of pyracy, Robery, or felony upon the sea, shall be given upon oath; and to call and assemble a Court of Admiralty on Ship board, or upon the land, when, and as often as occasion shall require, which Court shall consist of seven persons, at least. And it is further enacted, that if so many of the persons aforesaid cannot conveniently be assembled, any three of the aforesaid persons, whereof the President or Chief of some English factory, or the Govr., Lieut. Govr., or member of our Council, in any of the plantations or colonies aforesaid, or Commanders of some of our Ships, is always to be one, shall have full power and authority, by virtue of the said act, to call and assemble any other persons on Ship board, or upon the land, to make up the number of seven. And it is provided, that no persons but such as are known merchants, factors, or planters, or such as the Captains, Lieuts., or warrant officers, in any of our Ships war, or Captains, Masters or Mates, of some English Ship, shall be capable of being so called, and sitting and voting in the said Court.(a)

§ 145. "And it is further enacted, that such persons, called and assembled as aforesaid, shall have full power and authority, according to the course of the Admiralty, to issue warrants for bringing any persons accused of pyracy or Robery before them, to be tryed, heard, and adjudged, and to summon witnesses, and to take informations and Examinations of witnesses upon their oath, and to do all things necessary for the hearing and

---

(a) 6 Evan's Stat. 126.

final determination of any case of pyracy, robery and felony, and to give Sentence and Judgment of death, and to award execution of the offenders convicted and attainted as aforesaid, according to the will, acts, and the methods and rules of the Admiralty ; and that all and every person and persons so convicted and attainted of pyracy and robery, shall have and suffer such losses of lands, goods, and chattels, as if they had been attainted and convicted of any pyracies, felonies and roberies, according to a statute made in the 28th year of the reign of King Henry the Eighth, for tryalls of pyracies or Roberies upon the high sea.

§ 146. "Now Know Ye, that we, in pursuance of the said act of our special grace, certain knowledge and mere motion, have made, constituted and appointed, and by these presents do make, constitute and appoint you, the said Richard, Earl of Bellamont, and the Govr. or Commander in Chief of the said province of New York for the time being ; John Nanfan, and the Lieut. Govr. of the said province for the time being ; the Govr. of our Collony of Connecticut for the time being ; the Vice Admiral or Vice Admirals of our said province of New Yorke, East and West New Jersey, and Connecticut, for the time now, and for the time being ; Stephen Cortland, William Smith, Peter Schuyler, John Young, James Graham, A. Depyster, Robert Livingston, Saml. Staats, John Carbill, and Robert Walters, members of our Council in the said province of New Yorke, during their continuance in the said Council, and the members of our Council in the said province for the time being ; our Chief Justice in our said province of New York for the time being ; our Judge or Judges of the Vice Admiralty in the said provinces of New Yorke, East and West New Jersey and Connecticut, now and for the time being ; the Capt. and Commander of our Ships of War within the Admiralty Jurisdiction of the said provinces of New Yorke, East and West New Jerseys and Connecticut, now and for the time being ; the Secretary of the said province of New Yorke, now and for the time being ; Thomas Weaver, and the receiver of our revenue of the province of New York for the time being ; Patrick Mayne and Edward Randolph, and the Surveyor General of our Customs in America for the time

being ; our Collectors of our plantation duties in the said provinces of New York, and East and West New Jerseys and
Connecticut, for the time being, and George Larbin, to be our
Commissioners at the said several provinces of New York, East
and West New Jersey, and Connecticut, for the examining,
enquiring of, trying, hearing, and determining and adjudging,
according to the directions of the said act, in any place at sea,
or upon the land, at the said provinces of New York, East and
West New Jerseys, and Connecticut, all pyracies, fellonies, and
roberies, committed, or which shall be committed, in or upon
the sea, or within any haven, river, creek, or place where the
Admiral or Admirals have power, authority, or jurisdiction.
And you, the said Richard, Earl of Bellamont, and the Govr.
or Commander in Chief of the said province of New York for
the time being ; John Nanfan, and the Lieut. Govr. or Com-
mander in Chief of the said province for the time being ; the
Govr. of our Collony of Connecticut for the time being ; the
Vice Admiral or Vice Admirals of our said provinces of New
Yorke, East and West New Jersey, and Connecticut, now, and
for the time being ; Stephen Cortland, William Smith, Peter
Schuyler, John Young, James Graham, Abraham Depyster,
Robt. Livingston, Samuel Staats, John Carbill, and Robert
Walters, members of our Council in the said province, during
their continuance in the said Council, and the members of our
said Council in the said province for the time being ; our Chief
Justice in our said province of New York for the time being ;
our Judge or Judges of the Vice Admiralty in the said provinces
of New York, East and West New Jersey and Connecticut,
now and for the time being ; the Captains and Commanders of
our Shipps of War within the Admiralty Jurisdiction of the
said provinces of New York, East and West New Jerseys and
Connecticut, now and for the time being ; the Secretary of the
said province of New Yorke, now and for the time being ;
Thomas Weaver, and the receiver of our revenue of our said
province of New York for the time being ; Patrick Mayne and
Edward Randolph, and the Surveyors Genl. of our Customes
in America ; our Collectors of our plantation duties in the said
provinces of New Yorke, East and West New Jersey and Connecticut, for the time being ; George Larbin, our Commissioners

at the said provinces of New York, East and West New Jersey and Connecticut, for the purposes herein above mentioned ; we do make, ordain and constitute, by these presents :

§ 147. "Hereby giving and granting unto you, our said Commissioners, jointly or severally, or any one of you, by warrant under the hand and seal of you, or any one of you, full power and authority to committ to safe custody any person or persons against whom Information of pyracy, robery, or felony upon the sea, shall be given upon oath, which oath you, or any one of you, shall have full power, and are hereby required to administer to all, and assemble a Court of Admiralty on Ship board, or upon the land, when, and as often as occasion shall require, (which Court, our will and pleasure is,) shall consist of seven persons at the least, and if so many of you, our said Commissioners, cannot conveniently be assembled, any three or more of you, whereof you, the said Richard, Earl of Bellamont, or the Govr. or Commander in Chief of New Yorke, East and West New Jersey, or Connecticut, or either of the said places for the time being, always to be one, shall have full power and authority, by virtue of the said act and of these persons, to call and assemble any other persons on ship board, or upon the land, to make up the number of seven ; provided, that no persons but such as are known merchants, factors, or persons, or such as are Captains, Lieutenants, or warrant officers in any of our ships of war, Captains, Masters or Mates, of some English Ships, shall be capable of being so called, sitting and voting in the said court.

§ 148. "And our further will and pleasure is, and we do hereby expressly declare and command, that such persons, called and assembled as aforesaid, shall have full power and authority, according to the course of the Admiralty, to issue warrants for bringing any persons accused of pyracy or robery before them, to be tried, heard, and adjudged, and to summon witnesses, and to take informations and examinations of witnesses upon their oath, and to do all things necessary for the hearing and final determination of any case of pyracy, robery, or felony upon the sea, and to give sentence and judgment of death, and to award execution of the offenders, convicted and attainted as aforesaid, according to the civil laws and the methods and rules of the Admiralty; and that all and every person or persons so convicted or attainted of pyracies and robery, shall have and suffer such losses of lands, goods, and chattels, as if they had been attainted and convicted of any pyracies, felonies and roberies, according to the aforementioned statute made in the reign of King Henry the Eighth.

§ 149. "And our express will and pleasure is, and we do hereby direct and command, that so soon as any Court shall be assembled as aforesaid, either on ship board, or upon the land, this our commission shall first be openly read, and the said Court, then and there, shall be solemnly called and proclaimed, and then you, the said Richard, Earl of Bellamont, or the Govr. or Commander in Chief of New Yorke, East and West New Jersey or Connecticut, or either of the said places for the time being—shall, in the first place, publicly in open Court, take the oath appointed in the said act; and you, the said Richard, Earl of Bellamont, or the Govr. or Commander in Chief of New Yorke, East and West New Jersey or Connecticut, or either of the said places for the time being, having taken the oath in manner and form aforesaid, shall individually administer the same to every person who shall sit and have and give a voice in the said Court, upon the trial of such prisoner or prisoners as aforesaid. And lastly, we do hereby direct, impower and require you, our said Commissioners, to proceed, act, adjudge and determine in all things according to your powers, authority and directions of the above recited act, and of these presents; and the entry or enrollment thereof, shall be unto you, and each and every of you, for so doing, a sufficient warrant and discharge.

"In witness whereof, we have caused these our letters to be made patent. Witness ourself, at Westminster, the 23d day of November, in the twelfth year of our reign."

§ 150. The Commissions to the Judges of the Vice-Admiralty Courts, were equally full and explicit in their grant of jurisdiction, and it was under these commissions that the judicial powers of the Admiralty, in civil causes, were actually administered in the Colonies, from the beginning to the time of our Revolution.

The commission to Hon. Richard Morris, is dated 15th Oct. 1762, was as follows :

Commission of the Vice Admiralty Judge.

Letters patent granted to Richard Morris, Esq., for the office of Judge of the respective Courts of the Provinces and Colonys of New York, Connecticut, and East and West Jerseys, in America.

§ 151. "George the Third, by the grace of God, of Great Britain, France and Ireland, King, defender of the faith : To our beloved Richard Morris, Esquire, greeting : We do by these presents, make, ordain, nominate and appoint you, the said Richard Morris, Esquire, to be our Commissary in our provinces and colonies of New York, Connecticut, and East and West Jerseys, in America, and Territories thereunto belonging, in the room of the former judge, deceased, hereby granting unto you full power to take cognizance of, and proceed in all causes civil and maritime, and in complaints, contracts, offences, or suspected offences, crimes, pleas, debts, exchanges, policies of assurance, accounts, charter parties, agreements, bills of loading of ships, and all matters and contracts which, in any manner whatsoever, relate to freight due for ships, hired and let out, transport money or maritime usury, (otherwise bottomry,) or which do any ways concern suits, trespasses, injuries, extortions, demands, and affairs civil and maritime whatsoever, between merchants or between owners and proprietors of ships or other vessels and merchants, or other persons whomsoever, with such owners and proprietors of ships or other vessels whatsoever, employed or used, or between any other persons howsoever had, made, began, or contracted for any matter, cause or thing, business or injury whatsoever, done or to be done as well in, upon, or by the sea or public streams or fresh waters, ports, rivers, creeks, and places overflowed whatsoever; within the ebbing and flowing of the sea or high water mark, as upon any of the shores or banks adjoining to them or either of them, together with all and singular, their incidents, emergencies, dependencies annexed and connexed causes whatsover; and such causes, complaints, contracts and other the premises aforesaid, or any of them, howsoever the same may happen to arise, be contracted, had, or done, to hear and determine (according to the civil and maritime laws and customs of the High Court of Admiralty in England) in our said provinces and colonies of New York, Connecticut, and East and West Jerseys, in America, and territories thereunto belonging whatsoever, and also with power to sit and hold courts in any cities, towns, and places in our provinces and colonys of New York, Connecticut, and East and West Jerseys, in America aforesaid, for the having and determining of all such causes and businesses, together with all and singular, their incidents, emergencies, dependencies annexed and connexed causes whatsoever, and to proceed judicially and according to law, in administering justice therein.

§ 152. "And moreover, to compel witnesses, in case they withdraw themselves for interest, fear, favour, or ill-will, or any other cause whatsoever, to give evidence to the truth in all and every the causes above-mentioned, according to the exigencies of the law. And further, to take all manner of recognizances, cautions, obligations and stipulations, as well to our use, as at the instance of any parties for agreements or debts and other causes and businesses whatsoever, and to put the same in execution, and to cause and command them to be executed. Also, duly to search and enquire of and concerning all goods of traitors, pirates, manslayers, felons, fugitives and felons of themselves, and concerning the bodies of persons drowned, killed, or by any other means coming to their death in the sea, or in any ports, rivers, public streams, or creeks and places overflowed; and also concerning mayhem happening in the aforesaid places, and engines, toils and nets prohibited and unlawful, and the occupiers thereof. And moreover, concerning fishes royal, namely, whales, kiggs, grampusses, dolphins, sturgeons, and all other fishes whatsoever, which are of a great or very large bulk or fatness, by right or custom any ways used, belonging to us and to the office of our High Admiral of England.

§ 153. " And also of and concerning all casualties at sea, goods wrecked, flotzon, jetson, lagon, shares, things cast overboard and wreck of the sea, and all goods taken or to be taken as derelict, or by chance found or to be found ; and all other trespasses, misdemeanors, offences, enormities and maritime crimes whatsoever, done and committed or to be done and committed as well in and upon the high seas, as all ports, rivers, fresh waters, and creeks and shores of the sea to high water mark, from all first bridges towards the sea, in and throughout our said provinces and colonies of New York, Connecticut, and East and West Jerseys, in America, and maritime coasts thereunto belonging, howsoever, whensover, or by what means soever arising or happening.

§ 154. " And all such things as are discovered and found out, as also all fines, mulcts, amersements and compositions due and to be due in that behalf ; to tax, moderate, demand, collect and levy, and to cause the same to be demanded, levied, and collected, and according to law to compel and command them to be paid.

§ 155. " And also to proceed in all and every the causes and businesses above recited, and in all other contracts, causes, contempts and offences whatsoever, howsoever contracted or arising, (so that the goods or persons of the debtors may be found within the jurisdiction of the Vice-Admiralty in our provinces and colonys of New York, Connecticut, and East and West Jerseys, in America aforesaid,) according to the civil and maritime laws and customs of our said High Court of Admiralty of England, anciently used, and by all other lawful ways, means, and methods, according to the best of your skill and knowledge. And all such causes and contracts to hear, examine, discuss, and finally determine, saving, nevertheless, the right of appealing to our aforesaid High Court of Admiralty of England, and to the Judge or President of the said Court for the time being. And saving also the right of our said High Court of Admiralty of England, and also of the Judge and Register of the same Court, from whom, or either of them, it is not our intention in any thing to derogate by these presents.

§ 156. "And also to arrest, and cause and command to be arrested, all ships, persons, things, goods, wares and merchandizes for the premises, and every of them, and for other causes whatsoever, concerning the same, wheresoever they shall be met with or found within our provinces and colonys of New York, Connecticut, and East and West Jerseys, in America aforesaid, and territories thereof, either within liberties or without, and to compel all manner of persons in that behalf, as the case shall require, to appear and to answer with power of using any temporal coercion, and of inflicting any other penalty or mulct according to the laws and customs aforesaid ; and to do and minister justice according to the right order and course of the law, summarily and plainly, looking only into the truth of the fact.

§ 157. "And we impower you in this behalf, to fine, correct, punish, chastise, and reform, and imprison, and cause and command to be imprisoned, in any gaols, being within our provinces and colonys of New York, Connecticut, and East and West Jerseys, in America aforesaid, and maritime places of the same, the parties guilty and violators of the law and jurisdiction of our admiralty aforesaid, and usurpers, delinquents, and contumacious absentees, masters of ships, mariners, rowers, fishermen, shipwrights, and all other workmen and artificers whomsoever, exercising any kind of maritime affairs, as well according to the aforementioned civil and maritime laws and ordinances and customs aforesaid, and their demerits, as according to the statutes and ordinances aforesaid, and those of our kingdom of Great Britain, for the Admiralty of England, in that behalf made and provided.

§ 158. "And to deliver and absolutely discharge, and cause and command to be discharged, whatsoever persons imprisoned in such cases, who are to be delivered and to promulge and interpose all manner of sentences and decrees, and to put the same in execution with cognizance and jurisdiction of whatsoever other causes, civil and maritime, which relate to the sea, and which any manner of ways respect or concern the sea or passage over the same, or naval or maritime voyages performed, or to be performed, or the maritime jurisdiction above said, with power also to proceed in the same according to the civil and maritime laws and customs of our aforesaid Court, anciently used, as well those of mere office mixt or promoted, as at the instance of any party, as the case shall require and seem convenient.

§ 159. "And we do by these presents, (which are to continue during our royal will and pleasure only,) further give and grant unto you, Richard Morris, Esquire, our said Commissary, the power of taking and receiving all and every, the wages, fees, profits, advantages and commodities whatsoever, in any manner due and anciently belonging to the said office, according to the custom of our High Court of Admiralty of England, committing unto you our power and authority concerning all and singular, the premises in the several places above expressed, (saving in all things the prerogative of our High Court of Admiralty of England aforesaid,) together with power of deputing and surrogating in your place for and concerning the premises, one or more deputy or deputies, as often as you shall think fit.

§ 160. "Further, we do in our name command, and firmly and strictly charge, all and singular, our Governors, Commanders, Justices of the Peace, Mayors, Sheriffs, Marshals, Keepers of all our Gaols and Prisons, Bailiffs, Constables, and all other our officers and ministers and faithful liege subjects, in and throughout our aforesaid provinces and colonies of New York, Connecticut, and East and West Jerseys, in America, and the territories thereunto belonging; that in the execution of this our commission, they be from time to time aiding, assisting, and yield obedience in all things, as is fitting unto you and your deputy whomsoever, under pain of the law and the peril which will fall thereon. Given at London, in the High Court of our Admiralty aforesaid, under the great seal thereof, the sixteenth day of October, in the year of our Lord, one thousand seven hundred and sixty-two, and of our reign the second."

His predecessor, Hon. Lewis Morris, held the office from 1738, under a commission in the same words—and these commissions were translations of the commissions of the Hon. Roger Mompesson and the Hon. Francis Harrison, who had previously filled this office—and they embraced the colonies from Delaware to Massachusetts inclusive.(*a*)

§ 161. In these commissions and letters patent were found the source, extent, and definition of the admiralty and maritime jurisdiction in the colonies. I am not aware, that up to the Revolution, any British statute in relation to the admiralty jurisdiction named the colonies; and, the well known principles that statutes do not bind the colonies unless they are named, and that the King's commission runs through his whole dominions, are sufficient to make these commissions the legitimate source and law of the admiralty jurisdiction in the colonies. They declare that jurisdiction to extend to all causes, civil and maritime, embracing charter parties, bills of lading, policies of assurance, accounts, debts, exchanges, agreements, complaints, offences, and all matters which in any manner whatsoever relate to freight, transport money, maritime loans, bottomry, trespasses, injuries, extortions, demands, and affairs whatsoever, civil and maritime. These

---

(*a*) A memorandum of such other Commissions as I have seen, is here inserted, to show their territorial extent. They are to be found in the office of the Secretary of State of New York.

James, Duke of York, &c., to Thomas Dongan, Commission as Governor of New York and the Islands, dated September 30, 1682. His Commission, as Vice-Admiral for the same, is dated October 3, 1682.

James II, to Edmund Andross, Commission as Governor of New York and New England, April 7, 1688.

William and Mary, to Henry Sloughter, Commission as Governor, dated January 4th, 1689.

The same to Benj. Fletcher, Commission as Vice-Admiral of New York, East and West New Jersey, New Castle and dependencies, dated 1693.

William III, to the Earl of Bellamont, Commission of Vice-Admiral of New York, Massachusetts Bay, New Hampshire and dependencies, 1698.

Commission of Roger Mompesson, Judge of the Court of Vice-Admiralty in Massachusetts Bay, New Hampshire, Connecticut, Rhode Island, the Jerseys, New York and Pennsylvania, and dependencies, April 1, 1703.

George I., to Francis Harrison, Commission as Judge of the Court of Vice-Admiralty of New York, 13th February, 1721.

George II., to Lewis Morris, Commission as Judge of the Vice-Admiralty Courts of New York, Connecticut, and East and West Jerseys, 16th January, 1738.

general words are of the most comprehensive character, and include all matters which are in their nature maritime, while all those causes whose jurisdiction have been denied to the English Admiralty are especially enumerated as admiralty and maritime causes.(*a*)

§ 162. When we look, also, to the extent of this jurisdiction, so far as place is concerned, we find it equally extensive, extending to every thing done in, upon, or by the sea, or public streams, or fresh waters, ports, rivers, creeks, and places overflown whatsoever, within the ebbing and flowing of the sea, or high water mark, from all first bridges towards the sea.(*b*)

§ 163. So far as persons are concerned, it is also equally extensive, embracing all demands and affairs between merchants, or merchants and owners of ships or other vessels, and other persons whomsoever, for any matter, cause or thing, business, or injury whatsoever, done as well in, upon, or by the sea, or public streams, or fresh water, ports, rivers, creeks, and places overflowed whatsoever, within the ebbing and flowing of the sea, or high water mark, as upon any of the shores or banks adjoining to them. This plainly embraces all classes of persons having any relation to maritime transactions—those who build and furnish vessels—those who equip, man and supply them—those who load and unload them—those who freight them—those who are employed in their service, to navigate or to preserve them, or to perform the various functions necessary or convenient to be performed to enable the vessel in the best manner to answer the purposes to which she is devoted; and also those who injure her, or violate their duty or obligations to her;—a jurisdiction, to all intents and purposes, equal to that claimed by the Admiralty, and set forth in so much detail by Dr. Godolphin. Indeed, it is not possible for the English language to make the grant clearer, or broader, or stronger.(*c*)

§ 164. And these commissions were issued and acted under,

(*a*) Ante, § 48–50, 126, 127, 151, 158.   1 Black. Com. 106, 107, 108.
(*b*) Ante, §§ 26, 51, 158.   (*c*) §§ 126, 151, 158, 104–107.

in their widest interpretation, during all the period of colonial government, here and elsewhere. The actual business of the Vice-Admiralty Courts, as shown by their records, up to the time of the Revolution, shows that this extended jurisdiction, was not dormant but active.(*a*)

§ 165. It has indeed been said, that this extensive jurisdiction of the Admiralty in the Colonies was the subject of complaint at the time of the Revolution ; and it is undoubtedly true, that the extension of the Admiralty jurisdiction, beyond its ancient limits, was in some petitions and public documents stated, as one of the grievances of the colonies. The difficulty with the mother country, grew out of the imposition of taxes, and the collection of revenue ; and the whole of that jurisdiction was given to the Admiralty, as was also trespass on the King's lands, and other matters which were peculiarly offensive. " It was ordained," says the old Congress in their list of grievances, " that whenever offences should be committed in the colonies, against particular acts imposing duties and restrictions upon trade, the prosecutor might bring his action for the penalties in the Court of Admiralty." These were in no sense admiralty and maritime cases, and it was this recent extension beyond the ancient limits,—the limits of those commissions—of which the colonists complained, and not the proper exercise of admiralty and maritime jurisdiction which had been practised from the earliest times ; and the fact that the Constitution uses the words *all* cases of admiralty and maritime jurisdiction, taken in connection with those complaints, shows that the convention intended that the word *all* as well as the word *maritime* should have its proper signification.(*b*)

(*a*) Stokes' Const. of the Colonies, 270. Dunlap's Ad. Prac. 35, 37.   5 Mas. R. 472.
(*b*) 5 How. 456. Ibid. 484.

CHAPTER X.

The Jurisdiction of the State Courts of Admiralty.

§ 166. At the time of the Revolution, as has been before re-marked, each state became an independent nation, clothed with all the powers of sovereignty, including all judicial pow-ers in their greatest plenitude. In some of those in which an Admiralty Court had previously existed, the court was retained, the Judge being appointed by the newly constituted state, by a simple commission, as Judge of the Court of Admiralty. No statute had specified his powers, and his commission was si lent on the subject. He was appointed to exercise the same powers as the colonial courts had exercised. Such were Mas-sachusetts and New York. In some of the states, as in New York, the statute 15 Ric. 2, was enacted, and in others the juris-diction remained unchanged. Thus in different States, the constitutions of the Admiralty Courts and the limits of the Ad-miralty Jurisdiction were widely different, and in some of the States the court was abolished altogether ; and in others new courts were established with powers regulated by statute.(*a*)

§ 167. In Pennsylvania, an act for establishing a Court of Admiralty, was passed Sept. 9, 1778, and another for regula-ting and establishing Admiralty Jurisdiction in March, 1780. By this latter act, it was enacted that the Judge should "hold a Court of Admiralty, and therein have cognizance of all con-troversies, suits and pleas of Maritime Jurisdiction, not cogni-zable at the common law, offences and crimes other than con-tempts against said court only excepted, and thereupon shall pass sentence and decree according as the maritime law and the law of nations, and the laws of this commonwealth shall require."

By section 22, it was enacted that " all and every the proceed-ings of the Court of Admiralty of this commonwealth, shall be liable to the prohibition of the Supreme Court of Judicature

---

(*a*) Ante, § 24. 1 Greenl. Laws of N. Y. 11, 18, 150, 152, 338.

in like manner, and with like effect as the prohibition of the
Court of King's Bench in England, in like cases."(a)

§ 168. In New Jersey, an act regulating and establishing
Admiralty Jurisdiction, was passed in 1781, which provided
that the Judge of the Admiralty should " hold a Court of Admiralty, and therein have cognizance in all cases of prize capture and re-capture upon the water from enemies, or by way
of reprisal, or from pirates, and in general of all controversies,
suits and pleas of Maritime Jurisdiction, and thereupon the
said Judge shall pass sentence and decree according to the
maritime law and the law of nations, and the ordinances of the
Honorable, the Congress of the United States of America, and
the laws of this State."

The second section provided that all causes should be tried
by a jury. The 20th section established the same rule as to prohibitions as the Pennsylvania act.(b)

§ 159. In Maryland, a Court of Admiralty was established
in 1776, for the trial of captures and seizures with full power
to take cognizance of all libels on account of such captures and
seizures, and to proceed to a final determination, and decree
thereupon. " * * * The process and proceeding to be as
usual in Courts of Admiralty, but if either party demand a jury
on any material controverted fact," a jury was to be summoned.(c)

§ 170. Virginia passed an act in 1779, as follows :
Be it enacted by the General Assembly, the Court of Admiralty to consist of three Judges, two of whom are declared to be
a sufficent number to constitute a court, " shall have jurisdiction
of all maritime causes except those wherein parties may be accused of capital offences, now depending and hereafter to be
brought before them." It was expressly provided that such
court, was to be " governed in their proceedings and decisions
by the regulations of the Congress of the United States of Amer-

---

(a) Laws of Pennsylvania, 1778.
(b) Laws of New Jersey, 1781.
(c) Laws of Maryland,

ica, by the acts of the General Assembly,—by the *laws of Oleron and the Rhodian and Imperial Laws, so far as they have been heretofore observed in the English Courts of Admiralty, and by the laws of nature and nations,*—a wide and beneficial jurisdiction. No one can fail to observe how distinctly the ancient ordinances and maritime laws, the civil law, and the former practices of the English Admiralty, are adopted instead of the narrow limit observed by the English Admiralty at that time.(*a*)

§ 171. These being the only States whose early statutes were conveniently accessible to me, I have considered these references sufficient fully to establish that diversity which could hardly fail to exist in twelve different nations; which, although friendly and allied, were nevertheless independent of and foreign to each other.

With this diversity existing, it could hardly be contended that the phrase, all cases of admiralty and maritime jurisdiction, was to include only the cases so called in some particular State which was not pointed out, much less to perpetuate in each State its peculiar law of admiralty jurisdiction, thus making diversity instead of uniformity of admiralty jurisdiction, a portion of our organic law; and requiring the constitutional grant to the General Government to receive a different construction in the different States. Such a state of things must have made the judicial system of the United States entirely impracticable. In this view of the State Courts of Admiralty the grant must have been intended to embrace a general maritime jurisdiction.

If all the States, before the adoption of the Constitution, had re-enacted the Statute 15 Rich. 2, it is not perceived how it could have had any influence on the construction of the Constitution. If the States, without exception, had abolished their Courts of Admiralty, and swept away all their admiralty and maritime jurisdiction before the Constitution was framed, such legislation, instead of rendering useless or nugatory the grant in question, would only have rendered it so much the more neces-

---

(*a*) Laws of 1779, chap. 27. 10 Hen. Stat. 98. 5 How. 474. 5 Mas. R. 472. Dunlap's Pr. 36.

sary.   And on the same principle, any modification or limitation
of the state jurisdiction, would have no effect on the construction
of the constitutional grant.   Cases of a certain class would be
none the less maritime cases, and it would be none the less
important that they should be subject to the federal judiciary, to
secure that equal administration of the maritime law, and that
uniformity and nationalty of decision under it, which would
promote the harmony of the commercial world, of which the
States, being foreign to each other and to other nations, were an
important part.   And it would be none the less certain that a
grant to the General Government of jurisdiction in all such cases,
would make them all subjects of national jurisdiction to be distributed to such courts, and proceeded in, *in rem* or *in personam*,
with or without a jury, in such manner as the Congress should
provide.(*a*)

(*a*) 1 Wheat. 324, 5.   5 How. 461.   6 Ibid. 385.

CHAPTER XI.

The Admiralty and Maritime Jurisdiction of France and other portions of Continental Europe.

§ 172. The marine ordinances of France have always been held in deservedly high estimation. Her wisest statesmen and monarchs have all along, through many centuries, given the most profound attention to the subject of maritime law; and, under the administration of Courts of Admiralty, filled by the ablest judges, a system of maritime law has there been built up more perfectly than in any other country; and commentators and jurisconsults of most various learning, and most profound and practical reflection, have been, at the same time, the cause and the effect of this constant attention to the best interests of maritime commerce. The jurisdiction of the French Admiralty has always been of the widest and most salutary character.(a)

§ 173. The judges of the Admiralty shall take cognizance, preferably to all others, and between all persons of whatever quality or condition, even though privileged, French and strangers, as well in demanding as defending, of all that concerns the construction, tackle and furniture, arming, victualling, and manning, sale and adjudication of ships.

We declare them competent judges of all actions, proceeding from charter parties, freighting, bills of lading, freight, engaging and wages of seamen, and victuals furnished to them by order of the master during the manning of ships, together with policies of insurance and obligations of bottomry, and on the return of a voyage, and generally of all contracts concerning the commerce of the sea, notwithstanding all submissions to the contrary.(b)

(a) Ord. de la Marine, tit. 2, arts. 1 to 11.   Merville, Com. 13 to 25.   1 Valin, 112 to 151.   Cleirac, Les Us' et Coutumes de la Mer, Jurisdiction de la Marine, 315 to 501.

(b) This and the following three sections are a translation of the jurisdictional articles of the Ordonnance de la Marine, tit. 2, arts. 1 to 11.

§ 174. They shall likewise take cognizance of prizes taken at sea, wrecks, shipwrecks, and stranded ships, of ejecting and contributing average, and damages happened to ships and their lading, and also of inventories and deliverances of assets left in ships by persons dying at sea.

They shall likewise take cognizance of the dues for licenses, thirds, tenths, sea marks, anchorage and others belonging to the Admiral, and of those which shall be levied or pretended by the lords of manors, or other particular persons near the sea, upon the fisheries or fish, and upon goods or ships going out or coming into port.

The cognizance of fishing in the sea and salt water, and the mouths of rivers, shall likewise belong to them, and likewise that of parks and fisheries ; and they shall also take cognizance of nets and threads, and of the buying and selling of fish upon the shore, or in the boats, ports, or harbors.

§ 175. They shall likewise take cognizance of damages done by ships to the fisheries, either upon the coasts or in navigable rivers, and of those that the ships shall receive, and likewise of the ways appointed for hauling up ships coming from the sea, if there be no regulation, title, or possession to the contrary.

They shall also take cognizance of the damages done to the keys, banks, moles, palisadoes, and other works cast up, against the violence of the sea, and shall take care that the depth of the ports and roads be preserved and kept clean.

They shall take up the bodies of drowned persons, and shall draw up a verbal process of the condition of the corpses found at sea and on the sand, or in the ports, as likewise of the drowning of mariners sailing in navigable rivers.

§ 176. They shall assist at the musters and reviews of the inhabitants of the parishes subject to the sea watch, and shall take cognizance of all differences arising upon that account, and likewise of crimes committed by them that are upon the guard of the coasts, while they are under arms.

They shall also take cognizance of piracies and robberies, and desertions of seamen, and generally of all crimes and offences committed upon the sea or the coasts, and in the ports and harbors.(a)

§ 177. These various codes and systems cannot but have been familiar to the framers of the Constitution, and for the purpose of this treatise, it is not necessary to inquire further into the jurisdiction of the Admirals, or of the Admiralty Courts of the various commercial nations of the world. They will be found to differ considerably in the mere Admiralty law—the maritime regulations of the municipal code. There will be found, also, a great uniformity in their adoption of those principles and rules which constitute the general maritime law. Those which have been referred to, show the same difference in municipal regulation, and the same uniformity in general principles, which would appear on a more extended examination. A brief list of them is here given, for the double purpose of showing the universality of maritime codification in commercial nations, and of directing the student to the numerous and cognate sources of the maritime laws.

§ 178. Some of them are actual legislative enactments, others the ordinances of monarchs, and others are mere compilations, made up of extracts from well known ancient codes and ordinances. Others again, are mere essays and treatises on maritime subjects—which, in consequence of their practical wisdom, have, by long use and authority, came to be considered the highest evidence of marine law,—and others, are the voluntary regulations which persons, interested in shipping, have adopted for their own convenience; and which, in like manner, have ripened into law. They are to be found in the great work of Pardessus, in which he has collected the maritime laws of all commercial nations, and preceded each by a historical notice, valuable for the combined results of thorough historical and antiquarian research, careful and ingenious criticism, and liberal

---

(a) Ord. de la Marine, tit. 2, arts. 1 to 11. In the third part of the Us' et Coutumes de la Mer, Cleirac, in his learned and curious treatise, La Jurisdiction de la Marine ou de l'Admirautie, has extracted and collected the text of the royal ordinances of the Admiralty of France, from the earliest periods. Cleirac, 316.

and generous views of the true end and proper extent of the maritime law.(*a*)

§ 179. *The Maritime Law of the Rhodians.*(*b*)—This is the most ancient code of maritime law. It was promulgated about 900 years before the Christian era, and about seventy years after the time of Solomon. These laws being founded upon natural justice, entered largely into the maritime legislation of all the commercial nations of antiquity of whose laws we have any knowledge. They were generally received in the Mediterranean, and Greece and Rome acknowledged their authority. In the time of Julius Cæsar and of Augustus, the distinguished jurisconsults, O'Libius, Labeo, and Labinus, adopted them, especially in cases of jettison; and the Emperors Claudius, Vespasian, Trajan, Adrian and Antonius, confirmed those laws, and directed that all cases of maritime commerce should be decided according to them.(*c*)

§ 180. *The Maritime Laws of the Kingdom of Jerusalem.*— These laws date back to the existence of the Christian Kingdom of Jerusalem, established after the capture of the Holy City by Godfrey de Bouillon, in the first Crusade.(*d*)

§ 181. *The Rooles or Judgments of Oleron*—Commonly called the Laws of Oleron, take their name from the Island of Oleron. The English and the French have long disputed the honor of having produced these laws, and their real origin is undoubtedly obscured by a remote antiquity; and, by common consent, they are admitted to be the foundation of all the European maritime codes. The earliest French edition to which Pardessus refers, published in 1485, bears for a title, "Jugemens de la Mèr des Maisters, des Mariniers, des Marchants, et de tout leur estre"—a literal translation of which is the the title of

---

(*a*) Pardessus Loix. Maritimes, *passim.*

(*b*) Sea Laws, 76, 78. 1 Pard. Loix. Mar. 231.

(*c*) Encyc. de Jurisp. Art. Rhodien. 1 Boulay Paty. tit. prel. § 1 to 6. 2 Brow. Civ. and Ad. Law, 38. 3 Kent's Comm. 1 to 21.

(*d*) 1 Pard. 275.

the earliest English edition, published in the reign of Henry VIII.—" Judgment of the Sea of Masters, of Mariners, and Merchants, and all their doings.(*a*)

§ 182. *Les Jugemens de Damme ou Lois de Westcapelle.*— These are mainly a translation of the Laws of Oleron, made for Dam, a city of Austrian-Flanders, situated a short distance from the sea, near to Bruges.(*b*)

Coutumes d'Amsterdam, Enchuysen and Stavern.—These also, were substantially translated from the Laws of Oleron, and they were entitled,—" *Ordonnance que les patrons et les negocians observent entre eux sur le droit Maritime.*"(*c*)

Maritime laws of the Low Countries.(*d*)

§ 183. *Laws of Wisbuy.*—Wisbuy, in the island of Gothland, was the great maritime and commercial entrepot of the North of Europe, more than five hundred years ago, and her maritime code was then known as " *Dat hogeste und dat oldeste water rechte van Wisby.*" *The ancient and supreme water-law of Wisby.* " *The Gothland water-law established by the merchants and masters.*"(*e*)

§ 184. *Le Consulat de la Mer. Il Consulato del Mare.* — *The Consulate of the Sea.*—Grotius says, that the Consulate was made up of the various enactments of the Greek Emperors of Germany, of the kingdoms of France, of Spain, of Syria, of Cyprus, of Majorca, and of the republics of Venice and Genoa.

In an Italian edition, printed at Venice in 1539, it has this title, according to Pardessus, " Libro de consulato nuovamente

---

(*a*) Prynne, 107. Sea Laws, 116, 120. Cleirac, 1, 7. Malyne's Pet. Ad. Dec. Append. 1 Pardessus Loix. Mar. 283, 323. Brow. Civ. and Ad. Law. 39. Miege Anc. Sea Laws. 1 Boucher Consulat, chap. 18 to 27.

(*b*) 1 Pard. Loix. Mar. 371.

(*c*) 1 Pardessus Loix. Mar. 405.

(*d*) 4 Pard. Loix Mar. 1, 19, 185.

(*e*) 2 Brow. Civ. and Ad. 39. 1 Pard. Loix. Mar. 424, 463. Sea Laws, 174. Cleirac, 136, 139, 463, 524. Malyne's Pet. Ad. Dec. Append. Miege Anc. Sea Laws. 1 Boucher Cons. chap. 21 to 27.

stampato a ricoretto nel quale sono scritti capitoli a statuti e buone ordinationi, che le antichi ordinerono per li casi de mercantie et di mari et mercante et marinari et patroni di navilio."(a)

"Ici commence le livre du consulat, nouvellement corrige et imprimé, dans lequel sont contenus les loix et les ordonnances sur les actes maritimes et mercantiles."(b)

§ 185. *Le Guidon de la Mer.*—This is an ancient treatise entitled "Le Guidon pour ceux que font marchandize et qui mettent à la Mer ;" written in French for the use of the merchants of Rouen. It is devoted mainly to the law of Maritime Insurance, but Cleirac declares, that it is written with such consummate ability that, in explaining the contracts of insurance, the author has completely elucidated the whole subject of maritime contracts and naval commerce. It is a work of the highest authority.(c)

§ 186. *The Laws of the Hanse Towns.*—In the year 1254, Lubec, Brunswick, Dantzic, and Cologne, in Germany, and subsequently, Bruges in Flanders, London in England, and Novorgood in Russia, and the principal cities of the Rhine, and other portions of Europe, constituted a sort of maritime confederacy for the protection and promotion of their commercial interests ; and for that purpose, about the year 1597, formed a code of maritime law of the greatest respectability—embracing in its brief articles much of what had before existed in the separate codes of the Hanseatic and other cities, and the nations of Europe.

This code may be found in 3 Pard. 431, 455. Miege's Anc. Sea Laws. Brow. Civ. and Ad. 39. 3 Kent Comm. 1 to 21. Cleirac, 157, 166. Pet. Ad. Dec. Append. Sea Laws, 190, 195.

§ 187. The other maritime ordinances and codes which had

(a) 2 Pard. 1, 49. Grotius de Jur. Bel. & Par. Lib. 3, chap.   note 4. 5 Pard. Loix. Mar. 11.

(b) 2 Boucher Consulat, 1, title.

(c) 2 Pard. Loix. Mar. 369, 377. Cleirac, 181. Brown Civ. and Ad. 41.

existed before that time, were numerous, and are here briefly enumerated in the order in which maritime legislation or codification was commenced in each nation or city.

A. D. 940. The Maritime Law of Norway. 3 Pard. 1, 21.
" 1063. Maritime Law of the Two Sicilies. 5 Pard. 214, 237.
" 1117. Maritime Law of Iceland. 3 Pard. 45, 55.
" 1150. Maritime Law of Denmark. 3 Pard. 205, 229.
" 1158. Maritime Law of Lubec. 3 Pard. 391, 399.
" 1160. Maritime Law of Pisa and Florence. 4 Pard. 545, 569.
" 1224. Maritime Law of the Prussian States. 3 Pard. 447, 459.
" 1232. Maritime Law of Venice and Austria. 5 Pard. 1.
" 1243. Maritime Law of Catalonia, Aragon, Valence, and Majorca. 5 Pard. 321, 333.
" 1254. Maritime Law of Sweden. 3 Pard. 89, 111.
" 1270. Maritime Law of Hamburgh. 3 Pard. 329, 337.
" 1270. Maritime Law of Russia. 3 Pard. 489, 505.
" 1303. Maritime Law of Bremen. 3 Pard. 309, 317.
" " Maritime Law of the Papal States. 5 Pard. 99, 113.
" 1316. Maritime Law of Genoa. 5 Pard. 419, 439.
" " Maritime Law of Sardinia. 5 Pard. 267, 281.

CHAPTER XII.

"Admiralty" and "Maritime."

§ 188. In the foregoing brief review of the Admiralty and Maritime jurisdiction of the different portions of the British Empire, of the original States of an Union, and of the nations of Continental Europe, it has been shown that Admiralty and Maritime cases consist of many very numerous classes of cases every where distinctly characterized by their relation to ships and shipping. That of these numerous and various cases, the English Admiralty Court, at the time of the American Revolution, entertained jurisdiction of but very few—the Admiralty Courts of Scotland still more—the British Colonial Courts of Vice-Admiralty still more—the early English Admiralty still more—the French Admiralty Courts, and those of other continental nations, still more—and that the extent and the character of these various jurisdictions were plainly written in the known evidences of the law, when our constitution gave to the federal government jurisdiction of all cases of Admiralty and Maritime jurisdiction. With these various jurisdictions to choose from, if any one was to be adopted, it is hardly rational to suppose that that one would not have been specified or in some manner indicated. If no intention as to the extent of jurisdiction had been indicated, it would be evident that the matter was to be left to the Congress ; but it was important, in a national point of view, that all uncertainty should be removed, and the broadest grant was therefore made of *all* cases.

§ 189. It has been stated in another place, that the English language is the only link that connects the laws and institutions of the United States with those of Great Britain ; and that to the English law and to English Dictionaries, we must resort for the meaning of the words used in the Constitution. If we bring the Admiralty and Maritime grant in the Constitution to this test, we shall find that the words *Admiralty* and *Maritime* then had, as they now have, a well established signification entirely in harmony with their use by the great civilians who made the Admiralty and Maritime jurisdiction the study of their lives.(*a*)

ADMIRALTY.—A Court having cognizance in all Maritime affairs, civil as well as criminal. MARITIME.—Relating to the sea ; marine.

Johnson's Dic. edit. 1755. Barclay's Dic. Webster's Dic. Falconer's Maritime Dic. Corvell's Law Dic. Cunningham's Law Dic. Bell's Law Dic. Bouvier's Law Dic.

§ 190. It will be seen, also, that the words Admiralty and Maritime are of constant occurrence in the works of the jurists of Holland and Spain, as well as those of England, Scotland, and France ; and those words have thus acquired an established signification, of which the framers of the Constitution can not be supposed to have been ignorant. Nor can they be presumed to have used them in any narrower sense than that in which they have been used for centuries by the whole commercial world. On general principles, it cannot be presumed, that they were used in any local or merely municipal sense. The fact that the Admiralty Court of England was not permitted by the King's Bench to exercise jurisdiction in all Admiralty and Maritime cases, but was confined to a very few—the residue being monopolized by the common law courts—can in no manner affect the proper force and signification of those words. Common respect for the wisdom of our ancestors, prevents us from believing, that so paltry a class of cases as those which were left to the English Admiralty at the time of our Revolution, was deemed by them necessary to be embraced in the National Constitution, as unsafe to be trusted to the States, or of sufficient importance, in a national point of view, to be solemnly granted to the national judiciary.

They do not rise to the respectability of a class of cases, nor have they any national character, or general commercial importance, to distinguish them from the great mass of Admiralty

---

(*a*) § 32, 191.

and Maritime cases; nor have I been able to imagine any
reason whatever why those cases, alone, should have been
transferred to the general government; nor have I ever met
with even an alleged reason for supposing that they were transferred to the general government, because the English Court of
Admiralty entertained jurisdiction of them. It must have been
for a higher, more patriotic, and more international reason, that
the States surrendered the whole subject to the federal government.(a)

§ 191. If we examine the etymology or received use of the
words Admiralty and Maritime jurisdiction, we shall find that
they include the judicial jurisdiction of the admiral, and of all
maritime causes, or causes arising from things done upon and
relating to the sea; or, in other words, all transactions and proceedings relative to commerce and navigation, and to damages
or injuries upon the sea, or navigable waters of the nation, and
on the high seas. In the maritime codes, and their commentators, and in the writings of the greatest jurists, in all the great
maritime nations of Europe, the terms Admiralty jurisdiction
are uniformly applied to the courts exercising jurisdiction over
maritime contracts and concerns, and administering the general
maritime law. The judges of the common law courts in England, in a spirit which has been alluded to, use them in a narrower sense; but the distinguished men who practised and
presided in the Admiralty, and who made such subjects their
peculiar study, always used those words in their wider and
more appropriate sense; and there was no superior sanctity in
the decisions at common law upon the subject of the jurisdiction of those courts, which should entitle them to outweigh the
very able and learned decisions of the great civilians of the
Admiralty. In seeking for the proper signification of those
words even in England, where could we so properly search for
information on the subject as in the works of those jurists, who

---

(a) Ante, § 4, 5, 38, 39, 40. 2 Gall. 468. 5 How. 456, 7. 5 How. 452, 3. 6
How. 385. Ante, § 27, 28.

have adorned the maritime courts from age to age, and made its jurisdiction the pride and study of their lives.(*a*)

§ 192. It has been before remarked that the Constitution was formed after twelve years of actual independent nationality in the States, under the confederation—that the United States Government can, in no proper sense, be called an offset from that of Great Britain—that the existence of Great Britain is not alluded to in the Constitution, much less are any of her institutions adopted as the patterns or originals of our own, so that if the jurisdiction of the British Admiralty Courts—English, ancient and modern—Scotch—Colonial—had been always and every where the same, still that a grant of *all* admiralty and maritime cases could, on no rational principles, be construed as meaning, not all cases, but only such cases as one court of one nation had, by another court of the same nation, been permitted to take jurisdiction of for merely municipal reasons. Surely, if any British Court was to furnish the rule of our admiralty jurisdiction, it would be the Colonial Courts, whose jurisdiction was so fully set forth in their written commissions.(*b*)

(*a*) Ante, § 38, 39, 40, 41. 2 Gall. 469.
(*b*) Ante, §§ 30, 31. Ante, §§ 125, 126, 127, 151, 158.

CHAPTER XIII.

*Trial by Jury—Suits at Common Law—Suits in Personam—
Commerce.*

§ 193. It has been sometimes said that the 6th and 7th amendments to the Constitution securing the right of trial by jury, have the effect to restrict the general grant in the Constitution, for the reason that in Admiralty Courts causes are usually determined by the Court without the aid of a jury. " Depriving us in many cases of the benefit of trial by jury," was one of the grievances enumerated in the Declaration of Independence ; and the trial by jury has always been, to the American People, an object of deep interest and solicitude, and every encroachment upon it has been watched with great jealousy. The right to it is secured by all the State Constitutions, and the want of such an express security in the Constitution of the United States was one of the strongest objections taken against its adoption. To meet the public feeling on the subject the sixth and seventh amendments to that instrument were adopted in these words :(a)

(7.) " In suits at common law where the value in controversy shall exceed twenty dollars, the right of trial by jury shall be preserved, and no fact tried by a jury shall be otherwise re-examined in any court of the United States than according to the rules of the common law."

(6.) " In all criminal prosecutions the accused shall enjoy the right to a speedy and public trial by an impartial jury of the State or district wherein the crime shall have been committed, which district shall have been previously ascertained by law."

§ 194. Able jurists have contended, that in this view the admiralty jurisdiction should be considered as restricted, rather than extended by the frame of our judicial system. The most careful reflection, however, has not enabled me to perceive how

---

(a) 3 Pet. R. 446

the question of the jurisdiction of the Admiralty is in the remotest degree affected by their provisions. The sixth amendment is expressly limited to criminal prosecutions for crimes committed in some State or district of the United States. It would, therefore, hardly extend to crimes committed on the high seas, which would alone be the subject of admiralty jurisdiction, and if it could, there is nothing to prevent the Congress from doing what they have long since done, and what the British Parliament had done before them ; provided by law that the trial of maritime crimes in the admiralty shall be by jury.(a)

§ 195. So the seventh amendment is limited to suits at common law, which does not include either suits of equity, or of admiralty and maritime jurisdiction.(b)

§ 196. Indeed it seems quite plain, that while the People had the subject before them, fresh from the discussions in relation to the Constitution itself, they intended to confine the constitutional necessity for jury trials to crimes committed within the territorial limits of the United States, and to suits at common law; and to leave it to the wisdom of Congress to decide whether the jurisdiction over transactions so peculiar as those of the sea, should be exercised only by judges schooled in the principles and mystery of such transactions as had been done in all ages and nations before, or should be left to the uncertain chances of juries, familiar alone with the usages and necessities of the land. The Congress wisely gave to maritime offences a jury, but as wisely decided that in causes, civil and maritime, the court should decide the fact as well as the law.(c)

§ 197. The question whether any particular court has jurisdiction or whether a particular cause be within the judicial cognizance of the General Government, is totally different from any question of the manner in which the court shall proceed, and if the Congress should now pass a law that the trial of all

---

(a) 5 Howard, 493.　Edw. Ad. Jur. 153.　4 Black, 268.　5 How. 450. - 5 U. S. Stat. at Large, 726.　Conk. Ad. Jur. and Prac. 7,

(b) 3 Pet. 446, 7.

(c) 5 How. 441, 492, 3, 4.

causes in the courts of the United States should be by jury, it
would not in the slighest degree change or modify the jurisdiction of those courts, nor interfere with the grant to the Federal
Government, as will be readily perceived, by recurring to the
ninth section of the judiciary act giving jurisdiction to District
Courts. Had the exception in the last clause of the section
been omitted, admiralty and maritime cases would have been
triable by jury like all other cases, but the jurisdiction would
not have been changed. In some of the State Courts of Admiralty all causes were tried by a jury.(a)

§ 198. The phrase " Suits at common law," in the seventh
amendment to the Constitution, has also been made the foundation of an objection to the admiralty jurisdiction in all these
cases, which in England, at the time of the Revolution, could not
be tried in the Court of Admiralty, but must be brought in the
courts of common law—an objection which seems to have been
first raised by the late Judge Baldwin in the case of Bains v.
The Schr. James and Catharine.(b)

§ 199. The cases brought by the Constitution within the
judicial form of the United States are of four general classes.
1st. Cases of every description in law and equity arising under
the Constitution, laws and treaties of the United States—a jurisdiction necessary to enable the United States to execute and
enforce its own laws. 2d. Cases of every description affecting
ambassadors, other public ministers and consuls—a provision
obviously necessary to enable the Government of the United
States to regulate its intercourse with foreign nations, and to
secure the dispensing of justice to the agents of that intercourse.
3d. To all cases of admiralty and maritime jurisdiction—a provision necessary to enable the General Government to administer that branch of the law of nations known as the general
maritime law—embracing the system of laws which regulate the rights and duties of those engaged in maritime affairs

(a) 5 How. 459.   Ante, § 168, 169.
(b) Bald. 544.

or doing business on the common navigable highways of nations. 4th. To controversies between citizens of different States, &c.—a provision necessary to secure a due administration of justice in cases in which national prejudices, state pride or state interest might influence the decision of the state tribunals. This classification relates entirely to the jurisdiction, so far as it depends upon the subject matter.(*a*)

§ 200. There is also another classification of cases which is entirely independent of the question of jurisdiction, and depends solely upon the mode of proceeding, viz. common law cases, equity cases, and admiralty and maritime cases—these classes include all judicial cases. By cases in law are meant cases in which legal rights and duties and offences are to be ascertained in courts of law. By cases in equity are meant cases in which equitable rights and duties are to be ascertained in courts of equitable jurisdiction and proceeding; and by admiralty and maritime cases, are meant cases in which maritime rights, duties and offences become the subject of judicial cognizance in courts of admiralty and maritime jurisdiction.(*b*)

§ 201. Each of these courts has its own system of legal principles, and its own practice or course of procedure, so that a suit in law or suit in equity, and a suit in Admiralty, can hardly be said to resemble each other. It is not, however, to be understood, that the same substantial claim may not be a matter of controversy in courts of either class. A claim for mariner's wages may be prosecuted in a court of law, and it is then a case in law, or a suit at common law; and it is to be settled according to the rules which govern the court in which it is prosecuted. The same demand may also, by the necessity of a discovery, or of an injunction, or by the intervention of trustees, be brought within the range of equitable jurisdiction—it then becomes a case in equity, and the rules of that course of procedure must be applied to it. Or the same claim may seek

(*a*) Ante, § 27.
(*b*) Ante, § 27. 3 Pet. 446. 5 How. 460.

its more usual and appropriate forum, a Court of Admiralty; in which case, it is to be disposed of according to the course of Admiralty Courts. The Constitution nowhere provides what cases shall be within the one or the other class, nor what shall be the steps of proceeding. That is left to be settled by the courts, according to the established principles of judicial procedure, subject to the restrictions in the 6th and 7th amendments of the Constitution, which provide that in all criminal prosecutions, and in all suits in common law courts, involving more than twenty dollars, the right of trial by jury shall be preserved.(a)

§ 202. The fact that the Constitution provides only that all crimes shall be tried by a jury, and that in all suits at common law, where the value in controversy shall exceed twenty dollars, the right of trial by jury shall be preserved—and omits to include in the same provision Admiralty and Maritime civil cases, and cases in equity, shows that it was not intended to include them; and that the whole force of the 7th amendment is, that in all cases, except Equity and Admiralty cases, the parties shall have the right to a trial by jury, if they demand it.

§ 203. The learned judge seems to have overlooked the distinction between the Constitution and the acts of Congress, as well as the difference between the course of proceeding and the fundamental law of jurisdiction. The limit and extent of the judicial power of the United States, are fixed by the Constitution, which is inflexible and above the power of the Congress, while the mode of exercising that jurisdiction, the organization of the courts, and the course of procedure, are prescribed by the acts of the Congress, and are subject to be altered, modified and repealed, at the pleasure of the national legislature, which may at any time enact, that all cases of Admiralty and Maritime jurisdiction shall be tried by a jury. The forum would, nevertheless, remain the same.(b)

(a) 3 Pet. Ad. 446. 3 Swan. 605, 670. 1 Vernon, 54. 10 Ves. 155. 1 Cox, 264. 3 Beav. 409. 12 Mod. 16.
(b) Ante, § 18.

§ 204. It is not uncommon in the reports, to find counsel, and even judges, insisting that the court has not jurisdiction in a particular maritime cause of action *in personam*, while they admit the jurisdiction over the same cause of action *in rem.* And it has been sometimes very gravely asserted, that the Admiralty Courts have jurisdiction only *in rem*, or at most, but very rarely *in personam*, and only as ancillary to the jurisdiction *in rem.* A striking instance of this, is to be found in the late case of *Cutler* v. *Rae*, (7 How. R. 729,) where an action *in personam* was held to be not within the jurisdiction of the Admiralty, although the subject matter of the action—an average contribution—has, in all ages and nations out of England—*semper, ubique, ab omnibus*—been held to be most peculiarly a matter of Admiralty and Maritime jurisdiction. The readiest reference to the most common books of precedents and cases, will show that in the earlier periods of Admiralty practice, almost all the cases were *in personam.* This was the usual course of Admiralty proceedings, and it was not considered necessary to arrest the vessel, except in cases where the owners or master were absent, or where a mere question of privilege or preference was to be decided. But the distinction between proceedings *in rem* and *in personam*, has no proper relation to the question of jurisdiction. If mariner's wages, salvage, freight, and bottomry, are maritime causes of action, then the Court of Admiralty has jurisdiction of them, and may use any of its appointed modes to give the party any remedy to which the law entitles him. The substratum of the action, is the liability of one party to respond to another, and the court may enforce it against the person, or against a particular portion of his property, or against his property generally, as the law may have provided the right. If the cause of action be by law, a lien upon a vessel, or her cargo, or freight, or the proceeds thereof, or the remnants and surplus thereof, the court may enforce that lien by a suit *in rem*, or may allow the lien to remain, and compel the party himself to pay the demand, by imprisoning his person, or by selling his property on execution. In such cases, the question before the court, is not whether the court have jurisdiction, but whether the party have right; it is not a question in abatement, but a question of the merits of the action. "If the cause is a maritime cause, subject to Admiralty cognizance, jurisdiction is complete over the person as well as over the ship. It must in its nature be complete, for it cannot be confined to one of the remedies on the contract, when the contract itself is within its cognizance."(a)

§ 205. It has been sometimes insisted, that the Admiralty has not jurisdiction of any case of which the common law has jurisdiction. Indeed, as has been before remarked, such a rule was made a principal cause for restraining the English Admiralty Court. The jurisdiction of that Court especially extended to cases not maritime, arising beyond sea and with foreigners. A reason given for this jurisdiction, was that by the common law, the courts of common law could only take cognizance of matters arising within the counties of the realm, because every fact must be averred in the pleadings to have arisen or happened within some particular county of England. While this strictness prevailed, it is clear that cases arising beyond sea could not be tried in the common law courts. In process of time, however, the common law courts held the venue to be immaterial and not traversable, and hence a fictitious venue was laid, and all facts were averred to have arisen at Westminster, and then, and for that reason, they denied the jurisdiction of the Admiralty, it being no longer necessary. The test of happening within or without the body of a county, which should have been confined to cases (not necessarily maritime,) alleged to have happened beyond sea, was in process of time applied to maritime cases happening in the close seas of England, and finally the notion came to prevail, that all cases in which the common law gives a remedy, and in which the common law courts are easily accessible, are not within the Admiralty jurisdiction. It is extraordinary that it should be contended, that no cases which might be the subject of suits at common law, should be heard in the Admiralty—since seamen's wages, and almost all the subjects of English Admiralty jurisdiction, may be prose-

---

(a) 12 Wheat. 460. Dunlap Ad. Prac. 69. Bald. C. C. R. 544. 7 Howard, 729. 6 Howard. 392. Boyd's Proceedings, *passim.* Clerke's Praxis. *passim.* Hall's Adm. *passim.*

cuted in common law courts, even in England, and such a construction would annihilate the Admiralty jurisdiction in that country, and make the grant of it in our constitution quite unmeaning and nugatory.(a)

§ 206. It has however, with much less reason, been said in relation to the lakes and rivers, bays and harbors, in this country, that they are not within the Admiralty and maritime jurisdiction, because the common law courts on the shores are conveniently accessible and competent to give relief. This must be a fallacy, if it be true that the Admiralty and maritime jurisdiction is conferred upon the federal government, as has been before remarked, for national and international purposes, and not to supply deficiencies in the common law, nor to create a more accessible jurisdiction—especially since the same court of the United States is at the same time a common law court, as well as an Admiralty Court. It was because, by the common consent of civilized nations, maritime transactions, on the great highways of commerce, should be subjected to the *vera lex*, *recta ratio*—the equitable principles and rules of natural justice —which, without the enactment of any legislature, are acknowledged as the general maritime law—because the internal as well as external peace of the nation might be involved, and the rights of citizens of the different States might be subjected, not to a general and unbiassed tribunal, but to a local, a prejudiced or a partial one, that this jurisdiction was made national.

That there are local laws and local courts ready, and, in their own view, competent, to give redress, so far from being a reason why the Admiralty jurisdiction should be excluded, is one of the strongest reasons why it should be ample and accessible. In no other way can the maritime law be maintained or administered with uniformity and national consistency, and the equal rights of all the States be preserved on the waters washing the shores of different States. The constitution is full of evidence to show that the nationality of the States was to be preserved, in all matters in which the rights and interests

---

(a) Ware, 91.   5 How. 464.   3 Pet. 447.

of the particular States alone were to be concerned, but in every thing in which there was to be a common right and a common interest, there the rights of the States were to be preserved through the agency of the federal government. The navigable waters of the nation are not the exclusive property of any State, but are common to all.(*a*)

§ 207. Hence the Constitution conferred upon the General Government the power "To regulate Commerce with Foreign Nations, and among the Several States, and with the Indian Tribes"—a grant which covers the whole ground of commercial intercourse, but was accompanied by the limitations that "no tax or duty shall be laid on articles exported from any State— no preference shall be given by any regulation of commerce or revenue to the ports of one State over those of another—nor shall vessels bound to or from one State, be obliged to enter, clear, or pay duties in another." "All duties, imports, and excises shall be uniform throughout the United States." Subject to these limitations, the legislative power extends to all subjects of international commerce—the States being considered as nations. It surely cannot be denied, that the judicial power is coextensive with the legislative power. The want of a proper judicial power to enforce the national legislation, was one of the greatest evils under the Confederation.(*b*)

§ 208. The wisdom of our ancestors, in laying the foundations of the republic, is in nothing more evident than in our organic regulations in relation to commerce. For all commercial purposes, we must be one people—no protective, retaliatory, prohibitory systems of revenue or other restriction, can ever interfere with the bonds of our nationality—perfect freedom and equality of trade and navigation among ourselves, is constitutionally secure. If it had not been so, long before this time we should have been severed, divided, antagonistical and weak nations, the fragments of our original Union. How easy

---

(*a*) 5 How. 495. Ante, § 27. Federalist, No. 83. 5 How. 459.
(*b*) Const. Art 1, § 8. Subd. 1, 3. Ibid, § 9. Subd. 5.

it is to perceive that our harmony may be interrupted, and our strength impaired, if each state may adopt and enforce on its half of a river, its section of a lake—its short stretch of coast—in its own ports and harbors, and local waters, to which all the States have a common right of use—a system of commercial and maritime law, repealing or conflicting with that great system of commercial law which is known as the Admiralty and Maritime Law, and which alone can secure those equal State rights which it was one great object of the constitution to protect.(a)

Ante, § 4.

CHAPTER XIV.

The Maritime Law—Maritime Contracts.

§ 209. The maritime law, as has been before remarked, is not the law of any particular country, but a law common to all nations which are engaged in maritime commerce, and does not rest for its character or authority on the peculiar institutions and local customs of any particular country, but consists of certain principles of equity, and usages of trade, which general convenience, and a common sense of justice, have established, to regulate the dealing and intercourse of merchants and mariners, in matters relating to the sea, in all the commercial countries of the world.(*a*)

§ 210. The general maritime law is found, in its perfection of reason, broadly and fully laid down and discussed in the works of the celebrated and learned commentators upon the maritime codes, and of other elementary writers on maritime law, such as Selden, Grotius Stracha, Bynkershoek, Valin, Stypmanus, Loccenius, Casa Regis, Emerigon, Kuricke, Pothier, Roccus, Malynes, Cleirac, Boucher, Boulay Paty, Pardessus, Vinnius, Lubeck, Targa, and many others, whose works have been the universally known, and everywhere conceded evidence of the Admiralty and maritime law.(*b*)

§ 211. It would swell this treatise far beyond the limits which I intend to give it, were I to attempt an analysis or synopsis of those various codes and commentaries. It will be sufficient, here, to remark, that none of them adopt any rule at all analogous to the modern English rule, as narrowed down by the prohibitions of the King's Bench. The question, whether a cause of action arose within the limits of a county or in a har-

---

(*a*) Ante, § 41. Ware, 315. 3 Kent's Com. 3d edit. 1.
(*b*) I Boulay Paty, 96. 3 Kent's Com. 3d edit. 1 to 21.

bor—or was founded on an instrument sealed or unsealed—or made on shore or on ship board—in a usual or unusual form—appears never to have entered the minds of those legislators and jurists. They have always looked solely to the maritime nature and character of the transactions, which cannot depend upon any such considerations, and they treat of all cases of service, contract, tort, or accident relating to ships, shipping and maritime commerce.(*a*)

§ 212. While, however, the maritime law regulates and enforces all maritime contracts, it does not take cognizance of agreements not in themselves maritime, although they may be preliminary to maritime contracts, and have a direct reference to them. Thus, a marine policy of insurance is a maritime contract; but an agreement to make a particular policy, has been held to be not a maritime contract; so that if the agreement should be violated, and the policy should not be made, or being made, should differ in important particulars from that agreed upon, the Admiralty would not have jurisdiction of a suit for that violation, although it would entertain a suit on the policy actually made. So, too, the building of a ship is a maritime service, and the building contract is one within the cognizance of the Admiralty; but a mere undertaking to make a building contract for a ship, or to procure a person to build a ship, is not within the jurisdiction of the Admiralty. It is not a maritime contract. It is not subject to the regulation of the maritime law. The distinction in many cases will, undoubtedly, seem shadowy and unreal, still, in a large class of cases, it will be readily perceived, and its importance fully appreciated.(*b*)

§ 213. It is not always easy to determine, what is a maritime contract. The dividing line between causes maritime and not maritime, is not always strongly marked. It is believed that a sure guide in matters of contract, is to be found in the relation which the cause of action has to a ship, the great agent

---

(*a*) 3 Pard. Loix. Mar. 451.
(*b*) 2 Gall. 468.   3 Mason, 16.   Dunlap Prac. 43.   4 Mas. 380.

of maritime enterprize, and to these a highway of commerce. The languages of those nations in which the Admiralty and maritime jurisdiction has been longest acknowledged, and where the system of law which regulates maritime commerce has been most studied, furnish a brief illustration of the proper compass of the maritime law, in the significant descriptive names which they give to it in the vernacular tongue. *Sea Laws—Maritime Law—Law of Ships and Shipping—Laws of Naval Trade and Commerce—Droit Maritime— Water-rechte—Scip rechte—Scip rechts—Skip roet—Zee rechten— Gius Nautico—Leggi Maritimi—Jus Maritimi.*(a)   Much of which is briefly expressed in the title of the " Consulate Agreements, statutes, and good ordinances, which the ancients established for the cases of merchants and mariners and masters of vessels."(b)

We find no allusion to tides as affecting the law—no exceptions of ports or harbors, or narrow seas—or bodies of counties— or contracts in unusual form—or sealed or unsealed, with or without a penalty—made on land or on ship board. *The only question is, whether the transaction relate to ships and vessels, masters and mariners, as the agents of commerce, on great navigable waters. " Toutes les affaires relative à la navigation et aux navigateurs appatient au droit maritime.*"(c)

§ 214. At the hazard of unnecessary repetition, I shall here bring together further evidence, consisting of extracts from documents which have been already referred to, and which will show the uniformity or similarity of language which has been used on this subject in different ages and countries.

" To hold conusance of pleas, debts, bills of exchange, policies of assurance, accounts, charter parties, contractions, bills of lading, and all other contracts, which may any ways concern

---

(a) *Mare.*—The Sea; sometimes a great river. *Maritimus.*—Of or belonging to the Sea. *Nauta.*—A Sailor. *Nauticus.*—Belonging to ships or mariners. *Navis*—A ship or bark; any vessel of the sea or rivers. *Navalis.*—Belonging to ships.—AINSWORTH.

(b) 5 Pard. 11. Ante, § 184.

(c) 3 Pard. Loix. Mar. 451. 1 Boulay Paty, 99.

moneys due for freight of ships hired and let to hire, moneys lent to be paid beyond the seas at the hazard of the lender, and also of any cause, business, or injury whatsoever, had or done in or upon or through the seas, or public rivers, or fresh water, streams, havens, and places subject to overflowing whatsoever within the ebbing and flowing of the sea."(a)

" Also, touching all and singular other matters which concern merchants, owners and proprietors of ships, masters, shipmen, mariners, and shipwrights."(b)

" Agreements, statutes, and ordinances, established by the ancients for the cases of merchants and mariners and masters of vessels."(c)

" Laws of ships and navigators."(d)

" Judgments of the sea, of masters, of mariners, and merchants, and all their doings."(e)

" Ordinances that masters and merchants observe among themselves in subjects of maritime law."(f)

" Water-law,—as established by the merchants and masters."(g)

" Directions for those who pursue commerce and put to sea."(h)

" All business, civil and maritime, whatsoever, commenced, or to be commenced, between merchants, or between owners and proprietors of ships and other vessels, and merchants or others whomsoever, with such owners and proprietors of ships, and all other vessels whatsoever."(i)

" To take cognizance of, and proceed in all causes, civil and maritime, and in complaints, contracts, debts, exchanges, policies of assurance, accounts, charter parties, agreements, bills of lading of ships, and all matters and contracts which in any manner whatsoever, relate to freight due for ships hired and let out, transport money, bottomry, or which are affairs between merchants, or between owners and proprietors of ships or other

---

(a) Ante, § 48.

(b) Ante, § 50.

(c) Ante, § 84.

(d) 5 Pard. Loix. Mar. 7, 9.

(e) Ante, § 51, 181.

(f) Ante, § 182

(g) Ante, § 183.

(h) Ante, § 185.

(i) Ante, § 126.

vessels and merchants, or other persons with owners and proprietors of ships and all other vessels."(a)

It will be observed, that these are extracts from the earliest
and most authentic evidences of the maritime law throughout
the whole coast of modern civilization in Europe and America,
previous to one hundred years ago ; and the concurrence of
all these authorities cannot fail to show, that the maritime law
is, and always has been, The Law of Ships and Vessels and
Naval Commerce.

(a) Ante, § 151.

CHAPTER XV.

Ships and Vessels.

§ 215. Ship is a general term, and in the law is equivalent to vessel. It is defined, a locomotive machine adapted to transportation over rivers, seas and oceans.

" *Sub vocabulo navis omnia navigationum comprehenduntur.*

" *Navim accipere debemus sive marinam, sive fluviatliem, sive in aliquo stagno naviget.*"(a)

§ 216. Whether the old tradition, that the first idea of the canoe was suggested by a split reed floating on the water be true, or whether the simple raft was not the first instrument of maritime locomotion and transportation, it is not necessary to inquire; nor whether the tiny sail of the nautilus, or the web-foot of the water fowl, suggested the first means of propulsion. It is, however, certain that ships and vessels, in all their varieties of construction, and all their modes of propulsion, are but the more or less perfect combinations of the canoe and the raft, the sail and the paddle, as human ingenuity and science in the progress of civilization and art have removed old difficulties, and suggested new expedients, till vessels are the most perfect and wonderful productions of human art, and in all the stages of their progress, from the humble catamaran and balsa to the majestic steamer of our day, they have been the great agents of exploration and trade, and the formidable instruments of individual and national plunder, as well as of defence and legitimate conquest.(b)

§ 217. Questions have sometimes arisen, how far size, and

(a) Malynes, 123, 141. 1 Boulay Pat. 100, 101. 1 Pard. 97. Enc. Am. art. Ship.
(b) Falconer's Dic. art. Naval Architecture. Sea Laws, 446, 1 Molloy, 307. Falc. Dic. Catamaran.

capacity, and purpose, and mode of propulsion, must enter into the definition of a ship or vessel under the maritime law, and cases are found in the books in which ships or vessels are denied that character, because their size was small compared with the more capacious constructions of modern times, and because they were employed in the humble occupations of agricultural or agrestic commerce. Those can hardly be denied the character of ships and vessels which, in every particular, are superior to the ships and vessels of those countries and periods in which the great codes of maritime law were promulgated and enforced; nor can it make any difference whether the vessel is propelled by the wind or the tide, or paddles, or whether the paddles are moved by steam, by animals, or by the human arm.(a)

§ 218. Under the name "*navis*, ship," says Malynes, "is all kind of shipping understood, and *navigium*, vessel, is a general word, many times used for any kind of navigation. So that it is not of any moment to describe the diversity of ships, as carracks, galleons, galleasses, gallies, centauries, ships of war, fly boats, busses, and all other kinds of ships and vessels." Each nation has its mode of construction and rigging and navigation, and its kind of craft, but all are ships and vessels which are manned by a master and crew, and are devoted to the purposes of transportation and commerce, whether in the fisheries or in mere trade. A scow, a lighter, a ferry-boat, and probably a raft or timber ship, under certain circumstances, would be held to be a ship or vessel, and subject to the same maritime law as other vessels. It is not the form, the construction, the rig, the equipment, or the means of propulsion that establishes the jurisdiction, but the purpose and business of the craft as an instrument of naval transportation.(b)

§ 219. The statutes of the United States in various cases refer

---

(a) N. Y. Law Rep. 373. 9 Wheat. 1. Gilp. 525. 4 N. Y. Leg. Ob. 440.

(b) It would not be uninteresting to enter into some details of the extraordinary diversity which exists in the water craft of different nations and of different ages, nor would it fail to illustrate and enforce the remark in the text; but such an inquiry would be out of place here.

to the size of ships and vessels, and it must be held that vessels of the classes described as ships and vessels in the statutes are for the purposes of the maritime law ships and vessels. By the registry acts, all ships and vessels intended for the foreign trade, "whether ship, brigantine, scow, schooner, sloop, or whatever else,"(a) must be registered and recorded; and among others are mentioned vessels not exceeding fifty tons.

§ 220. Vessels engaged in the coasting trade, " on the sea coast or on a navigable river," including ferry boats,(b) as well as all other vessels, must be enrolled and licensed if they be of the burthen of five tons or upwards ;(c) and they are all uniformly spoken of in the statutes as " ships and vessels." And some of the ships of Columbus, in which he traversed an unknown ocean on the greatest maritime enterprize of the world,—of Cortes seeking to conquer a populous empire—of the buccanneers, the terror of armed fleets and of fortified cities, were inferior in size to the small craft that carry on commerce on our smaller lakes and rivers. " The first discoverers of America committed themselves to the unknown ocean in barks, one not above fifteen tons —Frobisher in two vessels of twenty or twenty-five tons—Sir Humphrey Gilbert in one of ten tons only.(d)

§ 221. And vessels devoted especially to the humbler commerce of agricultural productions, or of the homespun fabrics of the farm and the mechanics shop, are in the same manner to be considered ships and vessels, and subject to the maritime law. It can make no difference in the principle, whether the ship or vessel be loaded with tea from Canton, coffee from Rio, cotton from Mobile, tobacco from Richmond, flour from Baltimore, coal from Liverpool or Philadelphia, onions from Wethersfield, or with pork, poultry, butter, cheese, fruits, and other articles of produce from the farms and villages between the large

---

(a) 2 Bior. Laws U. S. 318, sec. 9.
(b) 2 Bior. Laws U. S. 337, secs. 12, 14.
(c) Id. 334, sec. 4, 344, sec. 26.
(d) Quarterly Review.

ports—all these are the agricultural products of their locạ-
lities.   And in the same manner silks, cashmeres, crapes, laces,
and cloths from the foreign looms, and liquors from abroad, are
no more cargo, or merchandize or goods, than boots and shoes,
home-made clothes, cider, whisky, wooden clocks, shoe pegs,
and other coarse articles of manufacture, which often fill the
sloops and schooners of the coasting trade of the rivers and
bays.   They are the manufactures of their localities, and the
vessels that carry them are the ships and vessels of the maritime law, even though they do not make the three years voyages of Solomon to Tarshish for " gold and silver, ivory, and apes
and peacocks."   The earlier as well as the later codes of maritime law, expressly embrace the vessels employed in this class
of commerce, and it is not easy to see how a doubt was ever
raised on the subject.(a)

§ 222. A ship is usually described as consisting of the ship,
her tackle, apparel and furniture, and in case of a steamer, her
engine.   This includes the hull and spars, which constitute the
ship—the rigging, which constitutes the tackle—the sails, which
are her apparel—the anchors, and numerous utensils for ships
use, which are the furniture.   This does not include the boats
nor the ballast.(b)

§ 223. A ship is always the same ship, although the original
materials of which it was composed may, by successive repairs
and alterations, have been in the course of time entirely changed, and if a ship be entirely taken to pieces, without the intention of reconstruction, should the same materials be reconstructed
into a ship in precisely the same manner, it would not be the
same, but another ship.(c)

(a) Gilp. 526. 2 Chron. 9, 21.
(b) Sea Laws, 444. 1 Hag. 124. 1 Molloy, 313.
(c) Sea Laws, 443–4. Malyne's, 123. 1 Boulay Paty, 102, 104. 1 Mol. 312.

CHAPTER XVI.

Seas—Lakes—Rivers.

§ 224. A ship is none the less or more a ship, because she is confined to fresh or salt water, or running or stagnant water. The phrases, the Sea—the High Sea—the High Seas—are frequently used in connection with the Admiralty jurisdiction. The High Sea—the Open Sea—are phrases used to distinguish the expanse and mass of any great body of water, from its margin or coast—its harbors, bays, creeks, inlets. High seas, in the plural number, more properly means the oceanic mass of waters, which is composed of many subdivisions of seas and oceans.(a)

§ 225. *The Sea,* what is it in the legal sense? It means when used by a nation or people, the large navigable waters on which that people have intercourse or commerce in ships and vessels. On islands in the ocean, it means the ocean—in the languages of the South of Europe, it means the Mediterranean—on the Baltic Sea, the White Sea—the Zuyder Zee—Sea of Geneva—the Black Sea—the Sea of Marmora—the Sea of Azoph—the Caspian Sea—the Sea of Aral—the Red Sea—the Dead Sea—the Sea of Gallilee, it means the waters of those seas respectively. In classic Latin and Greek, ancient and modern, and in the vernacular tongue of those who dwell on the shores of those seas, and carry on commerce on their waters, those waters are sea, and the vessels which navigate them are ships. In the 107th Psalm, the phrase, "those who go down to the sea in ships," is a strictly literal translation of the Greek of the Septuagint, and the Latin of the Vulgate, and in all these languages, precisely the same words are used for sea, and for ship as are used in Mark 4, 1, for the little sea of Gallilee, and the ves-

---

(a) 5 How. 462. Dunlap's Prac. 32.

sels in the port of Capernaum; and the same words are in constant use throughout the Scriptures, for all sorts of navigable waters and navigating vessels. Virgil uses *mare* for the river Timavus—and it was in common use by all writers in latin, for any large body of navigable waters, and an adjective was added to give it a specific use. Mare inferum—superum—Tyrhenum—Tuscum—Adriaticum—Ionicum. Mare Magnum—Mare Oceani.(*a*)

§ 226. The visible flux and reflux of the Tide is by no means necessary to constitute the sea. There are no visible tides in the Baltic, the Mediterranean, the Black, the Caspian, the Aral, the Marmora, the Azoph, the Dead Sea, or the Sea of Gallilee. I say visible tides, for if the tides be the result of the moon's attraction, then there must be a tide in all large bodies of water, for that attraction must be universal and irresistible—and although not easily perceptible because of the restless character of the fluid, still a tideometer might be constructed with such delicate arrangements as to show the attraction of the moon with as much certainty as the heat in her winter rays is measured by delicately constructed thermometers. If the jurisdiction of a court should be made to depend upon such a criterion, instead of the character of the controversy, such an instrument, instead of the arguments of counsel, would be necessary to enlighten the court.

§ 227. The Mediterranean sea was the great theatre of all the maritime commercial enterprize of the early ages, of which we have any knowledge. No one ever doubted that cases on that sea were cases of Admiralty and maritime jurisdiction—yet there is no tide, and always a current running the same way, as regularly as in the Mississippi—and the Baltic, the White, the Black, and the Caspian seas have no tide, but, like our inland seas, the great western lakes, they have at intervals, longer or shorter, a rise and fall of the water whose cause is unknown. They may be the result of atmospheric pressure—of the force

---

(*a*) 5 How. 462. Ains. Dic. Mare.

of winds—of uncertain and variable inflowing currents—and they may be the result of the ocean tides that, by irregular and obstructed subterranean channels, manifest their power in irregular spasmodic throes. If civilization and commerce had first had their harbors, and built their cities and their ships on the inland waters of the western continent, instead of the eastern, then our majestic rivers and lakes, the inland waters of America, would have had the glory of exhibiting the necessity, and establishing the principles of the maritime law of the world, as they have already been the theatre of some of the most brilliant naval and maritime exploits which have contributed to our national glory.(a)

§ 228. It is not difficult to see how the matter of the tides has risen to a rank in relation to jurisdiction, to which it is not entitled. At the first in England, the rise and fall of the tide was spoken of only in relation to the space between high and low watermark, in tide waters, which was declared to be within the ebb and flow of the tide, and so within the Admiralty jurisdiction, when the tide was in, but it had no relation to the general question of Admiralty jurisdiction. " As far as the tide ebbed and flowed," meant as far as high water mark on the shore, and not as far up the stream as the tide was perceptible. It had no relation to tideless waters. But in England, during the contests with the Admiralty, the common law courts, as has been shown, seized upon any thing for a pretext to further their views, and it was easy to make the flowing of the tide a limit as well in the navigable rivers as on the sea coast. In the general maritime law, there is nothing that confines maritime transactions or the maritime law, to tide waters or salt water. They are limited only to the affairs of ships and vessels, and those who sail, or own, or use, or injure them.(b)

§ 229. In Admiralty and maritime torts and offences, which depend entirely upon locality, the ebbing and flowing of the tide has

---

(a) Falcon's Dic 559–60. Silliman's Journal, 6 Am. Reg. 343.
(b) 7 Pet. 342. 11 Pet. 175. 12 Pet. 72. 5 How. 463. Ante, § 71.

been taken as an arbitrary limit to what is called the high sea; and in England, the common law courts have established the tide as the test of jurisdiction in British waters. But in the United States, even in matters which depend upon locality, such as seizures, navigability, instead of tide, is made the test. The Congress and the courts embrace within the Admiralty and maritime jurisdiction all seizures on waters navigable from the sea, by vessels of ten or more tons.(a)

§ 230. There can be nothing in the mere rise and fall of the water, which can affect the jurisdiction of courts, nor in the periodicity of the rise and fall, nor in the cause of that rise and fall. Periodical inundations and freshets exist in most rivers and lakes, and they are subject to some curious laws which are known, and to many others, which have hitherto eluded discovery. It is sufficient to say, that they would form quite as respectable a source of legal jurisdiction and maritime law, as any merely lunatic influence.

§ 231. The Rivers are properly, and philosophically speaking, a part of the sea. This fact of physical geography is not stated for the purpose of thereby establishing a maritime jurisdiction in all or in any rivers. For the purpose of this question, navigability is the true test. The jurisdiction does not depend upon the existence of tides or of salt, or the absence of currents— nor upon any of the characteristic points of distinction between rivers and oceans.

It may seem fanciful, and, perhaps, unprofessional, to devote even a paragraph or two to such a view of the subject; but when, by a strict construction, a narrow and exclusive sense is sought to be applied to words of a larger signification, it is not always useless to show that a still more strict and technical construction brings us practically to the same larger and more beneficial signification.

§ 232. The earth is made up of two great systems, if we may so say—the land system and the water system. "And God called the dry land earth, and the gathering together of the wa-

---

(a) Jud. Act, § 9. Conk. Treat. 2d edit. 136, 139, 350, 351.

ters called he seas." The land and the water are each made up of numerous subdivisions, having generic and specific characteristic definitions. They are, nevertheless, respectively, one in a general sense. The land is all connected together, though we do not sometimes see the connection. The mountain, the valley, and the plain, exist as well at the bottom of the ocean as on the visible dry ground; and capes and promontories, and isthmuses and peninsulas, and islands, are but portions of the land. So arms, inlets, bays, ports, rivers, straits, and lakes, are parts of the sea, as the branches of the tree, or the limbs of the human body are portions of the body. The waters of our little archipelago of New York, that wash the shores of Long Island, Staten Island, NewYork Island, Bedlow's Island, Governor's Island, Barn Island, Randall's Island, Blackwell's Island, &c., though they are all within counties of the State of New York, and within the harbor of New York, and are connected with the ocean in every direction by straits, not more than a pistol shot in width, do not lose their character as a part of the ocean, because those islands lie near each other, any more than the waters that surround the West India Islands, or the Islands of the Grecian archipelago, cease to be portions of the sea, because the Islands of the sea lie clustered in their bosom. The great ocean (for, in the general sense, there is but one ocean,) is but the great central mass of water, like the trunk of the tree. It is the great reservoir from which water departs in vapor, to be condensed on the land, and rolled back in rivers to its original source, the ocean. If we could take, in a panoramic view, the whole apparent aqueous system, we should see that the waters are all one mass, apparently, as well as really, with the exception of here and there a lake with a subterranean outlet, and a few rivers that lose themselves in bibulous sands. This is the geographical and philosophical view of this great fact of the unity of the waters. "The gathering together of the waters called he seas"—Genesis. If the ocean and all its rivers and arms could be dried, and again filled, not by the supplies from rivers, but by welling up from its own depths, it would present the same appearance as before—the great rivers would be shorter, but they would be there, and filled with the ocean brine, which would send its vapors to the land, and all the old channels of the rivers would be again filled with their currents, and the ne-ver ending circulation would be again in motion. It is all one mass of water, and it would be as rational to say that the peninsulas, promontories, isthmusses, and islands are no part of the land, so far as the Admiralty is concerned, as that the bays, creeks, channels, inlets, harbors and rivers, are no part of the sea. For practical purposes, however, in relation to the Admiralty and maritime law, we must be limited, not by any strict and technical limit, but by the purpose—the use—the subject matter, for the purposes of commerce—and navigability, so far as water is concerned, is, on principle, the only test of maritime jurisdiction.(a)

§ 233. The navigable rivers, up to the point of obstruction to the navigation, " *all navigable rivers beneath the first bridges*," that is, so far as they are navigable, even in England, have been held to be within the Admiralty and maritime jurisdiction, so far as those classes of cases are concerned, of which the English Admiralty had jurisdiction, even when arising on the ocean. In the Vice-Admiralty Courts of the Colonies, the jurisdiction extended to " *public streams, fresh waters, rivers and creeks*."

§ 234. The United States, by the first act of Congress, in relation to the judiciary passed Sept. 24, 1789, declared that the Admiralty and maritime jurisdiction extended to " *all waters navigable from the sea by vessels of ten or more tons burthen*"—and these early acts have been always held to be important contemporaneous constructions of the Constitution.(b)

§ 235. The Act for the Government and regulation of Seamen in the Merchant Service, passed July 20th, 1790, section 6, subjects all seamen and all ships and vessels " in the merchant service," (that is to say, not in the public naval service,) to the

---

(a) 5 How. 462.
(b) 5 How. 464.   Conk. Treat. 2d ed. 350, *n*.

jurisdiction of the Admiralty in cases of mariners wages, and it makes no allusion whatever to the sea or the tides. The act of July 16, 1798, for the relief of sick and disabled seamen, and the act of May 3, 1802, amending the same, expressly provide, that persons navigating coasting vessels, including " every boat, raft, or flat," going down the Mississippi, with the intention to proceed to New Orleans, shall be considered as *seamen* of the United States.

§ 236. The act " for enrolling and licensing ships or vessels to be employed in the coasting trade and fisheries, and for regu‧ lating the same," passed Feby. 18, 1793, and the previous act for registering and clearing vessels, &c., and the act of March 2d, 1819, supplementary to the acts concerning the coasting trade," and the act of May 2d, 1822, for the collection of duties on exports and tonnage in Florida, expressly includes all " the *navigable rivers of the United States.*"

§ 237. A uniform current of decisions and of practice in every court of the United States having Admiralty jurisdiction, from the first establishment of the courts, have settled the law, that all cases arising under these acts, are cases of Admiralty and maritime jurisdiction. It must, therefore, be conceded, that principle and practice, the law and the reason of it, the acts of Congress, and the decisions under them, all concur in declaring that navigable rivers are within the Admiralty and maritime jurisdiction, for certain purposes at least—and the force of these views seems to be fully felt by Judge Woodbury, in his dissenting opinion in the case of *Waring* v. *Clark*, where he expressly declares, that the maritime law of continental Europe would carry Admiralty jurisdiction over all navigable streams.(*a*)

§ 238. There is no difference between the Mississippi, or any other navigable river, at its mouth and far inland, or between the ports of Cincinnati, St. Louis, Natchez, New Orleans,

(*a*) Conk. Treat. 2d edit. 138, 139, 350, 351. 5 How. 475. Gilp. 203, 505. 6 How. 392. 4 N. Y. Leg. Ob. 450.

Georgetown, or the numerous other ports on the navigable
rivers, and other arms of the sea, except the tides and the currents, and the salt.   If any of these can affect the jurisdiction,
it must be, not the comparative strength of these elements, but
their absolute philosophical existence, no matter how feeble.
There cannot be jurisdiction more surely in the fearful tides of
the Bay of Fundy and the Solway, than in the gentler flow of
hardly perceptible tides—in a current of one mile an hour than in
one of ten—in the intense saltness of the Dead Sea and the Great
Salt Lake, than in the almost fresh waters of the Baltic and
the Black Sea.   Currents exist in a greater or less degree—and
chemical analysis detects saline particles—and the influence of
the Moon's attraction must be felt—in all large bodies of
water.

§ 239. The existence of perpetual currents, flowing always
the same way, has never been held to affect the jurisdiction of
the Admiralty.   Under the equator, currents in the Atlantic are
so violent that they carry vessels very speedily from Africa to
America, but absolutely prevent their return the same way.
This current performs a continual circulation, setting out from
the Guinea coast in Africa, for example, thence crossing straight
over the Atlantic Ocean, and so setting into the Gulf of Mexico
by the south side of it, then sweeping around by the bottom of
the Gulf, it issues out by the north side of it, and thence takes
a direction north-easterly along the coast of North America, till
it arrives near Newfoundland, when it is turned by a roundly
motion backwards across the Atlantic again upon the coast of
Europe, and from thence southward again to the coast of
Africa, from whence it set out.   It flows permanently, and in
some places at the rate of five miles an hour.   A boat not
acted on by the wind, would go from the Canaries to the coast
of Caraccas in thirteen months; in ten months would make
the tour of the Gulf of Mexico; and in forty or fifty days,
would go from Florida to the banks of Newfoundland.   It de-
posites on the coasts of Iceland and Norway, trees and fruits
belonging to the torrid zone; and remains of a vessel burnt at
Jamaica, were found on the coast of Scotland.   It is a great
river in the midst of the Ocean.   Other permanent currents, of

even greater force and regularity, exist in the Straits of Gibraltar, the Straits of Magellan, and St. George's Channel ; and strong, constant currents, and variable and periodical currents of great force, exist in most of the Straits and Channels of the Ocean, often, during their existence, entirely overcoming the tide.(a)

§ 240. The Dardanelles is thirty-three miles long, and varies in width from half a mile to a mile and a half. Cocks are heard crowing from the opposite shores. Lord Byron swam across it in an hour and five minutes, swimming more than four miles because of the current, which is so rapid that no boat can row directly across. It is but a river connecting two lakes. In ancient times it had its commerce and its ships. More than four hundred years before the Christian era, it was the scene of the greatest naval battle and victory known to ancient history. And, although it can be navigated against the current only by the force of strong, favorable winds, or by steam, in modern times, it floats an immense commerce, and ships of the line, of the largest class, and armed fleets, pass through it from sea to sea. The fearful currents in the Straits of Magellan, are known to all navigators. The great American rivers, those of a few furlongs width, and those of many leagues wide, pour down their majestic torrents with such force that their turbid waters are carried to an immense distance into the Ocean. They are rivers there as much as in the land. When steam shall have wrought out its destiny, and spread the triumphs of its great revolution throughout the world, these currents will be of no account whatever in navigation.

§ 241. It is universally conceded that the general principles of law must be applied to new kinds of property, as they spring into existence in the progress of society according to their nature and incidents, and the common sense of the community. In the early periods of maritime commerce, when the oar was the great agent of propulsion, vessels were entirely unlike those of

---

(a) Falc. 113, Art. Currents. Encyc. Am. Art. Currents.

modern times—and each nation and period has had its peculiar agents of commerce and navigation adapted to its own wants and its own waters, and the names and descriptions of ships and vessels are without number. Under the class of mariners in the armed ship are embraced the officers and privates of a little army. In the whale ship, the sealing vessel—the codfishing and herring fishing vessel—the lumber vessel—the freighting vessel—the passenger vessel—there are other functions besides these of mere navigation, and they are performed by men who know nothing of seamanship—and in the great invention of modern times, the steamboat, an entirely new set of operatives, are employed, yet at all times and in all countries, all the persons who have been necessarily or properly employed in a vessel as co-labourers to the great purpose of the voyage, have, by the law, been clothed with the legal rights of mariners— no matter what might be their sex, character, station or profession.(a)

§ 242. This has been because the maritime law does not stick in the bark of a literal and technical construction, but looks at its rules with a liberal and rational regard to the subject matter—to the substance and not to the form. Shall it not do so in relation to the waters, as well as the agents of commerce and the principles of law—shall the great inland waters of the American Continent be denied, the privileges which uniform judicial decision and immemorial usage, have always allowed to those of Europe, as soon as discovery found them and commerce penetrated them? Should modern science, art and adventure succeed in carrying profitable commerce through all parts of the frozen zones, and carry our ships to the very poles of the north and the south, would that commerce be denied the benefits of the maritime law and its judicial jurisdiction, because there are no tides at the polar centres? No more can we on principle deny the same benefits to the great waters which the discovery of Columbus, in process of time opened to a commerce out-valuing that of all antiquity. What is to be the commerce of American rivers, when those of thousands of

---

(a) 20 Wend. Rep. 648.   Falcon. Dic. word, Naval Architecture.   Gilp. 505, 524.   Ord. la. Mar. Liv. 2.

miles in length—like the shorter ones of the older settlements—shall have their shores covered with busy commercial cities, their rapid feeders with manufacturing towns, and their valleys with farms, and shall bear on their currents the merchandize, manufactures and agricultural products of what is now an unbroken wilderness. The maritime law will be just as appropriate and just and necessary to their wants as to those of the old world, and rational, sound, legal construction cannot fail to give the benefit of it to them as it has to the old world.

§ 243. The whole maritime commerce of the world at the time of the earlier and most universally acknowledged codes was not equal to the present maritime commerce of the American lakes and rivers. In 1846 (it has increased incalculably since,) the American registered, enrolled and licensed tonnage of the lakes was 106,386 tons, worth six million of dollars ; the number of clearances and entries, 15,845 ; and the amount of imports and exports, $3,861,088 ; the number of mariners was 6972. The river tonnage at the same period was 249,000 tons, employing 25,000 men, and carrying on a commerce a little short of $20,000,000. The line of lake coast is about 5000 miles in extent, 2000 of which is on the coast of a first rate power foreign to the United States, and of the remaining 3000 miles of lake coast, and of the 17,000 miles of navigable rivers, almost the whole lies at the same time in two or more States of our Union, which in all matters, independent of the National Constitution are foreign to each other.(a)

(a) [*From the Albany Evening Journal, April*, 1849.] LENGTH OF SEA COAST OF THE UNITED STATES.—The sea coast of the United States, according to a recent report of the land office, is five thousand one hundred and twenty miles, including the Atlantic, Gulf and Pacific, or a "shore line" following the irregularities of the shore and sea islands, according to an estimate of the superintendent of the coast survey of 33,063 miles.

From the northern limits of the United States to the Cape of Florida
on the Atlantic ocean, ... 1,900 miles.
From the Cape of Florida to the mouth of the Rio Grande on the Gulf
of Mexico, ... 1,600 "
From the boundary point one league south of the port of San Diego
on the Pacific, along the coast of Oregon and the Straits of Fuca to
the boundary point 49 deg. north latitude, ... 1,620 "
Making together the length of sea coast on the Atlantic, Gulf and
Pacific, ... 5,120 "

§ 244. On Lakes Champlain, Ontario, and Erie, the United States had more than forty armed vessels, from small craft of one gun, up to "tall admirals" of more than one hundred guns,—were they not Ships and Vessels? On those waters

---

Or a " shore line " following the irregularities of the shore and sea islands, according to an estimate of the superintendent of the coast survey, of . . . . 33,063 miles.

The *Buffalo Commercial* of April, 1849, contains a full list of all the shipping upon the Northern and Western Lakes, with the tonnage of each. The total number of each, and the valuation, is as follows:

Name.				Number.	Valuation.
Steamers,	.	.	.	. 95	$3,380,000
Propellers,	.	.	·	. 45	950,000
Sail Vessels,	.	.	.	. 774	7,868,000
Total,	.	.	·	. 914	$11,898,000

THE COMMERCIAL MARINE OF THE UNITED STATES.—The following astonishing statistics are from the report of the Secretary of the Treasury, of the commercial navigation of the United States for the last fiscal year.

The extraordinary commercial progress of our country is shown in the following table of the sum total of our tonnage, with the increase per cent, for four decimal periods:

1818, 1,225,284 tons; 1828, 1,741,391 tons, 42 per cent; 1838, 1,995,639 tons, 15 per cent; 1848, 3,154,051 tons, 56 per cent.

In thirty years the tonnage of the United States has increased 160 per cent, upon what it was in 1818.

The first six States, in point of ship building, are presented in their order, as follows:

Maine, 89,974 tons; New York, 68,434 tons; Massachusetts, 39,366 tons; Pennsylvania, 29,638 tons; Maryland, 17,480 tons; Ohio, 13,656 tons.

The following facts appear from the report:

One third of the ship-building of Pennsylvania is in the West—8,000 tons of New York ship building is on the lakes.

The State of Ohio, an entirely inland State, is the sixth in point of ship building.

The State of Ohio builds as much tonnage in vessels as all the States and ports from Chesapeake Bay to the Rio Grande.

Ohio builds double as much as Virginia, North Carolina, South Carolina and Florida.

The following is a view of the American tonnage of the lakes, as entered in the different marine districts:

Lake Champlain, 4,745 tons; Lake Ontario, 33,800 tons, Lake Erie, 115,960 tons ; Lake Michigan, 10,483 tons—Total, 164,997.

The tonnage of the western rivers, (exclusive of New Orleans,) is:

Pittsburgh, 30,970 tons; Wheeling, 2,660 tons; Cincinnati, 21,350 tons ; Louis-

Perry and McDonough immortalized themselves. Were they not Naval Heroes?—and their brave tars, were they not Mariners? Did they not take Prizes? Like the modern ocean, those lakes and rivers are now navigated by vessels of every size and description, from vessels of fifteen hundred tons burthen, down to the smallest commercial craft—clearing at custom houses a thousand miles from the ocean for all the ports of the States, and for foreign ports at the ends of the earth; and they pass from one State jurisdiction to another, back and forth, hundreds of times on a voyage from New Orleans to St. Louis. They transport millions of passengers bound from State to State, and from one nation to another, on the great errands of the infinitely diversified commerce of about ten millions of people on the shores of those waters—and they are freighted with but the first fruits from fields scattered here and there on the borders of a domain yet to be cultivated, reaching across seventeen degrees of latitude and sixty degrees of longitude, and of whose future yearly productions and maritime commerce, the human mind can form no adequate idea.(a)

§ 245. In all the arrangements of this lake and river commerce, there is nothing to distinguish it from the other maritime

---

ville, 8,822 tons; St. Louis, 36,512 tons; Nashville, 2,445 tons; Vicksburg, 588 tons—Total, 108,127.

The river tonnage entered at New Orleans is almost equal to the whole of the above, making a total of almost 200,000 tons of ship tonnage on the western rivers.

American Almanac.

(a) 5 Howard, 497.

[*From the New York Express, July,* 1849.] " Montreal, July 2.—In connection with the statements of my last letter on the Navigation of the St. Lawrence, I may mention that we have had in port during the week three American schooners, drawing eight feet water, with full cargoes, direct from Ohio, which will return with cargoes of salt, and I cut the following from the arrivals in the Quebec Shipping List :

" ' The propeller Western Miller, from Toronto, to Messrs. Gillespies & Co., arrived here on Wednesday evening. Her cargo consists of 2200 barrels of flour, 72 do. oatmeal, 73 do. cornmeal, 30 do. pot barley, 2199 bushels wheat, 55 barrels, split peas, 48 kegs butter. 12 bales wool, and 3 casks hams. It will be seen, on commerce of the world. There is not a contract, or a wrong, not a want, a right, or a duty, not a construction, or a contrivance, a utensil, a material, or a supply, nor an agent of commerce, animate or inanimate, that is met with on the widest, the stormiest, and the saltest ocean, that has not its double on those mighty rivers and lakes; and the same rules of law are to be applied to the controversies that spring up there. A salvage, an average, a bottomry, a case of wages, of freight, of pilotage, of wharfage, on Lake Erie, the Mississippi, or the St. Lawrence, are as clearly cases of Admiralty and Maritime jurisdiction, and as much subject to the Admiralty and Maritime law, as similar cases in the Black Sea or the Baltic, the Straits of Magellan, the Dardanelles, or Long Island Sound. Their nature is the same every where—they are maritime every where.(a) If the Admiral of ancient times existed here, with the jurisdiction and functions of his palmiest days, it would be now, as it was then, in the local waters alone—where his own nation claimed exclusive jurisdiction—in our close seas, our harbors, lakes and rivers, or over our own vessels, that his power and prerogative would be felt in the Admiralty law.

§ 246. The Congress in 1845, passed " An Act extending the jurisdiction of the District Courts to certain cases upon the lakes and navigable waters connecting the same." It is in these words:

---

reference to our advertising columns, that the Western Miller will leave again for Toronto to-morrow at noon '

" This vessel is a propeller which makes the passage back from Quebec to Montreal, 180 miles, against the current, in twenty-four hours. She is built to pass the Welland Canal, and may consequently navigate freely from Chicago to Quebec. The cargo above stated is equal to 3500 barrels, or more than the average cargoes of the brigs and schooners which clear from good Northern ports for the Gulf of Mexico, the West Indies, or the Spanish Main."

[*From the New York Tribune, October,* 1849] " MONTREAL, Oct. 9, 1849 — A bark has just left Chicago on its way to California, by the St. Lawrence. She has fifty-three passengers from the West, but will take her cargo from Quebec. Special permission was given to this vessel. Next session of Parliament will throw the St. Lawrence open to all vessels."

(a) 1 Doug. Mich. R. 154. 6 Ohio R. 71.

" *Be it enacted by the Senate and House of Representatives of the United States of America in Congress assembled,* That the District Courts of the United States shall have, possess, and exercise, the same jurisdiction in matters of contract and tort, arising in, upon, or concerning, steamboats and other vessels of twenty tons burden and upwards, enrolled and licensed for the coasting trade, and at the time employed in business of commerce and navigation between ports and places in different States and Territories upon the lakes and navigable waters connecting said lakes, as is now possessed and exercised by the said courts in cases of the like steamboats and other vessels employed in navigation and commerce upon the high seas, or tide waters, within the Admiralty and Maritime jurisdiction of the United States ; and in all suits brought in such courts in all such matters of contract or tort, the remedies, and the forms of process, and the modes of proceeding, shall be the same as are or may be used by such courts in cases of Admiralty and Maritime jurisdiction ; and the maritime law of the United States, so far as the same is or may be applicable thereto, shall constitute the rule of decision in such suits, in the same manner, and to the same extent, and with the same equities, as it now does in cases of Admiralty and Maritime jurisdiction ; saving, however, to the parties the right of trial by jury of all facts put in issue in such suits, where either party shall require it ; and saving also to the parties the right of a concurrent remedy at the common law, where it is competent to give it, and any concurrent remedy which may be given by the State laws, where such steamer or other vessel is employed in such business of commerce and navigation.

" *Approved,* February 26, 1845."(*a*)

§ 247. This act has been considered as extending the Admiralty jurisdiction to the internal waters mentioned in the act— and, in that point of view, its constitutionality has been doubted. And it is undoubtedly true, that if the language of the Constitution " All cases of Admiralty and Maritime jurisdiction,"

(*a*) Acts of 1845, 5 Stat. at Large, 726.

does not embrace cases arising on the navigable rivers and lakes, then no act of Congress could make such cases Admiralty or Maritime cases ; for no principle is better settled, than that the Congress cannot extend any more than they can destroy a provision of the Constitution. If, however, under any of the clauses of the Constitution the federal government has the power to regulate such cases, then it is equally clear, that the judicial determination of such cases may be conferred on such courts of the Union, and the proceedings in them may be regulated in such manner as the Congress may determine.(a)

§ 248. The power "to regulate commerce with foreign nations, and among the several States, and with the Indian tribes."

" To constitute tribunals inferior to the Supreme Court—to define and punish piracies and felonies committed on the high seas, and offences against the law of nations."

" To make all laws which shall be necessary and proper for carrying into execution the foregoing powers, and all other powers vested by the Constitution in the government of the United States," together with the judicial power, are amply sufficient to authorize the Congress to pass any laws which they may deem salutary in relation to the jurisdiction and mode of trial of any cases of aquatic commerce on the great navigable rivers and lakes.(b)

§ 249. The phraseology of the act of 1845, seems to indicate, that at the time of its passage, the Congress were impressed with the importance of extending the beneficial course of Admiralty proceedings to such cases, but were somewhat doubtful of their power to consider them as cases of Admiralty jurisdiction. The remark of Mr. Webster, the most profound expositor of the Constitution, after Chief Justice Marshall, on the subject of this act, seems to be true :—" The only objection to this necessary law, seems to be that Congress, in passing it, was

---

(a) Conk. Ad. Jur. and Prac. 4.
(b) 6 How. 392.

shivering and trembling under the apprehension of what might be the ultimate consequence of the decision of this court in the case of the Thomas Jefferson. It pitched the power upon a wrong location. Its proper home was in the Admiralty and maritime grant, as in all reason and in the common sense of all mankind, out of England, Admiralty and maritime jurisdiction ought to extend, and does extend to all navigable waters, fresh or salt."(a)

§ 250. So far as the cases embraced in the purview of the act, are concerned, it would hardly be doubted that the Congress might give jurisdiction of them to the Courts of the United States, and that being so, the process and proceedings are entirely under the control of the national Legislature. It cannot be doubted, that the Congress might provide, that in all suits in the Courts of the United States, the remedies and the forms of process, and the modes of proceeding, shall be the same as are or may be used in cases of Admiralty and maritime jurisdiction, saving to the parties the right of trial by jury, in the cases provided by the Constitution—and as has been before remarked, the trial by jury might be made compulsory in all Admiralty cases, if it were expedient.

When, therefore, the Congress enacts that, in certain classes of cases over which they have jurisdiction, the District Courts shall exercise the same jurisdiction—according to the same forms of process, and modes of proceeding—and apply the same rules of law as in cases of Admiralty and maritime jurisdiction, it is entirely immaterial whether those classes of cases be really Admiralty cases or not, according to any received definition. For all practical purposes of law and justice, they are Admiralty cases, even if they should arise in the depths of the mountain forests.

§ 251. This act, it will be observed, as to subject matter, embraces all matters of *contract* and *tort arising in, upon, or concerning steamboats or other vessels.* As to the kind of water

---

(a) Infra, § 255.   6 How. 378.   5 How. 475.   3 Dal. 297.

craft, it embraces *steamboats and other vessels*, enrolled and licensed for the coasting trade—as to the size of the vessels, it embraces vessels of *twenty tons burden and upwards*—as to the business in which the vessels are employed, it must be the business of *commerce and navigation between ports and places in different states and territories*—and as to the locality, it must be upon *the lakes and the navigable waters connecting said lakes.*

§ 252. It does not embrace the great navigable rivers, which do not connect the lakes. Thus, while it embraces the Niagara river, it does not embrace the Mississippi—a distinction for which it is difficult to perceive the cause. The commerce of the rivers is quite as important as that of the lakes, and if an act of Congress be necessary for the purpose, it is to be hoped that the navigable rivers may soon have the benefit of a similar enactment.(*a*)

§ 253. In the case of the Thomas Jefferson, 10 Wheat. 428, the Supreme Court held that the Admiralty had not jurisdiction in a case of seaman's wages, earned on the Ohio, Mississippi, and Missouri rivers, the whole voyage being above tide water. The case does not appear to have been argued, and Judge Story, in delivering the opinion of the Court, adverted to the old controversy between the English courts, and because the English Admiralty did not claim jurisdiction except in tide waters—this, he says, is the prescribed limit which it was not at liberty to transcend—seemed to suppose that the jurisdiction could not exist here. Neither the English Admiralty nor common law courts in those days, so far as I have been able to discover, ever adverted to the point, except to claim jurisdiction below the first bridges in all navigable rivers. He puts his opinion on the prescribed limit which the English Admiralty was not at liberty to transcend. He says, " In the great struggles between the courts of common law and the Admiralty, the latter never attempted to assert any jurisdiction except over ma-

---

(*a*) **Ante,** § 246, 247, 248, 249.

ritime contracts. In respect to contracts for the hire of seamen, the Admiralty never pretended to claim, nor could it rightfully exercise, any jurisdiction except in cases where the service was substantially performed or to be performed upon the sea, or upon waters within the ebb and flow of the tide. This is the prescribed limit which it was not at liberty to transcend." Thus placing his decision on what he supposes to be purely English ground, yet without citing any authority to show that the question, in the form in which he presents it, had ever been mooted in that country. The English Admiralty had certainly all along claimed jurisdiction in all navigable rivers below the first bridges, that is, up to the point of obstruction—and above the bridges, I know of no evidence that a case ever arose, or that there were then any ships or maritime commerce in which they could arise.(a)

§ 254. The Supreme Court had, before that time, decided, as they have since, that the jurisdiction, in case of contracts, does not depend on place, but on the nature of the transaction—and also that, so far as place was concerned, waters navigable from the sea, by vessels of only ten tons burthen, are by the statute, sec. 9, within the Admiralty jurisdiction. The criticism of the learned judge of the language of that statute and the Seaman's Act, seems to want his usual reflection. The clause in the first act is apparently declaratory, and the clause inserted to preclude a doubt, " all civil causes of Admiralty and maritime jurisdiction, including all seizures, under laws of import, navigation, or trade of the United States, when the seizures are made on waters which are navigable from the sea, by vessels of ten or more tons burthen, within their respective districts as well as upon the high seas." By the simple force of that language, all such cases, as well on the lakes and rivers as on the high seas, have been uniformly held to be within the Admiralty jurisdiction, and to be civil causes, triable by the court without a jury; so the Seaman's Act of 1790, in its title, embraces, all seamen " in the merchant service," its language is, " every seaman

---

(a) 10 Wheat. 428.   6 Cond. R. 173.   Dunlap's Prac. 32.

or mariner"—" any seaman or mariner"—" every ship or vessel"
—"any ship or vessel"—without any allusion to the tides—
mere navigability seems to be all that is necessary, and that is
left to be inferred from the fact, that the service is on board a
ship or vessel.(*a*)

§ 255. Notwithstanding this case of the Thomas Jefferson, at
a later period, the Supreme Court held a different doctrine.
They could not fail to be embarrassed by the narrow rule then
adopted on merely English grounds, for it would exclude the
Mississippi river and the port of New Orleans, a port thronged
with the largest ships, and carrying on a wider and more extensive maritime commerce than most of the ports of the world.
At that port the water is fresh and free from tide, but it would
shock the legal sense of every lawyer to exclude it from the
Admiralty and maritime jurisdiction; and the Supreme Court,
accordingly, held in the case of Peyroux v. Howard, and Waring
v. Clarke, and it is now well settled that it is within the Admiralty jurisdiction, although there is no ebb or flow, and its current always runs outwards, like the Mediterranean, and its
waters are fresh. The court, however, do homage to the
English rule, and place their decision on the ground, that
the river is influenced by the tide, and shows a sort of
irregular swell, which must be caused by the tide. The
learned judge, who delivered the opinion of the court, says
that "so far as Admiralty jurisdiction depends upon locality, it is bounded by the ebb and flow of the tide." But
in matters of contract, it does not depend upon locality, but
upon subject matter, as has been repeatedly decided, and is well
settled.(*b*)

§ 256. On principle, it clearly cannot be the moon's attraction, the presence or absence of the tide, which determines

---

(*a*) 5 How. 441. 6 How. 344. Conk. Treat. 2d edit. 136, 139, 350, 351.
7 Pet. 324.

(*b*) Ante, § 255. 7 Pet. 324. 5 How. 441. Ibid. 497-8. 7 Pet. 343. 5 How.
441. Gilp. 524.

the jurisdiction—nor upon the periodical rise and fall of the water.(*a*)—Nor the presence or absence of saline particles in the water.(*b*)—Nor the presence or absence of a current in the water.—Nor the size or character of the outlet, stream, or straight by which the lake or sea is connected with a larger body, or with the ocean.(*c*)—Nor that the water be an inland basin, land locked or land surrounded sea or lake.(*d*)—Nor that the water be a river.(*e*)—Nor upon place or locality in matters of contract, but on the subject matter.(*f*)—Nor upon its being in a harbor, or port, or body of a county.(*g*)—Nor upon the question, whether the common law has provided a remedy or not for similar cases.(*h*)—Nor upon the question, whether the local municipal laws and officers can be resorted to.(*i*)—Nor upon any British statute.(*j*)

It can depend upon nothing in matters of contract, but the subject matter, the nature and character of the controversy. If that be connected with ships and shipping—commerce and navigation—the Admiralty has jurisdiction, otherwise not. " Toutes les affairs relatives à la commerce et navigation et aux navigateurs appartient au droit maritime."(*k*)

(*a*) Ante, § 226, *et seq.*
(*b*) Ante, § 238, *et seq.*
(*c*) Ante, § 240, 247.
(*d*) Ante, § 226, 227.
(*e*) Ante, § 240.

(*f*) Infra, § 261. 5 How. 441.
(*g*) Ante, § 162, 232. 5 How. 464.
(*h*) Ante, § 205. 5 How. 459.
(*i*) Ante, § 206.
(*j*) Ante, § 14, 118, 161.

(*k*) 3 Pardessus Loix Mar. 451.

CHAPTER XVII.

The Question considered on Authority.

§ 257. The foregoing historical, legal, judicial and constitutional considerations, while they exhibit the ample jurisdiction of the maritime law, establish also the rule, that the law of jurisdiction of the English High Court of Admiralty, as acknowledged and restrained by the common law courts of England, at the time of the American Revolution, and since, is not the law of the jurisdiction of the American Admiralty; and that the decisions of the King's Bench and Common Pleas in England, restraining the Admiralty jurisdiction, are of no authority here.

§ 258. The same rule is established, by a weight of authority in this country, which would have rendered the present treatise unnecessary, were it not true, that while the general rule has been fortified by repeated decisions, in every court of the United States, and in every period of our judicial history, a large number of cases have also been decided on principles which can be maintained only on the authority of the narrower English rule; and this conflict of decisions has subjected the general rule to renewed attack and investigation, as new cases arise, apparently in the hope of establishing new exceptions, if not of destroying the rule altogether, and confining the American Admiralty to the modern English limits.(*a*)

§ 259. It is, however, true, that the more important the case

---

(*a*) 1 Pain. 673. Ware, 91, 152. 5 How. 441. 6 Id. 344. Davies' R. 93. While these sheets are passing through the press, a second volume of the decisions of Judge Ware of the Maine District, reported by Mr. Edward H. Davies, has been issued from the press. I invite attention to the interesting note commencing on page 93, in which the jurisdiction of the American Admiralty is placed on its true grounds, in a manner every way worthy of the distinguished jurist who has so long been an ornament to the Admiralty bench.

presented, and the greater the ability with which the question of jurisdiction has been argued at the bar, and the more carefully and learnedly has it been examined by the bench, the more surely has the jurisdiction of the Admiralty been sustained in that large and beneficial extent which alone makes it a valuable portion of the national jurisdiction. It is also true, that opinions have been pronounced in favor of the narrow English rule, which seem to be written in a spirit somewhat characteristic of Westminster Hall, in the days of Lord Coke, and which seem to treat the question as one of mere municipal importance, rather than as one of national interest.(a)

§ 260. From the case of the *Betsey*, in 1794, and *La Vengeance*, in 1796, down to the case of *Waring* v. *Clarke*, in 1847, and the case of *The New Jersey Steam Navigation Co.* v. *The Merchants Bank*, in 1848, the Supreme Court have uniformly held the same general principles on this subject. Many of the judges who presided in that tribunal during its earlier existence, and a large portion of the Congress that established our judicial system, had been members of the convention which formed the Constitution, and were thus well fitted to judge of the proper force of its language. While we cannot but admit that those members of the court who have dissented in a few instances from the opinion of the court, have been worthy of distinguished honor for the learning and ability which made them ornaments of the court, it is no disparagement of them to say, that those who have been first and always in the majority, embrace those immortal jurists, whose judicial career has shed the most lustre upon the nation. And the existence of three or four dissenting opinions in sixty years, in which the whole argument on the other side has been presented in the strongest light by judges of the most distinguished ability, after solemn argument, instead of throwing doubt upon the repeated decisions of the court, is, in truth, strong evidence in support of the soundness of the principles which have prevailed.(b)

(a) 6 How. 344, 389. 5 Id. 441. Ware, 91.

(b) 3 Dal. 6. Ibid. 297. 4 Wheat. 438. 5 How. 441. 6 Id. 344. 1 Gal. 468. Ware, 149. 2 Gal. 398. 1 Brockenborough R. 380. 2 Sumn. R. 157. 7 Peters, 324. 11 Id. 175. 12 Id. 72.

§ 261. It has thus been uniformly held :

1. That the grant in the Constitution, extending the judicial power to all cases of Admiralty and maritime jurisdiction, is neither to be limited to, nor to be interpreted by, what were cases of admiralty and maritime jurisdiction in England, when the Constitution was adopted. This rule, alone, considered in its proper force and effect, sweeps away the foundation of every objection that has been made to the general jurisdiction of the American Admiralty.

2. Another rule, equally well settled, furnishes as complete an answer to those objections. It has been always held, that the American Admiralty has a general maritime jurisdiction, embracing all maritime causes of action, as well in matters of contract as in matters of tort. That in matters of tort the jurisdiction depends upon the locality, and embraces all damages and injuries upon the sea. That in matters of contract, the jurisdiction depends upon the subject matter—the nature of the contract—and embraces all transactions and proceedings relative to naval commerce and navigation.

These rules have been so often laid down, and so uniformly held as general principles, that they must be considered as perfectly settled. Other less general rules, equally at war with the English decisions, have been fully established in our courts.

3. That the right of trial by jury does affect the question of the maritime jurisdiction.

4. The jurisdiction is not affected by the question, whether the courts of common law have jurisdiction in like cases, or whether the matter may have arisen within a port or harbor, or county of a state.

5. That the American Admiralty has jurisdiction of all cases of maritime lien.(a)

§ 262. Who can faill to perceive, that these principles and rules cover the whole subject. Considered in their proper light, and applied only in their necessary extent, they furnish a sufficient guide in settling all questions of jurisdiction in Admiralty

---

(a) Vide cases cited under § 260.

and maritime cases. For, from them, follows inevitably, another general principle, clearly stated by Du Ponceau. "In cases of Admiralty and maritime jurisdiction, a general authority is given to the courts of the United States, to administer in all cases that particular body of laws known as the Admiralty and maritime laws." If English law does not bind us, nor English decisions furnish us a guide, where can we look but to the general maritime law, for the definition and classification of cases of Admiralty and maritime jurisdiction.(a)

§ 263. It has been already remarked, that the true test of a maritime contract is to be found in its relation to a ship or vessel, the great agent of maritime enterprise—a test, at the same time simple, obvious, and easily applied. And I now propose, in closing this portion of this work, briefly to notice in detail the most numerous classes of maritime causes, in connection with the decided cases and other authorities. To those who look at the subject in the light of sound legal science, and examine its principles with a careful analysis of the substance, rather than of words and forms, it cannot fail to be apparent, that the classes and cases now to be noticed shed a light upon the whole subject, by which any other case may be easily referred to its proper class.

The great characteristic relations of maritime law are distributed by Pardessus in a manner, at the same time brief, simple, intelligible, and comprehensive, in his work on commercial law, as follows.(a)

"The transactions embraced in maritime commerce may be classified in a simple and intelligible order. Vessels, the only means by which navigation is carried on, cannot exist except as the property of some one, and all that concerns the vessels themselves, and every thing relating to the means of acquiring title to them, constitutes the first class.

"The management of the vessel is intrusted to a leader, usually known under the name of captain, and from this title and character are derived his rights and duties.

"The captain, and those who labor in the service of the ves-

(a) Duponceau on Jurisd. 9.   (b) 1 Pard. Droit Com. 81.

sels, in stations more or less subordinate, contract engagements in which the general principles of the hiring of services, are subjected to important modifications and extensions.

" Those to whom the vessels belong do not always employ them for their own personal use. They grant to others the right to transport goods in them, or they undertake, themselves, to make the transportation. Hence, necessarily, arise rules in relation to such engagements, and the application of the general principles which affect the responsibility of those engaged in transportation, and the necessary relations between the co-freighters in certain circumstances.

"The accidents to which navigation is exposed may occasion losses or sacrifices, known under the generic name of averages —and shipwrecks, in which it is necessary to provide for salvage.

" Maritime commerce being, in its nature, exposed to damages of every kind, speculators come to the aid of owners of ships and cargoes, and undertake to repair the losses which they suffer. This is the object of the contract of insurance.

" Maritime expeditions, sometimes giving rise to unforseen need of funds, which it is not always easy to procure by simple loans, and for the payment of which other security cannot be given, than the objects themselves, on which the advances are made, men have felt the need and acknowledged the advantages of associating the lender in the risks of navigation, so that the chance of loss may be compensated by the hope of a larger interest than his capital would produce in the commerce of the land, and this has given rise to the contract of bottomry.

" Maritime business is not confined solely to voyages and transportation of persons or merchandise ; the fisheries are an important branch of it, subject to special regulations, dictated by national and commercial interests."

§ 264. The first man who applies his service to making a ship available for the great purposes to which she is designed as a maritime agent, is the builder. He brings to the construction, skill, labor and capital, and incorporates all of them, in a greater or less degree, into the fabric. Without his aid she would perform none of her appropriate functions, for she could not exist. This service is eminently maritime, although it be all performed on land. It would be none the less so if much of it consisted in fitting and hewing the timber for her in their native forests, provided the labor was performed with a direct view to her construction. In the same manner if he supply capital to purchase that which is intended to enter and enters into her construction, and if he furnish neither labor, nor materials, nor money, but gives simply the skill which plans and directs, or the care which superintends the labor of others in her construction, he still performs a maritime service, although he may never have been, even for an instant, on the water. The building contract is a maritime contract, whether it be verbal or written, express or implied—" all matters that concern owners and proprietors of ships, as such, and shipwrights, are within the admiralty jurisdiction."(a)

§ 265. The builder may sue the owners *in personam* in the Admiralty, to recover whatever is due to him for his services in the construction of the vessel, or for violations of the building contract; and he has also a lien or privilege against the ship herself, which may be enforced in the Admiralty. The building contract being maritime, it is evident that the owner may sue the builder in the Admiralty, for violations of the contract. The distinction between maritime contracts and agreements leading to or preliminary to maritime contracts has been adverted to, and must not be lost sight of.(b)

§ 266. The ship, as has been remarked, consists of the hull and spars—the supplying her with tackle, apparel, furniture and boats to fit her for sea, although often included in the builders contract, is nevertheless the appropriate work of other classes of men, such as sail makers, riggers, chandlers, boat builders, all of whom when called in to contribute in their appropriate departments to the completion of the ship, her tackle, apparel,

---

(a) Gilp. R. 473, 536. Davies. R. 199. Ante, § 50, 95, 105, 151. Godol. 43.

(b) Ante, § 212.

&c., perform maritime service of the same nature as that of the builder, and equally cognizable in the Admiralty.(a)

§ 267. Next after the builder of the ship the material man applies his services to making her available for the great purpose for which she is created. Those are called material men who, at the time of the building of a vessel, or during her subsequent existence as a vessel, supply her at the express or implied request of the master or owner with necessary materials to build, fit, outfit, furnish or repair her. Those who thus furnish her with what is necessary to enable her to navigate the sea, and to pursue her voyage in safety, and to perform her appropriate functions, have a maritime demand against the master if he order them, and against the owner, and they have also a lien or privilege upon the ship herself, her tackle, apparel and furniture, unless the dealings of the parties show that an exclusive personal credit was given to the master or owners. Their demands are as strictly maritime as that of the ship builder, and sometimes even more so, in one sense, inasmuch as they are supplied to a vessel afloat, while much of the builders service is carried on ashore, and derives its maritime character only from its purpose and destination.(b)

§ 268. In the same manner, many others who supply the wants of a vessel may, by analogy, come under the head of material men. Necessaries for a vessel, are not merely those things which are physically material and absolutely necessary to her existence or preservation, which are incorporated with her, or used on board of her, but also those which a careful and provident owner would provide to enable her to perform well the functions which, as a maritime agent, she is destined to perform. Whatever is fit and proper at the time for the service in which the vessel is engaged. This may include money, labor and skill, personal services as well as goods, soliciting,

---

(a) Ante, § 171, 208.
(b) Edw. Ad. Jur. 4 Wash. 457. 4 Wheat. 438. 1 Sum. 73. 1 Pain. 620. 7 Rep. 324. Ante, § 50, 95, 106, 151.

procuring, and hiring a crew—seeking and securing or supplying a cargo, passengers or freight, a charter—factorage or brokerage for doing her business—towing, or otherwise removing her—have all been held to be maritime contracts ; and they are all in the nature of materials—they are supplies of her wants. It is the present, apparent want of the vessel, not the character of the thing supplied, which makes it a necessary. Thus anchors and cables are, in the general sense, necessaries ; but if the vessel is fully supplied with them, another anchor or cable is not necessary. If it be not furnished to supply a want of the vessel, it cannot properly be called materials or supplies.(a)

§ 269. The English Admiralty has, for a long course of years, been prohibited the exercise of this jurisdiction. But it is perfectly well settled in this country, that contracts of this sort are maritime contracts, and may be enforced in the Admiralty. It was first decided in the Supreme Court, in the case of the *General Smith*, in which Judge Story, delivering the opinion of the court, says, " No doubt is entertained by this court, that the Admiralty rightfully possesses a general jurisdiction in cases of material men ; and if this had been a suit *in personam*, there would not have been any hesitation in sustaining the jurisdiction of the court."

And the same principle has also been acknowledged and decided in numerous other cases.(b)

§ 270. Whenever the debt for materials, &c., *is* by law, no matter what law, or by contract, a lien on the vessel, then the

---

(a) Edw. Ad. Jur. 113. 1 W. Rob. 288, 346.

In the case of *Lane* v. *The Brig President*, water casks were held to be materials, but vinegar not. The reason of this distinction is not given, and the counsel waived the claim for vinegar. There was probably a reason which the report does not state, inasmuch as vinegar is a necessary article of ship stores, and is, by law, a part of the navy rations. 4 Wash. 457. Act of March 3d, 1801, § 3.

(b) 4 Wheat. 438. 2 Gal. 398. 2 Story, 176. Ware, 477. 5 Pet. 675. 4 Mas. 380. 7 Pet. 324. 4 Cond. 496. Gilpin, 477, 540. 1 Sum. 73. 1 Paine, 620. 9 Wheat. 409. 12 Ibid. 611. 4 Wash. 453. 3 Rob. 288. 1 Hag. Ad. R. 320.

vessel may be proceeded against *in rem ;* and in all cases the contracting parties may be proceeded against *in personam.*(*a*)

§ 271. By the civil law, those who built, repaired, or supplied a ship, had a privilege or lien upon the ship herself, for the amount of the debt thus contracted in creating her, or in keeping up her existence and usefulness; and the same principle is incorporated into all the codes of maritime law, and is a well settled rule of the general maritime law, and, as such, was acted on by the English Admiralty for centuries, till it was overthrown in the time of Charles II. by the courts of common law, which acknowledge no such privilege or lien, and only recognize the common law lien of the mechanic, who, by virtue of his possession, and not otherwise, is allowed a lien. The maritime lien is not accompanied by possession, and does not, in any manner, spring from possession. It is a sort of proprietary interest, springing from the nature of the transaction, and the beneficial service rendered to the ship, the great agent of maritime commerce, and it follows her for a longer or shorter period, into whosesoever hands she may go.(*b*)

§ 272. The civil law and the general maritime law, and the particular maritime codes, without exception, extend this lien or privilege to all ships and vessels without any distinction between foreign and domestic ships. Indeed, it is not easy to see how any difference can exist in principle—if one is a ship or vessel, so is the other—if one is a maritime contract, so must be the other—and the same law, and the same reason, which gives a lien in the one case, gives it in the other. It is for service, labor, materials and supplies, furnished to the ship, and in some sort made a part of her, for her benefit, that the lien attaches to her—still, the Supreme Court of the United States, in the case of the *General Smith,* made a broad distinction,

---

(*a*) 4 Wheat. 438.

(*b*) Dig. 42, 5, 6. Id. 134. 1 Hag. Ad. 320, 325. 3 Id. 136. Edw. Juris. 93 to 109. 1 Rol. Ab 533. Cro. Car. 296. 1 Vesey, 154. 2 Show. 338. Abb. on Ship, 143, 149, *n.* 1 Sum. 73, 81.

and declared that, unless the local law of the particular State, where the supplies, &c., are furnished, gives a lien, there is no lien in the case of domestic vessels. Since that case, numerous other cases have repeated and enforced this distinction ; and it is now so well settled, as practically to constitute a part of the law of the American Admiralty. It is, however, believed, that whenever the question shall come before the Supreme Court and be fully considered by that Court, after argument, the distinction between foreign and domestic vessels will be found to be no part of the law of the Admiralty. The mere residence of the owner would seem to have even less relation to maritime subject matter, than the pretexts of the time of Lord Coke. It is believed, that the decisions of the English Common Law Courts insensibly influenced the decision of the Supreme Court, although the ground upon which the Court puts the decision, is by no means the English ground. The Court seems to say that liens on domestic ships, are subject to the local law of the place where the ship belongs. It has not always been held, that the local legislatures have the power to repeal or modify the provisions of the general maritime law. The contrary has been held by Judge Story.(a) They have undoubtedly the power to declare what shall be the law of their own tribunals between their own citizens, but it is not so clear that they are authorized to declare what shall be the law of the United States, in cases of Admiralty and Maritime jurisdiction in the Courts of the United States.(b)

§ 273. Indeed it may be gravely questioned whether the States, as such, have any ships and vessels ; and whether all are not ships and vessels of the United States, and all American vessels domestic vessels. The port where the vessel belongs has no necessary reference to State or other limits. It is the place where the owner resides. And, on the other hand, if an American vessel is, in all cases, to be considered as belonging

---

(a) 2 Story C. C. R. 456.
(b) Daveis' R. 29. Ibid. 71. Ibid. 199. 4 Wheat. 438. 5 How. 475, 491, 495. 7 Pet. 324. 3 Wash. 313.

to the particular State where the owner resides, and the ports as such, are ports of the United States, and the States have no Admiralty and Maritime jurisdiction—then, so far as that jurisdiction is concerned, an American vessel in a port of the United States may be said to be in a foreign port; "foreign," in this regard, meaning simply another independent sovereignty, having its own peculiar laws, administered in its own way, by its own judicial system.(a)

§ 274. Ships and vessels being usually owned in shares by several persons, who are not otherwise partners, it is evident that often dissensions may arise between the owners as to the employment of the ship. In such cases, one party may employ the ship, on giving security to the other. The Court of Admiralty has jurisdiction to enforce the law between the part owners, and to compel the one or the other party to give the required security. Cases of licitation or sale, for the purpose of partition, are also within the power of the American Admiralty, as they are of the European Maritime Courts, out of England.(b)

§ 275. The Admiralty has jurisdiction of all matters that concern owners and proprietors of ships, as such. This embraces a large number of cases of almost every description. For the torts and contracts of the master, as such, the owners are liable—for whatever is a lien upon the vessel, the owners are liable by virtue of that lien, to the extent of the value of the vessel; and, in many cases, to the whole extent of the demand. For the contracts of each other as owners, they are liable to third persons to their full extent *in solido ;* and all these are cases of Admiralty and Maritime jurisdiction.

The Admiralty has also jurisdiction of possessory and petitiory actions.(c)

(a) 1 Wheat. 409. 5 Pet. Cond. Rep. 636.

(b) Bee, 2. Gilp. 10. Story on Part. 435, 436. 1 W. Rob. 278. Conk. Treat. 2d ed. 156. Dunlap Prac. 67, 69. Gilp. 11, 34.

The case of the Seneca, (Gilp. 10,) was reversed, by Judge Washington, in an able opinion, reported in 18 American Jurist, 486, and 6 Penn. Law Jour. 213.

(c) Ante, § 82. Godolph. 43. Ante, §§ 50, 105, 126, 151. 1 Hag. 306. 2 Pet.

§ 276. Possessory Actions are actions to recover ships or other property, to which a party is entitled by virtue of a maritime right, and which is withheld from him. They are analagous to the action of replevin or detinue at the common law, in which the specific property is recovered instead of damages. These actions are brought by owners to try the right to the posssession of a ship—by master or owners to recover possession. The English Admiralty Court is reluctant to take jurisdiction of such cases, and always confines itself to cases where possession is withheld from the party having the legal paper title to the ship. If the proprietor's right is disputed, the court will not attempt to decide upon it. In this country, the jurisdiction of the Admiralty over all this class of cases is well settled.(a)

§ 277. "Ships were originally invented for use and profit, to plough the seas, not to lie by the walls."(b) The ship being finished and furnished, her first want is a ship's company to navigate her. Without their strength, and knowledge, and skill, and intrepidity, she must rot at the wharf, or be hurried to destruction. The ship that by the agency of the most uncertain, capricious, and powerful elements, moves with a certainty and a security only surpassed by the beauty of her appearance, and the grace of her motion, when under the control of a well appointed crew—becomes in the hands of unpractised landsmen, the victim of the first peril, and their efforts only urge her the sooner to inevitable destruction. The services of the ship's company is, therefore, the maritime service which is entitled to the highest consideration and the greatest favor; and the jurisdiction of the Admiralty in cases of mariner's wages, is settled by a course of decisions of unbroken authority during centuries. The more fanatical enemies of the Admiralty jurisdiction have not, however, failed to perceive that

---

Ad. 288. 2 Brown Civil and Ad. 131. Ware, 188, 322. Gilp. 11. Daveis' R. 172.

(a) Ware, 233. 4 Rob. 275, 293. 18 Am. Jur. 486. 2 Dod. 42, 288.

(b) 1 Molloy, 308.

their principles are as fatal to this class of cases as to many others, and have accordingly declared that the Admiralty has been permitted to retain these cases only from usage springing from necessity or policy; and it is still held in England, that of cases on whaling contracts, or other contracts, not in the usual form, the Admiralty has no jurisdiction. The jurisdiction, however, is firmly established in this country on principle, and all cases of mariner's wages are, by eminence, maritime cases, and subject to the jurisdiction of the Admiralty; and this includes whaling, sealing and fishing voyages, and demands for subsistence, expenses of cure, &c., which are in the nature of wages.(a)

§ 278. The term mariner includes all persons employed on board ships and vessels during the voyage to assist in their navigation and preservation, or to promote the purposes of the voyage. Masters, mates, sailors, surveyors, carpenters, coopers, stewards, cooks, cabin boys, kitchen boys, engineers, pilots, firemen, deck hands, waiters,—women as well as men,—are mariners.(b)

§ 279. The mariners of the public vessels of the nation cannot proceed against them in the Admiralty, for the same reason that the government or sovereign cannot be sued. It is not because the court has not jurisdiction, but because there is no right of action against the government or its property. In like manner, the mariners of a public vessel of a foreign power within our jurisdiction, are not allowed to proceed against the vessel or officers. This is not because they are simply foreigners, but because by the common law, and universal consent of nations, the person, the ministers, and the vessels of a sovereign, retain their independent character, and their consequent immunities, wherever they are rightfully, in times of peace.(c)

(a) Ante, § 81. Dunlap Prac. 20, 24, 26. 1 Dod. 11. Dunlap Prac. 59, 60, 61, 62. 1 Sum. 384. Ware, 437. 5 Pet. 675. 2 Mas 544. 4 Mas. 380.

(b) 2 Rob. 261. 3 Mas. 91. Bee, 424. 2 Dod. 104. Dunlap Prac. 59.

(c) 2 Dod. 100. Bee, 112, 422. Dunlap Prac. 64. Gilp 203, 514.

§ 280. When an American seaman is discharged with his own consent in a foreign country, or the ship is sold in a foreign country, and her company discharged, and three months extra pay is, by law, required to be deposited in the hands of the consul, of which two-thirds are to be paid to the seamen, no action at common law will lie to recover these extra wages against the master if he neglect to pay them to the consul, but the Admiralty will entertain a suit, as well on the part of the seaman, as on the part of the United States, to recover such extra wages. The jurisdiction in similar cases is denied in England.(a)

§ 281. In the earliest periods of maritime commerce, a common form of compensating the mariner was by giving him, in one way or another, an interest in the success of the voyage. In modern times, fixed pecuniary wages have taken the place of a share of the earnings, except in cases of whaling, fishing and sealing voyages, in which the ancient mode of compensation still prevails. In England, none but contracts in the usual form are allowed to be prosecuted in the Admiralty, and a fixed rate of pecuniary wages is held to be the usual form. There cannot be a more striking illustration of the caprice and want of rational principle which has characterized the prohibitions of the English common law courts.(b)

§ 282. There have been attempts in England and in this country to establish an exemption in favor of the seamen of foreign merchant ships. It has been sometimes placed on the ground of the comity of nations—sometimes on the fancied ground that a vessel is part of the territory of the nation to which she belongs—sometimes on the ground that there can be no jurisdiction in such cases except by the consent of the consul, or other diplomatic representative of the foreign nation to which the seamen or the vessel belongs—all of which are fallacious. There is no such comity of nations—nothing within

---

(a) Act of Feb'y. 28. 1803, concerning Consuls, § 3. Dunlap Prac. 62, 63. 1 Mas. 45. 4 Mas. R. 541. Gilp. 193. Ed. Ad. Rep. 239. Daveis' Rep. 124.
(b) Cleirac, 66, 138.

the territory of a nation is without the jurisdiction, and no officer of a foreign government can grant or destroy the jurisdiction of our courts. Some exemptions are established by the Constitution, some by treaty, and some by the established and immemorial usage of nations, and they do not apply to persons and property engaged in the ordinary pursuits of commerce. In the present state of international intercourse and commerce, all persons in time of peace, have the right to resort to the tribunals of the nation where they may happen to be, for the protection of their rights. The jurisdiction of the courts over them is complete, except when it is excluded by treaty.(a)

§ 283. During the building, fitting, furnishing, supplying, loading and unloading, and repairing of a vessel, it is necessary that she should lie at a wharf, dock or pier, to be most conveniently and safely accessible. The pecuniary charge in the nature of rent to which vessels are liable for the use of a dock or wharf, is called wharfage or dockage, and it is the subject of Admiralty jurisdiction. The master and owner of the ship and the ship herself may be proceeded against in Admiralty to enforce the payment of wharfage, whether the vessel lie alongside the wharf or at a distance, and only use the wharf temporarily for boats or cargo. Of the same nature, is the charge for storing the sails or other furniture in a store-house on shore, and that kind of rent or storage is also the subject of a maritime action.(b)

§ 284. For the purposes of being finished and loading and unloading, under many circumstances, it is necessary or expedient that the vessel should be moored at a distance from the land, and that her tackle, apparel and furniture, her cargo and supplies, her passengers and crew should be transported in lighters, barges or other small craft. The service thus rendered is maritime, and lightermen, bargemen and water men, who thus render service to a vessel are all entitled to resort to

---

(a) Dunlap Prac. 66. Ante, § 14.
(b) Pet. Ad. 223. 2 Gal. 483. Gilp. 101. Ware, 354.

the Admiralty to enforce the payment of their demands, by proceeding *in personam* againt the master or *in rem* against the vessel herself.(*a*)

§ 285. To enable the vessel safely to transport her cargo, it is of the first importance that the vessel may keep her trim—that one portion of cargo may not injure another by collision, by leaking, by steam, heat, odor,—that storms may not break it loose and destroy it, it is of the first importance that it be well stowed; and the business of stowing ships has fallen into the hands of a separate class of artisans known as stevedores, French, *arrimeurs.* Their services are maritime, and they may enforce the payment of their demands by suits *in rem* against the vessel, or *in personam* against the master or owners. Stevedores are also often employed to break out and discharge the cargo of a vessel at the port of delivery. Doubts have been expressed whether this be a maritime service. It seems to be as necessary to the vessel, and to her commercial and maritime purposes, both in completing a past voyage and in getting ready for a new one, that her cargo should be discharged, as it is that it should be taken in. And the same principle which allows the sailor and the lighterman—him that scrapes her bottom, as well as him that sets up her rigging, or paints her sides, to resort to the Admiralty, will also allow the same privilege to him that performs the crowning act of maritime commerce, that for which all others labor, and to which all other acts are subordinate, and on which the right to freight depends, and which is, in fact, the great purpose, and the only ultimate purpose, of a ship, the delivery of the cargo.(*b*)

§ 286. The primary and principal purpose of a ship is transportation for hire. *Contracts of affreightment* are, therefore, within the admiralty and maritime jurisdiction. If the ship, her master and owners, do not faithfully and fully perform their contracts to carry goods or passengers, the ship is liable *in rem*,

---

(*a*) Gilp. 526. MSS. decision of Judge Betts.
(*b*) 2 Sumn. 151. Valin.

and the master and owners *in personam*, in Admiralty for the damages ; and in the same manner if the freight be not paid, the master and owners of the ship may proceed in the Admiralty against the goods *in rem*, or against the party liable for the freight *in personam*, to recover the freight. All agreements for the carriage of persons or property by vessels are contracts of affreightment, and all hire or reward for the use of vessels is freight, and these agreements may be in writing or merely verbal. The written acknowledgment of the reception on board of a particular quantity or parcel of goods in a particular vessel to be carried to a particular place, is a bill of lading. There is an usual, but not a necessary form, of a bill of lading, and any paper, containing the substantial elements of the usual bill of lading, is a bill of lading. Shipments are often made without any bill of lading, or written evidence of the transaction, or of the liabilities of the parties, and the law, and the jurisdiction is the same as if the whole were in writing. It is the fact that the goods are shipped, and not the written acknowledgment of it— the obligation to carry them safely, and not the written contract, that create the liability and fix the jurisdiction of the court.(*a*)

§ 287. When a ship, or a specified portion of it, is hired out in mass for a voyage or a portion of a voyage, for a gross sum, or so much a ton, a voyage, a month, or the like, the contract is usually called a chartering of the vessel. A charter party, strictly, is a deed in two parts, divided, *charta partita*. When not under seal it is called a memorandum of a charter ; when not in writing it is not properly a *charta*, but it is, nevertheless, usually spoken of as a charter. The jurisdiction and the law of the American Admiralty is the same, whether the agreement be a deed, a writing, or a mere verbal agreement. It is the substance of the undertaking of the party, and not the form of words that they use, that creates the liability and confers the jurisdiction. The jurisdiction of the Admiralty over cases of hiring of

---

(*a*) 2 Gall. 398. Ware, 149, 188, 263. 1 Sumn. 551. 2 id. 589. 3 Kent's Com. 220. Gilp. 184. Ware, 134, 138, 149, 156. 1 Pet. Ad. 206. Davies R. 82, 184. 2 N. Y. Legal Obs, 4. Ante, §§ 48, 52, 94, 126, 151.

vessels, and the carriage in vessels of persons and property, is too well settled to be questioned. The principles of law which control the rights and duties to the parties to such contracts will be found in the various maritime codes and in the commentaries upon them—in the treatises of Holt and Abbot, and in the cases already referred to in our courts.(a)

§ 288. It has been made a question whether contracts for the transportation of passengers, were within the jurisdiction of the Admiralty. There is nothing in principle to distinguish, in this respect, the transportation of human beings from that of other portions of animated nature. Men, as well as birds and beasts, and fishes, have, in all ages, been objects of maritime transportation. Ships, laden with soldiers and convicts, and emigrants, from the earliest periods, have traversed all the oceans and seas and other navigable waters—Naulage, nolis—from *naulum*, "the *freight* or fare paid for passage on the Sea in a ship," is found in the earliest books. " Passengers, those who pay *freight* for the carriage of their persons and baggage."(b) Passage money—is particularly mentioned as within the Admiralty jurisdiction, by Godolphin.(c) " Causes, civil and maritime, which respect or concern the sea, or passage over the same," are specified in the commission of the Vice-Admiralty Judges.(d) " Passenger ships and vessels," are regulated by Acts of Congress, in most important particulars,(e) and the business of the transportation of passengers for freight, is now one of the most important and lucrative branches of maritime commerce. The rights of passengers, in various forms, have been often the subject of suits in Admiralty, in the Southern District of New York—and the jurisdiction is there fully established, both in the District and Circuit Court.(f)

(a) Ware, 156. 3 Sumn. 144. Abbot on Ship. 316. 3 Kent's Com. 204. Ware Rep. 263. 3 Sumn. 144. 1 Hag. 6, 266. Ante, §§ 79, 94, 126, 151.

(b) Gilp. 184.

(c) Cleirac—Termes de la Marine, 510. Vid. The Consulate, 68, and the Continental Codes, *passim*. Pard. Droit Com. § 704.

(d) Ante, § 106.

(e) Ante, § 158.

(f) Act of March 2d, 1819.

§ 289. Cases for *pilotage*, are cases of Admiralty and Maritime jurisdiction.

The name of pilot, or steersman, is applied either to a particular officer serving on board the ship during the course of the voyage, and having the charge of the helm and of the ship's route—or to a person taken on board at a particular place, for the purpose of conducting a ship through a river, road, or channel, or from or into port. In the first case, the pilot is merely a mariner, and his rights are precisely the same as any other mariner. In the second case, the nature of the service is eminently maritime, and of a character especially entitled to favor. The pilot may proceed *in rem* against the vessel, or *in personam* against the owner or master. The jurisdiction of the Admiralty is fully established in this country and in England, and on the Continent of Europe.(*a*)

River and harbor pilotage, in English maritime affairs, is called loadmanage, from loadsman or lodesman, a kind of pilot established for the safe conduct of ships and vessels in and out of harbors, or up and down navigable rivers.(*b*)

§ 290. A ship is, of necessity, a wanderer. She visits places where her owners are not known, or are inaccessible. The master is not usually of sufficient pecuniary ability to respond to the demands of the voyage, and he is the fully authorized agent of the owners. These and other kindred characteristics of maritime commerce, have established the necessity of making the ship herself security, in many cases, to those who have demands against the master or owners. The contracts and the torts of the master and owners are, therefore, in numerous cases, a lien upon the vessel herself. All these are maritime liens, whether created by actual hypothecation, or by implication, or by operation of law.

Maritime Liens—Wherever there is a maritime lien, it may be enforced in the Admiralty. Maritime liens differ from common

---

(*a*) 1 Mas. 508. 6 Rob. 227, 350. 2 Dod. 498. 10 Pet. 108. Rule 14. Abbot, 265. 2 Wils. 214. Dunlap's Prac. 59.

(*b*) Falconer's Dictionary.

law liens in a very important point. A common law lien is always connected with a possession of the thing—it is simply a right to retain. On the other hand, a maritime lien does not in any manner depend upon a possession. It is a right affecting the thing, and giving a sort of proprietary interest in it, and a right to proceed against it, to recover that interest—the Admiralty has jurisdiction in all such cases. Wherever there is a maritime lien upon property, it adheres to the proceeds of that property, into whose hands soever they may go, and those proceeds may be attached in the Admiralty.(*a*)

§ 291. *Maritime loans* are within the Admiralty and Maritime jurisdiction, and have been so considered from the earliest periods, and in all commercial nations. The necessities of commerce so often call for such loans, that cases springing out of that class of transactions, abound wherever maritime commerce exists. In the civil law, and in the various maritime codes, and in the elementary writings of the most learned commentators, the law of these loans, principally known by the name of bottomry and respondentia, holds a prominent place.(*b*)

§ 292. *Bottomry loans* are those in which a sum of money is loaned for a particular voyage, on the security of the ship—the ship and freight—or the ship, freight, and cargo, on condition that if the voyage be performed safely, the money and interest shall be paid ; and if she do not so arrive, but is lost by a peril of the sea, then none shall be paid. These are within the Admiralty jurisdiction in England as well as in Continental Europe and in this country.(*c*)

§ 293. *Respondentia bonds* are bonds given to secure a loan,

---

(*a*) Ware, 149, 154, 188, 263, 322. 7 Howard, 731. 6 Pet. Rep. Gilp. 185.

(*b*) 2 Hag. 294. 3 Hag. R. 1, 7. 1 W. Rob. 1. 3 Rob. 240. 3 Mar. 255, 341. 2 Sum. 157. 1 Pet. 386. 2 Gall. 191, 398. 2 Pet. Ad. 295. Bee, 130–31, 157, 250. 2 Gall. 345. 1 Wash. 49, 293. 3 Wash. 12, 90, 404. 1 Wheat. 96. 1 Paine, 67, 572, 671. 1 Pet. 431.

(*c*) 2 Sum. 157. 2 Hag. Ad. R. 48. 1 Paine's R. 671. Pet. U. S. Dig. Bottomry. Curtis' Dig. Bottomry. Ed. Ad. Jur. 55. Ante, § 48, 52, 94, 126, 151.

made on the cargo instead of the ship, and they lack the element of maritime risk, the owner being personally responsible. The jurisdiction of the Admiralty over them has never been denied in the Courts of the United States.(*a*)

§ 294. The contract of *Insurance* against the perils of the sea, is one that was suggested by, and sprang from, the hazards peculiar to ships and vessels, in the pursuits of maritime commerce. In like manner, the rights, duties, and liabilities which are its characteristics, have always been regulated by the maritime law. Indeed, the investigation of a case of marine insurance, is but an inquiry into the facts, transactions, and perils of navigation, and the application of the principles and rules of the maritime law. It has always and everywhere been considered a maritime contract—and nowhere out of England has it ever been excluded from the Admiralty jurisdiction. And in all the grants of jurisdiction, even in England, it is specially mentioned as a matter of Admiralty jurisdiction.

The question of the jurisdiction of the American Admiralty, on policies of insurance, has never been submitted to the Supreme Court of the United States. It has, however, been distinctly presented, and the jurisdiction sustained by the Circuit Court, on principle, in the memorable case of *De Lovio* v. *Boit*, in which the Admiralty jurisdiction was so fully and learnedly discussed, and again in the case of *Andrews* v. *The Essex Fire and Marine Ins. Co.*(*b*)

§ 295. Cases of *average contribution* are cases of maritime jurisdiction. The whole subject is the creation of the maritime law, and it is perhaps more than any other subject, in all its relations and in every aspect, purely maritime; and from the time of Rhodian laws to the present, all codes and commentators have held the same language on the subject. When in peril of shipwreck, a sacrifice is made of a portion of the pro-

---

(*a*) 3 Kent. Com. 357. 4 Mas. 248. Pet. Dig. Bottomry.
(*b*) 2 Gall. 398. 3 Mason, 27. Ante, § 48, 107, 116, 151.

perty thus exposed to save the residue, every person whose property is saved is liable to contribute in proportion to his goods saved, to make up the loss of those whose goods have been sacrificed for the common benefit. This is called an average contribution. So entirely is this subject under the regulation of the maritime law, that it has been held that common law courts have no jurisdiction of it. And to bring it within the jurisdiction of the common law courts in England, as well as to make consignees liable, the practice has become general of requiring those who receive the goods, to execute a bond before taking their goods, binding them to pay their shares. It is now, however, well settled that " the contribution may be recovered either by a suit in equity or by an action at law, instituted by each individual entitled to receive against each individual that ought to pay for the amount of his share."(a) The subject matter of a demand for contribution being maritime, it is clearly a case of admiralty and maritime jurisdiction, and the court may resort to such of its modes of proceeding as may be appropriate to give the relief. If the demand be a lien upon any property within the reach of the court, the proceedings may be *in rem*. If the party liable to pay be within the reach of the court, the proceeding may be *in personam*.(b)

(a) Domat, lib. 11, tit. 9, § 2, art. 6, 9. Pard. Droit. Com. 742. Boulay Paty, 2. Valin, 211. Abbot. Ship. 507-8. I East, 220. 3 Kent. Com. 244. 3 B. & Adol. 523. Dunlap. Prac. 57. 4 Wheat. 78, 12 ibid. 16. 1 Doug. Mich. 154. Abbot Ship. Perkin's Edit. 507. 3 Kent. Com. 244. Ante, § 52, 106. 7 Haw. R. 722.

(b) Allusion has been made (Ante, § 204,) to the confusion of ideas which has some times been exhibited on the subject of jurisdiction *in personam*, and to a striking instance of it in the late case of *Cutler* v. *Rae*, 7 How. It is to be regretted, that the case was not argued as presenting a question of jurisdiction, inasmuch as what was there said by the distinguished Chief Justice, has been considered as going far to unsettle the principles of admiralty jurisdiction, as they have always been held by that court for more than half a century, and which are supposed to have received their impregnable fortification in the two great cases of *Waring* v. *Clarke*, in 5 Howard's Reports, and *The New Jersey S. Nav. Co.* v. *The Merchants Bank*, in 6 Howard's Reports, in which the best ability in the nation, at the bar and on the bench, had reviewed the whole subject and re-asserted the true principles of that jurisdiction.

The dissenting opinion of Mr. Justice Wayne justifies the brief comment which I shall make on that case.

§ 296. The jettison of cargo may give rise to other rights besides those of average contribution. Many contingencies arise in the progress of a voyage, which render it necessary to appropriate cargo to the use of the ship—to sell it to raise funds for the necessary purposes of the voyage. These are cases of Admiralty and maritime jurisdiction.(a)

§ 297. From the nature of maritime commerce and navigation, all practicable promptness and certainty are of the utmost

---

The case presented in the pleadings, as reported, was this : A vessel bound from New Orleans to Boston, with an asserted cargo, was overtaken by a storm, and was run ashore by the captain to save the lives of those on board, and to preserve the cargo which would otherwise have been lost. By this voluntary stranding the vessel was totally lost and the cargo saved to the amount of $5400. It was received by the defendant, who was the consignee—not the owner. The claim was for an average contribution. The defendant admitted these facts, but denied his liability as matter of law.

This, on all the principles which the court have upheld for half a century, and which have been acknowledged for centuries in all the maritime courts of Continental Europe, is a clear case of admiralty and maritime jurisdiction—nothing can be more thoroughly maritime or more universally regulated by the maritime law.

There was, however, a very grave question of legal liability entirely separate from any question of jurisdiction, and that was whether the defendant being consignee and not owner, and having received the property as wrecked—damaged and saved property—and not as preserved property, and without having undertaken, by bond or otherwise, to pay an average contribution was personally liable to pay it—a question, be it said, which under the maritime law, might well be considered as debateable. This was not in any view a question of jurisdiction. It was not in abatement, but in denial of the legal liability.

This was the question which the court actually decided. Briefly stated, the court decided that there is no such maritime lien in cases of average as would make the party liable, simply by receiving the property saved or its proceeds ; and that the owner of the goods himself, is not by the maritime law, personally liable for a contribution, if his property be delivered to him free from the universally acknowledged right of the master to detain it till its share of the contribution be paid. This is the whole decision. The court does indeed call it a question of jurisdiction, and in language treat it as such, but that fallacious use of language cannot alter principles. The cause was decided on two controlling points of the defence to the action, and the question of jurisdiction was really untouched.

It will not be considered disrespectful to the majority of the court to express the opinion, that if it had not been for that fallacious view of jurisdiction, they could hardly have failed to come to the conclusion on the merits which is set forth in the dissenting opinion of Judge Wayne.

(a) Ante, § 106. Laws of Oleron, art. 8. Cleirac, 30.

importance. The benefits of a careful study of markets, and of a wise forecast, may all be lost to the shrewdest merchant by negligent or wilful delays on the part of the ship. The master is always bound to proceed with dispatch. It is a necessary element of his undertaking to transport. In like manner the merchant is bound to give the ship all reasonable dispatch. Ships are made to plough the seas, and all who are connected with her may improperly delay or impede her progress. The master may neglect to perform his appropriate functions. The crew may be improperly absent, or they may refuse to perform their duty. The merchant may neglect to put his goods on board at the beginning, or to take them out at the end of the voyage. This hindrance or delaying of a vessel is compensated by demurrage, which is an allowance for the detention of the vessel. It is often a matter of express contract, but it is not necessarily so. In the Black Book of the Admiralty are found cases for demurrage. They are Admiralty and maritime cases.(a)

§ 298. Vessels engaged in the fisheries, in wrecking, in privateering, or other maritime employment in which association increases efficiency or security, often agree to make common cause in their enterprize ; such arrangements are agreements of *consortship*. They are maritime contracts—and are within the acknowledged jurisdiction of the Admiralty of this country.(b)

§ 299. The Admiralty has also jurisdiction of the *survey and sale* of vessels. In cases of distress or serious injury, in which a master, in a port away from his owners, finds it impracticable to repair, refit, or proceed on his voyage, the sale of the vessel and cargo seems to be his only resort, and nothing can be more fit and proper than that the maritime courts, administering the law of the sea, and in some sort the law of nations, should be held competent to examine into the circumstances, and order a sale. The master himself cannot fail to find in such a jurisdic-

---

(a) Gilpin, 90, 145. 9 Wheat. 362. 1 Gal. 318. 1 Rob. 286. 4 id. 71, 169, 185. 5 id. 33, 143, 152. 2 Hag. Ad. 317. 2 Dod. 58. Prynne Ad. 116. Rhod. Law, art. 101.

(b) 3 How. 568. Ante, § 106. 2 N. Y. Leg. Ob. 157.

tion a most reliable auxiliary, and to the owner and underwriter it must be a protectiona gainst fraud, improvidence, and indiscretion. Under the influence of English common law decisions, there has been some disposition to deny the Admiralty jurisdiction, but it may now be considered as established.(*a*)

§ 300. Cases of salvage are cases of Admiralty and maritime jurisdiction. Salvage is the compensation that is to be made to persons by whose assistance a ship or its lading has been saved from impending peril, or recovered after actual loss. It is of two kinds; military salvage consisting of recapture or rescue of a ship from an enemy; and civil salvage, consisting of saving in cases of property derelict and shipwrecked, or in peril. They are both within the Admiralty jurisdiction, both in England and this country.(*b*)

§ 301. For the protection of its commerce, for the collection of its revenues, and for the enforcement of all the regulations of its police in navigable waters, the United States, like all other commercial nations, find it necessary to impose penalties and forfeitures on goods afloat and on vessels, in relation to which the laws of trade, navigation and revenue, have been violated. In a great variety of such cases, the vessels and the goods are the only things within the reach of the courts and their process. Whenever, therefore, a penalty or forfeiture is attached to a ship or vessel, or goods on board of her, it is enforced by a seizure of the thing, and the proceeding to condemn it, is a suit in the District Court, in the name of the United States or other party, in whose favor the penalty or forfeiture is imposed.

An open, visible seizure, by an officer of the Government, authorized by law to seize, must precede the commencement of judicial proceedings. The seizures are usually made by the

---

(*a*) Dunlap's Ad. Prac. 48, 49. Abbot, 23. Esp. N. P. 65. Edward's Ad. Rep. 118. 2 Dod. 288–295. 10 Wheat. 412. 5 Mason, 465. 7 Wheat. 581.

(*b*) Dunlap's Prac. 57. Abbot on Shipping, 554. 2 Cranch, 240. 4 id. 347. Do. 1 Peters, 513. Daveis R. 20, 61. 8 Penn Law Jour. 529,—a case of salvage in Wisconsin.

revenue officers, or by the commanders of armed vessels on the high seas.(a)

§ 302. All seizures under laws of impost, navigation or trade of the United States, where the seizures are made on waters navigable from the sea by vessels of ten or more tons burthen, are civil cases of Admiralty and Maritime jurisdiction, and the proceedings to enforce them must be had in the District Court.(b)

§ 303. It is the place of seizure, and not the place of committing the offence, which decides the jurisdiction.(c) If the seizure be made in a foreign jurisdiction, or on the high seas, the District Court of the District to which the property is brought has the jurisdiction.(d) If the seizure be made within a judicial district of the United States, the District Court of that district has the jurisdiction. If the seizure be unlawful, the party has his redress by a suit *in personam* in the Admiralty ; and the jurisdiction in this class of torts is co-extensive with the jurisdiction of the seizure, and exists whether the seizure be on the high seas, in ports and harbors, or on the lakes and rivers of the interior.

Where there has been a condemnation in a revenue case of forfeiture, an informer entitled to a share of the proceeds, may institute an original suit in the Admiralty to recover them.(e)

§ 304. *Ransom* Bills are exclusively of Admiralty cognizance

---

(a) 5 How. 464. Collection Act of 1699, § 70. Collection Act of 1793, § 27. 3 Wheat. 246. 9 Cranch, 289. Slave Trade Act, May 10, 1800; March 2, 1807. Piracy Act, March 3, 1819. Bett's Prac. 68.

(b) 1 Cond. 11, 333. 2 Id. 168, 256, 437. Ware, 97. Jud. Act, § 9. 7 Cranch, 112. 4 Id. 240, 276, 443. 3 Wheat. 246. 9 Wheat. 391. 3 Dal. 297. 8 Wheat. 391. 12 Id. 1. 11 Id. 1.

(c) 1 Cond. 164. 2 Id. 265. 3 Id. 406. 5 Id. 472, 623. 4 Cranch, 443. 7 Id. 112.

(d) 5 Cond. 627, 641. 1 Mas. 361. 9 Wheat. 391.

(e) Dunlap Prac. 38, 41. 1 Cond. 152. 4 Id. 143, 150, 325. Conk. Treat. 2d ed. 136, 139, 350, 351. 7 Cranch, 112. 1 Cond. 12, 133. 2 Id. 168, 256, 431. 4 Wash. 492.

—they necessarily involve the question of prize or no prize, of the legality of the capture, and of the regularity of the commission and conduct of the captors, which questions are of Admiralty cognizance alone.(a)

§ 305. *Proceeds.*—Whenever there is a maritime lien, it is in the nature of a proprietary interest, and it adheres to the proceeds of the thing into whose hands soever they may go; and the ownership and possession of the proceeds, render the party himself liable personally for the demand, and he may be proceeded against *in personam.* The existence of this principle has led to the mistaken notion, that there is no jurisdiction *in personam*, except as ancillary to, or springing out of, a lien. But no principle is better settled, than that personal liability in a maritime cause of action, has no connection with or relation to lien. This lien upon proceeds extends often to the proceeds of a judicial sale in the registry of the court, it being a general rule, that before the proceeds are distributed, the court, on proper proceedings for that purpose, will adjudicate upon the claims to such proceeds arising from liens upon them.(b)

§ 306. Cases of Prize have always been held to be within the Admiralty and Maritime jurisdiction of the United States, and in all forms, *in rem* and *in personam*, for condemnation for military salvage, for restitution, and for damages, they have been, from the earliest periods, entertained by the courts sitting as Courts of Admiralty; and, by the act of Congress of June 26, 1812, § 6, they are expressly made civil causes of Admiralty and Maritime jurisdiction.(c)

§ 307. In Scotland, and in the continental nations of Europe, the Admiralty, by virtue of its general powers, exercises the

---

(a) 2 Gall. R. 104. 341, 343.   1 Pet. C. C. 142.   Ante, § 106.

(b) 5 Pet. 675.   Gilp. 185.   2 Gal. 483.

(c) 3 Dal. 6, 54.   Act of June 26, 1812, § 6.   Conk. Treat. 2d ed. 135.   3 Dal. R. 19.
8 Cranch, 137.   1 Wheat. 335.   1 Pet. Ad. Dec. 1.   1 Gal. 563.   9 Cranch. 3
Cond. R. 397.   5 Wheat. 385.

same jurisdiction, but in England the High Court of Admiralty has no such jurisdiction by virtue of its general power ; but the Prize Court is always constituted by virtue of a special commission.(*a*)

§ 308. The Court of Admiralty has jurisdiction over the whole subject matter of damage on the high seas.

Cases of torts on the high seas, *super altum mare*, have always been held, even in England, to be within the jurisdiction of the Admiralty. And the jurisdiction in such cases has usually been held to depend upon locality, embracing only civil torts and injuries done on sea, or on waters of the sea, where the tide ebbs and flows. It depends upon the place where the cause of action arises, and that place must be the sea or tide waters. In this country, under the influence of English authority, the same language has been held. It may, however, be doubted whether the civil jurisdiction, in cases of torts, does not depend upon the relation of the parties to a ship or vessel, embracing only those tortious violation of maritime right and duty which occur in vessels to which the Admiralty jurisdiction, in cases of contracts, applies. If one of several landsmen bathing in the sea, should assault, or imprison, or rob another, it has not been held here that the Admiralty would have jurisdiction of the action for the tort.(*b*)

§ 309. Cases of assault and battery, imprisonment, or other personal injury, or ill usage, arising between master or officers on the one hand, and seaman or passengers on the other, are clearly within the Admiralty and Maritime jurisdiction. The Admiralty entertains jurisdiction of personal torts committed by the master on a passenger, whether by direct force, as trespasses, or by consequential injuries. The contract of passengers with the master, is not for mere ship room and personal exis-

---

(*a*) Black. 237. Doug. 613.

(*b*) 1 W. Rob. 387. 3 Story on Const. 527, 530. 1 Wheat. 335. Dunlap's Ad. Prac. 43, 49. 1 Paine, 117. Ware, 91, 94. Vid. 4 Moore, 322. 4 C. Rob. 73. 7 Penn. Law Jour. 77.

tence on board, but for reasonable food, comforts, necessaries, and kindness. In respect to females, it proceeds yet further, and includes an implied stipulation against obscenity, immorality, and a wanton disregard of the feelings. A course of conduct oppressive and malicious in these particulars, will be punished by the Court, as well as personal assaults. By the 16th rule of the Supreme Court, it is provided, that in all suits for assault and battery, or beating, the suit must be *in personam* only.(*a*)

This is undoubtedly true, where the action is technically for the assault and battery, as a mere tort—but it would seem, on principle, that if the action be brought on the contract, as for not carrying a passenger safely and without injury, or for not treating with proper kindness a passenger or seaman, an assault or beating being the gravamen of the breach, the suit may be *in rem* against the vessel.

§ 310. Cases of spoliation and damage, are cases of Admiralty and Maritime jurisdiction. These include illegal seizures or depredations of vessels or goods afloat. This embraces the civil injury called piracy, which consists in an unwarrantable violation of property committed on the high seas. The injured party may proceed against the property or the proceeds of the property, to recover it, or against the person of the wrong doer for the damage.(*b*)

§ 311. Every violent dispossession of property on the ocean, is *prima facie* a maritime tort, and as such, it belongs to the Admiralty jurisdiction. Petitory as well as possessory suits, are cases of Admiralty and Maritime jurisdiction. They may be brought in all cases to reinstate the owners of ships, who have been wrongfully deprived of their property. This includes cases of restitution of captured property—of vessels ir-

---

(*a*) Rule 16. 3 Mason's R. 242. 7 N. Y. Leg. Ob. 342.

(*b*) 2 Dod. 369, 372. 2 Chit. Gen. Prac. 517. 1 Vent. 173. 2 Keb. 828. Bulst. 327. 4 Inst. 152. 3 Bulst. 27. 1 Rob. 530, c. 25. 1 Com. Dig. 272. 1 Hag. 142. 1 W. Rob. 433.

regularly or illegally condemned, and sold by the master without legal authority, or in an illegal or irregular manner.(*a*)

§ 312. Cases of collision of vessels, are cases of Admiralty and Maritime jurisdiction.

There have been attempts to exclude from the jurisdiction, in these cases, all cases arising within a county, a port, or a harbor, but the jurisdiction may now be considered as fully settled in all cases within waters affected by the ebb and flow of the tide, and on the great lakes and the rivers connecting them as well within ports, harbors, and counties, as on the open sea.(*b*)

§ 313. The extent of the political grant of judicial jurisdiction, in maritime cases, to the General Government, as an independent Sovereignty, has been thus treated at greater length than it would have been, but for the conviction, that the subject is one deserving all the importance which the founders of the Republic gave to it. The attempt to limit, and even to destroy, this jurisdiction, has entirely overlooked the great national reasons for which the grant was made, and was in the highest degree necessary to the respectability and usefulness of the General Government, and has confined itself to the narrow, local and municipal grounds which, in an age unlike our own, were taken in a paltry strife of judicial rivalry. I cannot help thinking that if all the judicial power vested in the United States, had, in all its details, been distributed in a judicial system, composed of subordinate judicial officers and courts, as well as of higher tribunals, fully adequate to all the wants of the people, in small matters as well as great, within the range of that grant of power, it would have been felt in the strength, and harmony, and peace and affection which would result from

(*a*) 1 Wheat. 238. 10 Wheat. 473. 5 Mas. 465. 1 Gal 585.
(*b*) Rule 15. 2 Dod. 83. 1 Hag. 109. Gilp. 579. 1 How. 89. 3 Hag. 321.
5 How. 441. Daveis' R. 193. Ibid. 360.

the increased security of the rights of the citizens of the different States. The national judiciary would thus have been visible everywhere, accessible everywhere, and everywhere the shield and the protection of the citizen and the stranger against local prejudices, sectional sympathies, and fanatical animosities. The mere moral effect of that judicial system, with its present limited extent, is of incalculable benefit to the nation, and it is the duty of all who love the honor of the country, to sustain it in its legal and proper extent.(a)

(a) Ante, § 27, 28.

CHAPTER XVIII.

Admiralty Practice.— The Organization of the Courts.

§ 314. The law of National jurisdiction or sovereignty in Admiralty and Maritime cases being ascertained, the next subject of inquiry, is the mode of administering justice in such cases.

Practice is the means by which justice is administered. And as the first step in providing for the administration of justice, is the creation of courts of justice, so the last step is the exercise of the powers of the court in executing its judgments.—Thus the whole of what is usually denominated Admiralty Practice, is the organization and jurisdiction of the Admiralty Courts, their forms, modes, and rules of procedure, and the duties and responsibilities of their various functionaries.

Admiralty Courts.

§ 315. There are no courts of the United States which are merely Admiralty Courts. The only Courts, except the Courts in the Territories, are—THE DISTRICT COURTS.——THE CIRCUIT COURTS.——THE SUPREME COURT.——And they have each of them Admiralty jurisdiction in certain cases, as well as Common law—civil and criminal—and Equity jurisdiction.

The District Court.

§ 316. The United States, exclusive of the Territories, was originally divided into as many districts as there were States. The great increase in population and business of some of the States, has made it necessary to divide them into two districts. In each of these districts is a court called a *District Court*, held by a single judge, who is called the District Judge, and in him all the judicial powers of that court are vested.

23

§ 317. The District Courts have exclusive original cognizance of all civil causes of Admiralty and Maritime jurisdiction, including all seizures under laws of impost, navigation or trade, of the United States, where the seizures are made on waters which are navigable from the sea by vessels of ten or more tons burthen, within their respective districts, as well as upon the high seas.(*a*)

§ 318. The judges of the District Court must reside within the districts for which they are appointed, and they are required to hold stated terms, at such times and places as are established by law.(*b*) The stated terms in the southern district of New York are held on the first Tuesday of every month. They are also authorized to hold special courts at their discretion, at such places in their respective districts as the nature of the business, and the discretion of the judge, shall direct. The character of maritime causes, and the necessities and occupations of many of the persons engaged in maritime transactions, and whose presence as parties or witnesses is often necessary to the administration of justice, renders delay, in many cases, equivalent to a denial of justice. It is with a view to speedy justice, that this power to hold special courts has been conferred on the courts ; and in the maritime portions of the country, it is the uniform practice to hold special courts frequently for the trial of causes. In the southern district of New York special terms are held on every Tuesday when the stated term is not in session.(*c*) And as the court is always open, and, wherever the judge is, there is a court, it is the practice to enter all orders in causes, in the vacation of the usual terms, as of a special term held on the day of entering the order.

§ 319. In case of the inability of the Judge of any District

(*a*) Jud. Act of 1789, § 9. Conk. Treat. 2d edit. 83, 129.
(*b*) Vide a full abstract of the terms of the District Courts throughout the United States, Conk Treat. 2d edit. 106, *et seq.*
(*c*) Jud. Act of 1789, § 3. Dunlap, 108.

Court to attend on the day appointed for holding a District Court, such court may, by virtue of a written order from the Judge thereof, directed to the Marshal of the district, be adjourned by the Marshal to the next stated term of said court, or to such day prior thereto as in the said order shall be appointed. And in case of the death of the said Judge, all process, pleadings and proceedings are continued of course, until the next stated session after the appointment and acceptance of the office by his successor.(a)

In case of the disability of the District Judge to perform the duties of his office, the cases before him are transferred to the Circuit Court, as is more fully stated in section 321.

The Circuit Court.

§ 320. An appointed number of Districts constitute a Circuit, of which a judge of the United States Supreme Court is Circuit Judge ; and in every District of said Circuit is held a Circuit Court, composed of two judges, the District Judge of the District, and the Circuit Judge of the Circuit. Either of the judges may hold the Circuit Court in all cases, except in appeals from the District Court, in which cases the District Judge cannot sit.

The Circuit Courts have no original civil Admiralty jurisdiction. In that class of cases, their jurisdiction is confined to appeals from the District Courts in their respective districts, and the court is composed of the Circuit Judge alone. In many of the Districts, the District Court is clothed with the powers of a Circuit Court, in which cases it is to be considered as a Circuit Court, in the exercise of those powers.

From final decrees in a District Court, in causes of Admiralty and Maritime jurisdiction, where the matter in dispute, exclusive of costs, exceeds the sum or value of fifty dollars, an appeal is allowed to the Circuit Court next to be holden in the District where the decree was rendered.(a)

(a) Act of March 26, 1804, § 1. Jud. Act of 1789, § 6. 1 Gal. 238. Act of Aug. 23, 1842, § 5.

(a) Conk. Treat. 2d edit. 96. Act of March 3d, 1803, § 2.

§ 321. In case of the disability of the District Judge to perform his duties, the business may be transferred to the Circuit Court, by virtue of the "Act further to amend the judicial system of the United States," passed March 2, 1807, which provides :——Sec. 1. That in case of the disability of the District Judge of either of the districts of the United States to hold a district court, and to perform the duties of his office, and satisfactory evidence thereof being shown to the Justice of the Supreme Court, allotted to that circuit in which such district court ought by law to be holden ; and on application of the District Attorney or Marshal of such district in writing to the said justice of the supreme court, said justice of the supreme court shall thereupon issue his order in the nature of a certiorari, directed to the clerk of such district court, requiring him forthwith to certify into the next circuit court to be holden in said district, all actions, suits causes, pleas or processes, civil or criminal, of what nature or kind soever, that may be depending in said district court and undetermined, with all the proceedings thereon, and all files and papers relating thereto ; which said order shall be immediately published in one or more newspapers, printed in said district, and at least thirty days before the session of such circuit court, and shall be deemed a sufficient notification to all concerned.   And the said circuit court shall thereupon have the same cognizance of all such actions, suits, causes, pleas or processes, civil or criminal, of what nature or kind soever, and in the like manner as the district court of said district by law might have, or the circuit court, had the same been originally commenced therein ; and shall proceed to hear and determine the same accordingly ; and the said justice of the supreme court during the continuance of such disability shall moreover be invested with and exercise all, and singular, the powers and authority, vested by law in the judge of the district court in said district.   And all bonds and recognizances taken for or returnable to such district court shall be construed and taken to be to the circuit court, to be holden thereafter, in pursuance of this act, and shall have the same force and effect in such circuit court, as they could have had in the district court to which they were taken : *Provided*, that nothing in this act contained shall be so construed as to require of the judge of the supreme court within whose circuit such district may lie, to hold any special court, or court of Admiralty, at any other time than the legal time for holding the circuit court of the United States in and for such district.——SEC. 2. That the clerk of such district court shall, during the continuance of the disability of the district judge, continue to certify as aforesaid, all suits or actions of what nature or kind soever, which may thereafter be brought to such district court, and the same transmit to the circuit court next thereafter to be holden in the same district; and the said circuit court shall have cognizance of the same in like manner as is herein before provided in this act, and shall proceed to hear and determine the same: *Provided nevertheless,* that when the disability of the district judge shall cease or be removed, all suits or actions then pending and undetermined in the circuit court, in which by law the district courts have an exclusive original cognizance, shall be remanded, and the clerk of the said circuit court shall transmit the same, pursuant to the order of said court, with all matters and things relating thereto, to the district court next thereafter to be holden in said district, and the same proceedings shall be had therein in said district court as would have been, had the same originated or been continued in the said district court.——SEC. 3. That in case of the district judge in any district being unable to discharge his duties, as aforesaid, the district clerk of such district shall be authorized and empowered, by leave or order of the circuit judge of the circuit in which such district is included, to take, during such disability of the district judge, all examinations and depositions of witnesses, and make all necessary rules and orders preparatory to the final hearing of all causes of admiralty and maritime jurisdiction.

§ 322. Under the 3d section of this act, the Hon. Judge Nelson, the Justice of the Supreme Court, allotted to the second circuit, has recently made the prescribed order in the following form:

"It having been satisfactorily shown to me, that the Hon. Samuel R. Betts, District Judge of the Southern District of New York, is disabled from ill health to discharge the duties of his office, it is ordered that James W. Metcalf, Esq., clerk of the said District Court, do take, during such disability of said District Judge, examinations and depositions of witnesses, and make all necessary rules and orders preparatory to the final hearing of all causes of admiralty and maritime jurisdiction, according to the act of Congress, March 2, 1809.

" SAMUEL NELSON.

" Washington, Jany. 28th, 1850."

This order is entered at length in the minutes of the District Court, and in pursuance of it, the clerk at the regular term of the court, calls the causes of Admiralty and maritime jurisdiction, in their order on the docket or calendar of causes, and performs all the functions of the judge in such causes, except to hear the arguments, and decide the cause. He takes down the testimony in writing, upon which, after hearing the parties, the Judge decides.

§ 323. In all suits and actions in any District Court of the United States, in which it shall appear that the judge of such court is any ways concerned in interest, or has been of counsel for either party, or is so related to or connected with either party, as to render it improper for him, in his opinion, to sit on the trial of such suit or action, it shall be the duty of such judge, on application of either party, to cause the fact to be entered on the records of the court; and, also, an order that an authenticated copy thereof, with all the proceedings in such suit or action, shall be forthwith certified to the next Circuit Court of the district; and if there be no Circuit Court in such district, to the next Circuit Court in the state ; and if there be no Circuit Court in such state, to the most convenient Circuit Court in an adjoining state; which Circuit Court shall, upon such record being filed with the clerk thereof, take cognizance thereof, in the like manner as if such suit or action had been originally commenced in that court, and shall proceed to hear and determine the same accordingly ; and the jurisdiction of such Circuit Court shall extend to all such cases so removed as were cognizable in the District Court from which the same was removed.

Supreme Court.

§ 324. The Supreme Court of the United States consists of a

Chief Justice, and eight associate judges. It has exclusively all such jurisdiction of all civil suits in Admiralty, against ambassadors or other public minister, or their domestics, or domestic servants, as a court of law can have, consistently with the law of nations. And also of all civil suits in Admiralty, when a state is a party, except between a state and its citizens, or citizens of other states, or aliens.

It has also original, but not exclusive, jurisdiction of civil suits in Admiralty, between a state and citizens of other states, or aliens—and suits brought by ambassadors or other public ministers, or in which a consul, or vice-consul, is a party.

The Supreme Court has also power to issue writs of prohibition to the District Courts, when proceeding as Courts of Admiralty and Maritime jurisdiction.

The Supreme Court has also jurisdiction, on appeal, from the Circuit Courts, in all cases of final decrees in Admiralty, when the matter in dispute, exclusive of costs, shall exceed the sum or value of two thousand dollars.(a)

§ 325. The judges of all these courts, are appointed by the President of the United States, by and with the advice of the Senate, to hold during good behavior. Before they proceed to execute the duties of their respective offices, they must take the following oath or affirmation:

"I, A. B., do solemnly swear or affirm, that I will administer justice without respect to persons, and do equal right to the poor and to the rich; and that I will faithfully and impartially discharge and perform all the duties incumbent on me as judge, &c., according to the best of my abilities and understanding, agreeably to the constitution and laws of the United States. So help me God."(b)

§ 326. Their commissions are issued from the Department of State—are simple appointments to the office, without any enumeration of duties, or grant of powers or privileges. Their com-

(a) Jud. Act of 1789, § 13.
(b) Const. art. 2, § 2, art. 3, § 1. Jud. Act of 1789, 8.

missions give the office, and it is to the laws of the Congress alone that they are to look for their duties, their powers, and their privileges. The commission is in the following form:

"John Quincy Adams, President of the United States of America—

"To all who shall see these presents, greeting.

"Know ye, that reposing special trust and confidence in the wisdom, uprightness, and learning of Samuel R. Betts, of New York, I have nominated, and by and with the advice and consent of the Senate, do appoint him Judge of the United States, for the southern district of New York, and do authorize and empower him to execute and fulfil the duties of that office, according to the constitution and laws of the said United States, and to have and to hold the said office, with all the powers, privileges, and emoluments to the same, of right appertaining unto him, the said Samuel R. Betts, during his good behavior.

"In testimony whereof, I have caused these letters to be made patent, and the seal of the United States to be hereunto affixed. Given under my hand, at the City
[L. s.] of Washington, the twenty-first day of December, A. D. 1826, and of the Independence of the United States the fifty-first.

"JOHN QUINCY ADAMS.

By the President,

" H. CLAY, *Secretary of State.*"

The commission of the Judge of the District Court is usually inserted at length in the minutes of the court, on the day of his taking his seat on the bench, preceded by an order as follows:

" The Honorable Samuel R. Betts having been appointed Judge of this Court, and having taken the oath required by law, took his seat upon the bench, and his commission was ordered to be entered at length in the minutes."

§ 327. They have no separate commission or constitution, as Courts of Admiralty. When sitting to try an Admiralty cause, the court is an Admiralty Court, and when sitting to try a criminal, it is a Criminal Court, and the court passes from the trial of an Admiralty cause to a common law cause, and *vice versa*, and becomes alternately, at the same sitting, according to the nature of the cause on trial, an Admiralty Court, an Equity Court, and a Common Law Court of civil or criminal jurisdiction, without any change of style or form, or officers or records, except that each case is conducted according to the established course of proceedings appropriate to its class. It is thus always the same court, whether acting in one class of causes or another. It is only as Admiralty Courts that they are here to be considered.

The judges are not allowed to exercise the profession or employment of counsel or attorney, or to be engaged in the practice of the law.(*a*)

§ 328. All these courts have power to issue all writs which may be necessary for the exercise of their respective jurisdictions, and agreeable to the principles and usages of law. They have also power to impose and administer all necessary oaths or affirmations, and to punish, by fine or imprisonment, at the discretion of the court, all contempts of authority in any cause or hearing before the court. Also, to make and establish all necessary rules for the orderly conducting business in said courts, provided such rules are not repugnant to the laws of the United States.(*b*)

§ 329. In the exercise of its appropriate jurisdiction, the Court of Admiralty exercises equitable as well as legal jurisdiction. If the subject be of a maritime nature, and so within the power of the court, and be of such a nature, that the relief must be in the nature of equitable relief, the court is entirely competent to give the equitable as well as the legal relief. It has the capacity of a court of law, and, in certain respects, the capacity of a court of equity. In its decisions upon the ultimate rights of parties, from considerations of conscience, justice and humanity,

---

(*a*) 6 Wheat. 452.   4 Cranch, 24.   Act of Dec. 18, 1812.
(*b*) Jud. Act of 1789, § 14.   Ibid, § 17.   7 Cr. 32.

it sometimes mitigates the severity of contracts, and moderates exorbitant demands.(a) The nature of maritime controversies; obviously, however, necessarily excludes from Courts of Admiralty, large classes of cases, such as specific performance—trusts, &c., which are of frequent occurrence in Courts of Equity. And the Court of Admiralty is not a Court of General Equity, nor has it the characteristic powers of a Court of Equity, but it is bound, by its nature and constitution, to determine the cases submitted to its cognizance, upon equitable principles, and according to the rules of natural justice. It cannot, in a technical sense, be called a Court of Equity. It is rather a Court of justice."(b)

§ 330. These courts, in the exercise of their admiralty jurisdiction, have three great classes of functions. They are *Prize Courts*, in which are adjudicated all the various admiralty and maritime questions relating to maritime prizes of war.

They are *Instance Courts*, in which are heard and determined civil suits of a maritime character between party and party; and they are *Criminal Courts*, in which are tried and punished those maritime officers of which the acts of Congress have given them jurisdiction.

As Prize Courts and Instance Courts, all causes are heard and determined by the court alone, without the aid of a jury. As Criminal Courts, they administer justice in Admiralty cases, with the aid of a grand jury and a petit jury, like the common law courts of criminal jurisdiction.

§ 331. *Clerks.*—Each of these courts has power to appoint its clerk. It is the Court, not the judge or judges that has the power of appointment, and the appointment is in the first instance properly made by the judge or judges, by a written certificate of appointment. The appointment should always be formally made by an order of the Court duly entered in the minutes. Each clerk before entering upon the execution of his office, must take the following oath :

(a) Edw. Ad. Jur. 31. Sup. § 358. 11 Pet. 175. 1 Sum. 388. 2 id. 443. 9 Cran. 125. 1 Wheat. 440. 2 Dod. 58. 1 Hag. 347. 2 id. 377. Bee. 106.

(b) 1 W. Rob. 182. 4 Rob. 250. 2 Dod. 6 Rob. 227.

" I, A. B. being appointed clerk of   , do solemnly swear, (or affirm,) that I will truly or faithfully enter and record all the orders, decrees, judgments and proceedings of the said court ; and that I will faithfully and impartially discharge and perform all the duties of my said office, according to the best of my ability and understanding, so help me God."

The clerks must also give a bond with sufficient sureties, (to be approved by the court,) to the United States, in the sum of $2000, faithfully to discharge the duties of their office, and seasonably to record the decrees, judgments and determinations of the court.(*a*)

§ 332. It is the duty of the clerk in Admiralty cases, to perform all those services which are usually performed by clerks of courts—to receive and mark its files—to keep and affix its seal—to issue its processes—to keep its minutes of proceedings and its records—and to administer oaths, take bail, &c., in court—being in all these matters the servant of the court whose power he aids. He has authority by statute, to take bail and depositions in certain cases—and to perform various duties in case of the inability of the judge, as has been before stated—and he keeps the account of the moneys deposited in court. He is bound at evey stated session of the court, to present an account to the court of all the moneys remaining therein subject to its order, stating particularly on account of what causes said moneys are deposited—which account, with the vouchers, must be filed. He may be attached for contempt, if he refuse or neglect to obey the orders of the court for depositing such moneys.(*b*)

§ 333. In the Southern District of New York, the clerk keeps, as one of the books of the court, an Admiralty Register, in which he enters the title of each Admiralty cause, a brief note of the cause of action, and the names of the proctors, as soon

---

(*a*) Jud. Act. § 7.

(*b*) Act of May 8, 1792, § 8 and 10. Ins. 45, Act of March 2, 1809. Ante, § 321. Act of March 3, 1817.

as the libel is filed, and chronological minutes of the steps in the cause, to its final determination.

Such a register so greatly promotes the convenience of the court, the clerk and the parties, and is so useful in preserving the due order of proceedings, and making them acceptable to all who may be entitled to know them, that it is almost a matter of necessity in courts having much Admiralty business, and is so useful in all cases, that it might well be required by a general rule of the Supreme Court, to be kept in all the courts of the United States.

§ 334. *Proctors and Advocates.*—In all the courts of the United States, the parties may plead and manage their own causes personally, or by the aid of such attorneys or counsel, as by the rules of the courts respectively, are permitted to manage and conduct causes therein. Attorneys in Admiralty Courts are called Proctors—from the Latin, *procurator*—French, *procureur*—after the usage of the civil law ; and counsellors are called Advocates. The modes and conditions of admission as Proctors and Advocates, are different in different districts, the whole matter being entirely subject to the rules of the respective courts.

It is the peculiar duty of the Proctor to conduct the proceedings out of court—process, pleadings, entries, stipulations, admissions, consents, settlements, and motions. He is the nominal representative of the party, and his name should appear in all the papers ; and all orders should be stated to have been made on his motion.

It is the peculiar duty of the Advocate to represent the party in court—to make motions, examine witnesses, address the court, and advocate the cause.(*a*)

§ 335. Proctors are more properly appointed by the party in writing ; but there is no legal necessity for a written proxy— a verbal appointment is sufficient ; and till denied, the court always presumes the Proctor who appears has proper authority.

(*a*) Judiciary Act of 1789, § 35. Bett's Prac. 9, 10, 12.

The court may always call upon him to state for whom he is authorized to appear.

If the party have a Proctor and Advocate, he cannot conduct the cause himself; nor can he call to his assistance one who is not a Proctor or Advocate of the court.

Both Proctor and Advocate, while the cause is pending, have full power over it. After final decree, they have no power, except to sue out execution and superintend and direct its enforcement. They have no power to discharge the decree, except on its performance, unless authorized by the party.(a)

§ 336. The power of the Proctor and Advocate is revocable by the party without cause assigned. It should be done by leave of the court on notice to the Proctor. And, on the application of the party, the general powers of the Proctor or Advocate may be restricted.

Proctors and Advocates are officers of the law—held to the strictest integrity, and the best faith and honor to their clients and the court. They are accountable to the court for their professional conduct, and are subject to be deprived of their privileges and office, and otherwise punished, by attachment, fine, or imprisonment by the court, for violation of professional duty, or for such moral delinquency as would bring into disrepute the administration of justice.(a)

§ 337. The United States are always represented in all cases in court, civil as well as criminal, by the District Attorney of the United States for the District in which the suit is pending, except in the Supreme Court. In that court, the Attorney General of the United States represents the Government.(b)

§ 338. *United States Commissioners.*—By the act of Feb. 20, 1812, chap. 25, the Circuit Courts of the United States are authorized, whenever the extent of their districts renders it

---

(a) Jud. Act of 1789, § 35. Betts' Prac. 11. 1 W. Rob. 337. 1 Hag. 223. 2 Hag. Ecc. 195. 1 W. Rob. 335. 3 Phill. 311. 3 Hagg. Ecc. 687. Ibid. 255. Betts' Prac. 13, 14.

(b) Jud. Act of 1789, § 35.

necessary, to appoint such and so many discreet persons within
the district as may be necessary, to take acknowledgments of
bail and affidavits, to have the like force and effect as if taken
before a judge of the court.   By the act of March 1st, 1817,
chapter 30, they are also authorized to take affidavits and bail
in civil causes in the District Courts; and are also, authorized
to take depositions under the 30th section of the Judiciary Act
of 1789.   By the act of August 23, 1842, chapter 188, they are
clothed with all the powers that a judge or justice of the peace
may exercise, under the sixth section of the act of July 20,
1790, on the government and regulation of seamen in the merchant service.   They are also empowered to exercise all the
powers that any justice of the peace, or other magistrate of any
of the United States, may exercise in respect to offenders for
any crime or offence, by arresting, imprisoning, or bailing the
same, under and by virtue of the 32d section of the Judiciary
Act of 1789, and to require and to take recognizances of witnesses.(a)

§ 339. By the rules of the Supreme Court, they are also
authorized to take bonds or stipulations in Admiralty cases,(b) and in cases where the court may deem it expedient or necessary, for the purposes of justice, the court may
refer any matters arising in the progress of the suit, to one
or more Commissioners, to hear the parties, and make report
therein, with all the power of Masters in Chancery, in references to them, including the power to administer oaths and examine parties and witnesses (c)   This rule unquestionably authorizes the courts to refer matters to any person who, by their
order of reference, may be appointed a commissioner for that
matter alone, but it is also the practice, under it, to refer matters
" to a commissioner," leaving the party to select such one of the
regularly appointed U. S. Commissioners, as he may prefer to
employ.

(a) 2 Stat. at Large, 679.   3 Ibid. 350.   5 Ibid. 516.
(b) Rule 5, 35.
(c) Rule, 44.

§ 340. *The Marshal.*—The Marshal of the District is the executive officer of the Supreme Court, the Circuit Courts and the District Courts, in the district for which he is appointed. He is appointed by the President, by and with the advice of the Senate, for four years, removable at the pleasure of the President; and before he enter on the duties of his office, he must become bound for the faithful performance of the same, by himself and by his deputies, before the judge of the District Court of the United States, jointly and severally, with two good and sufficient sureties, inhabitants and freeholders of the district, to be approved by the District Judge, in the sum of $20,000, and must take, before said judge, as must also his deputies, before they enter on the duties of their appointment, the following oath of office :

" I, A. B., do solemnly swear or affirm, that I will faithfully execute all lawful precepts directed to the Marshal of the district of under the authority of the United States, and true returns make, and in all things well and truly, and without malice or partiality, perform the duties of the office of Marshal, or Marshal's Deputy, (as the case may be,) of the district of during my continuance in said office, and take only my lawful fees. So help me God."(*a*)

§ 341. It is his duty to execute, throughout the district, all lawful precepts directed to him, and issued under the authority of the United States, and he has the same powers in executing the laws of the United States, as sheriffs and their deputies in the several states have by law, in executing the laws of the respective states. He has power to command all necessary assistance in the execution of his duty, and to appoint, as there shall be occasion, one or more deputies, who shall be removable from office by the judge of the District Court, or the Circuit Court sitting within the district, at the pleasure of either.(*b*)

(*a*) Jud. Act of '89, § 27. ' Conk. Treat. 2d edit. 116.
(*b*) Rule 41.   Act of February 28th, 1795, to Suppress Insurrections, § 9.

§ 342. If the Marshal or his deputy be a party to, or interested in, the suit or proceeding, the suits and precepts therein shall be directed to such disinterested person as the court or any justice or judge thereof, may appoint, and the person so appointed, is authorized to execute and return the same.

In case of the death of the Marshal, his deputies continue in office, unless otherwise specially removed, and execute the office in the name of the deceased, until another Marshal be appointed and sworn.

The defaults or misfeasances in office of the deputies, as well after as before the death of the Marshal, are breaches of the condition of the Marshal's bond, and the deputies are responsible to the executors or administrators of the Marshal, in the same manner as to him in his life time.(a)

§ 343. When the Marshal or his deputy is removed from office, or his term has expired, he has power to execute all such precepts as are in his hands at the time—and the Marshal is answerable for the delivery to his successor, of all prisoners in his custody. The removal does not take effect till notice of the appointment of the successor.(a)

§ 344. The United States, at the organization of the government, had no prisons, and by a joint resolution, passed September 23, 1789, recommended the legislators of the states to pass laws, making it the duty of the keepers of the state jails, to receive and keep the prisoners committed under the authority of the United States, the United States paying at the rate of fifty cents a month for each prisoner, during the time he should be confined, and also supporting prisoners committed for offences. If any state did not pass such law, and should retract it after passing it, the Marshal is authorized, under the direction of the Judge of the District, to have and fit up a convenient place for a temporary jail.(b)

(a) Jud. Act, '89, § 28.   Vid. Pet. C. C. R. 241.   Wallace, 119.

(b) Conk. Treat. 2d edit. 118, 124.   Reso. Sept. 23, '89.   Reso. March 3d, '91. Reso. March 3d, 1821.

After a prisoner is committed to the state jail, he is no longer in the custody of the Marshal, nor controllable by him ; and the Marshal is not liable for the escape of a debtor committed to a state jail.(*a*)

§ 345. If the Marshal or his deputies neglect or violate their duty, or disobey the order of the court, they may be attached as for a contempt.(*b*)

The Marshal may also, by order of the Court, compel the payment of his fees, by summary process of attachment against the party liable to pay them.(*c*)

(*a*) These provisions, by which all prisoners of the United States are transferred to the State Sheriff of the County, have saved the expense of providing jails of the United States ; but it may well be questioned whether the inconveniences, risks, and actual evils of thus placing the execution of the U. S. laws, and the protection of the rights of citizens of other States, under the control of State Officers, do not more than counterbalance the expense.

9 Cranch, 76.

(*b*) Act of March 3d, 1817. 7 N. Y. Leg. Ob. 174.

(*c*) 7 Cranch, 276. 2 Gall. 101.

CHAPTER XIX.

The Practice of the American Admiralty Courts, historically considered.

§ 346. It has been remarked, that the grant of the jurisdiction in all Admiralty and Maritime cases, was made total, because these cases are in some sort international, and at least are of such character, as to render it eminently proper that they should be subject to the legislation and control of the General Government, instead of being subject to the fluctuating and various regulations of the State Governments, which, from the necessity of the case, could have no common arbiter, and could not fail to be found disagreeing from, or conflicting with, that great system of maritime law which the interests of commerce require to be maintained in its unity and integrity. For an analogous reason, the Admiralty Courts of the United States could not fail to be more useful and more acceptable to the people, as their practice should be simplified, and made the same in every part of the United States.(*a*)

§ 347. The practice in the courts of the United States, sitting as courts of common law, was made to conform to that of the Supreme Courts of the respective states. As all the states had courts of common law, to which the citizen usually resorted, and with whose mode of proceeding he was acquainted, it was not desirable that the general government should, in that matter, introduce an inconvenient novelty, or establish a uniformity of practice which could hardly fail to be burdensome. On the other hand, the Admiralty and Maritime jurisdiction was, by the Constitution, entirely transferred from the states to the general government, and made a purely federal jurisdiction, of limited extent and peculiar character, and it was equally desirable that it should be uniform throughout the states, as well as conformable to the course of proceedings in the Admiralty Courts of

---

(*a*) Betts' Prac. Art. xiv.

other nations, and of the separate states, before the adoption of the Constitution.

§ 348. The act to establish the judicial system of the United States, was passed on the 24th September, 1789, and five days thereafter, on the 29th of the same month was passed the "Act to regulate the processes in the Courts of the United States." This act, adopted as the practice of the Courts of the United States, in the respective states, in suits at common law, the practice of the Supreme Courts of the states, and provided also that "The forms and modes of proceedings in causes of Equity and of Admiralty and Maritime jurisdiction, shall be *according to the course of the civil law*." This act was, by its own provision, to continue in force until the end of the next session of Congress, and no longer. Its necessary effect was, however, to start the courts on that system of practice, and really to impose upon them, in Admiralty and Maritime cases, the civil law practice, as that under which they must continue to administer justice, even after the expiration of that act, until further provision should be affirmatively made.(a)

§ 349. This adoption, however, of the course of the civil law, without modification or exception, could not fail to be somewhat embarrassing, by keeping the courts fettered by many rules and proceedings, which in the Admiralty and Maritime Courts of other countries to which ours were to be assimilated, had long before been directly abrogated or allowed by tacit neglect to give place to simpler and less technical proceedings; and might, in a measure, defeat the very unity and uniformity which it was intended to establish. Accordingly, in 1792, the Congress passed the act, "For regulating processes in the Courts of the United States," which provided that the forms of writs, executions and other process except their style, and the forms and modes of proceedings in suits of Admiralty and Maritime jurisdiction, should be *according to the principles, rules and usages which belong to Courts of Admiralty, as contradistinguished from courts of common law*. Subject, however, to

---

(a) Process Act of 1789, § 2. 2 Bior. Laws, U S. 72.

such alterations and additions, as the said courts should in their discretion deem expedient, or to such regulations as the Supreme Court of the United States should think proper from time to time, by rule to prescribe to any Circuit or District Court concerning the same.(*a*)

350. Under this act of 1772, the practice of the courts in admiralty and maritime cases has maintained its characteristic resemblance to the principles, rules and usages of Courts of Admiralty. The courts, however, in the different districts, have differed from each other in many of the less important details, quite as much as the whole have differed from the Admiralty Courts of other countries, while in all can be traced the evidence of their common descent from the practice of the civil law.

§ 351. The primitive Roman law suit had few details and little machinery. The plaintiff himself, without writ, seized his adversary by the neck, and took him by force before the Prætor. The plaintiff told his grievance ; the defendant his defence ; proof was taken if necessary ; the cause was decided without delay ; and if the deemed was not paid, the defendant was confined as a criminal, or payment was enforced by a forcible sale of his property. Necessity and convenience trans formed the power to arrest from the party himself, to officers of justice appointed for the purpose. The order of the judge then became necessary, which soon ripened into a process or citation. The judge required a written statement of the plaintiff's case, which soon became the libel. Security to appear and to pay the debt or bail, took the place of forcible detention; and a written statement of the defence was demanded instead of a verbal one. Delays ensued—ingenuity, and wisdom, and eloquence were put in requisition—and from thence sprung the legal profession, and from their acuteness and habits of analysis, grew inevitably and insensibly a complicated and technical system of proceedings which had come to the greatest perfection of strictness in the time of the Empire, many of the details of which are now unknown ; and although Brown asks with

---

(*a*) Dunlap Prac. 72, 79.   3 Dal. 320.   10 Wheat. 473.   6 Cond. 194.   Process Act of 1792, § 2.   2 Bior. Law U. S. 299.

emphasis—" How can the practice of the Admiralty Court be intelligible without knowing the practice of the civil law? And Lord Hardwicke says—" The Court of Admiralty always proceeds according to the rules of the civil law." This is true only in a very general sense.(a)

§ 352. The course of a law suit in ancient Rome, so far as it can be now ascertained, and even as it exists at this time in the countries subject to the civil law, after many centuries of modifications and meliorations is only of the same type with a suit in Admiralty, as conducted in modern days. And the study of that wonderfully refined and artificial mode of proceeding, in all its details of subdivision and systematic distribution of subjects, cannot fail to have a salutary effect upon the mind of the student in furnishing him a careful analysis and classification of all the elements of a complete system of remedies through the medium of courts of justice, and could not be without its advantage in showing him the origin of many actual rules of practice in Courts of Admiralty, still the deviation from that original type is so wide, and so great a proportion of the details have been wisely allowed to fall into disuse, that I shall not attempt to furnish even a synopsis of the Roman practice. Nor shall I attempt to elucidate, much less to cover up or encumber that which is in its nature, simple, intelligible and natural by the obsolete learning and multifarious technicalities of earlier periods or other countries ; I shall endeavor, only, in as simple and intelligible a manner as practicable, to give the actual practice of the courts of the United States in Admiralty and Maritime causes. In doing so, I shall not, however, attempt to collect the local rules of the various courts in which diversity exists.￼ Such a course would only tend to keep up a diversity which, in time, might lead to the establishment of several systems of Admiralty practice, instead of that thorough uniformity which should be established in all the Courts of Admiralty and Maritime jurisdiction.(b)

(a) Dunlap Prac. 73, 75. Ware, 299. 2 Brown, 507. 1 Atk. 295. Ware, 298.

(b) Dunlap Prac. 79.

§ 353. The actual Admiralty practice of modern times, is in truth, so natural and simple, that it is not easy to see why any diversity should exist in the established practice. The deviations from a universal and uniform system of proceedings which may be necessary in particular cases, may well enough be left to the discretion of the court, to be exercised as the circumstances of the case may demand, without, in any manner, affecting the general rule. The Congress seems to have felt the importance of this uniformity, and with a view more fully to secure it, to have passed the act of August 23, 1842. Sections six and seven are as follows :(a)

§ 354. " *Sec.* 6. That the Supreme Court shall have full power and authority, from time to time, to prescribe, and regulate, and alter, the forms of writs and other process to be used and issued in the District and Circuit Courts of the United States, and the forms and modes of framing and filing libels, bills, answers, and other proceedings and pleadings, in suits at common law or in Admiralty and in Equity pending in the said courts, and also the forms and modes of taking and obtaining evidence, and of obtaining discovery, and generally the forms and modes of proceeding to obtain relief, and the forms and modes of drawing up, entering and enrolling decrees, and the forms and modes of proceeding before trustees appointed by the court, and generally to regulate the whole practice of the said courts, so as to prevent delays, and to promote brevity and succinctness in all pleadings and proceedings therein, and to abolish all unnecessary costs and expenses in any suit therein.

§ 355. " *Sec.* 7. That, for the purpose of further diminishing the costs and expenses in suits and proceedings in the said courts, the Supreme Court shall have full power and authority, from time to time, to make and prescribe regulations to the said District and Circuit Courts, as to the taxation and payment of costs in all suits and proceedings therein ; and to make and prescribe a table of the various items of costs which shall be taxable and

---

(a) 5 Stat. at Large, 518.

allowed in all suits, to the parties, their attorneys, solicitors, and proctors, to the clerk of the court, to the marshal of the district, and his deputies, and other officers serving process, to witnesses, and to all other persons whose services are usually taxable in bills of costs. And the items so stated in the said table, and none others, shall be taxable or allowed in bills of costs; and they shall be fixed as low as they reasonably can be, with a due regard to the nature of the duties and services which shall be performed by the various officers and persons aforesaid, and shall in no case exceed the costs and expenses now authorized, where the same are provided for by existing laws."

§ 356. Under that act, the Supreme Court, in 1844, adopted "Rules of Practice of the Courts of the United States, in causes of Admiralty and Maritime Jurisdiction, on the Instance side of the Court—in pursance of the act of 23d August, 1842, chap. 188." These rules, although, in many respects, imperfect as a system of practice, lay down and establish the leading and characteristic outlines of the Admiralty practice, leaving the District and Circuit Courts, to regulate the practice of these courts, respectively, in such manner as they shall deem most expedient for the due administration of justice in suits in Admiralty, in all cases not provided for by the rules adopted by the Supreme Court.(a) Those rules, also, pre-suppose a knowledge of the general course of Admiralty practice, and of many of its details, as it has come to us from the civil law courts, on the Continent, modified in England by the practice of the Ecclesiastical Courts and the Court of Chancery, and to those who are already familiar with the course of Admiralty proceedings, those rules are the clear and easily understood introduction of a most salutary reform in the Admiralty practice—abolishing and rendering unnecessary many of the cumbrous and useless forms and proceedings which, in earlier periods, perhaps, were not without practical benefit. The power to regulate the costs and fees, conferred by the 7th section of the act, has not yet been exercised, although a general regulation and tariff of fees is greatly needed.

(a) Rule 46. These Rules are inserted at length in the Appendix—vid. Index.

§ 357. The publication of those rules seems to furnish an occasion for a simple commentary upon them, embracing a straightforward account of the proceedings in Admiralty suits, in which so much of the universal law and traditionary practice of the courts, should be united with the rules of the Supreme Court, and methodically arranged, as should be necessary to furnish a useful book of instruction for learners, and a convenient manual for the more experienced practiser, and, at the same time, tend to make the practice uniform throughout the United States.

It will be seen that they apply equally to all the courts of the United States, as well the Supreme and the Circuit Courts, as the District Courts, in Admiralty and Maritime cases. As has been observed, many matters of minor detail have been left to be prescribed by the courts themselves, by their own rules, and many others to be disposed of as they arise, according to the discretion of the sitting judge. In those matters of minor detail, instead of stating the practice of several districts, that of the Southern District of New York is alone given.(a) The Admiralty business of that district has hitherto been more than that of all the United States besides, and for about a quarter of a century, has been administered by a judge, "*singulari diligentia, incredibili industria*," who has derived, from his various learning and unequalled experience in such cases, that great practical wisdom which has characterized his decisions.

(a) The Rules of the District Court for the Southern District of New York, are inserted at length in the Appendix—vid. Index. In all cases in which the Rules of the Supreme Court have regulated the practice, those of the District Court are, of course, abrogated.

CHAPTER XX.

The General Character and Course of Admiralty Proceedings.

§ 358. This court, as before stated, is bound to determine the cases submitted to its cognizance, upon equitable principles, and according to the rules of natural justice. This principle of the maritime Law pervades also the whole Practice of the Admiralty in the United States. The grand object of doing justice between the parties is superior to technical rules and forms, and where the stricter practice of the English common law, or the civil law, would turn a party out of court, or defeat or pervert justice, by considering an arbitrary rule of proceeding as paramount to all other considerations, the American Admiralty finds, in the educated reason and cultivated discretion of the court, the means of defeating chicanery, rectifying mistakes, supplying deficiencies, and suggesting to the party the means of reconstructing his case, if necessary, without the loss of such real progress as he may have already made.(*a*)

§ 359. Suits and proceedings in Admiralty are divided into two great classes—suits and proceedings *in rem*, and suits and proceedings *in personam*.

Suits *in rem*, are against a thing itself, and the relief sought is confined to the thing itself, and does not extend to any persons. Suits *in personam*, on the other hand, are against a person, and the relief is sought against him without reference to any specific property or thing. In a suit *in rem*, unless some one intervenes and assumes the responsibilities of the controversy, the power and process of the court is confined to the thing itself, and does not reach either the person or the other

---

(*a*) Ante, § 41, 321. 8 Pet. 538. 1 Hag. 357. 3 Mas. 255. Ibid, 343. Ware, 355.

property of its owner. In a suit *in personam*, the court is confined to the rights and liabilities of the person, and, in its execution proceeds against his property generally, without any regard to its relation to the matter in controversy.(*a*)

§ 360. There are no criminal proceedings *in rem*. The only cases of *quasi* criminal and penal character, are those for the enforcement of the penalties and forfeitures which are imposed by law upon property afloat, under the navigation and revenue laws. They are, like other cases *in rem*, classed with civil causes, and are tried without the intervention of a jury.(*b*)

§ 361. In certain cases the proceedings *in rem* and the proceedings *in personam*, may be united in the same suit, for the purpose of more complete justice.

§ 362. One of the attempts to limit the jurisdiction of the Admiralty, consists of a denial of its power to entertain a suit *in personam*. In England, and in this country on English authority, it has been said, that since the venue has become immaterial, the courts of common law are competent to give relief in all personal actions ; and that when the common law can give relief, the Admiralty has no jurisdiction ; and that the Admiralty has jurisdiction *in rem* only because the common law has no power to proceed *in rem*. This point has been urged with some emphasis, although almost all the earliest English cases, and many of the latest, are cases *in personam*. Clerke, in his Practice, devotes the first and largest portion of the work to proceedings *in personam*. The same is true of Boyd, in his proceedings of the Scotch Admiralty. Suits *in personam* have always been of constant occurrence in the continental courts of Admiralty, and it is the usual mode of proceeding there ; and they constituted, in all periods, a large portion of the business of the British Colonial Courts of Vice-Admiralty, before the American Revolution ; and since that period, in the English Admiralty, at home, and in our own courts, suits *in*

(*a*) Dunlap Prac. 80.   (*b*) 7 Cranch, 112.

personam are of frequent occurrence. It is only remarkable that judges, of distinguished learning and acuteness, should ever have been mystified on the subject.

Wherever there is personal liability in a maritime cause of action, " personal contracts and injuries which concern navigation," the right may be enforced by a suit *in personam*, in the Admiralty.

Wherever there is a maritime lien on a thing, the lien may be enforced by a suit *in rem*, in the Admiralty.(*a*)

§ 363. The party complaining is called the Libellant—the party resisting is called the Claimant, in a suit *in rem*, because his right to appear or intervene, depends upon his claiming the property or some interest in it. In some cases, a party is brought in against whom no substantial relief is sought, but who, from his position or relation to the controversy, is bound to answer the libel ; in that case, he is more properly called the Respondent. In suits *in personam*, the party who defends is usually called the Defendant. Both parties are actors. The libellant is also sometimes called Promovent—Actor—Plaintiff. The defendant is sometimes called Reus Impugnant—Intervevant—Intervenor.(*b*)

§ 364. The familiar principle, that all the parties to a suit are bound by the decree, has its widest application in cases of Admiralty suits and proceedings *in rem*. The decree, as has been remarked, can only dispose of the thing, but so far as the thing is concerned, all the world are bound by the decree ; that is to say, a decree as to the title, or possession, or sale, or forfeiture of the thing, binds all the world. No man is allowed to come in and say, that the decree does not bind him, and that he will have the matter re-tried ; and this is because all the world are parties to the suit. By the regular process of the court, all parties who have any interest in the thing, are warned

---

(*a*) 2 Brow. Ad. Additional observations at the end of the volume. Ante, §§ 48, 55 to 59, 93 to 96, 104 to 107, 115, 116, 126, 151, 203.

(*b*) Dunlap Prac. 84. 4 Cranch, 2. 2 Brow. Civ. 428, 432. Wood Civ. 339. Ibid. 375.

to come in and defend it ; and it is therefore said that the whole world are parties in an Admiralty cause, and therefore, the whole world is bound by the decision.(*a*)

§ 365. The reason on which this dictum stands, will determine its extent. Every person may make himself a party, and appeal from the sentence. But notice of the controversy is necessary in order to become a party ; and it is a principle of natural justice of universal obligation, that before the rights of an individual be bound by a judicial sentence, he shall have notice, either actual or implied, of the proceeding against him. Where these proceedings are against the person, notice is served personally or by publication. Where they are *in rem*, notice is served upon the thing itself. This is, necessarily, notice to all those who have any interest in the thing ; and it is reasonable, because it is necessary, and because it is the part of common prudence for all those who have any interest in it, to guard that interest by persons who are in a situation to protect it. Every person, therefore, who can assert any title to a vessel, has constructive notice of her seizure, and may fairly be considered as a party to the libel, but those who have no interest in the vessel which could be asserted in a Court of Admiralty, have no notice of the seizure, and can, on no principle of justice, be considered as parties in the cause, so far as respects the vessel.(*b*)

§ 366. He that has a maritime suit to prosecute, sets forth, in writing, addressed to the judge of the court, his claim, circumstantially and intelligibly, with the greatest simplicity and conciseness, and closes with a prayer for the relief which he desires. This is called a Libel, from the latin *libellus*, a little book. It is signed by the party, and verified by his oath, and presented to the clerk of the court, with security when necessary, who files it and issues the proper process to the Marshal of the district, who executes it according to its direction, and takes the security required by law.(*c*)

(*a*) 3 Hagg. 132. 3 Price, 109. 9 Cranch, 144.

(*b*) 9 Cranch, 144.

(*c*) Betts' Prac. 16. Ware, 365.

§ 367. The defendant appears, and in the same circumstantial, simple, and concise manner, sets forth, in writing, what he has to say in answer and defence to the suit. This is called an Answer which being signed and sworn to, is also filed with the clerk. The libellant, then, if he desires to dispute the answer, files a general denial. This is called a Replication —and the cause is at issue.

§ 368. If, however, the defendant finds that, on the libel itself, the libellant ought not to have the relief for which he prays, or that the court have not jurisdiction, instead of answering the facts alleged in the libel, he may except to the libel, stating, in written exceptions, the points in which he considers the libellant's case defective. Or, if he have any single fact which should constitute a complete bar to the action, he may set that up alone, in an exceptive allegation, and rely upon it as a bar, or he may unite the whole in an answer—answering as to all the facts in the libel, and setting up others in avoidance or in bar, and stating his exceptions to the libel—and derive the same advantages from them as if he had set them up in separate pleadings. It was formerly held, that objections to the jurisdiction should be set up at the commencement of the proceedings, but it is now well settled, that objection to the jurisdiction may be taken at any stage of the proceedings.

This is true, however, in its full extent only, where the want of jurisdiction springs from the subject matter of the action. Where it is merely a matter of personal exemption or privilege, the court will, if practicable, hold that the appearance and answer of the defendant is a waiver of the exemption or privilege.(a) In like manner, the libellant may, instead of putting in a general replication, put in a special replication, setting up new matter—or he may, before putting in his replication, except to the answer for scandal, impertinence, or insufficiency, and submit its form or its substance to the decision of the court, before incurring the expense of a trial.

(a) Betts' Prac. 52. 7 Jur. 659. 1 Hag. Ec. 185. 3 Hag. 173. Ibid. 340. Ibid. 337. 1 W. Rob. 62. Ibid. 293. 7 Jur. 659. 1 Curties, 481. Ware, 332.

§ 369. Whenever a party desires the order of the court, regulating, correcting, modifying, or arresting the proceedings in a cause, or where any one desires to institute proceedings of an independent or summary character, without any formal suit or process—of which the exercise of Admiralty powers furnish many instances—a Petition or Motion is the usual mode of bringing the matter originally before the court, and the matter is carried to its final result, without the introduction of witnesses or the usual forms of a trial.

If, during any stages of the cause, security be required, it is usually given by stipulation, not under seal, instead of by bond or recognizance under seal.

§ 370. The rules of Pleading in Admiralty do not require all the technical precision and accuracy which is necessary in the practice of the courts of common law, but they require that the cause of action should be plainly and explicitly set forth, in clear and intelligible language, so that the adverse party may understand what is the precise charge which he is required to answer and make up an issue directly upon the charge. Since the evidence must be confined to the matters put in issue by the pleadings, and the decree must follow the allegations and proofs, the pleadings cannot fail to be of great importance, and good pleading is nowhere more important, or more characteristic of the best professional ability than in Admiralty.(a)

§ 371. There are no established or necessary Forms, to which the pleadings or other proceedings or entries must conform—a party is at liberty to adopt such form and such phraseology as may best suit his taste, taking care that, in appropriate language, he bring his matter fully and intelligibly before the court. It is, nevertheless, shown by universal experience, that well framed and appropriate forms, for the various steps of judicial proceedings, greatly contribute to the convenience of suitors and proctors, and promote that certainty, regularity, and

---

(a) Ware, 52. Ibid. 357.

intelligibility, which constitute the perfection of such proceedings, and that uniformity which is so desirable.(*a*)

There are inserted in the text only such characteristic forms as may be necessary, for the purpose of illustration and direction, and there is added, at the end of this volume, a more complete collection of forms, adapted to American Admiralty practice, than has been before brought together. Reference will be made to them, as the subjects are considered in the course of this work, and they will be referred to in the index.

(*a*) Betts' Prac. 17, 18.

CHAPTER XXI.

Practice of the District Court.—The Libel.

§ 372. No process can issue from the District Court till the libel is filed in the Clerk's office, from which the process is to issue. The principles of the practice in this respect being, that no process should issue except as the act of the court, and that the court cannot exercise a proper discretion in issuing the process till the cause of action is properly placed before it, under the solemnity of an oath, with a proper prayer for relief. The first proceeding is, therefore, the Libel or Information. It is called a Libel in suits by individuals—an Information or Libel of Information, in suits by the government. Libels on behalf of the government are not required to be sworn to.(*a*)

§ 373. The Libel is a statement of the case upon which the libellant founds his right to recover, closing with a prayer for the proper relief. It should contain—the address to the Court—a statement of the names of the parties—the general nature of the *action* —the *facts* which entitle the party to recover—a prayer for the relief which the party seeks—and for the process by which the adverse party or thing is to be brought before the court.(*b*)

The following is the form of a libel *in personam* :—

§ 374. "To the Honorable Samuel R. Betts, Judge of the District Court of the United States for the Southern District of New York:

"The Libel of Ebenezer N. Hinckley, of the city of New York, Mariner, against David L. Robinson, of the same city,

---

(*a*) S. C. Rule I. Dunlap Prac. 111, 113. Ware R 385.
(*b*) Betts' Prac. 18. Hall's Prac. 121. Dunlap Prac. 112.

Merchant, owner of the ship Majestic, in a cause of contract, civil and maritime, alleges as follows:

§ 375. "*First.* That said David L. Robinson was, at the time in this article mentioned, owner of the ship Majestic, of New York, and said ship was lying in said port; and being such owner, sometime in the month of December, in the year eighteen hundred and thirty-seven, the said Robinson employed the libellant to take charge of and command said vessel as master, for a voyage from New York to Antwerp in Belgium—thence to such other port or ports as might be deemed expedient, and back to a port of discharge in the United States, at the wages of sixty dollars per month. And that in pursuance thereof, the libellant entered on board, and took charge of said ship as master thereof, on or about the eighth day of the said month of December.

§ 376. "*Second.* That the said vessel having taken on board a cargo, the libellant as master proceeded with her for the port of Antwerp. That owing to the ice, they were entirely unable to reach Antwerp at that time, but were forced to put into Cowes in England, where they remained until they were enabled by the thawing of the ice, to reach Antwerp. That they safely arrived at Antwerp, and there discharged the cargo, and made freight. That the libellant then proceeded with said vessel in ballast, to the port of Bristol in England, and there took on board a cargo, and returned with said vessel to the port of New York, where she arrived, and discharged her cargo and made freight. And, on the 5th day of December, 1838, the said voyage for which the libellant had so engaged, being duly performed, the libellant was discharged from the said ship by said Robinson.

§ 377. "*Third.* That during the whole time the libellant was master of said ship, he well and truly performed his duty as such master; whereby he was entitled to receive from the said Robinson, owner as aforesaid, the balance of his wages, amounting to five hundred and ninety-eight dollars and up-

27

wards, over and above all payments and just deductions; but said Robinson has refused, and still refuses, to pay the same.

§ 378. "*Fourth.* That all and singular the premises are true, and within the Admiralty and Maritime jurisdiction of the United States, and of this Honorable Court.

"Wherefore, the libellant prays that a warrant of arrest, in due form of law, according to the course of this Honorable Court, in cases of Admiralty and Maritime jurisdiction, may issue against the said David L. Robinson, and that he may be required to answer on oath this libel, and the matters herein contained. And that this Honorable Court would be pleased to pronounce for the wages aforesaid; and to give the libellant such other relief in the premises as law and justice may require. And also to condemn the said David L. Robinson in costs.

"EBENEZER N. HINCKLEY.

"Sworn, Jan'y 10, 1838, before me,

"*George W. Morton,* U. S. Commissioner."

§ 379. The address to the judge of the court by his name and his official description, with which the libel should commence, is the same in libels of every class. The statement of the parties, and of the general nature of the action, varies according to the circumstances of each case. In libels *in rem* the simplest form is—

"The libel of A. B. of the city of Boston, merchant, against the ship Seabird, whereof C. D. is, or lately was master, her tackle, apparel and furniture, and also against all persons lawfully intervening for their interest therein, in a cause of contract civil and maritime, alleges as follow."(*a*)

Parties in the Libel.—Libellants.

§ 380. The party really entitled to the relief should always be made libellant. The practice of instituting a suit in the name of one person for the benefit of another, to whom the right

---

(*a*) S. C. Rule 33. Vide the various precedents of Libels referred to in the Index.

has been transferred, and of making one person libellant as the representative of many others, does not obtain in Admiralty— though in cases of salvage, and some other cases, something analogous to it occurs, as will be shown.

All persons entitled, on the same state of facts, to participate in the same relief, and no others, should be joined as libellants, whether the suit be *in personam* or *in rem.*(a)

§ 381. In cases of salvage service, in which usually many concur with various degrees of risk and merit, although each man's compensation depends upon the circumstances of his own comparative merit, and he must recover upon his own case, and although, usually from necessity, each must be a witness for his fellows, it is the uniform practice for all to unite in the same suit, as well those who actually labor in making the salvage, or those who are entitled to share in the compensation by virtue of their legal relation to the subject matter. Nor is there any objection to any one or more of salvors instituting the suit in their own names for the benefit of all others, who shall come in and contribute to the suit, or shall be ascertained to be entitled to share in the salvage. This is, in a measure, necessary because from the very nature of a salvage service, the salvage is but one thing, of which each man is entitled to a share always relative to that of the others and to the whole; and it is impossible that the court should properly ascertain any one man's share, without having the merits of all before it for definite adjudication.(b)

§ 382. In suits against a vessel for mariner's wages, in cases provided for by the act of Congress in relation to seamen in the merchants' service, all the seamen having like cause of complaint, are required to join in the same suit; and this too, although their cases are necessarily distinct, and each man must recover on his own contract and service, entirely independent of, and without any relation to, his fellows. This rule is

(a) Dunlap Prac. 84, 85.
(b) 1 Sum. 400. 8 Pet. 4.

imposed by the statute, and is supposed to have been established simply with a view to avoid unnecessary multiplicity of suits and accumulations of costs.(a)

§ 383. In cases of seizure, the suit must be brought in the name of the United States, unless otherwise expressly provided by statute, in which case the provisions of the statute must be complied with. Some officers of the United States are authorized to sue in their official name in certain cases.(b)

§ 384. The master's general agency for the owners in relation to the ship, and his special property in her and her cargo and freight, authorize him to bring in his own name actions which the owners have in relation to the ship, her cargo or freight.

There are also large classes of cases in which not only the owners, but other persons,—as the seamen, the shippers, the passengers—are also interested, which may be brought in the name of the master, in the behalf, and for the benefit of all. Such are prize cases—salvage cases—collision cases—average cases. In such cases, the libellant should add to his own name and description, in the statement of the parties, a statement that he sues for himself and for others, as the case may be, naming them.

This is one of the advantages of the Admiralty practice, inasmuch as instead of the multiplicity of suits and circuity of action, which in the common law courts are often required, one plea, trial, and decree, determine the whole controversy between all the parties to it.(c)

§ 385. All persons are presumed to have a right to sue in their own names till the contrary appear. There are, however, certain exceptions to this rule coming under another general rule, that parties having no independent will or discretion must be represented in court by other persons who are competent to act. Married women prosecute by their husbands or next

(a) Seaman's Act of July 20, 1790, § 6.   Dunlap, 85.
(b) Betts' Prac. 69.   (c) Dunlap, 85.

friends—minors by their guardians, tutors, or next friends—
lunatics and persons *non compotes mentis* by tutor, committee,
or *guardian ad litem.* The estates of deceased persons are
represented by executors, administrators, or other legal representatives.(*a*)

§ 386. Courts of Admiralty being in some degree international
courts, it seems that in them parties are allowed to proceed
by virtue of their right at the place of their domicil—in other
wards that the party may proceed according to his actual right.
If a married woman have a maritime right which, by law, she
enjoys and may enforce in her own name without the consent
or control of her husband, or against him as a party, she may
sue in her own name in Admiralty. If a party have any character as heir, executor, administrator, guardian, &c., as in which
he is entitled to sue by the law of his domicil, he may sue in
that character in the Admiralty here, in virtue of his character
at home.

When a party's right to sue as he does, depends upon any
character, office, duty or right, he must be so described in the
libel as to show his right.(*b*)

Parties in the Libel—Defendants.

§ 387. The libellant may in one form or another have his
action against all persons and things to which he has a right to
resort for relief. If there be a person or persons, or corporation
personally responsible to him jointly or severally in a maritime
cause of action, he may proceed against them by a libel *in
personam.* If they be only severally responsible, they must
be sued separately ; if they be only jointly responsible, they
must be sued jointly. If, however, joint debtors be liable each
for the whole debt, the libellant may properly institute his action
against them all by a general description, naming specifically
only those whose names are known to him or those who are

(*a*) Wood. Civ. Law, 339. Consett. Prac. 50. 1 Brown Civ. Law. 139. Betts,
18. 4 Mas. 380. 1 Mas. 45. Ware, 75, 91, 462.

(*b*) Ware, 91. Betts, 19. Dunlap, 88.

within the reach of the process of the court, and thus proceed to his decree against the parties thus brought, or such as choose to appear, leaving them to seek the proper contribution from their associates not actually brought in.

So, too, if there be a thing or things—vessel cargo—freight—merchandize—proceeds—against which the libellant has a maritime lien, or privilege, or right, no matter how acquired, he may enforce it by a libel *in rem*.

If the general owner or the special owner, that is to say, one having a special property—a right of possession and control—as the master or charterer (owner for the voyage) be, by virtue of his relation to the thing, personally responsible to the libellant for the demand which is a lien upon the thing, then the libellant may unite the two modes of proceeding, and may enforce his right by a libel *in personam* and *in rem.(a)*

§ 388. Whomsoever and whatsoever he proceeds against should be aptly and legally described in his libel in the introductory statement of the parties. A sufficient reason for this is found in the fact, that the real controversy is more quickly perceived, and the necessary facts are more readily and certainly arranged if the general relations of the parties be first distinctly understood.

The Supreme Court in the General Admiralty Rules have specified several cases of joinder of persons and things in a few of the classes of admiralty and maritime cases, and others are left to be governed by the principles of maritime responsibility.(b)

§ 389. In all suits by material men, for supplies, repairs, or other necessaries, for a foreign ship or for a domestic ship, when the local law gives a lien, the libellant may proceed against the ship and freight *in rem*, or against the master or the owner alone, *in personam.(c)*

(a) 2 Sum. 443.   5 Pet. 675.   7 How. 729.
(b) Vid. the precedents referred to in the Index.
(c) Rule 12.   Ante, § 267 to 273, and precedents.

§ 390. In all suits for mariner's wages, the libellant may proceed against the ship, freight and master, or against the ship and freight, or against the owner alone, or the master alone, *in personam.*(*a*)

§ 391. In all suits for pilotage, or for damage by collision, the libellant may proceed against the ship and master—or against the owner alone, or the master alone, *in personam* (*b*)

§ 392. In all suits for an assault and beating on the high seas, or elsewhere, within the Admiralty and Maritime jurisdiction, the suit must be *in personam* only.(*c*)

§ 393. In all suits against the ship or freight, founded on a mere maritime hypothecation, either express or implied, of the master, for moneys taken up in a foreign port, for supplies, or repairs, or other necessaries for the voyage, without any claim of marine interest, the libellant may proceed either *in rem* or against the master or the owner alone, *in personam.* In these cases, money is borrowed by the master, on the responsibility of the owner, and the ship is mortgaged as security. The ship, the master, and the owner are all liable for the debt, and may, on principle, be joined in the action.(*d*)

§ 394. There are other cases in which money is borrowed solely on the credit of the ship herself, in which marine interest is charged, and the money is put at the risk of the voyage and the safety of the ship—these are strict cases of bottomry, and in all suits on bottomry bonds, properly so called, the suit must be *in rem* only, against the property hypothecated or the proceeds of the property, in whosesoever hands the same may be found, unless some personal misconduct have raised a personal liability, as where the master has, without authority, given the

---

(*a*) 1 Mas. 508–12. 2 Story's R. 16, 99. 3 Hag. 114. 1 W. Rob. 155. 1 W. Rob. 383. Ante, § 277 to 281, and precedents.
(*b*) Rule 14, 15. Ante, § 289, 312, and precedents.
(*c*) Rule 16. Ante, § 309, and precedents.
(*d*) Rule 17. Ante, § 290 to 293, and precedents.

bottomry bond, or, by his fraud or misconduct, has avoided the same, or has subtracted the property, or unless the owner has, by his own misconduct, or money lent, or subtracted the property, in which cases the suit may be *in personam*, against the wrong-doer.(*a*)

§ 395. In all possessory or petitory suits between part owners or adverse proprietors, or by the owners of a ship, or the majority thereof, against the master of a ship, for the ascertainment of the title and delivery of the possession, or for the possession only, or by one or more part owners against the other, to obtain security for the return of the ship from any voyage undertaken without their consent, or by one or more part owners against the others, to obtain possession of the ship for any voyage, upon giving security for the safe return thereof, the process must be by an arrest of the ship and by a monition to the adverse party to appear and make answer to his suit.(*b*)

§ 396. The foregoing provisions, in form permissive, are not supposed to be exclusive of any other joinders of persons or property which may be authorized by sound principle. Thus, although the court in the 18th rule speak of following the proceeds of property only in cases of bottomry, is supposed that the general rule, uniformly held by the court, will still prevail, that wherever the property affected by a lien or privilege has been converted into proceeds, under such circumstances as not to destroy the lien or privilege, the proceeds in whosesoever hands they are, may be followed by suit, as effectually and as far as the thing itself might have been. In like manner, numerous familiar maritime causes of action are not mentioned—thus the court have always held that the admiralty has jurisdiction of the whole subject matter of damage on the high seas—every personal injury, every violent dispossession of property on the ocean belongs to the admiralty jurisdiction ; still within these great classes, the rules enumerate only the cases of collision and assault or beating—and similar omissions will be observed in

---

(*a*) Rule 18. Ante, § 292, and precedents.
(*b*) Rule 20. Ante, § 274, 311, and precedents.

other classes. The Supreme Court have not the power to exclude from the Admiralty jurisdiction cases which the Constitution and the laws have placed within that jurisdiction, and all who know the characteristic, cautious propriety of that court, know that they did not intend to exercise powers which did not belong to them.(a)

All rights against the thing to recover a demand are in the nature of a mortgage or hypothecation. The thing is pledged either by operation of law or by the act of the parties, and the rule of the civil law was that the party had his choice to proceed against the party, or the thing, or both.(b)

The specification of particular causes of action in Rules 12 to 20, inclusive, is therefore presumed not to exclude other causes of action, but to be intended only to lay down a rule in those enumerated cases, leaving others to the operation of analogous principles, or of the general rule.

§ 397. So the Admiralty rules of the Supreme Court, with regard to joinder of person and thing, it is presumed, cannot be considered as repealing or abrogating the sound and salutary principle, that, wherever the libellants cause of action gives him, at the same time, a lien or privilege against the thing, and a full personal right against the owner, then he may by a libel, properly framed, proceed against the person and the thing, and compel the owner to come in and submit to the decree of the court against him personally in the same suit, for any possible deficiency.

§ 398. If parties are improperly introduced, they may be struck out of the libel, on motion, or, more properly, the misjoinder may be made the subject of an exception to the libel.(c)

If new or further parties are found to be necessary, they may be added by order of the court on petition, or they may be added by a supplemental libel.(d)

(a) 5 Pet. 675. 6 Pet. Rep. 143. 7 How. 729. Ante, § 305, 308, 309, 310, 311.
(b) 5 Encyc. de Jurs. 103, art. Hypoth. Kauf. Mack. 396, note.
(c) Dunlap's Prac. 87. Ware. 53.
(d) Betts' Prac. 21. Dunlap, 87.

§ 399. In the statement of the parties in libels *in personam*, the names, occupation and places of residence of the parties should be stated, if they are known, and in libels *in rem*, it should be stated that the property is in the district.(*a*)

§ 400. After the statement of the parties, the nature of the cause should be shortly stated "*in a cause of contract, civil and maritime, or of tort or damage, or of salvage, or of possession, or of prize or forfeiture, or penalty, civil and maritime, as the case may be.*" The actions known to the civil law were classified in various modes, and the classes were almost as numerous as the transactions of men. That extreme classification is now considered unnecessary, and every civil cause of Admiralty and Maritime jurisdiction may be included in one or the other of the above classes.

The Statement of the Cause of Action.

§ 401. The libel must allege in distinct articles, the various allegations of facts upon which the libellant relies to support his suit, so that the defendant can answer, distinctly and separately, the several matters contained in each article. The amount claimed to be due should be stated, and it should be stated without unreasonable exaggeration. For the convenience of all parties the articles should be numbered article first, second, &c., in paragraphs, according to the subject matter, of greater or less length, as the orderly statement of the cause of action may require.(*b*)

§ 402. This statement should contain every fact necessary to give the court jurisdiction, and to entitle the libellant to the remedy or relief which he seeks, and it should contain nothing else. The statements of fact may be more or less detailed and amplified according to the taste of the pleader, but simplicity, compactness, orderly arrangement, and severe logical accuracy, in the common narrative style, are the perfection of pleading in Admiralty, and the court properly discourages the voluminous

---

(*a*) Ad. Rule 23.   Ware, 332.   Betts' Prac. 19.
(*b*) Ad. Rule 23.   Ware, 336.   1 Sum. 328.   8 Jur. 501.   Ware, 399.   Ad. Rule 27.

and involved statements, repetitious, exaggerated and cumulative epithets which discredit some systems of pleading.(a)

§ 403. In suits *in personam,* the libellant may join in the same libel any number of causes of action whether of contract or tort between the same parties. This is another advantage of the Admiralty course of proceeding, which the different forms of action, the different forms of pleas, the different modes of trial, and the different kinds of judgments and executions, all having their technical niceties, in common law proceedings, renders impracticable.

In like manner, if the suit be *in rem,* the libellant may join in the same libel any number of demands against the thing; indeed, it could seem that he must do so, inasmuch as he could hardly be permitted again to attach the thing in the innocent hands of a purchaser at his own sale. Each separate cause of action should be set forth in a distinct and orderly manner in a separate article.(b)

§ 404. In cases in which one party sues for himself and others, the stating part of the libel shonld contain facts to show that others are entitled, and who they are, and how they are entitled—and wherever several parties are joined, and the rights of the parties are distinct, separate and independent, there each libellant's case should be stated in an article by itself, not only with a view to the convenience of the opposite party and of the court, but also because, in such cases, the right to appeal is the individual right of each party, and the final decree should be for or against each individual, (or set of partners,) by name, and, so far as he is concerned, confined to him. In practice, this is often neglected, and, in case of several parties, a general joint libel and answer are put in, and a general decree made, which leads to embarrassment and needless expense, in case of an appeal by some and not all the parties, or separate appeals by all.(c)

(a) 8 Jur. 222. 1 Hag. 96. Ibid 133. Conk. Treat. 2d ed. 353 7 Cranch, 389. Betts' Prac. 19. 2 Sum. 1. Conk. Ad. 419.

(b) Dunlap's Prac 88. Betts' Prac. 20. Cont. Ware, 427.

(c) Ante, § 380, 381, 382, 384. 5 Pet 714. 6 Pet. 143.

§ 405. The libel should contain a distinct statement of the amount claimed with reasonable common accuracy and truth ; and the court disapproves of actions being entered in an amount disproportioned to any reasonable estimate of the amount justly recoverable ; and when that seems to have been done for any sinister purpose, the court will sometimes manifest its displeasure in disposing of the question of costs.

The court is not, however, bound by the amount of damages claimed in the libel. When it appears, on investigation, that the libellant has merits, and that justice requires a larger remuneration than he has demanded in his libel, the court is not precluded by any technical forms from doing full justice. Sir William Scott, in a case of salvage, when the libellant claimed £800, gave £2100, notwithstanding, the objection was made— the whole matter, says he, is before the court; and I think the court is by no means limited by any particular demand.(a)

§ 406. In cases of seizure for a breach of the revenue, or navigation, or other laws of the United States, the information or libel must state the place of seizure, whether it be on land or on the high seas, or on navigable waters within the Admiralty and Maritime jurisdiction of the United States, and the district within which the property is brought, and where it then is. The libel must also propound, in distinct articles, the matters relied on as grounds or causes of forfeiture, and aver the same to be contrary to the form of the statute or statutes of the United States, in such case made and provided, as the case may require.(b)

It is sufficient to describe the offence in the words of the statute, provided it be so described that if the allegation be true, the case must be within the law. It is, in no case, necessary to state any fact which is only matter of defence to the claimant,

---

(a) 8 Jur. 501.   Ware, 434.   5 Rob. 322.
(b) 2 Gal. 485, 497.   7 Cranch, 382, 389.   Ibid. 496.   Ibid. 570.   1 Wheat. 9. 8 Wheat. 380.   9 Wheat. 381, 591.   Conk. Treat. 2d ed. 352, 353, et seq.   Ad. Rule 22.

nor to negative exceptions introduced by way of proviso, or by subsequent statutes.(*a*)

§ 407. If the libellant desires to have his process contain a clause to attach the credits and effects of the defendant, in case he cannot be found, there should be inserted in the libel a statement, that the defendant has credits and effects in the hands of one or more persons, who should be named therein. This is necessary to enable the Marshal to summon the garnishee.(*b*)

§ 408. The judicial power of the United States being limited, the Courts of the United States are of limited jurisdiction, limited by the grant of judicial power in the Constitution, and limited by the Acts of Congress distributing that jurisdiction to the Courts. Their action extends, and must be confined to the cases, controversies, and parties over which both the Constitution and the laws have authorized them to act. It is therefore a cardinal rule, that the libel must, on its face, state a case which is within the jurisdiction of the Court. It is not enough, nor is it at all necessary to make the general statement that the case is within the jurisdiction, but the facts necessary to give jurisdiction must be set forth in the libel. In practice, however, the stating part of the libel usually closes with a general account that the facts are true, and within the jurisdiction of the court.(*c*)

The Prayer of the Libel.

§ 409. After the stating part of the libel, follows the prayer for the proper process to enforce the rights of the libellant, by · bringing the party or the property defendant before the court, and for such relief and redress as the court is competent to give in the premises. If the suit be *in personam* alone, the process and the relief must be merely personal. If the suit be *in rem* alone, the process and the relief are confined to the thing, and no person is under any legal obligation to appear and de-

---

(*a*) 1 Wheat. 9.   8 Wheat. 380.   9 Wheat. 381, 391.   7 Cranch, 382.   2 Gal. 485, 497.

(*b*) Ad. Rules, 2, 37.   (*c*) Ante, § 15. Betts' Prac. 16.

fend the suit, or will incur any personal liability by neglecting to do so. If the suit be *in personam* and *in rem*, then the prayer is for a process, which will bring before the court, both the person and the thing, for adjudication in the matter of the libel.(*a*)

§ 410. If the suit be *in personam* alone, the libellant may pray for a simple citation, in the nature of a summons to appear and answer to the suit, or for a simple warrant of arrest, in the nature of a *capias*—or for a warrant of arrest with a clause therein, if the defendant cannot be found to attach his goods and chattels to the amount sued for—or if such property cannot be found, to attach his credits and effects to the amount sued for, in the hands of garnishees, and to summon the garnishees to appear and answer, on oath or solemn affirmation, as to the debts, credits, and effects of the defendant, in his hands, and to such interrogatories touching the same, as may be propounded by the libellant. If the suit be *in rem*, the process prayed for, unless otherwise provided by statute, must be a warrant of arrest of the thing itself, and a monition to all persons interested, to appear by a day certain, and intervene for their interest.(*b*)

§ 411. Immediately after the prayer for process, follows the prayer for the specific and general relief which the libellant desires—in suits *in rem*, that the property may be condemned and sold, in seizure cases, as forfeited to the United States—or in other cases, may be condemned and sold to pay the demand of the libellant stated in the libel—or that the vessel may be decreed to belong to the libellant or delivered to him—or otherwise, as the case may be, according to the relief to which the party may be entitled—or in suits *in personam*, that the defendant may be decreed to pay the debt or damages claimed by the libellants—and in all cases, that the defendant may be condemned to pay the costs.

(*a*) Ante, § 396, 397. Betts' Prac. 20.

(*b*) Ad. Rules 2, 9, 37. Vid. the forms of prayers in the Precedents of Libels, in the Appendix.

§ 412. If the libellant desire to address himself to the conscience of the defendant, and to compel him to give testimony as to the matters in controversy, he may close his libel with interrogatories, touching all and singular the allegations in the libel, and demand that the defendant answer them on oath. The practice of thus inserting proper interrogations, tends greatly to the promotion of justice, and its prompt and economical administration, by reducing to the narrowest compass that portion of the cause which is to occupy the time of the judge, and the witnesses in court.(a)

(a) Conk. Treat. 2d ed. 356.   Vid. Precedents in the Index.   Ad. Rules 23, 37.

CHAPTER XXII.

Commencement of the Suit.

§ 413. The filing of the libel is the commencement of the suit. Before being filed, the libel should be signed by the party or his agent, and by his proctor, and verified by his oath. It is usually signed by an advocate—but this is not necessary. If the libel prays for only a citation or summons, without arrest, the libel need not be sworn to. It must be filed in the clerk's office from which the process is to issue, before the mesne process can be issued.

The District Courts in their own rules, provide in what cases and in what amounts security shall be given for costs, by the libellant, before commencing the suit. This is usually given by *stipulation*, which, as before stated, is the proper name for an undertaking of security in Admiralty, and not by bond under seal, although there is no legal objection to its being in the form of a bond. A stipulation with surety for costs, is required in the New York District in all cases, except those of American seamen prosecuting for mariner's wages. In suits *in personam* the amount of the stipulation is $100—*in rem*, $250.

These stipulations being undertakings in court, they are usually prepared by the clerk, and executed and acknowledged before him, but there is no legal objection to there being prepared by the proctor, and acknowledged before any United States Commissioner, or the judge. The surety must justify as bail, by a written affidavit on the stipulation, that he is worth twice the amount of his stipulation over and above his debts.(*a*)

§ 414. The stipulation for costs is in the following form :

" DISTRICT COURT OF THE UNITED STATES OF AMERICA, FOR THE SOUTHERN DISTRICT OF NEW YORK.

" STIPULATION

" *Entered into pursuant to the Rules of Practice of the Court.*

" WHEREAS a Libel was filed in this Court, on the tenth day

(*a*) Ware, 385, 427. Ad. Rule 1. Ware, 286. Ibid. 296. Ad. Rules 5, 38.

of January, in the year of our Lord one thousand eight hundred and forty-six, by Ebenezer N. Hinckley, against David L. Robinson, in a cause of contract, civil and maritime, for the reasons and causes in the said libel mentioned, and praying that a monition may issue against the said defendant—And James Jackson, of the city of New York, merchant, surety, and the said libellant, the parties hereto, hereby consenting and agreeing, that in case of default or contumacy on the part of the libellant or his surety, execution may issue against their goods, chattels and lands, for the sum of one hundred dollars:

"Now, THEREFORE, it is hereby stipulated and agreed for the benefit of whom it may concern, that the stipulators undersigned shall be, and are bound, in the sum of one hundred dollars, conditioned that the libellant above named, shall pay all such costs as shall be awarded against him by this court, or in case of appeal, by the Appellate Court.

"E. N. HINCKLEY,
"JAS. JACKSON."

"Taken and acknowledged, this 10th day of January, 1846, before me,

"GEORGE W. MORTON, *U. S. Commissioner.*"

"*Southern District of New York, ss.*—James Jackson, party to the above stipulation, being duly sworn, doth depose and say that he is worth the sum of two hundred dollars over and above all his just debts and liabilities.

"JAMES JACKSON,

"Sworn this 10th day of January, 1846, before me,

"GEORGE W. MORTON, *U. S. Commissioner.*"

§ 415. On filing the libel and the stipulation for costs, the process prayed for is issued by the clerk, as a matter of course, in most cases, but in suits *in personam* no warrant of arrest of the person or property of the defendant shall issue, for a sum exceeding $500, unless by the special order of the court, upon affidavit or other proper proof, showing the propriety thereof.(*a*)

(*a*) Ad. Rule 7. Betts' Prac. 23, 28.

§ 416. The order of the judge is endorsed on the libel in this form :—

" On filing the within libel, and otherwise complying with the rules of the court—let a warrant of arrest issue in this cause against the defendant, (naming him,) and let him be held to bail in   dollars.   (Signed by the Judge.)

In the Southern District of New York, the defendant is held to bail, in cases under $500, in $100 more than the amount sworn to be due. In the cases ordered by the judge, he fixes the bail in his discretion.

In all cases on filing the libel, the Clerk issues the process and endorses on it the amount in which the Marshal must take bail as follows :—

" The Marshal will take bail in the sum of   dollars."

The libel being prepared, let it be signed and sworn to by the libellant, or, in case of his absence, by his agent or attorney, before the Judge, or the Clerk, or a United States Commissioner, and signed also by the Proctor and the Advocate.

If it be a case for security for costs, either prepare the stipulation, and have it executed, and acknowledged and justified ; or let the surety go to the clerk's office, and execute one prepared there.

If the libel pray for an arrest, if the amount be over $500, apply to the Judge for an order that a warrant may issue. File the libel, and request the Clerk to issue the warrant, and mark it for bail.

CHAPTER XXIII.

Mesne Process.

§ 417. The court is always open for the test and return of process, as has been stated: but the convenience of the court, as well as of the officers and suitors, has induced each court by its rules to appoint certain general return days. In the Southern District of New York every Tuesday is a general return day. All Admiralty mesne process is tested on the day it is issued and made returnable on the next general return day, at the usual hour for the opening of the court, unless a certain time be necessary to intervene between the test and return, in which case it is made returnable at the earliest return day which will include that time.(*a*)

§ 418. The proper order and conduct of legal proceedings demands that the process of the court should be prepared with care and correctness, according to the rules and practice of the court, but in this matter, as in every other in Admiralty, the ends of justice is the paramount consideration, and common law technicalities of process are unknown. Any error, mistake, or oversight will, therefore, be corrected by the court, on application, always on such terms as may be just, and as matter of course when the party has not been prejudiced. The issuing of the process being the act of the clerk, the party or his proctor is not responsible for its imperfections.(*b*)

§ 419. The process issues in the name of the President of the United States—is directed to the Marshal of the District, and is tested in the name of the Judge of the court. It must be served by the Marshal or his deputy, unless he be interested, in which case, the court, on application *ex parte*, showing the interest,

---

(*a*) Act of Aug. 23d, 1842, § 5. Stat. at Large, 516.
(*b*) Jud. Act, of 1789, § 32. Betts' Prac. 24, 28.

will appoint a disinterested person, to whom the process will be directed, and by whom it will be served and returned.(*a*)

§ 420. The simple monition *in personam* is in the following form :

"THE PRESIDENT OF THE UNITED STATES OF AMERICA.

" *To the Marshal of the Southern District of New York,*
"*Greeting :*

WHEREAS a libel has been filed in the District Court of the United States of America, for the South-
[L. S.] ern District of New York, on the tenth day of January, in the year of our Lord one thousand eight hundred and forty-six, by Ebenezer N. Hinckley, against David L. Robinson, in a certain action civil and maritime for wages therein alleged to be due the said libellant, amounting to four hundred and ninety-eight dollars, and praying that a monition may issue against the said defendant pursuant to the rules and practice of this court,

" Now, therefore, we do hereby empower, and strictly charge and command you, the said Marshal, that you cite and admonish the said defendant, if he shall be found in your District, that he be and appear before the said District Court, on the first Tuesday of February instant, at eleven o'clock in the forenoon, at the city hall in the city of New York, then and there to answer the said libel, and to make his allegations in that behalf, and have you then and there this writ, with your return thereon.

" Witness the Honorable SAMUEL R. BETTS, Judge of said Court, this first day of February, in the year of our Lord one thousand eight hundred and forty-six, and of our Independence the seventieth.

" JOSEPH SMITH, *Proctor,*

"C. D. BETTS, *Clerk.*"

Take the process to the Marshal, and give him information when the party or the property to be served may be found.

(*a*) Ad. Rule 1. Betts' Prac. 29. Jud. Act of 1789, § 27.

§ 421. If the process be a simple monition or summons to appear and answer to the suit, it is the duty of the Marshal forthwith to serve it on the defendant, by delivering to him a copy thereof. It is a very useful measure of precaution, on the part of the marshal, to ask the defendant to sign on the back of the process his acknowledgment of the service ; but if he omit to do so, the service will be good, and in either case the Marshal returns the process to the clerk's office, with his return endorsed upon it "*Personally served.*" (Signed by the Marshal.)

§ 422. If the process be a simple warrant of arrest, it is the duty of the Marshal immediately to arrest the person of the defendant, and keep him in custody, unless he give bail, with sufficient sureties, by bond or stipulation, with condition that he will appear in the suit, and abide by all the orders of the court, interlocutory or final, in the cause, and pay the money awarded by the final decree rendered therein, in the court to which the process is returnable, or in any Appellate Court.(*a*)

It is the duty of the Marshal to see that the sureties are sufficient, and that the stipulation is duly made and executed, inasmuch as the libellant is not consulted, and has no power to meddle with the duty of the Marshal in the premises, who acts under the proper responsibility of his office.

The Marshal returns the process to the Clerk's office, with his true return endorsed upon it, and with the stipulation, if any, which he has taken.

§ 423. The following is the form of the stipulation :

" DISTRICT COURT OF THE UNITED STATES OF AMERICA FOR THE SOUTHERN DISTRICT OF NEW YORK.

STIPULATION

Entered into pursuant to the Rules and Practice of the Court.

Whereas, a Libel has been filed in the District Court of the United States of America for the Southern District of New

---

(*a*) Ad. Rule 3.   Ware, 286.   See the Forms of Warrants in the Appendix, vid. Index.

York, on the first day of June, 1849, by James Johnson, Libellant, against William Pratt, defendant, in a certain action civil and maritime, for pilotage, therein alleged to be due and owing to the said Libellant, amounting to fifty-six dollars—and Charles Jones, of the city of New York, ship chandler, surety, and the said defendant, parties hereto consenting and agreeing, that in case of default or contumacy on the part of the defendant, execution may issue against them, their goods, chattels and lands, for one hundred and fifty-six dollars—

Now, therefore, it is hereby stipulated and agreed, for the benefit of whom it may concern, that the said defendant shall appear in the said suit before the said District Court of the United States of America, for the Southern District of New York, on the first Tuesday of June, instant, at 11 o'clock in the forenoon, at the City Hall, in the city of New York, and abide by all orders of the court, interlocutory or final, in the said cause, and pay the money awarded by the final decree rendered therein in the said court, or any appellate court.

CHARLES JONES,
WILLIAM PRATT.

Taken and acknowledged, June 3, 1849,
  before me,
    R. M. Stilwell, U. S. Commissioner."

    (*Add affidavit of justification as in section* 414.)

In the Southern District of New York, the Marshal usually takes a penal bond under seal, instead of a stipulation. A stipulation is, however, more consistent with the course of Admiralty practice.(*a*)

§ 424. Imprisonment on mesne process having been abolished in most of the States, and to the same extent in the courts of the United States, a question has been made in several cases, whether the power to arrest in Admiralty be not abolished; and it has been uniformly held, that the right to arrest still exists under the Admiralty rules of the Supreme Court, if not under

---

(*a*) Ad. Rule, 3.

the general course of the Admiralty practice. There has been no act of Congress abolishing imprisonment, since the passage of the act of 1842, authorizing the Supreme Court to prescribe and regulate the process, &c., in Admiralty ; so that that act, and the rules adopted in pursuance of it, are the last, and, of course, the paramount legislation on the subject.(a)

It may well be questioned, whether the Congress in prescribing for the courts of the United States, the laws on the subject of imprisonment, passed by the respective States for the State Courts, could, by a reasonable construction, be held to embrace the Admiralty Courts, which, by the Constitution, cannot exist in the States. The whole course of the law on the subject of the Admiralty Courts, shows that the Congress have always considered them and their practice as peculiar, and not subject to the same laws and principles as other courts, and, especially, have provided that their process should be " According to the principles, rules and usages, which belong to the courts of Admiralty as contradistinguished from courts of law," at the same time that they provided, that the State practice in common law cases, shall prevail in the courts of the United States(b)—In the one case carefully insisting upon uniformity, and excluding the diversity of State practice, and in the other case, expressly prescribing that same diversity as a portion of the law of the United States. Indeed, it may well be asked, whether the peculiarities of maritime commerce, which have made courts of Admiralty necessary, do not also make the power to arrest persons, as well as things, a necessary element of their usefulness. The characteristic difference between the business of the land, and that of the water, is very striking. On the land, we contract with our neighbors, or those into whose character and responsibilities we can inquire—who have property, families, friends, reputation among us, which makes them visible, tangible, and reliable— or we can decline to give credit or deal for cash, or not at all— and we may, with great propriety, be compelled to stand the hazard which we have voluntarily taken. But in maritime

---

(a) 8 N. Y. Legal Observer, 45. 2 Law Rep. new series, 470.
(b) Process Act of 1789, § 2. Ante, § 349.

matters it is not so, but directly the reverse. We must deal with an impersonality, as it were, for the benefit and with the responsibility of whom it may concern. We cannot know with whom we deal, nor on whose responsibility we are ultimately to rely—we negociate with transient persons—we rely upon sea-rovers—we cannot demand cash—nor refuse to give credit— nor decline to deal at all. Contracts are made for us by others in one place, to be performed by us with others in another. What would become of maritime commerce, if no charter party or bill of lading was made on credit!—if sailors, before signing the shipping articles, must be paid in full for the voyage ! —Instead of contracting " with whomsoever may go as master," and whomsoever may be owners, as every where and always has been the policy of the law, must the seamen inquire out the owners, (no matter how far off,) and look into their affairs, or ask for an endorser ! What security could there be for the merchant in shipping, or the consignee in receiving his goods, the pilot, the lighterman, the wharfinger, the sailor, the material man, compelled to give credit, by public as well as private interests, and by the invincible necessities of maritime commerce, to transient persons, whose characters are unknown, and whose residences are inaccessible, and who, on being sued without arrest, would find a substantial defence in a fair wind and an open sea !,

§ 425. If the warrant of arrest contain a clause, if the defendant cannot be found, to attach his goods and chattels to the amount sued for, or, if such goods and property cannot be found, to attach his credits and effects to the amount sued for, in the hands of the garnishee named in the process—in such case, the process should direct that the garnishee upon whom the attachment is to be served, be summoned to appear and answer the interrogatories addressed to him in the libel.(a)

§ 426. Under such a process, it is the duty of the Marshal to arrest the party, if he can be found in his district, and he has

---

(a) Vid the Form in the Appendix. Vid. Index. Betts' Prac. 30.

no right to attach goods, chattels, or debts, credits, or effects, before he has endeavored to find the party himself. But inasmuch as the attachment of property will be immediately dissolved by the defendants appearing and giving bail, the Marshal should by no means, by devoting time to a fruitless search for the defendant, lose the opportunity of attaching his property. If, therefore, the party be not found at his usual place of business or abode, the Marshal should proceed to make the attachment. He should attach the goods and chattels of the defendant, if they can be found, to the amount sued for—and if they cannot be found, then he should attach the debts, credits, and effects of the defendant, in the hands of the garnishee named in the process, to the amount sued for, and summon the garnishee to appear on the return day of the process, and answer according to the requisition of the process. The garnishee may be summoned by serving upon him a copy of the warrant.

§ 427. If the goods and chattels of the defendant are attached, or if the garnishee have credits and effects in his hands, in either case the defendant can always have the attachment dissolved by order of the court, on his appearing in the suit, and giving a bond or stipulation, with sufficient sureties, to abide by all orders, interlocutory or final, of the court, and pay the amount awarded by the final decree rendered in the court to which the process is returnable, or in any Appellate Court. On such bail being given, the suit proceeds in the same manner as if the defendant had been originally arrested, and there had been no attachment.(a)

§ 428. The practice under the attachment clause in the warrant has been the subject of some uncertainty, and it is of sufficient importance to justify a reference to the principles and authorities which have regulated it. In the case of Smith v. Miln, garnishee, before Judge Betts, the libellant had proceeded to a personal execution against the garnishee, without any summons having been served on him. There had been only an

---

(a) Ad. Rule 4.

30

attachment of credits alleged to be in his hands. On a motion to set aside the proceedings, the judge examined the subject fully, and the result of his inquiries cannot be better given than in his own language.

§ 429. "The jurisprudence of all civilized countries, seems to embody the means of rendering the effects of a debtor liable to the claims of his creditors ; and, probably, no other tribunals than courts of common law have found themselves incapacitated to effect that end by their own inherent powers, without having first brought the debtor personally, under their authority. What then, in the English common law is an exception, limited to two small districts, is, in other systems, a common, pervading, and familiar principle.

"The proceeding by way of foreign attachment, resting, in England, only on the customs of London and Exeter, on the continent, in Scotland and the United States, takes its form from the high principle, that persons may be reached by justice through the medium of their property, both for the purpose of compelling their personal appearance and submission to the court, and also by sequestrating his property for the benefit of creditors.

"It is clearly demonstrated by the United States Supreme Court in Manro v. Almeida, (10 Wheat. 473,) that it is a well settled branch of Admiralty powers, not derived from the customs of London, but coming to that jurisdiction from the same sources which furnish the other elements of its power. That case also supplies rules sufficiently explicit and full to direct the use and application of this particular power.

"The object in the case under consideration was, by means of a foreign attachment, to compel the appearance of Montgomery to the suit instituted against him. The court consider it a familiar and authorized method to do so, by force of the remedy by attachment, and point out, very perspicuously, under what circumstances and in what manner, it is to be employed. (Id. 492, 493.)

§ 430. "The attachment may be of goods and chattels themselves, or of rights and credits, and by actual arrest of the goods,

or by notice to the person having either or both in his possession·
(Conk. Ad. P. 478.) When the service is by notice, and not by
actual levy on the goods, two things are necessarily implied : 1.
That the garnishee be apprized of what the process demands and
for what cause; and, 2. That he be warned of the time and place
to appear before the court, and discharge himself of the effect of
the citation, by showing that he holds nothing belonging to the
debtor, or by specifying exactly what it is, and submitting himself, in respect thereto, to the authority of the court.

"The term *garnishee* means one warned or vouched in
respect to the interest of third parties; (F. N. B. 106;) and *gar-
nishment* is a warning; (Jacob's L. Dict. Encycl. Amer. voce
Foreign Attachment.) Accordingly, under the custom of London, the garnishee must be warned not to pay the money to the
debtor, and to appear and answer to the plaintiff's suit. (Bohun's Customs and Priv. of London, 256; Comyn's Dig. Attachment, A.) So he may, it seems, plead to the general action
and deny the indebtedness of the defendant. (Comyn's Dig.
Attachment, E.) The same rule obtains in a trustee process.
(6 Dane's Ab. ch. 192, art. 1.)

"The garnishee, under the English law, may appear by attorney, and plead that he has no property of the defendant in his
hands, or confess it, or wage his law, or plead other special
matter. (Bohun, 256.) The general issue is, whether the garnishee, at the time of the attachment, or at any time after, had
any money or goods of the defendant in his hands. (Id. 255.)
The plaintiff is thus put to prove the garnishee had moneys in
his hands; and if this proof is not made, a verdict will be rendered for him. (Id. 258.) When the proceeding is for the purpose of bringing the defendant into court, and he makes default
on proclamation a *scire facias* issues against the garnishee.
(Comyn, For. Attachment, A.) On the appearance of the defendant, all proceedings against the garnishee cease. (Cro. El.
157, 593. Salk. 291.) And he must have notice of the foreign
attachment, to bind him in the allotment of his effects to the
debt. (Fisher *v.* Lane, 3 Wilson, 296.)

"In the states using the remedy of foreign attachment, its
effect is principally regulated by statute; but in all cases the
cardinal principle in the proceeding is, that the trustee or gar-

nishee shall, by summons or *scire facias*, be brought into court, with notice of the claim upon him, and have a full opportunity to oppose the demand. (6 Dane's Ab. 492, ch. 192, arts. 1 to 8.) And see the practice in various states, stated and explained. Graighle *v.* Wottagle et al. Pet. C. R. 345. Manken *v.* Chandler & Co., 2 Brockb. C. R. 125. Fisher *v.* Consequa, 2 Wash. C. R. 382. Franklin *v.* Ward, 3 Mason, 136, Ibid. 247. Pickquet *v.* Swan, 4 Mason, 443. Barry *v.* Fayles, 1 Peters' R. 315. Brasheer *v.* West, 7 Peters, 621, and 2 U. S. Digest, Supplement, 884.)

§ 431. "Although the Admiralty process of foreign attachment is not borrowed from that given by the custom of London, or the trustee processes in use in most of the states of the Union, yet, all being directed to a common object, and founded upon unity of principle, light is reflected from one upon the other, and we may accordingly recur to the practice of the law courts, serviceably, for explications of the methods by which the common design is best effected.

"We will consider, however, more specifically, how the law and practice, stands in the Court of Admiralty, on this head.

"Clerke's Praxis, as appears by the preface to the edition in Latin, was compiled in the reign of Elizabeth, and became a standard authority long before it was published; and the Scotland manuscripts were revised and arranged under the sanction of men of great eminence and experience in that branch of the law. It has always been accepted as the most authoritative exposition extant, of the early course and usages in Admiralty proceedings. (2 Brown Civ. & Ad. 396. 1 Atk. R. 296. 3 D. & E. 338.) Title 28, lays down the principle, and furnishes the outline of the form of the warrant, applicable to foreign attachments used to compel the appearance of a defendant; and art. 32, in connection with art. 28, renders the direction full and explicit, beyond all ambiguity, that both the debtor and garnishee are to be cited to appear in court and answer the matter of claim.

§ 432. "These chapters or articles of Clerke were recognized in the South Carolina District Court in 1802, as sufficient authority, for arresting property to compel the defendant's appearance, and although the form of the warrant in that case is not given, it is plainly to be implied that it conformed to the directions of Clerke. (Bee R. 186.) The rules of practice of this court, first compiled in 1828, and revised in 1838, provide, that if a party against whom a warrant of arrest issues, cannot be found, and return thereof be made, the plaintiff may have a warrant to attach the property of the defendant, and may also have inserted therein a clause of foreign attachment, according to the course of the Admiralty. (Rule 25.)

" The same practice prevails in the First Circuit. (Dunlap's Ad. Pr. 139, 140.) The foreign attachment sued out here must be according to the course of the Admiralty, and that has been amply shown to require notice or citation to the garnishee. The argument against this motion is, that by Rule 29 the garnishee was obliged, on the mere attachment of the goods of a debtor in his hands, to file his affidavit, giving a full statement of the property in his hands, or pay it into court, and that such service was, accordingly, all the notice or warning necessary to give him.

" The rule will not justify that interpretation. It does not regulate the manner of making out or serving a foreign attachment. These are supposed to have been conformably to the course of the Admiralty ; and then it supplies a summary and cheap method by which the holder of the property may become discharged from the cause, and whereby, also, his creditor may be secured the control of the property attached.

§ 433. "Rules 2 and 37 of the Supreme Court, adopted since the decision in 10 Wheat. 473, specify concisely the steps the creditor and garnishee are respectively to take. The process is described by which a defendant may be arrested in suits *in personam*. (Rule 2.) The mesne process may be by a simple warrant of arrest of the person, in the nature of a *capias*, or by a simple monition, in the nature of a summons, to appear and answer to the suit, as may be prayed for in the libel ; or the warrant for the arrest of the person may have a clause therein, that if he cannot be found, to attach his goods and chattels, or if such property cannot be found, to attach his credits and effects in the hands of the garnishees named therein.

" It is insisted, that the foreign attachment clause authorized by this rule, is not required to contain, also, a summons or notice to the garnishee to appear, and that accordingly no such citation need be made.

" The argument would equally prove, that it is not necessary to cite or summon the defendant himself, for, as he is absent, and cannot be arrested, if no citation is to be served on the holder of his property, the libellant would be allowed to seize the property and prosecute to a decree, without notification, to any person, of his acts.

" This, most manifestly, cannot be so, upon general principles; and Rule 37, instead of favoring that conclusion, in my judgment, most clearly implies, that the garnishee is before the court in the ordinary way of bringing in such party. It provides, that, in cases of foreign attachment, the garnishee shall be required to answer on oath as to the debts and effects in his hands, and to such interrogatories as may be propounded by the libellant; and if he refuse or neglect to do so, the court may award compulsory process, *in personam*, against him.

" A party is not placed in a predicament subjecting him to attachment, but in disobeying or counteracting some process or mandate of court; and this regulation imports, that he has been put within the jurisdiction of the cause and the court by service of process on him."

§ 434. If the suit be *in rem*, it is, in substance, a suit against all persons having any interest in the thing, to the extent of their interest in it. All the world are said to be parties to such a suit, and are bound by the decree, so far as the property proceeded against is concerned, and may intervene and make themselves actual and nominal parties to it, and bring their rights before the court. The process issued is a warrant to arrest the property, and usually contains, also, a monition to all persons interested, to appear on a day certain, and show cause why the property should not be condemned, to satisfy the demand of the libellant. On such a process, it is the duty of the Marshal to arrest the property described in the writ, and safely keep it, subject to the order and decree of the court—the warrant extends to sails and rigging taken ashore, as well as to the ship—and also, to give public notice of the arrest, and of the time assigned for the return of the process and the hearing of the cause. This must be given in such newspaper in the district, as the District Court shall order. And if there be no newspaper published therein, then in such other public places in the district, as the court shall direct. On the return day of the process, he must return the same into court, with his return endorsed, thereon stating what he has done under the writ. He has no right, on the arrest of property *in rem*, to take any bail for the property, but he must retain it specifically, and is responsible for its proper custody. For the purpose of detention and security, the Marshal may, if necessary, take off the sails of a vessel, or her rudder, or anchors, so that she cannot escape.(*a*)

§ 435. In cases of seizure, under the revenue laws, the court must cause fourteen days notice to be given of the seizure and libel, by causing the substance of the libel with the order of the court therein setting forth the time and place appointed for trial, to be inserted in some newspaper published near the place of seizure ; and also, by posting up the same in the most public manner for the space of fourteen days at or near the place of trial.

In analogy with this statute provision, it is the practice in the Southern District of New York to require the Marshal to make the same publication and action in civil cases between party and party, in all cases *in rem*, unless the court shall for sufficient cause order a shorter publication.(*b*)

§ 436. The usual attachment and monition, *in rem*, is in the following form :

" *Southern District of New York, ss.*
" THE PRESIDENT OF THE UNITED STATES OF AMERI-

(*a*) Ante, § 364, 365. Ware, 296. 1 Dods. 282. 1 Hag. 124. Act May 8, 1792, § 4. Conk. Treat, 2d edit. 120. Ad. Rule 9. Act of March 2, 1799, § 69. 13 Pet. 279. Sea Laws, 445. Boyd. Proc. 17. 4 Cran. 2.

(*b*) Ad. Rule 9. Act of March 2, 1799, § 59. Conk. Treat. 2d edit. 361.

ca, To the Marshal of the Southern District of New York,
Greeting :   Whereas a libel has been filed in the District
[L. s.] Court of the United States, for the Southern District of
New York, on the first day of June, in the year of our
Lord, one thousand eight hundred and forty-nine, by
William Robinson against the Bark Richard Alsop,
whereof George Johnson is or lately was master, her tackle,
apparel and furniture, in a cause of contract, civil and maritime,
for the reasons and causes in the said libel mentioned, and
praying the usual process and monition of the said court in that
behalf to be made, and that all persons interested in the said
vessel, her tackle, &c., may be cited in general and special, to
answer the premises, and due proceedings being had, that the
said vessel, her tackle, &c., may, for the causes in the said libel
mentioned, be condemned and sold to pay the demands of the
libellant.

"You are hereby commanded, to attach the said bark or vessel, her tackle, &c., and to detain the same in your custody,
until the further order of the court respecting the same, and to
give due notice to all persons claiming the same, or knowing
or having any thing to say why the same should not be condemned and sold, pursuant to the prayer of the said libel, that
they be and appear before the said court, to be held in and for
the Southern District of New York, on the third Tuesday of
June instant, at eleven o'clock in the forenoon of the same day,
if the same shall be a day of jurisdiction, otherwise on the next
day of jurisdiction thereafter, then and there to interpose a claim
for the same, and to make their allegations in that behalf. And
what you shall have done in the premises do you, then and
there, make return thereof, together with this writ.

" Witness, the Honorable Samuel R. Betts, Judge of the said
Court, at the city of New York, this first day of June, in the
year of our Lord, one thousand eight hundred and forty-nine, and
of our Independence the seventy-third.

"Jas. W. Metcalf, Clerk.

" W. R. Beebe, Proctor for Libellant."

§ 437. The Return of the Marshal should be endorsed on the
writ in the following form :

" In obedience to the within attachment and monition, I attached the property therein described, on the second day of June, instant, and have given due notice to all persons claiming the same, that this court will on the third Tuesday of June, instant, (if that day should be a day of jurisdiction, if not, on the next day of jurisdiction thereafter,) proceed to the trial and condemnation thereof, should no claim be interposed for the same.

" Henry F. Tallmadge, *U. S. Marshal.*

" Dated June 17th, 1849."

§ 438. The proceeding *in rem* is predicated on the assumption, that the owner and other persons interested in property, have it in their own charge, or have placed it under the control of others who will see that their interests will be protected, whenever any process shall be served upon it. The process commands the Marshal to notify all parties—it is his duty, therefore, to make the service openly—to leave a written notice with the person in possession, and to exercise his acts of custody and control, in such open and visible manner, by a keeper, or otherwise, that the persons having the same in charge, may take the necessary steps to protect the rights of all those interested.(*a*)

§ 439. Process *in rem* is founded on a right in the thing, and the object of the process is to obtain the thing itself, or a satisfaction out of it for some claim resting on a real or a quasi proprietary right in it. The court arrests the thing for the purposes of satisfaction. It holds its possession by its officers, and the property, in contemplation of law, is in the custody of the court itself. As the court has the legal possession for the purposes of justice and to that extent is clothed with the sovereignty of the country, it has, of course, the power to defend, and protect its possession, and to resume it, if it should be, by any means, divested. If, therefore, the thing be taken out of the possession of the officer, by a party to the suit or by a stranger,

---

Ante, § 364, 365. Betts' Prac. 33.

the court, on motion, will compel such person by attachment or other summary process, to re-deliver it. And if a purchaser obtain possession without paying the price, he may, in like manner, be compelled to pay the purchase money or re-deliver the property to the officer.(*a*)

§ 440. In all suits *in rem* against a ship, her tackle, sails, apparel, furniture, boats, and other appurtenances, if such tackle, apparel, sails, furniture, boats, or other appurtenances, are in the possession or custody of any third person, the court may, after a due monition or notice to such third person, and on hearing the cause, if any, why the same should not be delivered, award and decree, that the same be delivered into the custody of the Marshal, or other proper officer, if, upon the hearing, the same is required by law and justice. The rule of the Supreme Court mentions only the case of a ship, but the principle is one of general application, and under like circumstances, when a principal object is arrested, and some of its appurtenances are withheld from the Marshal by a third person, the court would, in the manner pointed out in the rule, compel its delivery to the Marshal. The proceeding can work no injustice, for such third person can immediately intervene in the suit, for his interest in the things so taken from him.(*b*)

§ 441. In cases of proceedings *in rem*, where freight or other proceeds of property are attached, or are bound by the suit, (as is often the case in suits for seamen's wages, bottomry, or salvage,) and such freight or other proceeds are in the hands or possession of any person, the court, upon application, by petition, of the party interested, may require the party charged with the possession thereof, to appear and show cause why the same should not be brought into court, to answer the exigency of the suit, and if no sufficient cause be shown, the court may order the same to be brought into court to answer the exigency of the suit, and upon failure of the party to comply with the order,

---

(*a*) 2 Mas. 409. Ware. 352.
(*b*) 1 Hag. 124. 1 Dod. 282, 381. Ad. Rule 8.

may award an attachment or other compulsory process, to compel obedience thereto.(a)

> *Draw a petition—stating briefly the facts—let it be sworn to before a United States Commissioner—serve copy and notice of presenting same, with time and place, on the party holding the property. For the precedents, see the Index.*

§ 442. It is also the duty of the Marshal to keep the property seized in such safe and secure manner, as to protect it from injury while in his custody; so that if it be condemned, or be restored to the owner, its value to the parties may be unimpaired, and the Marshal himself be not responsible for unnecessary deterioration or damage.

§ 443. If the suit be both *in rem* and *in personam*, there may be separate processes at different periods, or one process may combine the usual process *in personam* with the process *in rem*, in which case the Marshal executes it in the same manner as he would do the two if they were separate, and he makes on the united process a return of all that he has done in pursuance of the writ.

(a) Ad. Rule 38.   Ware, 296.   1 Curteis, 466.

CHAPTER XXIV.

Interlocutory Sale or Delivery of Property.

§ 444. If the property be in its nature perishable, or is liable to deterioration, decay, or injury, by being detained in custody, pending the suit, the court may, on the application of either party, in its discretion, order the same, or so much thereof as shall be perishable, or liable to deterioration, decay, or injury, to be sold, and the proceeds thereof, or so much thereof as shall be a full security to satisfy the decree, to be brought into court, to abide the event of the suit. Instead of a sale the court may, on the application of the claimant, order an appraisement of the property to be made, and order the same to be delivered to the claimant, on his depositing in court so much money as the court shall direct, or the court may order it to be delivered to him on his giving a stipulation, with sureties, in such sum as the court shall direct, to pay the money awarded, and abide by the final decree rendered by the court, or the Appellate Court, if any appeal be taken. These orders for sale, or delivery on bail, may be made at any time, as well in vacation as in term.(a) In such cases, the money deposited, the stipulation, or the proceeds of the sale, are a substitute for the thing itself, and to them the court resorts for satisfaction of the decree.

§ 445. The 89th section of the Collection Act of 1799, provides, that in cases of seizure, upon the prayer of any claimant of the seized property, or any part thereof, the same may be delivered to him, it shall be lawful for the court to appoint three proper persons to appraise the property, who shall be sworn in open court, for the faithful discharge of their duty; and such appraisement shall be made at the expense of the party on whose prayer it is granted; and on the return of such

---

(a) Ad. Rule 10. Conk. Treat. 2d edit. 363. Collection Act, 1799, § 89. 1 Gal. 148, 476. Act of April 5. 1843. Supra, § 448.

appraisement, the claimant, with one or more sureties, may give a bond for the appraised value ; and the court, on being furnished with the certificate of the collector of the district, that the duties are paid, may order the property to be delivered to the claimant, and the bond to be filed ; and if the goods are acquitted, the bond shall be cancelled ; but if judgment shall pass against the claimant for the whole or any part of the property, and the claimant shall not, within twenty days thereafter, pay into court, or to the proper officer thereof, the appraised value of the property condemned, with costs, judgment shall be granted on the bond, on motion in open court, without further delay. The same practice has been pursued in cases between individuals. Indeed, the statute was but an adaptation of the Admiralty practice to seizure cases, probably caused by a doubt springing out of the analogy between cases of seizure and those of prize, in which latter cases property is never delivered on bail, before decree, except by consent.

§ 446. Without adverting to the well settled principle, that the Court of Admiralty is always open, and that all proceedings in causes are entered as taking place in open court, it was supposed that a further act was necessary, and accordingly the act of April 5, 1832, was passed. providing, that such proceedings, in all cases, may take place as well in vacation as in term, and that the bail may be taken by the clerk, on the parties producing the certificate of the collector of the sufficiency of the sureties,—the collector and district attorney being reasonably notified in cases of the United States, and the party or counsel in all other cases.

The learned judge of the Northern District of New York has expressed a doubt whether an Admiralty stipulation without seal, would be a compliance with the act, which uses only the word *Bond ;* and whether the appraisers can be sworn before the clerk in vacation, in seizure cases. All the principles of Admiralty practice, and its rules of construction, seem to me to concur in removing such doubt. A stipulation is a Bond. It is that by which the party is bound.

The length of notice—mode of service, and other such details, can be regulated only by the judge of each district according to the circumstances of the district.(a)

§ 447. If a ship or vessel be arrested, the same may, upon the application of the claimant, be delivered to him, upon an appraisement under the direction of the court, upon his depositing in court so much money as the court shall order; or upon his giving a stipulation with sureties, as in the case of perishable goods; and the stipulation or money thereafter becomes a substitute for the thing itself. When a vessel is delivered on bail, the owner takes her *cum onere*. She still remains in his hands, liable to all the liens legally attaching on her.

The object of these various provisions is to enable parties to save themselves from those indirect consequences of litigation *in rem*, which are often destructive of the thing itself, and deeply injurious to the party, without any benefit whatever to the cause of justice, or to the proceedings in court; and, therefore, if the claimant decline to make any such reasonable application to meliorate the evils of delay, and allows the ship to lie in the custody of the Marshal, the court may in its discretion, on the application of either party, upon due cause shown, order a sale of the ship, and direct the proceeds to be brought into court, or otherwise disposed of, as it may deem most for the benefit of all concerned.(b)

§ 448. These applications for interlocutory or provisional relief, may be made at any time after the commencement of the suit, and before the decree, and as often and whenever the circumstances may require such relief, at chambers as well as in open court, in vacation as well as in term. It should, however, be observed, that no person is allowed to make an application to the court, in relation to the proceedings, unless he first by a claim or some stipulation or other regular proceeding, acquire an acknowledged legal relation to the cause. In the matter of

---

(a) Conk. Treat. 2d ed. 366. 1 Gal. 148, 476. Paine, 435. Pet. Cir. R. 235. Ware, 286.

(b) Conk. Treat. 2d ed. 363. Ware, 296. Ad Rule, 11. 3 C. Rob. 178. 2 Mason, 57.

the sale or delivery of property, mutual convenience, and the desire to save expense, induces the parties usually to consent to the proper order. If consent will not be given, application must be made to the court.

> *Draw Claim—have it sworn to before a U. S. Judge, Clerk, or Commissioner, and file it. Give stipulation for costs.*
>
> *Make an affidavit of the circumstances. Let it be sworn to as above. Serve copy, with notice of motion, on the opposite party. Get admission, or make proof of service, and make motion in open Court or at Chambers.*

For the precedents, see the index.

CHAPTER XXV.

Return of Process—Default—Appearance.

§ 449. At the opening of the court, on the return day of the process, the Marshal returns the process to the Clerk, and the Judge directs the defendant to be called. The proctor of the libellant should always be in court on the return day. The old practice of calling the defendant on three several days, and entering three several defaults if he did not appear, and practically not requiring him to appear till on the third day, has become, in modern times, an empty form, producing nothing but expense and delay, and, in the American Courts, has fallen into disuse. The crier now, by order of the Judge, if the suit be *in personam*, calls the defendant, and if he does not appear in person or by proctor, the court, on motion of the libellant's proctor, pronounces him in contumacy and default, and adjudges the libel to be taken *pro confesso* against him, and proceeds to hear the cause *ex parte*, and to decree therein as to law and justice may appertain. This *ex parte* hearing may take place at the time of the default, or on any future day in court, as the court may direct. The more usual course, when the libel is taken *pro confesso*, is to refer the matter to a Commissioner, to hear the parties and make report thereon to the court.(*a*)

The following is the form of the order:

"The process in this cause being returned personally served, the defendant is duly called, and does not appear; and on motion of   Proctor for the libellant, the said defendant is pronounced to be in contumacy and default, and the libel is adjudged to be taken, *pro confesso*, against him, and it is referred to   a Commissioner, to ascertain the amount due to the libellant, and to report the same to the Court, with all convenient speed."

(*a*) Ad. Rule, 29.   Collection Act of 1799, § 29.   Conk. Treat. 2d edit. 362. Ad. Rule, 4.   Betts' Prac. 35.

§ 450. After a decree of contumacy and default, the defendant, at any time before the final hearing and decree, may apply to the court to set aside the default, and allow him to come in, appear, and answer the libel, and the court may, in its discretion, permit him to do so, and may impose such terms as to costs as may be just, even to the payment of all the costs of the suit, up to the time of the application. The phraseology of the Admiralty rule of the Supreme Court has been said to require the payment of the whole costs, as a condition of relief, but so strict and hard a construction, in a court so liberal and equitable as the Admiralty, would not be adopted, unless a three-fold necessity should require it, and no violence is done to the language by giving the phrase, " the court may, in its discretion," its proper application to all that follows it, in the rule. Such applications to the favor or discretion of the court, must be founded on affidavit or other evidence of the grounds of the application.(*a*)

§ 451. In the same manner, in the discretion of the court, on motion of the defendant, and on payment of such costs, and complying with such orders and terms in the premises, as the court may direct, a final decree in contumacy and default may be rescinded, and the party allowed to appear, and a re-hearing granted at any time within ten days after the decree has been entered.(*b*)

Draw the affidavit of the facts—serve copy on the proctor of the opposite party, with such notice of making the application as is required by the rules of the court.

§ 452. If the suit be *in rem*, on motion of the libellant's proctor, proclamation is made by the crier for all persons having anything to say why the property should not be condemned and sold to answer the prayer of the libellant, to come forward and make their allegations in that behalf. If no one appears, on like

(*a*) Ad. Rule 29.
(*b*) Ad. Rule 40. 1 W. Rob. 21. Conk. Treat. 2d edit. 394.

motion, the defaults of all persons are entered, a decree of condemnation and sale is made, on a brief statement by the proctor, of the cause of action, and the suit proceeds *ex parte* to a final hearing and decree, then, or at a future day, or the court may refer the matter to a Commissioner to ascertain the amount and report it to the Court.(*a*)

The following is the order:

" The Marshal having returned that he has duly attached the brig Sea-Bird, her tackle, apparel, and furniture, and given due notice to all persons claiming the same, that this court will, on this day, proceed to the trial and condemnation thereof, should no claim be interposed for the same, on motion of Proctor of the libellant, proclamation is made for all persons having anything to say why the same should not be condemned and sold, to answer the prayer of the libellant, and no person appearing, on like notice it is ordered, that the defaults of all persons be entered, and that the said brig, her tackle, &c., be condemned and sold to answer the prayer of the libellant, and that a *venditioni exponas* issue accordingly ; and, on like motion, it is further ordered, that it be referred to a Commissioner, to ascertain the amount due to the libellant, and to report the same to the court with all convenient speed."

§ 453. It is not usual for the court to refer to a Commissioner matters of tort or uncertain damages, or mere questions of law, where the judgment and discretion of the court itself would be better informed by the actual hearing of the controversy, but there is no legal objection to making a reference in such cases, and it is sometimes done.

Commissioners, in matters referred to them, have all the usual powers of Masters in Chancery, in cases of reference, and may administer oaths, and examine parties and witnesses in proper cases.(*b*)

(*a*) Betts' Prac. 36. Ad. Rule, 44.
(*b*) Betts' Prac. 37. Ad Rule 44.

The Acts of Congress having provided for the appointment of commissioners to perform various semi-judicial duties, it is usual to make the references to them, as persons experienced in such matters, but there is no legal objection to referring a matter to one or more commissioners chosen by the parties, or appointed by the court, for the particular case alone.(a)

§ 454. In cases of seizure, when no one appears, the decree of condemnation is absolute—the only question being whether the property be forfeited or not. In such cases, it is usual for the District Attorney, on his motion for condemnation, to state briefly the substance of the libel and the cause of forfeiture.

§ 455. On the return day of the process or at any other time, when by the course and order of the court, it is the duty of the libellant to take any step in the cause, and he neglects to do so, the defendant appearing, the court may, on his motion, order the libellant to be called; and if he do not appear, may, on like motion, decree him to be in default and contumacy, and pronounce the suit to be deserted, and the same may be dismissed with costs. The Admiralty Rules of the Supreme Court do not as in case of the default of the defendant, say any thing of the power of the court to set aside the default. There cannot be any question, however, of the power of the court, on application in proper time, to set aside any default for not complying with the rules or orders of the court. There might be doubts of the power to set aside a regular final decree on the merits, although taken by default, and hence the propriety of the twenty-ninth and fortieth rules.(b)

The following is the form of the order :

" The libellant having failed to appear in this cause, and prosecute his suit according to the course and order of the court, on motion of   Proctor for the defendant, this

---

(a) Ad. Rule 44.
(b) Ad. Rule 39.   Ante, § 450, 451.

suit is pronounced to be deserted, and the libel is dismissed with costs."

§ 456. If the libellant appear on the return of the process, and move the usual proclamation, the defendant must then appear, put in his answer to the libel, if *in personam*, and his claim and answer, if *in rem*, or on motion obtain from the court such further time as may be necessary.

In suits *in personam*, the defendant is often arrested but a short period before the return of the process, and it is, almost, of course, therefore, to allow him time to procure a copy of the libel, examine his defence and prepare his answer. In cases of real defence, the court gives ample time, and the Practice in Admiralty is such, that proctors are rarely found to oppose the granting of all necessary indulgence.

It is not usual in the Southern District of New York for the proctor to give any written notice of his appearance. In the presence of the court, the defendant's proctor states *viva voce*, that he appears for the defendant, and files his answer or asks for time to do so. The more orderly practice, however, would be, to require the proctor for the defendant to furnish to the clerk to be filed, a written notice that he appears for the defendants, one or more of them—that the files and minutes of the court may always show who is the responsible representative of the defendant. A general rule of the Supreme Court prescribing such notice is desirable.(*a*)

The following is the form of the notice :

DISTRICT COURT—IN ADMIRALTY.

WILLIAM PRATT,   }
   vs.
JOHN JONES, and others.

Sir,—You will please to enter my appearance as Proctor for the defendants (or claimants) in this cause.
          June 2d, 1849.
                            A. B., *Proctor.*
To J. W. M., Esq., *Clerk.*

(*a*) Ad. Rule 23.

§ 457. In cases *in rem*, the process must usually be served fourteen days before the return day, and in many cases more, and there is not, so often, a necessity for further time to answer. If, however, there be any such necessity, the time is extended by the court, and it is usual, in such cases, to connect with the order allowing further time for appearance, an order that the defendant be in contumacy and default, unless his answer be put in within such further time. Further time to answer the libel is practically an extension of the return day of the process ; and on the further day, the defendant may take any course which he might have done, on the actual return day of the process, had he been then ready.

> *Make out and serve, on the Clerk and the libellant's Proctor, a notice of appearance, and make out your claim, answer or exception—have it properly verified, and file it with the proper stipulation, on or before the return of the process, or, at that time, attend Court and move for further time.*

§ 458. It is a general rule that appearance waives any objection, so far as respects the mere formality of the previous proceedings. But this only refers to the more full and deliberate intervening which is affected only by signing the necessary stipulations and putting in the necessary answer. If, therefore, there be any question of formality to be brought before the court, it should be done before perfecting the appearance. By the ancient practice, proctors were required to exhibit a proxy or instrument of appointment by the clients, but this strictness is now entirely obsolete. By the modern practice, for a period of at least 200 years past, proxies have been dispensed with, and a proctor is at liberty to commence or defend a suit on his own responsibility, without the production of any proxy. He is bound, however, to produce his parties before the court, when called on to do so ; and he is expected to be duly authorized to appear by the party for whom he intervenes. The court has a right to call upon the proctor at any period of the cause, to state not generally, but specifically by name, the whole of the parties for whom he is authorized to appear.(*a*)

§ 459. *Garnishee.*—The garnishee, or party holding the property attached, being served with the citation or monition, must appear in person, or by proctor, on the return day of the monition, and answer in writing, on oath, as to the property, goods, chattels, credits, and effects, of the defendant in his hands, and to such interrogatories touching the same, as may be propounded by the libellant. These interrogatories may be annexed to the libel, or put in separately, after the garnishee has appeared, and the answer must be filed in the cause.

If the party refuse or neglect to answer, the court may award compulsory process against him *in personam.*

If he admit any debts, credits, or effects, the same must be held in his hands, liable to answer the exigencies of the suit; and he will be held personally responsible for the demand of the libellant as decreed by the court, to the extent of what he has in his hands.

If the garnishee deny having debts, credits, or effects, in his hands, the libellant may reply to his answer, and the question will be tried by the court like any other issue.(*b*)

If the property of a third person be attached, he may intervene by claim for the protection of his property.

§ 460. In the original suit, when the defendant has not been served personally, but his property or credits have been attached to compel an appearance, on the return of the warrant, the defendant is called in the same manner as if he had been sued personally, and not appearing, he is pronounced in contumacy and default, and the matter of the libel taken *pro confesso* against him, and the amount ascertained, and the decree perfected, in the same manner as in other cases. And execution may issue against his person and property generally, and, espe-

---

(*a*) 1 Hag. Ecc. R. 185.　2 Dod. 369.　Clerke Praxis, 13, 15.　1 W. Rob. 337, 340.　2 Notes of Cases, 216.　4 C. Rob. 290.　Betts' Prac. 36, 47.

(*b*) Ad. Rule, 37.　Vide Precedents in the Appendix.　Hall Ad. 70 to 78.　Ante, § 425 to 423.

cially, against his property, credits, and effects, in the hands of the garnishee, and if the garnishee refuse to deliver or apply the same to the execution, then against the person and property of the garnishee, to the amount of the execution, or of the property, credits, and effects, in his hands.(a)

No person is allowed to intervene in a suit or proceeding *in rem*, unless he give a stipulation, with sureties, to abide by the final decree rendered in the cause, and to pay all such costs, expenses, and damages as shall be awarded by the court, upon the final decree, whether it is rendered in the original or appellate court. In practice it is usual to defer putting in the stipulation till the time of filing the claim, answer, or allegation, but in strictness, no party is allowed to make delay or expense to the libellant till he shall have given the necessary security. The appearance of the party is not perfected—he is not considered fully in court, till he has put in his claim or answer and stipulations.(b)

(a) Hall Ad. 70 to 77. Ante, § 426. Vide Precedents in the Appendix.

(b) Ad. Rule 34. Ware, 296. Betts' Prac. 41 to 45, 49, 50. Clerke Prax. tit. 38. Hall Ad. 78.

CHAPTER XXVI.

The Pleadings after the Libel.

§ 461. The pleadings on the part of the defendant are, the Claim—the Exception—the Answer.

Claim.—The claim is confined to proceedings *in rem* in which alone can there be any occasion to make a claim of property. It is a statement in proper form of the right of the party making it to the property attached by the process of the court. It has been before remarked, that all parties having an interest in the property attached, in a suit *in rem*, will be bound by the decree and, of course, are entitled to come in and make themselves parties to the suit, to defend their interest. Persons having liens upon the property thus intervene, a maritime lien being a sort of proprietary interest. All parties who thus intervene are bound, in the first place, to make their claim to the property—in other words, to state their interest in it, that the court and the libellant may know whether, and to what extent, they have a right to defend the suit; for it is quite as important to the cause of justice, that the libellant's rights should not be impaired by the unauthorized meddling of those who have no interest, as that the defendant's rights should not be impaired by his not being allowed to defend it in his own name. The claim is nothing but the statement of the party's right in the property, and its sole purpose is to show his right to appear and defend the suit and represent the property.(*a*)

No set form of words is necessary to form a claim. In this, as in other pleading, the court looks to the substance, rather than the form. It must state that the party is the true and *bona fide* owner of the interest which he represents, and that no other person is the owner thereof. It must be verified by the

---

(*a*) Admir. Rule 26. Ware, 104, 107. Betts' Prac. 56, 57. Clerke Prax. tit 3. Hall Ad. 78. 2 Mas. 409.

oath of the party or his agent or consignee. When it is verified by the oath of an agent or consignee, he must also swear that he is authorized to do so by the owner, or if the property be at the time of arrest in the possession of the master of a ship, that he is the lawful bailee thereof for the owner. As the putting in a claim and defending a suit may put the libellant to great expense—unnecessary and unjust if the claimant have no right—he must file a stipulation, at the time of putting in his claim, with sureties, in such sum as the court shall direct, for the payment of all costs and expenses which shall be awarded against him by the final decree of the court, or upon appeal by the appellate court. In the Southern District of New York the stipulation for costs is in $250. It may be increased by the court, if necessary, on motion.(*a*)

§ 462. The following is the form of a claim :

" To the Honorable Samuel R. Betts, Judge of the District Court of the United States for the Southern District of New York :

" David Rome and William B. King, of Eastport, in the County of Washington, State of Maine, owners of the Schooner Hornet, her tackle, apparel, and furniture, intervening for their interest in the said Schooner Hornet, her tackle, apparel, and furniture, appear before this Honorable Court, and claim the said schooner, her tackle, apparel, and furniture, and state that they are the true and *bona fide* owners thereof, and that no other person is the owner thereof.

" And thereupon, the said claimants pray, that this Honorable Court will be pleased to decree a restitution of the same to them, and otherwise right and justice to administer in the premises. " DAVID ROME,
" WILLIAM B. KING.

" Sworn, July 10, 1847, before me,
" *George W. Morton*, U. S. Commissioner."
W. R. Beebe, Proctor.

This claim may be put in immediately, without waiting for the return of the process.(*b*)

(*a*) Ad. Rule 26. Ware, 52. Betts' Prac. 56, 57.
(*b*) Ad. Rule, 26.

§ 463. Claimants of separate interests may appear separately and put in separate claims. The owners of the respective shares of the ship—the owners of the respective portions of the cargo—the government for its duties, or for a forfeiture—the underwriters when they have reason to believe that the property has been or may be abandoned to them—the consul of a foreign nation, if he have reason to believe that the citizens or subjects of his nation are interested—in short, any person or officer will be allowed to appear and make his claim, (first giving security for costs) whenever, in the opinion of the court, excluding him may lead to a failure of justice. Persons or officers, however, who appear by virtue of some general right, will not be allowed to receive the property or money awarded by the decree, unless the right of the principal party to receive it, and their right of the agent to represent him, be proved to the court.(a)

§ 464. If there be several libels against the same vessel or property, the claimant must put in his claim in each suit, and the libellants in each suit should also put in their claim in all the other suits, lest a decree of condemnation and sale by default, in one suit, should dispose of the property, without the power of redress.

§ 465. The merely putting in a claim, is not a defence to the libellant's claim. The property may belong to the claimant, and still the libellant have full title to the relief sought—indeed, his right to that relief often depends upon the claimant's being the owner of the property. After the claim is in, and the claimant is thus entitled to be heard for his interest, he must put before the court the grounds of his defence, in suitable allegations, that the court, as well as the opposite party, may be informed of the grounds of defence. These may be put forward in a separate defensive allegation, or they may be united with the answer, if one be required. If the libel does not pray for an answer, the defendant need not put in an answer, properly

---

(b) Dunlap, 88. 6 Wheat. 152. 10 Id. 66. 1 Mason, 14. Ante, § 325. Ware 104. Hinchliffe's Prac. 10. 1 Rob. 129–327. 2 id. 88, 92, 104. For precedents in the appendix, vid. Index.

so called; that is to say, he is not compelled to answer the facts set forth in the libel; but whatever may be the prayer of the libel, any party defending the suit, must spread before the court the grounds of his defence, or he will be debarred from making his defence—it being a primary rule in Admiralty, that the cause must be heard and decided according to the allegations, as well as the proofs in the cause.(a)

§ 466. *Exceptions.*—If any pleading or proceeding be irregular, insufficient, or objectionable, the proper mode of bringing before the court the objection, is by exceptions or exceptive allegations—which in their purpose and effect correspond with special demurrers and pleas in bar at common law, and they are properly classed with pleadings. Thus, if the libel—the answer—the replication—the interrogatories, or the answers to them—the report of the clerk, or commissioner, auditor, or assessor, to whom any matter is referred—be liable to just objection, it may be excepted to—and if not excepted to, the court will be slow to listen to any objections to its form or substance.(b)

In mere matters of form, exceptions should be made before answering in chief, or at the same time, or they will be considered as waived.

The following is the form of an exception :

§ 467. "To the Honorable, &c.

"The Exceptions of David Jones, defendant, to the libel of James Jackson, libellant, allege that the said libel is informal and insufficient, as follows :—

"*First Exception.*—That the same is not signed by the libellant, nor by any proctor of this court.

"*Second Exception.*—That the same does not allege that the libellant has sustained any damages in the matter of the libel ; nor that the defendant is indebted to the libellant in any sum.

(a) Ad. Rule, 34. 2 W. Rob. 204. Ibid. 227. 7 Jur. 1117. 3 Hag. Ecc. 97. Ware, 439.

(b) 2 Brow. Civ. and Ad. 361. Dunlap, 192, 193. Betts' Prac. 38, 57 to 59. See the precedents referred to in the Index.

"*Third Exception.*—That the third article thereof, is scandalous and impertinent.

　　　　　　　　　"E. F., *Proctor for Defendant.*"

§ 468. If on the libel itself, it appears that the libellant ought not to have the relief for which he prays, or that the court have not jurisdiction, instead of answering the facts alleged in the libel, he may except to the libel, stating in an exception the point in which he considers the libellant's case defective—or if there be any single fact on which the defendant chooses to rely as a bar to the libellant's demand—as a prior judgment or decree, or release—an accord and satisfaction—a forfeiture, or the like—he may set it up alone, and put his case upon that issue. It is not usual to adopt this course, because he may set up the subject matter of the plea in his answer, and have the same benefit of it, without losing his defence on the general merits, if he fail in the matter of the plea. The practice, therefore, prevails of uniting the matter of the plea and the answer in the same pleading. Pleas of this sort are called exceptions. If they set up matter in abatement merely, they are called dilatory exceptions,—if matter in bar, they are called peremptory exceptions.(*a*)

The following is the form of such plea or exception:

§ 469. "To the Honorable Samuel R. Betts, Judge of the District Court of the United States for the Southern District of New York:

"The Exception of David Jones, defendant, to the libel of James Jackson, libellant, alleges that, on the tenth day of June last, the said libellant, in consideration of one dollar to him paid, released the said defendant from the cause of action set forth in the said libel; and, therefore, the said defendant is not bound further to answer the same; and he prays that the said libel may be dismissed with costs."

　　　　　　　　　　　　　"David Jones."

"Sworn, &c.,
　　　　"E. F. *Proctor for Def't.*"

─────────────

(*a*) Betts' Prac. 48.

§ 470. The libellant may, in like manner, except to the sufficiency, or fullness, or distinctness, or relevancy, of the answer to the articles and interrogatories in the libel.

Exceptions must be carefully prepared, specifying in the simplest and clearest manner, in separate exceptions, the matter excepted to, each exception being numbered; and the exceptions must be put in without unnecessary delay—the time is usually fixed by the rules of the court. They must be filed with the clerk, and notice thereof given to the opposite party. He may then, at any time before the matter of the exceptions has been decided by the court, give notice that he submits to any or all of the exceptions, in which case, on filing such notice, the clerk will enter, of course, the proper order as to such exceptions—that the defendant answer further, or more fully, or more distinctly, or that the irrelevant matter be stricken out.(a)

§ 471. If there be any exceptions not submitted to, they are noticed for hearing before the court by either party, and each exception is overruled, or adjudged good and valid, by the court —and as to such as are adjudged good and valid, the court must order the defendant to answer the same within such time as the court shall in the order direct; and may also impose such costs on the defendant as may be reasonable. And the court may also, as a further sanction to its order, compel the defendant to make further answer, or it may direct the matter of the exception to be taken *pro confesso*, against the defendant to the full purport and effect of the article of the libel, to which it purports to answer, as if no answer had been put in thereto.(b)

§ 472. *Answer.*—If the libel, whether it be *in rem* or *in personam*, prays for an answer, then all parties intervening as defendants, must put in an answer to the allegations of the libel. This answer must be on oath, or solemn affirmation, and must be full, explicit, and distinct, to each separate article of the libel, and each separate allegation in the libel, in the same order as num-

(a) Ad. Rule, 28. Betts' Prac. 58, 59.
(b) Ad. Rule, 30.

bered in the libel—and must, in like manner, answer each interrogatory propounded at the close of the libel.(*a*)

§ 473. The following is the form of an answer:

" To the Honorable Samuel R. Betts, Judge of the District Court of the United States, for the Southern District of New York.

" The answer of John Richards, of Portland, in the State of Maine, intervening for his interest in the brig Spartan, to the libel of Edmund Kimball, junior, and George R. Sheldon, of the city of New York, merchants copartners, doing business under the name of Kimball and Sheldon, answers and alleges as follows :

" *First.* That this respondent is ignorant of the matter contained in the first, fourth, and fifth articles of the said libel, and as to the matters contained in the second and third articles of the said libel, he has no personal knowledge, but has understood and believes that the same are, in a great part, falsely alleged, and that the truth is as is hereafter alleged.

§ 474. " *Second.* That the said brig Spartan being in good order, and well and sufficiently equipped and manned, arrived in the bay of New York early in the evening of the 28th day of November, it being moonlight, and the wind and tide being favorable, but the wind being light, the vessel did not enter the East River before the moon had set, and it had become overcast and dark, so that it was difficult to see a vessel without a light, even at a short distance. That when about to anchor, the master and crew of the said brig Spartan, discovered a vessel which proved to be said brig Buenos Ayres, lying in the stream at single anchor, directly ahead of them, and but a short distance off, and by the force of the tide and wind, without any neglect, carelessness, or default of the master and crew of the Spartan, and notwithstanding every possible precaution, she was driven towards, and in contact with, the said brig Buenos

---

(*a*) Ad. Rule, 37. Ware, 385, 439. 1 Sum. 328. Ib. p84. 4 Mass. 511. Betts' Prac. 51. Dunlap's Prac. 197 to 210.

Ayres, and sustained damage to a large amount, to wit, to the amount of two hundred and fifty dollars and upwards.

§ 475. "*Third.* That at the time above mentioned, the brig Buenos Ayres was lying at anchor in the harbor of New York, in the channel of the East River, between the Fulton Ferry and the South Ferry, and had not a light set in her rigging, on deck, or elsewhere visible to those on board of the brig Spartan, and the said accident was occasioned by negligence and want of care in the master, officers and crew of the said brig Buenos Ayres, in anchoring the said brig without proper light in the channel of the East River, where inward bound vessels must pass.

"*Fourth.* That all and singular the premises are true.

"Wherefore the respondent prays that this honorable court would be pleased to pronounce against the libel aforesaid, and to condemn the libellant in costs, and otherwise law and justice to administer in the premises.

"BURR & BENEDICT,
Proctors for Respondent.

"Sworn, &c.

"E. BURR, *Advocate.*"

§ 476. The defendant is not, however, bound to answer any allegation or interrogatory contained in the libel, which will expose him to any prosecution or punishment for a crime, or any penalty, or any forfeiture of his property for any penal offence. He cannot pass by in silence such allegations or interrogatories, but must object to answer them on such grounds. If his objection covers the whole matter of the libel, he may set up his exemption in a single exception to the proceeding. In other cases, he may unite his exception with his answer.(a)

§ 477. *Interrogatories.*—As the libellant has the right to propose interrogatories to the defendant, so the defendant has the right to resort to the oath of the libellant, and may, at the close of his answer, propose to the libellant any interrogatories touch-

(a) Ad. Rule, 31.

ing any matters charged in the libel, or touching any matter of
defence set up in the answer. These interrogatories should
be numbered, and the libellant must answer in writing in detail, under oath or solemn affirmation, each interrogatory in the
order of their numbers. Like the defendant, the libellant is
not bound to answer any interrogatory which will expose him
to any prosecution or punishment for a crime, or any penalty,
or any forfeiture of his property for any penal offence.

Either party may, at any time, before hearing propose interrogatories to the other, and he is not compelled to annex them
to his pleading, or to put them in at the same time that he files
his pleading, although that is the usual course.(a)

The following is the form of interrogatories :

§ 478. "Interrogatories propounded to James B. Tucker, libellant, by Abraham Farmer and Timothy Ste-
vens, respondents, in a cause Civil and Maritime,
for wages, in the District Court of the United
States for the Southern District of New York.

"*First Interrogatory*. Did not Timothy Stevens above
named, sometime in the month of June last past, or at some
other time, and when in particular tender to you, or offer to
pay to you some, and how much money, which he admitted to
be due to you, for wages for services on board the ship Orbit ?

"*Second Interrogatory*. Did not said Stevens so tender or offer to pay to you the sum of twelve dollars and fifty cents ?

"*Third Interrogatory*. Did you not decline receiving the said
sum or some sum of money, tendered or offered to you by said
Stevens ?

"E. H. *Proctor*."

§ 479. In default of due answer, by the libellant, to any interrogatories, the defendant may except to his answer, in the

---

(a) Ad. Rule 32.   Conk. Treat. 2d edit. 356.   Dunlap's Prac. 125.   Ante, § 476.

same manner, as the libellant may except to the answers of the defendant; and on the hearing of the exceptions, the court may adjudge the libellant in default and dismiss the libel, or may by attachment compel a further answer within a time to be fixed by the court; or may take the subject matter of any interrogatory which is insufficiently answered *pro confesso*, in favor of the defendant, as the court, in its discretion, shall deem most fit to promote justice.(*a*)

§ 480. If the libellant or the defendant is out of the country, or unable from sickness or other casualty, to make an answer to any interrogatory on oath or solemn affirmation, at the proper time, the court may, in its discretion, in furtherance of the due administration of justice extend the time, award a commission to take the answer of the party when and as soon as it may be practicable, or may dispense with it altogether.(*b*)

§ 481. To the answer of the defendant, if the libellant does not admit its statements, he replies by a replication, which is usually in a general form, simply taking issue upon the answer. A general replication is put in without oath, and may be in this form:

" To the Honorable Samuel R. Betts, Judge of the District Court of the United States for the Southern District of New York:

" The Replication of Thomas G. Smith, libellant, to the answer of John P. Goodmanson, defendant, alleges, that he, the said libellant, will aver, maintain and prove his libel to be true, certain, and sufficient; and that the said answer of the said defendant is uncertain, untrue, and insufficient; and he humbly prays, as in and by his said libel he has already prayed.

" BURR & BENEDICT, *Proctors for Libellant.*"

§ 482. It is sometimes desirable to reply to an answer, setting

(*a*) Betts' Prac. 358, 359.   Ad. Rule, 32.
(*b*) Ad. Rule, 33.

up new. matter.   In that case, a special replication may be put
in, replying to such new matter.   A special replication should
be sworn to like an answer.

The pleadings may thus go on, by turns, so long as the mode
of pleading may require it.   They are called Replications, Du-
plications, Triplications, Quadruplications, and so on ; but they
are very rarely resorted to, and may be considered as obsolete.

As the libel may set forth many causes of action, so any of
the pleadings may set up as many distinct matters of defence,
avoidance, or reply, as the case may supply.(a)

(a) Betts' Prac. 48.

CHAPTER XXVII.

Amendments and Supplemental Pleadings.

§ 483. As has been before remarked, causes in Admiralty must be heard and decided according to the allegations of the parties, and the proofs under them ; and it has always been the practice of the American Admiralty Courts, to allow every facility to the parties to place fully before the court their whole case, and to enable the court to administer substantial justice between the parties, without circuity of action, or turning round in court, and never to allow a party to overcome his adversary by the man-traps and spring-guns of covert chicanery, or by the surprises and technicalities of mere pleading or practice. Therefore, on proper cause shown, omissions and deficiencies in pleadings may be supplied, and errors and mistakes in practice, in matters of substance, as well as of form, may be corrected, at any stage of the proceedings, for the furtherance of justice. The whole subject rests entirely in the discretion of the court, as well as in relation to the relief to be granted as to the terms on which it shall be granted. Amendments may be made, on application to the court at any time, as well after as before decree—and at any time, before the final decree, new counts or articles may be added, and new and supplemental allegations may be filed; and this may be done after the cause is in the Appellate Court, if the new allegations be confined to the original subject of controversy. A new subject of controversy cannot thus be inserted in the Appellate Court.(a)

§ 484. Before any pleading is answered or the opposite party /has taken any subsequent step in the cause, amendments may be made, of course, without previous notice to the opposite

---

(a) Ad. Rule 24. Ware. 52. 1 Wheat. 261. 12 Wheat. 1. Paine, 435. Betts Prac. 57. Jud. Act. § 32 Conk. Treat. 2d edit. 357, 360. Ware. 53, 437. 9 Cranch, 243. 3 Wash. 481. 11 Wheat. 1. Conk. Ad. 606.

party, or application to the court. In such cases, the amendment must be filed with the clerk, and if it be after the appearance of the opposite party, a copy of it should be served on him.

In case one of several plaintiffs or defendants die before final judgment, if the cause of action survive to or against his co-partners, the suit does not abate by such death, but a suggestion of the death is made on the record, and the suit proceeds in the name of the survivors.

In case a sole plaintiff or defendant die before final judgment, in case the cause of action, by law, survive, the executor or administrator of the deceased party has full power to prosecute or defend the suit to final judgment ; and the court and the opposite party is bound to consider the executor or administrator as the real party. The executor, however, is always entitled to a continuance of the cause, on motion till the next term, but the other party has not such right.(*a*)

§ 485. The Supreme Court have construed this section, in a common law case, holding, that after the order admitting the executor to appear, it is too late to contest the fact of his being an executor. It is apparent, therefore, that the motion to be so admitted, should be made on notice to the other party to enable him to contest that fact.

If the executor or administrator neglect or refuse to appear and make himself a party, the court may issue a process requiring him to show cause why the action should not proceed ; and if he fail to appear within twenty days after service of such process, then the court may proceed and render judgment against the deceased party, in the same manner, as if the executor or administrator had voluntarily made himself a party to the suit.(*b*)

(*a*) Betts' Prac. 58, 59, 110.   9 Cranch, 244.   1 Wheat. 261.   11 Wheat. 1.   7 Cranch, 496.   1 Gal. 123.   Ware. 51.   15 Pet. 40.   1 Sum. 328.   Jud. Act, § 31.   Dunlap, 87.   3 Cranch. 193.   1 Paine, 483.

(*b*) 3 Cranch. 193.   1 Paine, 483.   3 Cranch, 193.

§ 486. Answers as well as libels, and indeed all pleadings should state the matter with all due certainty and precision, In case of misconduct set up, there must be special allegation of the facts, with due certainty of time, place, and circumstances. Any responsive pleading should reply to each article, by a clear and exact admission or denial, or defence to the matter of it. Proper certainty and precision are of the greatest importance; for as the party cannot regularly prove that which is not properly alleged, so it is not sufficient that there are facts proved, which might have a material bearing, unless there are allegations suited to bring them before the court, as matters of plea and controversy.(a)

§ 487. The general rule is, that the whole substantive case of a party should be at once brought before the court, but supplemental pleadings (libel, answer, interrogatories or exceptions,) may be filed whenever new parties, new allegations, or a more full, definite, or accurate statement of the subject matter of the controversy may be necessary, and supplemental pleadings, and not affidavits, are the proper mode of bringing before the court such new matter.(b)

§ 488. When any pleading or paper is defective in form or substance, it may be amended, and any party may, at any time, thus correct his papers by further, or more full and regular, supplemental, amendatory, exceptive, or responsive allegations to be filed in the cause.

Parties are not required to furnish copies of original pleadings to the adverse party, but each party is required to take out copies from the clerk's office; in the case, however, of new, further, amendatory, or supplemental papers, they must be furnished to the opposite party.

When such further papers are put in, if they affect the proceedings in any material point, the opposite party will be entitled to the indulgence of the court in a continuance of the cause.

(a) 1 Sumn. 328, 384.

(b) 7 Jur. 1117. Betts' Prac. 21. 5 Howard's Rep. 441. 7 Ibid. 729. 3 Hag. Ec, 97. 2 W. Rob. 204. Ibid. 227.

CHAPTER XXVIII.

Stipulation and Bail.

§ 489. It has been before stated that the proper mode of giving security or bail in Admiralty is by stipulation, instead of the common law mode of bond or recognizance. No particular form of words is necessary to constitute a stipulation. It is sufficient if it appear that the party stipulating undertakes to respond, according the legal requisition; and a bond or recognizance would be held good in the American Admiralty courts. There have been doubts raised on the subject, but they have been based on some hypercritical application of English rules of jurisdiction, which have held that the Admiralty could not have jurisdiction of an action on an instrument under seal. The usual form of the Admiralty stipulation briefly recites the pendency of the suit, and closes by distinctly assuming the required obligation. It is executed without seal, and should be acknowledged by the party before the court, the clerk, or a commissioner.(a)

§ 490. Stipulations differ from other contracts in an important particular. In contracts between parties, it is the intention of the party, expressed in an instrument, which is to govern the construction, but the security which is taken in the progress of a suit in a court of Admiralty, for the purpose of sustaining and enforcing its jurisdiction and authority, is taken under the order of the court or of the law. Its terms are directed by the law or the court, and as the will of the party is not consulted as to the tenor of the obligation, so his will or intention is not regarded in its interpretation. If, therefore, there be an ambiguity in the terms of the stipulation, or if the construction of them be doubtful, it is not the intention of the party for which we are to in-

---

(a) Dunlap's Prac. 143. Ware, 286. Ency. de Jurisp. art. Stipulation. Dig. ib. 45. Conk. 427

quire, for the will of the party had nothing to do in determining its conditions—the doubt must be removed by consulting the intention of the court or the law which required the stipulation, and dictated its terms.(*a*)

§ 491. Instead of a stipulation with personal surety, the court will usually allow a deposit of money in the registry of the court, as security.

When personal sureties are given, they are required to swear to their responsibility to twice the amount of the sum for which they undertake, over and above all debts.

If any party in interest desire a more strict inquiry into the responsibility of the sureties, he may, by an exception and notice thereof to the opposite party, require that the sureties appear personally before the court or a commissioner, and submit to a strict examination as to their property and responsibility.(*b*)

§ 492. If either party put in insufficient sureties, or the sureties become irresponsible or insufficient, or remove out of the district, on proper application, the court will compel further security, under the penalty of a stay of the proceedings, in case of a libellant, or in case of defendants, by denying the right to the party further to appear and contest the suit.(*b*)

§ 493. The stipulations taken in the course of an Admiralty cause are of several kinds. Under the Roman practice they were classified in various divisions and subdivisions—according to their nature—according to the occasion calling for them, and according to their form; but this classification is obsolete—and the learning connected with it is of little practical utility.(*c*)

In the case of Lane *v.* Townsend, (Ware, 286, 304,) Judge Ware, with his characteristic learning and acuteness, has presented the subject very clearly and correctly, as the matter stood before the promulgation of the Admiralty Rules of the Supreme Court.

(*a*) Dig. 45, 1, 52. Ware, 292. 7 N. Y. Leg. Ob. 345.

(*b*) Ad. Rule, 6, 10, 11. Betts' Prac. 41.

(*c*) Ware, 283. Dunlap, 153.

In the American Admiralty now, the stipulations —for costs— for costs and damages—for value—to appear and abide the decree of the court, and pay the amount recovered,—are the only stipulations practically in use. They vary slightly in their form, to adapt them to the various purposes to which they are applied in the original and appellate courts.(*a*)

§ 494. The libellant's stipulation for costs *in personam* and *in rem*, is for the payment of all such costs and expenses as shall be awarded against him by the final decree of the court, or, upon an appeal, of the appellate court.(*b*)

In cases of libels *in personam*, when no bail has been taken, and no property has been attached to answer the exigency of the suit, the court may, in its discretion, require the defendant to give a stipulation with sureties, in such sum as the court may direct, to pay all costs and expenses which shall be awarded against him in the suit, upon the final adjudication thereof, or by any interlocutory order in the progress of the suit.(*c*) It is presumed that the court, in such cases, would make the giving the stipulation a condition of permitting the defendant to appear and contest the suit.

§ 495. In case of filing a mere claim to the property *in rem*, the claimant must file a stipulation, with sureties, in such sum as the court shall direct, for the payment of all costs and expenses which shall be awarded against him by the final decree of the court, or, upon appeal, by the appellate court.(*d*) The claimant's property being in custody, he is properly liable only for costs.

In case of intervention by a third person, in a suit or proceeding *in rem*, the stipulation is to abide by the final decree, and pay all such costs, expenses and damages, as shall be awarded by the court upon the final decree, whether it is rendered in the original or appellate court.(*e*) There are obvious reasons why

---

(*a*) Ad. Rules 3, 4, 10, 11, 25, 35.   (*b*) Id. 26.   (*c*) Id. 25.
(*d*) Id. 26.   (*e*) Id. 34.

a third person intervening should be responsible for damages as well as costs.

§ 496. The stipulation of bail to the action *in personam*, is given on the arrest of the party, or on his appearing in discharge of his property or credits attached. The stipulation is, that he will appear in the suit, and abide by all orders of the court, interlocutory or final, in the cause, and pay the money awarded by the final decree rendered in the court to which the process is returnable, or in any appellate court.(*a*) On this stipulation the bail have no right to surrender their principal, nor has the principal any right to surrender himself in discharge of the bail. The stipulation is an absolute undertaking to pay the decree.(*b*)

§ 497. The stipulation of bail to the action in a suit *in rem*, is given to procure the discharge of the property proceeded against. It has been before remarked, that on such a discharge the owner takes the property *cum onere*, and it remains in his hands, subject to all the liens which legally attach to it. It is only necessary, therefore, that he give security to pay what the libellant may recover, leaving all other persons to assert their demands by a new proceeding *in rem*, after the discharge. The owner is therefore required, before taking his property, to give a stipulation, with sureties, in such sum as the court shall direct, to abide by the decree, and pay the money awarded by the final decree rendered by the court, or, in case of appeal, by the appellate court.(*c*)

§ 498. The stipulation for value is given in a suit *in rem*, where the suit is brought, not to enforce a partial lien upon the property, but to recover the property, or to sell the property, as in cases of seizure, of licitation, of salvage, of possessory or petitory suits, or suits against recusant owners. In all such cases, where a party is entitled to have the property delivered on bail, he is bound to stipulate, with sureties, to pay the

---

(*a*) Ad. Rules, 3, 4. Vid. precedents in the Appendix.
(*b*) Ware, 297. Malynes, 88.
(*c*) Ante, § 447. 2 Mason, 57. Ad. Rules, 10, 11.

full value of the property.　And in any case, a party may have his property delivered to him on his giving the proper stipulation, with sureties, for the full value of the property.　This value may usually be fixed by the consent and agreement of parties; if not, then it is ascertained by an appraisement, by sworn appraisers, to be appointed by the court, on motion and hearing of the parties.　The value being ascertained, the claimant must give a stipulation, with sureties, in that amount, that he will, on the interlocutory or final order or decree of the court, or, in case of appeal, of the appellate court, on notice of such order or decree to the proctor for the claimant, to pay into court the sum ascertained as the value.(a)

§ 499.　The act of March 3, 1847, entitled " An act for the reduction of costs and expenses of proceedings in Admiralty against ships and vessels," requires a brief notice, in this connection.　The inconsistency, impracticability, and injustice of its provisions are such, that it has been productive of nothing but evil, by counteracting the laudable purpose expressed in its title.　It is unnecessary to speak of the motives or measures of those who imposed upon unsuspecting members of Congress, and induced them to hurry through both houses of Congress, in the confusion of the last day of the last session of that Congress, a law so excellent in its apparent purpose, and so lame and impotent in its provisions—further than to say that it was a covert attempt, practically, to deny justice to seamen, notwithstanding the favor with which all nations, and especially our own, regard their claims.　The balance due to a seaman is usually less than $50, and rarely exceeeds $100, and in case of dispute, they are the easy victims of oppression if they are without professional aid.　This act seeks to compel them, even when successful, to submit to a decree for their little debt *without costs*—a ruinous decree—while it leaves to the merchant, with his larger demand, the right to a full and just decree for his debt, *with costs.* The effect of such discrimination is apparent, as soon as it is understood.　It practically deprives the seaman of his time hon-

---

(a) Ware, 296.　Vid. the forms in the Appendix.

ored and sacred lien upon the vessel. It does not reduce the costs and expenses. They are untouched in amount. They are only thrown upon the innocent instead of the guilty parties. The clerk cannot refuse to perform his duties,—the marshal must assume his great responsibility of custody and care—pay for advertising—pay a keeper and other necessary disbursements, and neither have any fees or reimbursement unless the libellant recover and collect a sum so large that fifty per cent of it will pay all the fees of the witnesses and commissioner, and leave a residue to be divided, *pro rata*, between those responsible and necessary and involuntary officers of the government; and the proctor, who alone can pilot the seaman through the courts, is absolutely denied all costs, except from the pocket of the seamen.(*a*)

The act is as follows:

§ 500. "*An Act for the Reduction of the Costs and Expenses of Proceedings in Admiralty against Ships and Vessels.*

"Be it enacted by the Senate and House of Representatives of the United States of America in Congress assembled, That in any case brought in the courts of the United States, exercising jurisdiction in admiralty, where a warrant of arrest, or other process *in rem*, shall be issued, it shall be the duty of the marshal to stay the execution of such process, or to discharge the property arrested if the same has been levied, on receiving from the claimant of the same a bond or stipulation in double the amount claimed by the libellant, with sufficient surety, to be approved by the judge of the said court, or, in his absence, by the collector of the port, conditioned to abide and answer the decree of the court in such cause; and such bond or stipulation shall be returned to the said court, and judgment on the same, both against the principal and sureties may be recovered at the time of rendering the decree in the original cause: *Provided*, That the entire costs in any such case, in which the amount recovered by the libellant shall not exceed one hundred dollars, shall not be more than fifty per cent of the amount recovered in the same,

---

(*a*) Conk. 399, 445.

which costs shall be applied, first, to the payment of the usua
fees for witnesses, and the commissioner, where a commissioner
shall act on the case, and the residue to be divided, *pro rata*
between the clerk and marshal, under the direction of the judge
of the court where the cause may be tried : *Provided, further,*
That no attorney's or proctor's fees shall be allowed or paid out
of the said costs.

"Approved, March 3, 1847."

§ 501. Does the act intend to allow every person, even a stranger, to take possession of a libelled vessel, giving a bond to pay
the demand for which she is libelled—if not, how is the marshal
to discriminate; or does it only extend to a "claimant," as
known to the Admiralty practice, one who has filed his claim
showing his interest and given the necessary stipulation—if so,
is the claim to be filed with the marshal?   Does it embrace all
cases *in rem*, and transfer from the court to the marshal the important judicial power of staying proceedings in a cause, and disposing of the questions of delivering property on stipulation—
without appraisement—without notice to the libellant—without
orders or proceedings in court? How is the libellant to proceed to
a decree when no property is arrested, and no party appears? Of
what use is a bond to abide and answer a decree in "the original
cause," when that cause has but one party and he the libellant.
These and other pregnant questions must be answered by those
who seek to apply the act.   The practice under it is simple.

> *Prepare a bond—have it executed with surety, and ap-
> proved by the Judge or the Collector of the port—give
> it to the Marshal, and take the property—without fee
> or reward to amy one.(a)*

§ 502. If a libellant be unable to give security for costs, he is
not thereby denied justice, but he is, on application to the judge,
permitted to give the juratory caution, or security by his oath.
This is analogous to the common law practice of suing *in forma pauperis.* That is to say, he personally stipulates in the
necessary amount, to appear from time to time, as required by

---

(a) Conk. Ad. 446-8.   Vid. the form of the Bond, in the Appendix.

he court, and adds to it his oath that he will do so. The de
fendant may also, by order of the judge, be permitted to give the
juratory caution in proper cases, where he cannot procure bail.
This security is but rarely taken.

The juratory security for costs is in the following form :

" In the District Court of the United States for the Southern
District of New York.

" In a certain cause, civil and maritime, wherein A. B.
is libellant and C. D. is defendant,—on this tenth day of
February, 1849, the said A. B. personally appeared and stipulated in the sum of one hundred dollars, to prosecute this said
cause, and to pay all costs and expenses which may be awarded
against him herein, by the final decree of this court, and, in case
of appeal, of the appellate court ; and to appear on the twelfth day
of February instant, (the return day,) and as often afterwards
as he shall be ordered by the court. And the said A. B. made
oath that he would appear as aforesaid.   " A. B.

·" Taken, acknowledged, and sworn,
          February 10th, 1849, before me,
                    " CHAS. W. NEWTON, *U. S. Commissioner.*"

(a) Dunlap's Prac. 157.   Conk. Prac. 463, 538.   Marriot's Forms, 354.

CHAPTER XXIX.

Seamen's Wages.

§ 503. The character of seamen and the nature of their employment has induced the Congress to provide specially for the collection of their demands for wages. Seamen have always been considered as wards of the Admiralty, and the wages of their perilous service have been by all nations highly favored in the law. It was the great considerations of policy and justice connected with that humble but most useful class of citizens, that induced the English common law courts to leave to the Admiralty the undisputed cognizance of suits for seamen's wages, and to make those wages a lien upon the last plank of the ship. A cheap and summary mode has been, therefore, provided, for hearing the controversies in relation to their wages, which are usually of small absolute amount but of very great importance to the seaman.

§ 504. As soon as the voyage is ended, and the cargo or ballast discharged, the seaman is entitled to his wages. If there be any dispute as to his wages, or if he be discharged from the vessel, he may, without any delay, proceed to enforce payment. If the balance be admitted he must wait ten days, or, at least, a reasonable time, after the cargo is out, before he commence. If the vessel have left the port, when the voyage ended, without paying the wages, or is about to go to sea again before the expiration of the ten days, be proceeds by libel, in the first instance, and arrests the vessel—all the seamen joining in the same suit—and the suit proceeds like other suits *in rem.* In all other cases he proceeds by a preliminary summons before a magistrate, before whom the question of probable cause of suit is investigated.(*a*)

(*a*) Betts' Prac. 60, *et seq.* Seamen's Act of July 20, 1790.

§ 505. In such cases, the judge of the District, or a magistrate or United States commissioner, issues a summons to the master of the vessel, to appear before him and show cause why process should not issue against the vessel, according to the course of Admiralty, to answer for the wages. This summons should be founded on an affidavit, or a libel, showing a *prima facie* right to sue. On the return of the summons, if the master do not appear, the certificate of sufficient cause is given of course. If the master appear, he is permitted "to show that the wages are paid, or otherwise satisfied or forfeited," or to settle the dispute on the spot, without further suit. If he does neither, the magistrate gives a certificate that there is sufficient cause whereon to found Admiralty process, and the certificate, with the libel, is filed with the clerk, who issues the process against the vessel, and the suit proceeds in the regular manner, according to the course of Admiralty.(*a*)

§ 506. The suit being thus commenced, if there be any other seamen on the same voyage, having like cause of complaint, they are not compelled to repeat the preliminary proceeding, but by petition, stating their case, they are allowed to join in the suit, which is done by filing their petition and annexing it to the libel. They are then considered as original libellants, and the suit proceeds, in their collective names, to a decree. Their rights are entirely separate and independent. They are co-libellants, but not joint libellants, and they are competent witnesses for each other. Each man's case must be separately proved—should be separately passed upon by the court, and the decree should be separate for each, especially in cases in which the amount will justify an appeal.(*b*)

§ 507. The practice in these cases is founded on the "act for the government and regulation of seamen in the merchant service." This is believed to embrace all vessels not in the national naval service. The first three sections of the act relate to ves-

---

(*a*) Betts' Prac. 60, *et seq.* Vid. the precedents in the Appendix.
(*b*) 6 Peters' 143.

sels and voyages of a particular character, but other sections of
the act embrace " any ship or vessel," " any seaman or mariner,"
and the careful use of different phraseology for different purposes,
in the different sections, shows that the language, in every case,
was intended to have its appropriate force.(*a*)   The law as administered under this act, in the Southern District of New York
will be found very fully laid down in Betts' Practice, pages 59
to 68.

By the act of 1846, chap. 60, canal boats, navigated without
masts or steam, are not subject to be libelled for wages.

§ 508. The learned Judge of that District, with a desire to
promote expedition, and to reduce expense, in 1838 established for
that District a summary practice, in all cases when the demand
is under $50, and, of course, not subject to appeal. As that
practice is local, it will not be set forth here in detail. It will
be found in the rules of that court, which are given in the Appendix, and in the full commentary on those rules in Betts'
Practice, pages 16, 78 to 82. The statutory practice of the preliminary summons and this summary practice, greatly reduced
expenses. It is, however, much to be desired that the Congress,
or the Supreme Court, would enact a lower tariff of fees, in
plenary cases, arranged with a full knowledge of the course of
Admiralty proceedings and the wants of commerce in this behalf.

(*a*) Seamen's Act of July 20, 1790.   Acts of 1846, p 61.

CHAPTER XXX.

Prize Causes.

§ 509. By the prize act of June 26, 1812, it is provided, (sec. 4,) that all captures and prizes of vessels and property, shall be forfeited, and shall accrue to the owners, officers, and crews of the vessels by whom such captures and prizes shall be made; and, on due condemnation had, shall be distributed according to any written agreement which shall be made between them; and if there be no such agreement, then, one moiety to the owners and the other moiety to the officers and crew, to be distributed between the officers and crew, as nearly as may be, according to the rules for the distribution of prize money, by the "act for the better government of the navy of the United States," passed the 23d April, 1800.(a)

By section six it is provided, that before breaking bulk of any vessel which shall be captured as aforesaid, or other disposal or conversion thereof, or of any articles which shall be found on board of the same, such captured vessel, goods, or effects shall be brought into some port of the United States, or into some port of a nation in amity with the United States, and shall be proceeded against before a competent tribunal, and after condemnation and forfeiture thereof shall belong to the owners and captors thereof, and be distributed as aforesaid; and in the case of all captured vessels, goods, and effects which shall be brought within the jurisdiction of the United States, the District Courts of the United States shall have exclusive original cognizance thereof, as in civil causes of Admiralty and maritime jurisdiction. And the said courts, or the courts, being courts of the United States, into which such cases shall be removed, and in which they shall be finally decided, shall and may decree resti-

---

tution, in whole or in part, when the capture shall shall have been made without just cause. And if made without probable cause, or otherwise unnecessarily, may order and decree damages and costs to the party injured, and for which the owners and commanders of the vessels making such captures, and also the vessels, shall be liable. Other sections provide for military salvage on recapture. By virtue of these provisions, the District Courts have full jurisdiction *in personam* and *in rem*, of the questions of prize and its incidents.(*a*)

§ 510. It is not deemed necessary to enter into the details of the practice in prize cases, and only a brief note will be made of the proceedings exhibiting some of their peculiarities.

The District Courts, in time of war, appoint, by commission under the seal of the court, standing commissioners of prize, in the principal ports, who perform their duties under their general appointment and under the sanction of their general oath of office.

Whenever a prize is brought in, it is the duty of the captors immediately to give notice, in writing, to the judge of the District, or to one of the prize commissioners, of the arrival of the property, and where it may be found; and also to deliver under oath, in writing, all documents and writings found in the prize.

§ 511. As soon as a prize is thus reported, it is the duty of a commissioner to repair on board and take note of the condition of the prize, and proceed to take the preparatory examination of witnesses. For this purpose, the captors must produce before the commissioner one or more of the persons captured with the property, and he must examine them, with the other witnesses, on the standing interrogatories adopted by the court, for the purpose of having, at the earliest opportunity, in the form of depositions, the circumstances of the property and the capture. The commissioners have no authority to use any but the standing interrogatories except by the express direction of the court.

The witnesses are examined separately, and not in the presence of each other, under oath. Each witness is required to answer to each interrogatory, and when the deposition is complete he signs it, and the commissioner adds his jurat. The depositions being all completed, the commissioner seals up the depositions and the ship's papers and documents, and addressing the package to the court, with an indorsement showing what it is, sends it to the clerk of the court.

§ 512. The captors must also, without delay, libel the property in the District Court, for condemnation as lawful prize. The libel may be filed without waiting for the preparatory examinations. If the capture be made by a national vessel, then the District Attorney of the United States, in the name of the government, libels the property in their behalf and that of the captors.

In the case of captures by privateers, the commander employs his proctor and libels in behalf of himself and the other captors ; and, in like manner, in case of captures by individuals, they libel in their own names jointly, or one or more for themselves and others. After the libel is filed, the usual process of arrest and monition issues to the marshal, who arrests the property and keeps it till after condemnation and sale, unless the parties consent to a sale or delivery on stipulation. Parties put in their claims, and the suit proceeds to a decree in the same manner as a seizure case or other suit *in rem*. The preparatory depositions are opened by order of the court, and are evidence in the case.

After a decree of condemnation, the property is sold, and the proceeds divided according to law.

(a) Betts' Prac. 72, *et seq*. Marriott's Forms, 122, 130. Stokes' Col. 284, *et seq*. 2 Bro. Civ. and Ad. 444. For the precedents in the Appendix, vid the Index.

CHAPTER XXXI.

Hearing.

§ 513. The cause being ready for hearing, is noticed for hearing according to the rules established in the district where it is to be heard. The circumstances of the different districts vary so widely, that no general rule could well be adopted for all.

The libellant, and the claimant or respondent, are both actors, and either party may notice the cause, and bring on the hearing.(*a*)

§ 514. It has already been stated, that the defendant cannot be heard in his defence, nor introduce evidence in the cause, unless he have appeared in the cause and contested the suit, either by exceptions to the libel, or by answering it. If he does neither, the court will hear and adjudge the cause *ex parte*, upon the evidence offered by the libellant. If the neglect to answer has, however, been from ignorance or other sufficient cause, the court is not precluded from receiving evidence, and may exercise its discretion for the purposes of justice.(*b*)

§ 515. At the hearing, if either party be not in attendance, his adversary may take such decree as he would be entitled to if his pleading were confessed. If any postponement be desired by either party, on sufficient reason, it is granted by the judge, the whole matter being in his discretion. He may postpone for a longer or shorter period, absolutely, or on such terms and conditions as justice may demand. The nature of maritime transactions is such, that witnesses are often transient, and their convenience, as well as the necessities of the parties, often exercise an important influence in determining the mind of the

---

(*a*) 4 Cranch, 2.   (*b*) Ware, 495.

court in matters relating to the mere conduct of the hearing. The court sometimes commences the hearing to take the testimony of transient witnesses on either, or both sides, without regard to the usual order of proceeding, and then postpones the cause for a longer or shorter time, as may be necessary to take the other testimony and complete the hearing. Sometimes the testimony is all taken, and the cause is postponed to hear, at a future day, the arguments of counsel. Sometimes postponement is ordered only on condition, that the party asking it, shall consent to take the depositions of witnesses, in writing out of court, or to admit what is expected to be proved by them.

§ 516. It is this flexibility of a Court of Admiralty—its power to adapt itself to the circumstances of the parties and their witnesses, without prejudice, and often with signal advantage to the cause of justice—that constitutes one of its great points of superiority over the courts of common law and trials by jury.

The full and proper presentment of the facts—the careful consideration and arrangement of them in argument—the due deliberation and reflection upon the facts and the law, which are the usual characteristics of proceedings in an Admiralty Court—are often impossible in tribunals of which a necessary part is a jury, drawn by hazard from the community at large, taken forcibly from their private affairs, and without the practised powers of analysis, of memory and of judgment, which alone could enable them to detect fallacies, to unravel the tangled web of deceit, and resist the persuasives of eloquence, especially when compelled to a hurried unanimity in cases where the wisest are compelled to doubt.

§ 517. An Admiralty cause is to be decided according to the allegations and proofs—*secundum allegata et probata*—and the proofs must correspond to the allegations.(a) The allegations are to be found in the pleadings. On the hearing, therefore, the first thing to which the attention of the Court is called, is the pleadings. The advocate for the libellant opens his case by a very brief and general statement of the nature of his case, and

---

(a) 1 Sum. 328.

of the defence, and reads the libel—the advocate for the defendant reads the answer, and, if there be other pleadings, each party reads his own. The more circumstantial and careful opening, which the inexperience of jurors renders necessary in trials at common law, are out of place in an Admiralty Court. The pleadings being read, the proofs are introduced in the same general order which must prevail in all lawsuits, but with less strict adherence to the artificial rules which are sometimes made to constrain the parties in jury trials. The judge always exercises his discretion as to the order of calling and re-calling witnesses, and the course of examination.

Evidence.

§ 518. *Pleadings.*—What is the legal effect of an answer as evidence has been considered a matter of doubt, and it has been said, that if the answer be not contradicted by two witnesses, or circumstances and one witness, it must be taken as true in all matters, responsive to the libel. This is the rule in Chancery but not in Admiralty. The answer to the libel has no more force as evidence than the libel itself has. They are not evidence in the common sense of the word. Being, however, the solemn statement of facts, by the parties, under the solemnity of an oath, the court is bound to examine them carefully, and it is impossible that they should not influence the mind of the court—in many cases of nicely balanced proofs, the influence of the pleadings may well turn the scale.(a)

§ 519. *Answers to Interrogatories.*—The power to interrogate the parties furnishes an effectual means of bringing the party before the court, with great advantage, in abridging the more expensive and doubtful *viva voce* proof on trial. Either party, as has been stated, may interrogate the other, in writing, as to any matters of fact, which may be necessary to support the action, or maintain the defence, and the party interrogated is bound to answer, in writing, each interrogatory, unless his answer will expose him to prosecution or punishment for a crime, or to a penalty or forfeiture of his property for a penal offence. The

---

(a) Ware, 393. Ante, § 412, 417.

answers to these special interrogatories are evidence in the cause at the hearing, for both parties.(a)

§ 520. *Depositions de bene esse.*—The provision made by the act of Congress, for taking *testimony de bene esse,* in cases in the Courts of the United States, without a *commission, dedimus potestatem, or letters rogatory,* greatly promotes the convenience of suitors. The depositions are often taken *ex parte,* and they are for that reason exposed to criticism. No presumptions are made in their favor, and they will not be received in evidence unless the provisions of the act be strictly followed.

The authority conferred upon the Magistrate is special, and confined within certain limits and conditions, and the facts calling for the exercise of it should appear upon the face of the instrument, and not be left to parol proof.(b)

§ 521. They may be taken in the following cases :

When the testimony of any person shall be necessary in any civil cause depending in any district in the United States, who lives at a greater distance from the place of trial than one hundred miles—or is bound on a voyage to sea—or is about to go out of such district—or is about to go to a greater distance than one hundred miles before the time of trial—or is ancient—or is very infirm.

§ 522. They may be taken before the following officers :

Any Justice or Judge of any of the Courts of the United States—or before any Chancellor, Justice or Judge of a Supreme or Superior Court—any Mayor or Chief Magistrate of a city—or Judge of a County Court or Court of Common Pleas of any of the United States, who is not of counsel or attorney to either of the parties, or interested in the event of the cause, or any United States Commissioner.(c)

(a) Ad. Rule 23, 31, 32. 1 Story, 91. Ware, 497, 501, 504.

(b) Jud. Act of 1789. Vid. the Section of the Act in the Appendix. 8 Cranch, 70. 2 Wheat. 287. 2 Gal. 314. 1 Wash. 144. 3 Id. 243, 529. 4 Id. 215. 7 Wheat. 356. Pet. Cir. R. 235, 291. Paine, 358, 400. 4 Day, 121. N. Car. Cases, 81. 1 Pet. 355. 5 Pet. 604. 1 Brockenb. 367. 1 Stat. at Large, 73, § 30.

(c) Ibid. Act of March, 1817, ch. 30. 3 Stat. at Large, 350. Ante, § 338.

§ 523. They must be taken in the following manner :

A notification from the Magistrate or officer, before whom the deposition is to be taken, to the adverse party, to be present at the taking of the same, and to put interrogatories, if he think fit, must first be made out and served on the adverse party or his attorney, as either may be nearest, if either is within one hundred miles of the place of taking the deposition, allowing time for their attendance after being notified, not less than at the rate of one day for every twenty miles travel.   And in causes of Admiralty and Maritime jurisdiction, or other cases of seizure, where a libel shall be filed, in which an adverse party is not named, and depositions are taken before a claim is put in, the like notification must be given to the person having the agency or possession of the property libelled at the time of the capture or seizure, if known to the libellant.(a)

§ 524. This notification must be "made out and served," it must therefore be in writing.   It should be entitled in the cause, or with reasonable certainty describe the cause.   It must be "from the Magistrate" "to the adverse party"—it must therefore be signed by the Magistrate in his official character, and addressed to the party to be notified, by name—in suits *in personam*, to the party adverse to him on whose part the deposition is to be taken—in suits *in rem*, in which personal defendants, claimants, owners or possessors of the property, are named in the libel, before a claim is put in, it must be addressed to them—after a claim is put in, it must be addressed to the claimants.   If there be no such party named in the libel, and no claim is put in, then it must be addressed to the person having the agency or possession of the property, at the time of the seizure of it in the cause, if he be known to the libellant.

Any person may be compelled to appear, and depose in the same manner, as to appear and testify in court.   This is by the usual subpœna, served in the usual manner, and if he refuse or neglect to appear, the Magistrate may, on due proof of service of the subpœna, bring him before him, by attachment.

(a) Jud. Act of 1789, § 30.   1 Stat. at Large, 73.   7 How. 693.

§ 525. At the taking of the deposition, the witness must be carefully examined and cautioned, and sworn or affirmed to testify the whole truth. The deposition should have a proper title, showing the cause, and the official description of the officer. The witness may be examined by both parties, or their counsel, if present, and if the deposition be *ex parte*, the Magistrate should endeavor, by a careful examination, to get out the whole truth. The testimony must be reduced to writing, either by the Magistrate or by the deponent, in his presence—and it must be subscribed by the witness—and the magistrate should put his official jurat to it, with the date, and retain the depositions till he deliver them, with his own hand, into the court for which they are taken, or the magistrate may add his official certificate of the reason for taking the deposition, viz., that the witness resides more than one hundred miles—or is about to go to sea, or otherwise, according to the act, and of the notice, if any, given to the adverse party, stating the time given him to appear. It is well to annex a copy of the notice. The Magistrate should state, in his notice to the adverse party, as well as in his certificate, the reason for taking the deposition, and if he omit to do so, the deficiency cannot be supplied by other proof.(a) If no notice be given, it would be well to certify the reason why it was not given; also, that the officer was not counsel, or attorney, or interested—that the deposition was reduced to writing by the witness or the officer, and signed by the witness. If these documents be on separate pieces of paper, they should be properly annexed together, and referred to with reasonable certainty. They must then be sealed up by the Magistrate, in an envelope, and directed to the Court in which the cause was pending, and remain under his seal till opened in Court.(b)

They should be endorsed with the title of the cause, and marked "Depositions," and they may be forwarded by mail or by private hand.

As soon as they are received by the clerk, he marks their receipt, and presents them to the Judge in Court, who opens them,

(a) 7 How. 693. 4 Wash. 214. 4 Day, 121. N. Carolina Cas. 81.
(b) 1 Pet. 351. 5 Pet. 604. 8 Cranch, 70. 3 Cond. 35.

and the clerk enters the fact in the minutes of the Court, and files the depositions, and notifies the proctor of the party on whose behalf they are taken.(*a*)

§ 526. By a general rule of the District Court of the Southern District of New York, notice must be given to the Proctor of the opposite party, of the filing of the depositions, and all objections to the form or manner in which they were taken or returned, are deemed waived, unless such objections are specified in writing, in four days, unless further time be granted by the Judge. Exceptions taken thus early will sometimes enable the party to remove them, or retake the deposition before the trial.(*b*)

§ 527. When witnesses are examined on the hearing of a cause in the District Court, in a case in which an appeal will lie, the respective parties may, on satisfying the Court that they may not be able to produce their witnesses, on the hearing of the appeal before the Circuit, move to have their testimony taken down in writing, and it shall be done so by the Clerk of the Court. The testimony so taken down by the clerk, is taken also *de bene esse*, and is to be used on the hearing of the appeal only in case the witnesses are then dead, or gone more than one hundred miles from the place where the Court is sitting, or that by reason of age, sickness, bodily infirmity, or imprisonment, they are not able to travel and appear at court.

§ 528. The depositions themselves, sworn to and certified in form according to the act, will be *prima facie* evidence of the official character of the Magistrate, and of the truth of his certificate, and the regularity of the proceedings, to take them so far as they are certified to, but the opposite party will be always at liberty, before the depositions are read in evidence, to disprove any or all the facts necessary to establish their validity—and no necessary fact will be presumed, of which the certificates and depositions are silent.(*c*)

(*a*) Vid. the Forms in the Appendix.

(*b*) Betts' Prac. 86.

(*c*) Paine, 358. 1 Pet. 351. 5 Pet. 604, 617. 2 Wheat. 287. 1 Gal. 488. 3 Wash. 408. 1 Brock. 367. 2 Wood. & M. 136

If the party against whom the depositions are taken, is present at the examination, it is his duty to make all the objections to the examination which are known to him at the time.(*a*)

§ 529. It has been held, in the first Circuit, that depositions taken during the session of the Court, are inadmissible, even if regularly taken, it being the duty of the party and his counsel to be present in Court—and that the taking of the depositions without notice, was good cause for a continuance to enable the other party to cross-examine the witness or repel his testimony, and this is said to be the practice in most of the Circuits. Even at a greater distance than one hundred miles, if the adverse party have known counsel residing where the deposition is taken, he should be notified.(*b*)

§ 530. To authorize the party to read a deposition taken *de bene esse*, under the Act of Congress, he must show that the witness is dead, or gone out of the United States, or out of the district, to a greater distance than one hundred miles from the place where the Court is sitting, or on a voyage to sea, or that by reason of age, sickness, or bodily infirmity, he is unable to travel and appear in court.(*c*)

§ 531. *Commission or Dedimus potestatem.*—By the proviso to the 30th section of the Judiciary Act, every Court of the United States is clothed with the power to grant a *dedimus potestatem*, or commission to take depositions, according to the common usage, when it may be necessary to prevent a failure or delay of justice. This remedial proviso, with its beneficial purpose fully and distinctly set forth, cannot be construed otherwise than to give the courts the fullest power, in every manner usual in courts of justice, to depute their own power to take testimony in a cause where the ends of justice will be promoted by doing so. A commission to take testimony in an enemy's country, in prize cases, is not issued.(*d*)

(*a*) Paine, 400.   (*b*) 2 Wood. & M. 137, 138.   2 Gal. 314.
(*c*) 7 How. 693. Jud. Act of 1789, § 30.   4 Wheat. 508.
(*d*) Jud. Act of 1789, § 30.   2 Gall. 93.   Stat. at Large, 197, note.   1 Pet. C. C. R. 235. Hall's Ad. 37.

The circumstances under which, and the mode in which the application may be made to the Court, may be regulated by standing rules of the Court, or left to the discretion of the Court in each particular case. In the Southern District of New York, it is regulated by standing rules (*a*)

§ 532. Commissioners under a commission to take testimony, act under a special authority derived from the Court, which must be strictly pursued—and cannot be exercised by any one but the Commissioner named in the writ.

In executing a commission, all the interrogatories, direct and cross, must be put to the witnesses, and substantially answered. Within the United States and its territories, witnesses may be compelled to appear before the Commissioners, and produce books and papers, and testify pursuant to the act of January 24, 1827, which will be found in the appendix. The depositions are not in any sense *de bene esse,* and none of the peculiar requisites in case of depositions *de bene esse,* are material.(*b*)

§ 533. *Letters Rogatory—or Commissions sub mutuæ vicissitudinis.*—By the law of nations, the Courts of Justice of different countries are bound to be mutually aiding and assisting to each other for the furtherance of justice. Hence, when the testimony of witnesses who reside abroad, is necessary in a cause, the Court or Tribunal where the action is pending, may send to the Court or Tribunal within whose jurisdiction the witnesses reside, a writ patent or close, as they may think proper. They are usually called *letters rogatory,* but are sometimes denominated *sub mutuæ vicissitudinis,* from a clause which they generally contain. By that instrument, the Court abroad is informed that a certain claim is pending in which the testimony of certain witnesses who reside within its juris-

---

(*a*) Vid. the Rules in the Appendix.

(*b*) 4 Stat. at Large, 197. 2 Dal. 401. 5 Cranch, 335. 1 Gal. 166. 2 Id. 93. 1 Wash. 34. Ibid. 144. 2 Id. 7. Ibid. 34. Ibid. 223. Ibid. 356. Ibid. 563. 2 Wheat. 287. Ibid. 371. 4 Id. 508. 2 Pet. 613. 3 Ibid. 1. 3 Wash. 109. Ibid. 404. 4 Id. 715. Ibid. 186. Id. 323. Pet. Cir. R. 8. Ibid. 235. Ibid. 301.

diction is required, and it is requested to take their depositions, or cause them to be taken, in due course and form of law, for the furtherance of justice and *sub mutuæ vicissitudinis obten- tu :* that is, with an offer on the part of the Court, making the request to do the like for the other in a similar case. If these letters rogatory are received by an inferior Judge, he proceeds to call the witnesses before him, by the process commonly employ- ed within his jurisdiction, examine them on interrogatories or takes their depositions, as the case may be, and the proceedings being filed in the Registry of this Court, authentic copies thereof, duly certified, are transmitted to the Court *a quo*, and are legal evidence in the cause. If the letters are directed to a Court of superior jurisdiction, they appoint an examiner or commissioners for the purpose of executing them and the pro- ceedings are filed and returned in the same manner.(*a*)

§ 534. *Parties.*—In cases of salvage, mariners' wages, and prize, it usually happens that the parties are the only persons by whom the most important facts can be proved, as no others are present. They are, therefore, from the necessity of the case, as well as upon principles of public policy as private jus- tice, admitted as witnesses in their own favor, for each other to prove such facts, by special exception to the general rule of evi- dence.(*a*)

When parties are examined as witnesses, they are not to be examined as to any matters except those to which their compe- tency is limited.

§ 535. It has often been made a question whether a master of a vessel is a competent witness in suits by his seamen for their wa- ges, and conflicting decisions are found in the books,—but the principle to be drawn from them all is, that his competency de- pends upon the same principles as that of any other witness. He is not an exception to the general rule. And in Admiralty, the rules of the common law as to the competency and incompe-

(*a*) Hall's Ad. 37. 1 Pet. C. C. 235. Conk. Ad. 640.
(*b*) Ware, 37.

tency of witnesses, are adopted in instance causes, with the exceptions which have been noticed.(*a*)

§ 536. When the proofs of a party are imperfect, yet go far to establish his case, he may offer his own oath in corroboration of the other proofs. This practice is derived from the necessity of having more than one witness, by the civil law. Full proof of a fact could not be made by one witness, and in many cases, manifest injustice would be the necessary result of the absence of any second witness. In such cases the party was allowed to complete his proof by his own oath. This is what is called the suppletory oath. This oath may be prayed, and is granted in all maritime causes.(*b*)

By the suppletory oath the party himself testifies, " that, of his own certain knowledge, the facts stated in his allegation, (to which he offers his oath,) are true."

§ 537. In certain other cases, a party may be a witness in his own cause. The search for a paper, and its loss, may be proved by the party himself, to lay the foundation for secondary evidence. In suits for personal property—for the contents of a trunk or package, known to no one but the party himself, he may, from necessity, be a witness to prove the contents—the existence and situation of the trunk or package being proved by other testimony.(*b*)

§ 538. There is also the *oath decisory*, which either party may tender to the other, that is, offering further decision of the cause upon the oath of his adversary. The adversary is bound either to accept the offer, or make a similar proposition in return. This is a mode of proof known to the civil law, and is said to have been practised in Admiralty in the Massachusetts District. It is not in general use, but under the modifications which the law of evidence is now undergoing, it would not be surprising if something like it should come into use in all courts.(*c*)

(*a*) Binn. 328. 3 Wheat. 435. Conk. Ad. 643. Rosc. Ev. 87.
(*b*) Hall's Ad. 93. Ware. 505. Dunlap, 284-8. Greenleaf's Ev. 294.
(*c*) Greenleaf's Ev. 204 to 408.

§ 539. The testimony being concluded, the cause is argued at that time or a future day. The advocate of the libellant usually states the principal points of fact and of law upon which he relies, with his legal authorities. The advocate of the defendant then argues the case to the court, and the advocate of the libellant closes the discussion, and the cause is fully submitted to the judge for his decision, which may be given on the spot in cases in which there is not a possibility of doubt, or, as is usual, it is pronounced after re-examination and deliberation.(a)

It is usual for the advocates to submit to the court written points of fact and of law, with reference to the testimony, and the authorities, and also to furnish the court, at the argument, a draft of such decree as is deemed proper.

§ 540. Allusion has already been made to the power of the court to vary, interrupt, or postpone proceedings when the cause of justice may require it. So, after the hearing of the cause is concluded, on proper cause shown, the court will rescind the conclusion of the cause for the purpose of hearing further proofs. This is sometimes done on the suggestion or request of the judge himself, if, in his examination of the case, he finds that by the surprise of the party, or by his own exclusion of testimony, the case is so imperfectly before him that injustice may be done; and it is sometimes ordered on the application of the party when there is newly discovered evidence, or when it is necessary to enable him to supply omissions.(b)

(a) Betts' Prac. 92, 97.

(b) 2 Hag. Ec. Sup. 149. 1 Dod. 10. 1 Phil. 173. 2 Dod. 70. 3 Curteis, 786. 1 Hag. Ec. 88. 2 Act. 57, 58, a. 1 C. Rob. 168. 2 Dod. 78.

CHAPTER XXXII.

Decree.

§ 541. The cause being heard and submitted to the Court for decision, the Court pronounces its decree according to the facts and the law, in favor of the libellants, or the defendants, or some of the libellants and some of the defendants, and against the others with or without costs, distributively, for or against any or all the parties, as justice may require. The flexibility of the Admiralty proceedings in this respect greatly conduces to the cause of justice.

§ 542. The decree made upon the hearing may be interlocutory or final. It is final when it disposes of the whole controversy, and leaves nothing further for the court to do in the cause, as when the libel is dismissed with costs, or without costs,—or there is a decree for a sum certain, with or without costs.

But when by the decree something still remains to be done by the court before all the rights of the parties in the premises, are fixed, and the recovering party has an order for execution—then the decree is interlocutory, however much it may dispose of the merits of the cause.

§ 543. When the decree is against the libellant, whether the suit be *in personam* or *in rem*, the usual form of the decree is that the libel be dismissed, with costs or without costs.

If the decree be in favor of the libellant, in a suit for the recovery of money, and the amount be not ascertained, it is usual to decide the principles on which the amount is to be settled, and to refer it to a Commissioner to ascertain and report the amount to the Court in the same manner as on a default. In the Southern District of New York, long experience has fully established the practice of confining the testimony on the hearing in such cases to the right of the party to recover, and of leaving the details of the amount to be proved, and the sum or balance to be ascertained before a Commissioner, and reported by him to the Court.(*a*)

This not only renders it unnecessary that the time of the Court should be occupied with the small details of accounts and computations, and the multifarious testimony necessary to ascertain them, but it greatly promotes the interest of parties, by enabling them to bring their proofs before the commissioner, from time to time, as convenience may dictate.

§ 544. A copy of the order of reference should be served on the Commissioner and on the opposite party—and notice should be given of the time of proceeding with the reference. The Commissioner appoints the time. On the hearing, the testimony taken before Court, and any other testimony may be given. It is introduced as on a trial, and is taken down by the Commissioner. Commissioners have the usual powers of Masters in Chancery, and may administer oaths, and examine parties and witnesses in proper cases. They have also the power to summon witnesses, and compel their appearance to testify, and may adjourn the hearing from time to time, to give the parties time to put in their proofs.(*b*)

The hearing being closed, the Commissioner reports to the Court the result and conclusion to which he has arrived.

§ 545. The Report is in the following form:

DISTRICT COURT OF THE UNITED STATES, FOR THE SOUTHERN DISTRICT OF NEW YORK.

William Robinson, *vs.* The Barque *Richard Alsop*, her tackle, &c.	Commissioner's Report.

In pursuance of a decretal order made in this cause, on the first day of September, in the year of our Lord one thousand eight hundred and forty-nine, by which, among other

---

(*a*) Ante, § 449. Vid. the Forms of the Decrees in the Appendix.
(*b*) Ad. Rule 44.

things, it was referred to one of the Commissioners of this Court, to ascertain and compute the amount due to the libellant, for materials and repairs, and to report thereon to this Court with all convenient speed.

I, John W. Nelson, United States Commissioner, do report, that I have been attended by the Proctor for the libellant and the Proctor for the claimant, and have taken and examined the testimony offered by the Proctors respectively, and do find that there is due to the libellant, for the materials and repairs mentioned in the libel, the sum of one hundred and eighty-eight dollars and ten cents.

Dated the 20th day of September, A. D. 1849.

All which respectfully submitted,

JOHN W. NELSON,
U. S. Commissioner.

A. B., *Proctor for Libellant.*

On the request of either party, the Commissioner must report the testimony taken before him, fully, to the Court, and he may always report specially.

§ 546. If either party be dissatisfied with the conclusion to which the Commissioner has arrived, either on the principles of his report, or in the allowances which he has made, he may except to the report. If the report be special, and error appear on the face of the report, a written exception is not necessary.(a)

The following is the form of exceptions to the report:

A. B. ⎫
vs. ⎬
C. D. ⎭

Exceptions on the part of the libellant, to the Report of John W. Nelson, Esquire, a United States Commissioner in this cause, dated September, 1849:

First Exception. That the said Commissioner did not allow to the defendant fifty dollars and twenty-four cents, paid by him to the libellant.

Second Exception. That the said Commissioner allowed to

(a) Vid. other Forms of Reports in the Appendix.

the libellant, seventy-seven dollars, for said repairs, beyond the contract price for the same.

Third Exception. That the said Commissioner has reported a balance of $188 70, due to the libellant, instead of a balance of $60, as shown by the proofs.

A. B., *Proctor for Libellant.*

When there are no exceptions, the report being filed, is confirmed on motion, without notice. When there are exceptions, the party excepting files and serves his exceptions, and the cause is again put upon the docket or calendar for hearing. The following is the form of a decree thereon :

A. B.
vs.
C. D.

This cause coming on to be heard on the exceptions to the report of John W. Nelson, Esquire, the Commissioner to whom the same was referred, bearing date September 20th, 1849, and the advocates for the respective parties being heard, on motion of C. D., Proctor for the libellant, it is ordered, that said exceptions be overruled, and that the said report be in all things confirmed with costs—and that the libellant recover against the defendant the sum of $188 10, with costs, and have execution therefor.(*a*)

§ 547. If the suit be *in personam*, and the decree be for the libellant for a sum certain, the usual form of the decree is, that the libellant recover against the defendant and his stipulators the amount, with costs to be taxed, and that he have execution therefor. In cases *in rem*, it is usual to give a decree the same form as *in personam*, and also if the property be still in custody, to decree a condemnation and sale of the property, and that the proceeds be brought into court. If the property have been delivered on stipulation, then that the stipulators pay into court the amount of their stipulation, within a certain time after notice of the decree, or that a summary judgment be entered against them on their stipulation, and that execution issue thereon.

_____

(*a*) Vid other Forms of Exceptions and Decrees in the Appendix.

In a suit *in rem,* it is not usual to render a decree *in personam,* but if the case proved shows a clear right to recover *in personam,* the libellant may be permitted, after a decree *in rem,* to introduce the proper allegations *in personam,* and proceed upon them to a further decree against the person.(*a*)

§ 548. After the decree is made, it sometimes appears that, by accident, oversight, mistake, or misapprehension, the decree is erroneous. In such cases, the Court of Admiralty possesses the power of correcting or varying the decree. Such a variation, however, should be confined to the alteration of an error arising from the defect of knowledge or information upon a particular point in the case, and the error must be brought to the attention of the court with the utmost possible diligence.(*b*)

§ 549. *Costs.*-The costs in Admiralty are entirely under the control of the court, and they are, therefore, often made the means of amercing either of the parties for misconduct, and are a salutary check upon mischievous litigation. They are sometimes, from equitable considerations, denied to the party who recovers his demand, and they are sometimes given to a libellant who fails to recover any, when he was misled to commence the suit by the act of the other party. In prize cases and salvage cases, the property is sometimes acquitted on payment of costs by the claimant. In the Massachusetts District, in a hard case, the court decreed for a libellant for his whole demand, with costs, and then allowed a set-off of a demand against debt and costs, so that although the set-off was more than the debt, still the libellant had a large portion of the costs.(*c*)

It is evident that no system of rules can be laid down in a matter so purely in the discretion of the court. The general rule is, that costs follow the decree—and circumstances of equity, of hardship, of oppression, or of negligence, induce the court to depart from that rule in a great variety of cases.

(*a*) Betts' Prac. 99.   Boyd's Proc. 28.   Conk. Prac. 774, 775.

(*b*) Betts' Prac. 100.   2 Chit. Gen. Prac. 538.   1 W. Rob. 21.

(*c*) Ware 395.   Dunlap, 87.   Dunlap, 102.   Edw. 70.   2 W. Rob. 306.   2 Hag. 90.

Under ordinary circumstances, a demand of payment of a debt before suit brought, is so obviously required by fair dealing, that Courts of Admiralty, in the exercise of their practical equity powers, sometimes insist upon proof of such demand, before a decree for costs will be given.(a)

An unconscionable demand, or a demand pursued in a vexatious or unconscionable manner, will not usually carry costs. When a libellant has put forward a principal demand, which he makes no real attempt to enforce, or which he must know to be unfounded, and recovers only a comparatively trifling amount, which would not have been resisted, it is not usual to allow him costs. Costs are never decreed against the Government.(b)

§ 550. *Fees.*—There is no legal tariff of fees in Admiralty, and the Supreme Court could not render a greater service to the Admiralty Courts than to establish a moderate tariff of fees in all cases, making the practice in this respect uniform through out the United States. At present, there is a great diversity, springing, in some degree, from the fact, that where there is no fixed rate, there will always be a strong tendency to assimilate the rates to those in the State Courts of Common Law and Equity, although there cannot be found a statute in which the practice of the Admiralty Courts is named, where it is not evident that uniformity and not diversity is the purpose of the law, and where it is not equally evident that the Congress con-sidered the Admiralty practice as peculiar, and in no manner to be classed with, or likened to, the practice of the Courts of Common Law and Equity. The fees of Proctors and Advocates are now subject to the regulation of the courts, under their general power, to regulate the practice. The rates established in the Southern District of New York will be found in the appendix. They have always been less than the fees in common law and equity. They are, in a measure, made up from the fee bill of the Court of Admiralty of the State of New York, before the Constitution, as established by a statute of that

(a) Dunlap, 91, 92. 1 Chit. Plead 362.
(b) 1 W. Rob 328. 1 Notes of Cases, 305. 10 Jur. 506. 4 Notes of Cases, 571.

State, and, so far as that State was concerned, adopted by Congress in the first Process Act of September 29, 1789. The statute will be found in the Appendix, where it is re-printed as fit to furnish, in some manner, a guide to the judgment of the courts, in establishing a tariff of fees for the United States, in Admiralty causes.(*a*)

The fees of the Clerk and the Marshal are regulated by the Acts of Congress, and, in some cases by the discretion of the Court. Vid. the Process Act of September 29, 1789, continued in force till the Process Act of May 8, 1792. Also, the Admiralty Fee Bill, in the Act of March 1, 1793—the Act of 28th February, 1799—and the Civil Appropriation Act, of 3d March, 1841, (the proviso to the clause making judicial appropriations.)(*b*)

§ 551. Whenever there are several actions or processes against persons who might legally be joined in one action—and whenever there are several libels against any vessel or cargo which might legally be joined in one libel, only the costs of one suit can be allowed, except on special cause shown, for the multiplicity of suits. And in causes of like nature, or relative to the same question, the court has full power to make any orders with a view to avoiding unnecessary costs, and especially to consolidate causes. The order to consolidate will be made only on application to the court, on notice to the other party.

If Proctors, Advocates, or other persons managing or conducting causes, appear to have multiplied the proceedings, so as to increase costs unreasonably and vexatiously, they may be required, by order of the court, to satisfy any excess of costs so incurred ; and the court will protect the Proctor from a collusive settlement to the prejudice of his right to his costs.(*c*)

(*a*) Vid the Appendix.

(*b*) " The expenses in Courts of Admiralty, are frequently a subject of complaint by those who are not sufficiently acquainted with the proceedings there, and the manner in which they arise. Those sums, which seem most to startle by their large amount, relate solely to the custody of the property, a duty which does not devolve upon any other species of Courts of Justice." Stewart's R. 588. They are not higher than what are usually and voluntarily paid and received by merchants for like services. Ibid. 489.

(*c*) Act of July 29, 1813. Betts' Prac. 124. Ibid. 10. Ware, 476.

§ 552. The court discourages hard and sharp practice, either in the proceedings in court, or in the negotiations between the parties—hurrying up a suit without a demand of payment or reasonable indulgence—refusing to listen to officers of adjustment—making technical objections to a tender sufficient in amount—if brought before the court, are likely to be remembered in the decree upon the question of costs, and, in like manner, the court encourages efforts to settle, and a tender or offer to pay a reasonable sum, and will, under all circumstances, hold an offer to pay as equivalent to a technical tender, and a declaration in advance, that less than a certain sum will not be accepted, will be considered as waiving a formal tender.(a)

It is the common practice of Courts of Admiralty, to give counsel fees either in the shape of damages, or as a part of the costs.(b)

§ 553. It is often the case, from the peculiar form of Admiralty proceedings, that justice requires that costs should be apportioned—as, when the court discriminates between parties in its decree, and some appeal and others do not—and when the property is in custody in several causes, and the fees of the Marshal for the custody and keeping of the property, have accrued for a common benefit to unconnected parties—in such and similar cases, the court will sometimes apportion the costs.(c)

Costs are taxed by the clerk, on notice to the opposite party—subject to an appeal to the Judge—and when the costs are to be paid out of a fund in court, the taxed bill should be filed.

§ 554. The final decree of the court being pronounced, the Clerk enrols the decree. The enrolment consists of an engrossment of the pleadings, processes, stipulations, orders and evidence in the cause, arranged in chronological order, from the libel to the final decree, constituting a complete written history of the cause. The depositions, and exhibits, and documents, if there be any, are inserted at length in the enrolment, as a part of the evidence, and the testimony of the witnesses who are examined in court, is copied from the notes of testimony taken by the Judge.

(a) Dunlap, 104–5. Conk. Prac. 711.   (b) 9 Wheat. 362. 3 Pet. R. 307.
(c) 2 Law Rep. (new series,) 24.

CHAPTER XXXIII.

Execution.

§ 555. In all cases, the libellant may have an attachment to compel the defendant to perform the decree. This is obtained by order of the court on motion, and upon the attachment, the defendant may be arrested and committed to prison, until he performs the decree, or is otherwise discharged by law or by the order of the court. The court would therefore require cause to be shown why an attachment should issue in the first instance. In cases where the decree is for the mere payment of money, although the rule of the Supreme Court provides that the party may, at his election, have the attachment in such cases, that election is, of course, subject to the discretionary control of the court, who would not allow its process to be made a mere instrument of oppression. If it should appear that the party have goods and chattels, from which the money can be made by a levy, then the proper process is a writ of execution, combining the nature of a *capias*, and *fieri facias*, commanding the Marshal or his deputy to levy the amount, of the goods and chattels of the defendant, and for want thereof, to arrest his body to answer the exigency of the execution.(*a*)

§ 556. The following is the form of an execution :

THE PRESIDENT OF THE UNITED STATES OF AMERICA,

To the Marshal of the Southern District of New York,
    Greeting :
Whereas, a libel was filed in the District Court of the United
      States, for the Southern District of New York, on the
[L. s.] twenty-eighth day of October, one thousand eight hun-
      dred and forty-three, by Elisha Burgess, libellant, against

---

(*a*) Ad. Rule 21.

Ramon De Zaldo, and such proceedings were thereupon had; that by the judgment and decree of the said court in said cause, on the twenty-second day July last past, the said Ramon De Zaldo was required to pay to the said libellant the sum of five hundred and two dollars and three cents, besides his costs in this suit, to be taxed, and execution was ordered therefor : And whereas, the said costs have been duly taxed at the sum of one hundred and seventy-nine dollars and fifty-nine cents, as by the records and files of said Court fully appear.

Now, therefore, we command you, that of the goods and chattels of the said Ramon De Zaldo, in your district, and, in default of goods and chattels of him, then of the lands and tenements in your district, of which he is seized, on the day you shall receive this writ, or at any time afterwards, you cause to be made, the sum of six hundred and eighty-one dollars and sixty-two cents ; and further, that you have those moneys in said court, at the City Hall, in the City of New York, on the first day of June next, to render to the said libellant in satisfaction of said decree ; And in default of goods, chattels, or lands, then that you arrest the said defendant, if he be found in your district, and keep him under safe and secure arrest until he shall pay the said sum of six hundred and eighty-one dollars and sixty-two cents, with interest, from the said twenty-second day of July last past, and your fees, or until he be otherwise discharged by law or by the order of the court ; and that you duly return to the said court what you shall do in the premises, together with this writ.

Witness the Honorable Samuel R. Betts, Judge of the said court, in the Southern District of New York, this twenty-seventh day of May, one thousand eight hundred and forty-four, and of our independence the sixty-eighth.

JAMES W. METCALF, Clerk.

BURR & BENEDICT, <i>Proctors.</i>

Executions in favor of the United States may run throughout the United States, and, in cases of individuals, they may run throughout the State, even where there are two districts in the State; but they must, in all cases, be issued from, and returnable to, the court, where the decree is obtained.(a)

§ 557. In cases *in rem*, where there has been a decree of condemnation and sale, a *venditioni exponas* is the proper execution to issue, if the property be still in custody. If the property have been delivered on stipulation, an order is made that the stipulators perform the condition of their stipulation, and in default thereof, that a summary judgment be entered against them on their stipulation, on which an execution issues against them *in personam.*

§ 558. If the property is still in custody, and a *venditioni exponas* issues, the marshal, on proper public notice, sells the property and is bound to pay the proceeds forthwith into the hands of the clerk, to be paid into the registry of the court, to be disposed of by the court according to law.(b)

The following is the form of the writ:

"*Southern District of New York, ss.*

"The President of the United States of America, to the Marshal of the Southern District of New York, Greeeting: Whereas, a libel of information was filed in the District Court of the United States for the Southern District of New York, on the first day of March, in the year of our [L. s.] Lord one thousand eight hundred and forty-nine, against the ship Rover, her tackle, apparel, and furniture; praying that the same may be condemned and sold, for the causes alleged in the said libel of information. And whereas the said ship has been attached by the process issued out of the said District Court, in pursuance of the said libel of information, and is now in custody by virtue thereof: and such proceedings have been thereupon had, that by the final sentence and decree of the said court, in this cause made and pronounced, on the first Tuesday of June one thousand eight hundred and forty-nine, the said ship, her tackle, apparel, and furniture are condemned and ordered to be sold by you, the said Marshal,

---

(a) Stat. at Large, 184.   (b) Rule 41.

after giving six days notice of such sale, according to law.—
Therefore, you, the said Marshal, are hereby commanded to
cause the said ship, her tackle, &c., so condemned and ordered
to be sold, to be sold in manner and form, upon the notice and
at the time and place by law required. And that you have the
moneys arising from such sale, in said Court, at the city hall in
the city of New York, on the first Tuesday of July, one thousand
eight hundred and forty-nine, and that you then pay the same
to the clerk of the court, and have you also then and there this
writ.

"Witness, the Honorable Samuel R. Betts, Judge of the said
Court, at the city of New York, in the Southern District of New
York, this twenty-fourth day of June, in the year of our Lord
one thousand eight hundred and forty-nine, and of our independence the seventy-third.

"JAS. W. METCALF, Clerk.

"C. L. BENEDICT, <i>Proctor.</i>"

On which the marshal returns as follows:

"In obedience to the above precept, I have sold the said ship
Rover, her tackle, apparel, and furniture, and the proceeds of
such sale, amounting to thirteen thousand one hundred dollars, I have paid to the Clerk of this Court as I am above commanded.

"Dated this 15th day of July, 1849.

"HENRY F. TALLMADGE, U. S. Marshal."

§ 559. It is a great irregularity for the marshal to distribute
the money, or any part thereof, to the parties, even according to
the decree. His function, under a *venditioni exponas*, is solely
to sell the property for cash, and bring the proceeds of the sale
into court, deducting nothing but the expenses of the sale. The
flexibility of Admiralty process, of which mention has been
often made, renders it highly improper for any of the officers of
the court to meddle with that which may, in the end, be materially modified by the court.(a)

(a) 6 Wheat 194. Ante. § 398. Ware, 354, 358.

It often happens that there are liens upon the property sold,
accruing while the property is in custody of the law—such as
wharfage, storage, labor, &c.　These the marshal has no right
to pay without the order of the court; much less would he
have the right to discharge previously existing liens, of any description.(a

§ 560.　All moneys paid into the hands of the clerk, to be deposited in the registry of the court, must be immediately deposited, in the name of the court, in some bank designated by the
court as the depository of the registry, and that account must
always be kept by the bank, subject to the condition that no
money shall be drawn out, except by a check signed by a judge
of the court, and countersigned by the clerk, stating on whose
account and for whose use it is drawn, and in what suit, and
out of what fund, in particular, it is paid.(b)

It is the duty of the clerk to keep a regular book containing
a memorandum and copy of all the checks so drawn, and the
dates thereof, and it is his duty at every term to report to the
court in detail the moneys in the registry.　After the proceeds
of a sale are in the registry, there not unfrequently arise grave
questions in the matter of distributing the funds; for, in Admiralty, the principles of distribution vary according to circumstances.　They are sometimes distributed according to the order
in which the suits were commenced, and sometimes in the order
in which the liens were created, and sometimes in the reverse
of that order, and sometimes to all alike, rateably.　The order of
distribution, or marshalling the proceeds, is settled by the court
according to the legal priority, although the court sometimes
refers it to the clerk to report the claims and their order of pre-
ferences.　The clerk then gives the parties a hearing and makes
up his report in writing, to which any party may take exceptions, in the same manner, as to other such reports, and the
matter is thus brought before the court for argument, and final
and deliberate adjustment.(c)

(a) Ware, 354, 359.　　　　　　　(b) Ad. Rule 42.
(c) 4 Cranch, 328　1 Wend. R. 39.　Boyd's Proc. 45.

§ 561. *Proceeds in the Registry.*—Any person having an interest in any proceeds in the registry of the court may, by petition and summary proceedings, intervene for his interest for a delivery of them to him, notwithstanding the decree; and upon due notice to the opposite party, if any, the court will proceed summarily to hear and decide thereon, according to law and justice. If the party fail in his claim, or desert it, the court may award costs against him (*a*)

§ 562. *Remnants and Surplus.*—It is often the case in proceedings *in rem*, that after a condemnation and sale, and payment of the libellant, there remains in court an unappropriated balance of the proceeds; this is sometimes called remnants and surplus. The party entitled to the whole or any portion of the residue can obtain it only by petition or motion to the court.

The proceeds of property which was affected by a lien are still affected by it, in whosesoever hands they may be. The regular sale of property, under a decree of the court, gives a good title against all the world, and hence the proceeds are often subject to demands which were not embraced in the suit; and the court, on motion or petition, will adjudicate upon the rights of parties claiming an interest in the remnants and surplus.(*b*)

The party may also proceed against remnants by libel and monition in a new suit, if he have a lien upon them.

The notion prevailed, for a while, that a party might enforce, against proceeds or remnants and surplus in the registry, a demand which he could not enforce against the property by an original suit. It is now, however, well settled that a party will not be allowed to resort to the proceeds or remnants of the property to enforce a demand which was not a lien upon the property, and enforceable in the Admiralty.(*c*)

(*a*) Ware, 359. Gilp. 189.   (*b*) Gilp. 189, 549.
(*c*) 3 Hag Ad. 129. 1 Ves. sen. 154. Ed. Ad. Jur. 99 to 108.

CHAPTER XXXIV.

Petitions—Motions—Orders—Rules—Notices.

§ 563. There are proceedings of an independent character connected with the powers of a Court of Admiralty, which are not properly actions or suits. These are originally commenced by petition, and carried to their final determination by the simple orders of the court, without any formal suit or process.(*a*)

Such are proceedings for a survey, on the application of seamen alleging unseaworthiness—or, on the application of a master to authorize a sale by him, as master, or other proceedings, where a final decree or adjudication, *inter partes*, is not sought for, but where the aid of the court is sought, to authenticate, or give solemnity and impartiality to proceedings authorized by statute and by the general Admiralty law. And whenever a party desires the order of the court, regulating, correcting, modifying, or arresting the proceedings in the cause —or authorizing any incidental, ancillary, or provisional proceeding, he may apply to the court by petition or motion.(*b*)

§ 564. If a petition be resorted to, the petitioner must state briefly and clearly the facts on which the demand for the relief are founded, either by a full statement, or by reference to the pleadings, depositions, or other documents, and must close with a prayer for the relief desired, so framed as to inform the court and the opposite party, if there be one, of the relief demanded in the premises. The petition must be sworn to by the petitioner. A copy must be served on the Proctor of the opposite party, with such notice of the time of presenting the same, as is required by the rules of the court.

(*a*) Dunlap's Prac. 129. Betts' Prac. 117, 119.
(*b*) Seaman's Act, § 3. Ante, § 299. Betts' Prac. 117. Dunlap's Prac. 129.

§ 565. [In case a motion is resorted to, the facts must be brought before the court in affidavits, or by proper reference to the pleadings, depositions, or other documents.

Copies of the affidavits must be served, with a notice containing, like the prayer of the petition, an intelligible statement of the relief or order which the party desires.

The other party produces, at the hearing, without service of copies or notice, such proofs by affidavits or other documents, as may best answer his purpose.

On these two sets of papers, the court usually disposes of the matter, unless in the exercise of a sound discretion, time and liberty are given, by the court, to the moving party, to introduce rebutting 'or explanatory proofs. This is rarely done except in cases of urgent equity, of hardship or of surprise.

Wherever circumstances authorize or require an *ex parte* motion or petition, as is sometimes the case, the court always requires not only full proofs to justify the order asked for, but also proof of diligence in endeavoring to give notice to the other party, if it be a matter of which he is entitled to notice.

§ 566. In the English Admiralty, the court, in most cases, gives its directory orders, the form of a writ, under seal of the court. They are sometimes called commissions, and sometimes warrants—thus, there are commissions to take bail—to appraise, to sell, &c.—which are moved for by the party, ordered by the court, and issued by the clerk. In the American Admiralty Courts, with more simplicity and directness, the order of the court, made on motion or petition, takes the place of the commission or warrant—a copy certified by the clerk being sufficient evidence of the direction of the court.(*a*)

There is, however, no legal objection to the more cumbrous and expensive forms of the English practice.

§ 567. There are no common motions, orders and rules, in Admiralty. The rules of court may sometimes authorize orders, of course, but they are always to be entered by the clerk,

---

(*a*) Betts' Prac. 43, 44. Dunlap, 177.

as made in court, either as of the stated term of the court, or as of a special court of that day. There are many chamber orders, mere mandates of the Judge—staying proceedings for a provisional purpose—extending or enlarging time—directing the issue of process—fixing the amount of bail, &c. These are made *ex parte* by the Judge, on affidavit showing the necessity— they are not entered in the minutes of the court, but are served on the opposite party, by delivering him a copy. If he be of opinion that the order has been granted improvidently, or on mistaken suggestion, he may apply for a hearing upon it, on an *ex parte* order to show cause why it should not be vacated.(*a*)

§ 568. Each court prescribes what notice shall be given of the various steps in a cause to be brought before it. The different systems of common law and equity practice, in the courts of the States, which prevail in the Courts of the United States, in common law and equity causes, have caused, in some proceedings, diversity, where it ought not to exist. In the New York districts, no causes are put upon the docket or calendar, at any term of the court, except such as the parties shall notify the clerk to put upon the docket, and shall also notify the opposite party that they are to be so put on. In other districts, the clerk, from his own registers, entries, and files, makes up a docket or list of all the causes at issue, and no notices are given, by or to any one, on the subject. Each party is expected to attend court, and when his causes are called, either bring them on for trial, or, by the order of the court, or the consent of his adversary, have them continued; or if his adversary be not present, have them dismissed or decided by default. This latter practice is the proper Admiralty practice. It prevails in the Supreme Court of the United States, and might well be prescribed by that court for all the District and Circuit Courts in Admiralty causes.

All notices in the Southern District of New York, are notices of four days. In all matters except the hearing of causes, al-

(*a*) Vid. Precedents in the Appendix.

though the regular notice is four days, the court will, on sufficient cause shown, order a shorter notice.(*a*)

All notices and other papers to be served in a cause, are to be served on the proctor instead of the party, if a proctor have appeared in the cause.

§ 569. Each District Court and each Circuit Court may, by general rules, regulate their practice, in such manner as they shall deem most expedient for the due administration of justice, in suits in Admiralty, in all cases not provided for by the General Admiralty Rules of the Supreme Court—and such rules exist in most, if not all the districts, both in the Circuit Courts and the District Courts. Those of both courts, in the Southern District of New York, in Admiralty cases, will be found in the Appendix.(*b*)

(*a*) Vid. the Rules.

(*b*) Ad. Rule 46. Process Act of 1792, § 2.

CHAPTER XXXV.

Admiralty and Maritime Crimes.

§ 570. The grant in the Constitution, of judicial power, to the government of the United States, in all cases of Admiralty and maritime jurisdiction, is without limitation, and, of course, embraces criminal as well as civil cases. It is under this grant alone, that the federal government have the right to punish a large class of offences whose punishment is provided for, in the acts of Congress in relation to crimes and offences on the high seas. In these acts, the various offences are not classed or described as Admiralty cases, but they are indiscriminately arranged with other descriptions of crimes subject to the federal jurisdiction. They will be found in the crimes acts of 1790, of 1804, of 1820, of 1825, and of 1835, in various sections, providing for the punishment of crimes and offences committed " on the high seas, or in any arm of the sea, or in any river, harbor, creek, basin or bay, or in any other waters within the Admiralty and maritime jurisdiction of the United States." The power of the federal government to punish these offences, is derived from the Admiralty and maritime grant in the Constitution; and of all of them which are not capital, the District Court has jurisdiction. If committed within any district, the trial must be in that district; and if upon the high seas, out of a district, then in the district where the offender is apprehended, or into which he may be first brought.(a) Those who contend for the narrow jurisdiction of the Admiralty, have not always considered what would be its effect upon the criminal jurisdiction of the General Government.

§ 571. Under the general provisions that, in Admiralty and

(a) Const. art. 3, § 2. 1 Stat. at Large. 4 id. 115, 777. 5 id. 517. 6 Amend. to the Const. U. S.

maritime cases, the mode of proceeding should be according to the usages of courts of Admiralty, the trial of maritime offences must have been according to the usage of Admiralty courts,(a) had not the Constitution and amendments otherwise provided :

"The trial of all crimes, except in cases of impeachment, shall be by jury, and such trial shall be held in the state where the said crimes shall have been committed, but when not committed within any state, the trial shall be at such place or places as the Congress may, by law, have directed."(b)

"No person shall be held to answer for a capital, or otherwise infamous crime, unless on presentment or indictment of a grand jury, except in cases arising in the land or naval forces, or in the militia when in actual service, in time of war or public danger."(c)

"In all criminal prosecutions, the accused shall enjoy the right to a speedy and public trial by an impartial jury of the state and district where the crime shall have been committed, which district shall have been previously ascertained by law, and to be informed of the nature and cause of the accusation, to be confronted with the witnesses against him, to have compulsory process for obtaining witnesses in his favor, and to have the assistance of counsel for his defence."(d)

§ 572. The practical operation of these provisions, has been to make the practice of the Admiralty, in criminal cases, the same as the practice of the courts of common law, in like cases. The cases are none the less cases of Admiralty and maritime jurisdiction, although, like criminal cases in the English Admiralty, they are tried before a jury, and, from the beginning, conducted after the manner of trials at common law, in criminal cases. The proper effect of those provisions is not, however, to adopt, in such cases the practice of the state courts, but the practice must be according to the usage of Admiralty courts, subject to the limitations of the Constitution, the amendments, and the acts of Congress.(e)

(a) Act of May 8th, 1792, § 2.   (b) Const. art. 3, § 2.
(c) 5th Amendment.   (d) 6th Amendment.
(e) Conk. Treat. 395.

§ 573. The powers usually exercised by justices of the peace and other magistrates in the states, of issuing warrants for crimes, making preliminary examinations, and committing, are usually exercised by the United States' commissioners, by virtue of the act of August 23, 1842, which will be found in the Appendix.(*a*)

(*a*) 5 Stat. at Large, 516.

CHAPTER XXXVI.

Limitations.

§ 574. There is no fixed rule of limitation of the time in which Admiralty suits shall be brought, except in the cases of criminal suits, and suits *quasi* criminal. Statutes of limitation are founded entirely on public policy, rather than on sound principle. Indulgence to a debtor, and delay in prosecuting him, would seem not to form any good reason why the creditor should lose his debt. The policy of all nations has, however, fixed limits to that indulgence, in certain cases—longer in one nation than another, and almost as various as the classes of cases. These limitations have usually been subject to exceptions, one of which is in favor of persons beyond sea, and all of which have their foundation in the inconvenience or impracticability of sooner enforcing the demand.

§ 575. If the omission to enact any statute of limitations in civil cases of Admiralty and maritime jurisdiction, sprang from the peculiar character of the cases, and the pursuits of many of those employed in maritime commerce—a large portion of their time in foreign countries, on the seas, and beyond the seas—urged by the strongest incentives of commercial necessity, as well as of public policy, to pursue their avocations without interruptions, and without being the masters of their own steps—it would not be the only instance in which the founders of the republic, and the framers of her first system of laws, silently manifested their remarkable forecast and practical wisdom. I cannot help thinking, that in such cases, the matter of limitations is best left as it is, to the discretion of the court, who can but judge in view of all the circumstances, whether the demand be so stale as to be considered neglected and abandoned—availing themselves of that principle of limitation in the administration of every system of jurisprudence which is derived out of the nature of things, and which is admitted in the universal maxim,—"*vigilantibus non dormientibus subveniunt leges.*" This is the constant practice of courts of Admiralty. This discretion of the court is not mere caprice, nor will, nor arbitrary power. It is the sound legal discretion of cultivated reason, in which the circumstances of the parties and of the property, and of the transaction—the wants and convenience of commerce, and the demands of public policy—and, most especially, the analogies of the local laws of limitation, are fully to be considered and carefully weighed.(*a*)

§ 576. In criminal and penal cases, and cases of forfeiture, there are limitations fixed by the acts of Congress. No person shall be tried for treason, or other capital offence, wilful murder and forgery excepted, unless the indictment for the same be found by a grand jury within three years next after the commission of the offence ; nor shall any person be prosecuted, tried, or punished for any offence, not capital, unless the indictment or information for the same be found or instituted within two years from the time of committing the offence ; this does not, however, extend to persons fleeing from justice.(*b*)

§ 577. For a large number of offences against the revenue laws, ships and vessels and other property are specifically forfeited, and the forfeiture is enforced by proceedings *in rem* in Admiralty. By the custom house act of March 2, 1799, § 89, prosecutions for those forfeitures, as well as actions against persons for violations of that act, are limited to three years next after the penalty or forfeiture was incurred ; but by the act of March 26, 1804, § 3, the limitations in such cases, was extended to five years. The same period of limitations applies to prosecutions for the slave trade by the 9th section of the act of April 20, 1818.

(*a*) 2 Gall. 477.   3 Mas. 91.   5 C. Rob. 102.   2 Levin. 207, 212.   1 C. Rob. 180.   3 id. 235.   6 id. 46.   1 Dod. 463.   8 Sumn. 276.   1 Yo. & Col. 455.   8 Clark & Fin. 121.   2 Dod. 338.   Edw. Jur. 149.   Stat. 4 Anne, c. 16.   3 Hag. 117, 419. Howard, 234.

(*b*) Crimes Act of April 30, 1790, § 31.   2 Cranch, 336.   1 Gal. 397.

CHAPTER XXXVII.

THE CIRCUIT COURTS OF THE UNITED STATES.

The Jurisdiction and Practice in Admiralty and Maritime Cases.

§ 578. It has been already stated, that the circuit courts have no original civil Admiralty jurisdiction. It has also been shown in what cases and how, original cases, in the District Court, may be transferred to the Circuit Court for original hearing. The Circuit Court has also, concurrently with the District, a large criminal jurisdiction in Admiralty cases. In all these cases, the practice in the Circuit Court, is like that in the District Court, in like cases, and is set forth in the preceding sections of this work, and to them the reader is referred. The Admiralty rules of the Supreme Court, apply to the Circuit as well as the District Court. The practice of the Circuit Court, in cases of appeal, however, should be stated.(*a*)

§ 579. *Appeals.*—From all final decrees in a District Court an appeal, when the matter in dispute, exclusive of costs, shall exceed the sum or value of fifty dollars, is allowed to the Circuit Court next to be holden in the District.

The appeal can be taken only to a final decree. An interlocutory decree—an incidental decree—a decree in a matter of discretion, cannot be appealed from. The appeal from the final decree, however, brings up for review all the orders, decrees, and proceedings in the cause.(*b*)

§ 580. It is of great importance to the due administration of justice, that causes should not be carried up in fragments, upon

---

(*a*) Ante, §§ 320 to 323.
(*b*) Act of March 3, 1803.   6 Cranch, 206.   7 id. 152.   9 Wheat. 576.   11 id. 280.   2 How. 238.

successive appeals. It would occasion very great delays and oppressive expenses. It was to prevent such a cóurse, unquestionably, that the Congress limited appeals to final decrees, and in the same spirit, the courts have always held, that if one party appeals and the other party does not also appeal, he shall be bound by the decree of the court below, and also of the court above, and will not be permitted to ask that the decree be modified in his favor, nor to bring another appeal. We hence derive the true criterion of a final decree. The final decree is not that which decides upon the substantial merits of the action, but that which completes the decretal action of the court in the cause; and that an appeal will bring up for review, at once, all that the court has done in the cause, so far as it may injuriously affect the appellants. We also perceive the proper functions of an appeal, which is to bring up for rehearing and re-adjudication the whole action of the court below, so that the court above may, in all things, do what the court below should have done, or remand the cause, with directions, which shall render another appeal unnecessary.(a)

If, therefore, there remain to be made any order—for costs—for confirmation of a report—for distribution, or other order, which is but a consequence of the decree on the merits, the appeal can not be entered before such order is made—that is the final decree, —not till then is it in a state for execution, without further action of the court below.

§ 581. The matter in dispute must be fifty dollars, exclusive of costs, or an appeal will not lie. If, however, the amount authorizes an appeal, the question of costs is subject to review, as well as any other question.(b)

When the libellant appeals, the amount of the matter in dispute is the amount demanded in the libel. If there be no amount specifically demanded in the libel, the party will be permitted to show the amount by affidavit or otherwise. The courts, in deciding upon the question of amount, lean with a liberal con-

---

(a) 3 Pet. 318.   10 Wheat. 431, 502.   11 id. 429.
(b) 2 How. 210.   3 Pet. 307.

struction in favor of the right of appeal, and if the recovery can, by posssibility, be more than fifty dollars, an appeal will lie.(a)

Whenever the rights of the parties are separate, although they be co-libellants or co-defendants, and the decree is distributive, as in cases of salvage, mariners' wages, and such cases, the aggregate amount does not give the right to appeal, but no party will be allowed to appeal unless the amount in dispute, so far as he alone is concerned, exceeds fifty dollars.(b)

When the defendant or claimant appeals, the amount decreed against him is the matter in dispute.

Whenever one party appeals the other party may appeal, so as to bring up for review the whole decree. But either party may appeal from the whole or from any part of the decree.

§ 582. The appeal from the District Court must be made to the Circuit Court next to be holden in the District. The time limited for an appeal is, therefore, very brief. All appeals from the District Court to the Circuit Court must be made while the court is sitting, or within such other period as shall be designated by the District Court, by its general rules, or by an order specially made in the particular suit. If an appeal be not so made the decree may be executed.(c)

§ 583. An appeal should be made in writing, and filed in the District Court. No particular form of words is necessary to constitute an appeal. It will be held sufficient if it show clearly that the party appeals from the decree.

In the Southern District of New York the matter of appeals has assumed more regularity and form than in some of the other districts, and the practice there has been found conducive to a full rehearing of the cause, with the greatest economy of time, labor and expense. The practice in that District, therefore, will be alone stated. In any District where the practice is different, a recurrence to the rules of the courts there, will show in what respects this practice is to be modified or departed from.

(a) 4 Dal. 20.　4 Cranch, 216.　5 id. 13.　7 id. 276.　3 Peters, 33.　7 id. 453.
Gilp. 37.
(b) 8 Peters, 4.　6 id. 143,
(c) Ad. Rule 25.　3 Mas. 443.

The convenience of parties has been usually found to require that a few days time should be allowed, as a matter of course, in which the party may consider whether he will appeal. In England fifteen days are allowed. In the civil law practice, the time was ten days. By the rules of the District Court, ten days are allowed from the time when the decree is in a condition to be executed without further proceedings in that court.(a)

§ 584. So far as the District Court is concerned, a brief notice in writing to the clerk of the court, and to the opposite proctor, is a sufficient notice of the appeal, to operate as a stay of proceedings till security may be put in.

This notice is as follows :

"DISTRICT COURT OF THE UNITED STATES FOR THE SOUTHERN DISTRICT OF NEW YORK.

> "A. B.
> *vs.*
> C. D.

"SIR:—The defendant intends to appeal from the final decree of the court in this cause.

"Dated Oct. 1, 1848.

"E. T., Proctor for Def't.

"To J. W. M., Esq., Clerk."

This notice served on the clerk and the opposite proctor, will stay the execution of the decree, till the expiration of the time to put in the necessary security on the appeal, which is required by the rules of the District Court.

§ 585. Whenever an appeal is entered the appellant must give security for damages and costs within ten days after the appeal is entered, and if security is not given within that time, the decree may be executed as if there had been no appeal, unless the court allow further time. The appellant must give four days notice to the adverse party, or proctor if he have one, of the time

---

(a) Dist. Rules, 151, 152.

and place of giving the stipulation, and of the persons proposed as sureties, with their additions and description. The sureties must then justify, and submit to an examination as to their sufficiency. They must stipulate in double the decree for damages or debt and costs, when the defendant appeals, and in such sum as may be fixed by the court, if the appeal be by the libellant.(a)

The rules of the Circuit Court require that there should be an appeal in writing, more formal than the notice of appeal which has been mentioned, and that it should be returned with the other documents, as an important paper in the court above. It should briefly state the allegations and prayer of the parties in the proceedings in the District Court, and the decree, with the time of rendering the same.(b)

§ 586. It is the well settled practice of the Admiralty, that in the appellate court, the parties are permitted to allege what was not alleged, and to prove what was not proved, in the court below. This, however, must be taken with the limitation that new causes of action cannot thus be introduced in the appellate court, otherwise an appeal might be made the means of giving original jurisdiction to an appellate court.(c)

The effect of this practice has been to present appeals in three classes :

1. Appeals for a mere review of the action of the court below in which, on the same pleadings and the same proofs, the cause is to be re-argued in the court above.

2. Appeals in which, on the same pleadings or allegations, the cause is to be re-tried, on the testimony in the court below, and other testimony, introduced for the first time in the court above.

3. Appeals in which the whole proceeding is re-constructed, new pleadings or allegations are put in, and the cause proceeds in all respects as though it had never been heard in the court below.

§ 587. It is obvious, that the course of proceedings in the court

---

(a) Vid. the form of the stipulation in the Appendix.
(b) Circ. Court Rule, 118.
(c) Ante, § 483. Clerke Prax. tit. 60. Hall Ad. 110.

above, as well on the part of the court as of the parties, must vary materially, as the appeal shall be of one or the other of those classes. Appeals are usually of the first or second class. *Those of the third class are very rarely, if ever, necessary or expedient.

The appellant must, therefore, in his appeal, state what course he intends to pursue in this behalf in the court above, and he shall be concluded by the appeal.

This appeal must be signed by the party or his proctor, and filed in the District Court, within the time limited for appealing, and with it must be filed an affidavit of service of a copy of it on the proctor of the appellees in the court below.(a)

Nothing further is necessary to be done to complete the appeal. No answer need be made to the appeal, or issue taken upon it, and no process or order is necessary to bring the appellees into the Circuit Court. The appellant must, however, proceed to have the necessary documents transcribed without delay, and within twenty days, and by the first day of the term of the Circuit Court next after the appeal, unless a longer time is allowed by the judge.(b)

§ 588. Within four days after the documents are completed by the clerk of the District Court, the appellant must cause them to be filed in the Circuit Court, which is then deemed to be possessed of the cause. If the appellant do not have the documents thus returned, the appeal is not received, and is deemed deserted, which may be certified to the court below, and thereupon that court may proceed to execute its decree.(c)

After the Circuit Court is possessed of the cause, by the re-receipt of the return from the District Court, the cause is no longer in the District Court. That court can not make any order whatever in relation to it.(d)

If on the appeal it shall not be intended to make new allegations, nor to pray different relief, nor to seek a new decision

---

(a) Circ. Rule 119, 120. Vid. the form of an appeal in the Appendix.
(b) Circ. Rule, 118, 124, 127.
(c) Circ. Rule 124, 125.
(d) Gilp. 40. 1 Gal. 503. Wheat. 194.

of the facts, then the pleadings, evidence, and decree, with the stipulations and the clerk's account of the funds in court, and the appeal, must be certified to the circuit with the appeal—and, in all cases, the statement of facts agreed upon by the parties, or settled by the District Judge, and on file, according to the practice of that court, may be certified in place of the evidence at large.

If it be intended to seek only a new decision of the facts, then the pleadings, with the stipulations and the clerk's account of the funds in court, and the exhibits and depositions, and the appeal, are alone to be certified.

If it is intended to put in new pleadings and seek new relief, then the return will contain only the appeal, copies of the process and return, the clerk's account, and the depositions, exhibits, and stipulations in the cause.(a)

The return or record sent from the court below to the Appellate Court, is called Apostles, from the Greek ἀποσέλλειν to send away.(b)

§ 589. By an appeal from the District Court to the Circuit Court, the Circuit Court becomes possessed of the cause, which is no longer in the District Court. The Circuit Court alone can make orders in it, and executes its own judgment without any intervention of the District Court; and, on the other hand, if a further appeal be had, to the Supreme Court, that court does not execute its own judgments, but sends a special mandate to the Circuit Court, to award execution thereon. The regular order of proceedings, therefore, requires that the property should follow the cause into the Circuit Court, not only with a view to its own action, but also that of the Supreme Court.(c)

If, therefore, there be a vessel or other property in custody of the Marshal, he should, by a proper order, be directed to hold it, subject to the order of the Circuit Court instead of the District Court. If there be funds in the District Court, they must be transferred to the Circuit Court, and deposited subject to its order—and the original stipulations, taken in the District Court,

---

(a) Circ. Rule 121, 122, 123. Vid. the Forms in the Appendix.
(b) Consett Prac. 193. 2 Brow. Civ. Ad. 438.
(c) 6 Wheat. 194, and cases there cited. 5 Cond. 65.

must be sent up to the Circuit Court. In no other manner can the cause be entirely in the Circuit Court, and that court have the power to make a full decree, and execute its own decree. For in the District Court, as well as in the Circuit Court, all parties and stipulators are bound by the decree in the cause, and it operates directly upon the persons and property. The Circuit Court will, if necessary, by mandamus, compel the district clerk to make the necessary return.(a)

> *As soon after final decree as you have determined to appeal, and within the term allowed, give notice of appeal to the Clerk of the District and the opposite Proctor. Give the necessary stipulations. Prepare, with care, the formal appeal. Serve copy on opposite Proctor, and file the original in the District Clerk's office, with affidavit of service.*
>
> *Order the necessary transcripts and return to be made to the Circuit Court.*
>
> *See that they are actually returned and filed in the Circuit Court in due time.*
>
> *See that the property, money, and stipulation, are also transferred to the Circuit Court.*

§ 590. The enrolled decree remains in the District Court as the decree of that court, and, till reversed, it is binding upon all the parties, as an adjudication of the right. It is suspended or stayed in operation during the pending of the appeal.

It is properly said, in regard to Admiralty cases, that an appeal suspends the sentence below, altogether, and the language of some of the cases has been thought to justify the opinion, that an appeal entirely destroys the effect, if not the operative existence, of the decree appealed from. The extent of the principle, however, seems to be that, notwithstanding the decree below, the cause is to be heard and decided in the Appellate Court, according to the law, as it exists at the time of the hearing, in the Appellate Court, in the same manner as if no sentence had been pronounced. In other words, the question is not in the court above, whether the court below erred, but whe-

---

(a) Circ. Rule. 129.   Vid. the Form in the Appendix.

ther, by the existing law, the decree ought to stand or be modified or reversed.(a)

§ 591. The appeal itself suspends the sentence below, and prevents its execution—but should the District Court proceed after an appeal, the Circuit Court will, on notice and hearing the parties, issue an inhibition to the District Court.(b)

Should any District Court entertain jurisdiction of any cause of Admiralty and Maritime jurisdiction, of which it had properly no jurisdiction, the defendant is not compelled to take the slow and expensive process of an appeal to arrest the jurisdiction, but the Supreme Court of the United States has power to issue a prohibition.(b)

§ 592. The appeal being perfected, and the proper documents returned to the Circuit Court, the proctor of the appellant should notify the proctor of the appellee, that the same are so returned. The proctor for the appellee must then enter his appearance in the Circuit Court without delay, and within the first two days in the term next after he is notified that the return is filed; if not, the case may be brought on by the appellant.

The entry of appearance is by a written notice to the clerk of the Circuit Court, that the proctor appears for the appellee, and requests that his appearance be entered.(b)

§ 593. If the appeal is of that kind that requires new pleadings, the libellant files a new libel in the Circuit Court, within the time limited by the court, and the adverse party answers in the same manner, or his default may be taken, and the cause proceeds like an original cause in the District Court. The written depositions and answers to interrogatories, and other written testimony from the District Court, may be used in the Circuit Court.(c)

§ 594. In the Circuit Court the cause proceeds like a new trial of an original cause. In that court, as in the District Court, both parties are actors, and may give notice of hearing, and

---

(a) 5 Cranch, 281. 3 Pet. 57. Conk. Treat. 2d. ed. 157.

(b) 3 Dallas, 54. Circ. Rule 126, 128. Jud. Act of 1789, § 13. Vid. the Forms in the Appendix.

(c) Circ. Rule 123, 131, 132.

bring on the cause. And the libellant opens and closes the cause in the same manner as in the court below. It is, in truth; a new trial. What has been said in relation to decrees of the District Court, applies with equal force to decrees of the Circuit Court; and the same stay of execution for ten days, in appealable cases, is provided by the general rules of the court.(*a*)

§ 595. By the strict Admiralty practice, the clerk of the court takes down in writing the testimony of the witnesses, that the same may be returned in case of appeal. The practice has been found to be productive of great delay and expense, and it has become the practice in the Southern District of New York, to substitute the notes of the judge, instead of those of the clerk, and to excuse the clerk from taking the testimony. He accordingly never takes down the testimony in that district. The notes of the District Judge are returned precisely as he takes them, and are read in evidence, and each party introduces such other and further proof, by the same or other witnesses, as may be in his power. The practice would be more perfect if, in cases when an appeal is taken, the whole testimony taken below could be settled by the proctor of the appellant serving on the proctor of the appellee his statement of the testimony—the proctor of the appellee proposing amendments, if necessary, and the judge settling it—the same, when settled, to be filed in the District Court and returned to the Circuit as the testimony in the cause. Such is the practice in the Circuit Court as to the testimony there. It can hardly be doubted that the practice should be made uniform by the Supreme Court.(*b*)

§ 596. If there be any reason why the decree of the District Court should be carried into effect subject to the ultimate decision on appeal, the Circuit Court will, on the proper application, at any time after the cause is in court, on notice, order the decree to be carried into effect on such terms and conditions as may be just. If the security of the party is likely to be greatly impaired by any delay, the court will sometimes order the decree to be executed unless further security is put in.(*c*)

(*a*) Ante, § 580. Circ. Rule 133, 134.   (*b*) Id. 135.   (*c*) Id 133.

§ 597. In cases where an appeal lies from the decree of the Circuit Court, the final decree will not be executed till ten days have elapsed from the pronouncing or filing of the decision of the court; and if the appellant desires a stay of proceedings, he must proceed to file his appeal within the ten days.(*a*)

As soon as the appeal is made from the decree of the Circuit Court, the appellant must, within four days, or such further time, as the court may allow, make and serve on the adverse party a statement of the testimony on the trial, except such testimony as was in writing, which must be properly referred to. The other party, within four days, must propose amendments, or the statement will be considered as acquiesed in. And the statement, if not acquiesced in, and the amendments, must be submitted, by the appellant's proctor, to the judge who heard the cause, within four days, for settlement, and, when settled, they are engrossed by the clerk, and, with the written evidence, are deemed the proofs on which the decree was made. The statement, so settled, operates as a stay of further proceedings in the Circuit Court.(*b*)

As an appeal may be taken at any time within five years, there would be an evident propriety in requiring the statement of the testimony to be settled in all appealable cases, and filed in the cause immediately after the decree, while the facts are recent.

§ 598. After the cause has been heard and decided in the Supreme Court, on appeal, that court issues its remittitur and mandate to the Circuit Court, directing the decree to be entered and executed there. The Circuit Court adopts and enters the proper decree, and it is then treated and executed as an original decree of that court.

What has been said on the subject of executing the decree of the District Court has equal application to the Circuit Court; the forms of execution are also the same, *mutatis mutandis* (*c*)

(*a*) Circ. Rule, 134. Infra, § 602.   (*b*) Circ Rule, 135. Infra, § 605.
(*c*) Ante, § 555, *et seq.* Vid. the forms in the Appendix.

CHAPTER XXXVIII.

THE SUPREME COURT OF THE UNITED STATES.

Its Jurisdiction and Practice in Admiralty and Maritime Cases.

§ 599. The original jurisdiction of the Supreme Court in Admiralty and Maritime cases is confined to cases which will rarely, if ever, arise. It is believed that no such case has hitherto been brought before that court, and they are quite as little likely to arise hereafter. Whenever such cases arise, the same practice will be required in that court as exists in the Circuit and the District Courts in such cases, except where the practice is otherwise regulated by the Supreme Court in its rules.(*a*)

§ 600. From all final judgments or decrees rendered in a Circuit Court, or in a District Court, acting as a Circuit Court, in any cases of Admiralty and Maritime jurisdiction, and of prize or no prize, an appeal, where the matter in dispute, exclusive of costs, shall exceed the sum or value of two thousand dollars, is allowed to the Supreme Court.(*b*)

What has been already said in relation to the amount in dispute, and the character and criterion of the final decree, applies equally to cases in the Supreme Court, and will not be here repeated.(*c*)

§ 601. After the final decision of the Circuit Court is made, and the final decree entered, an appeal may be taken at any time within five years, but if the party against whom the decree is made, desires a stay of proceedings on the decree, he must appeal within the time allowed by the rules of the court,

---

(*a*) Ante, § 324.
(*b*) Act of March 3, 1803. 2 Stat. at Large, 244.
(*c*) Ante, § 581. Sup. Court, Rule 13.

or further time granted by the court, and lodge a copy of his appeal in the clerk's office for the opposite party. The first step is the Appeal—the second, the Security—the third, the Citation—the fourth, the Return—the fifth, the Bond for costs.(a)

§ 602. *The Appeal.*—The appeal is entitled in the cause in the Circuit Court, and signed by the appellant or his proctor. It should briefly recite the proceedings in the Circuit Court, and be filed with the clerk of the Circuit Court—a copy is also to be lodged there for the opposite party, within ten days, Sundays excepted, after the passing the decree complained of, if the appeal is to operate as a stay of execution. No allowance of the appeal is necessary (b)

§ 603. *The Security.*—The Judge, before signing a citation, must take good and sufficient security that the appellee shall prosecute his appeal to effect and answer all damages and costs, if he fails to make his plea good. If no stay of proceedings is required, the security is in such amount as in the opinion of the Judge shall be sufficient to answer all such costs, as upon affirmance of the decree, shall be decreed to the appellee.(c)

If the appeal is to stay execution, the security must be in a sufficient sum to secure the amount of debt, damages, and costs which may be covered by the decree of the appellate court.(d)

It is the duty of the Judge to be satisfied that the security is good and sufficient, and to show that by his approval, endorsed on the bond. The security is usually taken in the form of a penal bond, and the penalty should be, at least, double the amount recovered in the court below, including costs and damages.(e)

The bond is filed in the Circuit Court, and remains there— because the Supreme Court does not execute its own decree,

---

(a) 10 Wheat. 306. Vid. the Forms in the Appendix.

(b) Jud. Act of 1789, § 23. Ante, § 597.

(c) Act of 12th Dec. 1794, § 22.

(d) 9 Wheat. 553.

(e) Vid. the Form in the Appendix.

but remands the cause to the Circuit Court to execute the decree.(*a*)

If the appeal be taken within five years, the security required by law may be given after the expiration of that period.(*b*)

§ 604. *Citation.*—There must be a citation to the opposite party, signed by a Judge of the Circuit Court which rendered the decree, or a Judge of the Supreme Court, giving the opposite party at least thirty days notice. The effect of the notice is to prevent the cause being heard before thirty days after the party is notified, unless the appellee appear.(*c*)

The citation must be signed by the Judge, and served personally by a copy. The original citation must be filed in the clerk's office, to be returned with the record.(*d*)

§ 605. *The Return.*—The return must contain every thing necessary to place the whole cause before the Supreme Court, in a manner to be fully heard. No cause will be heard until a complete record is filed, containing, in itself, without reference *aliunde,* all the papers, exhibits, depositions, statement of the testimony as settled, and other proceedings,—as well those carried into the Circuit Court from the District Court, as those originating in the circuit—including the appeal and citation, with proof of the service of them ; and this record must contain all objections to the testimony taken below, as no objection is allowed to be taken to the admissibility of any deposition, deed, grant, or other exhibit found in the record, unless the objection was taken in the court below, and entered on the record, and the same will otherwise be deemed to have been admitted by consent.(*e*)

§ 606. *The Bond for Costs.*—On filing the return in the Supreme Court, the appellant must give to the clerk a bond, with

---

(*a*) Ante, § 598.
(*b*) 10 Wheat. 306.
(*c*) Vid. the Form in the Appendix. 1 Cranch, 365.
(*d*) 5 Cranch, 21, 321, 329.
(*e*) Sup. Court Rule 33. Ante, § 597.

competent security, to respond to costs, in the penalty of two hundred dollars, or deposite that amount in bank, subject to his draft. This provision is very strictly enforced, and the cause will not be docketed before the security is given, and must take its place on the docket as of that date. This security is necessary, because the proctors and parties are usually remote from the seat of Government where the clerk's office is kept, and the clerk incurs considerable expenses, beyond his fees, in preparing the papers. It is his duty to have the record printed, and he delivers the copies to the parties and the court.(*a*)

§ 607. Each party should enter his appearance in person or by proctor, immediately after the return of the appeal. If an appearance be not entered on the record for either party, on or before the second day of the term next after that in which the case is docketed, it will be dismissed at the costs of the appellant.(*b*)

The following is a notice to the clerk to enter an appearpearance :

SUPREME COURT OF THE UNITED STATES.

Isaac Newton, claimant of the
  Steamboat New Jersey,
                    Appellant.
        vs.
John H. Stebbins,
                    Appellee.

Sir—You will please to enter my appearance for the appellee in this cause.

December 3, 1849.

E. C. Benedict,
                    Proctor for Appellee.

To Wm. T. Carroll, Esq., *Clerk.*

§ 608. If the decree appealed from was rendered thirty days before the term to which the appeal is returnable, the appellant

---

(*a*) Sup. Court Rule 37.   7 How. 784.   10 Pet.
(*b*) Sup. Court Rule 54.

must file the record with the clerk of the court at Washington, and docket the cause within the first six days of the term. If he do not, the appellee may do so, and have the cause stand for argument, or he may have the appeal dismissed. After the six days, the appellant cannot docket the cause, except upon the terms that the cause shall stand for argument during the term, or be continued at the option of the appellee. After it has been once dismissed, the appellant cannot docket it, unless by consent, or by the order of the court. And if it be not docketed until thirty days, from the commencement of the term, it must be continued to the next term.(*a*)

§ 609. The most liberal principles prevail in reference to amendments, but a party will not be allowed, by amendment, to introduce a new subject of controversy—nor will a new claim be allowed. If justice requires that a new claim be put in, or that the pleadings be reformed, the court will remand the cause to the Circuit,· with directions to permit that to be done which is necessary.(*b*)

§ 610. If pending an appeal, either party die, his legal representatives may voluntarily come in, and be admitted parties, and the cause proceeds without interruption. If they do not voluntarily come in, the other party may suggest the death on the record, and, on motion, have an order, that unless they become parties within the first ten days of the ensuing term, the moving party, if appellee, may have the appeal dismissed, or, if appellant, may bring on the hearing. The order, however, must be printed in a newspaper, at Washington, in which the laws are published, by authority there, at least sixty days before the beginning of the next term of the Supreme Court.(*c*)

Hearing.

No notice of hearing from party to party is necessary, in ca-

---

(*a*) Sup Court Rule 30, 43.

(*b*) 15 Pet. 40.   4 Wheat. 1.   8 Id. 380.   4 Id. 32.   1 Id. 298.   9 Cranch, 209. 7 Cranch, 496.   Ante, § 483.

(*c*) Sup. Court Rule 28.   Ante, § 485.

ses on the docket, and, after the cause has been docketed, it is continued on the docket till disposed of.

If there be any special motion to be made, which is not to be put on the docket, notice must be given to the opposite party, with copies of the papers to be used on the motion. The notice must be for a reasonable time—the situation of the parties, and the nature of the motion, being considered.

§ 611. If there be any irregularity in the appeal—if the amount does not warrant an appeal—if there be a palpable want of jurisdiction, or any cause why the cause should not be heard on appeal, it is the practice to make a special motion to dismiss the appeal, without waiting for the call of the cause in its order on the docket.

When an appeal has been dismissed through mistake, it may be reinstated, or a new appeal may be taken within the five years.(*a*)

§ 612. *Motions.*—The court does not hear arguments on Saturday, (except for special cause,) but that day is devoted to the other business of the court, and on Friday in each week, during the sitting of the court, at any time before the hearing of a cause is commenced, special motions have the preference, and they should be made at that time.

§ 613. *Argument.*—On the second day in term, the court commences calling the cases for argument, in the order in which they stand on the docket, and proceeds, from day to day, except Saturday, in that order. Only ten causes are liable to be called on each day. If either of the parties is ready, the cause is heard. If neither party is ready, it goes to the foot of the docket, except good reason to the contrary be shown to the court. No cause is taken up out of its place, or set down for a particular day, except under special and peculiar circumstances. Every cause which has been twice called in its order, and put at the foot of the docket, if not again reached, is continued to the next term of the court.(*b*)

When a case is called for argument, at two successive terms,

(*a*) 12 Wheat. 1.   (*b*) Sup. Court Rule 36.

and, on the call at the second term, neither party is prepared to argue it, it will be dismissed, at the costs of the appellee, unless good cause be shown for a further postponement.(a)

The court will not hear any cause, until furnished, by the parties, with a printed abstract, containing the substance of all the material pleadings, facts, and documents on which they rely, and the points intended to be made, and the authorities intended to be cited in support of them, arranged under the respective points —and no book, or case not on the points, can be referred to in the argument. Any party omitting to file such statement, will not be heard, but the other party will be allowed to proceed *ex parte.*(b)

Only two counsel are permitted to argue for each party—and no counsel is permitted to speak more than two hours, without the special leave of the court, granted before the argument begins.(c)

§ 614. When new evidence is admissible, and depositions are necessary, the depositions cannot be taken *de bene esse,* except by consent. They must be taken by commission, issuing out of the Supreme Court, or out of any Circuit Court, upon interrogatories, to be filed by the party applying for the commission, on notice to the opposite party, to be served with a copy of the interrogatories, and a notice to file cross interrogatories within twenty days.(d)

If it should be necessary to inspect originial papers, the presiding Judge of the Circuit Court may order them sent to the Supreme Court for inspection, and they may then be used in evidence.(e)

Oral testimony may be given in open court, whenever it is by law admissible.

§ 615. If the counsel on either or both sides prefer to submit

---

(a) Sup. Court Rule 35.

(b) Sup. Court Rule 29, 53.

(c) Sup. Court Rule 23, 53.

(d) 7 Cranch, 22. Ibid. 107. 2 Wheat. 371. 8 Cranch, 434. Sup. Court Rules, 25, 27.

(e) Sup. Court Rule 26. 1 Wheat. 439.

a printed argument, the court will receive it. If a printed argument is filed, the case stands on the same footing as if there were an appearance by counsel. The written or printed arguments will not be received, unless they are signed by an attorney or counsellor of the Supreme Court.(a)

Cases may be submitted, on printed argument, until the first Monday in February in each term. They are submitted without regard to their order on the docket, and thus a preference is obtained by submitting a cause on printed argument, although it is questionable whether a cause thus submitted is so efficiently discussed as on an oral argument.(b)

§ 616. *Decree.*—In cases of affirmance, the appellee is entitled to costs, unless otherwise ordered by the court, and damages, at the rate of six per cent per annum, to the day of affirmance ; and if, in the opinion of the court, the appeal is brought merely for delay, the damages are ten per cent. The interest is included in the damages.(c)

In cases of dismissal, except for the want of jurisdiction, costs are allowed the appellee.(d)

In cases of reversal, except for want of jurisdiction, costs are allowed the appellant, unless otherwise ordered by the court.(e)

Costs are never given against the United States.

Subject to those general limitations, costs and counsel fees are in the discretion of the court. This is also true of the costs in the court below. The appellate court does not ordinarily interfere with that discretion.(f)

The court does not, however, always simply affirm or reverse the decree below, but often modifies it, or makes a new decree, such as the court below should have made.(g)

In all cases after the decree is made, including cases of dis-

---

(a) Sup. Court Rule 40, 51, 52.   (e) Sup. Court Rule 45.
(b) 7 How. 733.   (f) 3 Pet. 307. 2 How. 210.
(c) Sup. Court Rule 17, 18, 20, 45. (g) 3 Dal. 54.
(d) Sup. Court Rule 45.

missal, the clerk issues a mandate or other process to the court below, informing it of the proceedings in the Supreme Court, and in the mandate he inserts the amount of costs, and annexes the bill of items taxed in detail, which is filed in that court, and the decree is executed there.(*a*)

Sup. Court Rule 45. Ante, § 598.

APPENDIX.

ADMIRALTY RULES.

RULES OF THE SUPREME COURT OF THE UNITED STATES IN ADMIRALTY.

Rules of Practice of the Courts of the United States in Causes of Admiralty and Maritime Jurisdiction on the Instance Side of the Court, in pursuance of Act of the 23d of August, 1842, Ch. 188.

RULE I.

No *mesne process* shall issue from the District Court in any civil cause of admiralty and maritime jurisdiction, until the libel or libel of information shall be filed in the clerk's office, from which such process is to issue. All process shall be served by the marshal or by his deputy, or where he or they are interested, by some discreet and disinterested person appointed by the court.

RULE II.

In suits *in personam*, the *mesne process* may be by a simple warrant of arrest of the person of the defendant in the nature of a *capias*, or by a warrant of arrest of the person of the defendant with a clause therein, that if he cannot be found, to attach his goods and chattels to the amount sued for, or if such property cannot be found, to attach his credits and effects to the amount sued for in the hands of the garnishees named therein ; or, by a simple monition in the nature of a summons to appear and answer to the suit, as the libellant shall, in his libel or information, pray for, or elect.

RULE III.

In all suits *in personam*, where a simple warrant of arrest issues and is executed, the marshal may take bail with sufficient sureties from the party arrested by bond or stipulation, upon condition that he will appear in the suit and abide by all orders of the court, interlocutory or final, in the cause, and pay the money awarded by the final decree rendered therein, in the court, to which the process is returnable, or in any appellate court. And upon such bond or stipulation, summary process of execution may and shall be issued against the principal and sureties by the court to which such process is returnable, to enforce the final decree so rendered, or upon appeal, by the appellate court.

RULE IV.

In all suits *in personam*, where goods and chattels, · or credits and effects, are attached under such warrant authorizing the same, the attachment may be dissolved by order of the court to which the same warrant is returnable, upon the defendant, whose property is so attached, giving a bond or stipulation with sufficient sureties to abide by all orders, interlocutory or final, of the court, and pay the amount awarded by the final decree rendered in the court to which the process is returnable, or in any appellate court; and upon such bond or stipulation, summary process of execution shall and may be issued against the principal and sureties by the court to which such warrant is returnable to enforce the final decree so rendered, or upon appeal, by the appellate court.

RULE V.

Bonds or stipulations in admiralty suits may be given and taken in open court, or at chambers, or before any commissioner of the court who is authorized by the court to take affidavits and bail, and depositions in cases pending before the court.

RULE VI.

In all suits *in personam*, where bail is taken, the court may, upon motion for due cause shown, reduce the amount of the sum contained in the bond or stipulation therefor: and in all cases where a bond or stipulation is taken as bail, or upon dissolving an attachment of property as aforesaid, if either of the sureties shall become insolvent pending the suit, new sureties may be required by the order of the court to be given, upon motion and due proof thereof.

RULE VII.

In suits *in personam*, no warrant of arrest, either of the person or property of the defendant, shall issue for a sum exceeding five hundred dollars, unless by the special order of the court upon affidavit or other proper proof showing the propriety thereof.

RULE VIII.

In all suits *in rem* against a ship, her tackle, sails, apparel, furniture, boats, or other appurtenances, if such tackle, sails, apparel, furniture, boats or other appurtenances are in the possession or custody of any third person, the court may, after a due monition to such third person, and a hearing of the cause, if any, why the same should not be delivered over, award and decree that the same be delivered into the custody of the marshal or other proper officer, if upon the hearing the same is required by law and justice.

RULE IX.

In all cases of seizure and in other suits and proceedings *in rem*, the process, unless otherwise provided for by statute, shall be by a warrant of arrest of the ship, goods or other things to be arrested, and the marshal shall thereupon arrest and take the ship, goods or other things into his possession for safe custody ; and shall cause public notice thereof, and of the time assigned for the return of such process and the hearing of the cause, to be given in such newspaper within the district as the District Court shall order, and if there is no newspaper published therein, then in such other public places in the district as the court shall direct.

RULE X.

In all cases where any goods or other things are arrested, if the same are perishable, or are liable to deterioration, decay or injury by being detained in custody, pending the suit, the court may, upon the application of either party, in its discretion, order the same. or so much thereof to be sold, as shall be perishable or liable to depreciation, decay or injury, and the proceeds, or so much thereof as shall be a full security to satisfy the decree to be brought into court, to abide the event of the suit ; or the court may, upon the application of the claimant, order a delivery thereof to him upon a due appraisement to be had under its direction, either upon the claimant's depositing in court so much money as the court shall order, or upon his giving a stipulation with the sureties in such sum as the court shall direct, to abide by and pay the money awarded by the final decree rendered by the court or the appellate court, if any appeal intervenes, as the one or the other course shall be ordered by the court.

RULE XI.

In like manner, where any ship shall be arrested, the same may, upon the application of the claimant, be delivered to him upon a due appraisement to be had under the direction of the court, upon the claimant's depositing in court so much money as the court shall order, or upon his giving a stipulation with sureties as aforesaid ; and if the claimant shall decline any such application, then the court may in its discretion, upon the application of either party, upon due cause shown, order a sale of such ship, and the proceeds thereof to be brought into court, or otherwise disposed of as it may deem most for the benefit of all concerned.

RULE XII.

In all suits by material men for supplies or repairs, or other necessaries for a foreign ship, or for a ship in a foreign port, the libellant may proceed against the ship and freight *in rem*, or against the master or the owner alone *in personam*. And the like proceeding *in rem* shall apply to cases of domestic ships, where by the local law a lien is given to material men for supplies, repairs, or other necessaries.

RULE XIII.

In all suits for mariners' wages, the libellant may proceed against the ship, freight, and master, or against the ship and freight, or against the owner or master alone *in personam.*

RULE XIV.

In all suits for pilotage, the libellant may proceed against the ship and master, or against the ship, or against the owner alone, or the master alone, *in personam.*

RULE XV.

In all suits for damage by collision, the libellant may proceed against the ship and master, or against the ship alone, or against the master or the owner alone, *in personam.*

RULE XVI.

In all suits for an assault or beating on the high seas or elsewhere within the admiralty and maritime jurisdiction, the suit shall be *in personam* only.

RULE XVII.

In all suits against the ship or freight founded upon a mere maritime hypothecation, either express or implied, of the master for moneys taken up in a foreign port for supplies or repairs, or other necessaries for the voyage, without any claim of marine interest, the libellant may proceed either *in rem,* or against the master or the owner alone *in personam.*

RULE XVIII.

In all suits on bottomry bonds, properly so called, the suit shall be *in rem* only against the property hypothecated, or the proceeds of the property in whosesoever hands the same may be found, unless the master has without authority given the bottomry bond, or by his fraud or misconduct has avoided the same, or has subtracted the property, or unless the owner has by his own misconduct or wrong lost or subtracted the property, in which latter case the suit may be *in personam* against the wrongdoer.

RULE XIX.

In all suits for salvage, the suit may be *in rem* against the property saved, or the proceeds thereof, or *in personam* against the party at whose request and for whose benefit the salvage service has been performed.

RULE XX.

In all petitory or possessory suits between part owners or adverse proprietors, or by the owners of a ship or the majority thereof against the master of a ship for the ascertainment of the title and delivery of the possession, or for the possession only, or by one or more part owners against the others to obtain security for the return of the ship from any voyage undertaken without their consent, or by one or more part owners against the others to obtain possession of the ship for any voyage upon giving security for the safe return thereof, the process shall be by an arrest of the ship, and by a monition to the adverse party or parties to appear and make answer to the suit.

RULE XXI.

In all cases where the decree is for the payment of money, the libellant may, at his election, have an attachment to compel the defendant to perform the decree, or a writ of execution in the nature of a *capias* and of a *fieri facias*, commanding the marshal or his deputy to levy the amount thereof of the goods and chattels of the defendant, and for want thereof to arrest his body to answer the exigency of the execution. In all other cases the decree may be enforced by an attachment to compel the defendant to perform the decree: and upon such attachment the defendant may be arrested and committed to prison until he performs the decree, or is otherwise discharged by law, or by the order of the court.

RULE XXII.

All informations and libels of information upon seizures for any breach of the revenue or navigation or other laws of the United States, shall state the place of seizure, whether it be on land, or on the high seas, or on navigable waters within the admiralty and maritime jurisdiction of the United States; and the district within which the property is brought, and where it then is. The information or libel of information shall also propound in distinct articles the matters relied on as grounds or causes of forfeiture, and aver the same to be contrary to the form of the statute or statutes of the United States in such case provided, as the case may require, and shall conclude with a prayer of due process to enforce the forfeiture, and to give notice to all persons concerned in interest to appear and show cause at the return day of the process why the forfeiture should not be decreed.

RULE XXIII.

All libels in instance causes, civil or maritime, shall state the nature of the cause, as, for example, that it is a cause civil and maritime, of contract, or of tort or damage, or of salvage, or of possession, or otherwise, as the case may be; and if the libel be *in rem*, that the property is within the district; and if *in personam*, the names and occupations and places of residence of the parties. The libel shall also propound and articulate in distinct articles the various allegations of facts, upon which the libellant relies in support of his suit, so that the defendant may be enabled to answer distinctly and separately the several matters contained in each article; and it shall conclude with a prayer of the process to enforce his rights *in rem*, or *in personam*, (as the case may require,) and for such relief and redress as the court is competent to give in the premises. And the libellant may further require the defendant to answer on oath all interrogatories propounded by him touching all and singular the allegations in the libel at the close or conclusion thereof.

RULE XXIV.

In all informations and libels in causes of admiralty and maritime jurisdiction, amendments in matters of form may be made at any time on motion to the court as of course. And new counts may be filed and amendments in matters of substance may be made, upon motion at any time before the final decree, upon such terms as the court shall impose. And where any defect of form is set down by the defendant upon special exceptions, and is allowed, the court may, in granting leave to amend, impose terms upon the libellant.

RULE XXV.

In all cases of libels *in personam*, the court may in its discretion, upon the appearance of the defendant, where no bail has been taken and no attachment of property has been made to answer the exigency of the suit, require the defendant to give a stipulation with sureties in such sum as the court shall direct, to pay all costs and expenses, which shall be awarded against him in the suit upon the final adjudication thereof, or by any interlocutory order in the process of the suit.

RULE XXVI.

In suits *in rem*, the party claiming the property shall verify his claim on oath or solemn affirmation, stating that the claimant, by whom or on whose behalf the claim is made, is the true and *bona fide* owner, and that no other person is the owner thereof. And where the claim is put in by an agent or consignee, he shall also make oath, that he is duly authorized thereto by the owner, or if the property be at the time of the arrest in the possession of the master of a ship, that he is the lawful bailee thereof for the owner. And upon putting in such claim, the claimant shall file a stipulation with sureties in such sum as the court shall direct, for the payment of all costs and expenses which shall be awarded against him by the final decree of the court, or upon an appeal, by the appellate court.

RULE XXVII.

In all libels in causes of civil and maritime jurisdiction, whether *in rem* or *in personam*, the answer of the defendant to the allegations in the libel shall be on oath or solemn affirmation; and the answer shall be full and explicit and distinct to each separate article and separate allegation in the libel, in the same order as numbered in the libel; and shall also answer in like manner each interrogatory propounded at the close of the libel.

RULE XXVIII.

The libellant may except to the sufficiency or fullness or distinctness or relevancy of the answer to the article and interrogatories in the libel; and if the court shall adjudge the same exceptions or any of them to be good and valid, the court shall order the defendant forthwith, within such time as the court shall direct, to answer the same, and may further order the defendant to pay such costs as the court shall adjudge reasonable.

RULE XXIX.

If the defendant shall omit or refuse to make due answer to the libel upon the return-day of the process, or other day assigned by the court, the court shall pronounce him to be in contumacy and default, and thereupon the libel shall be adjudged to be taken *pro confesso* against him, and the court shall proceed to hear the cause *ex parte*, and adjudge therein as to law and justice shall appertain. But the court may in its discretion set aside the default, and upon the application of the defendant, admit him to make answer to the libel at any time before the final hearing and decree, upon his payment of all the costs of the suit up to the time of granting leave therefor.

RULE XXX.

In all cases where the defendant answers, but does not answer fully and explicitly and distinctly, to all the matters in any article of the libel, and exception is taken thereto by the libellant, and the exception is allowed, the court may, by attachment, compel the defendant to make further answer thereto, or may direct the matter of the exception to be taken *pro confesso* against the defendant, to the full purport and effect of the article to which it purports to answer, and as if no answer had been put in thereto.

RULE XXXI.

The defendant may object by his answer to answer any allegation or interrogatory contained in the libel, which will expose him to any prosecution or punishment for a crime, or for any penalty or any forfeiture of his property for any penalty offence.

RULE XXXII.

The defendant shall have a right to require the personal answer of the libellant, upon oath or solemn affirmation, to any interrogatories which he may at the close of his answer propound to the libellant touching any matters charged in the libel, or touching any matter of defence set up in the answer, subject to the like exception as to matters which shall expose the libellant to any prosecution or punishment or forfeiture, as is provided in the 31st Rule. In default of due answer by the libellant to such interrogatories, the court may adjudge the libellant to be in default and dismiss the libel, or may compel his answer in the premises by attachment, or take the subject-matter of the interrogatory *pro confesso* in favor of the defendant, as the court in its discretion shall deem most fit to promote public justice.

RULE XXXIII.

Where either the libellant or the defendant is out of the country, or unable from sickness or other casualty to make an answer to any interrogatory on oath or solemn affirmation at the proper time, the court may in its discretion, in furtherance of the due administration of justice, dispense therewith, or may award a commission to take the answer of the defendant when and as soon as it may be practicable.

44

RULE XXXIV.

If any third person shall intervene in any cause of admiralty and maritime jurisdiction *in rem*, for his own interest, and he is entitled, according to the course of admiralty proceedings to be heard for his own interest therein, he shall propound the matter in suitable allegations, to which, if admitted by the court, the other party or parties in the suit may be required by order of the court to make due answer, and such further proceedings shall be had and decree rendered by the court therein as to law and justice shall appertain. But every such intervenor shall be required, upon filing his allegations, to give a stipulation with sureties to abide by the final decree rendered in the cause, and to pay all such costs and expenses and damages as shall be awarded by the court upon the final decree, whether it is rendered in the original or appellate court.

RULE XXXV.

Stipulations in admiralty and maritime suits may be taken in open court, or by the proper judge at chambers, or under his order, by any commissioner of the court, who is a standing commissioner of the court, and is now by law authorized to take affidavits and bail, and also depositions in civil causes pending in the courts of the United States.

RULE XXXVI.

Exceptions may be taken to any libel, allegation or answer for surplusage, irrelevancy, impertinence or scandal, and if, upon reference to a master, the exception shall be reported to be so objectionable, and allowed by the court, the matter shall be expunged at the cost and expense of the party in whose libel or answer the same is found.

RULE XXXVII.

In cases of foreign attachment, the garnishee shall be required to answer on oath or solemn affirmation, as to the debts, credits or effects of the defendant in his hands, and to such interrogatories touching the same as may be propounded by the libellant; and if he shall refuse or neglect so to do, the court may award compulsory process *in personam* against him. If he admit any debts, credits or effects, the same shall be held in his hands liable to answer the exigency of the suit.

RULE XXXVIII.

In cases of mariners' wages, or bottomry, or salvage, or other proceedings *in rem*, where freight, or other proceeds of property are attached to or are bound by the suit, which are in the hands or possession of any person, the court may, upon due application by petition of the party interested, require the party charged with the possession thereof to appear and show cause, why the same should not be brought into court to answer the exigency of the suit; and if no sufficient cause be shown, the court may order the same to be brought into court to answer the exigency of the suit, and upon failure of the party to comply with the order, may award an attachment or other compulsive process to compel obedience thereto.

RULE XXXIX.

If in any admiralty suit, the libellant shall not appear and prosecute his suit according to the course and orders of the court, he shall be deemed in default and contumacy, and the court may, upon the application of the defendant, pronounce the suit to be deserted, and the same may be dismissed with costs.

RULE XL.

The court may in its discretion, upon the motion of the defendant and the payment of costs, rescind the decree in any suit in which on account of his contumacy and default the matter of the libel shall have been decreed against him, and grant a rehearing thereof, at any time within ten days after the decree has been entered, the defendant submitting to such further orders and terms in the premises as the court may direct.

RULE XLI.

All sales of property under any decree in admiralty shall be made by the marshal or his deputy, or other proper officer assigned by the court, where the marshal is a party in interest, in pursuance of the orders of the court; and the proceeds thereof, when sold, shall be forthwith paid into the registry of the court by the officer making the sale, to be disposed of by the court according to law.

RULE XLII.

All moneys paid into the registry of the court shall be deposited in some bank designated by the court, and shall be so deposited in the name of the court, and shall not be drawn out except by a check or checks signed by a judge of the court, and countersigned by the clerk, stating on whose account and for whose use it is drawn, and in what suit and out of what fund in particular it is paid. The clerk shall keep a regular book containing a memorandum and copy of all the checks so drawn and the date thereof.

RULE XLIII.

Any person having an interest in any proceeds in the registry of the court, shall have a right by petition and summary proceedings to intervene *per interesse suo,* for a delivery thereof to him ; and upon due notice to the adverse parties, if any, the court shall and may proceed summarily to hear and decide thereon, and to decree therein according to law and justice ; and if such petition or claim shall be deserted, or upon a hearing be dismissed, the court may in its discretion award costs against the petitioner in favor of the adverse party.

RULE XLIV.

In cases where the court shall deem it expedient or necessary for the purposes of justice, the court may refer any matters arising in the progress of the suit to one or more commissioners, to be appointed by the court, to hear the parties and make report therein. And such commissioner or commissioners shall have and possess all the powers in the premises which are usually given to or exercised by masters in chancery in reference to them, including the power to administer oaths to and examine the parties and witnesses touching the premises.

RULE XLV.

All appeals from the district to the circuit court must be made while the court is sitting, or within such other period as shall be designated by the district court by its general rules, or by an order specially made in the particular suit.

RULE XLVI.

In all cases not provided for by the foregoing rules, the district and circuit courts are to regulate the practice of said courts respectively, in such manner as they shall deem most expedient for the due administration of justice in suits in admiralty.

RULE XLVII.

These rules shall be in force in all the circuit and district courts of the United States from and after the first day of September next.

It is ordered by the court, that the foregoing rules be and they are adopted and promulgated as rules for the regulation and government of the practice of the circuit courts and district courts of the United States in suits in admiralty on the instance side of the courts; and that the reporter of the court do cause the same to be published in the next volume of his reports; and that he do cause such additional copies thereof to be published, as he may deem expedient for the due information of the bar and bench in the respective districts and circuits.

RULES OF THE SUPREME COURT.

RULES OF THE PRACTICE OF THE SUPREME COURT OF THE UNITED STATES.

RULES AND ORDERS.

1.—FEBRUARY 3, 1790.

Ordered, That JOHN TUCKER, Esq., of Boston, be the Clerk of this Court.

That he reside and keep his office at the seat of the National Government, and that he do not practice either as an Attorney or Counsellor in this Court while he shall continue to be Clerk of the same.

2.—FEBRUARY 5, 1790.

Ordered, That (until further orders) it shall be requisite to the admission of Attorneys or Counsellors to practice in this Court, that they shall have been such for three years past in the Supreme Court of the State to which they respectively belong, and that their private and professional character shall appear to be fair.

3.—FEBRUARY 5, 1790.

Ordered, That Counsellors shall not practice as Attorneys, nor Attorneys as Counsellors, in this Court. (*See Rule* 14.)

4.—FEBRUARY 5, 1790.

Ordered, That they shall respectively take the following oath, viz : " I ___ do solemnly swear that I will demean myself (as an Attorney or Counsellor of the Court) uprightly, and according to law ; and that I will support the Constitution of the United States." (*See Rule* 6.)

5.—FEBRYARY 5, 1790.

Ordered, That (unless and until it shall otherwise be provided by law) all process of this Court shall be in the name of the President of the United States.

6.—FEBRUARY 7, 1791.

Ordered, That the Counsellors and Attorneys admitted to practice in this Court, shall take either an oath, or in proper cases, an affirmation, of the tenor prescribed by the rule of this Court on that subject, made February Term, 1790, viz: "I,   do solemnly swear, (or affirm, as the case may be,) that I will demean myself, as an Attorney or Counsellor of this Court, uprightly, and according to law; and that I will support the Constitution of the United States."

7.—AUGUST 8, 1791.

The Chief Justice, in answer to the motion of the Attorney General, made yesterday, informs him and the Bar, that this Court consider the practice of the Courts of King's Bench, and of Chancery, in England, as affording outlines for the practice of this Court; and that they will, from time to time, make such alterations therein as circumstances may render necessary.

8.—FEBRUARY 4, 1795.

The Court gave notice to the gentlemen of the Bar, that hereafter they will expect to be furnished with a statement of the material points of the case from the Counsel on each side of a cause. (*See Rule* 29.)

9.—FEBRUARY 17, 1795.

The Court declared, that all evidence on motion for a discharge upon bail must be by way of *deposition*, and not *viva voce*.

10.—AUGUST 12, 1796.

Ordered, That when process at Common Law, or in Equity, shall issue against a State, the same shall be served on the Governor, or Chief Executive Magistrate, and Attorney General of such State.

Ordered, That process of subpœna, issuing out of this Court, in any suit in Equity, shall be served on the defendant sixty days before the return day of the said process; and further, that if the defendant, on such service of the subpœna, shall not appear at the return day contuined therein, the complainant shall be at liberty to proceed *ex parte*.

11.—FEBRUARY 13, 1797.

It is ordered by the Court, that the Clerk of the Court to which any writ of error shall be directed, make return of the same, by transmitting a true copy of the record, and of all proceedings in the cause, under his hand and the seal of the Court. (*See Rule* 35.)

12.—AUGUST 7, 1797.

It is ordered by the Court, that no record of the Court be suffered by the Clerk to be taken out of his office, but by the consent of the Court; otherwise, to be responsible for it. (*See Rule* 35.)

13.—AUGUST 15, 1800.

IN THE CASE OF COURSE *vs.* STEAD'S EXECUTORS.

Ordered, That the plaintiff in error be at liberty to show, to the satisfaction of this Court, that the matter in dispute exceeds the sum or value of two thousand dollars, exclusive of costs; this to be made appear by affidavit, on   days' notice to the opposite party, or their Counsel in Georgia.

Rule as to affidavits to be be mutual.

14.—August 12, 1801.

Ordered, That Counsellors may be obtained as Attorneys in this Court on taking the usual oath. (*See Rule* 3.)

15.—December 9, 1801.

It is ordered, That in every case where the defendant in error fails to appear, the plaintiff may proceed *ex parte.* (*See Rules* 19 *and* 30.)

16.—February Term, 1803.

It is ordered, That where the writ of error issues within thirty days before the meeting of the Court, the defendant in error is at liberty to enter his appearance, and proceed to trial; otherwise, the cause must be continued. (*See Rules* 19 *and* 30.)

17.—February Term, 1803.

In all cases where a writ of error shall delay the proceedings on the judgment of the Circuit Court, and shall appear to have been sued out merely for delay, damages shall be awarded, at the rate of *ten per centum per annum* on the amount of the judgment. (*See Rule* 20.)

18.—February Term, 1803.

In such cases, where there exists a real controversy, the damages shall be only at the rate of *six per centum per annum.* In both cases the interest is to be computed as part of the damages. (*See Rule* 20.)

19.—February Term, 1806.

All causes, the records in which shall be delivered to the Clerk on or before the sixth day of a term, shall be considered as for trial in the course of that term. Where the record shall be delivered after the sixth day of that term, either party will be entitled to a continuance. In all cases where a writ of error shall be a supersedeas to a judgment rendered in any Circuit Court of the United States, except that for the District of Columbia, at least thirty days previous to the commencement of any term of this Court, it shall be the duty of the plaintiff in error to lodge a copy of the record with the Clerk of this Court within the first six days of the term; and if he shall fail so to do, the defendant in error shall be permitted afterwards to lodge a copy of the record with the Clerk, and the cause shall stand for trial in like manner as if the record had come up within the first six days; or he may, on producing a certificate from the Clerk, stating the cause, and that a writ of error has been sued out, which operates as a supersedeas to the judgment, have the said writ of error docketed and dismissed. This rule shall apply to all judgments rendered by the Court for the District of Columbia at any time prior to a session of this Court.

In cases not put in issue at the August term, it shall be the duty of the plaintiff in error, if errors shall not have been assigned in the Court below, to assign them in this Court at the commencement of the term, or so soon thereafter as the record shall be filed with the Clerk, and the cause placed on the docket; and if he shall fail so to do, and shall also fail to assign them when the cause shall be called for trial, the writ of error may be dismissed at his costs; and if the defendant shall refuse to plead to issue, and the cause shall be called for trial, the court may proceed to hear an argument on the part of the plaintiff, and to give judgment according to the right of the cause; and that where there is no appearance for the plaintiff in error, the defendant may have the plaintiff called, and dismiss the writ of error; or may open the record, and pray for an affirmance. In such a case *costs go of course.* Montalet *vs.* Murray. (*See Rules* 30 *and* 43.)

20.—FEBRUARY TERM, 1807.

It is ordered, That where damages are given by the rule passed in February term, 1803, the said damages shall be calculated to the day of the affirmance of the judgment in this Court. (*See Rules* 17 *and* 18.)

21.—FEBRUARY TERM, 1808.

1st. *Ordered,* That all parties of this Court, not being residents of the United States, shall give security for the costs accruing in this Court, to be entered on the record.

2d. *Ordered,* That upon the Clerk of this Court producing satisfactory evidence, by affidavit, or the acknowledgment of the parties or their sureties, of having served a copy of the bill of costs due by them respectively, in this Court, on such parties or their sureties, an attachment shall issue against such parties or sureties respectively, to compel payment of the said costs.

22.—FEBRUARY TERM, 1810.

Ordered, That upon the reversal of a judgment or decree of the Circuit Court, the party in whose favor the reversal is shall recover his costs in the Circuit Court.

23.—FEBRUARY TERM, 1812.

It is ordered, That only two Counsel be permitted to argue for each party, plaintiff and defendant, in a cause.

24.—FEBRUARY TERM, 1812.

There having been two Associate Justices of the Court appointed since its last session, *It is ordered,* that the following allotment be made to the Chief Justice and the Associate Justices of the said Supreme Court, among the circuits, agreeably to the act of Congress in such case made and provided; and that such allotment be entered on record, viz:

For the first circuit—the HON. JOSEPH STORY.

*For the second circuit—the Hon. BROCKHOLST LIVINGSTON.
For the third circuit—the Hon. BUSHROD WASHINGTON.
For the fourth circuit—the Hon. GABRIEL DUVALL.
For the fifth circuit—the Hon. JOHN MARSHALL, *C. J.*
For the sixth circuit—the Hon. WILLIAM JOHNSON.
For the seventh circuit—the Hon. THOMAS TODD.

25.—FEBRUARY TERM, 1816.

It is ordered by the Court, That in all cases where further proof is ordered by the Court, the depositions which shall be taken shall be by a commission to be issued from this Court, or from any Circuit Court of the United States. (*See Rule 27.*)

26.—FEBRUARY TERM, 1817.

Whenever it shall be necessary or proper, in the opinion of the presiding judge in any Circuit Court, or District Court exercising Circuit Court jurisdiction, that original papers of any kind should be inspected in the Supreme Court, upon appeal, such presiding judge may make such rule or order for the safe keeping, transporting, and return of such original papers, as to him may seem proper; and this Court will receive and consider such original papers in connection with the transcript of the proceedings.

27.—FEBRUARY TERM, 1817.

In all cases of admiralty and maritime jurisdiction, where new evidence shall be admissible in this Court, the evidence by testimony of witnesses shall be taken under a commission to be issued from this Court, or from any Circuit Court of the United States, under the direction of any judge thereof; and no such commission shall issue but upon interrogatories to be filed by the party applying for the commission, and notice to the opposite party or his agent or attorney, accompanied with a copy of the interrogatories so filed, to file cross interrogatories within twenty days from the service of such notice: *Provided, however,* that nothing in this rule shall prevent any party from giving oral testimony in open court in cases where, by law, it is admissible. (*See Rule 25.*)

28.—FEBRUARY TERM, 1821.

Whenever, pending a writ of error or appeal in this Court, either party shall die, the proper representatives in the personalty or realty of the deceased party, according to the nature of the case, may voluntarily come in and be admitted parties to the suit, and thereupon the cause shall be heard

---

*The Honorable SMITH THOMPSON having been appointed Associate Justice of the Supreme Court, in the place of the Honorable BROCKHOLST LIVINGSTON, deceased, the President of the United States assigned to him the second circuit, by instrument dated the   day of
A. D. one thousand eight hundred and twenty-three.

and determined as in other cases; and if such representatives shall not voluntarily become parties, then the other party may suggest the death on the record, and thereupon, upon motion, obtain an order, that unless such representatives shall become parties within the first ten days of the ensuing term, the party moving for such order, if defendant in error, shall be entitled to have the writ of error or appeal dismissed; and if the party so moving shall be plaintiff in error, he shall be entitled to open the record, and on hearing have the same reversed if it be erroneous: *Provided, however*, that a copy of every such order shall be printed in some newspaper at the seat of Government in which the laws of the United States shall be printed by authority, for three successive weeks, at least sixty days before the beginning of the term of the Supreme Court then next ensuing.—*March* 8, 1821.

29.—February Term, 1821.

Ordered, After the present term no cause standing for argument will be heard by the Court until the parties shall have furnished the court with a printed brief or abstract of the cause, containing the substance of all the material pleadings, facts, and documents on which the parties rely, and the points of law and fact intended to be presented at the argnment.—*March* 10, 1821. (*See Rule* 8.)

30.—February Term, 1821.

In all cases where a writ of error or an appeal shall be brought to this Court from any judgment or decree rendered thirty days before the term to which such writ of error or appeal shall be returnable, it shall be the duty of the plaintiff in error, or appellant, as the case may be, to docket the cause, and file the record thereof with the Clerk of this Court within the first six days of the term; on failure to do which, the defendant in error, or appellee, as the case may be, may docket the cause, and file a copy of the record with the Clerk, and thereupon the cause shall stand for trial in like manner as if the record had been duly filed within the first six days of the term; or at his option he may have the cause docketed and dismissed, upon producing a certificate from the Clerk of the Court wherein the judgment or decree was rendered, stating the cause, and certifying that such writ of error or appeal had been duly sued out and allowed.—*March* 14, 1821. (*See Rules* 19 *and* 43.)

31.—March 14, 1823.

No cause will hereafter be heard until a complete record, containing in itself, without reference *aliunde*, all the papers, exhibits, depositions, and other proceedings which are necessary to the hearing in this Court, shall be filed. (*See Rule* 11.)

32.—February Term, 1824.

No certiorari for diminution of the record shall be hereafter awarded in any cause, unless a motion therefor shall be made in writing, and the facts on which the same is founded shall, if not admitted by the other party, be verified by affidavit.   And all motions for such certiorari shall be made at the first term of the entry of the cause; otherwise, the same shall not be granted, unless upon special cause shown to the Court, accounting satisfactorily for the delay.

33.—FEBRUARY TERM, 1824.

In all cases of equity and admiralty jurisdiction heard in this Court, no objection shall hereafter be allowed to be taken to the admissibility of any deposition, deed, grant, or other exhibit found in the record as evidence, unless objection was taken thereto in the Court below and entered of record; but the same shall otherwise be deemed to have been admitted by consent.

34.—FEBRUARY TERM, 1824.

(*Rescinded.*)—On Saturday of each week during the sitting of the Court, motions in cases not required by the rules of the Court to be put upon the docket shall be entitled to preference, if such motions shall be made before the Court shall have entered upon the hearing of a cause upon the docket. (*See Rule* 50.)

35.—FEBRUARY TERM, 1825.

Ordered, That after the present term no original record shall be taken from the Supreme Court Room, or from the office of the Clerk of this Court. —*February* 19.   (*See Rule* 12.)

36.—JANUARY TERM, 1830.

The Court, on the second day in each term hereafter, will commence calling the cases for argument in the order in which they stand on the docket, and proceed from day to day during the term, in the same order; and if the parties, or either of them, shall be ready when the case is called, the same will be heard; and if neither party shall be ready to proceed in the argument, the cause shall go down to the foot of the docket, unless some good and satisfactory reason to the contrary shall be shown to the Court. That ten causes only shall be considered as liable to be called on each day during the term, including the one under argument, if the same shall not be concluded on the preceding day.   No cause shall be taken up out of the order on the docket, or be set down for any particular day, except under special and peculiar circumstances to be shown to the Court.   Every cause which shall have been twice called in its order, and passed, and put at the foot of the docket, shall, if not again reached during the term it was called, be continued to the next term of the court.

37.—JANUARY TERM, 1831.

1. In all cases the Clerk shall take of the plaintiff a bond with competent security, to respond to costs, in the penalty of two hundred dollars; or a deposite of that amount to be placed in bank subject to his draft.

2. In all cases the Clerk shall have fifteen copies of the records printed for the Court, provided the Government will admit the item in the expenses of the Court.

3. In all cases the Clerk shall deliver a copy of the printed record to each party. And in cases of dismission (except for want of jurisdiction) or affirmance, one copy of the record shall be taxed against the plaintiff, which charge includes the charge for the copy furnished him.

In case of reversal and dismission for want of jurisdiction, each party shall be charged with one-half the legal fees for a copy.

38.—JANUARY TERM, 1832.

It is ordered by the Court, That hereafter, the Judges of the Circuit and District Courts do not allow any bill of exceptions, which shall contain the charge of the Court at large to the jury in trials at common law, upon any general exception to the whole of such charge. But that the party excepting be required to state distinctly the several matters of law in such charge to which he excepts; and that such matters of law, and those only, be inserted in the bill of exceptions, and allowed by the Court.

39.—JANUARY TERM, 1833.

1. *It is ordered by the Court,* That during the session of the Court, any gentleman of the bar having a cause on the docket, and wishing to use any book or books in the Law Library, shall be at liberty, upon application to the Clerk of the Court, to receive an order to take the same (not exceeding at any one time three) from the Library, he being thereby responsible for the due return of the same within a reasonable time, or when required by the Clerk. And it shall be the duty of the Clerk to keep, in a book for that purpose, a record of all books so delivered, which are to be charged against the party receiving the same. And in case the same shall not be so returned, the party receiving the same shall be responsible for, and forfeit and pay twice the value thereof; as also one dollar per day for each day's detention beyond the limited time.

2. *It is ordered by the Court,* That during the session of the Court, any Judge thereof may take from the Law Library any book or books he may think proper, he being responsible for the due return thereof.

40.—JANUARY TERM, 1833.

Whereas, It has been represented to the Court, that it would in many cases accommodate Counsel, and save expense to parties, to submit causes upon printed arguments. It is therefore

Ordered, That in all cases brought here on appeal, writ of error, or otherwise, the Court will receive printed arguments, if the Counsel on either or both sides shall chose so to submit the same. (*See Rules* 44 *and* 51.)

41.—1834.

Ordered, That the original opinions of the Court, delivered to the reporter, be filed in the office of the Clerk of the Court for preservation as soon as the volume of Reports for the term, at which they are delivered, shall be published.

42 —1835.

All the opinions delivered by the Court since the commencement of the term shall be forthwith delivered over to the Clerk to be recorded.

And all opinions hereafter delivered by the Court shall immediately, upon the delivery thereof, be in like manner delivered over to the Clerk to be recorded. And it shall be the duty of the Clerk to cause the same to be forthwith recorded, and to deliver the originals with a transcript of the judgment or decree of the Court thereon to the reporter, as soon as the same shall be recorded.

And all the opinions of the Court, as far as practicable, be recorded during the term, so that the publication of the reports may not be delayed thereby.

43.—1835.

1. In all cases where a writ of error, or an appeal, shall be brought to this Court from any judgment or decree rendered thirty days before the commencement of the term, it shall be the duty of the plaintiff in error, or appellant, as the case may be, to docket the cause and file the record thereof with the Clerk of this Court within the first six days of the term. If he shall fail so to do, the defendant in error, or appellee, as the case may be, may docket the cause and file a copy of the record with the Clerk, in which case it shall stand for argument at the term; or at his option he may have the cause docketed and dismissed upon producing a certificate from the Clerk of the Court, wherein the judgment or decree was rendered, stating the cause, and certifying that such writ of error or appeal, had been duly sued out and allowed.

2. No writ of error or appeal shall be docketed, or the record of the cause filed by the plaintiff in error, or appellant, after the first six days of the term, except upon the terms that the cause shall stand for argument during the term, or be continued at the option of the defendant in error, or appellee. But in no case shall the plaintiff in error, or appellant, be entitled to docket the cause and file the record, after the same shall have been docketed and dismissed in the manner provided for in the preceding rule, unless by order of the Court or with the consent of the opposite party.

3. In all cases where the cause shall not be docketed and the record filed with the Clerk by either party until after thirty days from the commencement of the term, the cause shall stand continued until the next term. (*See Rules* 19 *and* 30.)

44.—1837.

When a printed argument shall be filed for one or both parties, the case shall stand on the same footing as if there were an appearance by Counsel. (*See Rule* 51.)

45.—1838.

In all cases where any suit shall be dismissed in this Court, except where the dismissal shall be for want of jurisdiction, costs shall be allowed for the defendant in error, or appellee, as the case may be, unless otherwise agreed by the parties.

In all cases of affirmance of any judgment or decree in this Court, costs shall be allowed to the defendant in error or appellee, as the case may be, unless otherwise ordered by the Court.

In all cases of reversals of any judgment or decree in this Court, except where the reversal shall be for want of jurisdiction, costs shall be allowed in this Court for the plaintiff in error or appellant, as the case may be, unless otherwise ordered by the Court.

Neither of the foregoing rules shall apply to cases where the United States are a party; but in such cases no costs shall be allowed in this Court for or against the United States.

In all cases of the dismissal of any suit in this Court, it shall be the duty of the Clerk to issue a mandate, or other proper process, in the nature of a procedendo, to the Court-below, for the purpose of informing such Court of the proceedings in this Court, so that further proceedings may be had in such Court as to law and justice may appertain.

When costs are allowed in this Court, it shall be the duty of the Clerk to insert the amount thereof in the body of the mandate, or other proper process, sent to the Court below, and annex to the same the bill of items taxed in detail.

46.—1838.

All motions hereafter made to the Court shall be reduced to writing, and shall contain a brief statement of the facts and objects of the motion.

47.—1838.

The Court will, at every future session, announce on what day it will adjourn at least ten days before the time which shall be fixed upon; and the Court will take up no case for argument, nor receive any case upon printed briefs, within three days next before the day fixed upon for adjournment.

48.—1841.

Ordered, That the Clerk take charge of the books of the Court, together with such of the duplicate law books as Congress may direct to be transferred to the Court, and arrange them in the Conference room, which he shall have fitted up in a proper manner; and that he do not permit such books to be taken therefrom, by any one, except the judges of the court.

49.—1842.

(*Rescinded.*)—*Ordered*, That printed arguments will not be received under the fortieth rule of the court, unless filed within forty days from the commencement of the Term, except in cases which are reached in the regular call of the docket. (*See Rule 52.*)

50.—DECEMBER TERM, 1844.

Ordered, That the court will not hear arguments on Saturday, (unless for special cause it shall order to the contrary,) but will devote that day to the other business of the court; and that on Friday in each week, during the sitting of the Court, motions in cases not required by the Rules of the Court to be put on the docket shall be entitled to preference, if such motions shall be made before the Court shall have entered on the hearing of a cause upon the docket; and the Rule No. 34, adopted at February Term, 1824, be, and the same is hereby, rescinded.

51.—DECEMBER TERM, 1844.

Ordered, That no printed or written argument be hereafter received, unless thn same shall be signed by an attorney or counsellor of this court.

52.—DECEMBER TERM, 1844.

Ordered, That printed arguments, under the fortieth Rule, will be received hereafter, and at the present Term, until the first Monday in February in each and every term, while the Supreme Court continues to meet on the first Monday in December; and that the forty-ninth rule of the Court, adopted at January Term, 1842, be, and the same is hereby, rescinded.

53.

Ordered, That no counsel will be permitted to speak, on the argument of any case in this court, more than two hours, without the special leave of the court, granted before the argument begins.

Counsel will not be heard, unless a printed abstract of the case be first filed, together with the points intended to be made, and the authorities intended to be cited in support of them, arranged under their respective points, and no other book or case can be referred to in the argument.

If one of the parties omits to file such a statement he cannot be heard, and the case will be heard *ex parte*, upon the argument of the party by whom the statement is filed.

This rule to take effect on the first day of December Term, 1849.

Woodbury, J., does not concur in this rule.

54.—DECEMBER TERM, 1849.

Ordered, That where an appearance is not entered on the record for either the plaintiff or defendant on or before the second day of the term next succeeding that at which the case is docketed, it shall be dismissed at the costs of the plaintiff.

55.

Ordered, When a case is called for argument at two successive terms, and upon the call at the second term neither party is prepared to argue it, it shall be dismissed at the costs of the plaintiff, unless sufficient cause is shown for further postponement.

DISTRICT COURT RULES AND INDEX.

RULES

OF THE DISTRICT COURT OF THE UNITED STATES FOR THE SOUTHERN DISTRICT OF NEW YORK.

RULE 1.

A libel, information, or petition, must state plainly the facts upon which relief is sought, without any repetitions or amplification of charges.

RULE 2.

No process shall issue until the pleading or statement in writing upon which it is allowed be duly filed.

RULE 3.

Libels, (except on behalf of the United States,) praying an attachment *in personam* or *in rem*, or demanding the answer of any party on oath, shall be verified by oath, or affirmation.

RULE 4.

The oath, or affirmation, of the party himself, in all cases where one is necessary, shall be required to pleadings filed in his name, except as is here-after otherwise provided, or as shall be specially ordered by the judge.

RULE 5.

Libels, informations, or petitions, praying a monition or citation only without attachment, need not be sworn to.

RULE 6.

Libels, and other proceedings to be filed, shall be plainly and fairly en-grossed, without erasures or interlineations materially defacing them. If papers not conforming to this Rule are offered, the clerk shall require the *allocatur* of the judge to be endorsed thereon before he receives them on the files.

RULE 7.

Amendments, or supplementary matters, must be connected with the libel or other pleading by appropriate references, without a recapitulation or restatement of the pleading amended or added to.

RULE 8.

In suits for seamen's wages, any mariner in the same voyage not made a party, may by short petition to the court in any stage of the cause previous to the final distribution of the fund in court, or discharge of the defendant and his sureties, be joined as libellant in the cause, but no costs shall be allowed for the proceedings taken to make him a party.

RULE 9.

The proctor in the original cause shall not, however, be compelled to proceed in behalf of such petitioning mariner, unless a reasonable indemnity is offered for such costs as may be incurred in consequence of his being joined in the cause.

RULE 10.

In case of salvage and other causes civil and maritime, persons entitled to participate in the recovery, but not made parties in the original libel, may upon petition be admitted to prosecute as co-libellants on such terms as the court may deem reasonable.

RULE 11.

Process on libels or informations may be made returnable on any day at a stated or special term, but writs for the sale of property under any order or decree of the court, and all final process, shall be returnable at a stated term, unless upon cause shown an earlier day is specially appointed by the judge.

RULE 12.

Tuesday of each week is appointed as a special sessions of the court, (except the stated term be then in session,) at which the same proceedings may be taken, in causes of admiralty and maritime jurisdiction, as at a stated term.

RULE 13.

Process to be used in commencing suits shall be a *citation* or *monition*; an *attachment in rem*, united with a *monition*, or, by special allowance of the judge, with an *attachment in personam*; an *attachment in personam* and *a writ of foreign attachment.*

RULE 14.

Where no specific process is provided by the Rules, parties may have such process as is in use in like cases in the supreme court of the state.

RULE 15.

Where it is not desired to arrest a defendant, the clerk on filing a libel or information may at the instance of the actor issue a citation or monition, according to the usage in civil and admiralty proceedings.

Rule 16.

No process *in personam* for the arrest of any person, in cases of torts or unliquidated damages, shall issue, except upon the mandate of the judge.

Rule 17.

In cases of liquidated damages, when the certainty and amount of the demand appear upon the face of the libel, an attachment *in personam* may be issued by the clerk without an order. The attachment shall plainly express the cause of action and the amount of the demand, and the clerk shall endorse thereon the sum for which bail is required, not exceeding one hundred dollars above the sum sworn to be due and unpaid ; but no attachment or citation shall be issued until the libellant shall have filed a stipulation for costs in the sum of one hundred dollars, (except in suits by the United States.)

Rule 18.

On the return of a citation or warrant by the marshal "*served personally*," the party shall be deemed in court, and may be proceeded against accordingly.

Rule 19.

When the citation or monition in suits *in personam* is not served personally, the libellant may at his election pursue the defendant to a decree of contumacy, in which decree may be embraced an order for the attachment of the defendant as for contempt of process ; or, on verifying by oath the matters demanded by the libel, the libellant may have an attachment *in personam instanter*, on the return of the citation "*not served.*"

Rule 20.

In the latter case all subsequent proceedings may be as if the attachment had been sued out in the first instance.

Rule 21.

On warrants to arrest the person in admiralty and maritime causes, the marshall may take bail in the form of a stipulation and in the sum endorsed on the warrant, conditioned for the appearance of the party on the return day to answer to the libellant in a cause civil and maritime, according to the course of the court.

Rule 22.

The sureties having made oath thereon to their sufficiency, and the bail stipulation being filed, it shall have the same effect in favor of ths actor and against the defendant as if taken in court ; and the marshal shall be deemed discharged of all personal responsibility for the appearance of the respondent.

Rule 23.

In case the marshal does not file such stipulation, or the sureties, being required, refuse to justify, like proceedings may be taken to compel the marshal to bring in the party, as if no stipulation had been entered into.

RULE 24.

The condition of the stipulation shall be deemed satisfied if the party shall appear in person on the return day of the warrant and submit himself for commitment, or enter into the usual stipulation in the cause, according to the course of the court.

RULE 25.

If a party against whom a warrant of arrest issues cannot be found and return thereof be made, the plaintiff may upon the mandate of the judge have a warrant to attach the property of the defendant, and may also have inserted therein a clause of foreign attachment, according to the course of the admiralty.

RULE 26.

In all cases of attachment under admiralty process to compel an appearance, the attachment may be dissolved on the party's giving a stipulation with sureties, to the same effect as in cases of arrest.

RULE 27.

In cases of foreign attachment, if the defendant appear, the same proceedings may be had as is usual in suits *in personam*, and if he make default, the court will proceed *ex parte*, and pronounce the proper decree, unless the attachment is discharged at the instance of the garnishee.

RULE 28.

Process cannot issue against goods, *choses in action* or moneys in the hands of third persons, except by the order of the judge and upon due proof of the claim first made; and the names of such persons and also of the persons whose effects are to be attached, together with a specification of such effects, shall be expressed in the process.

RULE 29.

On the service of the attachment by arrest of property, the parties holding the property or funds attached, shall on the return day of such process file an affidavit containing a full and true statement of the property or funds in their hands belonging to the principal party at the time the attachment was served and at the time the deposition is made, and declare whether they have any, and if any, what claim to any and what part thereof; and shall then, on motion of the actor, pay into court such amount as they shall not claim, or as may be ordered by the court, or give stipulation, with sufficient surety to abide the further order or decree of the court in relation thereto; and on their default in this behalf a rule may be entered that an attachment issue against them unless they shall show cause in four days or on the first day the court is in session afterwards.

Rule 30.

When the property, effects or credits named in the process are not delivered up to the marshal by the garnishee or trustee, or are denied by him to be the property of the party, it shall be a sufficient service of such foreign attachment to leave a copy thereof with such trustee, or at his residence or usual place of business, unless the libellant shall by competent surety indemnify the marshal for arresting the property pointed out to him.

Rule 31.

On the return by the marshal of service of such attachment by notice and copy with the reason thereof, the libellant may move the court for a peremptory attachment or such order as the equity of the case may demand; or on proof satisfactory to the court that the property, &c. belongs to the defendant, may proceed to a hearing and final decree in the cause as if the property had been held in arrest.

Rule 32.

All process to the marshal shall be returned on the return day thereof, and if he shall not return the same in four days after being required in writing so to do, by any person or his proctor, upon affidavit of such requirement and of the delivery of the process to him, an order may be entered of course that he show cause why an attachment shall not issue against him; and in the case of process *in rem*, the return of the marshal shall express the day of the seizure of the property or the day of sale, if a process for that object.

Rule 33.

No process shall be received on file unless duly returned by the officer to whom directed.

Rule 34.

In case the court is not in session at the return of process requiring to be acted on in open court, proceedings shall be deemed continued to the next sitting of the court, (either stated or special,) at which time the like proceedings may be had thereupon as if then returnable.

Rule 35.

On proclamation after due return of process, the libellant shall be entitled to a decree of default or contumacy, according to the nature of the case, and the three proclamations heretofore used are abolished.

Rule 36.

In case of the attachment of property, or the arrest of the person in causes of civil and admiralty jurisdiction, (except in suits for seamen's wages when the attachment is issued upon certificate pursuant to the act of Congress of July 20, 1790,) the party arrested, or any person having a right to intervene in respect to the thing attached, may upon evidence showing any improper practices or a manifest want of equity on the part of the libellant, have a mandate from the judge for the libellant to show cause *instanter* why the arrest or attachment should not be vacated.

RULE 37.

Stipulations may be taken, in admiralty and maritime causes out of court before the clerk or a commissioner, under a *dedimus potestatem.* The officer taking the stipulation shall, if required by the opposite party, examine the sureties on oath and decide as to their competency. An appeal may be taken *instanter* to the judge, in case the decision is against the sufficiency of the sureties.

RULE 38.

The conditions of stipulations in causes *in personam* shall be that the principal, whenever required by this court or an appellate court in case of appeal, shall appear and answer to the cause or to interrogatories, and pay all costs that may be decreed against him, and by the respondent or defendant that he will also perform and abide all orders and decrees in the cause interlocutory or final, or deliver himself personally for commitment in execution of such orders, to the proper officer.

RULE 39.

The amount of stipulations on the part of the defendants in causes *in personam*, shall be the sum endorsed on the warrant, and *in rem* on the delivery of property attached the appraised or agreed value of the property seized, unless the sum in either case is modified or enlarged by order of the court.

RULE 40.

Application may be made instanter to the judge after an arrest *in personam*, to mitigate the amount of the bail stipulation ; and like application may be made at any time after property has been delivered on bail stipulation, upon facts occurring after such delivery, to discharge such stipulation or to reduce the amount according to the equity of the case, previous notice of the application having been given the proctor of the libellant.

RULE 41.

Two days' notice shall be given the proctor of the libellant, of applications for delivering up on stipulation property under attachment, specifying the sureties intended to be given and their occupations and places of residence and the officer before whom and the place where the stipulation will be offered, except in suits by seamen for wages, when such notice may be *instanter*.

RULE 42.

The stipulation or bond to be given upon releasing and delivering up property arrested by process of the court, shall be conditioned that the claimant and his sureties shall at any time upon the interlocutory order or decree of the court, or of any appellate court to which the cause may proceed, and on notice of such order to the proctor of the party to whom the property shall have been delivered bring into court the appraised or agreed value of such property or any part thereof so ordered or decreed. If no proctor is employed by such party, the order or decree shall be deemed peremptory two days after the same is entered.

RULE 43.

The clerk shall provide a book in which shall be registered all stipulations filed in causes civil and admiralty which shall be open to the examination of all parties interested.

RULE 44.

No process *in rem* shall be issued, nor shall any appearance or answer be received or third party be permitted to intervene and claim, (except on the part of the United States,) unless a stipulation in the sum of two hundred and fifty dollars shall be first entered into by the party and at least one surety resident in the district, conditioned that the principal shall pay all costs awarded against him by this court, or in case of appeal, by the appellate court.

RULE 45.

But seamen suing *in rem* for wages in their own right and for their own benefit for services on board American vessels, and salvors coming into port in possession of the property libelled, shall not be required to give such security in the first instance. The court on motion with notice to the libellants may, after the arrest of the property, for adequate cause order the usual stipulation to be given in these cases, or that the property arrested be discharged.

RULE 46.

Notice of the arrest of property by attachment *in rem*, in behalf of individual suitors, shall be published and affixed in the manner directed by act of Congress in cases of seizures on the part of the United States, except when the judge by special order directs a shorter notice than fourteen days; and except that, instead of the substance of the libel a short statement of its purport may be given.

RULE 47.

Notice of sale of property after condemnation in suits *in rem*, (except under the revenue laws and on seizure by the United States,) shall be six days, unless otherwise specially directed in the decree of condemnation and sale.

RULE 48.

All such notices shall be published in the manner directed by act of Congress, in the case of condemnation under the revenue laws.

Rule 49.

The marshal shall be allowed, (in conformity to the former usage of the court,) one dollar and fifty cents per day for the custody of a vessel, her tackle, apparel and furniture, seized by any officer of the revenue, and seized, libelled and prosecuted for forfeiture.

Rule 50.

He shall be allowed for the custody of goods so seized, on all sums not exceeding $5000, held in custody less than thirty days, two per cent; on all sums exceeding $5000, held in custody less than thirty days, one per cent, on all sums not exceeding $5000, held in custody over thirty days, two and a half per cent, and on all sums exceeding $5000, held in custody over thirty days, one and a half per cent: except on attachment of specie, bullion, jewelry or precious stones, the allowance to the marshal shall be specifically fixed by the court, having regard to the special circumstances of each case.

Rule 51.

The marshal may have like allowances taxed on all other attachments of property in causes of civil and admiralty jurisdiction.

Rule 52.

All the above allowances are, however, subject to alteration by the court on motion, due notice thereof being given the opposite party and adequate cause being shown therefor.

Rule 53.

The allowance to the marshal above appointed for the custody of goods, shall be computed upon the gross proceeds in case of sale; or upon the appraised or agreed value if bonded: but the marshal, in case of an agreed valuation between the parties not assented to by him, may have an appraisement in the usual mode.

Rule 54.

If attachments *in rem* are accompanied by written instructions to the marshal, specifying the sum demanded, (adding thereto $250 to cover costs,) he shall as in case of executions, only arrest so much of the goods or effects to be seized (when severable) as shall be sufficient to satisfy such amounts.

Rule 55.

In all cases of stipulations in civil and Admiralty causes, any party having an interest in the subject matter may move the court, on special cause shown, for greater or better security, giving the opposite party two days notice thereof, unless a shorter time is allowed by order of the judge.

Rule 56.

After a citation or monition or warrant of arrest in suits *in personam* returned " *served personally*," if the defendant do not appear at the return day he shall be deemed in contumacy and in default, and the libellant may take order for enforcement of the stipulation, (in case any is given,) or to compel the defendant's appearance, according to the course of Admiralty proceedings: or at his option may proceed to hearing *ex parte*, and obtain the proper decree, unless the court, for good cause, shall allow the defendant further time.

Rule 57.

In suits *in personam*, stipulators to the marshal on the arrest of the defendant may be discharged from their stipulation on the surrender of the principal, as in cases of bail at law.

Rule 58.

So also stipulators or *fide-jussores* after the return of the attachment, in suits *in personam*, may surrender their principal, or he may surrender himself, in discharge of the stipulation, as in cases of special bail at law : except in respect to costs in this court, or any other court to which the cause may be appealed.

Rule 59.

All stipulations in causes civil and maritime shall be executed by the principal party, (if within the district,) and at least one surety resident therein, and shall contain the consent of the stipulators, that in case of default or contumacy on the part of the principal or sureties, execution to the amount named in such stipulation may issue against the goods, chattels and lands of the stipulators.

The court will modify the execution as to the time it may stay and the amount to be collected, according to the equity of the case. Non-resident parties must supply at least two sureties.

Rule 60.

In case of seizure of property in behalf of the United States, an appraisement for the purpose of bonding the same may be had by any party in interest, on giving one day's previous notice of motion before the court, or the judge, in vacation, for the appointment of appraisers.

Rule 61.

If the parties, or their proctors, and the district attorney are present in court, such motion may be made *instanter* after seizure and without previous notice.

Rule 62.

Orders for the appraisement of property under arrest, at the suit of an individual, may be entered of course by the clerk at the instance of any party interested therein, or upon filing the consent of the proctors for the respective parties.

Rule 63.

Only one appraiser is to be appointed in suits by individuals, unless otherwise specially ordered by the judge, and if the respective parties do not agree in writing upon the appaiser to be appointed, the clerk shall forthwith name him, either party having a right of appeal *instanter* to the judge from such nomination, for adequate cause.

Rule 64.

In case vessels, their tackle or appurtenances, are to be appraised, the clerk shall name a warden of the port, and in case of merchandise, an appraiser or an assistant appraiser of the custom house, as appraiser.

Rule 65.

In suits *in rem* for seamen's wages, and in all other actions *in rem* for sums certain, the claimant or respondent may pay into court the amount sworn to be due in the libel, with interest computed thereon from the time it was due to the stated term next succeeding the return day of the attachment, and the costs of the officers of court already accrued, together with the sum of $250 to cover further costs, &c., &c.; or, at his option, may give stipulation to pay such sworn amount with interest, costs and damages, (first paying into court the costs of the officers of court already accrued,) and in either case may thereupon have an order entered *instanter* for delivery of the property arrested—without having the same appraised.

Rule 66.

Appraisers, before executing their trust, shall be sworn or affirmed to its faithful discharge before the clerk or his deputy, (who are hereby appointed commissioners for the qualification of appraisers,) and shall give one day's previous notice of the time and place of making the appraisement, by affixing the same in a conspicuous place adjacent to the United States' Courts Rooms, and where the marshal usually affixes his notices, to the end that all persons concerned may be informed thereof, and the appaisement when made shall be returned to the clerk's office.

Rule 67.

Appraisers acting under an order of this court shall be severally entitled to three dollars for each day necessarily employed in making the appraisement; to paid by the party at whose instance the same shall be ordered.

Rule 68.

No vessels, goods, wares or merchandise in the custody of the marshal shall be released from detention upon appraisement and surety, until the costs and charges of the officers of this court, so far as the same shall have accrued, shall first be paid into court by the party at whose instance the appraisement shall take place, to abide the decision of the court in respect to such costs.

Rule 69.

No property in the custody of any officer of the court shall be delivered up without the order of the court; but such order may be entered of course by the clerk on filing a written consent thereto by the proctor in whose behalf it is detained: and also, after appraisement and bond duly executed.

RULE 70.

If in *possessory* suits, after decrees for either party, the other shall make application to the court for a proceeding in a *petitory* suit, and file the proper stipulation, the property shall not be delivered over to the prevailing party until after an appraisement made, nor until he shall give a stipulation, with sureties, to restore the same property, without waste, in case his adversary shall prevail in the petitory suit, and also to abide as well all interlocutory orders and decrees, as the final sentence and decree of the District Court, and on appeal, of the appellate court.

RULE 71.

In all cases where a judgment or decree is entered on a bond or stipulation filed with the clerk for the appraised or agreed value of any property libelled in this court, the clerk shall receive in addition to the amount of the bond, interest at the rate of six per cent. per annum, for the time which shall intervene between the entry of the judgment, or date of the stipulation, and the day when the money shall be paid into court.

RULE 72.

A tender *inter partes* shall be of no avail on defence or in discharge of costs, unless on suit brought, and before answer, plea or claim filed, the same tender is deposited in court to abide the order or decree to be made in the matter.

RULE 73.

When tender is first made, after suit brought, it must include taxable costs then accrued.

RULE 74.

No third party can intervene by claim without proof of a subsisting interest in the subject matter of the claim. This proof may, in the first instance, be the oath of the claimant, but subject to denial and disproof on the part of the libellant, on issue thereto or on summary petition.

RULE 75.

Double pleas, or exceptions, replications to pleas, triplications or rejoinders, &c., may be filed without previous leave of the court, the pleading of several matters being restricted to cases in which the matters are distinct.

RULE 76.

Defence may be made by answer or claim, of matters of law or fact, without the employment of exceptions or special pleas usual in causes of civil and maritime jurisdiction, other than exceptions to the competency of the party, or the process or other matter of abatement.

RULE 77.

If matter of bar at law to the libel is set up by answer or claim and allowed by the court, no costs shall be taxed for any other part of the answer or claim than that stating such bar.

RULE 78.

When the answer alleges a bar in law to the whole libel, it may be treated as a plea and set down for hearing, without filing a replication other than to such bar or going into proofs upon the issues in fact.

RULE 79.

Where a party not required to answer intervenes by claim and answer, costs will be taxed for the claims only.

RULE 80.

When an answer is required in a suit *in rem* of a party having no interest in the subject matter, he may file an exceptive allegation or disclaimer, and notice the same *instanter* for hearing. If the decree of the court is an affirmance of his plea, he shall be discharged the action with costs.

RULE 81.

One improperly joined as defendant in an action *in personam*, may have a decree of discharge in the same manner ; provided, it is made satisfactorily to appear to the court that he can give material testimony as a witness in the cause.

RULE 82.

When the claim is in derogation of the right set up by the libel, it may form a general issue therewith by denying "that the libellant is entitled to the remedy and relief in the premises sought by him," without traversing or admitting the several articles of the libel.

RULE 83.

A general issue may be taken by answer in like manner when the answer is not required to be under oath.

RULE 84.

So also the libel may be contested affirmatively by a general issue instead of a formal demurrer.

RULE 85.

When a general issue is taken to the libel in open court on the return day of process, either party may have the cause placed upon the calendar *instanter*, and it may be called in its place for proofs without other notice.

RULE 86.

Each party is entitled to like proceedings in such case, as if the cause had been noticed by each, pursuant to the usual practice.

Rule 87.

A sworn answer is not to be deemed higher evidence than the libel or information to which it responds, unless made so by the act of the promovent. An answer need not be put in under oath unless so required by a sworn libel, or one filed by the United States.

Rule 88.

The matter set up by a sworn answer responsive to the allegations or interrogatories of the libel, shall be deemed admitted on the part of the libellant, unless within four days from the time the answer is perfected, or from the expiration of the time allowed for excepting thereto, replication is filed, or a written notice served on the proctor of the respondent, that on the trial of the cause proof will be offered on the part of the libellant in opposition to the allegations of the answer. No replication need be filed for any other purpose, to an answer taking an issue in fact upon the allegations of the libel.

Rule 89.

A claim or answer may be put in and filed at any time after the service of process and before defaults entered : and when it shall be put in at any other time than on making proclamation, notice of the time of filing it shall be given the libellant, otherwise he shall not be bound to regard it.

Rule 90.

If separate answers or claims are put in by the same proctor, or by different proctors being connected in business, all costs thereby unnecessarily incurred shall be disallowed on taxation.

Rule 91.

An answer or claim on the part of the United States is to be put in without oath by the district attorney, and is not subject to exception for insufficiency.

Rule 92.

In the case of bailable process *in personam,* unless the defendant appear and put in bail stipulation according to the rules of the court, his claim or answer may be treated as a nullity, and his defaults be entered. An answer in such case shall be deemed filed from the time bail becomes perfected.

Rule 93.

On due proof that a claimant or respondent is absent from the United States, or resides out of the district, and more than one hundred miles from the city of New York, a claim or answer to a libel may be sworn to by a proctor or attorney in fact in behalf of such party. And if thereupon the libellant, by written notice to the respondent, demands a personal answer verified by the oath of the party, proceedings shall stay a reasonable time to enable such answer to be taken by commission or *dedimus potestatem*.

The provisions of this rule may also be applied to the verification of a libel, by the oath of a proctor or attorney in fact.

Rule 94.

The defendant may on the return day of process and before answering, demurring or pleading, file an exception to the libel that is multifarious or ambiguous, or without plain allegations upon which issue can be taken, and if it be adjudged by the court insufficient for any of these causes, and be not amended by the libellant within two days thereafter, it shall be dismissed with costs.

Rule 95.

Proceedings upon such exceptions shall conform to those on exceptions to answers or other pleadings.

Rule 96.

The libellant may, within four days from the filing of the answer or claim, file exceptions thereto for insufficiency, irrelevancy or scandal, which exceptions shall briefly and clearly specify the parts excepted to by the line and page of the papers in the clerk's office: whereupon the party answering or claiming shall in four days either give notice to the libellant of his submitting to the exceptions, or set down the exceptions for hearing, and give four days notice thereof for the earliest day of jurisdiction afterwards. In default whereof the like order may be entered as if the exceptions had been allowed by the court.

Rule 97.

If a party submit to exceptions for insufficiency, he shall answer further within four days after notice of his submitting. If the exceptions are allowed on hearing, he shall answer further within such time as the court shall direct ; and if the hearing of the exceptions shall not be duly brought on, or the further answer duly put in, the claim or answer excepted to shall be treated as a nullity, and the default of the party be entered.

Rule 98.

If exceptions for irrelevancy be submitted to, or be allowed by the court, or the hearing be not duly brought on by the respondent, the matter excepted to shall be struck out of the claim or answer by the clerk.

Rule 99.

Either party may propound interrogatories to the other, within four days from the putting in of the claim, or answer, or other pleading, and the perfecting of the same, if excepted to.

Rule 100.

A copy of the interrogatories shall be served on the party for whom the same are intended, or his proctor, if one be employed; and if he object thereto, he shall notify the party serving the same, who shall on due notice submit the same to the judge for his allowance. The interrogatories allowed shall be filed with the clerk, and notice thereof be given, and the party shall file his answer thereto in ten days after such notice; in default whereof, if libellant, the libel shall be dismissed; if claimant or defendant, the claim or answer shall be treated as a nullity, and default may be entered against such party.

Rule 101.

Answers to interrogatories may be excepted to in the same manner as answers or claims put in by a defendant, and shall, in all respects, be subject to the provisions of the rules in relation to exceptions; and if the libellant making answers shall not perfect the same after exception, the libel shall be dismissed for want of prosecution. But this rule and the preceding one shall not in any case be deemed to require answers to interrogatories on the part of the United States in suits brought in their behalf.

Rule 102.

The oath of calumny shall not be required of any party in any stage of a cause.

Rule 103.

Suits may be joined or consolidated upon the same principle as in the practice of the court at common law.

Rule 104.

When various actions are pending, all resting upon the same matter of right or defence, the court by order at its discretion, will compel the parties to abide by the decision rendered in one case, and will enter a decree in the other causes conformably thereto, although there be no common interest between the parties.

Rule 105.

Commissions for taking testimony, if not sued out pursuant to the rules of the circuit court, shall be moved for in four days after the claim or answer is filed and perfected, (if the same shall have been excepted to,) but if interrogatories shall be propounded for the other party, by the party who moves for a commission, he shall have four days for moving after the answers to the interrogatories shall be perfected, otherwise such commissions shall not operate to stay proceedings; but, on a proper case shown, application for a commission may be made at any time after the action is commenced and before issue joined, or after a default or interlocutory decree.

Rule 106.

Affidavits on which a motion for a commission is made, shall specify the facts expected to be proved, and the shortest time within which the party believes the testimony may be taken and the commission returned.

RULE 107.

A commission will not be allowed to stay proceedings, if the opposite party admits in writing that the witnesses will depose to the facts stated in such affidavit; such affidavit, with the admission, may be read on the trial or hearing, and will have the same effect as a deposition to those facts by the witness or witnesses named.

RULE 108.

The motion may be noticed and made at term before the court, or in vacation before the judge out of court; and only one commissioner will be named, unless special cause is shown for appointing a greater number, nor will costs be taxed for the services of more than one, except where both parties require a greater number.

RULE 109.

Interrogatories for the direct and cross-examination, in case the parties disagree respecting them, shall be presented to the judge for his allowance at one time, and one day's notice of such reference shall be given by the party objecting to the opposite interrogatories.

RULE 110.

Cross-interrogatories shall be served within four days after the direct have been received, or they shall be regarded as assented to, and if no notice of reference to the judge is given within five days after both direct and cross interrogatories have been served, each party shall be deemed to have assented to the interrogatories served.

RULE 111.

The interrogatories, direct and cross, as agreed to by the parties or settled by the judge, shall be annexed to the commission.

RULE 112.

Directions as to the execution and return of the commission, signed by the clerk and the proctor of the party moving it, or of both parties, if both unite in the commission, or if both propose interrogatories, shall accompany the commission.

RULE 113.

Depositions taken under commissions or otherwise, shall be forwarded to the clerk immediately after they are taken, and be filed on their return to the clerk's office in term or vacation, and notice thereof shall be forthwith given by the party filing them, to the proctor of the opposite party. And all objections to the form or manner in which they were taken or returned, shall be deemed waived, unless such objections shall be specified in writing in four days after the same are opened, unless further time shall be granted by the judge.

RULE 114.

In suits between individuals, either may at any time after the commissions or depositions are deposited with the clerk, enter an order of course as of a special sessions, if in vacation, to open the same, and deliver copies thereof.

RULE 115.

In suits on seizures in which the United States are a party, such order may be entered on the written consent of the proctors or attorneys of the respective parties, or on motion to the court at a stated or special session.

RULE 116.

Opening such commissions or depositions shall not preclude either party from objecting to the competency or relevancy of the evidence when offered on trial.

RULE 117.

Exceptive allegations to the credibility or competency of witnesses examined on deposition or commission, may be filed within four days after the depositions or commissions are opened at the clerk's office, and notice shall be given forthwith of such exceptions.

RULE 118.

Testimony impeaching or supporting the witnesses may in such case be given by the parties respectively, on the hearing of the cause, and may be taken in the same manner as proofs in chief.

RULE 119.

Depositions *in perpetuam rei memoriam* to be used in this court, may be taken under a *dedimns potestatem,* or by any officer authorized by act of Congress to take depositions *de bene esse,* to be used in the Courts of the United States, in like cases and by like proceedings as is now authorized by the Supreme Court of the state of New York.

RULE 120.

Notices of trial, argument or hearing, may be for any day in term, the court being then sitting, (including days to which the court may stand adjourned,) upon a sufficient excuse for not giving notice for the first day of the term.

RULE 121.

In all issues brought to trial, argument or hearing, except as provided in these Rules, *four days* previous notice shall be served on the attorney or proctor of the opposite party, when the attorney or proctor resides in this city ; in all other cases, affixing such notice conspicuously in the clerk's office, shall be a sufficient service.

RULE 122.

A note of the pleadings and of the date of the issue shall be served on the clerk, with a notice of the hearing, four days before the time of hearing, and such notices shall also specify the pleadings, and whatever papers or documents in his office shall be required by the parties to be produced by the clerk at the trial.

RULE 123.

So soon as issue is joined, the respondent or claimant may notice the cause for hearing on his part, and be thereupon entitled to a decree dismissing the same with costs, or such other decree as the case may demand, unless the libellant shall also notice the cause for the same time, and proceed to trial or hearing, or obtain a continuance by order of the court, on proper cause shown.

RULE 124.

When either party shall require *viva voce* testimony given in open court, to be taken down by the clerk pursuant to the act of Congress, it shall be taken in the same manner as in jury trials on common law issues, and not *verbatim*, as in depositions *de bene esse*.

RULE 125.

The notes of the judge may, by assent of parties, be used as if taken down by the clerk.

RULE 126.

Either party, desiring to diminish, vary or enlarge the minutes of proofs taken by the clerk or judge, may, within two days after the trial, serve a statement of proofs on the proctor of the opposite party, and such statement, if assented to, or if no amendments are proposed thereto within two days thereafter by such proctor, shall be regarded the true minute of the testimony given, and the notes of the judge or clerk be corrected in conformity thereto.

RULE 127.

If amendments are proposed, and the parties do not agree therein, the statements and amendments shall be forthwith referred to the judge, and he shall settle or determine how the facts are, and the statement thus settled or adjusted, shall be filed as the true minutes of the testimony given.

RULE 128.

In cases of demands, arising not *ex delicto*, on a decree in favor of the libellant by default, or on hearing, it shall be referred to the clerk to compute and ascertain the amount due the libellant, but reference may also be made in cases of tort, or on allegations of incidental or consequential damages, if desired by either party.

Rule 129.

In case of the absence of the clerk, or his incompetency from interest or otherwise, or upon any sufficient cause shown, such reference may be made to assessors or otherwise, according to the course and custom of courts of civil and admiralty jurisdiction.

Rule 130.

On such reference either party may produce and use the pleadings and proofs filed in the cause or heard in court, and other competent proofs pertinent to the matter of reference.

Rule 131.

The clerk shall allow neither party longer than ten days from the order of reference to complete the proofs thereon without the special order of the judge.

Rule 132.

At the instance of either party the clerk shall report the additional testimony received by him, and the offer of testimony rejected (if any) by him.

Rule 133.

Either party may except to the clerk's report, and set down the exceptions for hearing, on two days' notice, at the first stated or special sessions after the report is filed.

Rule 134.

Upon the coming in of the report a decree of confirmation may be entered on motion without notice, unless otherwise ordered by the court, or the report shall be excepted to: and in the latter case, the exception shall be overruled or held abandoned, unless brought to a hearing the first stated or special sessions of the court for which it can be noticed.

Rule 135.

If the libellant takes no proceedings upon the report within four days after the filing thereof in open court, the respondent may move the court to dismiss the libel for want of due prosecution.

Rule 136.

If the promovent in a libel or information neglects to proceed in the cause with the despatch the course of the court admits, the respondent or claimant may have the libel or information dismissed on motion, unless the delay is by order of the judge, or the act of the respondent or claimant.

Rule 137.

Four days' notice shall be given of the application to dismiss the action, and a copy of an affidavit or certificate of the clerk, that no proceedings had been taken, be served at the same time.

Rule 138.

A special session of the court (besides the sittings on Tuesday each week) may be opened at any time *instanter*, on the allowance of the judge, for hearing and disposing of special motions, arguments or questions of law, and also for taking proofs, or hearing admiralty and maritime or revenue causes, and rendering interlocutory or final decrees therein.

Rule 139.

No party shall be compelled to take or meet proceedings at a special sessions, (without the order of the judge previously served on him,) in other than civil causes of admiralty and maritime jurisdiction.

Rule 140.

No special sessions will be held for the trial of jury causes, nor out of the city of New York, without a special order of the court, entered upon the minutes and published in a newspaper in the city of New York, and also in one nearest the place where the court is to be held, (if out of the city,) at least fifteen days previous to such sitting.

Rule 141.

A guardian *ad litem* will be appointed on a petition, verified by oath, stating a proper case for such appointment; and the guardian shall give stipulations for costs, &c., the same as if he was personally the party in interest.

Rule 142.

Infants may sue by *prochein ami*, to be first approved by the court; the *prochein ami* to give stipulations and be responsible for costs, in the same manner as the infant would be if of full age.

Rule 143.

Suits can only be prosecuted or defended in *forma pauperis* by express allowance of the court. In such case the pauper will be discharged of al stipulations or liabilities for costs.

Rule 144.

But the court, on satisfactory proof of the inability of a party to comply with the usual stipulations in a cause, may mitigate and modify such stipulations conformably to the equities or exigencies of the case.

Rule 145.

Where proceedings on a decree shall not be stayed by an appeal, and the decree shall not be fulfilled or satisfied in ten days after notice to the proctor of the party against whom it shall be rendered, it shall be of course to enter an order that the sureties of such party cause the engagement of their stipulation to be performed, or show cause in four days, or on the first day of jurisdiction afterwards, why execution should not issue against them, their lands, goods and chattels, according to their stipulation; and if no cause be then shown, due service having been made on the proctor of the party, a summary decree shall be rendered against them on their stipulations, and execution issue ; but the same may be discharged on the performance of the decree and payment of all costs.

RULE 146.

A party obtaining a decree of the court, may, at his election, have for the execution thereof like process as is now used in this state for like purposes, except that of personal attachment as for a contempt of court.

RULE 147.

The writ of *fieri facias* or *venditioni exponas* is adopted as final process in this court in all cases for the sale of property, and the proceedings thereon in admiralty cases shall be conformable to those on the common law side of the court.

RULE 148.

Whenever from the death of any of the parties, or changes of interest in the suit, defect in the pleadings or proceedings, or otherwise, new parties to the suit are necessary, the persons required to be made parties may be made such either by a petition on their part or by the adverse party.

RULE 149.

In either mode, it shall be sufficient to allege briefly the prayer of the original libel, the several proceedings in the cause and date thereof, and to pray that such persons required to be made parties to the suit may be made such parties.

RULE 150.

On service of a copy of such petitition and of notice of the presenting thereof, such order shall be made for the further proceeding in the cause as shall be proper for its speedy and convenient prosecution as to such new parties, and the same stipulations and security shall in all such cases be required and given, as in cases of persons becoming originally parties to a suit.

RULE 151.

A party shall not be held to enter his appeal from any decree or order of the court as final, unless the same is in a condition to be executed against him without further proceedings therein in court.

RULE 152.

Ten days from the time of rendering the decree shall be allowed to enter an appeal, within which time the decree shall not be executed. A brief notice in writing to the clerk and opposite proctor, that the party appeals in the cause, shall be a sufficient entry of the appeal, without any petition to the court for leave to enter the same.

Rule 153.

When an appeal shall be entered, the appellant shall, within ten days thereafter, give security for damages and costs ; and if security shall not be given within that time, the decree may be executed as if there had been no appeal, unless further time be allowed by the court.

Rule 154.

The appellant shall give four days' notice to the adverse party, or his proctor, of the person or persons proposed as his sureties, with their additions and descriptions, and of the time and place of giving the stipulation.

Rule 155.

When an appeal shall be entered the appellant shall cause the proceedings of the court, required by law to be transmitted to the Circuit Court, to be transcribed for that purpose within thirty days after the appeal shall be entered in this court: and in default thereof, the decree shall be executed as if there had been no appeal, unless the court shall, upon special motion of the appellant, otherwise order.

Rule 156.

A rehearing will not be granted in any matter in which a decree has been rendered, unless application is made at the term when the decree is pronounced, or there is a stay of proceedings by order of the judge.

Rule 157.

No libel of review will be entertained in cases subject to appeal, nor unless filed before the enrolment of the decree or return of final process issued in the cause.

Rule 158.

When any moneys shall come to the hands of the marshal under or by virtue of any order or process of the court, he shall forthwith pay over the gross amount thereof to the clerk, with a bill of his charges thereon, and a statement of the time of the receipt of the moneys by him, and upon the filing of such statements, and the taxation of such charges, the same shall be paid to the marshal out of such moneys ; and the general account of all property sold under the order or decree of this court shall be returned by the marshal, and filed in the clerk's office with the execution or other process under which the sale was made.

Rule 159.

All bills of costs and of charges to be paid under any order or decree of this court, shall be taxed and filed with the clerk before payment thereof: and if the same shall include charges for disbursements other than to the officers of the court, the proper and genuine vouchers, or an affidavit therefor, (in cases of loss of vouchers,) shall be exhibited and filed, and if such bill shall be taxed without four days' notice to all parties concerned, they shall be subject to a retaxation of course, on application by any such party, not having had notice, and at the charge of the party obtaining such taxation.

Rule 160.

The clerk is authorized to tax or certify bill of costs and to sign judgments and also take acknowledgments of the satisfaction of judgments and all affidavits and oaths out of court as in open court in all cases where the same are not required by law to be taken in open court.

Rule 161.

In case of the absence of the clerk from the city or his inability to transact business, his deputy or chief clerk is authorized to sign judgments, to tax or certify all bills of costs in this court, other than those of the clerk, and also to affix the seal of the court and certify proceedings or papers in the name of the clerk in all other cases than exemplifications of the records or files of the court, and perform duties appertaining to the clerk by appointment of the court, or the course of practice, which are not specifically appointed by statute to be performed by the clerk.

Rule 162.

The clerk is authorized to enter satisfaction of record of any judgment rendered in this court in behalf of the United States, on filing acknowledgment of satisfaction of the same duly made by the district attorney.

Rule 163.

All rules to which a party is entitled of course, or which are moved for upon the written consent of the parties, may be entered by the clerk in vacation, without the mandate of the judge, and be entitled as of a special court held on that day.

Rule 164.

Proctors of any circuit or district court of the United States, and attorneys of the supreme court of this state, and solicitors of the court of chancery, may be admitted attorneys or proctors of this court and counsellors of the said supreme court and court of chancery, and counsellors and advocates of such circuit or district courts may be admitted counsellors and advocates of this court of course, upon taking the oaths prescribed by the constitution and laws of the United States.

Rule 165.

In admiralty and maritime causes wherein the matter in demand does not exceed fifty dollars, the proceedings for recovery thereof may be *summary*.

Rule 166.

Instead of filing a libel, the promovent in suits by individuals may, by short petition, state the matter of his demand and the amount or value thereof, or present an account stated, or a bill of charges by items, on filing either of which, process may issue as on the filing of a libel in ordinary cases.

RULE 167.

The same petition or statement used on application for a summons pursuant to the act of Congress of July 20. 1799, sec. 6, shall when admiralty process is ordered by the judge or justice of the peace, be filed and may stand and be proceeded upon in lieu of the libel in form.

RULE 168.

Any party intervening may contest the petition on demand orally or in writing, by general denial or affirmance, or file a plea in bar or answer or claim.

RULE 169.

No costs shall be taxed the defendant, for any plea, answer or claim, other than a general issue to the actor's demand, unless an answer on oath be demanded.

RULE 170.

Either party may file interrogatories to be propounded to his adversary, which shall be answered on oath.

RULE 171.

The monition or citation or attachment may be made returnable the first day of a stated or special session of court next succeeding the service thereof—at least three days intervening between the service and return of process *in rem*, in suits by individuals, and fourteen in suits by the United States: and on the return of process in open court duly served, the cause may be put *instanter* upon the calendar, and either party without other notice may proceed therein to proofs and hearing. And the party obtaining a continuance of the cause, if *in rem*, shall bear all expenses taxed for keeping the thing attached, intermediate such continuance and the final hearing.

RULE 172.

The notices to be published in suits by individuals, need contain only the title of the suit, the cause of action, the amount demanded, and the day and place of the return of the monition, and be subscribed with the name of the marshal and proctor of the libellant. No more than the usual printer's charge for advertisements of like size shall be taxed for the publication.

RULE 173.

In summary proceedings *in rem*, in behalf of the United States, when the goods are under seizure by the collector and in his possession, the clerk, at the instance of the district attorney, may omit the attachment clause in the monition issued.

Rule 174.

If the monition also contains an attachment in such cases, and the marshal returns that the goods, &c., are in the custody of the collector, he shall stand acquitted of all responsibility for their safe keeping or production to answer the decree.

Rule 175.

In such case the service of the motion shall be by leaving a copy or notice thereof, with the collector or person having the goods in keeping, and also making like service on the owner, or his agent, if known to the marshal and resident in the city.

Rule 176.

The costs to be taxed the district attorney, proctor and advocate on either side in a summary cause, shall not exceed twelve dollars.

Rule 177.

Fees shall not be taxed for more than one witness to prove the same facts, unless it appears that the witness was impeached or his testimony contradicted. No charges for serving writs of subpœna shall be taxed against the opposite party when the writ is executed by the marshal. If a witness does not attend after regular summons, proceedings to attachment may be had against him, without the service of a writ of subpœna.

Rule 178.

The provisions of the twelve preceding rules, are limited to those cases of admiralty and maritime jurisdiction, in which no appeal lies from this court to the circuit court.

Rule 179.

Summary proceedings in all respects not specified in the preceding rules are to be governed by the general course of procedure of the court.

PRACTICE IN INFORMATIONS.

Rule 180.

Informations on seizures upon land or water are to be drawn in a plain and concise form, only referring to, without reciting, statutes or sections of statutes at large. The information should set forth the gravamen of the suit by plain and issuable allegations; and when *in rem* the property demanded as forfeited is to be specified, together with the alleged cause of forfeiture. Informations are subject to the same general rules as to their structure and amendment as ordinary libels.

Rule 181.

Proceedings *in rem* for a forfeiture, and *in personam* for an offence, fine, penalty or debt, may be joined in one information, when having relation to the same transaction.

Rule 182.

On filing an information *in personam* or *in rem*, the clerk shall issue process thereon corresponding as nearly as may be with that employed in the instance court of admiralty in similar cases. But process *in personam* may be in the first instance a capias, or attachment against goods to compel an appearance, or a monition, at the election of the complainant.

Rule 183.

No party shall be held to bail on an information *in personam*, without the mandate of the judge, except where bail is required or authorized by statute.

Rule 184.

All rules applicable to the service of, or proceedings in relation to process in plenary causes in admiralty, shall equally apply to process on informations.

Rule 185.

If the information filed is multifarious or ambiguous, or does not supply plain allegations upon which issue can be taken or a distinct reference to the statute upon which it is founded, the defendant or claimer may move the court to have it reformed, giving two days previous notice, together with a specification of the exceptive parts, to the district attorney or proctor in whose name it is filed. It may be amended of course in conformity to such notice: if not reformed within two days after pronounced defective by the court, the defendant may take an order of discharge from the action.

Rule 186.

Amendments may be had to informations in any stage of the cause; but if after an issue is formed between the parties, it shall be on payment of all costs which may have accrued by means of the amendment or the defective pleading.

Rule 187.

In informations *in rem*, a delivery on stipulation of property seized, or a sale of perishable articles may be had as in case of proceedings in the instance court of admiralty.

Rule 188.

The claimer shall appear and interpose his claim or plea on informations *in rem*, within the same time and in the same manner as in causes on the instance side of the court of admiralty; and shall appear and plead to informations *in personam* within the same time and in the same manner as in

49

causes at common law : but no plea other than in abatement the general issue, former recovery, pardon or remission of the offence, fine or forfeiture, shall be received.

Rule 189.

Instead of a traverse of each separate cause of forfeiture alleged in the information, the defendant may plead as a general issue to an information *in rem,* " that the several goods in the information mentioned did not, nor did any part thereof, become forfeited in manner and form as in the information in the behalf alleged."

Rule 190.

Putting in and justifying bail on behalf of the defendants on arrest, and the proceedings to and on trial and execution where a trial by jury must be had, shall be the same as in cases of common law jurisdiction.

ADDITIONAL RULES.

June Term—1849.

To prevent unnecessary multiplication of suits, and the accumulation of costs for the recovery of seamen's wages, the following additional Rules in summary actions are adopted :

Rule 1.

In suits *in personam* for wages, where the amount sworn to be due in the libel is less than fifty dollars, the clerk shall not issue process without the usual stipulation for costs, unless the libel be accompanied by satisfactory proof that the respondent is about to leave the district ; or by an allocatur of the Judge, or by a certificate of a Commissioner of the Court, that upon due service of a summons to the respondent to appear before him, sufficient cause of complaint whereon to found process appeared.

Rule 2.

Such summons shall be served at least one day previous to the day of hearing, therein mentioned, and if it shall appear on the hearing to the satisfaction of the Commissioner, that the wages claimed have been paid or forfeited, he shall refuse the certificate. And if a reasonable offer of compromise shall be made on such hearing by either party, and be rejected by the other, the Commissioner shall add a certificate of such fact, and in case of final recovery by the party rejecting such offer, he shall recover no costs. No costs shall be taxed for the proceeding, unless the Commissioner shall certify that a demand of wages was made by the seaman a reasonable time previous to taking out the summons, and then the proctor shall be allowed no more than $1 25-100, the ordinary fees for attendance and motion in Court.

RULE 3.

No fees shall be taxed to the marshal, clerk or witness on such proceedings unless by special mandate of the judge, a subpœna or attachment is issued to compel the attendance of witnesses.

RULE 4.

The Commissioner's fees for his services thereon shall not exceed one dollar for a single sitting, and every adjournment granted shall be at the expense of the party obtaining it; if, however, it is required by the parties that the Commissioner take down in writing the testimony heard in the summons, he shall be allowed therefor the customary fees for like services. Proofs so taken in writing may be used by either party on the hearing in Court, in case the suit is further prosecuted.

RULE 5.

No more than one process shall issue against the master or owners at the same time for wages claimed by a crew, or any part thereof for the same voyage, nor during the pendency of a suit therefor, nor shall costs be taxed for more than one retainer or libel, in such cases, unless an order of the judge on cause shown, be previously had, authorizing other suits therefor. Seamen claiming wages for the same voyage may file an affidavit stating the amount due them, and if such affidavit be filed before the issue of process, the clerk may order the respondent to be held to bail in a sum exceeding by $100, the whole amount of such claims.

RULE 6.

The bail or stipulation given by the master or owner on such process shall be conditioned to abide the order of the Court in the particular suit, and in favor of such other parties as the Court may grant leave to join therein.

PRIZE RULES.

RULE 1.

There shall be issued, under the seal and authority of this court, commissions to such persons as the court shall think fit, appointing them severally commissioners to take examinations of witnesses in prize causes in *preparatory*, on the standing interrogatories, which have been settled and adopted by this court, and all other depositions which they are empowered to require, and to discharge such other duties in relation to ships or vessels, or property brought into this district as prize, as shall be designated by the said commissioners and the rules and orders of this court.

Rule 2.

The captors of any property brought into this district as prize, or some one on their behalf, shall without delay give notice to the district judge, or to one of the commissioners aforesaid, of the arrival of the property, and of the place where the same may be found.

Rule 3.

Upon the receipt of notice thereof from the captors or district judge, a commissioner shall repair to the place where the said prize property then is; and if the same be a ship or vessel, or if the property be on board a ship or vessel, he shall cause the said ship or vessel to be safely moored in sufficient depth of water, or in soft ground.

Rule 4.

The commissioner shall, in case the prize be a ship or vessel, examine whether bulk has been broken; and if it be found that bulk has been broken, one of the said commissioners shall take information upon what occasion or what cause the same was done. If the property captured be not a ship or vessel, or in a ship or vessel, he shall examine the chests, packages, boxes or casks containing the subject captured, and shall ascertain whether the same has been opened, and shall in every case examine whether any of the property originally captured has been secreted or taken away subsequently to the capture.

Rule 5.

The commissioner in no case shall leave the captured property until he secure the same by seals upon the hatches, doors, chests, bales, boxes, casks, or packages, as the case may require, so that they cannot be opened without breaking the said seals; and the said seals shall not be broken, or the property removed, without the special order of the court, excepting in case of fire and tempest, or of absolute necessity.

Rule 6.

If the captured property be not a vessel, or on board a vessel, the commissioner shall take a detailed account of the particulars thereof, and shall cause the same to be deposited under the seals as aforesaid, in a place of safety, there to abide the order or decree of this court.

Rule 7.

If no notification shall, within reasonable time, be given by the captors, or by any person in their behalf, of any property which may be brought as prize within this district, and the commissioners, or either of them, shall become informed thereof, by any means, it shall be the duty of the said commissioners, or one of them, to repair to the place where such property is, and to proceed in respect to the same, as if notice had been given by the captors.

Rule 8.

The captor shall deliver to the judge at the time of such notice, or to the commissioner or commissioners, when he or they shall, conformably to the foregoing rule, repair to the place where such captured property is, or at such other time as the said commissioners, or either of them, shall require the same, all such papers, passes, sea-briefs, charters, bills of lading, cockets, letters and other documents and writings as shall have been found on board the captured ship, or which have any reference to, or connection with the captured property, and which are in the possession, custody, or power of the captors.

Rule 9.

The said papers, documents and writings, shall be regularly marked and numbered by a commissioner, and the captor, chief officer, or some other person who was present at the taking of the prize, and saw that such documents, papers and writings were found with the prize, must make a deposition before one of the said commissioners that they have delivered up the same to the judge or commissioner as they were found or received, without any fraud, subduction or embezzlement. If any documents, papers or writings, relative to or connected with the captured property are missing or wanting, the deponent shall, in his said deposition, account for the same according to the best of his knowledge, information and belief.

Rule 10.

The deponent must further swear, that if at any time thereafter, and before the final condemnation or acquittal of the said property, any further or other papers relating to the said captured property shall be found or discovered, to the knowledge of the deponent, they shall also be delivered up, or information thereof given to the commissioners, or to this court, which deposition shall be reduced to writing by the commissioner, and shall be transmitted to the clerk of the court, as hereinafter mentioned.

Rule 11.

When the said documents, papers and writings are delivered to a commissioner, he shall retain the same till after the examination *in preparatorio* shall have been made by him, as is hereafter provided, and then he shall transmit the same, with the same affidavit in relation thereto, the preparatory examinations, and the information he may have received in regard to the said captured property, under cover, and under his seal, to this court, addressed to the clerk thereof, and expressing on the said cover to what captured property the documents relate, or who claim to be the captors thereof, or from whom he received the information of the capture, which said cover shall not be opened without the order of the court.

Rule 12.

Within three days after the captured property shall have been brought within the jurisdiction of this court, the captor shall produce to one of the commissioners, three or four, if so many there be of the company or persons who were captured with, or who claim the said captured property, and in case the capture be a vessel, the master and mate or supercargo, if brought in, must always be two, in order that they may be examined by the commissioner *in preparatory*, upon the standing interrogatories.

Rule 13.

In the examination of witness *in preparatorio*, the commissioner shall use no other interrogatories but the standing interrogatories, unless special interrogatories are directed by the court. He shall write down the answer of every witness separately to each interrogatory, and not to several interrogatories together; and the parties may personally, or by their agents, attend the examination of witnesses before the commissioners; but they shall have no right to interfere with the examination, by putting questions, or objecting to questions; all objections to the regularity or legality of the proceedings of the commissioners must be made to the court.

Rule 14.

When a witness declares he cannot answer to any interrogatory, the commissioner shall admonish the witness, that by virtue of his oath taken to speak the truth, and nothing but the truth, he must answer to the best of his knowledge, or when he does not know absolutely, then to answer to the best of his belief concerning any one fact.

Rule 15.

The witnesses are to be examined separately, and not in presence of each other, and they may be kept from all communication with the parties, their agents or counsel, during the examination. The commissioners will see that every question is understood by the witness, and will take their exact, clear and explicit answers thereto: and if any witness refuses to answer at all, or to answer fully, the examining commissioner is forthwith to certify the fact to the court.

Rule 16.

The captors must produce all their witnesses in succession, and cannot, after the commissioners have transmitted the examination of a part of the crew to the judge, be allowed to have others examined without the special order of the court: and the examination of every witness shall be begun, continued and finished in the same day, and not at different times. Copies of the standing interrogatories shall not be returned by the commissioner with the examination, but it shall be sufficient for the answer of the witnesses to refer to the standing interrogatories by corresponding numbers.

Rule 17.

Before any witness shall be examined on the standing interrogatories the commissioner shall administer to him an oath in the following form: "You shall true answer make to all such questions as shall be asked of you on these interrogatories, and therein you shall speak the whole truth, and nothing but the truth, so help you God." If the witness is conscientiously averse to swearing, an affirmation to the same effect shall be administered to him.

Rule 18.

Whenever the ship's company, or any part thereof, of a captured vessel, are foreigners, or speak only a foreign language, the commissioner taking the examination·may summon before him competent interpreters, and put to them an oath well and truly to interpret to the witness the oath administered to him, and the interrogations propounded, and well and truly to interpret to the commissioners the answers given by the witness to the respective interrogatories.

Rule 19.

The examination of each witness on the standing interrogatories shall be returned according to the following form:

" Deposition of A. B., a witness produced, sworn and examined *in preparatorio*, on the   day of   in the year   at the house of   on the standing interrogatories established by the District Court of the United States, for the southern district of New York. The said witness having been produced for the purpose of such examination by C. D., in behalf of the captors of a certain ship or vessel called the   (or of certain goods, wares and merchandise, as the case may be.)

" 1st. To the first interrogatory, the deponent answers that he was born at   &c.

" 2d. To the second interrogatory the deponent answers that he was present at the time of the taking, &c."

Rule 20.

When the interrogatories have all been answered by a witness, he shall sign his deposition, and the commissioner shall put a certificate thereto in the usual form, and subscribe his name to the same.

Rule 21.

No person having or claiming any interest in the captured property, or having any interest in any ship having letters of marque or commissions of war, shall act as a commissioner. Nor shall a commissioner act either as proctor, advocate or counsel, either for captors or claimants in any prize cause whatever.

Rule 22.

If the captain or prize·master neglect or refuse to give up and deliver to the commissioners the documents, papers and writings relating to the captured property, according to these rules; or refuse or neglect to produce, or cause to be produced, witnesses to be examined *in preparatory*, within three days after the arrival of the captured property within the jurisdiction of this court, or shall otherwise unnecessarily delay the production of the said documents, papers or writings, the commissioners, or one of them nearest to the place where the captured property may be, or before whom the examination *in preparatorio* may have been already begun, shall give notice in writing to the delinquent to forthwith produce the said documents, papers and writings, and to bring forward his witnesses, and if he shall neglect or delay so to do for the period of twenty-four hours thereafter, such commissioner shall certify the same to this court, that such proceedings may therefore be had as justice may require.

RULE 23.

If within twenty-four hours after the arrival within this district, of any captured vessel, or of any property taken as prize, the captors or their agent shall not give notice to the judge or a commissioner, pursuant to the provisions herein made, or shall not, two days after such notice given, produce witnesses to be examined *in preparatorio*, then any person claiming the captured property and restoration thereof, may give notice to the judge or the commissioners as aforesaid, of the arrival of the said captured property, and thereupon such proceedings may be had by the commissioners in respect to the said property, and relative to the documents, papers and writings connected with the said capture, which the claimant may have in his possession, custody or power, and relative to the examination of witnesses *in preparatorio*, as near as may be, as is before provided for in cases where the captors shall give notice and examine *in preparatorio*. And the said claimant may, in such cases, file his libel for restitution, and proceed thereon according to the rules and practice of this court.

RULE 24.

As soon as may be convenient after the captured property shall have been brought within the jurisdiction of this court, a libel may be filed, and a monition shall thereupon be issued, and such proceedings shall be had as are usual in conformity to the practice of this court in cases of vessels, goods, wares and merchandise seized as forfeited in virtue of any revenue law of the United States.

RULE 25.

In all cases by consent of captor and claimant, or upon attestation exhibited upon the part of the claimant only, without consent of the captor, that the cargo or part thereof is perishing or perishable, the claimant specifying the quantity and quality of the cargo, may have the same delivered to him on giving bail to answer the value thereof if condemned, and further to abide the event of the suit, such bail to be approved of by the captor, or otherwise the persons who give security, swearing themselves to be severally and truly worth the sum for which they give security. If the parties cannot agree upon the value of the cargo, a decree or commission of appraisement may issue from the court to ascertain the value.

RULE 26.

In cases were there is no claim, an affidavit being exhibited on the part of the captor of such perishing or perishable cargo, specifying the quantity and quality thereof, the captor may have a decree or commission of appraisement and sale of such cargo, the proceeds thereof to be brought into court, to abide the further orders of the court.

RULE 27.

The name of each cause shall be entered by the clerk upon the calendar for hearing in their order, according to the dates of the returns of the monitions, and lists of the causes ready for hearing are to be constantly hung up in the court room and clerk's office for public inspection.

RULE 28.

In all cases where a decree or commission of appraisement and sale of any ship and cargo, or either of them, shall have issued, no question respecting the adjudication of such ship and goods, or either of them, as to freight or expenses, shall be heard till the said decree or commission shall be returned, with the account of sales, and the proceeds according to such account of sales be paid into court, to abide the order of the court in respect thereto.

RULE 29.

After the examination taken *in preparatory* on the standing interrogations are brought into the clerk's office, and the monition has issued, no further or other examinations upon the said interrogatories shall be taken, or affidavits received, without the special directions of the Judge upon due notice given.

RULE 30.

None but the captors can, in the first instance, invoke papers from one captured vessel to another, nor can it be done without the special mandate of the judge; and in case of its allowance, only extracts from the papers are to be used.

RULE 31.

The invocation shall only be allowed on affidavit on the part of the captors, satisfying the court that such papers are material and necessary.

RULE 32.

Application for permission to invoke must be on service, at least two days previously, of notice thereof, and copy of the affidavit on the claimants or their agent, (if known to be in this port,) and after invocation allowed to the captors, the claimants, by permission of the judge, for sufficient cause shown, may use other extracts of the same papers in explanation of the parts invoked.

RULE 33.

But when the same claimants intervene for different vessels or for goods wares or merchandise, captured on board different vessels, and proofs are taken in the respective causes, and the causes are on the dockets for trial at the same time, the captors may, on the hearing in court, invoke of course in either of such causes the proofs taken in any other of them; the claimants, after such invocation, having liberty to avail themselves also of the proofs in the cause invoked.

RULE 34.

In all motions for commissions and decrees of appraisement and sale, the time shall be specified within which it is prayed that the commissions or decrees shall be made returnable.

RULE 35.

The commissioners shall make regular returns on the days in which their commissions and decrees are returnable, stating the progress that has been made in the execution of the commission or decrees, and if necessary, praying an enlargement of the time for the completion of the business.

RULE 36.

The commissioners shall bring in the proceeds which have been collected at the time of their returns; and they may be required from time to time to make partial returns of such sums only as are necessary to cover expenses.

RULE 37.

On the returns of commissions or decrees, the commissioners or the marshal must bring in all the vouchers within their control.

RULE 38.

All moneys brought into court in prize causes, shall be forthwith paid into such Bank in the City of New York, as shall be appointed for keeping the moneys of the court, and shall only be drawn out on the specific orders of the court in favor of the persons respectively having right thereto, or their agents or representatives duly authorized to receive the same.

RULE 39.

At every stated term of the court, the clerk shall exhibit to the court a statement of all the moneys paid into court in prize cases, designating the amount paid in each particular case, and at what time.

RULE 40.

The statement when approved by the court, shall be filed of record in the clerk's office, and be open to the inspection of all parties interested, and certified copies thereof shall be furnished by the clerk, on request, to any party in interest, his proctor or advocate.

RULE 41.

When property seized as prize of war is delivered upon bail, a stipulation according to the course of the admiralty is to be taken for double its value.

RULE 42.

Every claim interposed must be by the parties in interest, if within convenient distance; or in their absence, by their agent or the principal officer of the captured ship, and must be accompanied by a test affidavit, stating briefly the facts respecting the claim and its verity, and how the deponent stands connected with or acquired knowledge of it. The same party who may intervene is also competent to attest to the affidavit.

RULE 43.

The captors of property brought in or held as prize, or which may have been carried into a foreign port, and there delivered upon bail by the captors, shall forthwith libel the same in fact, and sue out the proper process. The first process may, at the election of the party, be a warrant for the arrest of the property or person to compel a stipulation to abide the decree of the court, or a monition.

RULE 44.

The monitions shall be made returnable in twenty days, and if the property seized as prize is in port, shall be served in the same way as in the case of monitions issued on the instance side of the court of admiralty, on seizures for forfeiture under the revenue laws. In case the property claimed as prize is not in port, then the monition is to be served on the parties in interest, their agent or proctor if known to reside in the district, otherwise by publication daily in one of the newspapers of this city for fifteen successive days preceding the return thereof.

RULE 45.

Whenever the jurisdiction of the court is invoked upon matters as incident to prize, except as to the distribution of prize money, there must be distinct articles or allegations in that behalf in the original libel or claim on the part of the party seeking relief. But in case the matters have arisen, or become known to the party subsequent to presenting his libel or claim, the court will allow him to file the necessary amendments.

RULE 46.

No permission will be granted to either party to introduce further proofs until after the hearing of the cause upon the proofs originally taken.

RULE 47.

In case of captures by the public armed vessels of the United States, and a proceeding for condemnation against the property seized as prize *jure belli*, or in the nature of a prize of war, under any act of Congress, the name of the officer under whose authority the capture was made must be inserted in the libel.

Rule 48.

A decree of contumacy may be had against any party not obeying the orders or process of the court, duly served upon him ; and thereupon an attachment may be sued out against him. But no constructive service of a decree or process, *viis et modis,* or *publica citatio* will be sufficient, unless there has been a publication thereof in a daily paper in this city, at least fifteen days immediately preceding the motion for an attachment.

Rule 49.

When damages are awarded by the court, the party entitled thereto may move for the appointment of three commissioners to assess the same ; two persons approved by the court will thereupon be associated with the clerk or deputy clerk of this court, if not interested in the matter, whose duty it shall be to estimate and compute the damages in conformity to the principles of the decree, and return a specific report to the court of the amount of damages, and the particular items of which they are composed.

Rule 50.

Any party aggrieved may have such assessment of damages reviewed in a summary manner by the court before final decree rendered thereon, on giving two days' previous notice to the proctor of the party in whose favor the assessment is made, of the exceptions he intends taking, and causing to be brought before the court the evidence given the commissioners in relation to the particular excepted to.

Rule 51.

Every appeal from the decrees of this court must be made within ten days from the time the decree appealed from is entered, otherwise the party entitled thereto may proceed to have it executed. No appeal shall stay the execution of a decree unless the party, at the time of entering the appeal, gives a stipulation with two sureties to be approved by the clerk in the sum of two hundred and fifty dollars, to pay all costs and damages that may be awarded against him, and to prosecute the appeal to effect.

Rule 52.

If the party appealing is afterwards guilty of unreasonable delay in having the necessary transcripts and proceedings prepared for removing the cause, it will be competent to the other party to move the court for leave to execute the decree notwithstanding the appeal.

Rule 53.

In all cases of process *in rem* the property after arrest is deemed in the custody of the court, and the marshal cannot surrender it on bail, or otherwise, without the special order of the court.

INDEX TO DISTRICT COURT RULES.

INDEX TO RULES IN PRIZE CAUSES.

Note.—The foregoing Rules of the District Court for the Southern District of New York, were adopted in 1838. A very large portion of them must therefore be considered as superseded by the General Admiralty Rules of the Supreme Court, (ante, pp. 339 to 348,) which in all cases of conflict are the paramount Rules. In the absence of any authorized revision, it was necessary to insert the whole.

51

CIRCUIT COURT.

NEW YORK SOUTHERN DISTRICT.

ON APPEALS.

RULE 116.

An appeal can be taken from no other than final decrees.

RULE 117.

A decree shall be deemed final when in a state for execution without further action of the court below.

RULE 118.

Every appeal to the Circuit Court, in a cause of admiralty and maritime jurisdiction, shall be in writing, signed by the party, or his proctor, and delivered to the clerk of the District Court, from the decree of which the appeal shall be made : and it shall be returned to the court, with the necessary documents and proceeedings, within twenty days, and by the first day of the term next after the delivery thereof to the clerk, unless a longer time is allowed by the judge.

RULE 119.

The appeal shall briefly state the prayers, or allegations, of the parties to the suit, in the District Court, in the proceedings in that court, and the decree, with the time of rendering the same. It shall also state whether it is intended, on the appeal, to make new allegations, to pray different relief, or to seek a new decision on the facts, and the appellants shall be concluded in this behalf, by the appeal filed.

RULE 120.

A copy of the appeal shall, at the same time, be served on the proctor of the appellees, in the court below. And an affidavit, of the due service of such copy, shall be filed with the appeal. And no process, or order, shall be necessary to bring the appellees into this court.

RULE 121.

If in the appeal, it shall not be intended to make new allegations, to pray different relief, nor to seek a new decision of the facts, then the pleadings, evidence, and decree, in the District Court, with the stipulations in the cause, and the clerk's account of the funds in court, in the cause, if any, shall be certified to this court with the appeal. But in all cases the statement of facts agreed between the parties, or settled by the judge of the District

Court, and on file, according to the practice of that court, may be certified in the place of the evidence at large.

Rule 122.

If it shall be intended to seek only a new decision of the facts, then the pleadings of the parties, with the stipulations in the cause, and the clerk's account of the funds in court, if any, and the exhibits and depositions in the cause, shall be certified to this court with the appeal. But the proofs need not be certified, unless specially required by the appellant, or ordered by this court.

Rule 123.

If it shall be intended to make new allegations, or to seek new relief, then the return to the petition of appeal, shall only contain copies of the process issued upon the libel, and of the return thereof, the account of the clerk of the funds in court, in the cause, the depositions and exhibits, and the stipulations in the cause.

Rule 124.

The appellant shall cause the notice of appeal, and an affidavit of the service of a copy thereof, with the documents required to be returned with the appeal, to be filed in this court within four days after the return is completed by the clerk, otherwise the appeal shall not be received, and shall be deemed deserted; and a certificate in this behalf shall be made to the court from which the appeal is made, which may proceed to execution of its decree.

Rule 125.

This court shall be deemed possessed of the cause, from the time of filing the appeal, with the documents required to be returned therewith, in this court.

Rule 126.

If the appellee does not enter his appearance, within the two first days in term, succeeding the filing the appeal, and proceedings, and affidavit of service of notice thereof on him, the appellant may proceed *ex parte* in the cause, and have such decree as the nature of the case may demand.

Rule 127.

No answer, or issue, need be given to the appeal. Each party may notice the cause for hearing, for the term to which the appeal is made, (if made in term time,) or if made in vacation, for the term next succeeding.

Rule 128.

A writ of *inhibition* will be awarded, at the instance of the appellant, when circumstances require, to stay proceedings in the court below; notice of such application having been previously given.

Rule 129.

A *mandamus* may in like manner be obtained to compel a return of the appeal when unreasonably delayed by the clerk, or court below.

Rule 130.

If the appellee shall have any cause to show why new allegations, or proofs, should not be offered, or new relief prayed, on the appeal, he shall give four days' notice thereof, and serve a copy of the affidavit containing the cause intended to be shown : and such cause shall be shown within the two first days of the term; otherwise the appeal shall be allowed according to its terms.

Rule 131.

If new allegations are to be made, or different relief prayed, in this court, then the libellant in the District Court, shall exhibit, in this court, a libel, on oath within ten days, to which the adverse party shall, in twenty days, answer on oath, subject in each case to the extension of those periods, by order of either of the judges of this court; and on a default on this behalf, the court will, on motion, without notice, make such order for finally disposing of the cause, on the default of the party, as the nature of the case may require.

Rule 132.

After the libel and answer, whether newly filed in this court, or certified from the District Court, shall be filed in this court, the cause shall be proceeded in to a hearing, as in other cases. But where interrogatories have been answered in the District Court, or written testimony taken, the same may be used in this court.

Rule 133.

The appellee may move this court to have the decree made in the District Court, carried into effect, subject to the judgment of this court, or of the Supreme Court on appeal, upon giving his own stipulation to abide and perform the decree of such courts: and this court will make such order, unless the appellant shall give security by the stipulation of himself, and competent sureties, for payment of all damages and costs, on the appeal in this court, and in the Supreme Court, in such sums as this court shall direct.

Rule 134.

In cases where an appeal shall lie from the decree of this court, the final decree shall not be executed until ten days shall have elapsed from the pronouncing or filing of the decision of the court.

Rule 135.

When appeal shall be made from the decree of this court, the appellant shall, within four days from the pronouncing or filing of such decision, unless further time is allowed by the judge, make, and serve on the adverse party, a statement of the testimony on the trial, excepting such evidence as was in writing, which shall be properly referred to therein. The party on whom the same shall be served shall, in four days after such service, propose amendments thereto, or the statement shall be deemed acquiesced in, and the statement and amendments, unless acquiesced in, shall be submitted by the appellant to the judge, in four days afterwards, for settlement; and the same, when settled, shall be engrossed by the clerk, and with the written evidence, shall be deemed the proofs on which the decree is made, and shall operate as a stay of further proceedings in this court.

RULE 136.

In all cases, in civil causes of admiralty and maritime jurisdiction, not expressly provided for by the foregoing Rules of this Court, the Rules of Practice of the District Court for the Southern District of New York, being in force at the time, and whether established before or after these Rules, (not being inconsistent with these Rules,) are adopted, and are to be received as Rules of Practice in this Court.

CIRCUIT COURT.

NORTHERN DISTRICT OF NEW YORK.

Rules of the Circuit Court of the United States for the Northern District of New York, regulating appeals from the District Court.—June Term, 1848.

I.

The transcript to be sent to this court, on appeal thereto from a sentence or decree of the District Court, may be certified by the clerk of the latter court, under his hand and the seal of the court.

II.

Eight days' notice of hearing on appeal shall in all cases be given, by the service thereof on the adverse party, or on his proctor.

III.

When an appeal from a decree of the District Court is interposed twenty days before the next stated session of this court, it may be noticed for hearing at such session by either party.

IV.

When an appeal from a decree of the District Court is interposed less than twenty days before the next stated session of this court, the appellee may, at his option, notice the cause for hearing at such session, on the first or other day thereof; or have the cause continued until the next stated session.

V.

Transcripts of the depositions taken in any cause, in the District Court, according to law—whether *de bene esse* under the acts of Congress, or on commission—and read at the hearing of the cause in that court, may be transmitted to this court on appeal, and read by either party as evidence at the hearing of the cause in this court.

VI.

A copy of the notes taken by the judge, or under his direction by the clerk, of the District Court, of the evidence of witnesses examined orally therein, shall be certified and transmitted to this court on appeal, along with the transcript of the record and other proceedings in the cause, and shall be admitted to prove the evidence given by such witnesses; but nothing herein contained shall be construed to abridge the right of the parties to re-examine such witnesses in this court, if they shall see fit to do so.

DISTRICT COURT.—NORTHERN DISTRICT OF NEWYORK.

Rules of Practice of the District Court of the United States for the Northern District of New York, in causes arising under the Act of Congress, entitled " An Act extending the Jurisdiction of the District Courts to certain cases upon the Lakes and navigable waters connecting the same," passed February 26, 1845, *and in causes of Admiralty and Maritime Jurisdiction other than those of municipal seizure.—July Term,* 1848.

1.

The " Rules of Practice of the Courts of the United States, in causes of Admiralty and Maritime jurisdiction, on the instance side of the court," prescribed by the Supreme Court of the United States, at the January Term, 1845, are understood to be obligatory on this court, in all causes arising under the act of Congress, entitled " An Act extending the jurisdiction of the District Courts to certain cases upon the lakes and navigable waters connecting the same," passed February 26th, 1845 ; and the said Rules are hereby declared to be Rules of Practice in this court, in exercising the jurisdiction conferred by the said act.

2.

A special session of the court will be held at Auburn on the first Tuesday of every week, at ten o'clock in the forenoon ; at which special sessions all process must be made returnable, and all proceedings must be had, except trials by jury, which will not be held without a special order of the judge for that purpose, except at a stated term. And in case of the non-attendance of the judge at the time hereby appointed, or at any other time which may by special order be appointed, for any special session of the court, all process and proceedings shall be continued, without prejudice, to the next special session, or to some earlier day for that purpose appointed by the judge.

3.

All process shall bear test of the day on which it is sealed, and shall be made returnable before the judge at Auburn, on Tuesday of the week next after the test thereof, or of some succeeding week.

4.

The newspaper called the *Buffalo Commercial Advertiser*, printed at the city of Buffalo, is hereby designated, in pursuance of Rule IX. of the Rules of Practice in admiralty and maritime causes prescribed by the Supreme Court, as the newspaper in which all notices shall be printed, which are by the said rule required to be published in a newspaper, in all suits *in rem*, in which the arrest of the vessel, goods, or other thing proceeded against, has been made at or within the collection district of Buffalo Creek.

5.

The Cayuga County Bank, in the village of Auburn, is hereby designated, in pursuance of Rule XLII. of the same Rules, as the place of deposit for moneys paid into court.

6.

Libels, answers, and all other pleadings and papers to be filed, shall be so plainly written as to be readily legible, and shall be free, to all reasonable extent, from interlineations and erasures; and it shall be the duty of the clerk to reject all papers delivered to him to be filed, which are not in conformity with this rule.

7.

All libels praying process of arrest, whether *in rem* or *in personam*, shall be verified by the oath or solemn affirmation of the libellant, unless, for sufficient cause shown, such oath or affirmation shall be dispensed with by the special order of the judge. And all libels, answers and other pleadings shall be signed by the party in his own proper hand-writing, and in like manner by the proctor for the party in whose behalf they are filed, unless, for special cause shown, such signature shall be dispensed with by leave of the court.

8.

In suits *in rem*, the mesne process shall be served, and the required notices given, at least fourteen days before the return day of the process, unless a shorter time shall be prescribed by special order, founded upon the exigencies of the particular case.

9.

All process, and all notices for publication in a newspaper in pursuance of Rule IX. of the Rules of Practice in admiralty and maritime causes, prescribed by the Supreme Court, shall be drawn up by the clerk; and no process, except subpoenas, shall be issued by him in blank.

10.

The notice mentioned in the last preceding rule shall contain the title of the suit, a summary statement of the cause of action, the amount claimed by the libellant, and the day and place fixed for the return of the process; and shall have the name of the proctor of the libellant, and that of the marshal, or of his deputy by whom the arrest shall have been made, suffixed thereto.

11.

The amount of the debt or damages for which the action is brought shall be stated in the libel, and, with the addition thereto, for costs, of $250 in a suit *in rem.* and of $100 in a suit *in personam*, shall be endorsed on the mesne process, thus: " Action for $."

12.

When the libellant is not a resident of the district, he shall, at the time of commencing his suit, give a bond or stipulation, with one or more sufficient sureties, in the sum of at least one hundred dollars, if the suit is *in personam*; and in the sum of at least two hundred and fifty dollars, if the suit be *in rem* —conditioned that he will appear from time to time, and abide by all orders, interlocutory and final, of the court, and pay the costs and expenses, if any, which shall be awarded against him by the final decree of this court, or of any appellate court: *Provided,* however, that this regulation shall not extend to suits for seamen's wages, nor to suits for salvage when the salvors have come into port in possession of the property libelled.

13.

In all cases not embraced within the last preceding rule, on motion of the defendant or claimant, the court will, in its discretion, direct the libellant, on pain of dismissing his libel, to give the like security.

14.

Instead of the security specified in the two last preceding rules, the party from whom it is required may, at his option, deposit in court a sum of money of the like amount.

15.

If in any case a libel shall be filed in behalf of a libellant who is not a resident within the district, before security for costs and expenses shall be filed as required by Rule xii., the proctor for such libellant shall be liable for such costs and expenses to the amount specified in the said rule, until such security shall be filed; and the payment thereof may be enforced by summary process *in personam* against such proctor.

16.

When a proctor is retained to defend in any suit, before the return day of the mesne process therein, who resides or has his place of business more than three miles from the clerk's office, and not more than three miles from the residence or place of business of the proctor for the libellant, such proctor for the defendant may, at any time before the return day of the process, serve a notice of his retainer on the proctor for the libellant; and it shall thereupon be the duty of the proctor for the libellant, without delay, to serve on the proctor for the defendant a copy of the libel on file.

17.

When the defendant's answer, or any other pleading subsequent to the

52

libel, is put in by being simply filed in the clerk's office, instead of being given in open court, in presence of the proctor or advocate for the adverse party, a copy thereof, with notice of the time of filing the same, shall without delay be served on the proctor of such adverse party.

18.

When a decree is made in the absence of the proctor of either party to the suit, unless such proctor resides at the place where the clerk's office is kept, it shall be the duty of the clerk immediately to transmit to him by mail a copy of the decree; and such proctor and party shall be responsible to the clerk for the fees to which he may be entitled for such service, according to the usual rate of charge.

19.

Not less than six days' notice shall be given of the sale of property on final process; and when, in the opinion of the marshal or his deputy, by whom the sale is to be made, the circumstances of the case require a longer notice, he may, in his discretion, extend it to any time not exceeding twenty days.

20.

For the custody of vessels and other property while under arrest, the marshal shall be entitled to the same fees as are allowed by the 92d rule of this court in cases of municipal seizure ; subject, however, to alteration by the court in particular cases for special cause shown.

21.

When interrogatories are propounded by the defendant at the close of his answer, touching any matters charged in the libel, or touching any matter of defence set up in the answer, (according to Rule xxxii. of the Rules of Practice prescribed by the Supreme Court,) the libellant shall answer the same within twelve days, unless, for sufficient cause shown, he shall, by special order, be allowed a longer period ; and the court may, in its discretion, require such interrogatories to be answered within a shorter time, or *instanter*.

22.

When interrogatories are propounded to a garnishee (in pursuance of Rule xxxvii. of the Rules of Practice prescribed by the Supreme Court,) a copy thereof shall be served upon the garnishee personally, or, in case of his absence from his dwelling house or usual place of abode, by leaving such copy with some person of suitable age who is a member or resident of the family ; and the garnishee shall be required to answer the interrogatories within twelve days after such service, unless a longer period shall, for adequate cause shown, be by special order allowed for that purpose; and the court may also, in its discretion, prescribe a shorter period.

23.

Exceptions to the libel (taken in pursuance of Rule xxxvi. of the Rules of Practice prescribed by the Supreme Court,) for surplusage, irrelevancy, impertinence or scandal, may be taken *ore tenus*, on the return day of the mesne process; and exceptions to the answer or other allegation given by the defendant, taken for the like causes, in pursuance of the same rule, or in pursuance of Rule xxvii., for want of sufficiency, fulness or distinctness, may be taken in like manner, when the answer or allegation is put in in open court; and the court will thereupon, in its discretion, either decide upon the sufficiency of the exceptions so taken, *instanter* or direct the same to be drawn up in writing, and appoint a day to hear argument thereon, or refer the same to a commissioner.

24.

When, at the return of the mesne process, further time has been granted to answer the libel; and the answer, instead of being produced and offered in open court, in the presence and hearing of the advocate of the libellant, is simply filed with the clerk, a copy thereof shall, without delay, be served on the proctor for the libellant, personally, if he resides within three miles of the proctor for the defendant, otherwise either personally or by mail; and the proctor for the libellant may, within ten days after the service thereof, file and serve exceptions thereto. The defendant, within eight days after the service of such exceptions, may give a written notice of his submission to any or all of them; and if any of them are not submitted to within the time prescribed, the libellant may bring the same to a hearing before the court, by giving, at any time within six days, a notice of not less than six nor more than ten days, of such hearing. Every exception not submitted to, and which is not notified for hearing within the time specified, shall be considered as abandoned.

25.

When exceptions are referred to a commissioner, if the party who obtained the reference shall not procure and file the commissioner's report within fourteen days from the date of the order of reference, unless further time shall be allowed, for sufficient cause shown, by special order, the exceptions shall be considered as abandoned. The party by whom the reference was obtained shall have eight days after filing the report of the commissioner, to except thereto. On filing the report, he shall give notice of filing the same to the adverse proctor, who shall have eight days after such notice to except to the report. Exceptions to a commissioner's report may be noticed for argument by either party, and the notice shall be served at least six days before the day designated for the hearing.

26.

All appeals to the Circuit Court must be interposed within ten days from the date of the decree, or within such other period as shall be designated by special order made in the particular suit; and in cases where the right of appeal is allowed, no final process shall issue, before the expiration of the ten days, or other period prescribed.

27.

The regulations prescribed by law relative to the mode of serving notices and other papers, in suits prosecuted in the courts of the state of New York, are hereby adopted, *mutatis mutandis*, as rules of this court, in cases at law as well as in admiralty.

PRESENT FEE BILL

IN SOUTHERN DISTRICT OF NEW YORK.

Advocates' and Proctors' Costs usually taxed in this District.

ADVOCATES' FEES.

Retaining fee, ...	$3 75
Perusing, examining and signing a libel, answer, special pleading, interrogatories or exceptions, when the advocate is not the proctor in the cause, . . .	1 25
Attendance in court on every necessary proceeding in a cause,	62½
Arguing in court on any special motion actually litigated, .	1 25
Arguing every special plea, demurrer or exceptions, actually litigated, ...	2 50
Arguing on final hearing, on pleadings and proofs, when the cause is litigated on the merits and in no other case, .	5 00
Attending a judge or commissioner on taking testimony *de bene esse* out of court, but no allowance for more than one attendance, ...	5 00
Attendance before the clerk or assessors on reference by order of the court, but no allowance for more than one attendance, ...	3 00

No fees taxed for more than one advocate in the same cause.

PROCTORS' FEES.

Retaining fee ; (but when the same person acts both as advocate and proctor, no retaining fee allowed as proctor,) .	3 75
Drawing libel, plea, answer, claim, exceptions, necessary affidavits, &c., each folio of 100 words, . . .	25
Copy same for each folio, . . .	12½
Every necessary motion made in court, . . .	62½
Attendance in court on every necessary proceeding in a cause, (not being the advocate,) . . .	62½
Drawing interrogatories each folio of 100 words, . .	25
Copy same per folio, ...	12½
[But taxation is never to exceed $2 50 for draft, and $1 50 for copy of interrogatories.]	
Brief on special motion or petition argued in court on both sides,	1 12½

Brief on final argument in court upon the merits, . . $2 50
    [These briefs to include all abbreviations of pleadings,
      proofs, &c., and no separate allowances made therefor.]
Attending judge or commissioner on taking testimony *de bene esse*
    out of court, (if not the advocate,) . . 5 00
Attending clerk or assessors on reference and computation of da-
    mages, (if not the advocate,) . . . 3 00
    [But no more than one attendance taxed in either of the
      two last cases.]
Attending taxation of costs, when notice thereof has been given
    or received, ... 50
Copy of bill of costs for opposite party, . . . 37½
Every necessary notice actually given, . . . 37½
Arguing a motion or cause in court, (if not the advocate, and if
    the charge is not taxed for an advocate in the cause.) 1 25

ADVOCATES' AND PROCTORS' FEES ON PROCEEDINGS TO OBTAIN ORDER FOR
PROCESS FOR SEAMEN'S WAGES IN PLENARY CASES.

Drawing affidavit and ac. per folio of 100 words, . . 25
Copy, . .   "   " . 12½
Attendance before Judge, ... 62½
Summons for Judge, per fol. . . . 25
For copies, per folio, ... 12½
Motion for process, ... 62½
Arguing motion when opposed, ... 1 25
Copy costs for opposite party, . . . 37½
Attendance on taxation, ... 50
Witnesses fees per day, ... 1 25
Drawing affidavit of serving summons, per folio, . . 25
Copy, per folio, ... 12½
    And disbursements actually made.
    If before a U. S. Commissioner, or State officer, his fees are
    to be added. .

FEE BILL

OF THE NEW YORK STATE COURT OF ADMIRALTY,

BEFORE THE FORMATION OF THE CONSTITUTION OF THE UNITED STATES.

An act for regulating the Fees of the several Officers and Ministers of Justice within this State.

Passed February 18, 1789.

FEES IN THE COURT OF ADMIRALTY.

TO THE JUDGE.

For the seal of process, fifty cents.

The seal to exemplifications, one dollar twenty-five cents.

Every sentence, three dollars seventy-five cents.

Taking an affidavit, twelve one-half cents.

Taking every stipulation, fifty cents.

Swearing a defendant or witness, and certificate thereof, twenty-five cents.

Taxing every bill of costs, one dollar twenty-five cents.

THE ADVOCATES FEES.

For retaining fee, three dollars seventy-five cents.

Every motion made without effect, sixty-two one-half cents.

Attendance at every court, when anything is necessary to be done there, in the cause, sixty-two one half cents.

Arguing on the final hearing, where a cause is litigated and a full defence is made, but in no other case, five dollars.

Perusing, examining and signing a libel, answer, plea, demurrer, or any other special pleadings, interrogatories or exceptions, when the advocate is not the proctor in the cause, one dollar twenty-five cents

Arguing on any special motion, one dollar twenty-five cents.

Arguing every plea, demurrer or exceptions, two dollars fifty cents.

And no fees to be taxed for more than one advocate in the same cause.

FEES OF THE PROCTORS IN THE COURT OF ADMIRALTY.

For retaining fee, three dollars seventy-five cents; but when the same person acts both as advocate and proctor, no retaining shall be allowed as proctor.

Drawing every libel or information, answer, replication. or other pleading or exceptions, eighteen cents for each sheet containing ninety words; and for copies, nine cents for each sheet as aforesaid.

Every motion made with effect, when he acts as advocate, sixty-two one-half cents.

Attendance in every court, when any thing is done in the cause, sixty-two one-half cents; but no person shall be allowed for attendance both as proctor and advocate in the same cause at the same court.

Drawing interrogatories, eighteen cents for each sheet containing ninety words, and for a copy thereof, nine cents for each, as aforesaid; but if any one set of interrogatories shall exceed thirteen sheets, no more than two dollars and a-half shall be allowed for drawing the same; and no more than one dollar twenty-five cents for a copy thereof.

Every notice, copy and service, thirty-seven one-half cents.

Abbreviating pleadings, depositions and exhibits, three cents for each sheet containing ninety words.

Arguing on a final hearing when the proctor is not the advocate in the cause, one dollar eighty-seven one half cents.

Copy of a bill of costs for the opposite party, when necessary to be taxed, thirty-seven one-half cents.

For attending taxation of costs, fifty cents.

Arguing any demurrer of exceptions, when the proctor is not the advocate in the cause, one dollar twenty-five cents.

FEES OF THE REGISTER IN THE COURT OF ADMIRALTY.

For drawing every stipulation, process, monition, or subpœna, eighteen cents for each sheet containing ninety words; and nine cents for engrossing each sheet.

Entering the return of process. eighteen cents.

Filing every libel, claim, pleading or other paper, twelve one-half cents.

Reading each pleading, deposition and exhibit on hearing, twelve one-half cents.

Copies of the pleadings, interrogatories. depositions and exhibits, when required, nine cents for each sheet of ninety words.

Entering each proclamation, eighteen cents.

Entering each default, twelve one-half cents.

Entering every motion of the plaintiff or defendant, twelve one-half cents.

Entering every rule of court, eighteen cents.

Examining each witness, and drawing his deposition, eighteen cents for each sheet containing ninety words.

Certifying each exhibit or writing shown to a witness at his examination, twenty-five cents.

Drawing every decree or decretal order, eighteen cents for each sheet containing ninety words; and for entering the same in the minutes, nine cents fer each sheet as aforesaid.

Drawing a record or making a draft of apostles, eighteen cents for each sheet containing ninety words ; but no pleading, deposition, exhibit or other writing to be inserted therein verbatim, or in hæc verba, shall be computed as any part of such draft.

Entering a record in the register, or engrossing or copying apostles or records to be sealed or exemplified, nine cents for each sheet of ninety words, including all the pleadings, depositions, exhibits and writings inserted therein.

Every certificate, eighteen cents.

Entering return of appraisement or sales, nine cents for each sheet of ninety words.

Drawing commission to examine witnesses, eighteen cents for each sheet containing ninety words ; and for engrossing the same, if on parchment, twelve one-half cents, including the parchment ; and if on paper, nine cents for each sheet of ninety words.

All money deposited in court, six and a quarter cents in four dollars.

THE MARSHAL'S FEES IN THE COURT OF ADMIRALTY.

For summoning every witness or appraiser, twelve one-half cents.

Giving notice of holding the court to each proctor or advocate, twelve one-half cents.

Swearing each witness in court, six cents.

Making each proclamation, twelve one-half cents.

Serving every capias, attachment or summons, one dollar fifty cents.

Travelling each mile, going only, either to serve process or subpœna witnesses, twelve one-half cents.

Custody fees of a vessel, one dollar twenty-five cents per day.

Sales, six and a quarter cents per four dollars, for any sum under eight hundred dollars, and for any larger sum, three cents per four dollars.

STATUTES.

FEES OF MARSHAL AND CLERK.

*An act making appropriations for the civil and diplomatic expenses of the
Government for the year eighteen hundred and forty-one.*

Passed March 3, 1841.

For defraying the expenses of the Supreme, Circuit, and District courts
of the United States, including the District of Columbia; also for jurors
and witnesses, in aid of the funds arising from fines, penalties, and forfeitures,
incurred in the year eighteen hundred and forty-one, and preceding years;
and likewise for defraying the expenses of suits in which the United States
are concerned, and of prosecutions for offences committed against the United
States, and for the safe-keeping of prisoners, three hundred and twenty-five
thousand dollars: *Provided, however,* That hereafter, in lieu of all fees,
emoluments, and receipts not allowed in districts where present the entire
compensation of any of the officers hereinafter named shall exceed the sum
of one thousand five hundred dollars per annum, it shall and may be lawful
for the United States' clerks, attorneys, counsel, and marshals, in the district and circuit courts of the United States in the several States, to demand
and receive the same fees that now are, or hereafter may be, allowed by the
laws of the said States respectively where said courts are held, to the
clerks, attorneys, and counsel, and sheriffs, in the highest courts of the said
States in which like services are rendered; and no other fees or èmoluments,
except that the marshals shall receive in full, for summoning all the jurors
for any one court, thirty dollars; and shall receive, for every days actual
attendance at any court, five dollars per day; and for any services, including the compensation for mileage, performed by said officers in the discharge of
their official duty, for which no compensation is provided by the laws of said
States respectively, the said officers may receive such fees as are now allowed by law according to the existing usage and practice of said courts of
the United States; and every district attorney, except the district attorney
of the southern district of New York, shall receive, in addition to the above
fees, a salary of two hundred dollars per annum: *Provided,* That the fees
and emoluments retained by the district attorneys, marshals, and clerks, exclusive of any reasonable compensation to their deputies, to be allowed in
their accounts by the courts of the respective districts to which they belong,
and after the payment of such necessary office and other expenses as shall
be allowed by the Secretary of the Treasury, not to exceed, as to any one

of the said offices in the southern district of New York, the sum of three thousand dollars per annum, and in any other district, the sum of one thousand dollars per annum, shall in no case exceed, for the district attorneys and the marshals, or either of them, the sum of six thousand dollars for each; and those for each of the clerks shall not exceed, in any case, four thousand five hundred dollars; the overplus of fees and emoluments to be paid into the public Treasury, under such rules and regulations as may be prescribed by the Secretary of the Treasury, subject to the disposition of Congress.

UNITED STATES COMMISSIONERS.

An act for the more convenient taking of affidavits and bail in civil causes depending in the Courts of the United States.

Passed February 20, 1812.

Be it enacted by the Senate and House of Representatives of the United States of America, in Congress assembled, That it shall be lawful for the circuit court of the United States, to be holden in any district in which the present provision, by law, for taking bail and affidavits in civil causes, (in cases where such affidavits are, by law, admissible) is inadequate, or on account of the extent of such district, inconvenient, to appoint such and so many discreet persons, in different parts of the district as such court shall deem necessary, to take acknowledgments of bail and affidavits; which acknowledgments of bail and affidavits shall have the like force and effect as if taken before any judge of said court; and any person swearing falsely in and by any such affidavit, shall be liable to the same punishment as if the same affidavit had been made or taken before a judge of said court.

Sec. 2. *And be it further enacted,* That the like fees shall be allowed for taking such bail and affidavit as are allowed for the like services by the laws of the state, in which any such affidavit or bail shall be taken.

Sec. 3. *And be it further enacted,* That in any cause before a court of the United States, it shall be lawful for such court, in its discretion, to admit in evidence any deposition taken in perpetuam rei memoriam, which would be so admissible in a court of the state wherein such cause is pending according to the laws thereof.

An act in addition to an act, entitled, " An act for the more convenient taking of affidavits and bail in civil causes, depending in the courts of the United States.

Passed March 1, 1817.

Be it enacted by the Senate and House of Representatives of the United States of America, in Congress assembled, That the commissioners who now are, or hereafter may be, appointed by virtue of the act, entitled " An act for the more convenient taking of affidavits and bail in civil causes, depending in the courts of the United States," are hereby authorized to take affidavits and bail in civil causes, to be used in the several district courts of the United States, and shall and may exercise all the powers that a justice or judge of any of the courts of the United States may exercise by virtue of the thirtieth section of the act, entitled "An act to establish the judicial courts of the United States."

DEPOSITIONS DE BENE ESSE.

An act to establish the Judicial Courts of the United States.

Passed September 24th, 1789.

Sec. 30. *And be it further enacted,* That the mode of proof by oral testimony and examination of witnesses in open court shall be the same in all the courts of the United States, as well in the trial of causes in equity and of admiralty and maritime jurisdiction, as of actions at common law. And when the testimony of any person shall be necessary in any civil cause depending in any district in any court of the United States, who shall live at a greater distance from the place of trial than one hundred miles, or is bound on a voyage to sea, or is about to go out of the United States, or out of such district, and to a greater distance from the place of trial than as aforesaid, before the time of trial, or is ancient or very infirm, the deposition of such person may be taken *de bene esse* before any justice or judge of any of the courts of the United States, or before any chancellor, justice, or judge of a supreme or superior court, mayor or chief magistrate of a city, or judge of a county court or court of common pleas of any of the United States, not being of counsel or attorney to either of the parties, or interested in the event of the cause, provided that a notification from the magistrate before whom the deposition is to be taken to the adverse party, to be present at the taking of the same, and to put interrogatories, if he think fit, be first made out and served on the adverse party or his attorney as either may be nearest, if either is within one hundred miles of the place of such caption, allowing time for their attendance after notified, not less than at the rate of one day, Sundays exclusive, for every twenty miles travel. And in causes of admiralty and maritime jurisdiction, or other cases of seizure when a libel shall be filed, in which an adverse party is not named, and depositions of persons circumstanced as aforesaid shall be taken before a claim be put in, the like notification as aforesaid shall be given to the person having the agency or possession of the property libelled at the time of the capture or seizure of the same, if known to the libellant. And every person deposing as aforesaid shall be carefully examined and cautioned, and sworn or affirmed to testify the whole truth, and shall subscribe the testimony by him or her given after the same shall be reduced to writing, which shall be done only by the magistrate taking the deposition, or by the deponent in his presence. And the depositions so taken shall be retained by such magistrate until he deliver the same with his own hand into the court for which they are taken, or shall, together with a certificate of the reasons as aforesaid of their being taken, and of the notice if any given to the adverse party, be by him the said magistrate sealed up and directed to such court, and remain under his seal until opened in court. And any person may be compelled to appear and depose as aforesaid in the same manner as to appear and testify in court. And in the trial of any cause of admiralty or maritime jurisdiction in a district court, the decree in which may be appealed from, if either party shall suggest to and satisfy the court that probably it will not be in his power to produce the witnesses there testifying before the circuit court should an appeal be had, and shall move that their testimony be taken down in writing, it shall be so done by the clerk of the court. And if an appeal be had, such testimony may be used on the trial of the same, if it shall appear to the satisfaction of the court which shall try the appeal, that the witnesses are then dead or gone out of the United States, or to a greater distance than as aforesaid from the place where the court is sitting, or that by reason of age, sickness, bodily infirmity or imprisonment, they are unable to travel and appear at court, but not otherwise. And unless the same shall be made to appear on the trial of any cause, with respect to witnesses whose depositions may have been taken therein such depositions shall not be admitted or used in the cause. *Provided*, That nothing herein shall be construed to prevent any court of the United States from granting a *dedimus potestatem* to take depositions according to common usage, when it may be necessary to prevent a failure or delay of justice ; which power they shall severally possess, nor to extend to depositions taken in *perpetuam rei memoriam*, which if they relate to matters that may be cognizable in any court of the United States, a circuit court on application thereto made, as a court of equity may, according to the usages in chancery direct to be taken.

COMMISSIONS.

An Act to provide for taking evidence in the Courts of the United States, in certain cases.

Passed 14th January, 1827.

SECT. 1. Be it enacted by the Senate and House of Representatives of the United States of America in Congress assembled, That, whenever a commission shall be issued, by any court of the United States, for taking the testimony of a witness or witnesses, at any place within the United States, or the territories thereof, it shall be lawful for the clerk of any court of the

United States. for the district or territory within which such place may be,
and he is hereby enjoined and required, upon the application of either of the
parties in the suit, cause, action, or proceeding, in which such commission
shall have been issued, his, her, or their agent or agents, to issue a subpœna
or subpœnas, for such witness or witnesses, residing or being within the said
district or territory, as shall be named in the said commission, commanding
such witness or witnesses to appear and testify before the commissioner or
commissioners, in such commission named, at a time and place in the subpœna
to be stated, and if any witness. after being duly served with such subpœna,
shall refuse or neglect to appear, or, after appearing, shall refuse to testify,
(not being privileged from giving testimony,) such refusal or neglect being
proved to the satisfaction of any judge of the court, whose clerk shall have
issued such subpœna or subpœnas, he may thereupon proceed to enforce
obedience to the process, or to punish the disobedience, in like manner as any
court of the United States may do in case of disobedience to process of *subpœna ad testificandum*, issued by such court; and the witness or witnesses,
in such cases, shall be allowed the same compensation as is allowed to witnesses attending the courts of the United States : *Provided*, that no witnesses
shall be required to attend at any place out of the county in which he may
reside, nor more than forty miles from his place of residence, to give his or
her deposition, under this law.

SECT. 2. And be it further enacted, That whenever either of the parties
in such suit, cause, action, or proceeding, shall apply to any judge of a court
of the United States, in the district or territory of the United States, in which
the place for taking such testimony may be, for a *subpœna duces tecum*, commanding the witness, therein to be named, to appear and testify before the
said commissioner or commissioners, at the time and place in the said subpœna to be stated, and also to bring or carry with him or her, and produce
to such commissioner or commissioners, any paper, writing, or written instrument, or book, or other documents supposed to be in the possession or power
of such witness. such judge being satisfied, by the affidavit of the person applying. or otherwise, that there is reason to believe that such paper, writing,
written instrument, book, or other document, is in the possession or power of
the witness, and that the same, if produced, would be competent and material evidence for the party applying therefor, may order the clerk of the
court, of which he is a judge, to issue such *subpœna duces tecum*, accordingly,
and if such witness, after being duly served with such *subpœna duces tecum*,
shall fail to produce any such paper, writing, written instrument, book or
other document, being in the possession or power of such witness, and described in such *subpœna duces tecum*, before, and to such commissioner or
commissioners, at the time and place in such subpœna stated, such failure
being proved to the satisfaction of the said judge, he may proceed to enforce
obedience to the said process of *subpœna duces tecum*, or to punish the disobedience, in like manner as any court of the United States may do in case
of disobedience to a like process, issued by such court; and when any such

paper, writing, written instrument, book, or other document, shall be produced to such commissioner or commissioners, he or they shall, at the cost of the party requiring the same, cause to be made a fair and correct copy thereof, or of so much thereof as shall be required by either of the parties: *Provided*, that no witness shall be deemed guilty of contempt for disobeying any subpœna directed to him by virtue of this act, unless his fees for going to, returning from, and one day's attendance at the place of examination, shall be paid or tendered to him at the time of the service of the subpœna.

COMMISSIONERS TO ACT AS MAGISTRATES, &c.

An act further supplementary to an act entitled, " An act to establish the judicial courts of the United States," passed the twenty-fourth of September, seventeen hundred and eighty-nine.

Passed August 23, 1842.

Sec. 1. Be it enacted by the Senate and House of Representatives of the United States of America, in Congress assembled, That the commissioners who now are, or hereafter may be, appointed by the circuit courts of the United States to take acknowledgments of bail and affidavits, and also to take depositions of witnesses in civil causes, shall and may exercise all the powers that any justice of the peace, or other magistrate, of any of the United States may now exercise in respect to offenders for any crime or offence against the United States, by arresting, imprisoning, or bailing the same, under and by virtue of the thirty-third section of the act of the twenty-fourth of September, Anno Domini seventeen hundred and eighty-nine, entitled, " An act to establish the judicial courts of the United States ;" and who shall and may exercise all the powers that any judge or justice of the peace may exercise under and in virtue of the sixth section of the act passed the twentieth of July, Anno Domini seventeen hundred and ninety, entitled " An act for the government and regulation of seamen in the merchant service."

Sec. 2. And be it further enacted, That in all hearings before any justice or judge of the United States, or any commissioner appointed as aforesaid, under and in virtue of the said thirty-third section of the act entitled, " An act to establish the judicial courts of the United States," it shall be lawful for such justice, judge, or commissioner, where the crime or offence is charged to have been committed on the high seas or elsewhere within the admiralty and maritime jurisdiction of the United States, in his discretion, to require a recognizance of any witness produced in behalf of the accused, with such surety or sureties as he may judge necessary, as well as in behalf of the United States, for their appearing and giving testimony, at the trial of the cause, whose testimony, in his opinion, is important for the purposes of justice at the trial of the cause, and is in danger of being otherwise lost ;

and such witnesses shall be entitled to receive from the United States the usual compensation allowed to Government witnesses for their detention and attendance, if they shall appear and be ready to give testimony at the trial.

Sec. 3. And be it further enacted, That the district courts of the United States shall have concurrent jurisdiction with the circuit courts of all crimes and offences against the United States, the punishment of which is not capital. And in such of the districts where the business of the court may require it to be done for the purposes of justice, and to prevent undue expenses and delays in the trial of criminal causes, the said district courts shall hold monthly adjournments of the regular terms thereof for the trial and hearing of such causes.

Sec. 4. And be it further enacted, That, in lieu of the punishment now prescribed by the sixteenth section of the act of Congress, entitled, " An act for the punishment of certain crimes against the United States," passed on the thirtieth day of April, Anno Domini one thousand seven hundred and ninety, for the offences in the said section mentioned, the punishment of the offender, upon conviction thereof, shall be by fine not exceeding one thousand dollars, or by imprisonment not exceeding one year, or by both, according to the nature and aggravation of the offence.

Sec. 5. And be it further enacted, That the district courts as courts of admiralty, and the circuit courts as courts of equity, shall be deemed always open for the purpose of filing libels, bills, petitions, answers, pleas, and other pleadings, for issuing and returning mesne and final process and commissions, and for making and directing all interlocutory motions, orders, rules, and other proceedings whatever, preparatory to the hearing of all causes pending therein upon their merits. And it shall be competent for any judge of the court, upon reasonable notice to the parties, in the clerk's office or at chambers, and in vacation as well as in term, to make and direct, and award, all such process, commissions and interlocutory orders, rules, and other proceedings, whenever the same are not grantable of course according to the rules and practice of the court.

Sec. 6. And be it further enacted, That the Supreme Court shall have full power and authority, from time to time, to prescribe, and regulate, and alter, the forms of writs and other process to be used and issued in the district and circuit courts of the United States, and the forms and modes of framing and filing libels, bills, answers, and other proceedings and pleadings, in suits at common law or in admiralty and in equity pending in the said courts, and also the forms and modes of taking and obtaining evidence, and of obtaining discovery, and generally the forms and modes of proceeding to obtain relief, and the forms and modes of drawing up, entering, and enrolling decrees, and the forms and modes of proceeding before trustees appointed by the court, and generally to regulate the whole practice of the said courts, so as to prevent delays, and to promote brevity and succinctness in all pleadings and proceedings therein, and to abolish all unnecessary costs and expenses in any suit therein.

Sec. 7. And be it further enacted, That, for the purpose of further diminishing the costs and expenses in suits and proceedings in the said courts, the Supreme Court shall have full power and authority, from time to time, to make and prescribe regulations to the said district and circuit courts, as to the taxation and payment of costs in all suits and proceedings therein; and to make and prescribe a table of the various items of costs which shall be taxable and allowed in all suits, to the parties, their attorneys, solicitors, and proctors, to the clerk of the court, to the marshal of the district, and his deputies, and other officers serving process, to witnesses, and to all other persons whose services are usually taxable in bills of costs. And the items so stated in the said table, and none others, shall be taxable or allowed in bills of costs; and they shall be fixed as low as they reasonably can be, with a due regard to the nature of the duties and services which shall be performed by the various officers and persons aforesaid, and shall in no case exceed the costs and expenses now authorized, where the same are provided for by existing laws.

Sec. 8. And be it further enacted, That on all judgments in civil cases, hereafter recovered in the circuit or district courts of the United States, interest shall be allowed, and may be levied by the marshal, under process of execution issued thereon, in all cases where, by the law of the State in which such circuit or district court shall be held, interest may be levied under process of execution on judgments recovered in the courts of such State, to be calculated from the date of the judgment, and at such rate per annum, as is allowed by law, on judgments recovered in the courts of such State.

SUMMONS FOR WAGES.

An act for the government and regulation of Seamen in the merchants service.

Passed July 20, 1790.

Sec. 6. And be it further enacted, That every seaman or mariner shall be entitled to demand and receive from the master or commander of the ship or vessel to which they belong, one third part of the wages which shall be due to him at every port where such ship or vessel shall unlade and deliver her cargo before the voyage be ended, unless the contrary be expressly stipulated in the contract; and as soon as the voyage is ended, and the cargo or ballast be fully discharged at the last port of delivery, every seaman or mariner shall be entitled to the wages which shall be then due according to his contract; and if such wages shall not be paid within ten days after such discharge, or if any dispute shall arise between the master and seamen or mariners touching the said wages, it shall be lawful for the judge of the district where the said ship or vessel shall be, or in case his residence be more than three miles from the place, or of his absence from the place of his residence, then, for any judge or justice of the peace, to summon the master of such ship or vessel to appear before him, to show cause why process should not issue against such ship or vessel, her tackle, furniture, and apparel, according to the course of admiralty courts, to answer for the said wages : and if the master shall neglect to appear, or appearing, shall not show that the wages are paid, or otherwise satisfied or forfeited, and if the matter in dispute shall not be forthwith settled, in such case the judge or justice shall certify to the clerk of the court of the district, that there is sufficient cause of complaint whereon to found admiralty process, and thereupon the clerk of such court shall issue process against the said ship or vessel, and the suit shall be proceeded on in the said court, and final judgment be given according to the course of admiralty courts in such cases used ; and in such suit all the seamen or mariners (having cause of complaint of the like kind against the same ship or vessel) shall be joined as complainants ; and it shall be incumbent on the master or commander to produce the contract and log-book, if required, to ascertain any matters in dispute ; otherwise the complainants shall be permitted to state the contents thereof, and the proof of the contrary shall lie on the master or commander ; but nothing herein contained shall prevent any seaman or mariner from having or maintaining any action at common law for the recovery of his wages, or from immediate process out of any court having admiralty jurisdiction, wherever any ship or vessel may be found, in case she shall have left the port of delivery where her voyage ended, before payment of the wages, or in case she shall be about to proceed to sea before the end of the ten days next after the delivery of her cargo or ballast.

PRACTICAL FORMS.

THE following precedents, with a very few exceptions, have been selected from the accumulated papers of twenty years of my own practice. Names and dates are often changed, and the merely formal parts are reduced to a uniformity which did not exist in the original papers, but which was desirable in a body of precedents. In many instances, also, I have changed the phraseology, with a view to greater brevity and clearness. Subject to these remarks, they are the precedents of actual practice, prepared by myself and others.

In the first instance, the forms and proceedings in a suit in Admiralty will be given in consecutive chronological order, from the commencement of the suit to its final termination; and then, such other forms will be added as shall seem to be necessary.

Forms of proceedings in a suit *in rem*, against a ship and cargo, for salvage, with a suit against the same ship for a forfeiture, for being brought into a prohibited port:

No. 1.—LIBEL BY THE OWNER AND MASTER OF THE SAVING VESSEL, FOR THEMSELVES AND OTHERS, AGAINST THE SAVED VESSEL AND CARGO, FOR SALVAGE.

DISTRICT COURT OF THE UNITED STATES OF AMERICA.
SOUTHERN DISTRICT OF NEW YORK:—
    In Admiralty.—
                    To the Honorable Samuel R. Betts, Judge of the District Court of the United States in and for the Southern District of New York:

The libel of Peter Harmony, owner of the American brig Merced of New York, and of Eliphalet Kingsbury, master of the said brig, for themselves and all others entitled, against the ship Waterloo, her tackle, apparel and furniture, and cargo, and against all persons intervening for their interest therein, in a cause of salvage, civil and maritime, alleges as follows:

First. That on the twenty-seventh day of August last past, the said Eliphalet Kingsbury being on a voyage, in the said brig Merced, from Havana, in the Island of Cuba, to Cadiz, in Spain, discovered a ship dismasted and apparently deserted, whereupon he hauled up for and boarded her; that he found the said ship which proved to be the British ship Waterloo, of London, with twelve feet of water in her hold, totally dismasted and entirely abandoned by her captain and crew; that he found no papers on board the said ship, but she had a full cargo of rum, sugar, and other West India produce on board.

Second. That the said Eliphalet Kingsbury thereupon took the said ship Waterloo in tow and made for the port of New York, where he arrived with the said ship on the twelfth day of September instant, the crew of the brig being almost worn out with fatigue in pumping out the said ship, and other work done on board of her, and they are entitled to a reasonable share of said ship and cargo for the salvage thereof.

Third. That all and singular the premises are true, and within the Admiralty and maritime jurisdiction of the United States and of this Honorable Court.

Wherefore the libellants pray that process in due form of law, according to the course of this Honorable Court in cases of admiralty and maritime jurisdiction, may issue against the said ship Waterloo, her tackle, apparel, and furniture, and cargo, and that all persons claiming any interest therein, may be cited to appear and answer upon oath, all and singular the matters aforesaid, and that this honorable court will be pleased to decree to the libellants a reasonable and proper salvage, in proportion to the value of said vessel and cargo, and that the said ship, her tackle, apparel and furniture, and cargo, may be condemned and sold to pay said salvage, with costs, charges, and expenses, and that the libellants may have such other and further relief in the premises as in law and justice they may be entitled to receive.

Sworn, Sept. 16, 1829,   PETER HARMONY.
    before me,   ELIPHALET KINGSBURY.
        FRED J. BETTS, Clerk.
ISAAC A. JOHNSON, Proctor.
E. C. BENEDICT, Advocate.

No. 2.—STIPULATION FOR COSTS TO BE GIVEN BY THE LIBELLANTS ON FILING THE FOREGOING LIBEL.

DISTRICT COURT OF THE UNITED STATES
FOR THE SOUTHERN DISTRICT OF NEW YORK.

Stipulation entered into pursuant to the Rules and Practice of this Court.

Whereas a libel was filed in this court, on the 16th day of September, 1829, by Peter Harmony and Eliphalet Kingsbury, against the ship Waterloo, her tackle, apparel, and furniture, and cargo, for the reasons and causes in the said libel mentioned; and praying that the same may be condemned and sold to answer the prayer of the libellants; and the said libellants and George Jones, surety, the parties hereto, hereby consenting and agreeing that in case of default or contumacy on the part of the libellants or their surety, execution may issue against their goods, chattels and lands, for the sum of two hundred and fifty dollars—

Now, therefore, it is hereby stipulated and agreed, for the benefit of whom it may concern, that the stipulators undersigned shall be, and are bound, in the sum of two hundred and fifty dollars, conditioned that the libellants above named shall pay all such costs as shall be awarded against them by this court, or in case of appeal, by the Appellate Court.

Taken and acknowledged, this   PETER HARMONY.
16th day of September, 1829, be-   ELIPHALET KINGSBURY.
fore me,   GEORGE JONES.
    FRED. J. BETTS, Clerk.

No. 3.—JUSTIFICATION OF SURETY.

Southern District of New York, ss.—George Jones of the city of New York, merchant, party to the above stipulation, being duly sworn, deposes and says, that he resides at 21 New street, and that he is a householder in the Southern District of New York, and is worth the sum of five hundred dollars over and above all his debts.

Sworn this 16th day of September,   GEORGE JONES.
1829, before me,
    FRED. J. BETTS, Clerk.

No. 4.—ATTACHMENT AND MONITION AGAINST A SHIP AND CARGO IN REM, ON THE FOREGOING LIBEL.

SOUTHERN DISTRICT OF NEW YORK, ss.—

The President of the United States of America, to the Marshal of the Southern District of New York, Greeting: Whereas a libel hath been filed in the District Court of

[L. S.] the United States, for the Southern District of New York, on the 16th day of September, in the year of our Lord one thousand eight hundred and twenty-nine, by Peter Harmony and others, against the ship Waterloo, her tackle, apparel, and furniture, and cargo, in a cause of salvage civil and maritime, for the reasons and causes in the said libel mentioned, and praying the usual process and monition of the said court in that behalf to be made, and that all persons interested in the said ship or vessel, her tackle, &c., and cargo, may be cited in general and special, to answer the premises, and all proceedings being had that the said ship or vessel, her tackle, &c., and cargo, may, for the causes in the said libel mentioned, be condemned and sold to pay the demands of the libellant :

You are therfore hereby commanded, to attach the said ship or vessel, her tackle, &c., and cargo, and to detain the same in your custody, until the further order of the court respecting the same, and to give due notice to all persons claiming the same, or knowing or having any thing to say why the same should not be condemned and sold pursuant to the prayer of the said libel, that they be and appear before the said court, to be held in and for the Southern District of New York, on the first Tuesday of October next, at eleven o'clock in the forenoon of the same day, if the same shall be a day of jurisdiction, otherwise on the next day of jurisdiction thereafter, then and there to interpose a claim for the same, and to make their allegations in that behalf. And what you shall have done in the premises do you then and there make return thereof, together with this writ.

Witness, the Honorable SAMUEL R. BETTS, Judge of the said Court, at the city of New York, in the Southern District of New York, this 16th day of September, in the year of our Lord one thousand eight hundred and twenty-nine, and of our Independence the fifty-sixth.

FRED. J. BETTS, Clerk.

ISAAC A. JOHNSON, Proctor for Libellant.

No. 5.—NOTICE FOR PUBLICATION CONTAINING THE SUBSTANCE OF THE LIBEL.

UNITED STATES OF AMERICA.

Southern District of New York, ss :—

Whereas a libel has been filed in the District Court of the United States for the Southern District of New York, on the 16th day of September, 1829, by Peter Harmony, owner, and Eliphalet Kingsbury, master of the brig Merced, libellants, against the ship Waterloo, her tackle, apparel and furniture, and cargo, alleging, in substance, that on the twenty-seventh day of August last, said Eliphalet Kingsbury, being on a voyage from Havana to Cadiz in the said brig Merced, discovered and boarded the British ship Waterloo of London, with twelve feet of water in her hold, totally dismasted and entirely abandoned by her captain and crew; that he found no papers on board of her, but that she had a full cargo of rum, sugar, and other West India produce on board : that he thereupon took the said ship in tow, and brought her into the port of New York on the twelfth day of September instant, her crew being almost worn out with fatigue, and that they are entitled to a reasonable share of said ship and cargo for the salvage thereof. And praying process against said ship and cargo, and reasonable and proper salvage, and that the said ship, her tackle, apparel and furniture, and cargo, may be condemned and sold to pay such salvage, with costs, charges, and expenses.—

Now, therefore, in pursuance of the monition under the seal of the said court to me directed and delivered, I do hereby give public notice to all persons claiming the said ship, her tackle, apparel and furniture, and cargo, or in any manner interested therein, that they be and appear before the said District Court to be held at the city of New York in and for the Southern District of New York, on the first Tuesday of October next, at eleven o'clock in the forenoon of that day, (provided the same shall be a day of jurisdiction, otherwise, on the next day of jurisdiction thereafter,) then and there to interpose their claims, and to make their allegations in that behalf.

Dated the 16th day of September, 1829.

THOMAS MORRIS, U. S. Marshal.

ISAAC A, JOHNSON, Proctor for Libellants.

6.—THE MARSHAL'S RETURN TO THE FOREGOING WRIT.

In obedience to the within monition, I attached the vessel and cargo therein described, on the 16th day of September last, and I have given due notice to all persons claiming the same, that this Court will on the 5th day of October inst., (if that day should be a day of jurisdiction, if not, on the next day of jurisdiction thereafter,) proceed to the trial and condemnation thereof, should no claim be interposed for the same.

Dated October 5, 1829.

THOMAS MORRIS, U. S. Marshal.

No. 7.—PROCLAMATION ON THE RETURN OF PROCESS IN REM.

Hear ye! Hear ye! Peter Harmony and Eliphalet Kingsbury against the ship Waterloo, her tackle, apparel, and furniture, and cargo. All persons who have any thing to say why the ship Waterloo, her tackle, apparel, and furniture, and cargo, should not be condemned and sold to answer the prayer of the libellants in this cause, come forward and make your allegations in that behalf.

No. 8.—ORDER OF THE COURT ON THE RETURN OF MESNE PROCESS IN REM.

The marshal having returned, upon the monition in this cause, that he had attached the said ship, her tackle, &c., and cargo, and had given due notice to all persons claiming the same, that this Court would, on this day, proceed to the trial and condemnation thereof should no claim be interposed for the same :—On motion of Mr. Johnson, proctor for the libellants, proclamation was made for all persons having any thing to say why the said vessel and her cargo should not be condemned and sold to answer the prayer of the libellants, to appear ; and on like motion, ordered that the defaults of all persons who have not already filed their claims be entered.

No. 9.—CLAIM BY THE AGENTS OF FOREIGN UNDERWRITERS TO VESSEL AND CARGO, IN CASE OF SALVAGE OF A FOREIGN SHIP.

United States District Court for the Southern District of New York.

IN ADMIRALTY.

To the Honorable Samuel R. Betts, Judge of the District Court of the United States for the Southern District of New York.

The answer and claim of Henry Barclay and George Barclay, of the city of New York, merchants intervening for the interest of their principals, to the libel of Peter Harmony and Eliphalet Kingsbury, alleges as follows :

First. That these defendants admit, that on the twenty-seventh day of August last past, the said Eliphalet Kingsbury was the master of the brig Merced, of New York, and that he was then in the said brig on a voyage from Havana, in Cuba, to Cadiz, in Spain ; but whether he then discovered a ship dismasted and apparently deserted, and whether he then hauled up for her and boarded her, and whether he found the said ship with twelve feet water in her hold, and totally dismasted and entirely abandoned by her captain and crew, and whether the said ship proved to be the British ship Waterloo, of London, and whether the said Eliphalet Kingsbury found any papers in the said ship or not, these respondents know not, and therefore can neither admit nor deny, but leave the same to be proved by the said libellant.

Second. That they admit it to be true, that the said Eliphalet Kingsbury arrived at the port of New York, on the twelfth day of September, in the year of our Lord one thousand eight hundred and twenty-nine, and that he had the ship Waterloo, of London, in tow, and that the said ship had a full cargo of rum, sugar, and other West Indian produce on board, and that said ship, when so brought in, was dismasted and disabled, but whether the crew of the said brig Merced were or were not almost worn out with fatigue, in pumping out the said ship, and with other work done on board of her, these respondents know not, and therefore leave the same to be proved by the said libellants.

Third. That, by a commission, dated the second day of July, in the year of our Lord one thousand eight hundred and seventeen, and signed by Joseph Maryat, chairman, and John Bennet, junior, secretary of the committee for managing the affairs of the underwriters, at Lloyd's, in London, in that part of the United Kingdom of Great Britain and Ireland called England, these respondents were appointed to act as agents for the subscribers at Lloyd's, at the port of New York, and Custom-house district, subject to the instructions in the said commission mentioned : and that, by the said instructions, they are, amongst other things, directed, " When salvage or remuneration is claimed, for assistance rendered to vessels, to attend the meeting of the commissioners, magistrates, or other persons legally authorized to determine the amount, in order to rebut any exaggerated statements on the part of the salvors, by the evidence of the master and crew ;" and they are likewise authorized and empowered by the said commission to attend to the interests of the subscribers to Lloyd's in general ; as by the said commission now in the possession of these respondents, will more fully and at large appear, and to which, for greater certainty, these respondents pray leave to refer.

Fourth. That they are likewise the agents for the underwriters at Liverpool, in that part of the United Kingdom of Great Britain and Ireland called England ; and for the underwriters in Glasgow, in that part of the United Kingdom of Great Britain and Ireland, called Scotland, under two several commissions with the like authority and instructions as mentioned in the said commissions, from the underwriters, at Lloyd's, in London aforesaid, as by the said several commissions from the underwriters at Liverpool, and from the underwriters at Glasgow, reference being thereunto had, will more fully and at large appear, and to which, for greater certainty, these respondents pray leave to refer.

Fifth. That they have no doubt that the said ship Waterloo, or her cargo, or both, or some part thereof, were or was insured at some or one of the said places, by some or all of the underwriters therein, and they have no doubt but that the said vessel, or her cargo, or both, or some part thereof, have or hath been abandoned by the persons interested therein, to the said underwriters, or some or one of them; and that the right of ownership in the said ship and cargo, or both, or some part thereof, hath accrued to the said underwriters, or some, or one of them; but these respondents cannot speak on this point with absolute certainty, but only to the best of their belief, inasmuch as a sufficient time hath not elapsed since the twelfth day of September, eighteen hundred and twenty-nine, when the said ship was as aforesaid brought into the said port of New York, to communicate the circumstance to the said several insurers, or any of them, and to hear from the said several underwriters, or any of them, on the same subject.

Sixth. That immediately after the said vessel and her cargo were brought into the said port of New York, as aforesaid, they wrote to the said underwriters at London, informing them of the circumstances of the case, as far as was known to these respondents, and requesting information from the said underwriters, of their rights and interests in and to the said vessel and her cargo, or any part thereof. That, on the sixteenth day of September, in the year of our Lord 1829, these respondents received from Thomas Morris, Esquire, marshal of the United States for this district, a request that these respondents would enter the cargo of the said ship at the Custom-house at New York, and would become responsible for the payment of the duties that might be payable to the United States on the cargo of the said ship. That, in pursuance thereof, these respondents entered the said cargo, and secured the duties upon the same by bond, conditioned for the payment of the duties to be ascertained on the said cargo. That said duties have since been ascertained, and amount to twenty-one thousand six hundred and ninety-eight dollars and ninety-one cents. which these respondents have thereby become liable to pay ; also, certain foreign duties chargeable on said ship and cargo, besides Custom-house fees and expenses paid by these respondents. And therefore these respondents, on behalf of the said several underwriters, claim the said vessel and cargo, and pray that out of the proceeds of the sale of the said vessel and cargo, if sold, this court may, in the first place, order the said amount of duties secured by these respondents, and the said foreign duties and fees, to be paid to these respondents, and that this honorable court, after hearing proof and decreeing a reasonable salvage, should it seem proper so to do, may further decree, that the rest, residue and remainder of the said ship and her cargo, or of the proceeds

55

thereof, should the same be decreed to be sold, after payment of said amount of duties and fees, and of the salvage, may be retained in the custody of this Honorable Court, for such reasonable time as may seem proper; wherein the rights and interests of the above-mentioned underwriters may be ascertained; and that this Honorable Court may further decree, that the said ship and cargo, or the proceeds thereof, or a part thereof, as proof may be made of interest, may be delivered up to these respondents, upon due proof being made in manner and form as this Honorable Court may direct, that the said underwriters or any of them have an interest in, and a right to receive the same or any part thereof.

GEORGE BARCLAY.

Sworn this 5th day of October, 1829,
  before me,
    FRED. J. BETTS, Clerk.

ROBINSON & BETTS, Proctors.
BEVERLY ROBINSON, Advocate.

No. 10.—STIPULATION FOR COSTS TO BE GIVEN BY THE CLAIMANT ON PUTTING IN A CLAIM.

DISTRICT COURT OF THE UNITED STATES,

FOR THE SOUTHERN DISTRICT OF NEW YORK.

Stipulation entered into pursuant to the Rules and Practice of this Court.

Whereas a libel was filed in this court, on the 16th day of September, in the year of our Lord one thousand eight hundred and twenty-nine, by Peter Harmony and Eliphalet Kingsbury, against the ship Waterloo, her tackle, apparel and furniture, and cargo, for the reasons and causes in the said libel mentioned, and praying that the same may be condemned and sold, to answer the prayer of the libellants.—

And whereas, also, a claim has been filed in said cause by Henry Barclay and George Barclay—and the said claimants and James Jackson, surety, the parties hereto, hereby consenting that in case of default or contumacy on the part of the claimants or their surety, execution for the sum of two hundred and fifty dollars may issue against their goods, chattels and lands.—

Now, therefore, it is hereby stipulated and agreed, for the benefit of whom it may concern, that the stipulators undersigned shall be, and are hereby bound, in the sum of two hundred and fifty dollars, conditioned that the claimants above named, shall pay all costs and expenses which shall be awarded against them by the final decree of this Court, or upon an appeal, by the Appellate Court.

Taken and acknowledged, this 5th day
of October, 1829, before me,
    FRED. J. BETTS, Clerk.

HENRY BARCLAY.
GEORGE BARCLAY.
JAMES JACKSON.

No. 11.—JUSTIFICATION OF SURETY.

Southern District of New York, ss.—James Jackson, of the city of Brook-lyn, merchant, party to the above stipulation, being duly sworn, deposes and says, that he resides at No. 11 Fulton street, in the city of Brooklyn, in the Southern District of New York, and that he is worth the sum of five hundred dollars over and above all his just debts and liabilities.

JAMES JACKSON.

Sworn to, this 5th day of October,
 1829, before me.
FRED. J. BETTS, Clerk.

No. 12.—CLAIM BY A FOREIGN CONSUL FOR UNKNOWN OWNERS IN A CASE OF SALVAGE OF A SHIP AND CARGO OF HIS NATION.

DISTRICT COURT OF THE UNITED STATES,
FOR THE SOUTHERN DISTRICT OF NEW YORK.

In Admiralty.

To the Honorable Samuel R. Betts, Judge of the District Court of the United States for the Southern District of New York :

The claim and answer of James C. Buchanan, His Brittannic Majesty's vice-consul in and for the city and state of New York and eastern New Jersey, intervening for the interest of the owner or owners of the British ship Waterloo and her cargo, alleges as follows :

First. That the said ship Waterloo is, as alleged in the said libel, and as the said claimant believes to be true, British property ; and he believes the cargo of merchandise alleged to have been found on board of the said ship, to be in like manner British property :—And as such vice-consul, and in behalf of such British owners as may be entitled to the same, he claims the same as their property.

Second. That as to the facts alleged and set forth in the said libel, the said claimant neither admits nor denies the same, but leaves the same to be duly proved to the satisfaction of this court.

And the said claimant prays, on behalf of the owner or owners of the said ship Waterloo, and her aforesaid cargo, or of any other person or persons whom the same may concern, that the said ship, her tackle, apparel and furniture, and her cargo, aforesaid, may be sold, and out of the proceeds of the sale thereof, after the payment of all costs and charges incurred, that the said libellants, having duly proved as aforesaid the facts in their said libel set forth, may be allowed and paid such rate and amount of salvage, for their labor and exertions in bringing the said ship and her aforesaid cargo into this port, as by this court shall be deemed just and reasonable under the circumstances of the case, and that the surplus of the said proceeds, after payment of such salvage as aforesaid, may be adjudged and decreed to be paid to the said claimant, on behalf of the owner or owners of the said ship and her aforesaid cargo, or whomsoever the same may concern; or that such other order or decree may be made in relation to the same as this court shall deem proper.

J. C. BUCHANAN, H. M. Vice Consul.

H. & E. WILKES,

Proctors and Adv'cts. for Claimants.

Sworn this 5th day of October,

   1829, before me,

FRED J. BETTS, Clerk.

Stipulation for Costs, as ante, No. 10, *page* 434.

No. 13.—CLAIM BY THE U. S. ATTORNEY ON BEHALF OF THE U. STATES FOR FORFEITURE AND FOR DUTIES IN A CASE OF SALVAGE OF A FOREIGN SHIP AND CARGO.

District Court of the United States of America for the Southern District of New York.

IN ADMIRALTY.

To the Honorable Samuel R. Betts, Judge of the District Court of the United States for the Southern District of New York.

The claim of James A. Hamilton, District Attorney of the United States of America for the Southern District of New York, intervening for the interest of the said United States, in the said ship called the Waterloo, and her cargo, and the answer of the said attorney, on behalf of the said United States, to the libel of the said Peter Harmony and Eliphalet Kingsbury, alleges as follows:

First. That the said James A. Hamilton, District Attorney of the United States of America for the Southern District of New York, claims the said ship Waterloo, together with the cargo of the said ship laden on board of her, as stated and set forth in the said libel, as forfeited to the use of the said United States for the cause following—to wit, that the said ship Waterloo is a ship or vessel owned wholly or in part by a subject or subjects of his Brittanic majesty, and said ship or vessel. after the thirtieth day of September, one thousand eight hundred and eighteen, did come and arrive from a port or place in a colony or territory of his Brittanic majesty, to wit, from the port of Annatto Bay, in the island of Jamaica, in the West Indies, which said port is and was, at the time the said ship sailed from thence by the ordinary laws of navigation and trade, closed against vessels owned by citizens of the United States, and that the ports of the United States were, and are closed against the said ship or vessel called the Waterloo, which said ship or vessel being so excluded from the ports of the United States, did enter the same, to wit, the port of New York, in the Southern District of New York aforesaid, in violation of the acts of the Congress of the United States, in such cases made and provided. By force and virtue of the acts in such case made and provided, the said ship or vessel, her tackle, apparel, and furniture, together with the cargo on board of the said ship or vessel, became and are forfeited to the use of the said United States.

Second. That if this Honorable Court shall adjudge and decree that the said ship or vessel, with her cargo, or either, is not forfeited to the use of the United States, for the cause aforesaid, the said ship or vessel, together with the cargo on board of her, is liable to the payment of the duties imposed by the laws of the United States, on the arrival of the said ship or vessel within the United States, and on the importation of the cargo of merchandize on board of her, to wit, rum and sugar of the growth, produce, and manufacture of some foreign country, and which are subject to the payment of duties to the United States, on being brought or imported into the United States; wherefore the said attorney, on behalf of the said United States, prays this Honorable Court to decree the payment of the said duties to the United States according to law, if the said ship and the cargo on board of her as aforesaid, shall be adjudged not to be forfeited to the use of the said United States for the cause aforesaid, and that he may have his costs, &c. And the said attorney further insists upon and submits to this Honorable Court the rights and interest of the said United States of America, in the premises whatever they may be, to be decreed to them.

JAMES A. HAMILTON,
Attorney United States, &c.

The United States does not give a stipulation for costs.

No. 14.—REPLICATION TO CLAIM AND ANSWER.

To the Honorable Samuel R. Betts, Judge, &c.

The replication of Peter Harmony and Eliphalet Kingsbury, libellants, to the claim and answer of James Buchanan, claimant and respondent, alleges that they will aver, maintain, and prove their libel to be true, certain, and sufficient; and that the said claim and answer of the said claimant and respondent is uncertain, untrue, and insufficient, and they humbly pray, as in and by their libel they have already prayed.

ISAAC A. JOHNSON,
Proctor for Libellants.

Special Motion—for Interlocutory Sale.

No. 15.—AFFIDAVIT OF CIRCUMSTANCES TO MOVE FOR SALE OF SHIP AND CARGO.

District Court of the United States for the Southern District of New York.

PETER HARMONY and ELIPHALET KINGSBURY, *vs.* THE SHIP WATERLOO, &c. and CARGO.	

SOUTHERN DISTRICT OF NEW YORK. ss.:—

Peter Harmony, one of the libellants in this cause, being sworn, says—

that the ship Waterloo is now at the wharf in the port of New York, sub-ject to large and increasing expense for wharfage, keeper's fees, and other expenses. That she is in a damaged condition, and requires care and re-pairs. That a large portion of her cargo is perishable, being sugar, and in a wet and damaged condition. That the only claims that have been inter-posed are those of the United States, for a forfeiture and for duties—of the British Consul, for the probable rights of unknown British owners, and of the agents of the underwriters, at Lloyd's, for the contingent rights of such un-derwriters. That, in his opinion, the interests of all parties concerned will be promoted by a speedy judicial sale of said ship, her tackle, apparel, and furniture and cargo, the proceeds of such sale to be brought into court for the benefit of whom it may concern, subject to the further order of the court.

Sworn October 7th, 1829,　　　　　　　　　　　PETER HARMONY.
　　before me,
　　　　`FRED. J. BETTS, Clerk.

No. 16.—NOTICE OF MOTION ON THE FOREGOING AFFIDAVIT.

District Court of the U. S.—Southern District of N. Y.

| PETER HARMONY and ELIPHALET KINGSBURY,
vs.
THE SHIP WATERLOO and CARGO. | |

GENTLEMEN—You will please take notice that, on the libel and claims in this cause, and on an affidavit, of which the foregoing is a copy, a mo-tion will be made before his Honor, Samuel R. Betts, Judge of this Court, at his chambers, No. 5 Pine-street, in the city of New York, on Thursday, the 8th day of October, inst. at 11 o'clock in the forenoon of that day, for an order, that the ship Waterloo and her cargo above-men-tioned, be sold under the direction of the marshal, and the proceeds brought into court.

New York, 7th Oct. 1829.　　　　　Yours, &c.
　　　　　　　　　　　　　　　ISAAC A. JOHNSON,
To　　　　　　　　　　　　　　　Proctor for Libellants.
　　JAMES A. HAMILTON, Esq. Proctor for the U. S.
　　ROBINSON & BETTS, Esqrs. Proctors for the Underwriters, &c.
　　H. & E. WILKES, Esqrs. Proctors for the Owners.

No. 17—PROOF OF SERVICE—ADMISSION.

We admit due service of the within notice.
　　Oct. 7th, 1829.
　　　　　　　JAMES A. HAMILTON, District Attorney.
　　　　　　　ROBINSON & BETTS, Pts. for H. Barclay & Geo. Barclay.
　　　　　　　H. &. E. WILKES, for British Consul.

OR THIS:

AFFIDAVIT OF SERVICE OF PROCESS.

Southern District of New York, ss. :

John J Young, of the city of New York, student at law, being duly sworn, says, that on the 7th day of October, instant, he served copies of the foregoing affidavit and notice on James A. Hamilton, Robinson & Betts, and H. & E. Wilkes, Esquires, Proctors for the claimants in this cause, by leaving the same in their respective offices, with their clerks.

Sworn Oct. 7th, 1829,   JOHN J. YOUNG.

before me,

E. C. BENEDICT, U. S. Commissioner.

No. 18 —ORDER FOR INTERLOCUTORY SALE OF A SHIP AND CARGO.

PETER HARMONY and ELIPHALET
KINGSBURY,
vs.
The Ship WATERLOO, her tackle, &c.
and Cargo.

On reading and filing the affidavit of Peter Harmony, and the admission of the proctors for the respective claimants, and on motion of Mr. Johnson, proctors for the libellants, It is ordered, that the ship Waterloo, her tackle, apparel, and furniture and cargo, be sold by the marshal, on six days public notice, and that a *venditioni exponas* issue accordingly ; and it is further ordered, that the marshal bring the proceeds of such sale into this court, and pay the same to the clerk thereof.

No. 19.—VENDITIONI EXPONAS.

Southern District of New York, ss :

The President of the United States of America, to the Marshal of the Southern District of New York, Greeting: Whereas, a libel was filed in the district court of the [L. S.]   United States for the southern district of New York, on the sixteenth day of September, in the year of our Lord one thousand eight hundred and twenty-nine, by Peter Harmony and Eliphalet Kingsbury, against the ship Waterloo, her tackle, apparel, furniture and cargo, and praying that the same may be condemned and sold to answer the prayer of the said libellants. And whereas, the said ship and cargo have been attached by the process issued out of the said district court, in pursuance of the said libel, and are now in custody by virtue thereof; and such proceedings have been thereupon had, that by the interlocutory sentence and decree of the said court, in this cause made and pronounced, on the seventh day of November, one thousand eight hundred and twenty-nine, the said ship, her tackle, apparel, and furniture and cargo, were ordered to be sold by you the said marshal, after giving six days notice of such sale, according to law. Therefore you, the said marshal, are hereby commanded to cause the said ship Waterloo, her tackle, apparel, and furniture and cargo, so ordered to be sold, to be sold in manner and form, upon the notice, and at the time and place by law required, and that you have the moneys arising from such sale in said court, at the city of New York, on the third Tuesday of November next, and that you then pay the same to the clerk of the court ; and have you also then and there this writ.

Witness, the Honorable Samuel R. Betts, Judge of the said court, at the city of New York, in the Southern District of New York, this seventh day of November, in the year of our Lord one thousand eight hundred and twenty-nine, and of our independence the fifty-third.

Fred. J. Betts, Clerk.

● No 20.—The return of the marshal.

In obedience to the above precept, I have sold the ship Waterloo, her tackle, apparel, and furniture and cargo, and such sale amounts to thirty-nine thousand two hundred and sixty-two dollars and ninety cents, which sum I have paid to the clerk of this court as I am above commanded.

Dated this 22d day of February, 1830.

Thomas Morris, U. S. Marshal.

No. 21.—The clerk's receipt to the marshal.

United States District Court.

Peter Harmony, &c.,
vs.
The Ship Waterloo, &c.

New York, February 22, 1830.

Received, from Thomas Morris, Esq., marshal, thirty-nine thousand two hundred and sixty-two dollars, and ninety cents, the amount of the proceeds of the said ship and cargo, sold under the *venditioni exponas* in this cause.

Fred. J. Betts, District Clerk.

$39,262 90.

Special Motion.

No. 22.—Application by the marshal for leave to pay the duties on cargo sold by him.

District Court of the U. S. for the Southern District of N. Y.

Peter Harmony, &c.
vs.
The Ship Waterloo, &c.

Gentlemen—I shall apply to the court in this cause, on Wednesday, the

11th day of November instant, for leave to pay to the collector of the port the duties on the cargo, out of the proceeds of the sale thereof.
November 7th, 1829.

Yours, &c.

To
Thomas Morris, Marshall.

Isaac A. Johnson, Esq., Proctor for Libellant.
James A. Hamilton.
Robinson & Betts.
H. & E. Wilkes, Proctors for Claimants.

Due service admitted.

Isaac A. Johnson.
James A. Hamilton.
Robinson & Betts.
H. & E. Wilkes.

No. 23.—Order on the foregoing application.

It being made to appear to the court that on entering the said ship and cargo, the duties on said cargo were secured to be paid, and application being now made on the part of the marshal of the district for an order that he pay over to the collector of the port the amount of duties so secured to be paid, and due notice having been given to the respective parties before the court, and no opposition being made to the application, it is ordered, that the marshal forthwith pay to the said collector the amount of such duties, and that on filing the proper vouchers of such payment, the said vouchers be received as part of the return to the *venditioni exponas* issued in this cause.

No. 24.—Depositions de bene esse.—Affidavit of necessity.

DISTRICT COURT OF THE UNITED STATES.
Southern District of New York.

Peter Harmony and Eliphalet Kingsbury.

vs.

The ship Waterloo, her tackle, &c., and her cargo.

}

Southern District of New York, ss.—Eliphalet Kingsbury, one of the libellants above named, being sworn, saith, that he was master of the brig Merced, of New York, on her late voyage from Havana to Cadiz, in the course of which she fell in with the above mentioned ship Waterloo in distress, and the deponent further saith, that William N. Winnett was first mate, and Caleb L. Upshur was the second mate of the said brig, upon the

56

said voyage, and that William Jackson, James Porter, William Dyer, John Stivers, James Jamison, William Grant, Joseph Dominguez, and Nicholas Yanino, composed the residue of the company of the said brig, and Felix Martinez, who was working his passage in said brig, on the aforesaid voyage. The deponent further saith, that the said William N. Winnett, Caleb L. Upshur, William Jackson, James Porter, William Dyer, John Stivers, James Jamison, William Grant, Felix Martinez, Joseph Dominguez, and Nicholas Yanino are witnesses whose testimony is necessary for the libellants in the above cause, and that the said witnesses are all sea-faring men, and are bound on a voyage to sea, as he is informed and believes.

E. Kingsbury.

Sworn, October 7th, 1829,
    before me,
        E. C. Benedict,
           U. S. Commissioner, &c.

No. 25.—Notice from the magistrate to the adverse party of taking depositions de bene esse.

DISTRICT COURT OF THE UNITED STATES.

FOR THE SOUTHERN DISTRICT OF NEW YORK.

Peter Harmony and Eliphalet Kingsbury. *vs.* The ship Waterloo, her tackle, apparel, and furniture, and cargo.	} *Notice.*

Please to take notice, that William N. Winnett, Caleb L. Upshur, James Porter, William Dyer, John Stevens, James Jamison and William Grant, witnesses, whose testimony is necessary in this cause, and who are bound on a voyage to sea, will be examined (de bene esse) on the part of the libellants in this cause, before me, a Commissioner duly appointed by the Circuit Court of the United States for the Southern District of New York, at my office, No. 15 Pine street, in the city of New York, on the eighth day of October instant, at nine o'clock in the forenoon, at which time and place you are hereby notified to be present, and put interrogatories, if you shall think fit.

Dated, New York, the 7th day of October, A. D. 1829.
        Yours, &c.
           E. C. Benedict, U. S. Commissioner.

To James A. Hamilton, Esq.
    Robinson & Betts, Esqrs.
    H. & E. Wilkes, Esqrs.
        Proctors for the Claimants.

No. 26.—Proof of service.

Southern District of New York, ss. :—John J. Young, of the said city, student at law, being duly sworn, deposeth and saith, that on the seventh day of October instant, he served a copy of the annexed notice on James A Hamilton, Esq., proctor for the United States, by delivering the same to a man attending in the office of the said James A. Hamilton ; that on the same day he served a copy of the said notice on Robinson & Betts, Esqrs., proctors for the claimants Barclay, by delivering the same to a clerk in the office of the said Robinson & Betts ; and that on the same day he served a copy of the said notice on H. & E. Wilkes, Esqrs., proctors for the claimant Buchanan, by delivering the same to E. Wilkes, Esq., personally, and further he saith not.

JOHN J. YOUNG.

Sworn, this 8th day of October,
    1829, before me,
        E. C. BENEDICT,
            U. S. Commissioner, &c.

No. 27. Subpœna to testify before a commssioner.

THE PRESIDENT OF THE UNITED STATES OF AMERICA,

To William N. Winnett, Caleb L. Upshur, William Jackson, James Porter, William Dyer, John Stevens, James Jamison, [L. S.]   William Grant, Felix Martinez, Joseph Domingues, and Nicholas Yanino, Greeting: We command you, that all and singular business and excuses being laid aside, you and each of you be and appear in your proper persons, before Erastus C. Benedict, a Commissioner appointed by the Circuit Court of the United States of America for the Southern District of New York, at his office, No. 15 Pine street, in the city of New York, in the said Southern District of New York, on the 8th day of October, one thousand eight hundred and twenty-nine, at nine o'clock in the forenoon of the same day, to testify all and singular what you and each of you may know in a certain cause now depending undetermined in the District Court of the United States, for the Southern District of New York, wherein Peter Harmony and Eliphalet Kingsbury are libellants against the ship Waterloo, her tackle, &c., and cargo, on the part of the libellants.   And this you or either of you are not to omit, under the penalty upon each and every of you of two hundred and fifty dollars.

Witness, Samuel R. Betts, Esquire, Judge of the District Court of the United States, at the city of New York, the 7th day of October, in the year of our Lord one thousand eight hundred and twenty-nine.

FRED. J. BETTS, Clerk.

ISAAC A. JOHNSON, Proctor.

No. 28.—Subpœna ticket.

By virtue of a writ of subpœna, to you directed and herewith shown, you are commanded, and firmly enjoined, that, laying all other matters aside, and notwithstanding any excuse, you be and appear in your proper persons, before Erastus C. Benedict, a Commissioner duly appointed by the Circuit Court of the United States of America, for the Southern District of New York, at his office, No. 15 Pine street, in the city of New York, on the 8th day of October, inst., at 9 o'clock in the forenoon of the same day, to testify all and every thing which you may know in a certain cause now depending in the District Court of the United States for the Southern District of New York, wherein Peter Harmony and Eliphalet Kingsbury are libellants against the ship Waterloo, her tackle, &c., and cargo, on the part of the libellants. And this you are not to omit, under the penalty of two hundred and fifty dollars.

Dated this 7th day of October, 1829.

By the Court.

ISAAC A. JOHNSON.
Proctor for Libellants.

To WILLIAM F. WINNETT.

No. 29.—Deposition.

UNITED STATES OF AMERICA.

Southern District of New York, City, County, and State of New York, ss.

On this eighth day of October, in the year of our Lord one thousand eight hundred and twenty-nine, before me, Erastus C. Benedict, a Commissioner, duly appointed by the Circuit Court of the United States, for the Southern District of New York, under and by virtue of the act of Congress, "for the more convenient taking of affidavits and bail in civil causes, depending in the courts of the United States," passed February 20th, 1812, personally appeared at my office, in the city of New York, in the said Southern District of New York, William N. Winnett, Caleb L. Upshur, William Jackson James Porter, William Dyer, John Stevens, James Jamison, and William Grant, witnesses on the part of the libellants in a certain civil cause of admiralty and maritime jurisdiction, now depending and undetermined in the District Court of the United States, for the Southern District of New York, wherein Peter Harmony and Eliphalet Kingsbury are libellants against the ship Waterloo, her tackle, apparel, and furniture, and cargo, and James Buchanan, Henry Barclay, and George Barclay, and the United States of America, are claimants. And the said William N. Winnett having been by me first cautioned and sworn to testify the whole truth, did thereupon depose and say, that he is twenty-five years old ; that he was chief mate of the brig Merced, on her late voyage from Havana to New York, and that Eliphalet

Kingsbury was master of said brig; that the said brig is of about two hundred and sixty tons burthen. The said brig sailed from Havana on the nineteenth day of August last, bound to Cadiz, as he supposes, with a cargo of sugar, cochineal, and segars, that on the twenty-seventh day of August last, about half past two in the afternoon, (sea time,) in latitude 34° 4′ N., longitude 75° 15′ W., they fell in with the wreck of a ship which had the words " Waterloo of London" on her stern; that deponent, with four men from brig Merced, boarded said wreck with the boat of the Merced. The mainmast and the mizzen-mast were carried away by the board; that at that time the captain of the brig Orion and some of his men were on board, and the brig Orion close by; that the captain of the Orion represented himself to be the captain of the brig Orion of Baltimore; that the said master and men of the Orion appeared to be taking from the wreck whatever they thought of use to them, and easily movable. The captain of the Orion represented to deponent that the wreck was in a sinking state, and that it was sickly below; that his men could not remain below but a few minutes at a time. The captain of the Orion said that he did not intend taking out the cargo, as he supposed the ship would sink before morning, and he requested the deponent to give his compliments to Captain Kingsbury, and tell him that the vessel was in a sinking state, and that he (the captain of the Orion) would not take her in tow, because she would sink, and no one could live on board of her. Deponent went into the cabin of the wreck, but could not remain more than a few moments, because of the offensive smell, which was so offensive that he thinks a man could not live below deck, that even the rats were found dead below. That while on board the wreck, a cargo book was thrown up out of the cabin by one of the Orion's crew, and deponent picked it up as a prize, and put it in his hat. That none of the crew of the Waterloo were then on board of her, nor was any person there except the persons from the Orion and the Merced; that deponent remained on board the Waterloo about fifteen minutes, when he returned to the Merced with the said cargo book, which he delivered to Captain Kingsbury, together with the message from the captain of the Orion to Captain Kingsbury, and Captain Kingsbury thereupon went on board the Waterloo, and remained there about three-quarters of an hour, and then returned to the Merced; that the Merced remained about the wreck all that night. The next morning the brig Orion was not in sight, and her captain and men had abandoned the wreck, and the weather in the morning was very squally, and the Merced was under double reefed topsails. That in the morning the captain declared his intention of having the wreck again boarded, and thereupon called the brig's crew aft and stated to them that he believed the Waterloo and her cargo were of much value, and asked them if they were willing to obey his orders on board the wreck as well as on board the brig, and to assist in taking the wreck into some port, and they all expressed such willingness. And thereupon deponent, with four men of the Merced's crew, boarded the wreck, the sea being at that time tremendous rough—this was about eight o'clock in the morning. That, upon getting on board, he sounded the pumps, and found about twelve feet of water in the hold ; that after sounding the pumps, the next thing that was done was to get all the small lines that could be found on board the wreck, to take on board the Merced, to make a hauling line to draw the hawser from the Merced to the wreck. During that day the pumps were manned, and kept going, and during the whole time the wreck was so much by the head that the sea was up to her hawser holes, and none of the water pumped run out of the scuppers during the first day, but the same ran out of the hawser holes. That during that day they cut away all the rigging and spars that seemed to impede her. That the loss of the main-mast and mizzen-mast were evidently the effect of a heavy gale. That all the rigging on the larboard side had been cut away, square up to the bulwarks ; the vessel evidently having been on her beam ends. There were no boats belonging to the wreck, and the davits were carried away. The guard irons had been torn from the channels, and the chain bolts were badly wrenched, so much so as to cause her to leak badly. One of the ring bolts on deck had been torn out, and the camboose was entirely destroyed, and there were no cables on board. The bulwarks and rails were stove in on both sides, and were a complete wreck. The starboard side was much injured. The vessel itself was a complete wreck. That she appeared to have been thrown on her beam ends on the starboard side. That when deponent went on board in the morning she had a list to port. The rigging was hanging to the chain bolts on the starboard side, and the spars were lying about the deck. The main top mast breast back stay bolts and the top gallant back stay bolts torn out by the weight of the rigging. That they had great difficulty in getting the wreck in tow of the Merced. She was attached to the Merced by a hawser from the stern of the Merced to the ship's windlass, and also fastened to the windlass bits of the brig. The sea was running high at the time of making her fast ; several attempts were made to fasten her before they succeeded. This was attended with danger as well as difficulty, on account of the sea. They were obliged to get small lines from the ship and fasten them to the hawser. It took about two and a half or three hours to accomplish getting the wreck in tow ; the wind during all this time was fresh, and they were employed in a boat of the Merced, with considerable danger. In a day or two afterwards they attached the wreck by means of another hawser. That afterwards, during the time of bringing in said vessel, the crew of the Merced were constantly employed in pumping by turns. About eight days after taking her in tow, one of the pumps became choked, and but one could thereafter be used; the crew, by constant pumping, became entirely exhausted. The men relieved each other at the pumps, day and night, every half hour, till they took a pilot. They were so much exhausted that they were obliged to sit down at the pumps, and have field beds of old canvass alongside of the pumps to lie down on. That generally, while they had the wreck in tow, the weather was bad and the sea very high. The vessel labored and strained much. About the

third of September they experienced a heavy gale, which threw the Waterloo on her beam ends, and caused her to leak to an alarming extent, and in
order to right her they cut away the foremast, and the rigging attached to
it; cut away the starboard anchor, and cleared the decks of every thing movable, and succeeded, with much trouble, in righting her. Previous to her
being thrown on her beam ends, as last aforesaid, the water in her hold had
been reduced to about three feet; shortly afterwards the leak had increased
so much that she had seven feet of water in her hold. That they then
feared she would sink, and wore ship, and got the low side to the wind.
That the apprehensions of the men were so great that they all got into the
jolly boat to save their lives, and begged the deponent, for God's sake, to get
in too; deponent, however, persuaded them to return on board the ship.
That on or about the fifth of September they encountered a somewhat more
severe gale, which knocked the ship again on her beam ends. She lay so
low in the sea that the water came in on her poop deck, and the leak gained
three feet in one hour while she lay thus. They finally succeeded in righting her, with much difficulty. The sea made a complete breach over her
while she lay thus. That all the Merced's crew were then on board the
Waterloo, except the captain, the cook and steward, and two men, who were
invalids. That so few men were left on board the Merced that it took about
twelve hours to reduce her to her proper sails. Deponent saw Captain
Kingsbury on the topsail and lower yards reefing and furling sails himself.
The gale abated in about twenty-four hours, during which time the wreck
labored and strained very much, and the leak increased in spite of their exertions, making the situation of all on board very dangerous. They finally
arrived off Sandy Hook, September the eleventh, and took a pilot on board,
and arrived at the Quarantine ground on the twelfth of September. That
during all the time while on board the wreck, they were in constant danger
of sinking, and suffering every kind of privation. The pumps were kept
constantly going, and they had very little hope of bringing the vessel in.
They were constantly engaged in stopping leaks and making her as tight as
possible. They could not at any time carry any sail on the Waterloo.
When they took possession of her she drew about nineteen and a half feet
at the stern. She appears to be a ship of four or five hundred tons. The
cargo has been discharged since her arrival, and consisted of sugar, rum,
coffee, lance wood and arrow root. Deponent verily believes that the wreck
would have sunk in eight hours from the time the Merced took her had she
been left to herself. The crew of the Merced, including the captain and
one man who worked his passage, consisted of twelve persons, the said man
who worked his passage aided in saving the vessel as much as the other
men. Two or three of the men, from the excessive labor, had their feet
swelled, and were otherwise injured, and deponent verily believes that all
the crew of the Merced were injured in health by their exertions in saving
the Waterloo. They were constantly on deck, and never slept below while
the Waterloo was in tow. They were frequently in danger of being swept

from the deck by the sea breaking over them. That during the time that the Waterloo was in tow Captain Kingsbury exerted himself in navigating the Merced, doing the duty of a man before the mast in addition to his own duties. That the brig Merced was, in deponent's opinion, worth about eighteen thousand dollars. The brig Merced was not chafed, or strained, or hurt at all, by taking the Waterloo in tow, but was frequently in a dangerous situation. That it was a perilous undertaking for so small a vessel as the Merced to take such a wreck in tow.

Being cross-examined on the part of the claimants, Barclay, he says— That they were on the usual course to Cadiz, and were running with the Gulf Stream as usual, when they fell in with the Waterloo. That deponent knew of no intention, on the part of the Captain, to stop at New York or any other port. That they were on the same course which they would have been if going to New York, or any part of Europe. The captain and crew of the Orion left the Waterloo about sunset, to return to the Orion. That deponent discovered the next morning after they took possession of the Waterloo, that she floated lighter in the water, and that the pumping had reduced the water in her hold. That, on the day on which they took possession of the wreck, the deponent, after having cut away what would impede the Waterloo, set about looking for the leaks, and endeavored to stop them. The leaks were principally on the starboard side, in the wake of the main and mizen channels. The leaks were stopped from the outside, by slinging, in a bowline knot. The hatches were left open for four or five days to purify the air, and thus to enable deponent to stay below a few minutes at a time.

(Examination closed for this day ; adjourned till to-morrow, October 9th, at 9 o'clock, A. M.)

Oct. 12th, 1829.—The cross-examination of the deponent, William N. Winnett being resumed by the Proctor for the claimant, Barclay, he says— For two or three days previous to falling in with the Waterloo, they had strong symptoms of a very heavy gale. Deponent kept the log. In the morning of the day on which they fell in with the Waterloo, there was a moderate breeze and pleasant weather. Observation was taken that day ; they were in the Gulf Stream when they fell in with the wreck. The winds which they encountered, while bringing in the Waterloo, were principally head winds and blowing weather. The men had no specific sickness on their arrival, except their swelled hands and feet, and the consequences of their fatigue ; their eyes were sore from want of sleep. Deponent does not know that he was able to go on in the Merced and perform his duty, but he was not disposed to go on in her, had he been able. The Merced remained in New York ten days or a fortnight—not longer. Storms are frequent off Cape Hatteras. Deponent thinks they were towards Cape May on the third of September. Both the gales of the third and fifth of September were dead ahead. During their continuance the vessel lay close to the wind—made little or no headway and plenty of leeway.

On further direct examination he says—A ship is said to be on her beam ends, when her gunwales are under water. The Waterloo, in the two gales, was in that situation. The wreck, when they took possession of her, was two planks lower in the water forward than when they first fell in with her and boarded her.

WM. N. WINNETT.

Taken, subscribed and sworn, Oct. 8th, 1829,
　　before me,

E. C. BENEDICT.

And the said Caleb L. Upshur, having been by me, &c., &c. And so on with the other witnesses.

No. 30.—CERTIFICATE OF COMMISSIONER.

UNITED STATES OF AMERICA,

Southern District of New York, ss. :—

I, Erastus C. Benedict, a Commissioner duly appointed by the Circuit Court of the United States, for the Southern District of New York, under and by virtue of the "Act for the more convenient taking of affidavits and bail in civil causes, depending in the courts of the United States," passed February 20th, 1812, do hereby certify, that the reason for taking the foregoing deposition is, that the testimony of the witnesses aforesaid is necessary in the cause in the caption of the said deposition named, and that they are bound on a voyage to sea; that a notification of the time and place of taking the said depositions, signed by me, was made out and served on James A. Hamilton, Esquire, proctor for the United States, on Robinson & Betts, Esquires, proctors for the claimants Barclay, and on H. & E. Wilkes, Esqrs. proctors for the claimant Buchanan, all residing in the city of New York, on the seventh day of October instant, to be present at the taking of the depositions, and to put interrogatories, if they might think fit, of which notice a copy is hereto annexed, marked A.

That on the eighth day of October, in the year of our Lord one thousand eight hundred and twenty-nine, I was attended by the proctors aforesaid, and by Isaac A. Johnson, Esquire, the proctor for the libellants, and by the said witnesses; and each of the witnesses was by me carefully examined and cautioned, and sworn to testify the truth, and the testimony by him given was by me reduced to writing, and thereafter subscribed by the said witness in my presence. And, that I am not of counsel or attorney to either of the parties, nor in any way interested in the event of the cause named in the said caption.

E. C. BENEDICT,
U. S. Commissioner for the Southern District of New York.
57

No. 31.—ENDORSEMENT AND DIRECTION OF THE DEPOSITIONS AFTER BEING SEALED UP.

PETER HARMONY, &c., } Depositions on the part of the libellants.
vs.
The Ship WATERLOO, &c. } E. C. BENEDICT, U. S. Commissioner.

To the
District Court of the United States, for the Southern District of New York,
New York.

It is also proper that the Commissioner should write his name across the seal.

No. 32.—ORDER TO OPEN DEPOSITIONS IN COURT.

On motion of Mr. Johnson, Proctor for the libellants, ordered, that the depositions taken in this cause, and remaining under the seal of E. C. Benedict, Esq., the Commissioner, be now opened.

No. 33.—ORDER FOR COMMISSION OR DEDIMUS POTESTATEM.

PETER HARMONY, &c. }
vs.
The Ship WATERLOO, &c. }

On reading and filing a consent of the Proctors of the several claimants in this cause, and on motion of Mr. Johnson, Proctor for the libellants, ordered, that a commission issue therein to John Scott, John Glenn, and Robert Purviance, Esquires, of Baltimore, directing them to examine Cornelius F. Driscol, upon interrogatories to said commission annexed.

No. 34.—DEDIMUS POTESTATEM.

The President of the United States of America, to John Scott, John Glenn, and Robert Purviance, Esquires, of. Baltimore, Greeting :
Know ye, that we, in confidence of your prudence and fidelity, have appointed you, and by these presents do give you, or any two of you, full power and authority to examine Cornelius F. Driscol, now or lately the master of the brig Orion, of Baltimore, as a witness in a certain cause depending in the District Court of the United States for the Southern District of New York, wherein Peter Harmony and Eliphalet Kingsbury are libellants, against the ship Waterloo, her tackle, &c., and her cargo, on the part of the said libellants, upon oath upon the interrogatories annexed to this commission, and to return the same annexed to this commission unto the said

[L. S.]

court, with all convenient speed, closed up under the seals of you or any two of you, the said Commissioners.

Witness, Samuel R. Betts, Esquire, Judge of the said court, at the Southern District of New York, this sixth day of November, in the year of our Lord one thousand eight hundred and twenty-nine, and of our independence the fifty-fourth.

Fred. J. Betts, Clerk.

Isaac A. Johnson, Proctor.

No. 35.—The return of the commissioners.

The execution of this commission appears in certain schedules hereto annexed.

John Scott, } Commissioners.
John Glenn, }

No. 36.—Direct interrogatories.

United States District Court for the Southern District of New York.

Interrogatories to be adminstered to Driscoll, of Baltimore, in the State of Maryland, a witness to be produced, sworn, and examined in a certain cause of Admiralty and Maritime Jurisdiction, now pending in the District Court of the United States, in and for the Southern District of New York, wherein Peter Harmony and Eliphalet Kingsbury are libellants, against the ship Waterloo and her cargo, and Henry Barclay and George Barclay, and James C. Buchanan, and James A. Hamilton, District Attorney of the United States are claimants, on the part and behalf of the libellants before the Commissioners in the writ hereto annexed named.

First Interrogatory.—What is your name, age, place of residence, and business or profession ?

Second Interrogatory.—Were you, or were you not master of the brig Orion, on a voyage from Porto Cabello to Baltimore, in the month of August last ? If yea, at what time did you sail from Porto Cabello and when did you arrive at Baltimore ?

Third Interrogatory.—Did you or did you not during the voyage aforesaid, fall in with the wreck of the ship Waterloo of London ? if yea, on what day and in what latitude and longitude was the said ship Waterloo when you so fell in with her ? Did you or did you not board the said ship, and was she not entirely deserted and abandoned by her crew, or was any one or more of her crew on board of her ? Were any of her masts carried away, and which, if any ? Did the said masts appear to have been carried away by violence and stress of weather, or how otherwise ?— Was any and what injury done to her hull by the carrying away of the said masts ? Was there or not any, and if any, how much water in the hold of the said ship, and did she or did she not appear to be in a sinking condition ?

Was she down by the head, and if so, how low? Did you go below? if you did, how long did you remain there? Was there any sickly or offensive smell below, and could or could not any person remain below for any and what length of time? Could or could not any person have remained in the cabin over two or three minutes at a time, and if not, why? Were or were not any, and if any, how many of your men taken sick while on board the wreck, and what, according to your best judgment, opinion, and belief, was the cause of such sickness, and was it or not caused by the smell in and from the cabin and hold of the wreck or how otherwise? Was or was not the said ship a complete wreck, and did you or did you not abandon her in the belief that she was sinking, and did you or not conceive it possible to get the said wreck into any port? declare fully.

Fourth Interrogatory.—Did or did not the brig Merced, of New York, fall in with the said wreck at or about the time you did, and did or did not any, and if any, how many of the Merced's crew board the Waterloo while you were on board of her? Did you or not declare to them your intention of abandoning the ship, and did you or not express your belief that she would sink before morning, or what did you say in relation thereto? How long after leaving the wreck did you remain in sight of her, and was or was not the wreck in sight on the morning after you fell in with her?

Fifth Interrogatory.—Do you know of any other matter or thing material or necessary, or that may tend to the benefit and advantage of the libellants in this cause? if yea, state the same as fully and particularly as if you were thereunto specially interrogated.

Isaac A. Johnson, Proctor for Libellants.

David B. Ogden, Advocate for Libellants.

No. 37.—Cross Interrogatories.

District Court of the United States in and for the Southern District of New York.

Cross Interrogatories to be administered to Driscoll, of Baltimore, in the State of Maryland, a witness to be produced, sworn and examined in a certain cause of Admiralty and Maritime Jurisdiction, now pending in the District Court of the United States in and for the Southern District of New York, wherein James A. Hamilton, District Attorney of the United States on behalf of the United States, and others, are claimants, and Peter Harmony and Eliphalet Kingsbury are libellants, against the ship Waterloo and her cargo, on the part and behalf of the United States, before the Commissions in the writ hereunto annexed named.

First.—If in answer to the third direct interrogatory, you answer, that you did, in August last, fall in at sea with the wreck of the brig Waterloo, of London, state particularly, clearly, and explicitly, the latitude and longitude in which the said ship Waterloo was, when you fell in with her, and also what port was the next direct port from the place at which the said wreck was, and particularly the state and direction of the wind at the time you left the said wreck, and whether it would not have been easier and less hazardous to have taken the said wreck into one of the ports of some one of the West India Islands, or some other port not in the United States, than to have brought her into the port of New York.

Last Interrogatory.—If you know any other matter or thing material or necessary to the claimants, the United States, state the same as fully as if you had been particularly interrogated.

JAMES A. HAMILTON,

District Attorney of the U. S. for the Southern
District of New York.

PHILIP HAMILTON, of Counsel.

No. 38.—THE DEPOSITION.

Deposition of witnesses produced, sworn, and examined on the thirteenth day of November, in the year of our Lord eighteen hundred and twenty-nine, by virtue of a commission issued out of the District Court of the United States for the Southern District of New York, to us, the undersigned Commissioners directed, for the examination of Cornelius N. Driscoll, a witness in a certain cause there depending and at issue wherein Peter Harmony and Eliphalet Kingsbury, are libellants, against the ship Waterloo, her tackle, &c., and her cargo, on the part and behalf of libellants, as follows :

Cornelius F. Driscol, of the city of Baltimore, being produced, sworn and examined, on behalf of the libellants, doth depose as follows :

First.—To the first Interrogatory, he saith, that his name is Cornelius F. Driscoll, aged twenty-eight years, his place of residence is the city of Baltimore, and a mariner by profession.

Second.—To the second Interrogatory, he saith, that he was master of the brig Orion, on a voyage from Porto Cabello to Baltimore, in the month of August last. He sailed from Porto Cabello on the sixth of said month of August, and arrived at Baltimore about the twenty-eight or twenty-ninth of said month.

Third.—To the third Interrogatory he saith, that during the said voyage, and on the twenty-sixth of August aforesaid, he fell in with the wreck of the ship Waterloo, of London, the said ship was in the latitude of thirty-four degrees four minutes, and the longitude of seventy-five degrees and some minutes, when he so fell in with her. He boarded the said ship. She was entirely deserted and abandoned by her crew ; there were none of her crew on board of her. Her main and mizen masts were carried away by the board. The said masts appeared to be carried away by violence and stress of weather. Her bulwarks were gone entirely on her main decks and some of the chain bolts were drawn out in consequence of the carrying away of the masts. She did appear to be in a sinking condition, there was considerable water in her hold, but how much, deponent cannot say. Her fore channels were in the water with a heavy list-port, whereby the water was frequently rolled on the deck. Deponent went below six or seven times, and remained under the companion way where he could get fresh air, about ten minutes at a time. There was a very sickly and offensive smell below—so much so, that two of his men became sickly, being exposed to it, and it would have been impossible for any person to have continued below five minutes with safety, unless, like deponent, he was in a condition where he could receive a fresh supply of air. The said ship was a complete wreck, and deponent abandoned her in the belief that she was sinking, and he conceived it impossible to get the said ship into any port.

Fourth.—To the fourth interrogatory he saith, that the brig Merced, of New York, did fall in with the said wreck. Four of the said brig Merced's crew boarded the said wreck about an hour after deponent, and while he was on board the said wreck. Deponent observed to Captain Kingsbury that he thought the wreck would go down, but he would lay alongside of her till morning. About midnight a squall came up, and deponent bore up, and in the morning he had lost sight of the wreck and the Merced.

Fifth.—To the fifth Interrogatory he answers, that he does not recollect any other matter or thing material or necessary, or that may tend to the benefit and advantage of the libellants in this cause, except that, in his judgment, the said wreck, when left by deponent, was in a most shocking and desperate condition.

Cross Interrogatories.

First.—To the first Cross Interrogatory he saith, that he has particularly detailed the latitude and longitude in which the said ship Waterloo was when he fell in with her, in the answer to the Third Interrogatory on the part of libellants, to which he refers as part of this answer. Norfolk, in the State of Virginia, was the next direct port from the place at which the said ship was. The wind was from the south-west when he left the wreck, and was stiff and squally ; and deponent believes that it would not have been easier and less hazardous to have taken the said wreck into one of the ports of some one of the West India Islands or some other port not within the United States, than to have brought her into the port of New York.

Last.—To the last Cross Interrogatory, he answers, that he knows nothing else material or necessary to the claimants, the United States.

C. F. Driscoll.

Sworn and subscribed before

JOHN SCOTT, } Commissioners.
JOHN GLENN, }

No. 39.—ENDORSEMENT AND DIRECTION—*Same as No. 31, ante, page* 450.

No. 40.—ORDER TO OPEN THE COMMISSION—*Same as No. 32, ante, p.* 450.

No. 41.—NOTICE OF HEARING TO THE PARTIES.

District Court of the United States for the Southern District of New York.

PETER HARMONY and ELIPHALET KINGSBURY,
vs.
The Ship WATERLOO, her tackle. &c. }

GENTLEMEN—This cause will be brought on for hearing at the next term of this Court, to be held at the City Hall, in the city of New York, on the first Tuesday of December next.

Dated New York, Nov. 26th, 1829.

Yours, &c.

ISAAC A. JOHNSON,

To   Proctor for Libellants.

ROBINSON & BETTS, Esqrs.

H. & E. WILKES, Esqrs.

JAMES A. HAMILTON, Esq. Proctor for Claimants.

The notices from the Proctors of claimants to the Proctors of the libellant are in the same form *mutatis mutandis*.

No. 42.—NOTICE OF HEARING TO THE CLERK.

Title of the cause as before.

Libel in rem for Salvage.

Issue joined October 5, 1829.

ISAAC A. JOHNSON, Proctor for Libellants.

H. &. E. WILKES, for Claimant Buchanan.

ROBINSON & BETTS, for Claimants Barclay.

JAMES A. HAMILTON, for the United States.

SIR—This cause will be brought in for hearing at the December Term of this Court.

November 28, 1829.

Yours,

ISAAC A. JOHNSON,

To   Proctor for Libellants.

FRED. J. BETTS, Clerk.

No. 43.—NOTICE TO THE CLERK TO BRING THE PAPERS INTO COURT.

(*Title of the cause as before.*)

SIR.—On the hearing of this cause the papers on file therein will be required in court, and you will please to have them there accordingly.

Yours, &c.,

ISAAC A. JOHNSON, Proctor for Libellants.

To FRED. J. BETTS, Esq., Clerk.

No. 44.—Order for Hearing.

On motion of Mr. Johnson, Proctor for the Libellant, it is ordered that this cause be now brought on for hearing.

No. 45.—Hearing.

The libels and claims being read by the respective parties,

Mr. David B. Ogden, the Advocate for the Libellants, offered the depositions of William N. Winnett, mate, Caleb L. Upshur, 2nd mate, James Jemison, William Jackson and James Porter, seamen, on board of the Waterloo, taken *de bene esse*, and the testimony of Cornelius F. Driscoll, taken on a commission,

And called as a witness for the Libellants, John Jones.

The testimony being closed,

Mr. Betts argued for the claimants, Barclay,

Mr. Wilkes argued for the claimant, Buchanan,

Mr. Cutting argued for the captain and crew,

Mr. Hamilton, District Attorney, argued for the United States,

Mr. Ogden argued for the Libellant, Harmony.

The court takes time to consider its decree.

No. 46.—Decree on the merits, with a reference to the clerk.

PETER HARMONY and ELIPHALET
KINGSBURY
vs.
The ship WATERLOO, her tackle,
&c., and her cargo.

The court having taken time to advise as to its decree in this cause, and as to the amount, proportion and distribution of salvage; and counsel having been heard on the part of the libellants, and of the several claimants in the cause, and mature deliberation being had, it is now ordered, adjudged and decreed, by the court, that out of the gross proceeds of sales under the writ of *venditioni exponas* issued in this cause, the clerk of this court, pay the taxed bills of costs of the officers of court, including the charges and disbursements allowed for preserving and unlading the above ship and cargo, together with duties on the cargo and the tonnage duties on the ship; and it is further ordered, adjudged, and decreed as aforesaid, that two equal third parts of the nett amount of sales as aforesaid, remaining after deducting such payments as aforesaid, be paid by said clerk to the salvors in this cause; and that the same be distributed in the manner following, that is to say, two equal third parts thereof to be paid to the libellant, Peter Harmony; and the remaining one equal third part thereof, to be divided into twelve equal parts and one of such twelve equal parts to be paid to each of the persons employed in saving said ship and cargo, as follows, to wit: to Eliphalet Kingsbury, master of the brig Merced, one part; to William N. Winnett, first mate of said brig, one part; to Caleb L. Upshur, second mate of said brig, one part; to James Jamison, William Jackson, William Dyer, James Porter, John Stivers, William Grant, Joseph Dominguez and Nicholas Yanino, seamen on board said brig, and Felix Martinez, a passenger on board the same, each one part;—

And it is further ordered, adjudged and decreed, as aforesaid, that out of the remaining one third part of the nett proceeds as aforesaid, the said clerk pay to the Proctors of the Libellants, of the British Consul, and of the Claimants, Henry and George Barclay, their taxed costs in this cause; and to the several claimants in the cause of the United States of America against the said ship Waterloo, her tackle, &c., the taxed costs incident to their claims in the same.

And it is further ordered, that the clerk of this court ascertain and report in this case the amount due to each libellant, pursuant to the terms of this decree; and that the final decree be so drawn, as to express the specific sum payable to the libellants respectively.

And it is further ordered, that the balance of the said one third part of the nett proceeds as aforesaid, remaining after deducting the amount of the taxed bills of costs last aforesaid, be retained in the office of discount and deposit of the Bank of the United States in the city of New York, to the credit of this court, until the further order of the court respecting the same.

No. 47.—Clerk's Report.

DISTRICT COURT OF THE UNITED STATES.
Southern District of New York.

Peter Harmony and Eliphalet Kingsbury.
vs.
The ship Waterloo, her tackle, &c., and her cargo.

In pursuance of the decree of this court, entered in the above cause on the nineteenth day of February, instant, by which it was, amongst other things, referred to me to ascertain and report the amount due each libellant, pursuant to the terms of the said decree, I, Frederick J. Betts, Clerk of this Court, do report, that I have proceeded to make a computation of the amount due as aforesaid, pursuant to the terms of the said decree, and of the abovementioned order, and that the following is a detailed statement of such computation, and of the amount awarded to each of the said libellants, to wit,

Gross amount of sales, ...		$39,262 90

Deduct.

Marshal's taxed costs, including duties, disbursements, &c., . . .	$24,295 78	
Clerk's taxed costs, . .	360 37	24,656 15
	Nett proceeds	$14,606 75

Two-thirds of nett proceeds being the amount awarded libellants, ...		$9,737 83½
Peter Harmony two-thirds of last above am't,	$6,491 88⅔	
Eliphalet Kingsbury 1-12th of 1-3d of do.	270 49½	
William N. Winnett do. do.	270 49½	
Caleb L. Upshur do. do.	270 49½	
James Jamison do. do.	270 49½	
William Jackson do. do.	270 49½	
William Dyer do. do.	270 49½	
James Porter do. do.	270 49½	
John Stivers do. do.	270 49½	
William Grant do. do.	270 49½	
Joseph Dominguez do. do.	270 49½	
Nicholas Yanino do. do.	270 49½	
Felix Martinez do. do.	270 49½	9,737 83½
		$4,868 91½

All which is respectfully submitted,
New York, March 20th, 1830.

FRED. J. BETTS, Clerk.

No. 48.—FINAL DECREE.

On reading and filing the Clerk's Report in this cause, Ordered, on motion of Mr. J. A. Johnson, that the said report be, and the same is hereby confirmed, in all things: and it is further ordered, adjudged and decreed, that the libellants recover salvage as follows:

Peter Harmony, . . .	$6,491 88⅔
Eliphalet Kingsbury, . .	270 49½
William N. Winnett, . . .	270 49½
Caleb L. Upshur, . .	270 49½
James Jamison, . . :	270 49½
William Jackson . . .	270 49½
William Dyer, . . .	270 49½
James Porter, . . .	270 49½
John Stivers, . . .	270 49½

William Grant,	.	.	.	270	49½
Joseph Dominguez,	.	.	.	270	49½
Nicholas Yanino,	.	.	.	270	49½
Felix Martinez,	.	.	.	270	49½

Special Motion—Motion to attach the Marshal.

No. 49.—NOTICE TO MARSHAL TO RETURN THE VENDITIONI EXPONAS.

District Court of the United States for the Southern District of New York.

PETER HARMONY and ELIPHALET
  KINGSBURY,
        vs.
The Ship WATERLOO, her tackle, &c.
  and Cargo.

SIR—You will please to take notice, that you are hereby required to return the *venditioni exponas* heretofore delivered to you in the above entitled cause.

New York, 3d February, 1830.

                Yours,

To   ISAAC A. JOHNSON, Proctor for Libellants.

  THOMAS MORRIS, Esq., Marshal, &c.

No. 50.—AFFIDAVIT OF SERVICE OF THE NOTICE.

District Court of the U. S. for the Southern District of N. Y.

PETER HARMONY, &c.
      vs.
The Ship WATERLOO, &c.

Southern District of New York, ss.:

John J. Young, of the city of New York, student at law, being duly sworn, deposes and says, that on the third day of February, instant, he served a notice, of which the above is a copy, on Thomas Morris, Esq., marshal for the southern district of New York, by delivering the same to him personally—and further says not.

                JOHN J. YOUNG.

Sworn this 15th day of February, 1830,
  before me,

      FRED. J. BETTS, Clerk.

No. 51.—AFFIDAVIT FOR MOTION FOR ATTACHMENT FOR NOT RETURNING
VINDITIONI EXPONAS.

District Court of the U. S.—Southern District of N. Y.

PETER HARMONY and ELIPHALET
   KINGSBURY,
         vs.
THE SHIP WATERLOO, &c. and CARGO.

SOUTHERN DISTRICT OF NEW YORK, ss. :—

Isaac A. Johnson, proctor for the above libellants, being sworn, saith that on the eighth day of October last, a motion was made and an order thereupon granted in this cause, that the ship Waterloo, above mentioned, her tackle, apparel, &c., and her cargo, be sold, and the proceeds brought into court, and on the same day a *venditioni exponas* was issued in said cause, and delivered to the Marshal of the Southern District of New York, returnable on the 19th day of October last ; that the said property was sold under the said writ of *venditioni exponas*, on certain days between the 15th and 31st days of October last, as this defendant has been informed and believes, but that said process has not been returned into this court to the knowledge or belief of this deponent.

                                     ISAAC A. JOHNSON.

Sworn this 15th day of February, 1830,
  before me,
        FRED. J. BETTS, Clerk.

No. 52.—ORDER FOR MARSHAL TO SHOW CAUSE WHY ATTACHMENT
SHOULD NOT ISSUE.

*District Court of the United States of America for the Southern District of
New York.*

PETER HARMONY and ELIPHALET
   KINGSBURY,
        vs.
THE SHIP WATERLOO and CARGO. .

On reading a notice to the Marshal of the Southern District of New York, to return the *venditioni exponas*, issued in this cause, and also on reading an affidavit of the service of said notice, and an affidavit of the Proctor of the libellants, showing that a writ of *venditioni exponas* has been issued and delivered to said Marshal, returnable on the nineteenth day of October last past, and that said writ was not returned, which papers were filed on the fifteenth instant ; and on motion of Isaac A. Johnson, Esquire, for libellants, ordered, that said Marshal show cause before this court, at the City Hall, in the city of New York, on the 22d day of Febrnry, instant, why an attachment should not issue against him for not returning said writ.

No. 53.—ADMISSION OF SERVICE.

I admit due service of the above order on me, this 17th February, 1830.

THOMAS MORRIS.

No. 54.—ORDER THAT ATTACHMENT ISSUE AGAINST THE MARSHAL FOR NOT RETURNING A VENDITIONI EXPONAS.

On reading and filing a certified copy of an order that the Marshal show cause why an attachment should not issue against him, and his admission of the service of the same, on motion of David B. Ogden, ordered, that an attachment issue against Thomas Morris, Esq., Marshal of the District for not returning the *venditioni exponas* in this cause.

No. 55.—ORDER TO PAY OVER THE SURPLUS AND REMNANTS.

DITRICT COURT OF THE UNITED STATES OF AMERICA.
FOR THE SOUTHERN DISTRICT OF NEW YORK.

• In the matter of the petition of the several owners of the ship Waterloo, and owners and consignees of her cargo, (former claimants in this Court in respect thereto,) for the remainder of the proceeds of the said ship and cargo, now remaining in Court ;

Mr. Wm. Betts, Proctor and Advocate for the promovents, now presents in Court, a power of attorney duly executed by the said parties, constituting George Barclay and Henry Barclay, of the city of New York, merchants, their attorneys in fact, with full powers to act jointly or severally in this behalf, praying, that the moneys aforesaid may be paid over to the said George and Henry Barclay, for the benefit of the parties concerned. And this Court being satisfied of the full right and authority of the promovents in this matter, the said power of attorney, and accompanying evidences and authentications being filed in Court, it is ordered and decreed by this Court, that the Clerk pay over to the said George and Henry Barclay, or to either of them, or their Proctor in this behalf, the proceeds of the said ship Waterloo and her cargo, now remaining undisposed of in Court, first deducting therefrom the legal fees and charges of the officers of Court, chargeable thereon, and to be certified by the Court.

Proceedings on Libel of Information.

No 55.—A LIBEL OF INFORMATION AGAINST A WRECK BROUGHT IN BY SALVORS, FOR A FORFEITURE, FOR A VIOLATION OF THE NAVIGATION ACTS—BEING BROUGHT INTO A PROHIBITED PORT.

DISTRICT COURT OF THE UNITED STATES,

FOR THE SOUTHERN DISTRICT OF NEW YORK.

In Admiralty.

To the Honorable Samuel R. Betts, Judge of the District Court of the United States for the Southern District of New York:

The libel of information of James A. Hamilton, attorney of the said United States, for the Southern District of New York, who prosecutes on behalf of the said United States, and being present here in court in his proper person, in the name and on the behalf of the said United States, against the ship Waterloo, her tackle, apparel, and furniture, and against all persons intervening for their interest therein, in a cause of forfeiture, alleges and informs as follows:

First. That Mordecai M. Noah, Surveyor of the Customs for the district of the city of New York, heretofore, to wit, on the twelfth day of October, in the year of our Lord one thousand eight hundred and twenty-nine, at the city of New York, and within the Southern District of New York, on waters that are navigable from the sea by vessels of ten or more tons burthen, seized as forfeited to the use of the said United States, the ship, or vessel commonly called a ship, the Waterloo, her tackle, apparel, and furniture, being the property of some person or persons to the said attorney unknown,

Second. That the said ship Waterloo is a ship or vessel owned wholly or in part by a subject or subjects of His Britannic Majesty, and which said ship or vessel, after the thirtieth day of September, in the year one thousand eight hundred and eight, and also after the thirtieth day of September, in the year one thousand eight hundred and twenty, did come and arrive from a port or place in a colony or territory of His Britannic Majesty, to wit, from Anatto Bay in the island of Jamaica, in the West Indies, which said port is, and was at the time the said ship sailed from thence, and also at the time of the arrival of the said ship at the port of New York, as is hereinafter mentioned, by the ordinary laws of navigation and trade, closed against vessels owned by citizens of the United States—and that the ports of the United States were, at the time of the arrival of the said ship at the port of New York, and still are, closed against the said ship or vessel called the Waterloo, which said ship or vessel being so excluded from the ports of the United States, did enter the same, to wit, the port of New York, in the Southern District of New York aforesaid, in violation of the acts of the Congress of the United States, in such cases made and provided. And that by force and virtue of the said acts of Congress, in such case made and provided, the said ship or vessel, her tackle, apparel and furniture, became and are forfeited to the use of the said United States,—and that the same are now in custody of the marshal of this court in the suit of certain persons claiming salvage.

And the said attorney saith that by reason of all and singular the premises aforesaid, and by force of the statute in such case made and provided, the aforementioned and described ship or vessel, her tackle, apparel, and furniture, became and are forfeited to the use of the said United States.

Lastly. That all and singular, the premises aforesaid, are, and were, true, and within the admiralty and maritime jurisdiction of the United States and of this Honorable Court, whereupon the said attorney prays the usual process and monition of this Honorable Court in this behalf to be made, and that all persons interested in the before mentioned and described ship or vessel, may be cited in general and special to answer the premises, and all due proceedings being had, that the said ship or vessel, her tackle, &c, may, for the causes aforesaid, and others appearing, be condemned by the definitive sentence and decree of this Honorable Court, as forfeited to the use of the said United States, according to the form of the statute of the said United States in such cases made and provided.

JAMES A. HAMILTON, Attorney U. S.
for the Southern District of New York.

No. 56.—NOTICE FOR PUBLICATION CONTAINING THE SUBSTANCE OF THE LIBEL.

UNITED STATES OF AMERICA;

Southern District of New York, ss.—

Whereas a libel of information has been filed in the District Court of the United States of America, for the Southern District of New York, on the fifteenth day of October, in the year of our Lord one thousand eight hundred and twenty-nine, by James A. Hamilton, Esq., Attorney of the United States, in behalf of the United States, against the ship Waterloo, her tackle, apparel, and furniture, alleging, in substance, that Mordecai M. Noah, Surveyor of the Customs, for the district of the city of New York, on the 12th day of October, 1829, on waters navigable from the sea by vessels of ten or more tons burthen, seized said vessel and cargo as forfeited to the use of the United States; that said vessel is owned wholly or in part by a subject or subjects of the King of Great Britain, and after the 30th day of September, 1820, did come and arrive from Annatto Bay in the island of Jamaica, in the West Indies, a port, by the ordinary laws of navigation and trade, closed against vessels owned by citizens of the United States, and that the ports of the United States were, and are, closed against said ship or vessel; and that said vessel did enter the port of New York, in violation of the acts of the Congress of the United States in such cases made and provided; and that said vessel, her tackle, apparel, and furniture became thereby forfeited to the use of the United States.   And praying that the same may be condemned as forfeited as aforesaid.

Now, therefore, in pursuance of the monition under the seal of the said court to me directed and delivered, I do hereby give public notice to all persons claiming the said ship, her tackle, &c., or in any manner interested therein, that they be and appear before the said District Court to be held at the city of New York, in and for the said Southern District of New York on the first Tuesday of November next, at eleven o'clock in the forenoon of that day, (provided the same shall be a day of jurisdiction, otherwise on the next day of jurisdiction thereafter,) then and there to interpose their claims, and to make their allegations in that behalf.

Dated this 15th day of October, 1829.

THOMAS MORRIS, U. S. Marshal, &c.
ISAAC A. JOHNSON, Proctor for Libellant.

No. 57.—ORDER FOR PROCESS IN REM IN A LIBEL OF INFORMATION.

On filing a libel of information on behalf of the United States by James A. Hamilton, Esq., U. S. District Attorney, it is ordered that a monition and attachment issue against the ship Waterloo, her tackle, apparel, and furniture, and cargo.

No. 58.—MONITION AND ATTACHMENT IN REM ON A LIBEL OF INFORM-MATION.—(As, ante, No. 4, page 429.)

No. 59.—CLAIM AND ANSWER OF THE OWNER OF A SAVING VESSEL TO A LIBEL OF INFORMATION AGAINST A WRECK FOR A FORFEITURE.

District Court of the U. S. for the Southern District of New York.

To the Honorable Samuel R. Betts, Judge of the District Court of the United States for the Southern District of New York.

The answer and claim of Peter Harmony, of the city of New York, intervening for his interest to the libel of information filed by James A. Hamilton, Esquire, District Attorney of the United States of America, for the Southern District of New York, against the said ship Waterloo, her tackle, apparel and furniture, alleges as follows :

First. That the brig Merced, of New York, owned by and belonging to the said claimant, being on a voyage from Havana, in the Island of Cuba, to Cadiz, in Spain, the master of the said brig Merced, on the twenty-seventh day of August last past, discovered a ship in distress, dismasted, and apparently deserted ; that he boarded said ship, and found her to be the British ship Waterloo, of London, having twelve feet water in her hold, being dismasted, and abandoned by her captain and crew, and having on board a cargo of rum, sugar, coffee, arrow root, and lancewood spars.

Second. That the master of the said brig Merced took the said ship Waterloo in tow, and made for the port of New York, where he arrived with the said ship on the twelfth day of September, last past.

Third. That on or about the sixteenth day of September last past, he, the said claimant, together with Eliphalet Kingsbury, the master of the brig Merced, for themselves and all others entitled, exhibited their libel in this Honorable Court, against the said ship Waterloo, her tackle, apparel, furniture and cargo, therein stating in substance the matters hereinbefore set forth, and praying that the said ship and cargo might be attached and taken by the process of this Honorable Court, and a reasonable salvage thereout decreed to the said libellants; and thereupon the said ship Waterloo and her cargo were attached and taken by the Marshal of the United States for the Southern District of New York, under and by virtue of the process and monition of this Court, and such proceedings were afterwards had. that the said ship Waterloo was, by an order and decree of this Honorable Court, made on or about the eighth day of October last past, ordered to be sold, and the proceeds brought into and deposited in Court; and the same have been accordingly sold by or under the direction of the said Marshal.

Fourth. That he is entitled, as owner of the said brig Merced, to a reasonable salvage out of the proceeds of the said ship Waterloo, and therefore he claims the same, and humbly prays, that the premises being considered, this Honorable Court may adjudge and decree such reasonable salvage to be paid to this claimant out of the proceeds of the said ship Waterloo, as to the Court may seem proper.

And the said claimant denies that the said ship Waterloo, her tackle, apparel and furniture, or the proceeds thereof, so far as regards the rights of this claimant to his salvage as aforesaid, are forfeited to the use of the United States, in manner and form as in the said libel is alleged; and the said claimant humbly prays, that his reasonable costs, in this behalf sustained, may be adjudged to him &c.

Isaac A. Johnson, Proctor, &c.

Sworn Oct. 3d, 1829,
before me,

Fred J. Betts, Clerk.

D. B. Ogden, Advocate.

No. 60.—Stipulation for costs—*as ante,* No. 10, *page* 434.

No. 61.—Claim and answer of salvors to a libel of information for a forfeiture.

District Court of the United States for the Southern District of New York.

To the Honorable Samuel R. Betts, Judge of the District Court of the United States in and for the Southern District of New York :

The answer and claim of Eliphalet Kingsbury, of the city of New York, shipmaster, on behalf of himself, and the officers and crew of the brig Merced, of New York, intervening for their interest in the ship Waterloo, her tackle, &c. and cargo, to the libel of information filed by James A. Hamilton, Esquire,

District Attorney of the United States of America for the Southern District of New York, against the said ship Waterloo, her tackle, apparel and furniture, alleges as follows:

First. That on or about the twenty-seventh day of August last past, this claimant being then master of the brig Merced, of New York, whereof Peter Harmony, of the said city, merchant, then was and still is owner, together with William Winnett, the first mate thereof, Caleb L. Upshur, the second officer thereof, and William Jackson, James Porter, William Dyer, John Stivers, James Jamison, William Grant, Felix Martinez, Joseph Dominguez, and Nicholas Yanino, the crew of the said brig Merced, in latitude thirty-four degrees north, and longitude seventy-five degrees, fifteen minutes west, discovered a ship in distress, with the main mast and mizen mast thereof carried away. That this claimant, together with part of the crew of the said brig Merced, boarded the said ship, and found her to be the British ship Waterloo, of London, having twelve feet water in her hold, in a sinking condition, dismasted as aforesaid, and entirely deserted, and left a derelict on the ocean. That from a cargo book which was found on board the said wreck, the cargo on board of her appeared to consist of rum, sugar, arrow root and lancewood spars. That this claimant, and the officers and crew of the said brig Merced, took the said ship Waterloo in tow, and made for the port of New York, where this claimant, after great difficulties, dangers and privations, arrived with the said ship Waterloo, on the twelfth day of Sept. last past.

Second. That on or about the sixteenth day of September, last past, the said Peter Harmony, together with this claimant, for themselves and all others entitled, exhibited their libel in this Honorable Court, against the said ship Waterloo, her tackle, apparel, furniture, and cargo, therein stating in substance the matters hereinbefore set forth, and praying that the said ship and cargo might be attached and taken by the process of this Honorable Court, and a reasonable salvage thereout decreed to the said libellants; and thereupon the said ship Waterloo and her cargo were attached and taken by the Marshal of the United States for the Southern District of New York, under and by virtue of the process and monition of this Court, and such proceedings were afterwards had, that the said ship Waterloo and her cargo were, by an order and decree of this Honorable Court, made on or about the eighth day of October, last past, ordered to be sold, and the same were accordingly sold by or under the direction of the said Marshal, and the proceeds thereof ordered to be brought into and deposited in this Honorable Court.

Third. And the said claimant further answering says—That he, together with the officers and crew of the said brig Merced, are entitled to a reasonable salvage out of the proceeds of the said ship Waterloo; and therefore the said Eliphalet Kingsbury claims the same. And this claimant further saith, that the said officers and crew, before the filing of the libel of the said the United States, as far as this claimant has been able to ascertain, left the city of New York on foreign voyages, and have left with this claimant their letter of attorney, authorizing him to appear for them in all courts and places on their behalf in relation to the said ship Waterloo and her cargo, in order to protect their interests and claims therein. And this claimant further answering, denies that the said ship Waterloo, her tackle, apparel and furniture, or the proceeds thereof, so far as regards the rights of this claimant, and the officers and crew of the said brig Merced, to their salvage as aforesaid, are forfeited to the use of the United States, in manner and form as in the said libel is alleged. And this claimant humbly prays, that the premises being considered, this Honorable Court may adjudge and decree such reasonable salvage to be paid to this claimant and the officers and crew of the said brig Merced, out of the proceeds of the said ship Waterloo, as to the said Court may seem proper, with costs.

And the said claimant humbly prays, that his reasonable costs in this behalf sustained, may be adjudged to him, &c.

E. KINGSBURY.

Sworn by E. Kingsbury, this 4th
   day of Nov. 1829.
        FRED. J. BETTS, Clerk.
    F. B. CUTTING, Proctor for Claimant.
    F. R. TILLOU, of Counsel.

No. 62.—STIPULATION FOR COSTS—*as ante, No.* 10, *page* 434.

No. 63.—ANSWER AND CLAIM OF A CONSUL TO A LIBEL OF INFORMATION AGAINST A WRECK FOR A FORFEITURE.

DISTRICT COURT OF THE UNITED STATES.

FOR THE SOUTHERN DISTRICT OF NEW YORK.

To the Honorable Samuel R. Betts, Judge of the District Court of the United States for the Southern District of New York.

The claim and answer of James C. Buchanan, his Britannic Majesty's Vice Consul in and for the City and State of New York, and Eastern New Jersey, intervening for the interest of the owners of the British ship Waterloo, her tackle, apparel, and furniture, to the libel of information of the United States of America, alleges as follows:

First. That the said ship Waterloo is, as stated in the second article of the said libel, and as the said claimant believes to be true British property, and that the said claimant claims the same on behalf of the owner or owners of the said ship.

Second. That he does not know, and therefore cannot say, whether the said ship Waterloo came and arrrived in the said port of New York from Anatto Bay, in the Island of Jamaica, in the West Indies, as stated and set forth in the said libel, nor if the fact be so, whether a forfeiture of the said ship Waterloo, her tackle, apparel and furniture, was incurred in consequence thereof, as stated in the said libel.

Third. That the said ship Waterloo was found dismasted and derelict at sea, by a certain brig or vessel called the Merced, said ship having been abandoned by the master and crew thereof, and that the said ship Waterloo, being a wreck, was taken possession of by the captain and crew of the said brig Merced, and brought into the said port of New York, without any act of intention or volition on the part of the said ship Waterloo, her captain, officers, or crew.

And the said claimant prays that the said ship Waterloo, her tackle, apparel and furniture, may be restored to the said claimant, and that he may be hence dismissed with his reasonable costs and charges in this benalf sustained.

J. C. BUCHANAN.

Sworn this 3d day of November, 1829,
    before me,
        FRED. J. BETTS, Clerk.

H. & E. WILKES,
Proctors and Advocates.

No. 64.—STIPULATION FOR COSTS—*as ante, No.* 10, *page* 434.

No. 65.—ANSWER AND CLAIM OF THE AGENTS OF FOREIGN UNDERWRITERS TO A LIBEL OF INFORMATION FOR A FORFEITURE.

DISTRICT COURT OF THE UNITED STATES,

FOR THE SOUTHERN DISTRICT OF NEW YORK.

IN ADMIRALTY.

To the Honorable Samuel R. Betts, Judge of the District Court of the United States for the Southern District of New York:

The answer and claim of Henry Barclay and George Barclay of the city of New York, merchants, intervening for the interest of their principals, to the libel of information of James A. Hamilton, Esquire, Attorney of the United States, for the Southern District of New York, filed on behalf of the said United States, alleges as follows:

First. That these respondents admit, that the said ship Waterloo is a ship or vessel owned wholly or in part by a subject or subjects of his Brittannic Majesty; and that the said ship or vessel, after the thirtieth day of September, eighteen hundred and eighteen, and also after the thirtieth day of September, eighteen hundred and twenty, did come from a port or place in a colony or territory of his Brittannic Majesty, to wit, from Anatto Bay in the island of Jamaica, in the West Indies; which said port is, and was at the time the said vessel sailed from thence, and also at the time of the arrival of the said ship at the port of New York, by the ordinary laws of navigation and trade, closed against vessels owned by citizens of the United States. But these respondents deny that the ports of the United States were, at the time of the arrival of the said ship at the port of New York, or at any time afterwards, closed against the said ship or vessel called the Waterloo, or that the said ship was excluded from the said port of New York. And they deny that the said ship did enter the said port of New York in the said district, in violation of the acts of the Congress of the United States in such cases made and provided, and that, by virtue of the said acts, the said ship or vessel, her tackle, apparel, and furniture, became forfeited to the use of the said United States.

Second. That the said vessel, on or about the twenty-seventh day of August, eighteen hundred and twenty-nine, was found by the captain and crew of the brig Merced of New York upon the high seas, and without the jurisdiction of the United States, totally disabled, a wreck, and entirely abandoned by her captain and crew; and that the said ship or vessel was then, and there taken in tow by the said brig Merced and brought into the port of New York. And these respondents deny that the said wreck, so brought as aforesaid into the port of New York, was, or was intended to be, comprehended in the provisions of the said navigation acts; but they insist and charge, that the said navigation acts were intended to apply, and in fact do apply solely, to vessels voluntarily entering the ports of the United States for purposes of trade and navigation.

Third. That by a commission dated the second day of July, in the year of our Lord one thousand eight hundred and seventeen, and signed by Joseph Marryat, Chairman, and John Bennet, junior, Secretary of the committee for managing the affairs of the underwriters at Lloyd's in London, in that part of the United Kingdom of Great Britain and Ireland called England, these respondents were appointed to act as agents for the subscribers to Lloyd's at the port of New York and custom house district, subject to the instructions in the said commission mentioned; and that by the said commission, they are authorized and empowered to attend to the interests of the subscribers to Lloyd's in general, as by the said commission, now in the possession of these respondents, will more fully and at large appear, and to which, for greater certainty, these respondents pray leave to refer.

And these respondents, further answering, say, that they are likewise the agents for the underwriters at Liverpool, in that part of the United Kingdom of Great Britain and Ireland, called England; and for the underwriters in Glasgow, in that part of the said United Kingdom called Scotland, under two several commissions, with the like authority and instructions as mentioned in the said commission from the underwriters at Lloyd's in London aforesaid, as by the said several commissions from the underwriters at Liverpool, and from the underwriters at Glasgow, reference being thereunto had, will more fully and at large appear, and to which, for greater certainty these respondents pray leave to refer.

And these respondents, further answering, say, that they have no doubt that the said ship Waterloo, or some part thereof, was insured at some or one of the said places by some or all of the said underwriters therein; and they have no doubt but that the said vessel, or some part thereof, hath been abandoned by the persons interested therein to the said underwriters, or some or one of them, and that the right of ownership in the said ship, or some part thereof, hath accrued to the said underwriters, or some or one of them ; but these respondents cannot speak on this point with absolute certainty, but only to the best of their belief, inasmuch as a sufficient time hath not elapsed since the twelfth day of September, eighteen hundred and twenty-nine, when the said ship was, as aforesaid, brought into the said port of New York, to communicate the circumstance to the said several underwriters, or any of them, and obtain their answer. That immediately after the said vessel was brought into the port of New York, as aforesaid, they wrote to the said underwriters at London, informing them of the circumstances of the case as far as known to these respondents, and requesting information from the said underwriters of their rights and interests in and to the said vessel, or any part thereof, to which they have, for the reason aforesaid, obtained no answer.

Fourth. That a 'libel hath been filed in this Honorable Court by Peter Harmony, the owner, and Eliphalet Kingsbury, the captain of the said brig Merced, against the said ship Waterloo, claiming salvage for having brought the said ship Waterloo into this port ; and these respondents insist, that if any portion of the said ship be forfeitable under the acts of navigation aforesaid, the salvage that may be adjudged to the said owner and captain is alone forfeitable, as they alone had any agency in the alleged infraction of the said acts.

And, therefore, these respondents, on behalf of the said several underwriters, claim the said vessel, and pray that the said vessel, or the proceeds thereof, over and above the salvage that may be decreed, may be detained in the custody of this Honorable Court, for such reasonable time as may seem proper, wherein the rights and interests of the above mentioned underwriters may be ascertained; and that this Honorable Court may further decree that the said surplus proceeds, over and above the salvage that may be awarded by this Honorable Court, may be paid to these respondents, upon due proof being made in manner and form as this Honorable Court may direct, that the said underwriters, or any of them, have an interest in and a right to receive the same, or such part thereof as they shall appear to be entitled to.

And these respondents will ever pray, &c.

GEORGE BARCLAY.

Sworn this 3d of November, 1829,
          before me,
     FRED. J. BETTS, Clerk.
          ROBINSON & BETTS,
               Prs. and Advs. for Claim'ts.

No. 66.—STIPULATION FOR COSTS—*As ante, No.* 10, *page* 434.

No. 67.—Order for default on return of process in rem on a libel of information.

The libel having been read, and the marshal having returned,—(*as ante, No.* 8, *page* 431.

———

No. 68.—Notices of hearing, to party and clerk—*Same as Nos.* 41, 42, 43, *ante, page* 455.

———

No. 69 —Final decree dismissing a libel of information.

This cause having been brought on for hearing, and the advocates of the respective parties being heard, and due deliberation being had, on motion of Mr. Johnson, Proctor for the defendant Harmony, It is ordered, adjudged, and decreed, that the libel in this case be dismissed.

———

No. 70.—Libel in rem by a ship-builder for a portion of the price.

To the Honorable Samuel R. Betts, Judge of the District Court of the United States for the Southern District of New York.

The libel of A. B. of the city of New York, ship builder, against the ship or vessel Madison, whereof C. D. is, or lately was master, her tackle, apparel and furniture, and against all persons intervening for their interest therein, in a cause of contract, civil and maritime, alleges as follows:

First. That, on the first day of March last, he was employed by E. F., of the city of Boston, merchant, to furnish the materials and build for him, as owner, the ship since called the Madison, of about seven hundred tons burthen, and now in the port of New York, for the sum of eighteen thousand dollars, payable as the work should progress, the final payment of three thousand dollars to be made when the said vessel should be launched.

Second. That he proceeded to build the said vessel, and in all things faithfully performed his contract, and the said ship was safely launched on the fourth day of December, instant, and delivered to the said E. F. and accepted by him.

Third. That the said E. F. now refuses to pay to the libellant the said final payment of three thousand dollars, which is justly due to him according to his contract.

Fourth. That all and singular the premises are true, and within the Admiralty and Maritime jurisdiction of the United States and of this Honorable Court.

Whereupon the libellant prays that process in due form of law, according to the course of this Honorable Court in causes of Admiralty and Maritime jurisdiction, may issue against the said vessel, her tackle, apparel and furniture, and that all persons claiming any right in said vessel, and especially the said E F., may be cited to appear and answer all the matters aforesaid, and that the said ship may be condemned and sold to pay the amount which shall be due to the libellant, on his contract aforesaid, with interest and costs, and that he may have such other and further relief as in law and justice he is entitled to receive.

A. B.

Sworn, &c., before me,

G. H., U. S. Commissioner.

J. B., Proctor.

E. L., Advocate.

No 71.—LIBEL

For the same cause in personam—against the owner.

To the Honorable, &c., *as in the last precedent.*

The libel of A. B. of the city of New York, shipbuilder, against C. D., of the city of Boston, merchant, owner of the ship or vessel Madison, in a cause of contract, civil and maritime, alleges as follows:

(First, second, third and fourth articles, as in the last precedent.)

Whereupon the libellant prays, that a warrant of arrest in due form of law, according to the course of this Honorable Court in causes of Admiralty and Maritime jurisdiction, may issue against the said C. D., and that he may be required to answer on oath this libel, and the matters herein contained, and that this Honorable Court will be pleased to decree to the libellant the payment of the amount which shall be due to him for building said ship, with interest and costs, and to give him such other and further relief as in law and justice he may be entitled to receive.

(*To be signed and sworn to as before.*)

No. 72.—LIBEL IN REM BY A SUPERINTENDENT OF THE BUILDING OF A SHIP FOR HIS COMPENSATION.

To the Honorable, &c., (*the address and statement of parties as in No.* 70, *ante, page* 471.)

First. That in the month of March last, he was employed by E. F., of the city of New Haven, to purchase materials, employ mechanics, and direct and superintend the building of a brig or vessel, in the city of New York, the funds to be furnished, and payments made by the said C. D., for the salary or wages, of seven hundred and fifty dollars, for the time between the laying the keel and the launching of said ship.

Second. That the libellant proceeded without delay faithfully to perform his duties under his said contract, and the keel of said ship was laid on the 4th day of June last, and the work has proceeded with all practicable despatch, and the said vessel would have been ready to be launched on the first day of October last, had the necessary funds been supplied to make the necessary payments and complete the work.

Third. That on the tenth day of September last, the said C. D. sold the said unfinished vessel to one E. F. of the city of New York, subject to the payment of the libellant, and ceased to furnish funds and to make the necessary payments, and the said E. F. declined to proceed with finishing the said vessel, and discharged the libellant, and both said C. D. and E. F. refuse to pay the libellant for his said services, and the whole of his said compensation is now due to him, amounting to seven hundred and fifty dollars, besides interest.

Fourth. That his demand for his said services is, by the law of the state of New York, a lien upon the said vessel. That the said vessel is still unfinished, and has not yet received a name, and is intended to be of about one thousand tons burthen.

Fifth. That all and singular the premises are true, and within the Admiralty and Maritime jurisdiction of the United States, and of this Court.

Wherefore the libellant prays, that process in due form of law, according to the course of this Honorable Court, in causes of Admiralty and Maritime jurisdiction, may issue against said unfinished vessel, and that all persons claiming any right in said vessel, and especially the said C. D. and E. F., may be cited to appear and answer all the matters aforesaid, and that the said unfinished vessel may be condemned and sold to pay the amount which shall be due to the libellant, on his contract aforesaid, with interest and costs, and that he may have such other and further relief as in law and justice he is entitled to receive.

(*To be signed and sworn to as No. 70, ante, page 471.*)

No. 73.—THE SAME IN PERSONAM—*The statement of the parties and the prayer, like No. 71, and the articles the same as No. 72, ante, page 472.*

No. 74.—LIBELS BY THE OWNER AGAINST THE BUILDER, WHEN THERE IS AN ADMIRALTY CAUSE OF ACTION—*Can be easily framed from the foregoing precedents.*

No. 75.—LIBEL IN REM BY A MATERIAL MAN FOR MATERIALS FOR TACKLE, APPAREL, OR FURNITURE, TO BUILD OR FINISH A VESSEL.

To the Honorable, &c.

The libel of A. B., of the city of Troy,   against the sloop or vessel Coaster, whereof C. D. is, or lately was master, her tackle, apparel and furniture, and against all persons intervening for their interest therein, in a cause of contract, civil and maritime, alleges as follows:

First. That some time in the month of May last, E. F. of the city of Albany,   being then, as owner, building a sloop or vessel since called the Coaster, and having employed the said C. D., her intended master, to act as his agent in building the same, applied, by the said master, to the libellant to furnish the   for building said vessel.

Second. That the libellant accordingly furnished, on the order of said master and builder, the various articles of   set forth in the account or schedule hereto annexed, at the prices mentioned in said account, which are the market prices therefor, and are reasonable and just, and the said articles were delivered to said vessel at Albany aforesaid, to be used in building and completing her, and the value thereof was, by the maritime law, and the law of the State of New York, a lien upon said vessel, her tackle, apparel, and furniture.

Third. That the said E. F. paid to the libellant, from time to time, on account, the sums credited in said account, leaving due the balance thereof, amounting to   dollars, with interest, which the said E. F. has neglected and refused to pay.

Fourth. That the said vessel is now at Albany, within the Northern District of New York, where she was built, which port she has never left.

Fifth. That all and singular the premises are true and within the Admiralty and Maritime jurisdiction of the United States, and of this Honorable Court.

Whereupon the libellant prays, &c.

(*Prayer, and signatures, and jurat as in No.* 70, *ante, page* 471.)

No. 76.—Libel for the same cause in personam against the owner—*with a clause for the attachment of his goods, chattels, credits, and effects.*

To the Honorable, &c.

The libel of A. B. of the city of Troy,   against E. F. of Albany, owner of the sloop Coaster, in a cause of contract civil and maritime.

(First, second, third, fourth, and fifth articles as in the last precedent.)

Sixth. That the said E. F. has absconded from this district, or is concealed, or cannot be found therein, and has goods and chattels in this district, and credits and effects in the hands of J. K. of the city of Buffalo.

Whereupon the libellant prays that a warrant of arrest, in due form of law, according to the course of this Honorable Court in causes of Admiralty and Maritime jurisdiction may issue against the said E. F. and that he may be required to answer on oath this libel and the matters herein contained, and that if he cannot be found, then that his goods and chattels in this district may be attached to a sufficient amount to answer the libellant, and if sufficient goods and chattels cannot be found in this district, then that his credits and effects, in the hands of said J. K. of Buffalo, may be attached to a sufficient amount to answer the libellant, and that said J. K. may be cited to appear and answer such interrogatories as may be propounded to him by the libellant, and that this Honorable Court will be pleased to decree to the libellant the payment of the amount which shall be due to him for the cause aforesaid, with interest and costs, and to give him such other and further relief as in law and justice he may be entitled to receive.

A. B.

Sworn, &c. before me,

   GEORGE W. MORTON,

     U. S. Commissioner.

J. B., Proctor.

E. L., Advocate.

No. 77.—LIBEL IN REM BY THE OWNERS OF A VESSEL TO OBTAIN POSSESSION OF HER.

To the Honorable, &c.

The libel of A. B. and C. D., of Bath, merchants, owners of the schooner or vessel the Sea Gull, her tackle, apparel and furniture, and against all persons intervening for their interest therein, in a cause of possession, civil and maritime, alleges as follows :

First. That they are the true and only owners of the schooner Sea Gull, her tackle, apparel and furniture, and being such owners, on or about the tenth day of May, 1846, appointed one E. F. master of said vessel, to navigate and sail her for them, at the wages agreed upon between them, and the said E. F. continued to be such master till the fifth day of August, instant, when the libellants removed him as master, and appointed another master in his place.

Second. That when the new master, so appointed by the libellants, went on board said vessel, by their orders, to enter upon his duties as such master, the said E. F. refused to give up the possession or the papers of said vessel to the said master, or to the libellants, who have demanded the same—to the great damage of the libellant.

Third. That all and singular the premises are true, and within the admiralty and maritime jurisdiction of the United States and of this Honorable Court.

Whereupon the libellants pray that process in due form of law, according to the course of this Honorable Court, in causes of Admiralty and maritime jurisdiction, may issue against the said vessel, her tackle, apparel and furniture, and that the said E. F. may be personally cited to appear and answer all the matters aforesaid, and that the said vessel, her tackle, apparel and furniture, may be delivered to the libellants, and that the said E. F. may be condemned to pay to the libellants their damages and costs in the premises, and that they may have such other and further relief in the premises as in law and justice they may be entitled to receive.

A. B.
C. D.

Sworn, &c.

J. B., Proctor.

C. L., Advocate.

No. 78. Libel in rem against merchandise for possession.

To the Honorable, &c.

The libel of H. B. of the city of New York, merchant, against nine cases of merchandise, marked A, 1 to 9, and against C. D., master of the ship or vessel the Carrier, in a cause of possession, civil and maritime, alleges as follows:

First. That heretofore, while the said vessel was lying in the port of Liverpool in England, and about to sail for the port of Philadelphia, John Brown, of Liverpool aforesaid, shipped on board said vessel, consigned to the libellant, nine cases of merchandise, marked A, 1 to 9, and the said master signed the usual bill of lading for the same, whereby he agreed to deliver the same to the libellant, in New York, on payment of the freight for the same at the rate of twenty cents per cubic foot.

Second. That the said ship having arrived in the said port of New York, the libellant paid to the said master his freight on the said merchandise, and demanded the delivery thereof, but the said master refused to deliver the same to him unless the libellant would pay one hundred and fifty dollars as an average contribution, which the libellant was not bound to pay, not being liable therefor, and the said master still refuses to deliver to him the said nine cases, and each of them which are of the value of two thousand dollars and upward, to the great damage of the libellant.

Third. That all and singular the premises are true, and within the Admiralty and maritime jurisdiction of the United States, and of this Honorable Court.

Wherefore, the libellant prays that process in due form of law, according to the course of this Honorable Court in causes of Admiralty and maritime jurisdiction, may issue against the said nine cases of merchandise, and that the said C. D. may be personally cited to appear and answer all the matters aforesaid, and that the said merchandise may be delivered to the libellant, and that the said C. D may be condemned to pay to the libellant his damages and costs in the premises, and that he may have such other and further relief in the premises as in law and justice he may be entitled to receive.

A. B.

Sworn, &c., before me,

   J. W. M., Clerk.

J. B., Proctor.

W. M., Advocate.

No. 79.—A libel in rem by the owner to recover a vessel witthheld on a claim of title.

To the Honorable Samuel R. Betts, Judge of the District Court of the United States, for the Southern District of New York:

The libel of Alfred Peabody, of Salem, in the Commonwealth of Massachusetts, merchant, against the schooner Lucinda Snow, whereof Stubbs, of　　　　　　　　now is or late was master, her tackle, apparel, and furniture, and against the said　　　　　　Stubbs. master, and against Rogers, of　　　　　　　in the State of Maine, and against all other persons lawfully intervening for their interest in the said schooner, in a cause of possession, civil and maritime, alleges as follows :

First. That the libellant is the true and lawful owner, absolutely of one half, and the lawful owner by way of mortgage of the remaining half of the said schooner Lucinda Snow, of ninety-nine tons burthen, now lying in the port of New York, and had the possession and employment thereof as such owner, till deprived of her as herein set forth.

Second. That the said schooner is wrongfully withheld from the libellant by the said Stubbs and said Rogers, on an alleged ground of title, depending upon a pretended sale by one Dawson Lincoln, now deceased, as master of said schooner Lucinda Snow, which sale was unauthorized, without any necessity and without any legal survey or condemnation of said schooner, in violation of the duty of the said Dawson Lincoln as master in fraud of the libellant, and is utterly void.

Third. That on or about the early part of the month of December last past, the libellant and the said Dawson Lincoln purchased the said schooner then lying in the port of Boston, for the sum of $2,400. and the libellant paid the sum of $600, on account of his half thereof, and the said Lincoln paid $600 on account of his half, and for remaining $1200 the libellant became surety, and signed a joint note for $1200 with said Lincoln, for the balance of such purchase money. That. upon such purchase being made, a bill of sale was duly executed and delivered by the then owners of said schooner to the libellant and the said Lincoln, whereby the libellant became the legal owner of one-half, and the said Lincoln became the owner of the remaining half of said schooner, and said schooner was duly registered according to the act of Congress in such case made and provided, as belonging, one-half to the libellant and one-half to said Lincoln.

That upon such purchase being made as aforesaid, and before sailing from Boston, the said schooner was thoroughly repaired at an expense of about $1000, and fitted for a three years voyage, which said expense was wholly supplied by the libellant; and to secure the libellant for the one-half of such expense, and for one-half of said note for a part of the said purchase money, and for one-half of any loss that might arise on her voyage from Boston to Galveston, hereinafter mentioned, the said Dawson Lincoln, on or about the 21st day of December, 1846, executed to the libellant a bill of sale of his one-half of said schooner, a copy whereof is hereto annexed, marked B. That such schooner was, at that time, six years old, in excellent condition, and worth at least the sum of $3.500.

Fourth. That the libellant purchased and supplied, from his own means, a cargo on joint account with the said Dawson Lincoln, who was then appointed master of said schooner, and with said cargo, and a freight of about

$160, the said schooner sailed from the port of Boston, on or about the 26th day of December last past, with the said Lincoln as Captain, bound to Galveston, Texas, where she arrived on or about the 27th day of January last past, in excellent order and condition, and discharged her cargo, and received a full freight at Galveston, for the mouth of the Rio Grande, where she arrived on or about the latter part of February last, and discharged her cargo, for which the said Captain Lincoln received the freight, amounting, as the libellant has been informed and believes, to more than $500. That while said schooner was so at the Rio Grande, in the early part of March last, she was chartered by the Government of the United States for the sum of $1200 a month, and proceeded to Vera Cruz, and lay at or near Sacrificios, and the said Lincoln received from the said Government, the sum of about $1500 and upwards on account of such charter ; that on or about the 2d day of April last, the said Captain Lincoln wrote in substance, from Vera Cruz to the libellant, that the first months charter of said schooner, amounting to $1200, would be due on the 10th day of April, and that he would remit that amount, together with $400, freight and proceeds of cargo sold by him to the agent of the libellant, at Salem, but the said Lincoln wholly failed to make any remittance whatever, and the libellant is credibly informed, and believes and states that the said Captain Lincoln, after his arrival at Vera Cruz, in neglect of his duty as master of said schooner, and of the interest of the libellant, embarked largely in the business of purchasing wrecked vessels on the shore, and in getting them off, without the authority or knowledge of the libellant, and had, some time before the said schooner ran on shore, as hereinafter mentioned, actually purchased a brig for about $1600, stranded on the shore, and a barque for about $800, also stranded on the shore, and was busily engaged in getting them off, up to the time the said schooner went ashore. That no remittance whatever having been at any time made by the said Captain Lincoln to the libellant or his agent, no reasonable doubt can exist that the said Lincoln, who was a man of little or no means, converted the proceeds of the cargo, freights and charter, or the greater part thereof, received by him, amounting to at least $1600, to purchase of said wrecks.

Fifth. That on or about Sunday, the 2d day of May last, the said Capt. Lincoln left the said schooner anchored at or near Sacrificios, with only the mate on board, and with all of the crew of the said schooner, went some ten miles down the coast in the schooner's boat, for the purpose of wrecking, and while so absent, a squall from the Northward came up in the early part of the day, and parted one of the schooners chains, and was driving her towards the shore directly on some old wrecks, when the mate, finding that she continued dragging her remaining anchor, and that she would inevitably go ashore in the vicinity of the old wrecks, slipped the remaining chain, and succeeded in running her on a smooth, clear beach, sustaining no injury to said schooner, except the loss of a few sheets of copper from her bottom, and although the said Lincoln returned with his crew from the wrecking expedition on the evening of the same day, he allowed said schooner to remain ashore, although only slightly grounded, from Sunday until the Friday following, without making an effort to relieve her, although she was uninjured, and could have been easily hove off with a very trifling expense, and although he had a sufficient chain and anchor convenient, on board of the brig he had purchased, to enable him to get her off, and although he could have applied the said monies in his hands, or could have raised money on the said brig or barque, or by bottomry on said schooner, more than sufficient to meet his expenses in getting her off; That on the said Friday, as the libellant is informed and believes, the said Captain Lincoln called a survey, and on the following day (Saturday) exposed said schooner for sale at auction, and after considerable competition at said sale, the said Rogers bid her in at such sale, at the sum of $1,750, and now alleges that he thereby became the legal owner of said schooner, and the libellant is informed and believes that the said Lincoln authorized and requested a person to bid for him, said Lincoln, at said auction sale, the sum of $1,700, or about that sum, for said schooner, if she could not be purchased at a less sum ; and the libellant states that no necessity existed for said sale, and that the same was fraudulent, collusive, illegal and void, and conferred no title whatever on the said Rogers, That on or about the third day after the alleged purchase at said sale, the said Rogers hove off the said schooner, with anchors and chains, at a very trifling expense, not to exceed, as the libellent believes, the sum of $50 or $100, and when so hove off, the said schooner had sustained no damage in her hull, spars, sails, rigging, or otherwise, except the loss of a few sheets of copper off her bottom, and a little caulking necessary on her wales, and a chain and anchor. That being supplied with this slight amount of caulking, and one chain and anchor, she proceeded in a few days thereafter, without any other repairs, to New Orleans, a distance of about 800 or 1000 miles, and there took in a full cargo of corn and proceeded to New York, where she arrived in safety after a quick passage of fourteen days in a good and sound condition, on or about the 6th day of August, instant, without receiving any repairs except as aforesaid. That a full cargo of corn, from its dense weight, and liability to shift and great strain in a vessel could not be brought, and would not be entrusted in any vessel except she were sound, staunch, and in good condition, and that, as the libellant is informed and believes, the said Rogers now values said schooner, at tho sum of $3,500, and the libellant states that it must have been quite apparent to the said Rogers and to the said Lincoln, at the time of said pretended auction sale, that said schooner was in no peril or danger, and no necessity existed for her sale, and that she could have been easily got off, as the one bid the sum of $1750, and the other authorized a bid of $1700 for said schooner, (50 per cent of her value when safely in port,) which bids would not have been made, had any real necessity for a sale existed.

Sixth. That after the said sale the said Lincoln continued his business of wrecking at Vera Cruz as aforesaid, and got off the said barque purchased by him, and, as the libellant is informed and believes, also purchased another stranded vessel and got her off. That the said Lincoln retained the entire proceeds of said auction sale, as well as the said moneys so received as aforesaid from the sale of cargo, freight and charter, amounting together to at least the sum of $3,300, no part of which has ever been received by the libellant, or by any person for his account, although he has paid for the whole of said outfits at Boston, and has paid said note so given by said Lincoln on account of the purchase money of one-half of said schooner, and has paid insurance and other running expenses of said schooner to the amount of about $300.

That the cargo shipped on joint account as aforesaid will barely reimburse the libellant for its cost, freight and expenses, and no profit has or will be made therein, and that the only freight received by the libellant since said schooner left Boston, in December, 1846, was about the sum of $60 received at Galveston on account of freight, which sum was credited to the schooner and the balance of said freight from Boston, being the sum of $100, was received by said Lincoln for his family.

.Seventh. That the libellant first heard of his schooner being ashore on or about the 25th day of May last, while he was at New Orleans, but he was in so critical a state of health that he was unable to go to Vera Cruz to look after his interests, and had to leave for the north on account of his bad health on or about the 3d day of June last, and that up to the time of leaving for the north as aforesaid, he had not received any letter, information, or communication whatever from the said Captain Lincoln, except the said letter of the 2d day of April hereinbefore mentioned. That the said Captain Lincoln died at Vera Cruz on or about the 17th day of July last.

Wherefore the libellant prays that process in due form of law, according to the course of this Honorable Court in causes of Admiralty and Maritime jurisdiction, may issue against the said schooner Lucinda Snow, her tackle, apparel and furniture, and that the said   Stubbs and Rogers, and all other persons having any interest in said schooner, may be cited to appear before this Honorable Court and to show cause why possession of the said schooner should not be delivered to the libellant as having full title to the possession thereof, against the said   Stubbs and   Rogers, and that this Honorable Court would be pleased to decree the said schooner to be delivered to the libellant, and that the said Stubbs and Rogers may be decreed to pay unto the libellant all freight and freights earned by said schooner while in their possession, or in the possession of either of them, with damages and costs, and that the libellants may have such other and further relief in the premises as in law and justice he may be entitled to receive.

ALFRED PEABODY.

Sworn, &c., before me,
    JAS. W. METCALF, Clerk.
    MARTIN STRONG & A. F. SMITH, Proctors.
        F. SMITH, Advocate.

No. 80.—LIBEL IN REM BY A MINORITY OWNER TO OBTAIN SECURITY. FOR THE RETURN OF A VESSEL, OR FOR A SALE.

To the Honorable Samuel R. Betts, District Judge of the United States for the Southern District of New York:

The libel of A. B., of the city of New York, part owner of the brig Packet against the said brig, her tackle, apparel and furniture, and against all persons intervening for their interest therein, and especially against C. D., part owner of said brig, in a cause of possession, civil and maritime, alleges as follows:

First. That the libellant is the true and lawful owner of one-quarter of the brig Packet, of the burthen of 200 tons, her tackle, apparel and furniture, and boats, and the said C. D. is the owner of the remaining three-quarters of said brig, and no other person is owner of said vessel or any portion thereof, and the said brig is now lying in the port of Hudson, in the Southern District of New York.

Second. That the said C. D. has hitherto acted as ship's husband of said vessel, and has now the possession thereof, and declares his intention of despatching said vessel on a sealing voyage to the Pacific Ocean. That the libellant has expressed to said C. D. his dissent from said voyage, and has remonstrated with him on the subject, and still dissents from the same, but the said C. D. persists in his determination to send her on said voyage, and is now procuring her outfit and crew.

Third. That all and singular the premises are true, and within the Admiralty and Maritime jurisdiction of the United States and of this Honorable Court.

Wherefore the libellant prays that process in due form of law, according to the course of this Honorable Court in cases of Admiralty and Maritime jurisdiction, may issue against the said vessel, her tackle, apparel, furniture and boats, and that all persons claiming any right in said vessel, and especially the said C. D., three-quarters owner as aforesaid, may be cited to appear and answer the matters aforesaid, and to show cause why the said C. D. should not be restrained from sending the said vessel on the said voyage until good and sufficient security shall be given in this court to the full value of the libellant's interest in said vessel, her tackle, apparel, furniture and boats, for the safe return of said vessel to the said port of Hudson, where she belongs, and that this Honorable Court will be pleased to decree that such security be given or the possession of said vessel, her tackle, &c., be delivered to the libellant, with costs, and that the said vessel, her tackle, &c., may be sold under the direction of this Honorable Court, and the proceeds of such sale brought into this court, to be divided according to law; and that the libellant may have such other and further relief in the premises as in law and justice he may be entitled to receive.

Sworn, &c., before me,   A. B.

J. W. NELSON, U. S. Commissioner.

E. J., Proctor.

T. H., Advocate.

No. 81.—A LIBEL IN REM BY A PART OWNER FOR A SALE OF THE VESSEL.

[*Address and statement of parties as in the last precedent—then proceed*] —in a cause of licitation or partition, alleges as follows:

First. That he is two-fifths owner of the brigantine Red Rover, her tackle, apparel, furniture and boats; that C. D. is owner of two-fifths and E. F. is owner of one-fifth, and is also master of said vessel, and she is now in the port of New York.

Second. That in consequence of diversity of opinion and interest in relation to the employment of said vessel, which is irreconcilable, the said owners are unable to agree upon any voyage or business for said vessel. That the libellant has named a reasonable price for said vessel, at which he is willing to sell his share, or buy the shares of his co-owners, but they refuse either to buy or sell, and, in consequence of their impracticability and obstinacy, he is unable to sell to any other person.

Third. That all and singular the premises are true, and within the Admiralty and Maritime jurisdiction of the United States and of this Honorable Court.

Wherefore the libellant prays that process in due form of law, according to the course of this Honorable Court in cases of Admiralty and Maritime jurisdiction, may issue against the said brigantine, her tackle, apparel, furniture and boats, and that all persons claiming any right in said vessel, and especially the said C. D. and E. F., part owners and master as aforesaid, may be cited to appear and answer the matters aforesaid, and that the said vessel, her tackle, &c., may be sold under the direction of this Honorable Court, and the proceeds thereof brought into court to be divided and distributed according to law, and that the libellant may have such other and further relief in the premises as in law and justice he may be entitled to receive.

                                                                    A. B.

Sworn, &c., before me,
             CHAS. W. NEWTON, U. S. Commissioner.
     E. B., Proctor.
     A. S., Advocate.

———

No. 82.—LIBEL IN REM AGAINST A DOMESTIC VESSEL BY A SHIP JOINER FOR LABOR AND MATERIALS—TO ENFORCE A STATE LIEN.

To the Honorable Samuel R. Betts, Judge of the District Court of the United States for the Southern District of New York:

The libel of William Robinson, of said district, ship joiner, against the barque Richard Alsop, (whereof   now is or late was master,) her tackle, apparel and furniture, and against all persons intervening for their interest in said barque, in a cause of contract, civil and maritime, alleges as follows:

First. That the said barque Richard Alsop, is a domestic ship, and is now owned, or was, at the time hereinafter mentioned, owned by some persons who are resident in the State of New York, who are to the libellant unknown, but who, as he is informed and believes, reside in the city of New York.

Second. That the said barque, in the month of July last, being in the port of New York, in the district aforesaid, the libellant furnished certain materials and performed certain labor as a ship joiner, (the particulars of which are mentioned and set forth in the schedule hereto annexed,) towards the altering, equipping, and finishing the said barque, at the request of the said master, and at the prices in the said schedule mentioned. That the charges in said account are just and reasonable, and that said materials furnished, and such labor done upon the said vessel, were necessary and proper, to the altering, equipping, and finishing the said barque.

Third. That the said labor was performed upon the said vessel, and that said materials so furnished, have gone into the said barque, and have become part thereof—and that the amount of said repairs done, labor performed, and materials furnished, amount to the sum of one hundred and eighty-eight dollars and seventy-nine cents, and that the labor was done and materials furnished upon the credit of said vessel, as well as of the master and owners thereof.

Fourth. That the amount due for said labor performed upon the said vessel, and such materials furnished to her, are, by the law of the State of New York, a lien upon the said vessel, her tackle, apparel, and furniture—and the said vessel is now in the Southern District of New York.

Fifth. That the libellant has repeatedly requested the said master to pay him the said sum of one hundred and eighty-eight dollars and seventy-nine cents, but that the said master has not paid the same, and still neglects and refuses so to do, and that the said sum now remains entirely due and unpaid.

Sixth. That all and singular the premises are true, and within the Admiralty and Maritime jurisdiction of the United States, and of this Honorable Court.

Wherefore the libellant prays, that process in due form of law, according to the course of this Honorable Court in cases of Admiralty and Maritime jurisdiction, may issue against the said barque, her tackle, apparel, and furniture; and that the said master, and all persons claiming any right, title, or interest in the said barque, may be cited to appear and answer upon oath all and singular, the matters aforesaid, and that the said vessel may be condemned and sold to pay the amount due to the libellant, with interest and costs, and that the libellant may have such other and further relief as in law and justice he may be entitled to receive.

WILLIAM ROBINSON.

Sworn, &c.

BURR & BENEDICT, Proctors.

E. BURR, Advocate.

(*Schedule :—A Copy of the Bill of Items.*)

No. 83.—LIBEL IN PERSONAM BY A SHIP CHANDLER AGAINST THE
OWNER FOR SUPPLIES—WITH ATTACHMENT CLAUSE.

To the Honorable Samuel R. Betts, Judge of the District Court of the
United States for the Southern District of New York.

The libel of George W. Quintard, of said District, late ship chandler,
against Peter S. J. Talbot, now or late owner of the schooner Mary, in a
cause of contract, civil and maritime, alleges as follows:

First. That in the month of June, one thousand eight hundred and forty-
seven, said schooner then being owned by the said Peter S. J. Talbot, and
lying• in the port of New York, and under the command of one Captain
Chase, and standing in need of provisions and stores—the libellant, at the
request of the said master, furnished to and for the use of the said schooner,
the provisions and stores contained in the schedule hereto annexed, amounting to the sum of sixty-eight dollars thirty-five cents, and that the same was
furnished at the prices in said schedule stated.

Second. That said stores were necessary to enable said schooner to perform her intended voyage or voyages, and were furnished on the credit of
the said schooner, as well as of the master and owners thereof.

Third. That the said owners have been requested to pay the said bill,
but have hitherto wholly neglected and refused to pay the same, and the
sum of seventy-three dollars and thirteen cents, including interest, is now
justly due and owing to the libellant for the same.

Fourth. That the libellant has been informed and believes that the respondent has credits and effects in the hands of Brett & Vose, of the city of
New York.

Fifth. That all and singular the premises are true, and within the Admiralty and Maritime jurisdiction of the United States and of this Honorable
Court.

Wherefore the libellant prays, that a warrant of arrest may issue against
the said Peter S. J. Talbot, and in case he cannot be found, then that his
goods and chattels be attached to the amount sued for; and if sufficient
goods and chattels cannot be found, then that his credits and effects be attached in the hands of Brett & Vose, garnishees; and that he may be required to answer all the matters aforesaid; and that this Honorable Court
would be pleased to decree the payment of the amount due to your libellant, as
aforesaid, with costs, and that he may have such other and further relief in
the premises as in law and justice he may be entitled to receive.

GEORGE W. QUINTARD.

Sworn before me,
   this 23d Sept. 1848,
        J. W. NELSON, U. S. Comm'r.
BURR & BENEDICT, Proctors.
E. BURR, Advocate.

SCHEDULE:
(A Copy of the Bill of Items.)

No. 84.—Libel in rem against a steamboat for repairs and wharfage.

To the Honorable Samuel R. Betts, Judge of the District Court of the Southern District of New York.

The libel of Maelzaer Howell, and Joseph E. Coffee, of the city of New York, manufacturers, and doing business as copartners in the said city, under the name and style of Howell & Coffee, against the steamboat Fanny, whereof J. Latson is now or late was master, her tackle and furniture, and also against all persons intervening for their interest therein, in a cause of contract, civil and maritime, alleges as follows:

First. The said steamboat or vessel Fanny, of the burthen of about one hundred tons, belonging to the port of New York, and for some time past and now lying in the port of New York, and, being in need of repairs, the said libellants furnished necessary materials for said steamboat or vessel, and did necessary work and labor upon the same to make her seaworthy, which said materials, and work and labor are particularly mentioned in a schedule hereunto annexed, that the same materials furnished, and work and labor done and performed by these libellants, amounts to sixty-seven dollars and forty-five cents, and also said libellants furnished a berth for said steamboat to lie at one of the wharves of the said city of New York, the wharfage whereof amounts to thirty-six dollars, and that all of said materials furnished, and work and labor done and performed upon said steamboat or vessel, and said berth or wharfage were necessary for said steamboat or vessel, and that said work, labor and wharfage together amounts to $113 45.

Second. That the master of said steamboat or vessel, and her owners, have never yet paid to these libellants said sums of money, or either of them, or any part thereof, but have hitherto wholly neglected and refused so to do, and said steamboat is now in the Southern District of New York.

Third. That all and singular the premises are true, and within the Admiralty and Maritime jurisdiction of the United States and of this Honorable Court.

Whereupon these libellants pray, that process in due form of law, according to the course of this Honorable Court in cases of Admiralty and Maritime jurisdiction, may issue against the said steamboat Fanny, her tackle, apparel, and furniture, that all persons claiming any right, title, or interest in the said steamboat or vessel may be cited to appear and answer all and singular, the matters aforesaid, and that the said steamboat may be condemned and sold to pay the demands and claims aforesaid, with interests and costs, and that the libellant may have such other and further relief as in law and justice he may be entitled to demand.

JOSEPH E. COFFEE,

Sworn, &c.   One of the Firm of Howell & Coffee.

D. E. WHEELER, Proctor.

J. Q. MORTON, Advocate.

SCHEDULE :

(A Copy of the Bill of Items.)

No. 85.—A LIBEL IN REM AGAINST THE SHIP AND FREIGHT FOR MONEYS
ADVANCED TO PAY REPAIRS.

To the Honorable Samuel R. Betts, Judge of the District Court of the
United States for the Southern District of New York:

The libel of Hiram Benner of Key West, in the territory of Florida, merchant, against the brig Joseph Gorham of the port of Charleston, in the
state of South Carolina, now lying in the port of New York, (whereof John
Williams now is, or late was, master,) her tackle, apparel, furniture and
freight, and also against all persons lawfully intervening for their interest in
the said brig, in a cause of contract, civil and maritime, alleges as follows:

First. That the said brig Joseph Gorham, of the burthen of one hundred
and forty-six tons, or thereabouts, is now owned, and was at the time hereinafter mentioned owned, by some persons resident out of the state of New
York, who are to the libellant unknown, but one of whom, as he is informed
and believes, resides in the State of South Carolina, and the others in the
state of Connecticut, and that the said brig belongs to the port of Charleston
in the said state of South Carolina.

Second. That the said brig, sometime in the early part of June last, sailed
from the said port of Charleston, bound to the said port of Key West, under
the command of the said John Williams as master. And that in the course
of the said voyage, and sometime on or about the twentieth day of June last,
the said brig got on shore on the Florida Reef, and suffered great damage.
That the said brig was subsequently got off and carried into Key West,
where it was found that it was necessary that she should undergo a course
of thorough and expensive repairs and be furnished with certain supplies, in
order to render her seaworthy and fit to go to sea.

Third. That the said John Williams, master as aforesaid, accordingly
went on and repaired said brig, and purchased said supplies, and that the
expenses of such repairs and supplies necessarily amounted to about twenty-
one hundred dollars. That the said master, not having the funds to pay for
the said repairs and supplies, applied to this libellant at Key West aforesaid
for a loan of part of the amount necessary for that purpose. And that this
libellant accordingly advanced to the said John Williams, for the use of the
said brig, and on her credit and that of her said master and owners, on the
eighth day of July last, the sum of sixteen hundred and six dollars and
seventy-five cents, to be repaid to this libellant on the arrival of the said brig
at New York, (to which port she was destined from Key West aforesaid,)
and that the said sum of sixteen hundred and six dollars and seventy-five
cents was applied by the said John Williams towards payment of the said
repairs and supplies.

Fourth. That shortly after the making of the said advance by this libellant, the said brig sailed from Key West for the port of New York, where
she arrived some two or three days since. That after her arrival at the said
port of New York this libellant applied to the said John Williams, master as
aforesaid, for re-payment of the said amount so advanced by him as afore-

said, which the said master declined, on the ground that he was utterly unable so to do. And that the said brig has now been taken possession of by one of her said owners, who refuses to recognize the said debt, or make any provision therefor, to the damage of this libellant of the full sum of sixteen hundred and six dollars and seventy-five cents.

Fifth. That the said brig, on her said voyage from Key West to New York, brought a cargo on freight, the whole or the greater part of which is now on board of the said brig, and the freight whereof is still uncollected.

Sixth. That all and singular the premises are true, and within the admiralty and maritime jurisdiction of the United States and of this Honorable Court. Wherefore the libellant prays that process in due form of law, according to the course of this Honorable Court in causes of admiralty and maritime jurisdiction, may issue against the said brig, her tackle, apparel, furniture and freight, wheresoever the same shall be found, and that all persons claiming any right, title, or interest therein may be cited to appear and to answer, upon oath, all and singular the matters aforesaid, and that this Honorable Court would be pleased to decree the payment of the amount so due to the libellant, with costs, and that the libellant may have such other and further relief as in law and justice he may be entitled to receive.

WILLIAM BENNER.

Sworn, &c.

GRIFFIN & HAVENS,
    Proctors for Libellant.

GEORGE GRIFFIN,
    Advocate for Libellant.

No. 86.—A LIBEL IN PERSONAM AGAINST THE OWNERS FOR SUPPLIES ORDERED BY THE MASTER IN A FOREIGN PORT.

To the Honorable Samuel R. Betts, Judge of the District Court of the United States for the Southern District of New York:

The libel of Simeon H. Lewis and John C. Clapp of Boston, in the state of Massachusetts, grocers, against Gilbert Hatfield and James T. Bertine now or late owners of the brig or vessel called the Gulielma of New York, in a cause of contract, civil and maritime, alleges as follows:

First. That at various times during the year eighteen hundred and forty-one the said brig Gulielma, then under the command of Richard Smith, and owned by the said Gilbert Hatfield and James F. Bertine, was lying at Boston aforesaid, and standing in need of stores, provisions, and other necessaries, to enable her to perform her intended voyage or voyages, and the libellants, at the request of the said master of the said brig, did furnish to and for the use of the said brig, provisions, stores and other necessaries, to enable said brig to perform her said intended voyage or voyages, to the amount of four hundred and twenty-five dollars and five cents, which said bill is hereunto annexed, signed and approved by the said master; and the said provisions, stores, and other necessaries were furnished on the credit of the said brig, and the master and owners thereof.

Second. That the libellants have repeatedly requested the said master and the said owners to pay them the said sum of money so due the libellants, for the provisions, stores, and other necessaries so furnished as aforesaid, but that the said master and owners have hitherto neglected and refused to pay the same, and still neglect and refuse so to do. And that the sum of one hundred and sixty-nine dollars and five cents, with the interest, are still due to the libellant over and above all payments and deductions.

Third. That all and singular the premises are true, and within the admiralty and maritime jurisdiction of the United States and of this Honorable Court.

Wherefore the libellants pray, that process in due form of law, according to the course of this Honorable Court in causes of admiralty and maritime jurisdiction, may issue against the said Gilbert Hatfield and James F. Bertine, owners as aforesaid, and that they may be required to answer all and singular the matters aforesaid, and that this Honorable Court would be pleased to decree the payment of the amount due as aforesaid, with interest and costs, and that the libellants may have such other and further relief as in law and justice they are entitled to receive.

SIMEON H. LEWIS,
JOHN CLAPP,
by the Attorney in fact,
A. B.

BURR & BENEDICT, Proctors.
E. C. BENEDICT, Advocate.

No. 87.—JURAT BY AN ATTORNEY IN FACT.

Southern District of New York, ss.—A. B. of said district being duly sworn, says that he is the attorney in fact for the libellants above named, who reside in Boston, and that the foregoing libel is true, according to his best knowledge and belief.

A. B.

Sworn before me,
J. W. NELSON, U. S. Commissioner.

SCHEDULE.
(*A copy of the bill of items.*)

No. 88.—A LIBEL IN PERSONAM BY A BUTCHER AGAINST THE OWNERS OF A PASSENGER BOAT ON THE HUDSON RIVER FOR SUPPLIES OF MEAT FROM DAY TO DAY.

To the Honorable Samuel R. Betts, Judge of the District Court of the United States in and for the Southern District of New York:

The libel of James McCur of the city of New York, butcher, against Ancram Livingston and Charles H. Hedges, owners of the steamboat Hudson, in a cause of contract, civil and maritime, alleges as follows:

First. That during the month of January, February, March, April, May, June, and July of the year one thousand eight hundred and forty-six, the said steamboat, whereof the said Livingston and Hedges were owners, being a passenger steamboat, and engaged in making trips on the Hudson River to and from the ports of New York and Hudson, this libellant did furnish meats from time to time to said steamboat, at the request of the master thereof, a full account of which is contained in the schedule hereunto annexed, amounting in the whole to the sum of one hundred and eighty-eight dollars and fifteen cents, over and above all credits.

Second. That the said meats were furnished for the use of said steamboat for the daily consumption of her passengers, officers, and crew, and were necessary to enable her properly to make her said trips and earn passage money.

Third. That although often requested, the said owners have not paid the said amount, nor any part thereof, to this libellant, and that the same is now justly due him.

Fourth. That all and singular the premises are true, and within the admiralty and maritime jurisdiction of the United States and of this Honorable Court.

Wherefore the libellant prays that a warrant of arrest, according to the course of this Honorable Court in cases of admiralty and maritime jurisdiction, may issue against the said defendants, and that they may be required to answer all and singular the matters aforesaid, and that this Honorable Court would be pleased to decree the payment of the amount so due to the libellants, with costs, and that the libellant may have such other and further relief as in law and justice he may be entitled to receive.

J. McCur.

Sworn before me this   day
  of December, 1847,
    John W. Nelson, U. S. Commissioner.
 Burr & Benedict, Proctors.
 E. C. Benedigt, Advocate.

Schedule.
(*Copy bill of items.*)

No. 89.—Affidavit to obtain summons.

Brig Lowell, Captain Wm. Lawrence, and Owners,

To Bernard Glancy, Dr.

To wages as second mate, from July 10, 1843, to January 20,
 1844. at $20 a month, $126 66

	Brought forward,		$126 66
CREDIT.			
By one month's advance,	$20 00		
Cash in Gibraltar,	15 00		
Cash in Messina,	30 00		
Hospital money, 6 months,	1 20	$66 20	

Balance due, $60 46

SOUTHERN DISTRICT OF NEW YORK, ss. :—

Bernard Glancy, late mariner on board the brig Lowell, being duly sworn says—That in July, 1843, he shipped on board brig Lowell, whereof William Lawrence was, and still is master, then lying in the port of New York, as second mate, (*or ordinary seaman, or mate, or cook, as the case may be,*) at the wages of twenty dollars a month, to perform a voyage to one or more ports in the Mediterranean, and back to the United States, and signed the usual shipping articles for said voyage, which are retained by the said master. That the deponent performed said voyage, and in all respects did his duty as such second mate, till the arrival of said vessel in the port of Palermo, where, without cause, he was turned ashore from said vessel by the said master, and prevented from performing the remainder of the voyage. That he returned to the United States as passenger in another vessel, and said brig Lowell arrived at the port of New York on the 20th day of Jan'y inst. where she now is. That there is now due to him, for his wages on said voyage, a balance of sixty dollars and upwards, as shown by the above schedule, which is just and true, which balance the said master has refused to pay.

BERNARD GLANCY.

Sworn Jany. 30th, 1844,
    before me,
        GEORGE W. MORTON, U. S. Commissioner.
    (*Or Justice of the Peace, or District Judge,
        as the case may be.*)

No. 90.—PRELIMINARY SUMMONS FOR SEAMAN'S WAGES.

To the Master and Owners of the Brig Lowell :

I, George W. Morton, United States Commissioner, do hereby summon you to be and appear before me, at my office, at the United States Courts, in the City Hall, in the City of New York, on the 31st day of January, instant, at 10 o'clock in the forenoon of that day, then and there to show cause, if any you have, why process of attachment should not issue from the District Court of this District against the brig Lowell, her tackle, apparel and furniture, according to the course of Admiralty Courts, to answer the claims of Bernard Glancy, for mariners wages.

Given under my hand, this 30th day of January, in the year of our Lord one thousand eight hundred and forty-five.

GEO. W. MORTON, U. S. Commissioner.

BURR & BENEDICT, Proctors.

No. 91.—AFFIDAVIT OF SERVICE OF THE SUMMONS.

Southern District of N. Y. ss.:

John C. Magrath, of the City of New York, clerk, being duly sworn, says—That on the thirteenth day of January, instant, he served the summons, of which the within is a copy, by delivering the same to the master of the brig Lowel, therein named. (Or by leaving the same on board the brig Lowel, within named, with the persons in charge thereof, the master being absent. Or, by fastening the same in a conspicuous place on the mast of said vessel, no person being on board in charge thereof.)

J. C. MAGRATH.

Sworn January 31, 1844,
    before me,
        GEO. W. MORTON, U. S. Commissioner.

No. 92.—CERTIFICATE OF THE MAGISTRATE.

I hereby certify to the Clerk of the District Court for the Southern District of New York, that there is sufficient cause of complaint whereon to found Admiralty Process against the brig Lowell, her tackle, apparel and furniture, to answer for the wages of Bernard Glancy.

January 31, 1844.

GEO. W. MORTON, U. S. Commissioner.

No. 93.—LIBEL IN REM FOR SEAMAN'S WAGES, AFTER PRELIMINARY SUMMONS BEFORE A MAGISTRATE.

To the Honorable Samuel R. Betts, Judge of the District Court of the United States for the Southern District of New York.

The libel of Bernard Glancy, mariner, formerly second mate of the brig Lowell, whereof Wm. Lawrence then was and is master, against the said brig Lowell, her tackle, apparel and furniture, and against all persons lawfully intervening for their interest therein, in a cause of wages, civil and maritime, alleges as follows:

First. That some time in the month of July, one thousand eight hundred and forty-three, the said vessel being in the port of New York, and bound on a voyage thence to one or more ports in the Mediterranean sea, and back to the United States, the said master, by himself or his agent, did ship and hire the libellant to serve as second mate on board the said vessel for the said voyage, at the wages of twenty dollars per month. That, for the due performance of the said voyage, the libellant signed shipping articles, which are now in the possession, or under the control of the said master, and which the libellant prays may be produced to this Honorable Court, for further certainty in the premises, and for the benefit of the libellant; and that, in pursuance of the said agreement, the libellant entered into the service of the said brig, as such second mate, on or about the tenth day of the month of July, in the year aforesaid.

Second. That the said brig having taken on board a cargo. proceeded therewith, and with the libellant on board, for the port of Gibraltar, where she safely arrived and discharged her cargo, and made freight. That she proceeded thence to Sardinia with certain specie on board, where she safely arrived; and that she proceeded thence to Messina, where she safely arrived, and discharged the said specie, and having taken on board another cargo, she proceeded therewith. and with the libellant on board, for the port of Palermo, where she safely arrived, and where she completed her cargo.

Third. That while the said vessel was lying at Palermo aforesaid, on the tenth day of December, 1843, the said master unjustly, and without any cause, and without the consent of the libellant, and against his will, turned him on shore, and would not permit him to perform the remainder of the voyage, and the said brig completed said voyage, and arrived at the port of New York on the 29th day of January, 1844, where she now is.

Fourth. That during the whole time the libellant was on board the said brig, to wit, from the time of his entering on board thereof, to the time of his discharge therefrom, he well and faithfully performed his duty as such second mate, and was obedient to all lawful commands of the said master, and the master of the said brig, whereby he became entitled to demand wages for the whole voyage of said vessel till her return to the United States; and at the time of his arrival in New York, there was due to him the sum of sixty dollars and upwards, over and above all just deductions.

Fifth. That all and singular the premises are true, and within the Admiralty and Maritime jurisdiction of the United States and of this Honorable Court.

Wherefore the libellant prays that process in due form of law, according to the course of this Honorable Court in cases of Admiralty and Maritime jurisdiction, may issue against the said brig Lowell, her tackle, apparel and furniture, and that all persons claiming any right or interest therein, may be cited to appear and answer all and singular, the matters aforesaid, and that this Honorable Court would be pleased to decree the payment of wages aforesaid, with costs, and that the said vessel may be condemned and sold to pay the same; and that the libellant may have such other and further relief in the premises, as in law and justice he may be entitled to receive.

BERNARD GLANCY.

Sworn January 30th, 1844,
before me, ,
 GEORGE W. MORTON,
  U. S. Commissioner.
BURR & BENEDICT, Proctors for Lib't.
BURR, Advocate.

No. 94.—LIBEL IN REM BY A SEAMAN FOR WAGES WHEN THE VESSEL HAS LEFT THE PORT WHERE HIS VOYAGE ENDED—OR IS ABOUT TO LEAVE—IN WHICH CASES IMMEDIATE PROCESS MAY ISSUE WITHOUT A SUMMONS.

To the Honorable Samuel R. Betts, Judge of the District Court of the United States for the Southern District of New York :

The libel of John Graham, of said District, late seaman on board the schooner State Rights, whereof Silvanus Cummings now is, or lately was, master, against the said schooner, her tackle, apparel and furniture, and against all persons lawfully intervening for their interest in said schooner, in a cause of wages, civil and maritime, alleges as follows :

First. That, some time in the month of January last, said schooner, then lying in the port of Charleston, and bound on a voyage thence to Murfreesborough in North Carolina and back, the said master, by himself or his agent hired the libellant to serve as seaman on board the said vessel, during the said voyage, at the wages of sixteen dollars per month, by verbal agreement, the libellant having signed no shipping articles. That in pursuance of said agreement the libellant entered on board and into the service of the said ship as such seaman, on or about the twenty-ninth day of the said month of January.

Second. That the said schooner having taken on board a cargo, proceeded therewith, and with the libellant on board, for Murfreesborough, where she safely arrived and discharged her cargo, and made freight. That having taken on board another cargo, she proceeded therewith, and with the libellant on board, for the port of Charleston, where she safely arrived and discharged her cargo, and made freight, and her voyage ended.

Third. That at the request of said master, the libellant continued on board the said schooner, at the wages aforesaid, and the said schooner having taken on board another cargo, proceeded therewith, and with the libellant on board, for the port of Jericho in the state of Georgia, where she safely arrived and discharged cargo, and made freight. That having taken on board a cargo of live oak, she proceeded therewith, and with the libellant on board, for the port of Norfolk, where she safely arrived and discharged a portion of her cargo, and made freight. That she proceeded from thence with the residue of her cargo, and the libellant on board, for the port of Philadelphia, where she safely arrived and discharged her cargo, and made freight. That having taken on board another cargo, she proceeded therewith, and with the libellant on board, for the port of New York, where she safely arrived, and the libellant was duly discharged on the seventh day of August last, and the said schooner has since made another voyage.

Fourth. That during the whole time he was on board of said vessel to the time of his discharge therefrom, he well and faithfully performed his duty as such seaman, and was obedient to all lawful commands of the said master, and the other officers of the said schooner, and was entitled to be paid his wages which were then due, and amounted to the sum of eighty-nine dollars and upwards, over and above all just deductions.

Fifth. That the said schooner has left the port of delivery, where the said voyage ended, without paying to the libellant the balance of wages due to him as aforesaid.

[*Or this, if it be true.*—

[*Fifth.* That the said schooner is about to proceed to sea before the end of ten days next after the delivery of her cargo or ballast]

Sixth. That all and singular the premises are true, and within the admiralty and maritime jurisdiction of the United States and of this Honorable Court.

Wherefore the libellant prays, that process in due form of law, according to the course of courts of Admiralty, and of this Honorable Court, in cases of Admiralty and Maritime jurisdiction, may issue against the said schooner, her tackle, apparel and furniture, and that all persons claiming any right, title, or interest therein, may be cited to appear and answer upon oath all the matters aforesaid, and that this Honorable Court will be pleased to decree the payment of the wages aforesaid, and with costs, and that the said vessel may be condemned and sold to pay the same, and that the libellant may have such other and further relief in the premises as in law and justice he may be entitled to receive.

JOHN GRAHAM.

Sworn, October 5, 1846,
    before me,
        ALEXANDER GARDINER,
           U. S. Commissioner.
BURR & BENEDICT, Proctor.
BURR, Advocate.

No. 95.—A LIBEL IN REM AND IN PERSONAM BY SEVERAL SEAMEN AGAINST A SHIP, FREIGHT AND MASTER, FOR WAGES AND SHORT ALLOWANCE OF BREAD.

To the Honorable Samuel R. Betts, Judge of the District Court of the United States for the Southern District of New York.

The libel of John C. Duffie, Alfred Sandford, Alexander Wilson, Benjamin Hoffman, Robert Twiss, and Charles M'Carty, of said district, mari-

ners, late seamen on board the barque Childe Harold, whereof one
Crosby now is, or lately was master, against the said barque, her tackle,
apparel and furniture, and the freight due for her cargo, now or lately laden
therein; also, against all persons lawfully intervening for their interest in
said vessel, and against   Crosby, master of said vessel, in a cause of
wages, civil and maritime, alleges as follows:

First. That some time in the month of November, one thousand eight
hundred and forty-four, the barque Childe Harold, whereof the said
Crosby was master, then lying in the port of New York, and bound on a
voyage from the said port of New York, to one or more ports in South
America, and back to a port of discharge in the United States; the said
master, by himself or his agent, hired the libellants, the said Duffie, Hoffman, Wilson, Sandford, M'Carthy and Twiss, to serve as seamen, and the
libellant, Howland, to serve as an ordinary seaman on board said vessel, for
and during the voyage, at and after the rate of wages of eleven dollars per
month to each of the libellants, except the libellant Howland, who was to
receive the wages of seven dollars per month. That, for the due performance of the said voyage, the libellants signed shipping articles, which are
now in the possession or under the control of the master or owners of the
said vessel, and which the libellants pray may be produced to this Honorable Court, for further certainty in the premises, and for the benefit of the
libellants. That in pursuance of the said agreement, the libellants entered
into the service of the said vessel as such seamen as aforesaid, on or about
the thirteenth day of the month of November, in the year aforesaid.

Second. That the said vessel having taken on board a cargo, proceeded
therewith, and with the libellants on board, for the port of Callao, where
she safely arrived, and delivered her cargo and made freight. That the
said vessel having taken ballast on board, proceeded therewith, and with
the libellants on board, for the port of Aquico, where she safely arrived.
That having there taken on board a cargo, she proceeded therewith, and
with the libellants on board, for the port of Arica, where she safely arrived,
and where she took on board some additional cargo, and proceeded to the
port of New York, where she safely arrived, on or about the 4th day of
October instant, where she now is, and where, since the arrival of the said
vessel, the libellants have all been duly discharged from the service
thereof.

Third. That during the voyage from New York to Callao, and for about
one month and a-half, the libellants were on a short allowance of good and
wholesome ship bread, the bread which was furnished to the libellants being mouldy, rotten and wormy, and unfit to be eaten; and that during all
the voyage from the port of Callao to Aquico, and from thence till the return of the vessel to this port, and for the period of about six months and
a-half, they were on a short allowance of good and wholesome ship bread,
(the bread that was furnished to the libellants being of the same description
as that furnished for their use on the passage to Callao,) the said master

having neglected to put on board the requisite quantity of provisions for the said voyage, according to the act of Congress in such case made and provided.

Fourth. That during the whole time the libellants were on board the said vessel, they well and faithfully performed their duty as such seamen, as aforesaid, and were obedient to all lawful commands of the said master and the other officers of the vessel, whereby and by reason of being put on such short allowance as aforesaid, they became entitled to demand from the said vessel as follows :—The libellant Duffie, for his wages and short allowance, the sum of one hundred and forty-six dollars and upwards, and each of the libellants Hoffman, Wilson, Sandford, Twiss, and M'Carthy, the sum of eighty-eight dollars, and to the libellant Howland, the sum of fifty-six dollars.

Fifth. That all and singular the premises are true, and within the Admiralty and Maritime jurisdiction of the United States and of this Honorable Court.

Wherefore the libellants pray that process in due form of law, according to the course of this Honorable Court in cases of Admiralty and Maritime jurisdiction, may issue against the said barque Childe Harold, her tackle, apparel and furniture, and her freight aforesaid ; and that the said Crosby, master of the said vessel, and all persons having any right, title, or interest in said barque, her tackle, apparel and furniture, may be cited to appear and answer all the matters aforesaid, and that this Honorable Court would be pleased to decree the payment of the wages and short allowance aforesaid, with costs, and that the said vessel may be condemned and sold to pay the same, and that the libellants may have such other and further relief in the premises, as in law and justice they may be entitled to receive.

(*Signed by the Libellants.*)

Sworn, &c.

BURR & BENEDICT, Proctors for Libellants.
E. BURR, Advocate.

No. 96.—LIBEL IN REM BY THE SEAMEN OF A CHINESE JUNK FOR WAGES, EXPENSES, AND PASSAGE MONEY HOME.

To the Honorable Samuel R. Betts, Dissrict Judge of the United States for the Southern District of New York.

The libel of Hia Siang, Ungti, Lin Chengsi, Koesing Thiane, Chien Atia, Lim Akeing, Kho per le, Lip hap, Sim agu¹ Chien ten yeng, Lia lai, Tan Sam Seng, Ungtian yong, Yer Achin, Lim ale, Gobun hap, Chen asn, Chwa Ackun, Lim tai Cheng, Chia a soey, Ong a Hiong, Tan a lak, Chew ate, Khoto Sun, Ung aiong, Sio a chiok, Chinese mariners of the province of Canton, in China, against the Chinese junk Keying, her tackle, apparel and furniture, and against all persons intervening for their interest therein, in a cause of wages, civil and maritime, alleges as follows:

First. That they were shipped as mariners at Whampoa, near Canton, in China, in a certain vessel called a Chinese junk, bearing the name Keying, now lying in the port of New York, by one   Kellet, who assumed to be the master thereof, for a voyage to Batavia or Singapore, for sugar or opium, and then to Chusan, or any other port, but the voyage was to continue only eight months, after which they were to continue with the ship or not, as they pleased; and whatever port they went to, they were to be sent back to Canton or Whampoa by the said Kellet, as master of the said vessel, who was to pay all their expenses in such foreign ports. That they were so shipped on the fourteenth day of September last, by a written contract, which was retained by said Kellet.

Second. That they all then entered on board the said junk, and the said junk sailed from Whampoa with them on board as the crew thereof, and they continued on board, working as such crew, until they arrived at New York some time since, and have continued on board of the said junk, as the crew thereof, until the sixth day of September instant, when they quit the same.

Third. That the said vessel did not stop at Batavia nor Singapore, nor procure any cargo of sugar or opium, or other cargo, but they were forced to come in the vessel to this port of New York, and there the voyage appeared to have been for the purpose of exhibiting the junk, its fixtures and crew, as a curiosity, and for hire, by which the said Kellet, and those who have been connected with him, have made large sums of money.

Fourth. That on the voyage they were greatly dissatisfied, and expressed such dissatisfaction to the said Kellet, when they found that they had passed Java and Singapore, but were forced by violence and severity, by blows and stripes, to work the junk on her voyage.

Fifth. That since their arrival at New York, they have become anxious to return home to China, where they have families, and are destitute of all means of support, and of all means of getting home to China, and are unprovided with clothing or necessaries for resisting the weather of the cold climate of this country.

Sixth. That the said junk is now ready for sea, having been lately made ready for that purpose, and is about proceeding on some voyage on the high seas, to these libellants unknown, without providing them with the means of returning home, or of support in the mean time, and they are no longer bound to continue with the said junk.

Seventh. That the monthly wages which they were to receive were at the following rates :—Hia Siang, eleven dollars; Sim agu and Ungti, each nine dollars; Ling Chensi, Kho Sing thiam, Lia lai, Leina Kung, Khor per le, Lip hap, Chin ten yeng, Tam Sam seng, Ungtian Yong, Chein a tai, each eight dollars a month; and Yer a chin, Lim a lee, Gobun hap, Cheva asa, Chiva Achan, Lim tai chong, Tan a lak, Chia Assey, Ong a Hiong, Chien ate, Khote sun, Ung a cong, Sio a chiok, were each to receive six dollars, all which wages were due to them, to be computed from the time of sailing to the sixth day of September instant, only deducting three months wages in advance paid to each, and the further sum of twelve dollars each, since their arrival here, which was for their expenditures while here; and your libellant, Hia Siang, receiving four months advance wages at Whampoa.

Eighth. That they are severally entitled to wages from the time of their shipping and sailing in the said junk to the last mentioned date; and also to money sufficient to procure a passage back to China, and to support in the mean time, until they can procure such passage, which will cost between one and two hundred dollars for each man.

Ninth. That all and singular the premises are true, and within the admiralty and maritime jurisdiction of the United States and of this Honorable Court.

Wherefore your libellants pray that process in due form of law, according to the course of this Honorable Court, in causes of Admiralty and maritime jurisdiction, may issue against the said vessel the Chinese junk Keying, her tackle, apparel and furniture, and that all persons claiming any right in said vessel, and especially the said Kellet, may be cited to appear and answer this libel, and all the matters aforesaid, and that the said vessel, her tackle, apparel and furniture, may be condemned and sold to pay the amount due to the libellants, with interest and costs, and that the libellants may have such other and further relief in the premises as in law and justice they are entitled to receive.

(Signed,)

Ong Ahiong,	Chien Atai,	Yea Achin,
Chew Ati,	Lim Akeing,	Lim Ale,
Khote Sun,	Kho per le,	Gobun Hap,
Ung Aiong,	Lip hap,	Chiva Asn,
Sio a Chiok,	Sim agu,	Chiva Achan,
Hia Siang,	Chien ten yeng,	Limtai Chong,
Ung ti,	Lia lai,	Tan a la,
Lin Cheng Li,	Tam Sam seng,	Chia Assey.
Koesing Thiam,	Ung tian yong,	

Sworn Sept. 7th, 1847,
    before me,
        CHARLES W. MORTON,
            U. S. Commissioner.

D. D. LORD, Proctor.
D. LORD, Advocate.

No. 97.—LIBEL IN PERSONAM AGAINST AN OWNER FOR THE TWO MONTHS EXTRA PAY PAYABLE TO THE CONSUL ON DISCHARGE.

To the Honorable Samuel R. Betts Judge of the District Court of the United States for the Southern District of New York:

The libel and complaint of Thomas Tucker, of said District, late mate, and William Caron, late cook and steward, on board the brig Caroline whereof Oliver Jenkins late was master and Frederick J. Henop, owner, against the said Frederick J. Henop, owner as aforesaid, in a cause of wages, civil and maritime, alleges as follows:

First. That some time in the month of February last past, the said brig, then lying in the port of New York, and bound on a voyage thence to the port of Liverpool, and thence to such ports or places as the master might direct, and back to a port of discharge in the United States, the said master, by himself or his agent, hired the libellant, Thomas Tucker, to serve as mate on board the said brig for and during the said voyage, at and after the rate of wages of thirty dollars per month; and the libellant, William Carver, as cook and steward, for said voyage, at and after the rate of wages of twenty dollars per month. And that for the due performance of the said voyage the libellants signed shipping articles, which the libellants pray may be produced to this Honorable Court by the said owner, for further certainty in the premises, and for the benefit of the libellants. And that in pursuance of the said contract the libellants entered into the service of the said brig as aforesaid on the seventeenth day of the said month of February.

Second. That the said brig having taken on board a cargo, proceeded therewith, and with the libellants on board, for the port of Liverpool, where she safely arrived and delivered her cargo, and made freight. That having taken on board another cargo of divers goods and merchandise, she proceeded therewith, and with the libellants on board, for the port of New York. That the said brig leaked badly soon after leaving the said port of Liverpool, whereupon the said master put into the Cove of Cork, where the said vessel was sold, and the libellant, Thomas Tucker, was discharged from the said brig by the said master, and he proceeded thence to Liverpool, where he entered as a passenger, without wages, on board the ship Europe, bound for New York, where he arrived on the second day of June instant. And your libellant, William Carver, was also discharged by the said master, and returned to the port of New York in the bark Governor Douglas, where he arrived on the said second day of June instant.'

Third. That said brig was an American vessel, in the merchant service, and owned by a citizen or citizens of the United States, and that the libellants were described in the crew list of said brig as American seamen.

Fourth. That at the time the libellants were discharged from the said brig the said master did not pay into the hands of the libellants, nor into the hands of the American consul at that port, nor into the hands of any other person for the use of the libellants, the three months extra pay, by the act of Congress in such case made and provided, directed to be paid to a seaman in an American vessel on his discharge in a foreign port.

Fifth. That libellants are each entitled to demand from the owner of the said brig such two month's extra pay; your libellant, Thomas Tucker, the sum of sixty dollars, and your libellant William Carver the sum of forty dollars.

Sixth. That all and singular the premises are true, and within the Admiralty and Maritime jurisdiction of the United States, and of this Honorable Court.

Wherefore the libellant prays, that process in due form of law, according to the course of this Honorable Court, in causes of Admiralty and Maritime jurisdiction, may issue against said Frederick J. Henop, owner as aforesaid, that he may be compelled to answer all the matters aforesaid, and that this Honorable Court would be pleased to decree the payment of the extra wages aforesaid, and that the libellant may have such other and further relief in the remises as in law and justice he may be entitled to receive.

Sworn, &c.

THOMAS TUCKER,
his
WILLIAM ⋈ CARVER.
mark.

BURR & BENEDICT, Proctors.
E. BURR, Advocate.

No. 98.—A LIBEL IN REM BY THE PILOT OF A PROPELLER ENGAGED IN TOWING ON THE HUDSON RIVER, THE CHAMPLAIN CANAL, AND LAKE CHÁMPLAIN, FOR WAGES.

To the Honorable Samuel R. Betts, Judge of the District Court of the United States, for the Southern District of New York:

The libel of George Mygatt, of said District, mariner, against the steam propeller Pilot, whereof David Farr now is, or late was, master, her engine, tackle, apparel, and furniture, and against James W. Low and Francis Dow, owners of said steam propeller Pilot, and against all persons intervening for their interest in said boat, in a cause of wages, civil and maritime, alleges as follows:

First. That some time in the month of November last the above named owners did, by themselves or their agents, hire the libellant to serve as pilot on board of such steam propéller as the said owners should designate in the line of propellers running from New York, on the Hudson river, and thence by the way of the canal and Lake Champlain, to St. Johns in Lower Canada, for the season then next ensuing, at the usual and customary wages, and the wages for which the libellant, in previous years, had served as pilot, being twenty-five dollars per month. That in pursuance of such agreement, the libellant first entered on board and into the service of the steam propeller Phœnix, one of said line, as such pilot as aforesaid, on the thirteenth day of April last.

Second. That the libellant continued on board said boat Phœnix, as such pilot, until the tenth day of June following, when, by the orders of the said owners, or their agent, he was transferred on board the steam propeller Pilot, another of said line, and continued to navigate her as pilot, being engaged in carrying cargo, and towing boats, and earning freight, between the places and on the river aforesaid, until the twenty-fifth day of November instant, when the season ended, and the boat was laid up, and the libellant discharged.

Third. That during the whole time the libellant was on board the said steam propeller Pilot, to wit, from the time of his entering on board thereof to the time of his discharge therefrom, he well and faithfully performed his duty as such pilot as aforesaid, and was obedient to all lawful commands of the said master, whereby he became entitled to demand and have of and from the said boat Pilot and her owners, the sum of one hundred and fourteen dollars and upwards, over and above all just deductions.

Fourth. That all and singular the premises are true, and within the Admiralty and maritime jurisdiction of the United States, and of this Honorable Court.

Wherefore, the libellant prays that process in due form of law, according to the course of this Honorable Court in cases of Admiralty and maritime jurisdiction, may issue against the said steam propeller Pilot, her tackle, apparel and furniture, and that the said owners, and all persons intervening for their interest in said boat, may be cited to appear and answer all the matters aforesaid, and that the said vessel may be condemned and sold to pay the wages aforesaid, and that the libellant may have such other and further relief as in law and justice he may be entitled to receive.

GEORGE MYGATT.

Sworn, &c., before me,
JOHN W. NELSON,
U. S. Commissioner.

BURR & BENEDICT, Proctors.
E. C. BENEDICT, Advocate.

No. 99.—LIBEL IN PERSONAM BY A MASTER AGAINST THE OWNER FOR WAGES—*vid. the form ante, page* 208.

No. 100.—LIBEL AGAINST OWNERS FOR PILOTAGE.

To the Honorable Samuel R. Betts, Judge of the District Court of the United States for the Southern District of New York:

The libel of Martin Gray, of said district, pilot, against Russel H. Post, William Layton, Noah Stokeley, and Richard P. Williams, now or late owners of the ship Elizabeth Dennison, in a cause of pilotage, civil and maritime, alleges as follows:

First. That sometime in the month of July, A. D. 1848, the said ship then being in the port of N. Y., under the command of one   Spencer, the said owners by themselves, or their agents, employed the libellant to take the said vessel to sea, from the port of N. Y., as pilot. That accordingly the libellant went on board said vessel, and took charge of the same, and did pilot her to sea on or about the twenty-fifth day of July aforesaid.

Second. That the libellant is a regular pilot, and did his duty faithfully and according to the best of his ability, as the pilot of said vessel, and is entitled to the regular and lawful fees for such service, which amount to the sum of thirty dollars and sixty-three cents, which sum the said master has admitted to be due, and promised to pay from time to time, but which is still due and unpaid.

Third. That all and singular the premises are true, and within the Admiralty and Maritime jurisdiction of the United States and of this Honorable Court.

Wherefore the libellant prays that a warrant of arrest, in due form of law, according to the practice and course of this Honorable Court, in cases of Admiralty and Maritime jurisdiction, may issue against the said Russel H. Post, William Layton, Noah Stokeley, and Richard P. Williams, and that they be cited to appear and answer upon oath all and singular the premises aforesaid, and that this Honorable Court will be pleased to decree the payment of the amount due to him aforesaid, with interest and costs, and that he may have such other and further relief as in law and justice he may be entitled to receive.

Sworn to before me, this   day
    of Nov. 1849,
        CHARLES W. NEWTON,
            U. S. Commissioner.
C. L. BENEDICT, Proctor.
E. C. BENEDICT, Advocate.

No. 101.—LIBEL BY THE HOLDER OF A BOTTOMRY BOND AGAINST SHIP, FREIGHT AND CARGO.

To the Honorable Samuel R. Betts, Judge of the District Court of the United States for the Southern District of New York:

The libel of Charles C. Keyser, of Pensacola, in the territory of Florida, against the brig Bridgeton, (whereof William A. Benedict now is, or lately was master and part owner,) her tackle, apparel, and furniture, and against all persons lawfully intervening for their interest therein, in a cause of bottomry, civil and maritime, alleges as follows:

First. That the said brig Bridgeton, while on a voyage from Laguira to the port of New York, during the month of August last, encountered a severe storm and gale, which injured the said brig, so that they were obliged to bear away for Pensacola, to refit the said brig, and to procure repairs, supplies, and necessaries to enable the said brig to perform her intended voyage to New York. That the said William A. Benedict being a stranger at Pensacola, and being in want of money to pay for the repairs of said brig and fit her for sea, and furnish her with provisions and other supplies necessary for the prosecution of his intended voyage, and having no other means of procuring the same, borrowed from the libellant, with the commission thereon, the sum of two thousand one hundred and seventy-nine dollars and eighteen cents upon the bottomry and hypothecation of the said brig, cargo, and freight, and that the said sum was advanced and paid accordingly.

Second. That in consideration of the said advance, and in fulfilment of the agreement of bottomry and hypothecation as aforesaid, he, the said William A. Benedict, the master, did, by a certain bond or instrument of bottomry and hypothecation, a copy of which is hereto annexed, bearing date at Pensacola, the seventeenth day of September, A. D. 1842, by him signed and duly executed, in the presence of two credible witnesses who have subscribed their names thereto as witnesses of the due execution thereof, bind the said brig, the tackle, apparel and furniture of the same, and also the freight now due and which might become due hereafter, to the owners of the said brig, for her then present voyage, and also the cargo then on board, and about to be put on board said brig, as security for the payment of a certain bill of exchange drawn by the said William A. Benedict on John R. Tatem, of Philadelphia, payable at sight, for the said sum of twenty-one hundred and seventy-nine dollars and eighteen cents, in favor of the said libellant, for the said advance so made, to repair and refit the said brig as aforesaid; and the said master did further agree in and by the said bond, that the said brig, her tackle, apparel and furniture, her freight and cargo, should be at all times liable and chargeable for the payment of the said bill of exchange until the payment thereof.

Third. That the said bill of exchange having been presented in due time to the said J. R. Tatem, was not accepted nor paid, and was duly protested on the twentieth day of October instant.

Fourth. That the said sum of twenty-one hundred and seventy-nine dollars and eighteen cents was so advanced and paid by the libellants to the said master, for the purpose aforesaid, and was necessary therefor, and that the said brig could not have sailed from Pensacola, if the same had not been advanced and paid as aforesaid; that the said brig, upon being so repaired, proceeded to the port of New York, where she arrived in the present month of October, to wit, on the sixteenth day of the same month.

Fifth. That the libellant has not received the aforesaid sum of twenty-one hundred and seventy-nine dollars and eighteen cents, though the same has been demanded from the said J. R. Tatem, and the payment thereof frequently requested of the said master, and that the said bill of exchange and the said bottomry and hypothecation remain entirely unsatisfied, to the great damage of the libellant.

Sixth. That all and singular the premises are true, and within the Admiralty and Maritime jurisdiction of the United States, and of this Honorable Court.

Wherefore the libellant prays that process in due form of law, according to the course of this Honorable Court in cases of Admiralty and Maritime jurisdiction, may issue against the said brig Bridgeton, her tackle, apparel and furniture, and her freight and cargo, and that all persons having, or pretending to have any right, title or interest therein, may be cited to appear and answer all and singular the matters aforesaid, and that this Honorable Court would be pleased to decree the payment of the amount so due, with interest and costs, and that the said brig, her tackle, apparel and furniture, and freight and cargo, may be condemned to pay the same; and that the libellant may have such other and further relief as in law and justice he may be entitled to receive.

Charles C. Keyser.
By C. R. Robert, his Att'y.

Burr & Benedict,
    Proctors for Libellant.

E. Burr, Advocate.

Southern District of New York, ss.:

Christopher R. Roberts being sworn, says—That he is the Attorney in fact and agent of the libellant, Charles C. Keyser, who resides at Pensacola. That he has read the foregoing libel, and knows the contents thereof, and that the same is true, to the best of his knowledge, information and belief.

C. R. Robert.

Subscribed and sworn to this 28th day
    of October, 1842, before me,
        George W. Morton,
            U. S. Commissioner.

COPY BOND.

To all men to whom these presents shall come:

I, William A. Benedict, mariner and master of the brig Bridgeton, of New York, of the burthen of 126 51–45ths tons, now at anchor in the bay of Pensacola, send greeting: Whereas, I, the said William A. Benedict, master of the aforesaid brig, now in prosecution of a voyage from Laguira to New York, having put into Pensacola Bay for the purpose of making repairs and other expenses, have drawn a bill of exchange of even date with these presents, upon J. R. Tatem, Esquire, of Philadelphia, for the sum of twenty-one hundred and seventy-nine dollars and eighteen cents, in favor of Charles C. Keyser, Esq., of Pensacola, in the territory of Florida, which amount of said bill of exchange was at my request, and to fit the said brig for going to sea, advanced and expended by the said Charles C. Keyser: Now know ye, that I, the said William A. Benedict, for and in consideration of the premises and of one dollar in hand paid, by these presents, do bind myself, my heirs, executors, and administrators, and also the owners of the said brig, to the just and true payment of the said bill of exchange, as well as the said brig Bridgeton, the tackle and apparel of the same, together with the freight now due, and which may become due hereafter to the owners of the said brig Bridgeton for her present voyage, and also the cargo now being on board of said brig, and about to be put on board of the same, pledging and hypothecating all and singular the same to the said Charles C. Keyser, his heirs, executors and administrators, for the payment in full of the said bill of exchange, according to its terms and tenor. And the said William A. Benedict doth covenant with the said Charles C. Keyser, that I am the master of the said brig Bridgeton, and have authority to charge the same, her freight and cargo as aforesaid, and that the same shall at all times be liable and chargeable for the payment of the said bill of exchange until the payment thereof, according to the true intent and meaning of these presents.

In witness whereof, I have hereto set my hand and seal to three bonds of this tenor and date, one of which being satisfied, the other is to be null and void at Pensacola, this 17th day of September, A. D. 1842.

WM. AMOS BENEDICT, [L. S.]

Witnesses—

    H. F. INGRAHAM.
    WILLIAM LIDERS.

No. 102.—LIBEL IN REM AGAINST A SHIP BY A CONSIGNEE OF GOODS, ON A BILL OF LADING, FOR NOT DELIVERING THE GOODS IN GOOD ORDER.

To the Honorable Samuel R. Betts, Judge of the District Court of the United States for the Southern District of New York:

The libel of Herman Boker, of the city of New York, merchant, against the Norwegian brig or vessel called the Aurora, whereof Cord Hjorth was and is master, her tackle, apparel and furniture, and all persons intervening for their interest therein, in a cause of contract, civil and maritime, alleges as follows:

First. That some time in the month March, one thousand eight hundred and forty-seven, Maurice Harting shipped on board said brig, then lying in the port of Antwerp, in the kingdom of Belgium, and bound to the port of New York, in good order and well conditioned, to be carried and transported in said brig to the port of New York and delivered to the libellant in like good order, eigthy-seven packages of merchandise, for the freight of three and a half dollars per ton of one thousand kilograms, and average accustomed to be paid by the libellant, the said Maurice Harting receiving therefor, from the said master, a bill of lading, a receipt and contract, whereby and wherein the said master charged his body and goods, and also the said vessel, her tackle, apparel, and furniture, for the performance of said contract, a copy of which is hereto annexed.

Second. That said brig sailed from the said port of Antwerp for the port of New York, with the said merchandise on board, where she arrived on or about the twentieth day of May, 1847, and now is; but notwithstanding the libellant has been at all times ready and willing, and still is ready and willing, to receive the said merchandise in good order, and on so receiving the

64

same to pay the freight thereon, yet the said master has not yet delivered the said merchandise to the libellant in good order and well conditioned; but owing to the careless, negligent, and improper manner in which the said merchandise was stowed, and the want of proper care on the part of the said master, his officers and crew, and persons employed by him or them, and by reason of permitting the passengers and other persons to throw water and filth on and among the cargo, and on a false and open deck, the same ran through upon the said cargo and damaged seventeen packages containing cutlery and other hardware and iron goods, greatly, whereby the libellant has sustained damage to the amount of twelve hundred dollars.

Third. That said brig is a foreign vessel, and is taking in cargo, and is about to leave this port and the United States, and the said master has refused, and refuses, to pay said damage and to deliver said merchandise in good order, so that the libellant will be without remedy unless by proceedings against said vessel, her tackle, apparel and furniture.

Fourth. That all and singular the premises are true, and within the admiralty and maritime jurisdiction of the United States and of this Honorable Court.

Wherefore the libellant prays that process in due form of law, according to the course of this court in cases of admiralty and maritime jurisdiction, may issue against the said master and against the said brig, her tackle, apparel, and furniture, and that all persons claiming any interest therein may be cited to appear and answer, all and singular the matters aforesaid, and that this Honorable Court would be pleased to decree the payment of the damages aforesaid, with costs, and that the said vessel may be condemned and sold to pay the same, and that the libellant may have such other and further relief in the premises as in law and justice he may be entitled to receive.

HERMAN BOKER.

Sworn to before me, this
   10th June, 1847,
       J. W. NELSON, U. S. Commissioner.
  BURR, BENEDICT & BEEBE, Proctors.
  BENEDICT, Advocate.

(Annex a Copy of the Bill of Lading.)

No. 103.—A LIBEL IN PERSONAM AGAINST A CONSIGNEE FOR FREIGHT ON
BILL OF LADING.

To the Honorable Samuel R. Betts, Judge of the District Court of the United States for the Southern District of New York:

Tht libel of A. F. Jenness, William Chase and Edward Leavitt, composing the firm of Jenness, Chase & Co., owners of the bark Ranger, her tackle, apparel, and furniture, against Christopher R. Robert and Howell L. Williams, composing the firm of Robert & Williams, of the city of New

York, merchants, in a cause of contract, civil and maritime, alleges as follows:

First. That they were, at the times hereinafter mentioned, and still are, the owners of the bark Ranger, and that Woodbury Dyer was then the master thereof.

Second. That some time in the month of May last, the said bark, then lying in the port of Cardenas, and destined on a voyage thence to the port of New York, A. B. shipped on board the said vessel twenty hogsheads of sugar, weight and contents unknown, to be therein carried from the said port of Cardenas to the port of New York, and there to be delivered, the dangers of the seas only excepted, in like good order as they were received, to the defendants, Robert & Williams, or to their assigns, he or they paying freight for the same at the rate of four dollars and fifty cents per hogshead, without primage and average accustomed. And, accordingly, the said master, at the port of Cardenas, on the sixteenth day of May, one thousand eight hundred and forty-nine, affirmed to the usual bills of lading, and delivered the same to the shippers of said cargo, a copy of which bill of lading is hereto annexed, marked " Schedule A."

Third. That in the same month said A. B. also shipped on board the said bark for the same voyage, eighty hogsheads of Muscavado sugar and seventy-nine hogsheads of molasses, on deck, weight and contents unknown, to be likewise delivered at the port of New York to the respondents, or to their assigns, he or they paying freight for the same at the rate of four dollars and seventy-five cents for each hogshead of sugar, and two dollars and fifty cents for each one hundred and ten gallons, gross custom house guage of the casks delivered, of molasses, in New York, without primage and average accustomed. And the said master, on the seventeenth day of May, signed the usual bills of lading, and delivered the same to the shippers, a copy of which is also hereto annexed, marked " Schedule B."

Fourth. That soon after the said bark, with the said cargo on board, set sail from Cardenas for New York, and there in due time safely arrived, and the said sugar and molasses were duly delivered to the said Robert & Williams, and were by them accepted and received.

Fifth. That by reason of the premises, the said Robert & Williams became bound to pay to these libellants the freight for the said merchandise, which amounted in the whole to the sum of seven hundred and eighteen dollars and twenty-seven cents, as is more particularly set forth in the schedule hereto annexed, marked C.

Sixth. That the said Robert & Williams, notwithstanding they have accepted and received the said merchandise, and that in like good order and condition as it was shipped, have refused to pay the freight for the same, although often thereto requested ; and there is now due the libellants for the freight on said merchandise, the sum of seven hundred and eighteen dollars and twenty-seven cents, with interest.

Seventh. That all and singular the premises are true, and within the Admiralty and Maritime jurisdiction of the United States and of this Honorable Court.

Wherefore the libellant prays, that a citation in due form of law, according to the course of this Honorable Court in cases of Admiralty and Maritime jurisdiction, may issue against the said Robert & Williams, and they be cited to appear and answer upon oath, all and singular, the matters aforesaid, and that this Honorable Court would be pleased to decree payment of the freight aforesaid, with interest and costs, and that the libellants may have such other and further relief in the premises as in law and justice they may be entitled to receive.

A. F. Jenness.

Sworn, July 8, 1849,
  before me,
   J. W. Nelson,
    U. S. Commissioner.
 C. A. Benedict, Proctor.
 E. C. Benedict, Advocate.

Schedule A.

Shipped in good order and condition, by   on board the bark called the Ranger, whereof Dyer is master, now lying at the port of Cardenas and bound for New York, To say, twenty hhds. sugar, with 33,219 lbs. nett, being marked and numbered as in the margin, and are to be delivered in the like order and condition at the port of New York, the dangers of the sea only excepted unto Messrs. Robert & Williams, or to their assigns, he or they paying freight for the said, four dollars and fifty cents per each hhd., without primage and average accustomed. In witness whereof the master or purser of the said vessel hath affirmed to four bills of lading, all of this tenor and date, one of which being accomplished the others to stand void.

Union.
No. 1—20.

Dated in Cardenas, the 16th day of May, 1849.

Woodbury Dyer.

Schedule B.

Shipped, in good order and well conditioned, by   in and upon the good bark called the Ranger, whereof Woodbury Dyer is master, for this present voyage, and now lying in the port of Cardenas, and bound for New York, eighty hhds. of Muscovado sugars, containing one hundred and eighteen thousand six hundred and twenty-six pounds, nett.

Seventy-nine hhds. of molasses, containing eleven thousand three hundred and seventy-four gallons, of which seventy-nine hhds, are on deck, being marked and numbered as in the margin, and to be delivered in the like good order and condition at the aforesaid port of New York, all and every the dangers and accidents of seas and navigation of whatever nature or kind excepted unto Messrs. Robert & Williams, or to their assigns, he or they paying freight for the said goods four dollars and seventy-five cents per each hhd.

R. W.
80 hhds. of
Muscv. Sugar
79 hhds. Molasses on
deck.

of sugar, and two dollars and fifty cents per each one hundred and ten gallons, gross custom house guage, of the casks delivered of molasses in New York, without primage and average accustomed. In witness whereof the master or purser of the said bark has affirmed to three bills of lading, all of this tenor and date, one of which being accomplished the other to stand void.

Dated in Cardenas, the 17th May, 1849.

Weight and contents unknown.

WOODBURY DYER.

Schedule C.

Messrs. ROBERT & WILLIAMS,

		To Bark RANGER	DR.
	To Freight from Cardenas,		
	20 hhds. Sugar	at $4 50	$ 90 00
Union.	80 " "	4 75	380 00
R. W	79 " Molasses, 10,924 galls. gross		
	guage casks, at $2 50 pr. 110 galls.		248 27
			$718 27

New York, *June* 19, 1849.

No. 104.—LIBEL IN PERSONAM ON A CHARTER PARTY AGAINST THE CHARTERER FOR CHARTER MONEY.

To the Honorable Samuel R. Betts, Judge of the District Court of the United States for the Southern District of New York:

The libel of Henry M. Allen, master, part owner, and agent of the brig Josephus of Mattapoisetts against George Whitaker of the city of New York, merchant, in a cause of contract, civil and maritime, alleges as follows:

First. That some time in the month of March, one thousand eight hundred and forty-five, the said brig being then in the port of New York, the said libellant made and concluded with the respondent, a charter party, (a copy of which is hereto annexed, and to which the libellant craves leave to refer,) bearing date the tenth day of March, in the year aforesaid, by which the libellant, for and in consideration of the covenants and agreements, thereinafter mentioned, to be kept and performed by the said respondent, did covenant and agree on the freighting and chartering of the said brig unto the said respondent for a voyage from the port of New York to Antigua, La Guayra, and Puerto Cabello, and back to New York, on the terms in the said charter party mentioned, that is to say,

1st. The said libellant engaged that the said brig, in and during the said voyage, should be kept tight, staunch, well fitted, tackled, and provided with every requisite, and with men and provisions for such a voyage.

2nd. The said libellant engaged that the whole of the said brig, (with the exception of the cabin, and the necessary room for the accommodation of the crew and the stowage of the sails, cables and provisions,) should be at the sole use and disposal of the said respondent during the voyage aforesaid. And that no goods or merchandise whatever should be laden on board otherwise than for the respondent, or his agent, without his consent, on pain of forfeiture of the amount of freight agreed upon for the same.

3d. The libellant further engaged to take and receive on board the said brig, during the aforesaid voyage, all such lawful goods and merchandise as the said respondent or his agent might think proper to ship.

Second. That, among other things, it was by the said charter party covenanted and agreed that the said respondent, for and in consideration of the covenants and agreements to be kept and performed by the said libellant, chartered and hired the said brig on the terms following, therein mentioned, that is to say,

1st. The said respondent engaged to provide and furnish to the said brig the necssary cargoes or ballast for her lading at the several ports aforesaid.

2nd. The said respondent further engaged to pay to the said libellant, or his agent, for the charter or freight of the said brig during the voyage aforesaid, in the manner therein following, that is to say,

Five hundred and ten (510) dollars per calendar month for each and every month, and pro rata for any unexpired month that said vessel might be employed, payable in current money of the United States, also to pay all the brig's foreign port charges, lighterage and pilotage.

The master to have what money he might require in foreign ports for disbursements, and the balance payable on discharge of the cargo in New York.

Third. And the libellant further alleges and propounds, that afterwards, to wit, on the twentieth day of March, in the year aforesaid, at the said port of New York, the said brig being then and there tight, staunch, well fitted, tackled, and provided with every requisite, and with men and provisions necessary for such a voyage as in said charter party mentioned, the said libellant and R. Gray, master of the brig aforesaid, loaded and received on board of the said brig, a full cargo of lawful goods, with which the said master immediately set sail and proceeded to the port of Antigua aforesaid, where being afterwards, to wit, on the third day of April, in the year aforesaid, arrived, the said master then and there made a delivery of such part of said cargo as was destined for Antigua aforesaid, to the agents or consignees of the said respondent.

Fourth. That the said master afterwards, to wit, on the twelfth day of April, in the year aforesaid, set sail and proceeded from the said port of Antigua to the port of La Guayra aforesaid, where being afterwards arrived, to wit, on the sixteenth day of April, in the year aforesaid, the said master then and there made a delivery of such part of said cargo as was destined to La Guayra aforesaid, and also took, loaded, and received on board of said brig five hundred bags of coffee, to be conveyed to New York.

Fifth. That the said master afterwards, to wit, on the twenty-fifth day of April, in the year aforesaid, set sail and proceeded from the port of La Guayra aforesaid, to the port of Puerto Cabello aforesaid, where being afterwards, to wit, on the twenty-sixth day of April, in the year aforesaid, arrived, the said master then and there made a delivery of the articles and residue of the said outward cargo, and afterwards, to wit, on the sixth day of May, in the year aforesaid, at Puerto Cabello aforesaid, took on board the said brig a further cargo of lawful goods, with which the said master set sail and proceeded to the port of New York aforesaid, where he afterwards, to wit, on the twenty-second day of May, one thousand eight hundred and forty-five, arrived, and delivered said homeward cargo to the said respondent or his agents at said port.

Sixth. That the libellant has always since the making of the said charter party, well and truly performed and kept all and singular the covenants and undertakings on his part, according to the said charter party, to be performed and kept, but the said respondent has not well and truly performed, and kept all and singular the covenants and undertakings on his part, according to the said charter party, to be performed and kept as is hereinafter more particularly propounded.

Seventh. That on the discharge of the said homeward cargo at the port of New York aforesaid, the sum of one thousand two hundred and forty-one dollars and upwards, for freight, foreign port charges, lighterage, and pilotage, (after deducting   dollars received by said master in foreign ports for disbursements,) became and was due and payable from the said respondent to the libellant, according to the said charter party and the agreement of the said respondent, as is alleged in the second article of this libel.

Eighth. That the said respondent has paid to the libellant the sum of six hundred and forty-one dollars on account of the said charter, and no more, and has not paid a balance of six hundred dollars due thereon, from the respondent to the libellant, on the discharge of the said cargo at the said port of New York, although often requested thereto, and now utterly neglects and refuses so to do, to the damage of the said libellant, the full sum of seven hundred and twenty-five dollars and upwards.

Ninth. That all and singular the premises are true, and within the admiralty and maritime jurisdiction of the United States and of this Honorable Court.

Wherefore the libellants pray, that a warrant of arrest, according to the course of this Honorable Court in cases of admiralty and maritime jurisdiction, may issue against the said respondent, and he be cited to appear and answer upon oath all and singular the matters so particularly propounded, and that this Honorable Court would be pleased to decree the payment of the damages aforesaid, with costs, and that the libellants may have such other and further relief as in law and justice they are entitled to receive.

HENRY M. ALLEN.

Sworn this   day of July, 1849,
    before me,
       GEORGE W. MORTON,
           U. S. Commissioner.
CHARLES L. BENEDICT, Proctor.
E. C. BENEDICT, Advocate.

No. 105.—LIBEL IN REM AND IN PERSONAM AGAINST A VESSEL AND OWNER OR A CHARTER PARTY FOR THE VIOLATION OF THE CHARTER.

To the Honorable Samuel R. Betts, Judge of the District Court of the United States within and for the Southern District of New York:

The libel of William Doughty, of the city of Washington, in the district of Columbia, against the schooner William Seymour, of New York, her tackle, apparel and furniture, and against Walter Carpenter, and all persons lawfully intervening for their interest in the said schooner, in a cause of contract, civil and maritime, alleges as follows:

First. That the said Walter Carpenter having, on the sixth day of January, one thousand eight hundred and forty-one, as master and owner of the schooner William Seymour, of New York, of the burthen of 127 tons, or thereabouts, then lying in the harbor of New York, chartered the said vessel unto the libellant, for a voyage from the port of New York, to such landing or landings in Atachapala bay, or waters emptying into the same, as the libellant might designate—there to take on board a full cargo of live oak timber, and return to the navy yard, at Brooklyn, New York, in the port and harbor of New York, on the following terms, that is to say : First—The said Walter Carpenter engaged that the said vessel, during said voyage, should be kept tight, staunch, well fitted, tackled and provided with every requisite, and with men and·provisions necessary for such a voyage. Second—That the whole of said vessel, with the exception of the cabin and the necessary room for the accommodation of the crew, and of the sails, cables and provisions, should be at the sole use and disposal of the libellant during the voyage aforesaid. Third—That he would take and receive on board the said vessel, during the aforesaid voyage, all such lawful goods and merchandize as the libellant or his agent might think proper to ship, excepting lime, and all other extra hazardous articles; and a gang of men not exceeding twelve in number, and to find them in good, wholesome provisions, one of whom was to have cabin accommodations, and the others to have steerage fare only ; and the libellant agreed with the said Walter Carpenter to charter and hire the said vessel as aforesaid on the following terms, that is to say : First—The libellant engaged to provide and furnish to the said vessel outward, one hundred barrels more or less of heavy freight, and from eight to twelve passengers, who were to be accommodated in the manner aforesaid ; also, to furnish a full return cargo of live oak timber. Second—To pay to the said Walter Carpenter, or his agent, for the charter or freight of said vessel, during the voyage aforesaid, for each passenger, the sum of ten dollars ; for the outward freight, nothing ; and for the return cargo, the sums particularly mentioned in the said charter party ; and it was further understood and expressly agreed in and by the said charter party, that said vessel should be ready to receive said outward freight, the fourth day of January, 1841, and should sail on such voyage the seventh day of January, 1841, and that the said charter should commence the fourth day of January, 1841 ; and that said Walter Carpenter should have the privilege of filling with freight, for his own special benefit, such part of said vessel as might not be required by the libellant, on her outward voyage, provided there should be no detention on that account ; and that on the signing of the said charter party, the libellant should pay the passage money aforesaid, and should advance a further sum, in all amounting to three hundred and fifty dollars ; and to the true and faithful performance of the said charter party, the said Walter Carpenter and the libellant, each to the other, bound themselves and their heirs, executors, administrators and assigns, and also the said vessel, her freight, tackle and appurtenances, and the merchandize to be laden on board, in the penal sum of one thousand dollars.

Second. That at and immediately after the making of the said charter party, the libellant provided and furnished to the said vessel, for her said outward voyage, one hundred barrels more or less of heavy freight, the same not consisting of lime nor of other extra hazardous articles, and also ten passengers, to be accommodated in the manner provided by said charter party, and paid to the said Walter Carpenter for each of the said passengers, the sum of ten dollars, the same being in advance for their passage money ; and did also advance to the said Walter Carpenter the further sum of two hundred and fifty dollars on account of the said charter party, and to be deducted from the amount of freight money, on the return of the said Walter Carpenter to New York, making in all the sum of three hundred and fifty dollars, as required by the said charter party.

Third. That the libellant has well and truly performed and kept all the covenants and undertakings on his part, in the said charter party to be performed and kept ; but neither the said Walter Carpenter nor the said vessel, has well and truly performed and kept the covenants and undertakings on the part of the said Walter Carpenter and of the said vessel, according to the said charter party to be performed and kept.

Fourth. That after the libellant had provided and furnished the said freight and passengers for the outward voyage aforesaid, and had paid and advanced the said sums of money, as hereinbefore mentioned, the said Walter Carpenter did not, nor did the said vessel sail on the said voyage, on the 7th day of January, 1841, nor with reasonable despatch, but, without any just or reasonable cause, delayed and remained in the port of New York, until the 19th day of January, 1841, to the great injury and risk of loss of the libellant.

Fifth. That the said Walter Carpenter, under pretence that a part of said vessel was not required by the libellant on her outward voyage, took on board, for his own special benefit, a large quantity of goods and merchandize other than those provided and furnished by the libellant; and the whole of the said vessel, with the exception of the cabin and the necessary room for the accommodation of the crew, and of the sails, cables, and provisions, was not at the sole use and disposal of the libellant during the voyage aforesaid.

Sixth. That the said Walter Carpenter detained the said vessel for the purpose of taking on board of the said vessel, for his own special benefit on her outward passage, goods and merchandize other than those provided and furnished by the libellant; and by so taking on board of the said vessel for his own special benefit, goods and merchandize other than those provided and furnished by the libellant, impeded her voyage and subjected the vessel to the difficulties which afterwards occurred.

Seventh. And the libellant further alleges and propounds, that Atachapala bay, in the said charter party mentioned, otherwise called Atchafalaya bay, is situate on the coast of the State of Louisiana, and the said vessel ought to have performed her voyage thither from the port of New York in a period of time not exceeding thirty days from her departure; but that the said Walter Carpenter and the said vessel left the port of New York on the nineteenth day of January, 1841; and on the fifth day of March, 1841, the said vessel put into the port of Savannah, not having performed one-half of her said outward voyage.

Eighth. That the course and conduct of the said Walter Carpenter, and the management of the said vessel was such, that all the said passengers, furnished by the libellant as aforesaid, either left the said vessel at Savannah for good cause, or were discharged by the said Walter Carpenter, who made no offer of carrying them forward on the said voyage, whereby the libellant was deprived of all the gains and advantages which he should, and ought, and would have obtained from the carriage of the said passengers.

Ninth. That on the arrival of the said vessel at Savannah, and between the 5th and 11th of March, 1841, the said Walter Carpenter caused a large part of the goods and merchandize so supplied and put on board of said vessel by the libellant, to be sold, and received the proceeds thereof, but has not rendered any account thereof to the libellant, nor paid for the same; which goods and merchandize so sold were of the value to the libellant of at least four hundred dollars.

Tenth. That the said Walter Carpenter, on or about the fifth day of April, 1841, caused other parts of the goods and merchandize so supplied and put on board of said vessel by the libellant, to be shipped from Savannah, to Samuel W. Dewey, of New York, the agent of said Walter Carpenter, but directed said agent not to deliver the same to the libellant, except upon the payment of freight, whereby the libellant is required to pay a large sum as freight, in order to obtain possession of said goods.

Eleventh. That on the arrival of said vessel at Savannah as aforesaid, the said Walter Carpenter refused to proceed on the said voyage, before January, 1842, and wholly broke up the said voyage; nor did he offer to proceed before that time, nor to carry said passengers or freight; nor did the libellant accept said goods at that port; nor did the said Walter Carpenter earn any part of the freight, either for the said passengers or the said goods supplied by the libellant, nor become entitled to the same; but became and is liable to refund the sum so paid by the libellant as aforesaid, and also became liable to pay for the said goods so shipped by the libellant, and also the said sum of one thousand dollars mentioned and stipulated in the said charter party.

Twelfth. That the said vessel having brought on a cargo from Savannah to Baltimore, and taken in a cargo at Baltimore, for New York, arrived in the port of New York, on the nineteenth day of May instant, and neither the said Walter Carpenter, nor any one on his behalf, nor in behalf of the said vessel, has paid to the libellant any part of the said sum of three hundred and fifty dollars, nor the said sum of one thousand dollars, or any part thereof, nor any sum whatever on account of the said charter party, or the damages for the violation thereof, nor on account of the sale and conversion of the articles belonging to the libellant, nor returned said articles to the libellant, nor in any way afforded him any satisfaction in the premises.

Thirteenth. That all and singular the premises are true, and within the admiralty and maritime jurisdiction of the United States and of this Honorable Court.

Wherefore the libellant prays, that process in due form of law, according to the course of this Honorable Court, in cases of Admiralty and Maritime jurisdiction, may issue against the said schooner, William Seymour, her tackle, apparel and furniture, and that the said Walter Carpenter, and all other persons having or pretending to have any interest in the said vessel, may be cited to appear and answer the matters aforesaid, and that this Honorable Court will be pleased to decree to the libellant such sum for damages for the violation of said charter party as may be just against the said Walter Carpenter and the said vessel, with costs, and that the said vessel may be condemned and sold to pay the same, and that the libellant may have such other and further relief in the premises as in law and justice he may be entitled to receive.

CHARLES B. MOORE, Proctor for Libellant.
D. E. WHEELER, Advocate.

NO. 106.—JURAT BY LIBELLANT'S PROCTOR.

Southern District of New York, ss:

Charles B. Moore, of the city of New York, Proctor for the libellant in the foregoing libels, being duly sworn, says—That the said libellant, as deponent is informed and believes, resides in the district of Columbia, and is now absent from the State of New York, having been in the State of Louisiana when last heard from. That the matters set forth in the foregoing libel are derived principally from original documents ; that deponent has read the said libel, and knows the contents thereof, and that the matters therein stated are true, to the best of the knowledge, information and belief of this deponent.

Chas. B. Moore.

Sworn to this 20th day of May, 1841,
    before me,
        George W. Morton,
           U. S. Commissioner.

No. 107.—A libel in rem by a seaman, on a whaling contract, for his share of the voyage, and the expenses of his cure, being injured in the service of the ship.

To the Honorable Samuel R. Betts, Judge of the District Court of the United States for the Southern District of New York.

The libel of George W. Stotesbury, late a seaman on board the ship Atlantic, whereof Thomas Wilcox now is, or late was, master, against the said ship, her tackle, apparel, and furniture, in a cause of wages, civil and maritime. And thereupon the said libellant alleges as follows :

First. That some time in the month of July, one thousand eight hundred and forty-five, the said ship Atlantic, then lying in the port of New London, and destined on a three years whaling voyage to the North-West Coast, the then master, William Beck, by himself or his agent, hired this libellant as green hand on board the said ship for the voyage aforesaid, on the two hundred and twenty-fifth lay or share of what should be taken, as wages, and this libellant signed the shipping articles, wherein the contract is fully set forth, and which he prays may be produced by the said master, as this Honorable Court shall direct.

Second. That on or about the fourth day of August, one thousand eight hundred and forty-five, this libellant went on board and into the service of the said vessel as a green hand, and the said ship, with the libellant on board, proceeded on her intended voyage, and cruized about the Western Islands and other places for the period of about seven months, when the said ship had arrived at Maui, in the Sandwich Islands.

Third. That as the said ship was going out of the harbor at Maui, on or about the sixteenth day of March, one thousand eight hundred and forty-eight, the libellant engaged in the service of said vessel, while doing his duty and obeying the commands of the master, fell from the main top sail yard, and was so severely injured that he was taken ashore to the hospital, where he remained confined to his bed for the space of about twenty-one months, or thereabouts.

Fourth. That while this libellant was so confined in the hospital the said ship went to the North-West, and cruized thereabouts until the month of November, one thousand eight hundred and forty-seven, when she started for home, and on her way touched at Maui on or about the twentieth day of the said month, and took this libellant on board, and then proceeded directly to the port of New London, where she arrived on or about the twentieth day of April last, and has since come to this port, where he now is.

Fifth. That during the said voyage the said ship took a cargo of oil and bone of great value, being, as the libellant is informed and believes, four thousand seven hundred barrels of right whale, between forty and fifty barrels of sperm, and forty-seven thousand pounds of bone ; and the libellant claims to be entitled to demand and have of and from the said ship, her master and owners, his share or lay of the said cargo, being the two hundred and twenty-fifth part thereof, worth, as this libellant verily believes, the sum of three hundred dollars and upwards, which the master and owners of the said ship have hitherto refused and still refuse to pay, to the great damage of the libellant.

Sixth. That by reason of the injuries so received in the service of the said vessel, as above stated, the libellant has lost the use of one of his legs, and one of his arms is rendered almost useless, and by reason thereof has been put to great expense already for medical advice, and before he can be restored must undergo an operation involving further expense to a large amount, and he claims to be entitled to demand and have of the said ship his reasonable expenses already incurred, and hereafter to be incurred, in and about his cure, and his reasonable support since his said injury, and till he shall be cured.

Seventh. That all and singular the premises are true, and within the Admiralty and Maritime jurisdiction of this Honorable Court, in verification whereof, if denied, the libellant craves leave to refer to the deposition and other proofs to be by him exhibited in this cause.

Wherefore the libellant prays that process in due form of law, according to the course of this Honorable Court in cases of Admiralty and Maritime jurisdiction, may issue against the said vessel, her tackle, apparel, and furniture, and that all persons having or pretending to have any right, title, or interest therein, may be cited to appear and to answer all and singular the matters hereinbefore set forth, and that this Honorable Court would be pleased to decree the payment of the wages aforesaid, with costs, and that the libellant may have such other relief in the premises as in law and justice he may be entitled to receive.

Eras. C. Benedict,
One of the Proctors for the Libellant,
Libellant being absent and sick.

Sworn to, before me this   day
   of July, 1848, as to best of deponent's knowledge and belief.
                GEO. W. MORTON,
                      U. S. Commissioner.
      BURR & BENEDICT,
                Proctors for Libellant.
      BEEBE, Advocate.

————

No. 108.—JURAT BY THE LIBELLANT'S PROCTOR.

SOUTHERN DISTRICT OF NEW YORK, ss. :—Erastus C. Benedict, one of the
proctors for the libellant, being sworn, says that the libellant in this cause is
absent from this district, and sick, and deponent is authorized to act for him
herein, and that the foregoing libel is true, according to his information and
belief.
                                        E. C. BENEDICT.

   Sworn July, 5th, 1848,
      before me,
      GEORGE W. MORTON, U. S. Commissioner.

————

No. 109.—A LIBEL BY SHIP'S HUSBAND AGAINST THE CHARTERERS, FOR DEMURRAGE.

To the Honorable Samuel R. Betts, Judge of the District Court of the United States for the Southern District of New York.

   The libel of Sylvester Baxter, part owner and agent, and ship's husband,
of the bark Arethusa of Barnstable, against David S. Draper and John B.
Develin, merchants, composing the firm of Draper & Develin, of the city of
New York, in a cause of contract civil and maritime, alleges as follows :

   First. That some time in the month of August, in the year one thousand
eight hundred and forty-seven, the said bark then being in the port of New
York, the said libellant made and concluded with the respondents a charter
party, a copy of which is hereto annexed, bearing date the twentieth day of
August aforesaid, by which the libellants, for and in consideration of the covenants and agreements hereinafter mentioned, to be kept and performed by
the said respondents, did covenant and agree on the freighting and chartering of the said bark unto the said respondents for a voyage from New York
to Lisbon, Cadiz, Marseilles, or Trieste—one only—and from the port of
discharge to proceed to Palermo and load back for New York, for the charter money and on the terms and conditions mentioned in the said charter
party.

   Second. That, among other things, it was therein and thereby agreed between the libellant and the respondents that the respondents should have
fifteen lay days in New York within which to load and despatch the said

bark from the port of New York. And in case the vessel should be longer detained, the said respondents agreed to pay to the said libellant demurrage at the rate of thirty-five Spanish milled dollars per day, for each and every day so detained, provided such detention should happen by default of the said respondents or their agent. And it was further understood and agreed that the cargo should be received and delivered alongside, within reach of the vessel's tackles. And it was therein and thereby further understood and agreed that the said charter, and the said fifteen days, should commence when the said vessel was ready to receive cargo at New York, her place of loading, and notice thereof given to the said respondent or to their agent.

Third. That the said bark having been put in readiness to perform the aforesaid voyage, and ready to receive cargo at New York, the said libellant, on the twenty-third day of August, one thousand eight hundred and forty-seven, caused notice thereof to be given to the respondents, pursuant to the terms of the said charter party. And the said respondents commenced to furnish the cargo. But notwithstanding such notice was duly given to the respondents, and notwithstanding the said bark was, from that time, at the direction and disposal of the said respondents, and notwithstanding there was no fault or remissness on the part of the libellant, the said respondents, by their own default, did not load the said bark and give her despatch from the port of New York within fifteen days, but delayed her, contrary to the terms of the said charter party, until the eleventh day of September thereafter, when she sailed, and the libellant became thereby entitled to demand from the respondents demurrage for five days, at the rate of thirty-five Spanish milled dollars per day, amounting to the sum of one hundred and seventy-five dollars over and above all just deductions.

Fourth. That said vessel well and faithfully performed said voyage, and the respondents paid the charter money therein stipulated except said demurrage. But notwithstanding the said respondents have been frequently requested to pay the said sum of one hundred and seventy-five dollars, the demurrage aforesaid, they have refused, and still refuse, so to do.

Fifth. That all and singular the premises are true, and within the Admiralty and Maritime jurisdiction of the United States and of this Honorable Court.

Wherefore the libellant prays that a monition or citation, according to the course and practice of this Honorable Court in admiralty and maritime cases, may issue against the said respondents, and that they be cited to appear and answer all and singular the matters aforesaid, and that this Honorable Court would be pleased to decree the payment of the demurrage aforesaid, with costs, and that the libellant may have such other and further relief as in law and justice he is entitled to receive.

S. Baxter,
By John A. Baxter.

Burr & Benedict, Proctors.
Beebe, Advocate.

No 110.—JURAT BY AN ATTORNEY IN FACT.

Southern District of New York, ss :—

John A. Baxter being sworn, says that he is agent or attorney in fact of Sylvester Baxter, the libellant above named. That said libellant is absent from the district, being. as deponent believes, in the state of Massachusetts. That the above libel is true according to the best of his knowledge and belief.

Sworn, May 10th, 1848,   JOHN A. BAXTER.
     before me,
         JOHN W. NELSON,
               U. S. Commissioner.
   BURR & BENEDICT, Proctors.
   E. C. BENEDICT, Advocate.

No. 111.—A LIBEL BY THE OWNERS OF A VESSEL IN PERSONAM AGAINST THE CONSIGNEE OF THE CARGO FOR UNREASONABLY DETAINING THE VESSEL.

To the Honorable Samuel R. Betts, District Judge of the United States for the Southern District of New York.

The libel of James Sprague, Charles Keen, David Crowell, and Daniel Butler, owners of the schooner John R. Watson, against J. Selby West, of said district, coal dealer, in a cause of contract, civil and maritime, alleges as follows:

First. That in the month of December last, the said schooner lying at Philadelphia, and destined on a voyage to New York, Richard Jones & Co., shipped on board the said schooner one hundred and ninety-four tons of coal, or thereabouts, to be therein carried from Philadelphia to New York, and there delivered in like good order and condition (the dangers of the sea only excepted,) to J. Selby West, or his assigns, to whom the same belonged, he or they paying freight for the same, at the rate of ninety cents per ton ; and accordingly the master of said schooner, at Philadelphia, on the fifteenth day of December last, signed the usual bill of lading, a copy of which is hereto annexed.

Second. That shortly after, the said schooner set sail from Philadelphia to New York, with the said coal on board, and there safely arrived on or about the nineteenth day of December ; and on the next day Jas. Sprague, the master of said vessel, caused a written notice to be served upon J. Selby West, the consignee and owner of the coal, as follows :

New York, Dec. 20th, 1848.

SIR—You will please to take notice, that the schooner John R. Watson, under my command, and loaded with coal consigned to you, was ready to discharge cargo this morning, of which fact you have been duly notified.

And you will further take notice, that demurrage will be demanded for every day she is detained.

Yours, &c.,

JAMES SPRAGUE.

To J. SELBY WEST, Esq.

Third. That the said West accepted the said cargo, and commenced to receive the said coal, but refused to take it save in very small quantities, and at irregular times, capriciously and vexatiously, and when urged and requested to take the same more expeditiously, replied, that he would take it when it suited him, and no faster, and would keep the schooner as long as he wanted to, for the captain could not help himself, and in accordance with such threat, he detained the said schooner until the fourth day of January, instant, on which day fifty tons of coal were still on board, and were taken out by him and his agents, and the schooner completely discharged.

Fourth. That during the whole time the said schooner was so detained, she was obliged to lie at the foot of forty-second street, in the North River, that being the place designated by the bill of lading, in danger of being frozen up and compelled to winter here, and her whole crew were detained, at the expense of the vessel, and two extra men and a horse were kept constantly waiting on the dock during very severe and cold weather, ready to deliver the coal whenever the said West should take it away. And the said West was often notified by the master of the said schooner that said master was constantly ready to deliver said coal, and that the expense and damage of such detention would be demanded of him.

Fifth. That the usual and sufficient time to discharge such a cargo of coal is four days, and these libellants claim to be entitled to have of the said West the damages sustained by them by reason of the unjust detion of said vessel beyond that time, which they allege amounts to the sum of two hundred and thirty-one dollars and upwards.

Sixth. That all and singular the premises are true, and within the Admiralty and Maritime jurisdiction of the United States, and of this Honorable Court.

Wherefore these libellants pray that a warrant of arrest, in due form of law, according to the course of this Honorable Court, in Admiralty and Maritime cases, may issue against the said J. Selby West, and that he may be compelled to answer upon oath all and singular the matters aforesaid, and that this Honorable Court would be pleased to decree the payment of the damages aforesaid, with costs, and that he may have such other relief as in law and justice he may be entitled to receive.

JAMES SPRAGUE.

Sworn to before me, this 9th day
of Jan'y, 1848,

GEO. W. MORTON, U. S. Commissioner.

BURR & BENEDICT, Proctors.

E. BURR, Advocate.

66

No. 112.—A LIBEL IN REM BY A MASTER AGAINST HIS VESSEL FOR ADVAN-
CES TO PAY CHARGES AND LIENS UPON HER.

To the Honorable Samuel R. Betts, Judge of the District Court of the
United States for the Southern District of New York.

The libel of Herman Schultze, master of the schooner Oscar Jones,
against the said schooner, her tackle, apparel and furniture, and against all
persons intervening for their interest, in a cause of contract, civil and maritime, alleges as follows :

First. That in the month of July, 1848, Mr. F. C. Costanze, of New Orleans, the then owner of said schooner, employed the libellant to take charge
of the said vessel, as master, on a voyage she was then about to make, and
other voyages in search of freight.

Second. That accordingly on or about the first day of July aforesaid,
the libellant went on board said vessel as master, and on the sixteenth of
July aforesaid, sailed from New Orleans to Terragona, thence to London,
thence to Newcastle-upon-Tyne, thence to Gibraltar, then to Malaga, thence
back to Gibraltar again, and thence to the port of New York, where he safely arrived on or about the 28th day of April last.

Third. That during the voyages aforesaid he was obliged, at various
times, to make large advances to and for the said vessel, to enable her to
proceed on her voyage and earn freight, and paid various carpenter's bills
for repairs, and bought provisions, tackle, apparel and furniture for the said
vessel, and paid large sums to the seamen employed on board thereof for
their wages, and made other advances more particularly set forth in the
schedule hereto annexed, amounting, in the whole, to the sum of one thousand nine hundred and nineteen dollars and fifty-two cents.

Fourth. That the said advances were necessary to enable the said schooner to prosecute her intended voyage and earn freight, and were made in
ports and places where the vessel did not belong, and where the owner did
not reside, and were made on the credit of the said vessel, as well as of the
owner thereof, and were to pay charges and demands which were at the
time a lien on said vessel, and by the payment thereof he became in law
subrogated in place of the parties to whom he made such payments, and
became entitled to hold, and prosecute, and enforce the lien of said demands
for his own reimbursement.

Fifth. That there is now due the libellant, from the said vessel, the sum
of four hundred and seventeen dollars and eighty-five cents for his said advances over and above all just deductions, and the said schooner is now in
the port of New York.

Sixth. That all and singular the premises are true, and within the Admiralty and Maritime jurisdiction of the United States and of this Honorable
Court.

Wherefore, the libellant prays that process in due form of law, according
to the course and practice of this Honorable Court in cases of Admiralty

and maritime jurisdiction, may issue against the said schooner, her tackle, apparel and furniture, and that all persons having any interest therein, may be cited to appear and answer upon oath all and singular the matters aforesaid, and that this Honorable Court would be pleased to decree the payment of the amount due to the libellant in the premises, with costs, and that the said vessel may be condemned and sold to pay the same, and that the libellant may have such other relief as in law and justice he may be entitled to receive.

H. Schultze.

Sworn this   day of May, 1849,
   before me,
      G. W. Morton, U. S. Commissioner.
  C. L. Benedict, Proctor.
  E. C. Benedict, Advocate.

SCHEDULE.

Payments and advances by Herman Schultze, master of the schooner Oscar Jones, for and on account of said vessel and owners.

	$	
3 bbls. potatoes in Mississippi,	7	50
Discharging cargo in Terragona,	30	50
Paid charges and consular dues,	112	54
Carpenter's bills,	186	66
Block and hulk for heaving down,	12	80
Galley and forecastle scuttle,	26	80
Blacksmith's bill,	7	00
Tinsmith's bill,	9	40
Labor for heaving down,	16	00
Warps and running ropes,	12	00
Paid ship chandler,	172	00
Do. do.	14	10
Paints, oil, varnish, rosin, and sulphur,	42	00
300 lbs. salt meat,	30	00
Stevedore's bill,	29	20
1 basket raisins,	1	00

	£	s.	d.
Pilotage,	9	4	7
Tonnage,	5	0	0
Provisions,	8	16	6
Rope, paint, and oil,	6	10	10
Wharfage and mooring,		12	6
Towage and pilotage to carpenter's yard,	1	2	0
Carpenter's bill,		16	0
Labor in discharging,	1	10	0
Sugar and coffee,	2	2	0

	£	s.	d.
Butcher's bills,	3	5	0
Vegetables, &c., bills	1	14	0
Towage down the river,	1	10	0
Landing the pilot,		18	0
Steward's wages,	3	8	8
The crew received	13	6	0
Wages of the mate,	29	16	0

	£	s.	d.
Mr. Anderson's bill,	13	17	10
Taking out ballast,		6	0
5 galls. rum,		17	6
40 lbs. molasses,		11	8
Market and baker's bill,	1	16	0
Towage and pilotage,	2	11	0

Paid wages of crew,	$201	00
Ballast and coals,	20	50
Barrel of flour,	6	36
Cartage on the above,		25
Joseph Battiner for port charges at Gibraltar, the 2nd time,	37	45
Mate's wages for twenty-three days,	23	00
Ship chandler's bills	46	35
Do. do.	1	50
Port charges and bill of health,	12	00
Medicine,	3	00
Two barrels of pork and two of beef,	50	92

Pilotage,	5	12
Consular fees and port charges,	48	12
Stevedore's bill,	15	60
Discharging ballast,	7	00
Consul's certificate,	2	00
Ship chandler's bill,	44	40
Crew received	13	10
Butter, and liquor, and tonnage from Captain Laughlin,	13	00
Market money,	1	35

Cash paid at Custom House for entrance fees,	$27	80
Pilotage from sea,	20	00
Towage,	10	00
State hospital money,	5	00

8 boxes raisins, short,	.	.	.	.	6 00
The crew, on acct. of wages,		.	.	.	5 99
Telegraph and postage,		.	.	.	2 75

No. 113.—LIBEL IN REM BY THE OWNER OF A STEAMER AGAINST A CANAL BOAT FOR TOWING HER.

To the Honorable Samuel R. Betts, Judge of the District Court of the United States, for the Southern District of New York:

The libel and complaint of Reuben Smith, jr., and Philemon H. Smith, owners of the American vessel known as the steamboat Metamora, whereof said P. H. Smith is master, against the canal boat W. Arnott, her tackle, apparel, and furniture, now in this district, and against all persons lawfully intervening for their interest, in a cause of contract, civil and maritime.

First. That the said libellants were, and now are, the owners of the American steamer Metamora, and that, at the instance and request of one Captain Best, master and owner of said canal boat, by said steamer, towed the said canal boat from the port of Albany to the port of New York, between the 9th and 11th days of November, 1846; and by agreement with the said Captain Best, were to receive for the towing the said canal boat the sum of twenty dollars; and the said canal boat is now in the Southern District of New York; and the said libellants have demaded the said twenty dollars, and the said captain has refused to pay the same.

Second. That all and singular the premises are true, and within the Admiralty and Maritime jurisdiction of the United States, and of this Honorable Court.

Wherefore the libellant prays, that process in due form of law, according to the course of this Honorable Court, in cases of Admiralty and Maritime jurisdiction, may issue against said vessel, her tackle, apparel, and furniture, and that all persons having any interest therein, may be cited to appear and to answer all and singular the matters hereinbefore set forth, and that this Honorable Court would be pleased to decree the payment of said sum, with costs, and that said canal boat may be condemned and sold to pay the same, and that the libellant may have such other and further relief in the premises as in law and justice he may be entitled to receive.

P. H. SMITH,
R. SMITH, JR.

Sworn November 11, 1846,
before me,
GEO. W. MORTON,
U. S. Commissioner.
WM. JAY HASKETT,
Proc. pro Libel'ts.
R. SCOTT, Advocate.

No. 114.—A LIBEL IN PERSONAM BY THE OWNER OF A WHARF AND A STORE AGAINST A MASTER FOR WHARFAGE AND STORAGE.

To the Honorable Samuel R. Betts, Judge of the District Court of the United States for the Southern District of New York.

The libel of Daniel Jones, of the city of New York, merchant, against Asa White, master of the ship Ajax, of Bristol, England, in a cause of contract, civil and maritime, alleges as follows:

First. That the libellant is the owner of a wharf in the city of New York, and he is entitled to recover wharfage from all vessels lying at said wharf. That on the tenth day of November last, the said Asa White placed the said ship Ajax at the wharf of the libellant, where she remained for the period of ninety-one days, for which the libellant is entitled to receive the sum of one hundred and eighty-two dollars, which the said master has refused to pay.

Second. That the libellant is also the owner of a store-house in the city of New York, and that said master stored in said store-house at the usual rates of storage, the sails and rigging of the said ship while the said ship was undergoing repairs, and the libellant is entitled to receeive for such storage the sum of twenty-one dollars, which the said master has refused to pay.

Third. That all and singular the premises are true, and within the Admiralty and Maritime jurisdiction of the United States and of this Honorable Court.

Wherefore the libellant prays that a warrant of arrest in due form of law, according to the course of this Honorable Court in causes of Admiralty and Maritime jurisdiction, may issue against the said Asa White, master, as aforesaid, and that he may be required to answer on oath this libel and the matters herein contained, and that this Honorable Court will be pleased to decree to the libellant the payment of said wharfage and said storage, amounting to two hundred and three dollars, with interest and costs, and that he may have such other and further relief as in law and justice he may be entitled to receive.

DANIEL JONES.

Sworn March 1, 1840,
    before me,
        GEORGE W. MORTON,
            U. S. Commissioner.
A. B. Proctor.
C. D. Advocate.

———

No. 115.—LIBEL AGAINST SHIP AND OWNERS BY A PASSENGER FOR A VIOLATION OF CONTRACT.

To the Honorable Samuel R. Betts, Judge of the District Court of the United States for the Southern District of New York:

The libel of Elon C. Galusha, against the ship Pacific, her tackle, apparel and furniture, and against H. J. Tibbetts, master and part owner, and Frederick Griffing, the other part owner of the said ship, and all persons lawfully intervening for their interest in the said ship, her tackle, apparel and furniture, in a cause of contract, civil and maritime, alleges as follows:

First. That the said ship at the several times hereinafter stated has been and is yet lying in this port bound on a distant voyage around Cape Horn to California. And the said H. J. Tibbetts and Frederick Griffing were and are the sole owners of the said ship, her tackle, apparel and furniture, and are about to sail in the said ship on such voyage, and the said H. J. Tibbett's was and is the master of said ship; and that the said owners and master employed Joseph Kissam as their agent to obtain passengers for the said ship in such voyage, and otherwise to act for them as their agent in respect to the said ship.

Second. That the libellant and other persons having seen that the said ship was advertised to sail, for California, and being desirous to go to that place with despatch, they either in person or through their agent or agents, applied to the said Joseph Kissam for information in regard to the terms and accommodations of the said ship, and also as to the time of her sailing from this port, whereupon the said Joseph Kissam, so acting as agent for the ship, then and there represented and stated to the said libellant or his agents that the said vessel was of the very best class and condition, and a fast sailer, and in order that the cabin passengers might have all the comfort desired and plenty of space for exercise and air, that the said owners engaged not to take more than fifty cabin passengers, and that the passage money by reason thereof would be three hundred dollars a passenger, instead of two hundred and fifty dollars the usual charge for such a voyage; whereupon the name of the libellant or his agent was left and taken, and a refusal or option given to him to go in such vessel upon such terms. That shortly thereafter the libellant or his agent again called, whereupon the said Kissam represented to him that another party, called the "Morgan party," had taken 26 berths (meaning had engaged passage for 26 persons) and that there were other persons speaking for the remainder of the berths, and if the libellant and his friends desired passages they must engage the same without delay.

Third. That the libellant or his agents after seeing the said agent, examined the ship, found the said Tibetts, the captain and part owner, went on board the said vessel with him, and thereupon the said captain and part owner exhibited to the libellant or his agents parts of the vessel between the decks, where state rooms and separate apartments for each two passengers were about to be hastily prepared, the vessel having a small cabin as a freighting vessel, and thereupon the said captain and part owner represented and stated to the libellant or his agents that accommodation would be prepared for fifty passengers, and that the passengers should not be crowded, and he marked out and represented to the said libellant or his agents where the said state rooms were to be, and the size of the same, and certain spaces which were to be left between the same for air and exercise, and represented that such state rooms were to consist of a range of separate apartments in each side of the said vessel, each of which were to be at least six feet square well lighted and ventilated, and between the same an open space or hall was to be left for ventilation and for promenade. That he also marked and showed the libellant or his agents, how and where the bulkhead was to be built separating the cabin from the steerage, and that only fifty cabin passengers were to be taken, and that such passengers should have an equal and impartial chance of drawing for berths, which were also to be made so nearly equal in accommodation as to afford but little, if any, choice. And that the said master and owners would not take freight to the inconvenience of the passengers, and that the said vessel would sail on or about the fifth day of January 1849, and that in consequence of the pressure of passengers it was necessary for the libellant to engage his passage without delay.

Fourth. That relying upon such representations and other like deceptive and unfair representations, this libellant proceeded to enter his name at $300 for a passage, and it being thereupon represented to the libellant that he must actually pay his passage money to insure his passage, that such was the custom, and that many others had paid; the libellants or his agents, shortly afterwards and on or about the 2nd day of January instant, paid to the said owners or their agents, the sum of three hundred dollars, as and for the passage money in advance as a cabin passenger.

Fifth. That the libellant being a resident of Lockport in this State, relying upon the representations aforesaid, prepared himself at much expense for such contemplated voyage; and after being so prepared, was in attendance in this city at the time appointed for the departure of the said vessel, and has been subjected to inconvenience, expense and risk of loss, besides the loss of his time by the delay of the said vessel; and since his arrival at this port he has ascertained, and alleges to be the fact, that the said owners have broken their positive agreement with the libellant in various particulars; and that the representations aforesaid were deceptive, and calculated and intended to induce the libellant and others to pay or deposit their money as aforesaid, at a high price, and then to deprive them of the means of redress; relying upon the known anxiety of the said libellant and others to proceed without delay to induce them to overlook the many variations from and neglects of the matters so represented to the libellant. That the said owners have made and fitted up in the ship aforesaid, between decks, (calling it a cabin,) a number of berths and pretended state rooms, or separate divisions, greater than the number so represented, and have filled up therewith the entire centre part of the vessel, which was to have been left open, preventing ventilation, and rendering them close, confined, and unhealthy, and have engaged to take and transport in and on board of the said vessel as cabin passengers, seventy-two persons, rendering it uncomfortable, and unsafe for the libellant to proceeed in such vessel upon the said voyage. And many of said passengers, who are represented to have paid, or to have engaged berths at three hundred dollars each, have been in part permitted to become passengers paying or engaging to pay for such passages only such $275, which circumstance of itself has contributed to crowd the vessel, and is contrary to the engagement made with the libellant or his agent, and the said vessel has also been over crowded with cargo and the passengers greatly inconvenienced thereby.

Sixth. That the libellant or his agents, and various others of the said passengers, on discovery of the matters, have demanded a return of the said passage money paid by them respectively, on failure to obtain a compliance with the representations and engagements aforesaid, but the same have been refused. That the libellant is unwilling to go in said vessel under such circumstances, and has sustained and will sustain damages, as he believes, beyond the amount of said passage money, to the amount of one thousand dollars.

Seventh. That all and singular the premises are true, and within the admiralty and maritime jurisdiction of the United States and of this Honorable Court.

Wherefore the libellant prays that process in due form of law, according to the course of this Honorable Court, in cases of Admiralty and maritime jurisdiction, may issue against the said ship, her tackle, apparel and furniture, and that the said H. J. Tibbetts and Frederick Griffing, and all persons claiming any right, title or interest in the said ship, may be cited to appear and answer upon oath all and singular the matters aforesaid, and that the Court will be pleased to decree the return of said passage money, with interest and costs, and payment of the damages aforesaid ; and that the libellant may have such other and further relief as in law and justice he is entitled to receive; and that the said ship, her tackle, apparel and furniture, may be condemned and sold to pay the libellant's demands.

E. C. GALUSHA.

Sworn, &c.

E. H. OWEN, Proctor.

F. B. CUTTING, Advocate.

No. 116.—A LIBEL IN REM BY A PASSENGER AGAINST A SHIP FOR DAMAGES IN NOT BEING SUPPLIED WITH PROVISIONS.

To the Honorable Samuel R. Betts, Judge of the District Court of the United States for the Southern District of New York :

The libel of Peter M'Donald, of the city of New York, who prosecutes for himself and on behalf of his wife, Alicia M'Donald, and also his children, Martin M'Donald, James M'Donald, Alicia M'Donald, Margaret M'Donald, and Catherine M'Donald, who are all infants under the age of twenty-one years, who were late passengers on board the British vessel known as the Aberfoyle, of Liverpool, whereof Thomas Jones was master, against the said vessel, her tackle, apparel and furniture, and against all

67

persons lawfully intervening for interest therein, in a cause of damage, civil and maritime, alleges as follows:

First. That in the month of December, in the year one thousand eight hundred and forty-six, the said vessel, whereof the said Thomas Jones was master, being at the port of Liverpool, in England, destined on a voyage from thence to the port of New York; the said libellants embarked on board of said vessel, as passengers, and paid their freight from the said port of Liverpool to the said port of New York, and the agreement under which the said libellants embarked as passengers on board the said vessel, was in substance as follows :—That in consideration of the sum of twenty-two pounds sterling paid, the said libellant and his family were to be provided with a steerage passage from Liverpool to New York, in the ship Aberfoyle, with not less than ten cubic feet for luggage for each statute adult, and that three quarts of water per day, during said voyage, should be furnished to each adult ; and that there should be furnished to each of said libellants to be computed as adults, per week, during said voyage, seven pounds of bread biscuit, flour, oatmeal or rice, or a proportionate quantity of potatoes, (five pounds of potatoes being computed as equal to one pound of the other articles,) one-half of the quantity to be biscuit, to be issued not less often than twice a week, two children under fourteen years of age, and over one year, being computed as one adult ; and the libellants state that they are all statute adults excepting the libellants, Ann M'Donald, Maria M'Donald, Alicia M'Donald, Margaret M'Donald, and Catharine M'Donald, who are all over one year and under fourteen years of age.

Second. That said voyage commenced about the twenty-sixth day of December last, and continued for about sixty-nine days, when the said vessel arrived at the said port of New York, where she now is. That shortly after the sailing of the said vessel, he, the said Thomas Jones, by himself or his agents, on the high seas, withheld from, and refused to furnish to the said libellant and his family, the said water and the said provisions so as aforesaid by the said agreement to be furnished, whereby the said libellant and his family, during the said voyage or passage as aforesaid, suffered great want, hunger and thirst, and starvation, to the great injury of the health, and deprivation of the comfort of the libellant and his family, and the libellant claims five hundred dollars damages.

Third. That all and singular the premises are true, and within the Admiralty and Maritime jurisdiction of the United States and of this Honorable Court.

Wherefore the libellants pray, that process in due form of law, according to the course of this Honorable Court in cases of Admiralty and Maritime jurisdiction, may issue against the said vessel, her tackle, apparel and furniture ; and that all persons having any interest therein may be cited to appear and answer all and singular, the matters hereinbefore set forth ; and that this Honorable Court would be pleased to decree payment of the damages aforesaid, with costs, and that the said vessel may be condemned and sold to pay the same, and that the libellant may have such other and further relief in the premises as in law and justice he may be entitled to receive.

PETER M'DONALD.

Sworn, April 1, 1847,
    before me,
        GEORGE W. MORTON,
            U. S. Commissioner.
    WILLIAM M. ALLEN, Proctor for Lib'ts.
    HORACE DRESSER, Advocate.

———

No. 117.—LIBEL IN PERSONAM BY A FEMALE PASSENGER AGAINST THE
        MASTER OF A VESSEL, FOR INSULT AND INDECENCY.

To the Honorable Samuel R. Betts, Judge of the District Court of the
United States for the Southern District of New York:

The libel of J. E., now a resident of the city and county of New York,
late a passenger on board the ship   whereof I— B——, also of
the city of New York, now is, or late was, master and part owner, against
the said I— B——, in a cause of damage, civil and maritime, alleges as
follows :

First. That on or about the fourth day of September, one thousand eight
hundred and forty-eight, this libellant being in the port of Liverpool, in the
United Kingdom of Great Britain and Ireland, and wishing to embark for
the United States of America, made application to the said I— B——, then
commanding the American packet ship   then lying in said port,
for a cabin passage to the port of New York, and thereupon engaged such
passage, paying therefor the sum of £31 10s. for a cabin passage for herself
and child, that being the highest price for the first class of passengers.

Second. That said B—— told this libellant, at the time of engaging
such passage, that he was a married man, that one of his sons was to accompany him on the voyage, and that this libellant should receive from him
every fatherly care, attention, and protection, and should be under his especial charge.

Third. That said ship left said port of Liverpool on or about the seventh
day of said September, and on the morning of the ninth of said month, while
this libellant was asleep in the state room allotted to her, (there being no key
to the door of the same,) said Captain B—— entered said state room,
awoke this libellant out of her sleep, and made indecent and insulting proposals to this libellant, and upon this libellant ordering said B—— out of
her said room, said B—— threatened that if this libellant revealed to the
other passengers what had passed he would denounce her as a whore, and
used other indecent and vulgar expressions to her. That this libellant afterwards, and in the course of about three hours after such occurrence, requested said B—— to provide a key for said state room door, which he refused to do.

Fourth. That for several days in succession after the last mentioned occurrence, said B——— wsa in the habit of coming into said libellant's room, awakening her out of her sleep, attempting violence to her person, and using indecent and vulgar expressions, and exposing his person in a disgusting manner; that upon this libellant ordering said B——— from her presence and room, and threatening to inform the other cabin passengers of his conduct towards her, said B——— shortly afterwards, and in the hearing of the other cabin passengers, ordered this libellant to remain in her room, and not to leave the same, for if the libellant attempted so to do he would send her amongst the steerage passengers. That this libellant was closely confined to her said state room for the space of two weeks, having her meals sent to her by said B———'s orders. That said B——— was also in the habit of falsely and maliciously slandering this libellant to other of the said passengers on board said ship during such voyage.

Fifth. That this libellant was much injured in health, fretted and annoyed in body and mind in consequence of such confinement and conduct of said B——— and was quite sick for some time after her arrival in said city of New York, and is damnified in the sum of three thousand five hundred dollars.

Sixth. That all and singular the premises are true, and within the admiralty and maritime jurisdiction of the United States and of this Honorable Court.

Wherefore she prays, that a warrant of arrest, in due form of law, according to the course of this Honorable Court in causes of admiralty and maritime jurisdiction, may issue against the said I— B———. and that he may be required to answer, upon oath, this libel, and all and singular the matters aforesaid, and that this Honorable Court will be pleased to decree the payment of the damages aforesaid, with costs, and that the libellant may have such other and further relief as in law and justice she may be entitled to receive.

J— E—.

Sworn, July 3d, 1849,
 before me,
  George W. Morton,
   U. S. Commissioner.
Thomas W. Smith,
  Proctor for Libellant.
W. Q. Morton, Advocate.

No.118.—Libel in personam by a seaman against a master and mate for a joint assault and battery.

To the Honorable Samuel R. Betts, Judge of the District Court of the United States, for the Southern District of New York.

The libel of Charles Grayman, late seaman on board the ship Louvre, whereof   Weeks was master, and   Whittlesey chief mate, against the master and mate in a cause of personal damage, civil and maritime, alleges as follows:

First. That sometime in the month of March, in the year one thousand eight hundred and forty eight, the libellant shipped on board the said ship Louvre for a voyage from New York to Roterdam, and back to New York.

That on or about the twenty-fifth day of March, while on the high seas, the libellant having been kept on deck longer than was usual, by reason of the illness of the cook, whose place he had volunteered to fill, in addition to his other duties, was lying in his berth in the forecastle while it was his watch below, and while there heard the mate call him to come upon deck, whereupon he immediately arose, but before he had fairly got out of the berth the mate sprang down into the forecastle, and seizing the libellant by the throat began to drag him along the floor, and the said master having come down with an iron belaying pin endeavored to strike the libellant with the same, but the libellant to avoid a blow with such a dangerous weapon escaped from the hands of the master, and ran upon deck, and the master and mate followed him, and coming up with him near the galley the said master endeavored again to strike the libellant with the iron belaying pin, and the libellant not being able to escape from his reach was obliged to ward of the blow with his arm and hand, and in so doing received a severe stroke with the said iron belaying pin upon the back of his hand, whereby the same was much injured, and to this day bears the marks of the blows so received : that upon another occasion, while engaged in hauling upon a rope, the said mate without the least cause or provocation, and without the slightest warning to the libellant, fell upon the libellant and beat him severely with his fist about the head and face, and the said master coming from the other side of the deck took a wooden belaying pin from the rail, and holding the libellant by the neck, struck the libellant five or six times on the head with the belaying pin, and with the assistance of the mate, then beat him with the same about his legs and body for some minutes; that by reason of such beating, the face and head of the libellant was very much bruised, and his body also injured; that he still feels the effects of such beating. And the libellant by reason of the premises claims to be entitled to demand of the said master and mate, damages to the amount of five hundred dollars and upwards.

Second. That on the arrival of the said ship in this port the libellant took out a warrant from the marine court of the State of New York, against the said Weeks and Whittlesey, for the above mentioned assaults, but that they have fled from the jurisdiction of that court, or so concealed themselves that they cannot be taken, and this libellant is wholly without remedy unless by process from this court.

Third. That the said defendants have goods and chattels in this district and credits in the hands of E. D. Hurlburt & Co., of the city of New York, merchants.

Fourth. That all and singular the premises are true, and within the admiralty and Maritime jurisdiction of the United States, and of this Honorable Court.

Whereupon the libellant prays that a warrant of arrest, in due form of law, according to the course of this Honorable Court in cases of Admiralty and Maritime jurisdiction may issue against the said Weeks and Whittlesey, and that they may be required to appear and answer on oath, this libel, and all and singular the matters aforesaid, and that if they cannot be found, that their goods and chattles, and if none be found, that their credits and effects in the hands of E. D. Hurlburt & Co., of the City of New York, merchants, garnishees, may be attached, to the amount sued for, and costs. And that this Honorable Court would be pleased to decree the payment of the damages sustained by the libellant, with costs, and that he may have such other and further relief as in law and justice he may be entitled to receive.

CHARLES GRAYMAN.

Sworn July 1, 1848,
  before me,
    CHAS. W. NEWTON,
      U. S. Commissioner.
W. R. BEEBE, Proctor.
E. C. BENEDICT, Advocate.

No. 119.—LIBEL IN REM FOR COLLISION.

To the Honorable Samuel R. Betts, Judge of the District Court of the United States for the Southern District of New York:

The libel of Robert Schuyler and George L. Schuyler, both of the city of New York, against the brig Sea, her tackle, apparel, and other furniture, and all persons lawfully intervening for their interest in the same, in a cause of collision, civil and maritime, alleges as follows:

First. That your libellants, before and at the time of the collision hereinafter in the third article mentioned, were the owners and proprietors of a certain steamboat called the Niagara, with her steam engine, boilers, machinery, tackle, apparel, and other furniture; which said steamboat your libellants used and employed in transporting passengers and freight between the port of New York and the port of Bridgeport in the state of Connecticut and between which said ports she was regularly run, daily and every day, Sundays excepted, for the purposes aforesaid.

Second. That on Sunday, the ninth day of January, in the year 1848, the said steamboat Niagara, with her steam engine, boilers, fixtures, apparel and other furniture on board thereof was safely moored, and lying at her usual berth alongside of the pier or dock at the foot of Market street, East River, in said city of New York, where she had a perfect right to be; the said steamboat being then, and also at the time when she was run into as hereinafter mentioned, tight, staunch, strong, and in every respect well manned, tackled, appareled and appointed, and having the usual and necessary complement of officers and men, and that the master and crew engaged on board were on the look out for the protection and safety of said vessel.

Third. That, on the morning of the said day, and while the said steam boat was safely moored as aforesaid, the said brig Sea, whereof Norton was master, on her way from Havre, in the kingdom of France, to her destination at said city of New York, came up the East River, between the Battery and Governor's Island, passing at the distance of about four or five hundred feet from the docks of said city on said river, with a strong wind from west-south-west, and with a flood tide; and then and there with great force and violence ran into and upon the said steamboat, and did thereby cause great damage and injury to the said Niagara, her guards, hull, and stern, and remained foul of and upon the said Niagara for some time, and until she (the brig Sea) swayed round, when she cleared and passed on.

Fourth. That the said brig Sea, before and at the time of the said collision, on a voyage from Havre to New York, was coming up the East River without a pilot, and with the design of anchoring or mooring in said river; that she was moving along rapidly, with the aid of wind and tide, carrying her fore and main-top sails; that from the improper and unskilful management of the persons navigating said brig, the anchors were not let go in due time to check her headway, and bring her round into the tide, nor were her sails properly and in season furled and clewed up so as to lessen her speed, but, on the contrary, the said brig was so improperly and unskilfully managed and navigated, in the particulars above mentioned, that she was driven upon and into the said steamboat as aforesaid.

Fifth. That the persons navigating the said brig Sea let one anchor go about abreast, or in the neighborhood of, the Fulton street slip or pier, which partially checked her headway, but, notwithstanding, she continued to drift up the stream with the tide, heading partly across it, and in the direction of the Brooklyn shore; that the second anchor not being shackled, or otherwise in readiness, as it should have been, was not cast off into the stream until the said brig had drifted up to about opposite Catharine street pier, and at a distance of three hundred feet or thereabouts from the said Niagara, and before a sufficient scope of cable had run out, or the two anchors had checked her headway, she ran into and afoul of the said Niagara, the stern of said brig striking with great force and violence against the starboard side of said steamboat, twenty-five feet from the bows, and cutting in the deck beams, fender-piece, and plank shears, besides twisting round and damaging her stern; that at the time of the striking, the said brig was heading round into the stream and towards the Brooklyn shore, and that the collision aforesaid was occasioned by the negligence, inattention, and want of proper care and skill on the part of said brig, her master and crew, and not from any fault, omission, or neglect on the part of the said Niagara, her master and crew.

Sixth. That the said brig Sea had not before, or at the time of the collision, a proper look out and watch to guard against the danger of a collision in a crowded port; that the crew of said brig were occupied on the forward part of the vessel—while she was drifting up as above mentioned, after having let go the first anchor—in shackleing or otherwise preparing the second anchor to be cast into the stream ; that the collision would not have occurred if both of said achors had been in readiness, or had been suffered to run in due season, which would have checked her headway, or if the position of her yards had been changed, by hauling on the larboard braces,—which would have forced her off from the docks towards the middle of the stream ; and that the master and crew of the Niagara, fearful, from the course pursued by those navigating the brig that she would run into and upon their vessel, did every thing in their power, by getting out additional fasts to the wharf, and heeling their vessel over, to diminish the extent of the injury and damage to be caused by the blow.

Seventh. That the said steamboat Niagara, was so injured and disabled by the force and violence with which she was struck by the said brig Sea, as to render it necessary to take her to the Dry Dock for repairs, at a time when her services on the line in which she was engaged, were particularly valuable to her owners ; and that the libellants, in consequence of the Niagara having been run into and foul of as aforesaid, have sustained damages for the hire and expenses of a steamboat to supply her place ; for repairs to the said Niagara, and to her fixtures for her loss of time, for expenses of her master and crew, and otherwise, to the amount of one thousand dollars— which said damages were occasioned by the negligence, want of skill, and improper conduct of the persons navigating the said brig Sea, and not by or through any fault, negligence, or improper conduct on the part of the persons on board the Niagara, her master and crew.

Eighth. That since the said Niagara was so run foul of and into as aforesaid, these libellants have applied to the firm of John Ewell & Company, the consignees of said brig—the owners of said brig residing, as these libellants are informed and believe, in the town of Warren, and State of Rhode Island, where said brig belongs—and requested them to settle with these libellants for the damages sustained by them as above mentioned ; but the said consignees deny that there is any liability on the part of said brig for the said damages, or any part thereof.

Ninth. That the said brig Sea is now lying in the port of New York, and within the jurisdiction of this Court.

Tenth. That all and singular the premises are true, and within the Admiralty and Maritime jurisdiction of the United States and of this Honorable Court.

Wherefore the libellant prays that process in due form of law, according to the course of this Honorable Court in cases of Admiralty and Maritime jurisdiction, may issue against the said brig Sea, her tackle, apparel, and other furniture, and that all persons having any interest therein, may be cited to appear and answer all and singular the matters aforesaid ; and that this Honorable Court would be pleased to decree the payment of the damages as aforesaid, and that the said vessel may be condemned and sold to pay the same, and that the libellants may have such other and further relief as in law and justice they may be entitled to receive.

GEORGE L. SHUYLER.

Sworn, &c.,

ALEXANDER HAMILTON, JR.,
Proctor for Libellants.

W. Q. MORTON, Advocate.

No. 120.—LIBEL IN PERSONAM AGAINST THE OWNER OF A SHIP, FOR SALVAGE.

To the Honorable Samuel R. Betts, Judge of the District Court of the United States for the Southern District of New York.

The libel of William Peters, master of the ship Amiable, for himself, and all others entitled, against John Jones, owner of the ship Hercules, in a cause of salvage, civil and maritime, alleges as follows:

First. That the libellant being at sea, and bound to the port of New York in the said ship Amiable, of which he was master, observed a brig with a signal of distress flying, and he immediately made for said vessel, when he discovered that she was aground on the beach, on the south side of Long Island, and being hailed by the master thereof, was informed that she was the brig Rover, of New York, and had been aground for several hours, and had, by force of the wind and tide, worked so far into the sand, that he feared she would not float at high water without assistance, and asked the libellant to assist him.

Second. That the libellant thereupon consented to render such assistance as was in his power, and for that purpose let go his anchor and lay by her, and got out hawsers to her, and, by constant heaving of himself and his whole ship's company, prevented her working further up into the sand, and at high water, succeeded in heaving her off without injury—whereupon the said master informed the libellant that he had no means of paying him there—that he was bound to sea, and was very desirous of not being delayed, and that he would give the libellant a letter to his owner, the said John Jones, who would pay him his reasonable salvage. That said master thereupon gave the libellant a letter to said owner, informing him that the libellant had rendered him valuable assistance, whereby the said brig had been saved from probable loss, and was entitled to salvage.

Third. That the libellant therefore consented to allow the said brig to pursue her voyage, and on his arrival in the port of New York, he presented said letter to said owner, and for himself and his ship's company; and his owners, whose ship had been perilled in rendering said assistance, offered to accept the sum of five hundred dollars, if paid without delay or trouble to the libellant, although, as he had previously been informed, said brig and cargo were worth the sum of thirty thousand dollars, and the said sum of five hundred dollars was an inadequate salvage compensation, but said owner refused to pay the same, and to pay any more than fifty dollars.

68

Fourth. That all and singular the premises are true, and within the admiralty and maritime jurisdiction of the United States and of this Honorable Court.

Wherefore the libellant prays that the said John Jones may be cited to appear and answer the matters aforesaid, and may be decreed to pay to the libellant, and the others so entitled, a full reasonable salvage compensation for the said assistance so rendered, and that they may have such other and further relief as in law and justice they may be entitled to receive.

WILLIAM PETERS.

Sworn, &c.

A. B., Proctor and Advocate for Libellant.

No. 121.—LIBEL IN REM BY THE SEAMEN OF A GOVERNMENT VESSEL AGAINST A VESSEL AND CARGO FOR SALVAGE.

To the Honorable Samuel R. Betts, Judge of the District Court of the United States for the Southern District of New York.

The libel of Joseph Smith, of said district, mariner, for himself and others interested as salvors against the schooner Josephine, her tackle, apparel and furniture, and cargo, in a cause of salvage, civil and maritime, alleges as follows:

First. That the United States sloop of war Plymouth, being on her passage from Rio Janeiro, and being tight, staunch, and well found, and manned with a crew of about two hundred and fifty men, on or about the thirtieth day of September, and while on the high seas, the said ship then being on her passage to the port of Boston, and about eight or nine o'clock in the evening of that day, fell in with the wreck of the schooner Josephine, about four or five hundred miles from the port of New York, said schooner then drifting about at the mercy of the waves, and entirely abandoned by her crew, and being derelict, and having the appearance of having been broken open and partly plundered.

Second. That after the discovery of said wreck, a boat was lowered from the said sloop, and a boat's crew sent on board to take possession of the said wreck so abandoned, and that after considerable exertion, made fast to the said schooner with hawsers, and altering the course of the said sloop of war, she proceeded to the port of New York with the said schooner and cargo in tow, and continued to tow her for about four days, when, having arrived at the port of New York, and in perfect safety, she was put in charge of the steamboat Hercules, who towed her to the wharf, in said port, where she now lies.

Third. That said schooner was at the time loaded with an assorted cargo, and was, at the time of her wreck, bound from Richmond to the West Indies, and had it not been for the assistance so rendered to the said schooner and cargo, the same would have been entirely lost.

Fourth. That the libellant was on board said sloop at the time of saving said schooner, and assisted in saving her and her cargo.

Fifth. That the captain, officers and crew of the said sloop of war, by reason of the service they so performed, and the risk and hazard they run in saving the said schooner and her cargo, deserve and are justly entitled to meet and competent salvage for such service, and to so much as has been and actually is usually allotted by this Court to persons doing and performing the like service, with all charges and expenses attending the same.

Sixth. That all and singular the premises are true, and within the Admiralty and Maritime jurisdiction of the United States, and of this Honorable Court.

Wherefore the libellant prays, that process in due form of law, according to the course of this Honorable Court, in cases of Admiralty and Maritime jurisdiction, may issue against the said schooner, her tackle, apparel and furniture, and the cargo laden therein, and that all persons having or pretending to have any right, title, or interest therein, may be cited to appear and answer all and singular the matters aforesaid, and that this Honorable Court would be pleased to decree such a sum of money, or proportion of the value of the said schooner Josephine and her cargo, to be due to the libellant and others, salvors, as a compensation for their salvage service, as shall seem meet and reasonable, together with their costs and expenses in this behalf sustained, and that the said schooner, her tackle, apparel and furniture, and the cargo laden therein, may be condemned and sold to pay the same, and that the libellants may have such other and further relief as in law and justice they may be entitled to receive.

Joseph Smith.

Sworn to before me, this 8th day
of Oct., 1846,
  Geo. W. Morton,
    U. S. Commissioner.
Burr & Benedict,
  Proctors and Advocates.

No. 122.—Libel against a ship and cargo for military salvage.

(From Hall's Admiralty.)

To the Honorable Richard Peters, Esq., Judge of the District Court of the United States, in and for the District of Pennsylvania:

The libel of John Christian Breevoor, master, and John Schier Seaman, agent of the ship Fair American, now riding at anchor in the port of Philadelphia, respectfully showeth:

First. That the said ship set sail from the port of Philadelphia, in the United States of America, on the 22d day of September, in the year of our Lord 1798, and proceeding on her voyage from the port aforesaid to the port of Havana, to wit, on the eighth day of October in the year aforesaid, between the hours of nine and ten in the morning, being then, to the best of their judgment, between five and six miles from the aforesaid port of Havana, was brought to and captured by a French privateer schooner L'enfant de la Grande Revenche, armed and cruizing against the property of the citizens of the United States, commanded by Captain Roullis. That the commander of the aforesaid privateer and his officers, after looking over the papers of the Fair American, declared said ship and cargo good prize, and took from the ship fair American, sailing as aforesaid, her officers and seamen, all except your libellants and Anthony Fachtman the cook, who were suffered to remain on board the said ship, and put on board from the said schooner, a prize master with six white men and two negroes, and ordered her course to be altered for Cape Francais.

Second. That on the 16th day of October in the same year, between the hours of nine and ten in the morning, the said ship Fair American being then in latitude 28° 45' North, and longitude 80° 30' West, under the command of the said French prize master, seamen and negroes, and having been under their command and control upwards of forty-eight hours, your libellants then and there, being and remaining on board the said ship Fair American, assisted by the aforesaid Anthony Fachtman the cook, did, by great labor and enterprise, and at the manifest risk of their lives, re-capture and take from the hands and control of the said French prize master, seamen and negroes, the said ship Fair American, and did alter her course for the port of Charleston, in the state of South Carolina, being the nearest port in the United States, where the said ship arrived in perfect safety on the 26th day of October, in the year aforesaid. By reason whereof the said ship and cargo were saved to the owners and all others concerned, having received nevertheless considerable damage in her rigging and sails, &c., while in possession of the French prize master and crew aforesaid.

Third. That the said ship Fair American, her tackle, &c., and cargo were valued and estimated in the policies of insurance effected in Philadelphia at the time the said ship set sail from the port aforesaid, at the sum of thirty-eight thousand dollars or thereabouts, and that after the said ship arrived at the port of Charleston aforesaid, she was valued and estimated, with her cargo together, at the sum of thirty thousand one hundred and one dollars or thereabouts. That the cargo of the said ship alone amounted, by just valuation, to the sum of twenty-five thousand and fifty-one dollars or thereabouts; that the cargo aforesaid has been sold or disposed of, so that your libellants cannot now take benefit of process of your Honorable Court against the same.

Whereupon your libellants pray that the process of this Honorable Court may issue to attach and seize the said ship Fair American, now belonging to Stephen E. Dutilh, of Philadelphia, and that by a definitive sentence the said ship may be condemned and sold, and that such adequate and reasonable proportion may be awarded to your libellants for their labor in the premises as shall be found due to your libellants by the laws of the United States, or by the laws of nations in such cases esteemed and used. And your libellants further pray, that process of your Honorable Court may also issue to call in Stephen E. Dutilh, owner of the said ship Fair American and part of the cargo aforesaid, and John Gourgon of Philadelphia, owner of the other part, and that they may be condemned to pay your libellants such reasonable salvage as to your Honor may deem just and proper.

J. INGERSOLL,

Proctor for Libellants.

No. 123.—LIBEL AGAINST A VESSEL AND CARGO AS PRIZE.

(From Hall's Admiralty.)

To the Honorable John Sloss Hobart, Esquire, Judge of the District Court of the United States for the New York District.

The libel of Silas Talbot, Esquire, Commander of the United States ship of war the Constitution, on behalf as well of the United States as of himself and the officers and crew of the said ship, against the ship Amelia, her tackle, apparel, furniture and cargo :

The said libellant for and on behalf as aforesaid, doth hereby propound, allege and declare to this Honorable Court, as followeth :

First. That pursuant to instructions for that purpose from the President of the United States, the libellant in and with the said United States ship of war the Constitution and her officers and crew, did subdue, seize and take upon the high seas, the said ship or vessel called the Amelia of the burthen of about 370 tons, with her apparel, guns, and appurtenances, and a valuable cargo on board of the same, consisting of cotton, sugar, and dry goods in bales, and hath brought the said ship or vessel and her cargo into the port of New York, where they now are.

Second. That the said ship or vessel called the Amelia, at the time of the said capture thereof, was armed with eight carriage guns, and was under the command of Citoyen Etienne Prevost, a French officer of Marine, and had on board besides the said Commander thereof, eleven French mariners ; that as this libellant hath been informed, the said ship or vessel with her said cargo, being the property of some person or persons to the said libellant unknown, sailed some time since from Calcutta, an English port in the East Indies, bound for some port in Europe : That upon her said voyage she was met with and captured as a prize by a French national corvette, called La Diligente, commanded by L. T. Dubois, who took out of her the captain and crew of the said ship Amelia, with all the papers relating to her and her cargo, and placed the said Etienne Prevost and the said French mariners on board of her, and ordered her to St. Domingo for adjudication, as a good and lawful prize ; and that she remained in the full and peaceable possession of the French from the time of the capture thereof by them, for the space of ten days, whereby this libellant is advised that as well by the laws of nations, as by the particular law of France, the said ship became and was to be considered as a French ship.

Third. This proponent doth allege, propound and declare, that all and singular the premises are and were true, public and notorious, of which due proof being made, he humbly prays the usual process and monition of this Court in this behalf to be made, and that the said Ettienne Prevost, and all other persons having or claiming any interest in the said ship Amelia, her apparel, guns, appurtenances and cargo, or any part thereof, may be cited in general and special, to answer the premises, and that right and justice may be duly administered in this behalf, and all due proceedings being had, that the same ship or vessel, her apparel, guns, appurtenances and cargo, for the causes aforesaid, and others appearing, may, by the definitive sentence and decree of this Honorable Court be condemned as forfeited, to be distributed as by law is provided respecting the captures made by the public armed vessels of the United States; or if it shall appear that the same or any part or parcel thereof ought to be restored to any person or persons, as the former owner or owners thereof, then that the same may be so restored upon the payment of such salvage as by law ought to be paid for the same.

RICHARD HARRISON,
Proctor and Advocate for the libellant.

No. 124.—LIBEL FOR RESTITUTION OF A CAPTURED SHIP AND CARGO.
(From Hall's Admiralty.)

To the Honorable Richard Peters, Esq., &c.

The libel of Robert Findley, &c.

First. That your libellants are the true owners of the ship William, James Leggat master, now lying in the port of Philadelphia, and within the jurisdiction of this Honorable Court.

Second. That on the third day of May last, the said ship being on her voyage from Bremen to Potomac river, in the state of Maryland, and within nine miles of the sea coast of the United States, received an American pilot on board for the purpose of conducting her safely up the Chesapeake Bay to the place of her destination, and after receiving the said pilot she continued on the same course until she had arrived within about two miles of Cape Henry, the southern promontory of Chesapeake Bay, in five fathom water, and as near the shore as the pilot thought it proper to go; when she was forcibly seized and taken into possession by a number of armed men under the command of Peter Joanene, captain of an armed schooner then coming out of Chesapeake Bay, called the Citizen Genet, and bearing the national colors of the republic of France, as a prize to the said schooner, and hath since been detained and now is in the possession of the said Peter Joanene, who also then and there made prisoners of the captain, officers and crew of the said ship William, and them as prisoners doth detain.

Third. That not admitting that the said schooner the Citizen Genet, was duly commissioned and authorized to make prizes of vessels belonging to British subjects, which they pray may be inquired of, humbly insist that according to the premises, the said ship William was, at the time of her being so taken, upon neutral ground, within the territorial jurisdiction and under the protection of the United States, who are now at peace with the king and people of Great Britain, and that the said Peter Joanene and the persons under his command had no permission or authority from or under the United States to capture British vessels within that distance from the sea coast, to which by the laws of nations and the laws of the United States, the right and jurisdiction of the United States extended.

Inasmuch, then, as the said capture and detention of the said ship William and the captain, officers and crew thereof, are manifestly unjust and contrary to the laws of nations and the laws of the United States, your libellants humbly pray that the said ship William, her cargo, tackle, apparel and furniture, and all other things belonging to her may, by the sentence and decree of this Honorable Court, be restored to your libellants. That the said captain, officers and crew thereof may be relieved from imprisonment for the purpose of navigating her to her destined port, and that full satisfaction may be made by the said Peter Joanene and all others concerned, as well for the said unlawful capture and detention of the said ship, as for the imprisonment of the said captain, officers and crew thereof, and all damages, charges and expenses incurred thereby.

For which end your libellants humbly pray process of attachment, arrest and monition as in like cases is customary.

RAWLE,
Proctor pro Libellant.

No. 125.—LIBEL OF INFORMATION FOR A FORFEITURE FOR BEING FITTED OUT FOR THE SLAVE TRADE.

To the Honorable Samuel R. Betts, Judge of the District Court of the United States for the Southern District of New York.

The libel and information of Benjamin F. Butler, attorney of said United States for the said Southern District of New York, who prosecutes in this behalf for the said United States, and being present here in Court in his own proper person, in the name and on behalf of the said United States, against the schooner Patuxent, her tackle, apparel, furniture, guns, and appurtenances, and goods and effects found on board thereof, in a certain cause of seizure and forfeiture, alleges and informs as follows:

First. That a certain schooner or vessel called the Patuxent, of the burthen of ninety-five tons, and fifty ninety-fifth parts of a ton or thereabouts, being the property of a citizen or citizens of the United States, was heretofore, to wit, on or about the twenty-fifth day of June, in the year of our Lord one thousand eight hundred and forty-five, by some person or persons being a citizen or citizens of the said United States, or residing within the same, to the said attorney unknown, for himself or themselves, or for some other person or persons, either as master, factor or factors, owner or owners, fitted, equipped, and prepared, within a port of the United States, that is to say, within the port of New York, in the said Southern District of New York, and within the jurisdiction of the United States, for the purpose of carrying on trade or traffic in slaves to some foreign country, to the said attorney unknown, contrary to the provisions of the first section-of the act of Congress, approved on the 22d day of March, 1794, entitled, " An act to prohibit the carrying on the slave trade, from the United States to any foreign place or country."

Second. That the said schooner called the Patuxent, being the property of a citizen of the United States, was heretofore, to wit, on or about the said twenty-fifth day of June, in the year of our Lord one thousand eight hundred and forty-five, by the said Nathaniel T. Davis, as master, for himself, fitted, equipped and prepared, within the port of New York, in the said Southern District of New York, for the purpose of carrying on trade or traffic in slaves to some foreign country, to the said attorney unknown, contrary to the provisions of the first section of the act of Congress, in the preceding article mentioned.

Third. That the said schooner called the Patuxent, (so owned as in the second article aforesaid specified,) was heretofore, to wit, on or about the twenty-sixth day of June, in the year of our Lord one thousand eight hundred and forty-five, by the said Nathaniel T. Davis so being a citizen of the United States, caused to sail from the said port of New York, for the purpose of carrying on trade or traffic in slaves to some foreign country to the said attorney unknown, contrary to the provisions of the first section of the said act of Congress, in the first article of this libel mentioned.

Fourth. That the said schooner called the Patuxent, being the property of the said Nathaniel T. Davis, a citizen of the United States, was heretofore, to wit, on or about the twenty-fifth day of June, in the year of our Lord one thousand eight hundred and forty-five, by the said Nathaniel T. Davis, for himself as master of said schooner, fitted, equipped and prepared within the said port of New York, for the purpose of procuring from some foreign kingdom, place or country, to the said attorney unknown, the inhabitants of such kingdom, place or country, to be transported to some foreign country, port or place, to the said attorney unknown, and to be sold and disposed of as slaves, contrary to the provisions of the first section of the act of Congress, in the said first article of this libel mentioned.

Fifth. That the said schooner called the Patuxent, so owned as in the fourth article of this libel mentioned, was, on or about the said twenty-fifth day of June, in the year of our Lord one thousand eight hundred and forty-five, by the said Nathaniel T. Davis, caused to sail from the said port of New York, for the purpose of procuring from some foreign kingdom, place or country to the said attorney unknown, the inhabitants of such kingdom, place or country, to be transported to some foreign country, port or place to the said attorney unknown, and to be sold or disposed of as slaves, contrary to the form of the statute in such case made and provided, being the first section of the aforesaid act of Congress, approved on the 22d day of March, 1794.

Sixth. That the said schooner called the Patuxent, so owned by the said Nathaniel T. Davis, a citizen of the United States, was heretofore, to wit, on or about the twenty-fifth day of September, in the year of our Lord one thousand eight hundred and forty-five, employed and made use of by the said Nathaniel T. Davis, so being a citizen of the United States, in the transportation and carrying of slaves, from some foreign country or place, to the said attorney unknown, to some other foreign country or place to the said attorney unknown, contrary to the provisions of the first section of the act of Congress, approved on the 10th day of May, 1800, entitled, " An act in addition to the act entitled, ' An act to prohibit the carrying on the slave trade from the United States to any foreign place or country." '

Seventh. That the said schooner called the Patuxent, so owned by the said Nathaniel T. Davis, a citizen of the United States, heretofore, to wit, on the twenty-fifth day of June, in the year of our Lord one thousand eight hundred and forty-five, was by him the said Nathaniel T. Davis, for himself as owner, fitted, equipped, and prepared in the port of New York, in the Southern District of New York, and within the jurisdiction of the United States, for the purpose of procuring negroes, mulattoes, or persons of color from some foreign kingdom, place or country, to the said attorney unknown, to be transported to some other port or place to the said attorney unknown, to be held, sold, or otherwise disposed of as slaves, or to be held to service or labor, contrary to the provisions of the second section of the act of Congress, approved on the 20th day of April, 1818, entitled, " An act in addition to an act to prohibit the introduction of slaves into any port or place within the jurisdiction of the United States, from and after the first day of January, in the year of our Lord one thousand eight hundred and eight ;" and to repeal certain parts of the same.

Eighth. That the said schooner or vessel so owned as aforesaid, was heretofore to wit, on the twenty-sixth day of June, in the year of our Lord one thousand eight hundred and forty-five, by the said Nathaniel T. Davis fitted, equipped, and prepared, and caused to sail from the said port of New York, for the purpose of procuring negroes, mulattoes, and persons of color, from some foreign kingdom, place, and country to the said attorney unknown, to be transported to some port or place to the said attorney unknown, to be held, sold, or otherwise disposed of as slaves, or to be held to service or labor, contrary to the provisions of the second section of the act of Congress in the seventh article of this libel mentioned.

Ninth. That the ship Yorktown, being a commissioned and armed vessel of the United States of America, commanded by Charles H. Bell, of the navy of the United States, was, during the month of September, in the year of our Lord one thousand eight hundred and forty-five, cruising on the coast of Africa, and while so cruising, to wit, on the 27th day of September, 1845, at or near Cape Mount, on said coast, seized and took the said schooner called the Patuxent, the said schooner then and there being employed

69

in carrying on trade, business and traffic contrary to the true intent and meaning of the acts of Congress aforesaid, approved respectively on the 22d day of March, 1794, and May 10th, 1800, and that said schooner has been sent to the United States for adjudication, and is now lying within the Southern District of New York, and within the jurisdiction of this Court.

Tenth. That by reason of the premises, and by force of the statutes in such case made and provided, the said schooner called the Patuxent, together with her tackle, apparel, furniture, appurtenances, guns, and the goods and effects found on board thereof, have become forfeited.

Eleventh. That all and singular the premises are and were true, and within the Admiralty and Maritime jurisdiction of the United States, and of this Honorable Court.

Wherefore the said attorney prays the usual process of attachment against said schooner, her tackle, apparel and furniture, and appurtenances and goods and effects, and the monition of this Honorable Court, in this behalf to be made, and that all persons interested in the said schooner, or in her tackle, apparel, furniture, guns, appurtenances, or the goods and effects found on board thereof, may be cited to answer the premises, and all due proceedings being had, that the said schooner, with her tackle, apparel, furniture, guns, appurtenances and goods and effects found on board thereof, may, for the causes aforesaid, and others appearing, be condemned by the definitive sentence and decree of this Honorable Court, as forfeited to the use of the said United States, according to the form of the statutes in such case made and provided.

B. F BUTLER, U. S. District Attorney.

No. 126.—LIBEL OF INFORMATION IN REM AGAINST A STEAMBOAT, TO RECOVER PENALTIES FOR NON-INSPECTION OF BOILERS, &c.

To the Honorable Samuel R. Betts, Judge of the District Court of the United States for the Southern District of New York.

The libel of information of J. Prescott Hall, Attorney of the United States for the said Southern District of New York, who prosecutes for the said United States in this behalf, and being present here in Court, in his own proper person, in the name and on behalf of the said United States against the steamboat Harlequin, her tackel, apparel and furniture, in a cause of seizure, alleges and informs as follows:

First. That by an act of Congress of the United States of America, approved on the seventh day of July, in the year one thousand eight hundred and thirty eight, entitled "An act to provide for the better security of the lives of passengers on board of vessels propelled in whole or in part, by steam;" it was among other things provided, that it should be the duty of the owners and masters of steamboats, to cause the inspection required by the fourth section of said act, to wit, an inspection of the hull of such steamboats, to be made at least once in every twelve months. And the examination required by the fifth section of said act, to wit, an exam-

¡ nation of the boilers and machinery of such steamboats, to be made at least once in every six months.

That after the passage of the said act, to wit, on divers days and times, between the fifth day of June, in the year of our Lord. one thousand eight hundred and forty nine, and the twentieth day of June, in the year last aforesaid, a certain vessel being a steamboat called the Harlequin, then being owned in whole or in part, by a citizen or citizens of the said United States, to the said attorney unknown, was used and employed in the transportation of passengers, and did carry passengers on the navigable waters of the said United States, to wit, from Port Richmond in the State of New York, in the said Southern District of New York, and Bergen Point in the State of New Jersey, the hull of said steamboat not having been inspected pursuant to the provisions of the fourth section of said act of Congress, at any time within twelve months prior to the said fifth day of June, or the said twentieth day of June, or any day intervening between the said fifth day of June, and the said twentieth day of June, in the year one thousand eight hundred and forty nine. By reason whereof, and by virtue of the said act of Congress, the owner or owners, and master of the said Steamboat, being a vessel propelled in whole or in part by steam, forfeited and became liable to pay to the said United States the sum of five hundred dollars, for the payment of which sum, the said steamboat hath become liable to be seized and proceeded against summarily by way of libel, and for the recovery of which, this civil and maritime cause is now instituted.

Second. That after the passage of the aforesaid act of Congress, to wit, on divers days and times, between the fifth and twentieth days of June, in the year of our Lord one thousand eight hundred and forty nine, a certain vessel being a steamboat, called the Harlequin, propelled in whole or in part by steam, then being owned by a certain person or persons to the said attorney unknown, then and still being a citizen or citizens of the United States, was used and employed in the transportation of passengers, and did carry passengers on the navigable waters of the United States, that is to say, between Port Richmond in the State of New York, in the Southern District of New York aforesaid, and Bergen Point in the State of New Jersey ; the boilers and machinery of said steamboat not having been examined pursuant to the provisions of the fifth section of said act of Congress, at any time within six months prior to the said fifth day of June, or the said twentieth day of June or any day intervening between the said fifth day of June, and the said twentieth day of June, in the year one thousand eight hundred and forty nine. By reason whereof and by virtue of the said act of Congress, the owner or owners and master of the said steamboat called the Harlequin, forfeited and became liable to pay to the said United States the further sum of five hundred dollars, for the payment of which sum the said steamboat hath become liable to be seized and proceeded against summarily by way of libel, and for the recovery of which this civil and maritime cause is now instituted.

Third. That after the passage of the said act, to wit, on the twentieth day of June, in the year one thousand eight hundred and forty nine, the owner or owners of a certain vessel being a steamboat, called the Harlequin, propelled in whole or in part by steam, did transport passengers, in and on board of said vessel, upon the navigable waters of the said United States, to wit, on waters between Port Richmond in the State of New York, in the said Southern District of New York, and Bergen Point in the State of New Jersey, without having first obtained from the proper officer, to wit, the Collector of the Customs for the Port and District of the city of New York, a license under the laws of the United States, existing at the time of the passage of said act.   That by reason of the premises, and by virtue of the said act, the owner or owners of the said steamboat, forfeited and became liable to pay to the said United States the further sum of five hundred dollars, for the payment of which sum the said steamboat hath become liable to be proceeded against summarily by way of libel, and for the recovery of which this civil and maritime cause is instituted.

Fourth. That all and singular the premises aforesaid are true, and within the Admiralty and Maritime jurisdiction of the United States and of this Honorable Court.

Wherefore the said Attorney of the said United States, on behalf of the said United States prays the usual process and monition against the said steamboat, and her tackle, apparel and furniture in this behalf to be made, and that all persons interested in the said steamboat and her tackle, apparel and furniture, may be cited to answer the premises, and that this Honorable Court may be pleased to decree for the penalties aforesaid, and that the said steamboat may be condemned and sold to pay the several penalties aforesaid with costs, and for such other relief as shall to law and justice appertain.

J. Prescott Hall,
U. S. Dist. Attorney.

No. 127.—A libel of information in rem against a vessel seized by a government vessel for being engaged in the slave trade.

To the Honorable Samuel R. Betts, Judge of the District Court of the United States for the Southern District of New York:

The libel of information of J. Prescott Hall, Attorney of the said United States for the said Southern District of New York, who prosecutes in this behalf for the said United States, and being present here in court in his own proper person, in the name and on behalf of the said United States, against the brig Susan, her tackle, apparel, and furniture, and against all persons intervening for their interest therein, in a cause of seizure and forfeiture, alleges and informs as follows:

First. That the brig Perry, a commissioned vessel of the United States of America, and belonging to the navy thereof, heretofore, to wit, on the fifth day of February, in the year 1849, being under the command of John A.

Davis, a lieutenant commanding in the navy of the United States, did, on the high seas, off the coast of Brazil, that is to say, about three miles outside of Round Island near Rio de Janeiro, on said coast of Brazil, seize and take a certain brig or vessel called the Susan, belonging to a citizen or citizens of the United States, of the burthen of two hundred and sixty tons or thereabouts; which said brig or vessel was then and there employed in carrying on trade, business and traffic in slaves, contrary to the true intent and meaning of the act of Congress of the said United States, approved on the tenth day of May, in the year of our Lord eighteen hundred, entitled " An act in addition to the act intituled ' An act to prohibit the carrying on the slave trade from the United States to any foreign place or country,' " and that by reason of the premises in this article stated, and by force of the fourth section of the said act of Congress, the said brig Susan, together with her tackle, apparel, and guns, and the goods and effects (other than slaves) found on board thereof, became and were forfeited.

Second. That the said brig Perry, being commissioned, belonging to the navy, and commanded as in the preceding article is alleged, did, heretofore, on the fifth day of February, in the year 1849, on the high seas, and at or about the point or place in said preceding article mentioned, seize and take the said brig Susan, which said brig was then and there employed in carrying on trade, business, and traffic in slaves, contrary to the true intent and meaning of the act of Congress of the said United States, approved on the 22nd day of March, in the year 1794, entitled " An act to prohibit the carrying on of the slave trade from the United States to any foreign place or country, and that by reason of the premises in this article stated, and by force of the before mentioned fourth section of the said act of Congress, approved on the tenth day of May, in the year 1800, the said brig Susan, together with her tackle, apparel, and guns, and the goods and effects (other than slaves) found on board thereof, became and were forfeited.

Third. That on board said brig Susan were found two blacks or mulattoes, supposed to be, or at and before the time of said seizure before alleged, to have been slaves.

Fourth. That the said brig Susan was heretofore, on or about the eighth day of July, in the year 1848, by some person or persons, being a citizen or citizens of the said United States, or resident within the same, to the said attorney unknown, fitted out within the port of New York in the South ern District of New York, and caused to sail from and out of said port, for the purpose of carrying on trade and traffic in slaves, to some foreign country, to the said attorney unknown, and for the purpose of procuring from some foreign country, to the said attorney unknown, the inhabitants of which country to be transported to some other foreign country, to said attorney also unknown, contrary to the provisions of the first section of the act of Congress of the said United States, approved on the 22d day of March, in the year 1794, entitled " An act to prohibit the carrying on the slave trade from the United States to any foreign place or country."

Fifth. That the said brig Susan being the property of and owned by a certain person or certain persons being a citizen or citizens of said United States, or residing therein, was heretofore, to wit, on the fifth day of February, in the year 1849, employed and made use of by some person or persons being a citizen or citizens of said United States, or residing within the same, to the said attorney unknown, in the transportation and carrying of slaves from some foreign country or place, to the said attorney unknown, to some other foreign country or place, to the said attorney unknown, contrary to the provisions of the first section of the act of the Congress of the said United States, approved on the tenth day of May, in the year 1800, entitled "An act in addition to the act intituled ' An act to prohibit the carrying on the slave trade from the United States to any foreign place or country.' "

Sixth. That the said brig Susan, being the property of and owned by citizens of the said United States was heretofore, on the fifth day of February, in the year 1849, employed and made use of in the transportation and carrying of slaves, from some foreign country or place to the said attorney unknown, to some other foreign country or place to the said attorney also unknown, contrary to the provisions of the said first section of the act of Congress in the preceding article specified.

Seventh. That the said brig Susan, being the property of and owned by citizens of the said United States, was heretofore, on the fifth day of February, in the year 1849, employed and made use of in the transportation and carrying of slaves from some foreign country or place, to wit, from the coast of Africa, to some other foreign country or place, to wit, to the empire of Brazil, and, to wit, from the empire of Brazil to the coast of Africa, contrary to the provisions and the form and effect of the said first section of the said act of Congress in the fifth article of this libel mentioned.

Eighth. That the said brig Susan, together with her tackle, apparel, furniture appurtenances, guns, and the goods and effects found on board thereof, having been so seized as aforesaid, has been sent to the United States for adjudication, and is now lying within the Southern District of New York and within the jurisdiction of this Court.

Ninth. That by reason of all and singular the premises aforesaid, and by force of the statutes in such case made and provided, the aforementioned brig Susan, together with her tackle, apparel, furniture, appurtenances, guns, and the said goods and effects became and are forfeited to the United States.

Tenth. That all and singular the premises aforesaid are and were true, and within the Admiralty and maritime jurisdiction of the United States, and of this Honorable Court.

Wherefore the said attorney prays the usual process of attachment against the said brig, her tackle, apparel, furniture, appurtenances and guns, and the goods and effects on board of her, and the monition of this Honorable Court in this behalf to be made, and that all persons interested in the before mentioned brig, her tackle, apparel, furniture, appurtenances, guns and the said goods and effects found on board thereof, may be cited to answer the premises, and all due proceedings being had thereon, that the said brig, her tackle, apparel, furniture, appurtenances, guns and the goods and effects found on board thereof, may, for the causes aforesaid, and, others appearing, be condemned by the definitive sentence and decree of this Honorable Court as forfeited to the United States, according to the form of the statutes of said United States in such case made and provided, and that the said brig, her tackle, apparel, furniture, appurtenances, guns and the goods and effects found on board thereof, may be sold and the proceeds thereof distributed and disposed of according to law.

J. Prescott Hall,
U. S. Dist. Att'y.

No. 128.—Libel in personam by a charterer on a verbal charter.

To the Honorable Samuel R. Betts, Judge of the District Court of the United States for the Southern District of New York:

The libel and complaint of William Quirk of Wilmington, North Carolina, against Peter Clinton and John G. Attridge, in a case of contract, civil and maritime, and thereupon the said William Quirk alleges and articulately propounds as follows:

First. That the said Peter Clinton being part owner, and the said John G. Attridge part owner and master of the brig Growler, of New York, on or about the sixteenth day of June, 1848, by James Smith, his agent and broker, chartered said brig to the libellant for a voyage from the port of New York to Wilmington, North Carolina, and thence to London, to be provided with, and to carry a full cargo of turpentine under and on deck, from Wilmington to London, at the freight of four shillings sterling per barrel for turpentine under deck, and three shillings and sixpence sterling per barrel on deck, and primage of five per cent on the amount of freight, the amount of the charter to be paid on the discharge of the cargo in London; 15 running lay days in Wilmington, for loading, and 14 running lay days in London, for discharging. The vessel to leave New York for Wilmington on or before the 20th day of June, then instant, and in case there should not be thirteen feet of water on the bar at Wilmington, the libellant was to pay lighterage on the cargo, sufficient to load her to thirteen feet draft, and the vessel to be consigned in Wilmington to J. & D. McRea, and in London to Charles Briggs.

Second. That said charter was made verbally and not in writing; and a few days after the same was so agreed on, the said defendants having had a better offer for said vessel, as the libellant has been informed and believes, chartered her to other persons for a different voyage, and refused to complete and fulfil said charter to the libellants.

Third. That the libellants lost and sustained damage to the amount of six hundred and twenty-dollars and upwards, which he insists the said defendants are bound in law to pay him, but which the defendants refuse to pay.

Fourth. That all and singular the premises are true, and within the admiralty and maritime jurisdiction of the United States and of this Honorable Court.

Wherefore the libellant prays, that a warrant of arrest, in due form of law, according to the course of this Honorable Court, in cases of Admiralty and maritime jurisdiction, may issue against the said Peter Clinton and John G. Attridge, and that they may be compelled to appear and answer upon oath all and singular the matters aforesaid, and if they cannot be found, that an attachment may issue against their goods and chattels, and if none be found, that their credits and effects in the hands of Mathew Clinton and Peter Clinton, of said district, garnishees, be attached, and that this Honorable Court would be pleased to decree payment of the damages aforesaid, with costs, and that the libellant may have such other and further relief as he may be entitled to receive.

WILLIAM QUIRK,
By JAMES SMITH,
His Attorney and Agent.

Sworn to this 2d day of August, by
James Smith, the Attorney in fact
and Agent of the libellant, who is
absent more than 100 miles from
the city of New York, before me,

GEORGE W. MORTON,
U. S. Commissioner.

BURR & BENEDICT, Proctors.

No. 129.—ORDER FOR WARRANT OF ARREST.—*Vid. ante, page* 226.

No. 130.—MARKING OF PROCESS FOR BAIL—*Vid. ante, page* 226.

No. 131.—LIBELLANT'S STIPULATION FOR COSTS IN REM—*Vid. No.* 2, *ante, page* 428.

No. 132.—LIBELLANT'S STIPULATION FOR COSTS IN PERSONAM—*Vid. ante, page* 224.

Mesne Process.

No. 133.—WARRANT OF ARREST IN PERSONAM.

THE PRESIDENT OF THE UNITED STATES OF AMERICA,

To the Marshal of the Southern District of New York, Greeting :

Whereas, a libel has been filed in the District Court of the United States

[L. S.]   of America, for the Southern District of New York, on the   day of   in the year of our Lord one thousand eight hundred and   by A. B. against C. D., in a certain action, civil and maritime, for freight, therein alleged to be due to the said libellant, amounting to two hundred and fifty-two dollars, and praying that a warrant of arrest may issue against the said defendant. Now, therefore, we do hereby empower, and strictly charge and command you, the said Marshal, that you take and arrest the said defendant, if he shall be found in your district, and him safely keep, so that you may have his body before the said District Court, on the   day of   at the City Hall, in the City of New York, then and there to answer the said libel, and to make his allegations in that behalf: and have you then and there this writ, with your return thereon.

Witness the Honorable Samuel R. Betts, Judge of said Court, this   day of   in the year of our Lord one thousand eight hundred and   and of our independence the seventy

                                           E. F., Clerk.

G. H., Proctor.

No. 134.—MARK FOR BAIL.

The Marshal will hold the respondent to bail in the sum of   hundred and   dollars.

Dated   18

                                           Clerk.

No. 135.—MARSHALL'S DEPUTATION TO HIS DEPUTY OR BAILIFF.

I hereby depute   to execute the within process.

Dated   18

                               U. S. Marshal.

No. 136.—MARSHALL'S RETURN.

Defendant taken.

                                   Marshal.

No. 137—THE LIKE, WITH ATTACHMENT AGAINST GOODS AND CHATTELS, AND ITS EFFECTS, AND SUMMONS TO GARNISHEE.

The President of the United States of America *to the Marshal of the Southern District of New York, Greeting*: Whereas a libel has been filed in the District Court of the United States of America, for the Southern District of New York, on the

70

[L. S.]   nineteenth day of May, in the year of our Lord one thous-
            and eight hundred and forty eight, by Thomas Gould,
            libellant, against John Gibons master of the ship Mount
            Vernon, in a certain action, civil maritime, for certain as-
saults and batteries therein alleged to have been committed on the said libellant, to his damage of five hundred dollars, and praying that a warrant
of arrest may issue against the said defendant, and that he may be held to
bail, pursuant to the rules and practice of this Court. Now, therefore, we
do hereby empower, and strictly charge and command you, the said Marshal, that you take and arrest the said defendant, if he shall be found in
your District, and him safely keep, so that you may have his body before
the said District Court on the 23d day of May inst, at the City Hall in the
City of New York, then and there to answer the said libel, and to make his
allegations in that behalf; and if the said defendant cannot be found in your
District, that you attach his goods and chattels in your District to the
amount sued for, and if no goods and chattels can be found, that you attach
his credits and effects to the amount sued for, in the hands of the Garnishees
John Elwell & Co., and St. George Givins; and that you summon the said
Garnishees, to appear before the said District Court on the said 23d day of
May instant, to do and abide what may be required of them in this behalf,
and have you then and there this writ; with your return thereon.

Witness the Honorable Samuel R. Betts, Judge of said Court, this 19th
day of May, in the year of our Lord one thousand eight hundred and forty
eight, and of our independence the seventy second.

J. W. METCALF, Clerk.

A. NASH, Proctor.

No. 138.—MARSHAL'S RETURN.

The defendant is not found in the District, and I have attached the following goods and chattels of said defendant.

OR:

The credits and effects of the said defendant, in the hands of John Elwell
& Co., and St. George Givins, garnishees, and have summoned the said
garnishees as within commanded.

HENRY F. TALLMADGE, Marshal.

No. 139.—CITATION AND MONITION IN PERSONAM, WITH MARSHAL'S RETURN.

The President of the United States of America, *to the Marshal of the
Southern District of New York, greeting:*—Whereas a libel has
been filed in the District Court of the United States of
America, for the Southern District of New York, on

[L. S.]   the   day of   in the year of our
            Lord one thousand eight hundred and
by A. B., against C. D., in a certain action, civil and mari-

time, for wages therein alleged to be due to the said libellant, amounting to seventy-five dollars, and praying that a citation may issue against the said defendant, pursuant to the rules and practice of this court.

Now, therefore, we do hereby empower, and strictly charge and command you, the said Marshal,   that you cite and admonish the said defendant if he shall be found in your district, that he be and appear before the said District Court, on the   day of   at the city hall in the city of New York, then and there to answer the said libel, and to make his allegations in that behalf; and have you then and there this writ, with your return thereon.

Witness the Honorable Samuel R. Betts, Judge of said Court, this   day of   in the year of our Lord one thousand eight hundred and   and of our Independence the seventy

                                                                J. W. M., Clerk.

E. F., Proctor.

No. 139.—RETURN OF MARSHAL.

Personally served.

                                        H. F. T., Marshal.

No. 140.—WARRANT OF ARREST OR ATTACHMENT AGAINST A SHIP, WITH A MONITION AND A WARRANT OF ARREST AGAINST THE MASTER OR OWNER.

Southern District of New York, ss.—

                        The President of the United States of America, to the Marshal of the Southern District of New York, greeting:

[L. S.]   Whereas a libel *in rem* and *personam* hath been filed in the District Court of the United States for the Southern District of New York, on the   day of   in the year of our Lord one thousand eight hundred and forty   by A. B., against the ship or vessel called the Rover, her tackle, &c., (or other property, describing it, as the case may be,) for the reasons and causes in the said libel mentioned, and praying the usual process and monition of the said court in that behalf to be made, and that all persons interested in the said ship or vessel, her tackle, &c., may be cited to answer the premises, and all proceedings being had that the said ship or vessel, her tackle, &c., may, for the causes in the said libel mentioned, be condemned and sold to pay the demands of the libellant.

You are therefore hereby commanded, to attach the said ship or vessel, her tackle, &c., and to detain the same in your custody, until the further order of the court respecting the same, and to give due notice to all persons claiming the same, or knowing or having any thing to say why the same should not be condemned and sold pursuant to the prayer of the said libel, that they be and appear before the said court, to be held in and for the Southern District of New York, on the   day of at eleven o'clock in the forenoon of the same day, if the same shall be a day of jurisdiction, otherwise on the next day of jurisdiction thereafter, then and there to interpose a claim for the same, and to make their allegations in that behalf.

[We do hereby further empower, and strictly charge and command you the said Marshal, that you arrest the said owner or master, if he shall be found in your district and have his body before the said District Court, on the   day of   at the city hall in the city of New York, then and there to answer the said libel, and to make his allegations in that behalf;] and have you then and there this writ, with your return thereon.

Witness the Honorable Samuel R. Betts, Judge of said Court, this   day of   in the year of our Lord one thousand eight hundred and   and of our Independence the

J. W. M., Clerk.

E. F., Proctor.

[*If the process be in rem only, the form is the same, omitting the last clause in brackets.*]

No. 142.—RETURN OF THE MARSHAL.

As within commanded, I attached the   therein described, on the   day of   and have given due notice to all persons claiming the same, that this court will on the   day of   inst., if that day should be a day of jurisdiction, if not, on the next day of jurisdiction thereafter, proceed to the trial and condemnation thereof, should no claim be interposed for the same, [and I have arrested the defendant within named.]

U. S. Marshal.

[*If the process be in rem only, the return is the same, omitting the clause in brackets.*]

No. 143.—THE LIKE, AGAINST A SHIP AND OWNER AND THE EXECUTOR OF ANOTHER OWNER.

Southern District of New York, ss:

The President of the United States of America, *To the Marshal of the Southern District of New York*, Greeting: Whereas, a libel hath been filed in the District Court of the United States, for the Southern District of New York, on the twenty-third [L. S.]   day of November, in the year of our Lord one thousand eight hundred and forty-one, by Robert Gordon, against the ship Hilah, her tackle, apparel and furniture, and against Edmund Hammond, master and owner, and against Thomas E. Lyde, executor of the last will and testament of Abraham Tanner, owner, deceased, for the reasons and causes in the said libel mentioned, and praying the usual process and monition of the said Court in that behalf to be made, and that all persons interested in the said ship Hilah, her tackle, &c., may be cited in general and special, to answer the premises, and all proceedings being had, that the said ship Hilah, her tackle, &c., may for the causes in the said libel mentioned, be condemned and sold to pay the demand of the libellant. You are therefore hereby commanded to attach the said ship Hilah, her tackle, &c., and to detain the same in your custody until the further order of the Court respecting the same, and to give due notice to all persons claiming the same, or knowing or having any thing to say why the same should not be condemned and sold, pursuant to the prayer of the said libel, that they be and appear before the said Court, to be held in and for the Southern District of New York, on the fourteenth day of December next, at eleven o'clock in the forenoon of the same day, if the same shall be a day of jurisdiction, otherwise on the next day of jurisdiction thereafter, then and there to interpose a claim for the same, and to make their allegations in that behalf. And you are hereby further empowered and commanded to cite and monish the said Edmund Hammond and Thomas E. Lyde, executor of Abraham Tanner, owner of said vessel, lately deceased, if they shall be found in your district, that they appear before the said Court, on the day herein above last mentioned, to answer the matters contained in the said libel, and to stand to and abide such order and decree as may be made by the Court in the premises ; and that you cite the said Edmund Hammond, master and owner, and Thomas E. Lyde, executor of the last will and testament of Abraham Tanner, owner, deceased, and all other persons having any interest in the said ship Hilah, her tackle, apparel, &c., that they be and appear before the said Court, on the said fourteenth day of December next, then and there to interpose their claims for the same, and to make their allegations in this behalf. And what you shall have done in the premises, do you then and there make return thereof, together with this writ.

Witness the Honorable Samuel R. Betts, Judge of the said Court, this twenty-third day of November, in the year of our Lord one thousand eight hundred and forty-one, and of the independence of the United States the sixty-sixth.

Chas. D. Betts, Clerk.

S. B., Proctor.

No. 144.—The like, in a cause of possession or restitution.

Southern District of New York, ss :—

The President of the United States of America, *To the Marshal of the Southern District of New York, Greeting :* Whereas, a libel *in rem* and *personam* hath been filed in the District Court of the

United States, for the Southern District of New York,

[L. S.] on the eighteenth day of August, in the year of our Lord one thousand eight hundred and forty-seven, by Alfred Peabody, libellant, against the schooner Lucinda Snow, her tackle, &c., and against Stubbs and Rogers, in an action, civil and maritime, for said vessel and her freight, for the reasons and causes in the said libel mentioned, and praying the usual process and monition of the said Court in that behalf to be made, and that all persons interested in the said schooner or vessel, her tackle, &c., may be cited in general and special, to answer the premises, and all proceedings being had that the said schooner or vessel, her tackle, &c., may, for the causes in the said libel mentioned, be delivered to the libellant.

You are therefore hereby commanded, to attach the said schooner or vessel, her tackle, &c., and to detain the same in your custody, until the further order of the Court respecting the same, and to give due notice to all persons claiming the same, or knowing or having any thing to say why the same should not be delivered to the libellant, pursuant to the prayer of the said libel, that they be and appear before the said Court, to be held in and for the Southern District of New York, on the first Tuesday of September next, at eleven o'clock in the forenoon of the same day, if the same shall be a day of jurisdiction, otherwise on the next day of jurisdiction thereafter, then and there to interpose a claim for the same, and to make their allegations in that behalf. And the libellant having prayed that the said Stubbs and Rogers may be cited to appear before the said Court, we do hereby further empower, and strictly charge and command you the said Marshal, that you cite and admonish the said Stubbs and Rogers, if they shall be found in your district, that they and each of them appear before the said District Court, on the seventh day of September next, at the City Hall, in the City of New York, then and there to answer the said libel, and to make their allegations in that behalf; and have you then there this writ, with your return thereon.

Witness the Honorable Samuel R. Betts, Judge of said Court, this nineteenth day of August, in the year of our Lord one thousand eight hundred and forty-seven, and of our independence the sixty-sixth.

J. W. METCALF, Clerk.

MARTIN STRONG & A. F. SMITH,
Proctors.

No. 145.—RETURN OF THE MARSHAL AS WITHIN COMMANDED.

I attached the   therein described, on the   day of
and have given due notice to all persons claiming the same, that this Court will, on the   day of   inst , if that day should be a day of jurisdiction, if not, on the next day of jurisdiction thereafter, proceed to the trial and condemnation thereof, should no claim be interposed for the same, and

I have cited the defendant Rogers within named, and the defendant Stubbs is not found in this district.

U. S. Marshal.

Dated 184

No. 146.—THE LIKE AGAINST SHIP, FREIGHT AND MASTER, FOR SEAMEN'S WAGES.

Southern District of New York, ss :

 .The President of the United States of America, *to the Marshal of the Southern District of New York, Greeting :* Whereas a libel in rem and personam, hath been filed in the District Court of the United States, for the Southern District of New York, on

[L. S.] the day of in the year of our Lord one thousand eight hundred and forty seven, by John C. Duffie, Alferd Sandford, Alexander Wilson, Benjamin Hoffman, Robert Fruss, and Charles McCarty, against the barque Childe Harold, and against the freights due for the cargo now or lately laden therein, and against Crosby master of said barque, for the reasons and causes in the said libel mentioned, and praying the usual process and monition of the said Court in that behalf to be made, and that the said master and all persons interested in the said barque or vessel, her tackle, &c. may be cited to answer the premises, and all proceedings being had, that the said barque or vessel, her tackle, &c. and freight may, for the causes in the said libel mentioned, be condemned to pay the demands of the libellant.

You are therefore hereby commanded, to attach the said barque or vessel, her tackle, &c. and to detain the same in your custody, until the further order of the Court respecting the same, and to attach said freight, and to give due notice to all persons claiming the said vessel and freight, or knowing or having any thing to say why the same should not be condemned pursuant to the prayer of the said libel, that they be and appear before the said Court, to be held in and for the Southern District of New York, on the day of at eleven o'clock in the forenoon of the same day, if the same shall be a day of jurisdiction, otherwise on the next day of jurisdiction thereafter, then and there to interpose a claim for the same, and to make their allegations in that behalf; and we do hereby further empower, and strictly charge and command you the said Marshal, that you cite the said Crosby, master of said vessel if he shall be found in your District, to be and appear before the said District Court, on the day of at the City Hall in the City of New York, then and there to answer the said libel, and to make his allegations in that behalf; and have you then there this writ, with your return thereon.

Witness the Honorable Samuel R. Betts, Judge of said Court, this day of in the year of our Lord one thousand eight hundred and and of our Independence the

A. B. Clerk.

C. D. Proctor.

No. 147—ATTACHMENT TO COMPEL OBEDIENCE TO AN ORDER OR DECREE.

The President of the United States to the Marshal of the Southern District of New York, greeting :—

Whereas in a certain cause, civil and maritime, in the District Court of the United States for the Southern District of New York, where A. B. is libellant against C. D., [or the ship or vessel, &c.,] the said court did, on the   day of   1850, by a decree made on that day, order and direct that [set forth the order] and whereas the said   neglected and refused to obey said decretal order, and thereupon the said court ordered and decreed that an attachment should issue against him to compel him to perform and obey the said decretal order. You are therefore commanded to attach and arrest the said   and him safely keep until he obey and perform the said decretal order, and [here specify the particular acts to be done,] and to return to the said Court what shall do in the premises, with this writ.

Witness, [teste as in other process.]
Proctor.   Clerk.

No. 148.—MARSHAL'S RETURN.

I have attached and arrested the within named   and have him now in my custody.

HENRY F. TALLMADGE, Marshal.

Stipulations.

No. 149.—LIBELLANT'S STIPULATION FOR COSTS AND EXPENSES.

District Court of the United States for the Southern District of New York.

STIPULATION ENTERED INTO PURSUANT TO THE RULES AND PRACTICE OF THIS COURT.

Whereas a libel was filed in this court, on the   day of   in the year of our Lord one thousand eight hundred and   by A. B., against   for the reasons and causes in the said libel mentioned, and the said A. B., and C. D. and E. F., his sureties, the parties hereto hereby consenting, that in case of default or contumacy on the part of the libellant or his sureties, execution for the sum of $100 (or $250) may issue against their goods, chattels and lands.

Now, therefore, it is hereby stipulated and agreed, for the benefit of whom it may concern, that the stipulalators undersigned are, and each of them is, hereby bound, in the sum of $100, (or $250,) conditioned that the libellant above named shall pay all costs and expenses which shall be awarded against him by the final decree of this court, or upon an appeal, by the Appellate Court.

A. B.
C. D.
E. F.

Taken and acknowledged, this   day $\rangle$
of   184 , before me, $\}$

Southern District of New York, ss :—

              party to the above stipulation, being duly sworn deposes and says that he is worth the sum of two (or five) hundred dollars over and above all his just debts and liabilities.

    Sworn this   day $\rangle$
    of.   185 , before me, $\}$

No. 150.—Defendant's stipulations for costs and expenses under the 25th rule.

District Court of the United States, for the Southern District of New York.

STIPULATION ENTERED INTO PURSUANT TO THE RULES AND PRACTICE OF THIS COURT.

Whereas a libel was filed in this Court, on the   day   of   in the year of our Lord one thousand eight hundred and by A. B. against C. D. for the reasons and causes in the said libel mentioned ; and whereas the said C. D. has appeared in said suit and the said C. D. and E. F., his surety, the parties hereto hereby consenting and agreeing, that, in case of default or contumacy on the part of the defendant or his sureties, execution may issue against their goods, chattels and lands, for the sum of   hundred   dollars :

    Now, therefore, it is hereby stipulated and agreed for the benefit of whom it may concern, that the stipulators undersigned shall be, and are bound in the sum of   hundred   dollars, conditioned that the defendant above named chall pay all costs and expenses which shall be awarded against him in the suit upon the final adjudication thereof or by any interlocutory order in the process of this suit.

    Taken and acknowledged, this   day $\rangle$
    of   185 before me, $\}$

Southern District of New York, ss.

          party to the above stipulation, being duly sworn, deposes and says that he is worth the sum of   dollars over and above all his just debts and liabilities.

    Sworn this   day   of   185 , before me,

No. 151.—Claimant's stipulation for costs and expenses.

District Court of the United States for the Southern District of New York.

STIPULATION ENTERED INTO PURSUANT TO THE RULES AND PRACTICE OF THIS COURT.

Whereas a libel was filed in this Court, on the   day of   in the the year of our Lord one thousand eight hundred

and   by A. B , against   for the reasons and
causes in the said libel mentioned, and whereas a claim has been filed in the
said cause by C. D., and the said C. D. and E. F. his surety, the parties
hereto hereby consenting, that in case of default or contumacy on the part
of the claimant or his sureties, execution for the sum of $250 may issue
against their goods, chattels and lands.

Now, therefore, it is hereby stipulated and agreed for the benefit of whom
it may concern, that the stipulators undersigned are, and each of them is,
hereby bound, in the sum of $250, conditioned that the claimant above
named, shall pay all costs and expenses which shall be awarded against
him by the final decree of this Court, or upon an appeal, by the Appellate
Court.

A B.

C. D.

E. F.

Taken and acknowledged, this   day ⎰
    of   185 , before me,   ⎱

Southern District of New York, ss. :—

                          party to the above stipulation, being duly sworn
deposes and says that he is worth the sum of five hundred dollars over and
above all his just debts and liabilities.

    Sworn this   day ⎰
      of   18s   , before me, ⎱

No. 152.—INTERVENOR'S STIPULATION FOR COSTS, EXPENSES, AND DA-
MAGES.

District Court of the United States for the Southern District of New York.

STIPULATION ENTERED INTO PURSUANT TO THE RULES AND PRACTICE OF THIS
COURT.

Whereas a libel was filed in this Court, on the   day
of   in the year of our Lord one thousand eight hundred
and   by A. B., against   for the reasons and
causes in the said libel mentioned, and whereas C. D. has intervened for his
interest, and the said C. D. and E. F. his surety, the parties hereto, hereby consenting and agreeing, that in case of default or contumacy on the
part of the said intervenor or his sureties, execution may issue against their
goods, chattels and lands, for the sum of $250.

Now, therefore, it is hereby stipulated and agreed, for the benefit of whom
it may concern, that the stipulators undersigned are, and each of them is,
bound, in the sum of $250, conditioned that the intervenor above named
shall abide by the final decree rendered in the cause, and shall pay all such

costs, expenses and damages as shall be awarded against him by the fina
decree of this Court, or of the Appellate Court.

A. B.
C. D.
E. F.

Taken and acknowledged, this   day }
    of   185   , before me,   }

Southern District of New York, ss. :—

         party to the above stipulation, being duly sworn
deposes and says that he is worth the sum of five hundred dollars over and
above all his just debts and liabilities.

    Sworn this   day }
    of   185   , before me,   }

No. 153.—Defendant's stipulation to appear and pay the decree—
given on arrest or appearance.

District Court of the United States for the Southern District of New York.

STIPULATION ENTERED INTO PURSUANT TO THE RULES AND PRACTICE OF THIS
COURT.

Whereas a libel was filed in this Court, on the   day
of   in the year of our Lord one thousand eight hundred
and   by A. B., against C. D. for the reasons and
causes in the said libel mentioned, and the said C. D. and E. F. and G. H.,
his sureties, the parties hereto, hereby consenting and agreeing, that in case
of default or contumacy on the part of the said defendant or his sureties,
execution may issue against their goods, chattels and lands, for the sum of
     dollars :

Now, therefore, it is hereby stipulated and agreed, for the benefit of whom
it may concern, that the stipulators undersigned are, and each of them is,
bound in the sum of   dollars, conditioned that the defendant above named, shall appear in the suit and abide by all orders of the
court, interlocutory or final, in the cause, and pay the money awarded by
the final decree rendered therein in this Court, or in any Appellate Court.

A. B.
C. D.
E. F.

Taken and acknowledged, this   day }
    of   185   , before me,   }

Southern District of New York, ss. :—

         parties to the above stipulation, being duly sworn,
depose and say each for himself that he is worth the sum of   hundred
dollars over and above all his just debts and liabilities.

    Sworn this   day }
    of   185   , before me,   }

No. 154.—Claimant's stipulation to abide by and pay the decree.

District Court of the United States, for the Southern District of New York.

STIPULATION ENTERED INTO PURSUANT TO THE RULES AND PRACTICE
OF THIS COURT.

Whereas, a libel was filed in this Court, on the   day of   in the year of our Lord one thousand eight hundred and   by A. B. against   for the reasons and causes in the said libel mentioned, and a claim has been filed by C. D., and the said claimant, and E. F. and G. H. his sureties, the parties hereto hereby consenting and agreeing, that in case of default or contumacy on the part of the claimant or his sureties, execution may issue against their goods, chattels and lands, for the sum of dollars.

Now, therefore, it is hereby stipulated and agreed for the benefit of whom it may concern, that the stipulators undersigned are, and each of them is bound, in the sum of   dollars, conditioned that claimant above named, shall abide by, and pay the money awarded by the final decree rendered in the cause by this Court, or in case of appeal, by the Appellate Court.

Taken and acknowledged, this   day   }
of   185   , before me, } ·

Southern District of New York, ss :

                 parties to the above stipulation, being duly sworn depose and say each for himself that he is worth the sum of   hundred dollars over and above all his just debts and liabilities.

Sworn this   day }
of   185   , before me, }

No. 155.—Stipulation for agreed or appraised value.

District Court of the United States for the Southern District of New York.

In Admiralty.

STIPULATION ENTERED INTO PURSUANT TO THE RULES AND PRACTICE OF
THIS COURT.

Whereas, a libel was filed on the   day of   in the year of our Lord one thousand eight hundred and   by A. B. against   for the reasons and causes in the said libel mentioned ; and whereas the same is now in the custody of the Marshal, under the process issued in pursuance of the prayer of said libel, and is of the value of   dollars, as appears by a consent (*or appraisement*) now on file in said Court ; and the parties hereto hereby consenting and agreeing that, in case of default or contumacy on the part of the claimant or his sureties, execution may issue against their goods, chattels and lands :

Now, therefore, it is hereby stipulated, for the benefit of whom it may concern, that the stipulators undersigned, and each of them, is bound in the sum of dollars, conditioned that they shall at any time, upon the interlocutory and final order or Decree of the said District Court, or of any Appellate Court to which the above-named suit may proceed, and upon notice of such order or decree, to said claimant, or Esquire, his proctor, pay into Court the full value aforesaid, and abide by, and pay the money awarded by the final decree rendered by this Court or the Appellate Court, if any appeal intervene.

Taken and Acknowledged, this ·day
of 185 before me, $\}$

U. S. Commissioner.

Southern District of New York, ss :

party to the above Stipulation, being duly sworn deposes and says that he is worth the sum of
dollars, over and above all his just debts and liabilities.

to, this day
185 before me, $\}$

U. S. Commissioner.

No. 156.—PENAL BOND TO THE MARSHAL ON ARREST OF THE PERSON.

Know all men by these presents, that we, C. D., E. F., and G. H., are held and firmly bound unto Henry F. Tallmadge, Marshal of the Southern District of New York, in the sum of dollars, lawful money of the United States of America, to be paid to the said Henry F. Tallmadge, his executors, administrators or assigns; to which payment, well and truly to be made, we bind ourselves and each of us, jointly and severally, our and each of our heirs, executors and administrators, firmly by these presents. Sealed with our seals. Dated this day of in the year of our Lord one thousand eight hundred and

Whereas, a libel has been filed in the District Court of the United States for the Southern District of New York, on the day of 185 by A. B. against the above bounden C. D., in a certain action, civil and maritime, for wages, therein alleged to be due and owing to the said libellant, amounting to twenty-seven dollars.

The condition of this obligation is such, that if the above bounden C. D. shall appear in the said suit, before the said District Court of the United States for the Southern District of New York, on the day of at the City Hall, in the City of New York, and abide by all orders of the Court, interlocutory or final in the cause, and pay the money awarded by the final decree rendered therein, in the said Court, or in any Appellate

Court, then the above obligation to be void, otherwise to remain in full force and virtue.

Sealed and delivered in }
   the presence of   }

No. 157.—JUSTIFICATION OF BAIL.

Southern District of New York, ss :

        being duly sworn, says, that he resides at No. and that he is worth the sum of over and above all his just debts and liabilities.

Sworn before me, this }
   day of   185   }

No. 158.—BOND UNDER THE ACT OF 1847.

Know all men by these presents, That we, C. D., E. F. and G. H., are held and firmly bound unto (*the libellant*) in the sum of (*double the amount claimed in the libel*) dollars lawful money of the United States of America, to be paid to the said   his executors, administrators or assigns; to which payment, well and truly to be made, we bind ourselves and each of us, jointly and severally, our and each of our heirs, executors and administrators, firmly by these presents. Sealed with our seals. Dated this   day   in the year of our Lord one thousand eight hundred and

Whereas, a libel has been filed in the District Court of the United States for the Southern District of New York, on the   day of   185   by   against the ship or vessel,   in a certain action, &c. civil and maritime, for   therein alleged to be due and owing to the said libellant, amounting to (*the amount claimed in the libel.*)

The condition of this obligation is such, that if the above bounden shall abide and answer the decree of the Court in such cause, then the above obligation to be void, otherwise to remain in full force and virtue.

Sealed and delivered }
   in the presence of }

No. 159—JUSTIFICATION.

Southern District of New York, ss.

       being duly sworn says, that he resides at No.   and that he is worth the sum of   over and above all his just debts and liabilities.

Sworn before me, this   day of   185

No. 160.—Certificate of approval by the judge, or the collector of this port.

I hereby approve of the sureties in the within bond.
Dated, &c.

(*Signed by the Judge or the Collector.*)

No. 161.—Stipulation for the safe return of a vessel in a suit by a part owner.

District Court of the United States for the Southern District of New York.

Filed the   day of   185

STIPULATION FOR LIBELLANT'S COSTS ENTERED INTO PURSUANT TO THE RULES OF PRACTICE OF THIS COURT.

Whereas, a libel was filed in this Court, on the   day of
in the year of our Lord one thousand eight hundred and fifty
by A. B., owner of   of the ship or vessel called the   her
tackle, &c., against the said ship or vessel, her tackle, &c., for the reasons
and causes in the said libel mentioned, which said vessel, her tackle, &c., is
of the value of   dollars, as appears by the consent (*or appraisement*) on file in said cause, and C. D. and E. F. the other owners of
said vessel, and G. H. and I. J. their sureties, parties hereto, hereby consenting and agreeing, that in case of default on the part of the libellant or his
sureties, execution may issue against their goods, chattels and lands, for the
sum of   dollars.

Now, therefore, it is hereby stipulated and agreed for the benefit of whom
it may concern, that the stipulators undersigned are, and each of them is
bound, in the sum of (*double the value of libellant's share,*)   dollars,
conditioned that the said vessel shall safely return from her present intended
voyage, to the port of New York.

Taken and Acknowledged, this   day
of   185 , before me,

U. S. Commissioner.

Southern District of New York, ss:

            parties to the above stipulation, being duly
depose and say each for himself that he is worth the sum of
hundred dollars over and above all his just debts and liabilities.

to, this   day
of   185   before me,

U. S. Commissioner.

No. 162.—Consent to stipulate for property without process.

District Court of the United States for the Southern District of New York.

John Jones,
vs.
The Steamer Eureka, her engine, tackle, &c.

A libel having been filed in this cause, I hereby consent that no process issue thereon to arrest the said vessel, provided that, in the course of this day, A. B., the owner thereof, file a claim, and with C. D., as surety, enter into the usual stipulations in the same manner as if the said vessel were arrested, and were to be discharged on stipulation.

Dec. 4, 1849.

\E. F., Proctor for Libellant.

No. 163.—The like, in a different form.

Title of the Cause.

A libel having been filed in this cause, and A. B., the owner of said vessel, having, without process, filed his claim to the same, and with C. D., as surety, having entered into the usual stipulations, it is agreed that the said cause shall, in all things, proceed as if the said vessel had been arrested and regularly discharged on stipulation.

Dec. 4, 1849.

E. F., Proctor for Libellant.
G. H., Proctor for Claimant.

No. 164.—Consent that a vessel be discharged on stipulation.

Title of the Cause.

The ship Wallace having been arrested on the process issued in this cause, we consent that, on filing the usual stipulation for costs, and the usual stipulation to appear, abide, and perform the decree in the sum of   dollars, to be entered into by A. B., the owner or master of said ship, and C. D. and E. F., as sureties, and on filing a claim, and on complying with the rules of the Court as to the fees of the officers of Court, the said ship be discharged from custody and arrest.

Dec. 5, 1849.

G. H., Proctor for Libellants.

No. 165.—Consent to fixing the value without appraisement and discharging the property from custody.

Title of the Cause.

I hereby consent that the value of the brig Rover, her tackle, apparel, and furniture, be fixed at six thousand dollars, without appraisement, and that, on filing a claim and the necessary stipulations for costs and value, &c., complying with the rules of the Court as to fees, the said brig be discharged from custody.

G. H., Proctor for Libellant.

No. 166.—Claim to a portion of the cargo.

To the Honorable Samuel R. Betts, Judge of the District Court of the United States for the Southern District of New York :

The claim of David Jones, of the city of New York, merchant, to nine cases of merchandise marked D. J., 1 to 9, a portion of the cargo of the brig Roarer, now in custody of the marshal of this district at the suit of John Livingston and others, alleges as follows:

That he is the true and bona fide owner of said nine cases of merchandise, and that no other person is the owner thereof.

And thereupon the said claimant prays that this Honorable Court will be pleased to decree a restitution of the same to him, and otherwise right and justice to administer in the premises.

DAVID JONES.

Sworn May 5th, 1843,
   before me,
      GEO. W. MORTON, U. S. Commissioner.
   A. B., Proctor and Advocate.

No. 167.—Claim to a vessel—*Vid. ante, page* 257.

No. 168.—A claim by the united states on the ground of forfeiture —*Vid ante, No.* 13, *page* 436.

No. 169.—An answer—*ante, page* 262.

No. 170·—A claim and answer—*ante, No.* 9, *page* 431 ; *No.* 12, *page* 435; *No.* 59, *page* 464 ; *No.* 61, *page* 465 ; *No.* 63, *page* 467 ; *No.* 65, *page* 468.

No. 171.—A claim, answer and exception to the jurisdiction.

To the Honorable Samuel R. Betts, Judge of the District Court of the United States, for the Southern District of New York.

The claim, answer and exceptions of Herman Schultze of said district master of the schooner Oscar Jones, intervening for his interest in the said schooner, her tackle, apparel and furniture to the libel of —— Cammerden, alleges as follows :

First. That the said Schultze as master, claims the said schooner, her tackle, apparel and furniture, and further alleges and answers as follows :

Second. That he is entirely ignorant of the matters alleged in the first and second articles of said libel contained.

72

Third. That at the time the said vessel was seized by reason of the libel of the said Cammerden, he had and still has an interest in the said vessel, to the amount of five hundred and sixty dollars and forty nine cents, inasmuch as he had served on board the said schooner, as mate from the   day of   one thousand eight hundred and forty   to the day of   one thousand eight hundred and forty   at the wages of   dollars per month, amounting in the whole to the sum of one thousand and forty two dollars and   cents, which has never been paid to him, and is still due. And also for certain moneys advanced by this claimant to pay the wages of the crew of the said schooner, and other necessary advances during the voyage now broken up by the process of this Court, amounting to the sum of four hundred and seventeen dollars and eighty five cents, which wages and advances were a lien on said schooner and this defendant having advanced the same is subrogated to the rights of said seamen, and he has filed his libel in this Honorable Court to enforce his said lien.

Fourth. That this Honorable Court has no jurisdiction of the matters contained in the said libel, the same not being matters of Admiralty and Maritime jurisdiction, the said libel being filed in this Court to enforce a certain decree or judgement rendered by a State Court of the City of New Orleans in Louisiana, in a suit on promissory notes in a personal action at law, and not by any Court of Admiralty, nor in a cause within the Admiralty and Maritime jurisdiction, nor on or for any cause, civil and maritime; and this claimant and respondent prays the same advantage thereof as if the same were separately, and formally pleaded to said libel.

Fifth. That the privilege and preference on the said schooner granted in the aforesaid decree, if any such exist or was granted, was so granted without said schooner being attached or in the possession or custody of said Court, and while the said schooner was absent at sea in foreign waters, ports and places, and the same could not and did not affect said schooner or any person except her owner, nor could it have any effect to give the plaintiff therein any preference over other persons, nor be enforced except within the jurisdiction of said Court which rendered the same and by the process thereof.

Sixth. That if the said claim of the said libellant be a lien on said vessel, the same is to be deferred to the claims of this claimant, which are for services rendered to said vessel in navigating and preserving her and bringing her safely to the United States, and the lien by hypothecation, decree or otherwise, in said promissory notes was subject to the payment of such wages and advances, and his said wages as mate were a lien prior in point of time to the said promissory notes and the decree thereon.

HERMAN SHULTZE.

Sworn to before me this   day of May 1849.

GEORGE W. MORTON, U. S. Commissioner.

C. L. BENEDICT, Proctor.

E. C. BENEDICT, Advocate.

No. 172.—Answer of a garnishee denying the possession of goods or credits.

To the Honorable Samuel R. Betts, Judge of the District Court of the United States for the Southern District of New York:

The answer of James W. Elwell, surviving partner of the firm of Elwell & Co., garnishee in the libel and complaint of Thomas Gould against John Gwin, in a cause of damage, civil and maritime, alleges as follows:

That it is not true that this respondent ever aided or assisted in concealing or seeking to conceal the said John Gwin or his property, and that it is not true that he held, at the time of the service of the process in this suit, or at any time since, any goods, chattels, choses in action, property, credits, or effects in his hands or under his control, belonging to the said John Gwin, or in which he has any interest.

Wherefore this respondent prays that he may be hence dismissed, and that his costs and expenses may be decreed to him.

No. 173.—Replication to an answer by a garnishee.

To the Honorable, &c.,

The replication of Thomas Gould, libellant, to the answer of James W. Elwell, survivor of Elwell & Co., alleges that he will aver, maintain, and prove his said libel to be true, certain, and sufficient, and that the said James W. Elwell, survivor, &c., at the time of the service of the process in this suit, in his hands goods, chattels, credits, and effects of said John Given, and he prays as in his said libel he has already prayed.

A. Nash,
Proctor for Libellant.

No. 174.—Interrogatories to be propounded to a garnishee.

Interrogatories to be propounded to James W. Elwell, garnishee in the libel of Thomas Goold against John Given.

First Interrogatory.—What is your name, place of residence, and occupation?

Second Interrogatory.—Do you know the defendant John Given, and how long have you known him, and what has been his occupation since you first knew him?

Third Interrogatory.—Have you not, during your acquaintance with him, been his consignee, merchant and agent in the city of New York, and has he not deposited in your hands, from time to time, sums of money, freights, and passage money, belonging to him? state the same fully and particularly.

Fourth Interrogatory.—Did he not leave in your hands, on a previous voyage, a sum of money as security to you, for your liability for him as bail, and is not the same still in your hands ?

Fifth Interrogatory.—Did he not leave in your hands this present voyage his chronometer and other nautical instruments for safe keeping, while he remained in port, and were they not, or some of the same, in your possession at the time of the service of the process in this cause upon you ?

Sixth Interrogatory.—Have you not in your possession, or under your control, some other property, goods, chattels, or funds, belonging to the said John Given?—State fully and particularly.

Seventh Interrogatory.—Have you not in your hands, or under your control, some notes, drafts, or other bills receivable, or debts, or choses in action, or credits, belonging to said John Given, or in which he is interested ?—State fully and particularly.

Eighth Interrogatory.—Is not the said Given part owner of some vessel, and have you not in your hands funds or property belonging to the owners of said vessel ?—State fully and particularly.

A. NASH,

Proctor for Libellant.

No. 175.—ANSWERS BY A GARNISHEE TO INTERROGATORIES PROPOUNDED TO HIM.

Answers of James W. Elwell, garnishee, to the interrogatories of Thomas Goold.

To the first interrogatory.—My names is James W. Elwell—I reside in New York, and am a merchant.

To the second interrogatory.—I have known the defendant two years, during which time he has been a ship master.

—And so on, answering fully and truly to each interrogatory.

JAMES W. ELWELL.

Sworn, June 10th, 1848,
    before me,

GEORGE W. MORTON, Commissioner.

No. 176.—AMENDMENTS.

To the Honorable Samuel R. Betts, Judge of the District Court of the United States for the Southern District of New York.

Amendments to the libel of William Bonell, against the ship Henry Clay, her tackle, apparel and furniture, and against Henry Schrever, late master in a cause of wages, civil and maritime.

First. Insert, after the word " October," in the fifth article, the words following—" and before the expiration of the voyage contracted for by your libellant."

Second. Add at the conclusion of the fifth article the words following—

" and when the said ship Henry Clay having performed her above mentioned intended voyage, arrived in safety on the ⟶ day of February last."

Third. Insert, after the word "vessel," in the sixth article, the words following—" and the said master, wages during the voyage aforesaid, and until the arrival of the said ship in New York " And

Fourth. Strike out the words " seventy-four," in the sixth article, and insert in lieu thereof " ninety-three."

BURR & BENEDICT, Proctors.

BURR, Advocate.

No. 177.—A SUPPLEMENTAL AND AMENDATORY LIBEL.

To the Honorable Samuel R. Betts, &c.

The supplemental and amendatory libel of A. B. against the brig Lowel, her tackle, &c., and against all persons intervening, &c., and against E. F., master, alleges as follows :

First, &c —(*Allege the facts as amended, in articles, and add prayer as amended, in same form as an original libel.*)

(*Sign and verify like original answer.*)

Orders Ex Parte.

No. 178.—THE ORDER OF THE JUDGE FOR BAIL, TO BE ENDORSED ON THE LIBEL.

Title of the Cause.

On filing the within libel, and otherwise complying with the rules of the Court, let a warrant of arrest issue in this cause against the defendant, and let him be held to bail in five hundred dollars.

SAM'L R. BETTS, Judge.

Dec. 18, 1849.

No. 179.—ORDER STAYING PROCEEDINGS TO GIVE TIME TO MAKE A MOTION.

Title of the Cause.

On the foregoing affidavit and notice of motion, let all proceedings in this cause, on the part of the libellant, be stayed for a sufficient time to make said motion, and have the order of the Court thereon.

SAM'L R. BETTS, Judge.

June 5, 1849.

No. 180.—ORDER ENLARGING TIME.

Title of the Cause.

Let the time to answer the libel——(*to reply—to answer the interrogatories—to except to the libel, or answer, or interrogatories*)—be extended days.

June 8, 1849. ⟶ SAM'L R. BETTS, Judge.

No. 181.—The caption of orders and decrees.

At a stated (or special) term of the District Court of the United States of America, for the Southern District of New York, held at the City Hall, in the City of New York, on Tuesday, the third day of January, in the year of our Lord one thousand eight hundred and forty-three.

Present—The Honorable Samuel R. Betts, District Judge.

A. B.,
  vs.
C. D. }

No. 182.—Order of condemnation by default and reference to a commissioner.

The marshal having returned, on the monition issued in the above entitled cause, that he had attached the said vessel, her tackle, apparel and furniture, and had given due notice to all persons claiming the same, that the court would, on this day, proceed to the trial and condemnation of the said vessel, her tackle, &c., should no claim be interposed for the same : whereupon, on motion of   Esquire, proctor for the libellants, proclamation was made for all persons interested in the said vessel, her tackle, &c., to appear and interpose their claims; and no person appearing, on like motion it was further ordered, that the defaults of all persons be and the same are accordingly hereby entered, and that the said vessel, her tackle, &c., be condemned to pay the demands of the libellant.

And it is further ordered, that it be referred to a Commissioner of this Court to ascertain and compute the amount due the libellant, for freight (*or other cause*) and to report the same to this Court, with all convenient speed.

No. 183.—Decree for the libellant on hearing with reference to compute.

This cause having been heard on the pleadings and proofs, and due deliberation being had, it is ordered, adjudged and decreed, that the libellant recover the amount of his wages [or freight, or materials, &c.,] in this cause ; and it is further ordered, that it be referred to a commissioner to ascertain and compute the amount due to the libellant in the premises, and that he report the same to this Court, with all convenient speed.

No. 184.—The like in a cause of damage, with reference to take and report the testimony on the amount of damage.

This cause having been heard on the pleadings and proofs, and due deliberation being had, it is ordered, adjudged and decreed, that the libellant recover his damages for the assault and battery [or collision, or other cause,] mentioned in the libel, and that it be referred to a commissioner to take the testimony of the amount of such damages, and to report the same to this Court with all convenient speed.

No. 185.—Order of confrmation of the report of a commissioner, and final decree, with judgment against the bail.

On reading and filing the report of George W. Morton, United States Commissioner, to whom the above matter was referred, by which there is reported due the libellant for the wages [*or freights, or other cause,*] de-- manded in the libel, the sum of dollars: On motion of Proctor for the libellant, it is ordered that the report be in all things confirmed, and that the defendant pay to the libellant in this action the amount so reported due to him, together with his costs to be taxed.

And on like motion, it is further ordered, that a summary judgment be and the same is hereby entered against the said A. B., the principal and C. D , the surety, for the sum of dollars, the amount of the bond and stipulation given to the Marshal, on the arrest of the defendant; aud that the libellant have execution thereon to satisfy this decree.

No. 186.—Final decree for a sum certain, with costs.

This case having been heard on the pleadings and proofs, and having been argued by the advocates for the respective parties, and due deliberation being had in the premises, it is now ordered, adjudged and decreed, by the Court, that the defendant pay to the libellant the sum of two hundred dollars, with his costs to be taxed.

No. 187—Decree on the merits with reference to a commissioner.

This cause having been heard on the pleadings in the cause, and having been argued by the advocates of the respective parties, and due deliberation being had, it is now ordered, adjudged and decreed, that the libellant recover against the defendant the amount due by the charter party, [or bill of lading —or bottomry—or respondentia bond—or for the materials—or for the supplies mentioned in the pleadings,] and that it be referred to a commissioner to ascertain the amount so due, after making all proper allowances, and that he report the same to the Court, with all convenient speed.

No. 188.—Final decree of forfeiture on a libel of information.

The monition issued in this cause, having been heretofore returned, and the usual proclamation having been made, and the default of all persons being duly entered, it is thereupon, on motion of Ogden Hoffman, Esq.,

Attorney for the United States, ordered, sentenced, and decreed, by the Court now here, and his Honor the District Judge, by virtue of the power and authority in him vested, doth hereby order, sentence and decree, that the four cases of broad cloths, mentioned in the libel in this cause, be, and the same accordingly are condemned as forfeited to the United States.

And upon like motion, it is further ordered, sentenced, and decreed, that the Clerk of this Court issue a decree of *venditioni exponas* to the Marshal of the district, returnable upon the   day of   next. And that upon the return thereof, the Clerk distribute the proceeds according to law.

No. 189.—FINAL DECREE FOR THE DEFENDANT IN A POSSESSORY AND PETITORY SUIT.

This cause having been heard on the pleadings and proofs, and argued by the Advocates of the respective parties, and due deliberation being had in the premises, and it appearing to the Court that the claimant has made out a sufficient and valid title to the vessel, it is now ordered, adjudged and decreed by the Court, that the libel filed in the cause be dismissed, with costs, to be taxed against the libellant. And on motion of the Proctors for the claimant, it is further ordered, that unless an appeal be taken to this de-cree, within the time limited and prescribed by the rules of this Court, the claimant's stipulations be cancelled.

No. 190.—FINAL DECREE ON A PEREMPTORY EXCEPTION TO THE LIBEL.

This cause having been heard on exceptions filed by the libellant to the plea interposed by the respondent, and having been argued by the Advocates for the respective parties, and on due deliberation, the Court doth now order, adjudge and decree, that the exceptions filed by the libellant to the plea of the respondent of a former trial and decree, upon the subject matter of this suit, be overruled with costs to be taxed, and that the libel of the libellant be decreed, barred, and be dismissed, with costs to be taxed, unless the libellant shall elect to reply to said plea, and in that case, that he have leave to file a replication thereto, within ten days, on payment of the costs created by such exception to be taxed.

No. 191.—DECREE OVERRULING EXCEPTIONS TO AN ANSWER.

This cause coming on to be heard on exceptions filed by the libellant to the answer of the respondent, and having been argued by the Advocates for the respective parties, and due deliberation having been had in the pre-mises, it is now ordered and decreed by the Court, that the exceptions of the libellant to the answer of the respondent be disallowed and overruled, with costs to be taxed.

No. 192.—DECREE SETTLING PRIORITY IN DISTRIBUTION OF PROCEEDS
IN COURT, IN SEVERAL CAUSES.

*Titles of all the Causes affecting
the proceeds in Court.*

No exception being taken to the Clerk's Reports in either of the above cases, and the question being agitated which, if any, of the parties is entitled to priority of payment, and also, whether costs are to have precedence in satisfaction, where the debts are only entitled to *pro rata* payment, and the Court having been moved to decree a distribution of the proceeds of the brig Triumph, her tackle, &c., now in the registry, and Advocates for the respective parties having been heard, and due deliberation had in the premises, it is ordered and decreed, that the demand of Elisha B. Baker, for services rendered as pilot, together with his taxed costs, be first paid out of the fund in Court; that then the amounts reported due the several libellants in the suits on which the vessel was arrested, be paid them respectively, together with their taxed costs, according to the order in which their attachments were served on the vessel. And that the several petitioners be afterwards paid rateably out of the surplus, after satisfaction of the other suitors, together with their costs to be taxed.

No. 193.—DECREE FOR LIBELLANT ON A CHARTER PARTY.

This cause having been heard upon the pleadings and proofs, and the premises being considered, and it appearing to the Court that the cargo of the brig Virginia, was well and securely stowed, and was, on her arrival at this port, delivered to the respondent, pursuant to the tenor and effect of the charter party in the pleading mentioned, and in good condition, except 4500 segars, injured by the dangers of the sea: and it further appearing to the Court that the libellant brought in the said vessel from Havana to New York, boxes of segars and bales of tobacco laden in the cabin of the said vessel, and not embraced within the provisions of the charter party, it is therefore considered by the Court, that the libellant recover his affreightment, in this case due and stipulated by the said charter party, and also the accustomed freight for the said boxes of segars and bales of tobacco, laden in the cabin of said vessel; and that it be referred to the Clerk to ascertain and compute the amount due according to the tenor of this decree; and it is further ordered, that in taking such account, the Clerk allow the respondent all proper credits for payments made pursuant to the charter party, and also credit for the value at Havana of one quarter box of segars, laden in the cabin, unless the respondent elects to take the one quarter box delivered from the vessel to the public store, it not having the proper mark of the respondent, corresponding with the bill of lading. It is further ordered, that the libellant recover his costs to be taxed.

73

No. 194.—Decree on special motion dismissing libel when process had improvidently issued.

Mr. Burr, Proctor for the claimants, reads and files affidavit of notice of motion, and affidavit of service, and moves that the vessel be discharged from custody.

Mr. Zabriskie, Proctor for the libellant, reads and files two affidavits, and argues in opposition to the motion.

Ordered, that the libel be dismissed and the vessel discharged from custody of the Marshal forthwith.

No. 195.—Decree for wages and short allowance for a part of the voyage, and forfeiture of the residue.

This cause having been re-argued upon the merits, by consent of the counsel for both the parties, and due deliberation being had in the premises, it is now ordered, adjudged, and decreed, that the libellant recover for the eight months service on board the vessel, up to his payment, in Hamburgh, the sum of eighty dollars, and for short allowance during that period, thirteen 33-100ths dollars—in the whole, ninety-three 33-100ths dollars, deducting therefrom his advance of twelve dollars, and nine dollars paid him as per receipt, amounting to the sum of twenty-one dollars, and that the defendant pay to the libellant the balance, amounting to seventy-two 33-100ths dollars, together with his costs to be taxed. And that the libellant's wages earned on the circuitous voyage from Hamburgh to Buenos Ayres, be decreed forfeited for desertion at the latter place.

No. 196.—Notice of reference.

District Court of the United States for the Southern District New of York.

A. B,
  vs.   } *Notice of Reference.*
C. D.

In conformity with the order entered in the above entitled cause, you will please to take notice, that the reference ordered therein, will be proceeded with, before me, at my office at the United States Courts, on the   day of   at   o'clock in the   noon of that day, at which time and place you are hereby notified to attend with the testimony you may have to offer in the matter referred.

  Dated, New-York, the   day of   A. D. 18.

           Yours, &c.,

                George W. Morton,

                    U. S. Commissioner.

To E. F., Proctor for Libellant.
G. H., Proctor for Defendant.

No. 197.—REPORT OF COMMISSIONER ON A GENERAL ORDER TO COMPUTE.

District Court of the United States for the Southern District of New York.

A. B.,
    vs.   } *Commissioner's Report.*
C. D.

In pursuance of a decretal order made in the above entitled cause, on the day of   in the year of our Lord one thousand eight hundred and   by which, among other things, it was referred to the undersigned, one of the Commissioners of this Court, to ascertain and compute the amount due the libellant for materials, [*or other cause,*] and to report thereon to this Court with all convenient speed.

I, Charles W. Newton, the Commissioner to whom the matter was referred, do report that I have been attended by the Proctor for the libellant and the Proctor for the defendant, and have taken and examined the testimony offered in support of the libellant's claim, and also that offered in reduction thereof, and do find that there is due to the libellant the sum of   dollars.

Dated the   day of   A. D. 18

All which is respectfully submitted.

CHAS. W. NEWTON,
U. S. Commissioner.

E. F., Proctor for Libellant.

No. 198.—REPORT OF A COMMISSIONER ON AN ORDER OF REFERENCE TO TAKE AND REPORT THE TESTIMONY AS TO THE AMOUNT OF DAMAGES.

District Court of the United States for the Southern District of New York.

A. B.,
    vs.   }
C. D.

I, George W. Morton, a Commissioner to whom it was referred, to take and report the testimony of the amount of damages in this cause, do report that I have been attended by the Proctors for the respective parties, and have examined all the witnesses which have been produced before me, and they gave the following testimony :

John Jones, a witness for the libellant, being sworn, testified that, &c.—*and so on with the other witnesses.*

All which is respectfully submitted.

GEORGE W. MORTON,
U. S. Commissioner.

E. F., Proctor for Libellant.

No. 199.—REPORT OF A COMMISSIONER ON A SPECIAL ORDER OF REFERENCE—REPORTING THE TESTIMONY.

U. S. District Court.

VALENTINE LARA, *vs.* The brig HENRY BUCK, her tackle, &c.	*Commissioner's Report, under the order of Court, of June,* 1847.

In pursuance of a decretal order made in the above entitled cause, by which, among other things, it was referred to a Commissioner to ascertain and report the amount due to the libellant, and it was ordered, that the claimant have leave to strike the name of David Woodside from the claim and answer filed in the cause, and also have leave to examine him as a witness on the reference in this cause, before the Commissioner, subject to all legal exceptions :

I, George W. Morton, the Commissioner before whom the reference was had, do report, that I have been attended by the Proctors for the libellant and the claimant, and have taken and examined the testimony offered by the respective parties, and do find, on the testimony of David Woodside, that the claimants are entitled to credits sufficient, with the amount paid into Court by them, to cover the amount decreed the libellant, and that there is nothing due the libellant beyond the amount paid into Court by the claimants.

At the request of the Proctor for the claimants, I have annexed to this report all the testimony taken under the orders of reference in the cause, together with a copy of the Judge's minutes of testimony taken on the hearing.

Dated December 4th, 1847.

All which is respectfully submitted.

GEORGE W. MORTON,
U. S. Commissioner.

A. NASH, Proctor for the Libellant.

Exceptions.

No. 200.—EXCEPTIONS BY THE LIBELLANTS TO THE FOREGOING REPORT.

U. S. District Court.

VALENTINE LARA, *vs.* The brig HENRY BUCK, &c.	*Exceptions to Commissioner's Report.*

The libellant excepts to the Commissioner's Report made under the order of the Court, entered in this cause, in June last.

First. Because the witness, David Woodside, who was examined before the said Commissioner, as a witness for the claimants, was, at the time of his examination and cross-examination, a part owner of the vessel, and therefore an incompetent witness for the vessel,

Second. Because the witness, David Woodside, was interested in the event of the suit.

Third. Because the said Commissioner has not in his said Report, stated the amount of the credits which he allowed to the claimants, on the testimony of said Woodside.

BURR & BENEDICT,
Proctors for Libellants.

No 201.—EXCEPTIONS BY A DEFENDANT TO THE REPORT OF THE CLERK OR A COMMISSIONER.

United States District Court.

RAMAN DE ZALDO, *ads.* ELISHA BURGESS.

The respondent hereby excepts to the report of the Clerk made herein, and by him this day filed, for the following causes, that is to say—

First. Because the said Clerk hath not in his said report, allowed as a credit to him, the said respondent, the sum of twenty-five dollars, duly paid to Captain Farnham, by him the said respondent, as appears by the testimony taken in this cause.

Second. Because the said Clerk hath not, in his said report, allowed as a credit to him the said respondent, the sum of one hundred and six dollars and seventy-five cents, duly paid to Captain Farnham, by the agent and consignee of this respondent, at Havana, in the Island of Cuba, as appears by the like testimony.

March 5th, 1844.

EDGAR LOGAN,
Proctor for Respondent.
A. D. LOGAN, Advocate.

No. 202.—A DILATORY EXCEPTION TO A LIBEL—*Vid. ante, page* 259.

No. 203.—A PEREMPTORY EXCEPTION TO A LIBEL—*Vid. ante, page* 260.

No. 204.—EXCEPTIONS TO A LIBEL FOR MISJOINDER.

United States District Court.

The Schr. NAOMI, &c., and JOHN W. HALL *ads.* DAVID J. BROWN.

John W. Hall, the respondent, excepts to the libel in this cause for this:—

First. That it misjoins in the same cause a suit in rem against the schooner Naomi and a suit in personam against John W. Hall, the master thereof.

Second. That it misjoins an alleged cause of action against the vessel for a violation of a charter party, and also an alleged cause of action against John W. Hall for the appropriating certain property by the said John W. Hall.

Third. That it misjoins parties who cannot rightfully be joined in such a suit, and misjoins causes of action which cannot be rightfully joined in such a suit.

C. L. BENEDICT, Proctor.
E. C. BENEDICT, Advocate.

No. 205.—EXCEPTIONS TO AN ANSWER FOR SCANDAL AND IMPERTINENCE.

District Court of the United States.

EBENEZER N. HINCKLEY,
        vs.
DAVID H. ROBERTSON.

Exceptions taken by the libellant to the answer of David H. Robertson, respondent in this cause.

First Exception. For that the allegations in the said answer, in the words following, to wit: " That during the time the libellant was at Antwerp, the captain of one of the deponent's vessels, the Henry Kneeland, at Antwerp the same time as the libellant, wrote to respondent, advising him as follows: ' I very much fear the voyage of the Majestic will turn out even worse than the Kneeland's, having met with an accident on her voyage; the ship is yet here, but ought to have been gone hence at least a week ago. Her commander is one of the last men that ought to be entrusted with the command of a ship; I have every reason for saying so, and feel it my duty to apprise you of it, and if not fully insured would recommend being so, as I think the ship not safe under the present command; and it is the opinion of the masters of ships here that I should apprise you of it; he is never seen about the ship, and appears to have lost himself altogether;' " are scandalous and impertinent and ought to be expunged.

Second Exception. For that the allegations in the said answer immediately following the matter quoted in the first exception, that is to say, " That deponent is informed and believes the libellant's neglect of duty was notorious at Antwerp at the time, and respondent was constantly informed of the same by persons subsequently arriving from that place," are scandalous and impertinent and ought to be expunged.

Third Exception. For that the allegation in the said answer, in the words following, to wit: " That, as the respondent is informed and believes, at the time the Majestic was loading at Newport, the agent of the cargo, before a notary public, protested against the libellant's incapacity and negligence is impertinent and ought to be expunged.

Fourth Exception. For that the allegation in the said answer, in the words following, to wit; " That the vessels owned by respondent which sailed with the same orders as libellant's, and were at Antwerp at the same time, made good voyages, and arrived at this port in the spring of the year, and have since proceeded on other voyages," is impertinent and ought to be expunged.

In all which particulars the said libellant humbly insists that the respondent's said answer is irrelevant, impertinent and scandalous; wherefore the libellant excepts thereto, and humbly prays that the impertinence and scandal of the said answer excepted to as aforesaid may be expunged, with costs.

BURR & BENEDICT,
Proctors for Libellant.
BURR, Advocate.

No. 206.—EXCEPTIONS TO AN ANSWER FOR INSUFFICIENCY.

District Court of the United States.

RAMON DE ZALDO
vs.
The brig ALDEBARON, her tackle, &c.,
and EBENEZER WHEELRIGHT.

Exceptions taken by the libellant to the answer of Ebenezer Wheelright, respondent to the libel and complaint of the said Ramon de Zaldo, filed in this cause.

First Exception. For that the said respondent has not well and sufficiently answered and set forth whether the agent of the libellant made and entered into an agreement with the said George C. Prior, as master and agent for the owners of said brig, on or about the 26th day of October, 1844, that the said brig should proceed to and take in a cargo at the port of Havana, and that the libellant or his agent should pay therefor the sum of one hundred dollars in addition to the compensation mentioned in the charter party ; and the sum of one hundred dollars was paid in pursuance of said agreement by this libellant's agent to the said master, as is alleged by the libellant's libel on file, in article 4th, page 5, lines 8, 9, 10, 11, 12, 13, 14, 15, 16, 17, 18, and 19.

Second Exception. For that the said respondent has not well and sufficiently answered and set forth whether, in pursuance of the last mentioned agreement, the said brig set sail from Cienfuegos to Havana, as is alleged in the libellant's libel, on file, in article 5th, page 5, lines 28, 29, and 30.

In all which particulars the said answer of the said respondent is imperfect,

584   APPENDIX.

insufficient and evasive, and the libellant therefore excepts thereto, and prays that the said respondent may put in a further and better answer to the said libel.

J. B. PURROY,
Proctor for Libellant.
NATH'L F. WARING,
Advocate.

No. 207.—EXCEPTIONS TO INTERROGATORIES TO A PARTY OR GARNISHEE.

District Court of the United States.—

A. B.
vs.
C. D.

Exceptions to the interrogatories addressed to the libellant [or defendant, or E. F., garnishee.]

First. The said libellant [or defendant, or garnishee,] excepts to the fourth interrogatory, for the reason that the answer thereto will expose him to a prosecution for a penalty, and he is not by law obliged to answer the same.

Second. He excepts to the seventh interrogatory, for the reason that it only inquires in relation to hearsay and the declarations of third persons, which are not competent evidence.

E. F., Proctor and Advocate for Libellants, &c.

No. 208.—EXCEPTIONS TO ANSWERS OF A PARTY OR GARNISHEE TO INTERROGATORIES.

District Court.

A. B.
vs.
C. D.

Exceptions to the answers of the libellant [or the defendant, or E. F., garnishee,] to the interrogatories addressed to him.

First. The defendant [or libellant, or garnishee,] excepts to the answer to the first interrogatory, for the reason that instead of answering the interrogatory fully, directly and positively, it answers the same evasively and indirectly, so far as it does answer the same, and omits wholly to answer how long the said defendant was confined in irons in the hold of said brig.

Second. He excepts to the answer to the fifth interrogatory, for the reason that said answer is impertinent and scandalous.

E. F., Proctor and Advocate for Def't, &c.

No. 209.—Exceptions to a deposition de bene esse.

U. S. District Court.

Thomas Davis, and others, }
vs.
Francis Hathaway, et al. }

Sir—You will please to take notice, that we object to the deposition of Charles E. Prescott, taken *ex parte de bene esse*, in this cause, because—

1st. It was not sealed up nor kept by the magistrate, nor delivered by him into Court, according to law, but the contrary appears.

2d. It is without date or jurat.

3d. It is not accompanied by the proper certificate of the Commissioner.

4th. The witness was not properly cautioned and sworn.

5th. There is no evidence of the reasons for taking the deposition, or of the facts that rendered it proper or necessary to take it.

6th. It is impossible to tell which deposition the certificate of the Commissioner refers to.

7th. The certificate appears not to have been given at the time of the taking of the deposition, but a long period afterwards; and it does not appear whether the facts certified relate to the time of the taking the one deposition or the other, or of the certificate.

Dated Dec. 16th, 1842.

Yours, &c.

Burr & Benedict,

Proctors for Libellants.

To Daniel Lord, Esq., and George B. Butler, Esq.,

Proctors for Defendants.

No. 210.—Interrogatories propounded to a party.

If the Interrogatories are annexed to a Pleading—let them follow immediately after the signatures and jurat to the Pleadings, with the following caption :

Interrogatories propounded to the defendant, (*or the libellant*) which he is required to answer in writing, under oath.

If the interrogatories are propounded independently of any pleading, let them be entitled in the cause as follows:

District Court of the United States.

A. B., }
vs. }
C. D. }

Interrogatories propounded to the libellant, (*or the defendant*) which he is required to answer in writing under oath.

First Interrogatory. What was the date of the arrival of the said ship

M. Howes, at Londonderry? and when did she arrive at the usual place of discharge in said port?

Second. How soon after the arrival of said ship at such port, did the master notify the consignees of said ship of his arrival?

Third. How soon after such arrival was the discharge of the cargo commenced? Why was it not commenced sooner? When was the vessel fully discharged? On what days was any part of the cargo discharged? How much was discharged on each of those days respectively? During how many days, or parts thereof, was the weather so stormy or bad as to render the cargo liable to damage, if delivered? When did the vessel leave the said port, on her return voyage? Why did she not leave sooner?

Fourth. Was not a part of the cargo in a damaged state on arrival, and if yea, how much? Was not two hundred bushels of corn and upwards so damaged? Was not such damage owing to the master or persons in charge of her, having stowed the quantity so damaged in bulk, instead of in bags, as required by the agreement between the libellants and defendants, and by the bill of lading?

Fifth. Were there not some disputes between the said consignees and the said master in relation to said damaged cargo and the freight, and if yea, were not the disputes submitted to arbitration? What were the subjects which were submitted to arbitration, and what was the award?

Sixth. Where was the master of said vessel when she was ready for sea, and if he was not at Londonderry, how soon after she was ready for sea did he return to Londonderry? Was the said master at Londonderry each and every day from the time said vessel arrived at said port, till she left on her return voyage? and if you answer in the negative, state particularly on what day or days, and what parts thereof, he was absent during the said time.

Seventh. Were you not aware, at the time the agreement to him was made, that the defendants were acting as agents, and who they were acting for, and that the defendants were not the principals in the charter.

S. L. M. BARLOW,
Proctor for Defendants.

New York, June 26, 1849.

No. 211.—ANSWER BY A PARTY TO INTERROGATORIES.

District Court of the United States.

A. B.,
vs.
C. D.

Answers of A. B., libellant, (or of C. D., defendant,) to the interrogatories propounded to him in this cause.

To the first interrogatory, he says, &c.

The answer must be signed by the party answering, and be sworn to as follows:

Southern District of New York, ss :

A. B., the foregoing respondent, being sworn, says—That the foregoing answers subscribed by him are true.

A. B.

Sworn January 4, 1850,
 before me,
  GEORGE W. MORTON,
   U. S. Commissioner.

Interrogatories to be annexed to a Commission, ante, No. 36, page 451.

Answers to same, ante, No. 38, page 453.

Cross Interrogatories, to be annexed to a Commission, ante, No. 37, page 452.

Answers to same, ante. page 454.

Interrogatories to a garnishee, ante, No. 174. page 571.

Answers to same, ante, No. 175, page 572.

No. 212.—PREPARATORY IRTERROGATORIES IN PRIZE CASES.

District Court of the United States.

Interrogatories administered to witnesses *in preparatorio*, touching and concerning the seizure and taking of a certain schooner, named Princess of Orange, alias Flying Fish, whereof Casparus Wyneburgh was master, by the private schooner of war Mary, whereof Edward Richards is commander.

1. Where was you born, and where do you now live; and how long have you lived there, and where have you lived for seven years last past ? Are you subject to the crown of Great Britain, or of what prince or state are you a subject ?

2. When, where, and by whom was the schooner and lading, goods, and merchandises, concerning which you are now examined, taken and seized, and into what place or port were the same carried ? whether was there any resistance made, or any guns fired against the said schooner, or persons who seized and took the same, and what and how many, and by whom?

3. Whether was you present at the time of the taking or seizing the schooner and her lading, goods, and merchandises, concerning which you are now examined, or how and when was you first made acquainted thereof ? Whether was the said schooner and goods taken by a man of war, or a private man of war, and to whom did such man of war, or private man of war

belong ? Had they any commission to act as such, and from and by whom, and by what particular vessel, or by whom was or were the said schooner seized and taken ? To what kingdom, country, or nation did the said schooner so seized and taken belong, and under the colors of what kingdom, country, or nation did she sail at the time she was so seized and taken ? Was the said schooner, which was taken, a man of war, privateer, or merchantman ?

4. Upon what pretence was the said schooner seized and taken ? To what port or place was she afterwards carried ? Whether was she condemned, and upon what account, and for what reason was she condemned, and by whom, and by what authority was she so condemned ?

5. Who by name was the master of the vessel concerning which you are now examined, at the time she was taken and seized ? How long have you known the said master ? Who first appointed him to be master of the said schooner, and when did he take possession thereof, and who by name delivered the same to him ? Where is the said master's fixed place of habitation with his wife and family, and how long has he lived there ? What countryman is he by birth, and to what prince or state subject ?

6. What number of mariners belonged to the said schooner at the time she was taken and seized ? What countrymen are they, and where did they all come on board ? Whether had you, or any of the officers or company, or mariners belonging to the said schooner or vessel, any part, share, or interest in the said schooner concerning which you are now examined, and what in particular, and the value thereof, at the time the said schooner was so taken, or the said goods seized ?

7. Whether did you belong to the schooner or vessel concerning which you are now examined, at the time she was taken and seized ? How long had you known her ? When and where did you first see her ? Of what burthen was she ? How many guns did she carry ? and how many or what number of men did belong to, or were on board the said schooner at the time she was taken, or at the beginning of the engagement before she was taken ? And of what country building was she ? What was her name, and how long had she been so called ? Whether do you know of any other name she was called by, and what were such names, as you know or have heard ?

8. To what ports and places was the said schooner or vessel concerning which you are now examined, bound, the voyage wherein she was taken and seized ? To and from what ports or places did she sail the said voyage before she was taken and seized ? Where did the voyage begin, and where was the voyage to have ended ? What sort of lading did she carry at the time of her first setting out on the said voyage, and what particular sort of lading and goods had she on board at the time she was taken and seized, proceeding upon a lawful trade ? Had she at that time any, and what prohibited goods on board her ?

9. Who were the owners of the said schooner and vessel, and goods, con-

cerning which you are now examined, at the time she was taken and seized ? How do you know they were the the owners of the said schooner and goods at that time ? Of what nation are they by birth, and where do they live with their wives and families, and to what prince or state are they subjects ?

10. Was there any bill of sale made to the owners of the said schooner ? In what month or year, and where and before what witnesses was the same made, and when did you last see it, and what is become thereof?

11. In what port or place was the lading, which was on board the schooner at the time she was taken and seized, first put on board the said schooner ? In what month and year was the lading so put on board ? What were the several qualities and quantities, and particulars thereof? Whether were the same laden and put on board the said schooner in one port, or at one time, or in several ports and places, and how many by name, and at how many several times, and what particulars and what quantity at each port ? Who by name were the several laders or owners thereof, and what country-men are they ? Where were the said goods to be delivered, and for whose account, and to whom by name did they then really belong ?

12. How many bills of lading were signed for the goods seized on board the said schooner ? Whether were the same colorable, and whether were any bills of lading signed which were of a different tenor with those which were on board the said schooner at the time she was seized and taken, and what were the contents of such other bills of lading, and what are become thereof ?

13. What bills of lading, invoices, letters, or any instruments in writing, or papers, have you to prove your own property, or the property of any other person, and of whom, in the schooner and goods concerning which you are now examined ?—produce the same, and set forth the particular times when, and how, and in what manner, and upon what account, and for what consideration, you became possessed thereof.

14. In what particular port or place, and in what degree of latitude were or was the schooner, concerning which you are now examined, taken and seized ? At what time, and upon what day of the month, and in what year, was or were the said schooner so taken and seized ?

15. Whether was there any charter party signed for the voyage wherein the schooner, concerning which you are now examined, was taken and seized ? What is become thereof ? when, where, and between whom was the same made ? What were the contents thereof ?

16. What papers, bills of lading, letters, or other writings, any way concerning or relating to the schooner concerning which you are now examined, were on board the said schoner at the time of the seizure of the said schooner ? Were any of the papers thrown overboard by any person, and whom, and when, and by whose orders ?

17. What loss or damage have you sustained by reason of the seizing and taking of the said schooner, concerning which you are now examined ? To what value does such loss or damages amount, and how and after what

manner do you compute such loss and damage ? Have you received any and what satisfaction for such the loss and damage which you have sustained, and when, and from whom did you receive the same ?

No. 213.—DEPOSITIONS OF WITNESSES IN PREPARATORIO IN PRIZE CASES.

District Court, &c.

The examination and depositions of witnesses *in preparatorio*, touching the capture and seizure of the schooner Flying Fish, and the goods and merchandises on board of her, made by the privateer schooner of war, Mary, Edward Richards, commander.

To the first interrogatory, Joseph Lopez, the deponent, says—That he was born, &c., *and so on through the interrogatories.*

JOSEPH LOPEZ.

Sworn August 6th, 1813,
      before me,

A. B., U. S. Commissioner.

No. 214.—THE OATH TO BE ADMINISTERED TO WITNESSES IN PREPA-
RATORIO.

" You shall true answers make to all such questions as shall be asked of you in these interrogatories, and therein you shall speak the truth, the whole truth, and nothing but the truth, so help you God."

No. 215.—OATH TO AN INTERPRETER.

You shall well and truly interpret to the witness the oath administered to him, and the interrogatories propounded to him ; and you shall well and truly interpret to the Commissioners the answers given by the witness to the respective interrogatories, so help you God.

No. 216.—LETTERS ROGATORY TO A FOREIGN JUDGE OR TRIBUNAL.

The President of the United States of America, to any Judge or Tribunal having jurisdiction of civil causes, at Havana, in the island of Cuba.

Whereas, a certain suit is pending in our District Court of the United States for the Southern District of New York, in which James Jones is li-bellant, and John D. Nelson, Henry Abbot, and Joseph E. Tatem are claimants of the schooner perseverance, her tackle, apparel, furniture and cargo, and it has been suggested to us that there are witnesses residing within your jurisdiction, without whose testimony, justice cannot be completely done between the said parties : We therefore request you that in furtherance of justice, you will, by the proper and usual process of your court, cause such witness or witnesses as shall be named or pointed out to you by the said parties or either of them, to appear before you, or some competent person by you for that purpose to be appointed and authorized, at a precise time by you to be fixed, and there to answer on their oaths or affirmations to the several interrogatories hereunto annexed, and that you will cause their depositions to be committed to writing, and returned to us under cover, duly closed and sealed up, together with these presents. And we shall be ready and willing to do the same for you in a similar case, when required.

Witness, the Honorable Samuel R. Betts, Judge of the said Court, at the city of New York, the tenth day of May, in the year of our Lord, one thousand eight hundred and twenty, and of our independence the forty-fourth.

A. B., Clerk.

C. D., Proctor for Libellant.
E. F., Proctor for Claimant.

Execution.

No. 217.—VENDITIONI EXPONAS IN A CASE OF SALVAGE, ON AN INTER-
LOCUTORY ORDER—*Vid. ante, No.* 19, *page* 439.

No. 218.—VENDITIONI EXPONAS ON A LIBEL OF INFORMATION—*Vid.
ante, page* 306.

No. 219.—AN EXECUTION IN THE NATURE OF A FIERI FACIAS AND A
CAPIAS—*Vid. ante, page* 304.

No. 220.—ATTACHMENT TO COMPEL THE DEFENDANT TO PERFORM A
DECREE—*Ante, No.* 147, *page* 360.

No. 221.—A FIERI FACIAS AGAINST GOODS, CHATTELS AND LANDS.

The President of the United States of America to the Marshal of the Southern District of New York, greeting :

Whereas a libel was filed in the District Court of the United States for the Southern District of New York, on the eighteenth day of October, eighteen hundred and forty-one, by Thomas Davis, James Williams, James Collins, and Charles E. Trescott, against Francis Hathaway and Edward Faucon. And such proceedings were thereupon had that by the judgment and decree of the said Court in the said cause entered, on the fifth day of October, one thousand eight hundred and forty-three, the said Francis Hathaway and Edward Faucon were required to pay to the libellant, James Williams, the sum of ninety-six dollars and eighty cents, and to the libellant Thomas Davis, fifty-nine dollars and twenty cents, besides their costs in this suit, to be taxed, and execution was ordered therefor. And whereas the said costs have been taxed at   as by the records and files of said Court fully appear. Now, therefore, we command you, that of the goods and chattels of the said Francis Hathaway and Edward Faucon in your District, and in default of goods and chattels of them, then of the lands and tenements in your District of which they were seised on the day you shall receive this writ, you cause to be made the sum of and further, that you have those moneys in said Court at the city hall in the city of New York, on the third Tuesday of June instant, to render to the libellants in satisfaction of said decree.

Witness the Honorable Samuel R. Betts, Judge of the said Court, the first Tuesday of June, 1845.

Clerk.

BURR & BENEDICT, Proctors.

No. 222.—THE MARSHAL'S RETURN.

No goods, chattels, or lands.
H. F. T., Marshal.

OR THIS:

I have made on the within execution the sum of   being the within amount, with interest.

Dated July,   1849.

H. F. T., Marshal.

Appeals.
No. 223.—NOTICE OF APPEAL—*ante, page* 322.

No. 224.—STIPULATION FOR DAMAGES AND COSTS IN THE DISTRICT COURT
ON APPEAL.

*District Court of the United States for the Southern District of New York.
In Admiralty.*

STIPULATION ENTERED INTO PURSUANT TO THE RULES AND PRACTICE OF THIS
COURT.

Whereas an appeal has been taken from the decree of this Court made on the   day of   in the year of our Lord one thousand eight hundred and forty-five, in a certain cause wherein A. B. is libellant against the brig Rover, her tackle, &c , and C. D., claimant, [or against C. D., defendant,] by the said libellant, [or the said claimant or defendant.]

Now, therefore, the stipulators undersigned hereby stipulate, in the sum of   dollars, to pay all damages and costs which shall be awarded against the said appellant by the final decree rendered by the Appellate Court.

A. B.
C. D.

Taken and acknowledged, this   day ⎫
of   185 , before me,   ⎬
         U. S. Commissioner.

Southern District of New York, ss. :—

                 party to the above stipulation, being duly sworn, deposes and says that he is worth the sum of   dollars over and above all his just debts and liabilities.

          to, this   day ⎫
of   185 , before me,   ⎬
         U. S. Commissioner.

No. 225—Appeal from the District Court to the Circuit Court.

Circuit Court of the United States.
Southern District of New York.

Francis Hathaway owner, and
Edward Faucon, master of the
Barque Florida, Appellants,
          vs.
Charles E. Trescott, James
Williams & Thomas Davis
Libellants.

To the Honorable the Circuit Court of the United States for the Southern District of New York, in the Second Circuit.

The appeal of the above named appellants respectfully showeth that on or about the eighteenth day of October, in the year one thousand eight hundred and forty-one, the above named libellants, Charles E. Trescott, James Williams and Thomas Davis, exhibited their libel in the District Court of the United States for the Southern District of New York, against the appellants, each claiming over fifty dollars, praying among other things for the reasons set forth in said libel, that these appellants might be condemned to pay the demands of said libellants, and costs in said libel mentioned, which libel was afterwards amended.

That process issued out of said court having been served on these appellants, Francis Hathaway and Edward Faucon, they did, on or about the twenty-first day of December, in the year one thousand eight hundred and forty-one, file their separate answers to the said libel, in the said District Court, praying that the said libel be dismissed with their costs in that behalf as by reference to said libel, and the said answers may more fully appear.

That the said cause came on to be heard before the Honorable Samuel R. Betts, Judge of the said District Court, on or about the 21st, 26th and 27th days of December, A.D. 1842, upon the depositions and proofs taken in said cause, and the testimony and proofs adduced by the respective parties, and the said judge having advised thereon on the 28th day of March, in the year 1843, made a decree or sentence in said cause, whereby it was among other things sentenced and decreed, that the libellants in said cause recover against these appellants their wages for the entire voyage for which in the said libel, they claim the same, up to the time of their discharge by the said Edward Faucon, master of the said barque, as by reference to the said decree, may more fully appear under which decree a reference was had to the clerk of this court, who reported that there was due to Charles E. Trescott the sum of $148, to the said James Williams the sum of $96 80, and to the said Thomas Davis the sum of $53, which report on the 5th day of October, was confirmed by the said court by the final decree thereof.

And these appellants are advised and insist that the said decrees are erroneous, inasmuch as the said libellants were not entitled to any wages in the premises.

And these appellants, for these and other reasons, appeal from the whole of the said decree in favor of said Trescott, Williams and Davis, to the next Circuit Court, to be held in the said District, (and on the said appeal they intend only to have the said cause heard anew, on the same pleadings and the same proofs;) and he prays that the said decree, and every part thereof, may be reversed with costs, or such other decrees thereupon made, as to the said Circuit Court, shall seem just, and that the said appellees be condemned to pay to these appellants their costs and damages in the premises.

or,

(And on the said appeal they intend to have said cause heard anew, in the Circuit Court, on the pleadings and proofs in the District Court, and other proofs to be introduced in the said Circuit Court)

or,

(And on said appeal they intend to make new allegations in the Circuit Court, and introduce the same and new and further proofs)

And he prays that the record and proceedings may be returned to the said Circuit Court, and that the said decree may be reversed or such other decree thereon be made. as to said Circuit Court shall seem just, and that the appellees may be condemned to pay to the appellants their costs and damages in the premises.

> A. B., Proctor.
> C. D., Advocate.

No. 226—Affidavit of service of a copy of the appeal.

Southern District of New York, ss.

A. B., of the city of New York, clerk, being duly sworn, says, that on the tenth day of October, 1843, he served a copy of the foregoing appeal on C. Van Santvoord, Esq., the proctor of the appellees, by delivering the same to him personally, [or by leaving the same in his office with the person in charge thereof.]

> A. B.

Sworn, Oct. 10th, 1843,
 before me,

GEORGE W. MORTON, U. S. Commissioner.

No. 227.—NOTICE OF PUTTING IN STIPULATION ON APPEAL.

United States Circuit Court for the Southern District of New York.

RAMON DE ZALDO, Appellant,

vs.

ELISHA BURGESS, Appellee.

GENTLEMEN :—Please take notice, that the stipulation to be filed by the above named appellant on the appeal made herein, will be executed and given by Andrew P. de la Pena, merchant, of No. 81 Front street, and whose residence is at No. 207½ William street, in the city of New York,— and Charles de Zaldo, merchant, of No. 81 Front street, and whose residence is at No. 74 Walker street, in said city.

And please further take notice, that the aforesaid sureties will severally attend at the office of the clerk of this Court, on Tuesday next, the sixth day of August instant, at 11 o'clock in the forenoon of that day, to execute said stipulation; and that they will at the same time and place justify as good and sufficient sureties herein.

Yours, &c.

New York, August 2d, 1844.   EDGAR LOGAN.
                                              Proctor for Appellant.

To BURR & BENEDICT, Esqrs.,
   Proctors for Appellee.

No. 228.—CERTIFICATE OF THE DISTRICT CLERK TO THE DOCUMENTS.

United States of America, Southern District of New York, ss.

[L. S.]   I, James W. Metcalf, Clerk of the District Court of the United States of America for the Southern District of New York, do hereby certify that the writings annexed to this certificate are true copies of their respective originals, on file, and remaining of record in my office in the cause within mentioned.

In testimony whereof I have caused the seal of the said Court to be hereunto affixed, at the city of New York, in the Southern District of New York, this second day of April, in the year of our Lord one thousand eight hundred and forty-eight, and of the Independence of the said United States, the sixty-second.

J. W. METCALF, Clerk.

No. 229.—INHIBITION FROM THE CIRCUIT COURT TO THE DISTRICT COURT.

The President of the United States to the Judge of the District Court of the United States for the Southern District of New York, greeting :

[L. S.]   Whereas in a certain cause of salvage, civil and maritime, in the District Court of the United States for the Southern District of New York, in which A. B. is libellant against the brig Roarer, her tackle, apparel and furniture, and cargo, and C. D., its claimant, the said District Court made a final decree on the   day of   last, and the said C. D. thereupon appealed to the Circuit Court of the United States next to be held in said District : Now, therefore, we inhibit and command you, that you do not further proceed in said cause, or attempt, or do, or cause, or procure to be attempted or done, any thing to the prejudice of said party appellant during the pendency of his said appeal, so long as the same shall remain undetermined in judgment, so that he may have full and free liberty and power to prosecute the same, under pain of the law and contempt thereof.

Witness the Honorable Brockholst Livingston, Justice of the Supreme Court of the United States, and Judge of the Circuit Court of the United States for the Southern District of New York, in the Second Circuit, the   day of   in the year of our Lord one thousand eight hundered and   and of our Independence the

                                         Clerk.

G. F., Proctor.

No. 230.—APPELLEE'S STIPULATION TO PERFORM THE DECREE, WITHOUT SURETY.

Circuit Court of the United States for the Southern District New of York.

In Admiralty.

STIPULATION ENTERED INTO PURSUANT TO THE RULES AND PRACTICE OF THIS COURT.

Whereas, in an appeal to this Court in a certain cause wherein A. B. is appellant, against C. D., appellee, on motion of the said C. D. it has been ordered, that the decree of the District Court be carried into effect, subject to the judgment af this Court, or of the Supreme Court, on appeal, upon his stipulating to abide and perform the decree of such Courts.

Now, therefore, the stipulator undersigned, the appellee aforesaid, hereby stipulates to abide by and perform the decree rendered in this cause, by this Court or the Supreme Court, on appeal, if any appeal shall intervene.

Taken and Acknowledged, this   day }
of   185   , before me, }
         G. W. M., U. S. Commissioner.

No. 231.—Appellant's stipulation, with sureties, to pay damages and costs on appeal.

Circuit Court of the United States for the Southern District of New York.

In Admiralty.

STIPULATION ENTERED INTO PURSUANT TO THE RULES AND PRACTICE OF THIS COURT.

Whereas, an appeal has been taken to this Court, from the District Court of the United States, in the Southern District of New York, in a certain cause wherein A. B. was libellant, against the brig Roarer, her tackle, &c., C. D. claimant, by the said claimant, and the said appellant has been ordered to give security by the stipulation of himself and competent sureties, in the sum of   dollars, for the payment of all damages and costs on the appeal in this Court and in the Supreme Court.

Now, therefore, the stipulators undersigned, hereby stipulate in the said sum of   dollars, to pay all damages and costs on the appeal in this Court and in the Supreme Court, in case such appeal shall intervene.

Taken and acknowledged, this   day }
  of   185 , before me,   }

  G. W. M., U. S. Commissioner.

Southern District of New York, ss:

                    party to the above stipulation, being duly deposes and says that he is worth the ˌsum of   dollars over and above all his just debts and liabilities.

          to, this   day }
  of   185   before me, }

  G. W. M., U. S. Commissioner.

No. 232.—Notice of hearing of appeal to party and clerk.

Circuit Court of the United States.

IN ADMIRALTY, ON APPEAL.

A. B., Appellant. }
    vs.   }
C. D., Appellee. }

Sir—The appeal in this cause will be brought on for hearing before the Honorable Samuel Nelson, at the next term of this Court, to be held at the City Hall, in the City of New York, on the first Monday of April next.

Dated March 22d, 1849.

                    Yours, &c.
                    E. F., Proctor for Appellant.

To G. H , Proctor for Appellee.

[The like to the Clerk of the Court—in all respects except the address.]

No. 233.—Appeal from the circuit court to the supreme court.

The Steamboat New Jersey, her tackle, apparel, &c.
Isaac Newton, claimant and appellant,
vs.
John H. Stebbins, respondent.

To the Honorable the Supreme Court of the United States:

The appeal of Isaac Newton, the above named claimant and appellant, respectfully showeth that on the fourteenth day of November, 1845, the above named John H. Stebbins filed his libel in the District Court of the United States, for the Southern District of New York, against the Steamboat New Jersey, her tackle, apparel, &c., in a cause civil and maritime, for the recovery of damages alleged to have been sustained by him to the sloop Hamlet and her cargo, by collision with the said Steamboat New Jersey, on the Hudson river, in the State of New York, and that the said Steamboat New Jersey was arrested upon process issued upon said libel, and was discharged on your petitioner's filing his claim and entering into stipulations, and your petitioner thereupon filed his answer to said libel, and the said libellant replied thereto, and such proceedings were had in the said cause that, on the fourteenth day of October, 1846, a final decree was made and pronounced therein by the said district court, wherein it was in substance adjudged that the said libellant recover against the Steamboat New Jersey, her tackle, &c. the sum of two thousand four hundred and three dollars and seventy-five cents, together with costs.

And that, after such final decree, your petitioner duly appealed therefrom to the Circuit Court of the United States, for the Southern District of New York, and the said cause was removed thereby into the said Circuit Court, and there tried anew ; and such proceedings were had in the said Circuit Court, that afterwards, on the eleventh day of November, 1847, the said Circuit Court made a final decree in the said cause, whereby it was decreed that the said decree of the District Court be in all things affirmed, with costs, and that the said appellee have execution, and that the stipulators cause their stipulations to be fulfilled ; which said decree of the said Circuit Court is, as this appellant is advised, erroneous, and ought to be reversed.

Wherefore, this appellant appeals from the whole of said decree of said Circuit Court to the Supreme Court of the United States, and respectfully prays that the said decree of the said Circuit Court, and the libel, answer, pleadings, depositions, evidence and proceedings, in the said cause may be sent to the Supreme Court of the United States without delay, and that the said Supreme Court will proceed to hear the said cause anew, and that the said decree of the Circuit Court, and every part thereof, may be reversed, and a decree made dismissing said libel, with costs, or such other decree as to the said Supreme Court shall seem just.

I. NEWTON.

Dated, New York, Nov'r 20, 1847.

C. VANSANTVOORD, Proctor for appellant.
H. S. DODGE, Advocate.

No. 234—BOND ON APPEAL.

Circuit Court of the U. S. of America,
Southern District of New York, in the Second Circuit.

The STEAMBOAT NEW JERSEY, her tackle, &c., ⎫
   Isaac Newton, claimant and appellant, ⎬
           vs. ⎪
JOHN H. STEBBINS, libellant and appellee. ⎭

Know all men by these presents, that we, Isaac Newton and Daniel Drew, of the city of New York, and Elijah Peck, of Flushing, in the county of Queens, are held and firmly bound, unto the above named John H. Stebbins, in the sum of five thousand dollars, to be paid to the said appellee ; for the payment of which, well and truly to be made, we bind ourselves, and each of us, our and each of our heirs, executors, and administrators, jointly and severally, firmly by these presents. Sealed with our seals, and dated the twentieth day of November, in the year of our Lord one thousand eight hundred and forty-seven.

Whereas, the above named appellant has prosecuted an appeal to the Supreme Court of the United States, at the city of Washington, in the District of Columbia, to reverse the decree rendered in the above suit by the Circuit Court of the United States, for the Southern District of New York:

Now, therefore, the condition of this obligation is such, that if the above named appellant shall prosecute his appeal to effect, and answer all damages and costs if he fail to make his appeal good, then this obligation shall be void, otherwise the same shall be and remain in full force and virtue.

I. NEWTON,   [SEAL.]
DANIEL DREW, [SEAL.]
ELIJAH PECK. [SEAL.]

Sealed and delivered, and taken and acknowledged, this 20th day of November, 1847, before me,

DAVID L. GARDINER, U. S. Commissioner.

United States of America,
   Southern District of New York, ss :

Daniel Drew and Elijah Peck, being duly sworn, depose and say, and each for himself saith, that he is worth the sum of five thousand dollars over and above all his just debts and liabilities.

DANIEL DREW,
ELIJAH PECK.

Sworn to, this twentieth day of November, A.D. 1847, before me,
DAVID L. GARDINER, U. S. Commissioner.

I approve the above bond and the sufficiency of the sureties thereto,
SAM'L R. BETTS.
Nov. 20, 1847.

No. 235.—CITATION.

By the Honorable Samuel R. Betts, one of the Judges of the Circuit Court of the United States, for the Southern District of New York, in the second circuit,

To John H. Stebbins:

Whereas, Isaac Newton, claimant, of the Steamboat New Jersey, her tackle, &c., has lately appealed to the Supreme Court of the United States, from a decree lately rendered in the Circuit Court of the United States, for the Southern District of New York, in the second circuit, made in favor of you, the said John H. Stebbins, against the said Steamboat New Jersey, her tackle, &c., and has filed the security required by law; you are, therefore, hereby cited to appear before the said Supreme Court, at the city of Washington, on the 22d day of December next, to do and receive what may appertain to justice to be done in the premises.

Given under my hand, at the city of New York, in the Southern District of New York, in the second circuit, the 22d day of November, in the year of our Lord 1847, and of the independence of the United States the seventy-second.

SAM'L R. BETTS.

No. 236.—AFFIDAVIT OF SERVICE OF CITATION AND APPEAL.

Southern District of New York, ss :

Andrew H. Hitchcock being duly sworn, saith that he served on the appellee, John H. Stebbins, on the 22d day of November, 1847, a copy of the appeal and a copy of the citation, filed in this cause with the clerk of the Circuit Court, in and for the Southern District of New York, on said twenty-second day of November, by delivering said copy of the citation to the said appellee personally, and by leaving said copy appeal for said appellee in the clerk's office of the Circuit Court aforesaid.

A. H. HITCHCOCK.

Sworn to, this 4th day of December, 1848, before me,
J. W. NELSON, U. S. Com'r.

No. 237.—RETURN, FROM THE CIRCUIT COURT TO THE SUPREME COURT.

United States of America,
    Southern District of New York, ss. :—

I, Alexander Gardiner, clerk of the Circuit Court of the United States of
        America, for the Southern District of New York, in the second
[SEAL.] circuit, do hereby certify, that the writings annexed to this certifi-
        cate are true copies of their respective originals, on file and remain-
ing of record in my office, in the cause within named.

In testimony whereof I have caused the seal of the said court to be hereunto affixed, at the city of New York, in the Southern District of New York,
in the second circuit, this fourth day of December, in the year of our Lord
one thousand eight hundred and forty-eight, and of the independence of the
said United States the seventy-third.

ALEX. GARDINER.

No. 238.—BOND TO THE CLERK FOR COSTS.

Supreme Court of the United States of America.

A. B., claimant of the schooner SEA FLOWER, her tackle, &c.,
            Appellant.
     vs.
 C. D.,
       Libellant and Appellee.
	Bond for Costs.

Know all Men by these Presents, That we, E. F. and G. H., are held
and firmly bound unto William T. Carrol, Esq., Clerk of the Supreme
Court of the United States in the sum of two hundred dollars, to be paid
to the said clerk, for the payment of which, well and truly to be made, we
bind ourselves, and each of us, our and each of our heirs, executors, and
administrators, jointly and severally, firmly by these presents.

Sealed with our seals, and dated the   day of   in the
year of our Lord one thousand eight hundred and

Whereas, the above named appellant has prosecuted an appeal from the
Circuit Court of the United States for the Southern District of New York,
to this court, to reverse the final decree rendered in the above entitled suit,
by the Circuit Court of the United States for the Southern District of New
York, in the second circuit:

Now, therefore, the condition of this obligation is such, that if the above
named appellant shall pay to said clerk all costs which he may be entitled to

demand of said appellant in this cause, then this obligation shall be otherwise the same shall be and remain in full force and virtue.

E.

G.]

Sealed and delivered, and taken and ⎫
  acknowledged this   day of   ⎬
  184 , before me,   ⎭

RICHARD E. STILWELL,

U. S. Commissioner.

United States of America,
    Southern District of New York, ss:

E. F. and G. H., the within obligors, being duly sworn, depose and say each for himself, that he is worth the sum of four hundred dollars over and above all his just debts and liabilities.

Sworn to, this   day ⎱
  of   A. D. 184 , before me, ⎰

RICHARD E. STILWELL,

U. S. Commissioner.

No. 239.—NOTICE OF APPEARANCE—*Ante, page* 333.

No. 240.—DECREE OF THE CIRCUIT COURT, AFTER THE REMITTITUR FROM
THE SUPREME COURT.

On reading and filing the remittitur and mandate of the Supreme Court, and on motion of Mr.   Proctor for the libellant, (or the defendant, or the claimant:) It is ordered, adjudged, and decreed, (according to the mandate,) and that the said   have execution of this decree.

No. 241.—A SUGGESTION TO THE SUPREME COURT OF THE UNITED STATES,
PRAYING FOR A PROHIBITION TO A DISTRICT COURT PROCEEDING IN AD-
MIRALTY.

To the Honorable the Supreme Court of the United States of America.

The suggestion of Samuel B. Davis, against the District Court of the United States for the District of Pennsylvania, respectfully alleges:

That he is a lieutenant in the navy of the French Republic, and commander of the Cassius, a vessel of war of the Republic, in her service, and duly commissioned to cruise against her enemies and make prizes of their ships and goods, as is proved by his commission, which he offers to produce to the Court.

That by the laws of nations, and by treaties between the French Republic and the United States, trials of captures on the high seas, of vessels brought within the jurisdiction of the Republic, and all questions incidental thereto, belong exclusively to the tribunals of the Republic, and to no other tribunals, and the vessels of war of the Republic, and the officers commanding them, cannot of right be sued or arrested in the ports of the United States for captures made on the high seas, and brought for legal adjudication into the ports of the Republic; and the District Courts of the United States ought not to entertain jurisdiction, or hold pleas of such captures. That by the laws of nations, the vessels of war of belligerent powers may take, as prizes of war, the ships and goods of their enemies, and bring them into the ports of the Sovereign under whom they act, and the commanders of such vessels of war are not amenable before the tribunals of neutral powers for their conduct therein, but only to their own sovereign under whom they act.

Yet one James Yard, a citizen of the State of Pennsylvania, as owner of the schooner William Lindsay, and her cargo, has filed his libel in the District Court of the United States for the District of Pennsylvania, proceeding as a Court of Admiralty and Maritime jurisdiction, against the said vessel of war the Cassius, and against the said Samuel B. Davis, her commander, and has caused them to be arrested by the process of said Court to answer for damages for capturing the said schooner on the high seas, and carrying her into the Port de Paix, a part of the French Republic

Wherefore the said Samuel B. Davis, respectfully requests that a writ of Prohibition may be issued out of this Honorable Court to the Judge of the District Court of the United States for the District of Pennsylvania, prohibiting him from holding the plea aforesaid concerning the premises aforesaid, anywise further before him.

SAMUEL B. DAVIS.

A. B., Proctor and Advocate.

No. 242.—A WRIT OF PROHIBITION, FROM THE SUPREME COURT OF THE UNITED STATES TO A DISTRICT COURT PROCEEDING, AS A COURT OF ADMIRALTY.

The President of the United States of America, to the Honorable Richard Peters, Judge of the United States for the District of Pennsylvania: Greeting:

Whereas, James Yard, a citizen of the state of Pennsylvania, has filed his libel in the District Court of the United States for the District Court of Pennsylvania, proceeding as a Court of Admiralty and Maritime jurisdiction, against the vessel of war the Cassius, belonging to the French Republic, and against Samuel B. Davis, her commander, a lieutenant of the French Republic, and has caused them to be arrested by process issuing out of said Court on the said libel, to answer for damages for capturing, on the high seas, the schooner William Lindsay, and her cargo, and carrying them into a port of the said Republic, as prize of war, of which cause the said District Court, proceeding as a Court of Admiralty and Maritime jurisdiction, has not jurisdiction :

Now, therefore, we do prohibit you, that you do not hold the plea aforesaid, concerning the premises aforesaid, anywise further before you.

Witness the Honorable John Jay, Chief Justice of the Supreme Court of the United States, the 10th day of August, in the year of our Lord one thousand seven hundred and ninety-five, and of the independence of the United States of America the eleventh.

JOHN TUCKER, Clerk.

A. B , Proctor and Advocate.

JUDICIARY OF THE UNITED STATES.

The names and residence of the Judges and Clerks, and the times and places of holding the Courts.

SUPREME COURT OF THE UNITED STATES.

Chief Justice.

Hon. ROGER B. TANEY, of Baltimore, Md.

Associate Justices.

Hon. JOHN McLEAN, of Cincinnati, Ohio.
Hon. JAMES M. WAYNE, of Savannah, Ga.
Hon. JOHN CATRON, of Nashville, Tenn.
Hon. JOHN McKINLEY, of Louisville, Ky.
Hon. PETER V. DANIEL, of Richmond, Va.
Hon. SAMUEL NELSON, of Cooperstown, N. Y.
Hon. LEVI WOODBURY, of Portsmouth, N. H.
Hon. ROBERT C. GRIER, of Pittsburg, Pa.

Reporter.

BENJAMIN C. HOWARD, of Baltimore, Md.

Clerk.

WILLIAM T. CARROL, of Washington, D. C.

The only session of the court is held at the Capitol in Washington, on the first Monday of December, every year.

CIRCUIT COURTS.

With the times and places of holding their sessions.

First Circuit.—(Mr. Justice WOODBURY.)
   Maine.—Portland, 23d April and September.
   New Hampshire.—Portsmouth, 8th May ; Exeter, 8th October.
   Massachusetts.—Boston, 15th May and October.
   Rhode Island.—Newport, 15th June ; Providence, 15th November.

Note.—The terms of the Courts are often changed by Act of Congress.

Second Circuit.—(Mr. Justice NELSON.)

    Vermont.—Windsor, 21st May ; Rutland, 3d October.

    Connecticut.—New Haven, 4th Tuesday in April; Hartford, 3d Tuesday in September.

    New York.—S. District, last Monday in February, first Monday in April, 3d Monday in October.—N. District, Albany, 3d Tuesday in October and May; Canandaigua, Tuesday next after 3d Monday in June.

Third Circuit.—(Mr. Justice GRIER.)

    New Jersey.—Trenton, 4th Tuesday in March and September.

    Pennsylvania.—E. District, Philadelphia, 11th April and 11th October. —W. District, Pittsburg, 3d Monday in May and November; Williamsport, 3d Monday in June and September.

Fourth Circuit.—(Mr. Chief Justice TANEY.)

    Delaware.—Newcastle, Tuesday following 4th Monday in May ; Dover, Tuesday following 3d Monday in October.

    Maryland—Baltimore, 1st Monday in April and November.

    Virginia.—E. District, Richmond, 1st Monday in May and 4th Monday in November.—W. District, Lewisburgh, 1st Monday in August.

Fifth Circuit.—(Mr. Justice McKINLEY.)

    Alabama.—Mobile, 2d Monday in April and 4th Monday in December.

    Louisiana.—New Orleans, 4th Monday in April and 3d Monday in December.

Sixth Circuit.—(Mr. Justice WAYNE.)

    N. Carolina.—Raleigh, 1st Monday in June and last Monday in November.

    S. Carolina.—Charleston, Wednesday preceding the 4th Monday in March; Columbia, 4th Monday in November.

    Georgia.—N. District, Marietta, 2d Monday in March and September. —S. District, Savannah, 2d Monday in April ; Milledgeville, Thursday after the 1st Monday in November.

Seventh Circuit.—(Mr. Justice McLEAN.)

    Ohio.—Columbus, 3d Monday in July and 2d Monday in November.

    Indiana.—Indianapolis, 3d Monday in May and 1st Monday in December.

    Illinois.—Springfield, 1st Monday in June and last Monday in November ; Chicago, 1st Monday in July.

    Michigan.—Detroit, 3d Monday in June and 2d Monday in October.

Eighth Circuit.—(Mr. Justice CATRON.)

    Kentucky.—Frankfort, 3d Monday in May and October.

    Tennessee.—Nashville, 1st Monday in March and September; Knoxville, 3d Monday in April and October; Jackson, 2d Monday in October and April.

    Missouri.—St. Louis, 1st Monday in April.

Ninth Circuit —(Mr. Justice DANIEL.)

Mississippi, Jackson, 1st Monday in May and November.

Arkansas, Little Rock, 2d Monday in April.

Dist. of Columbia, Hon. Wm. Cranch, Washington, 4th Monday in March, and 3d Monday in October.

DISTRICT COURTS.

Alabama —Judge, Hon. John Gayle, Mobile; Clerks, A. A. Gooch, Tuscaloosa; John Pitts, Mobile.

Montgomery.—4th Monday in May, and 1st Monday after the 4th Monday in November.

Mobile.—1st Monday in May, and 2d Monday in December.

Arkansas.—Judge, Hon. Benjamin Johnson, Little Rock; Clerk, William Field, Little Rock.

Little Rock.—1st Monday in April and November.

Connecticut.—Judge, Hon. Andrew T. Judson, Canterbury; Clerk, John J. Cleaveland, New Haven.

New Haven.—4th Tuesday in August and February.

Hartford.—4th Tuesday in May and November.

Delaware.—Judge, Hon. Willard Hall, Wilmington; Clerk, W. A. Mendenhall, Wilmington.

Newcastle.—3d Tuesday in June and 2d Tuesday in December.

Dover.—Tuesday next following the 3d Monday of March, and the Tuesday next following the 4th Monday of September.

District of Columbia.—Judge, Hon. William Cranch, Washington.

Washington.—1st Monday in June and December.

Florida.—Judge, Hon. Isaac H. Bronson, St. Augustine; William H. Marvin, Key West; Clerks, R. B. Hilton, Tallahassee; C. N. Jordan, Pensacola; Joseph S. May, Apalachicola; R. B. Smith, Tallahassee.

Tallahassee.—1st Monday in January. Apalachicola, 1st Monday in February. Pensacola, 1st Monday in March. St. Augustine, 1st Monday in April. Key West, 1st Monday in May and November.

Georgia.—Judge, Hon. John C. Nicoll, Savannah; Clerks, George Glenn, Savannah. W. H. Hunt, Marietta.

Marietta.—2d Monday in March and September.

Savannah.—2d Tuesday in February, May, August and November.

Indiana.—Judge, Hon. E. M. Huntington, Cannelton; Clerk, Horace Basset, Indianapolis.

Indianapolis.—3d Monday in May and 1st Monday in December.

Iowa.—Judge, Hon. John S. Dyer, Dubuque; Clerk, T. S. Parvin, Muscatine.

Dubuque.—1st Monday in January. Iowa City, 1st Monday in October. Burlington, 1st Monday in June.

Kentucky.—Judge, Hon. Thomas B. Monroe, Frankfort; Clerk, John H. Hanna, Frankfort.

Frankfort.—3d Monday in May and October.

Louisiana.—Judges, Hon. Theo. H. McCaleb, New Orleans; Hon. Henry Boyce, Alexandria; Clerk, N. R. Jennings, New Orleans.

New Orleans.—2d Monday in December and 1st Monday in January. Opelousas.—1st Monday in August. Alexandria, 1st Monday in September. Shreveport, 1st Monday in October. Munroe, 1st Monday in November.

Maine.—Judge, Hon. Asher Ware, Portland; Clerk, George F. Emery, Portland.

Wiscasset.—1st Tuesday in September. Portland, 1st Tuesday in February and December. Bangor, 4th Tuesday in June.

Maryland.—Judge, Hon. Upton S. Heath, Baltimore; Clerk, Thomas Spicer, Baltimore.

Baltimore.—1st Tuesday in March, June, September and November.

Massachusetts.—Judge, Hon. Peleg Sprague, Boston; Clerk, Seth E. Sprague, Boston.

Boston.—3d Tuesday in March, 4th Tuesday in June, 2d Tuesday in September and 1st Tuesday in December.

Michigan.—Judge, Hon. Ross Wilkins, Detroit; Clerk, John Winda, Detroit.

Detroit.—3d Monday in June and 2d Monday in October.

Mississippi.—Judge, Hon. Samuel J. Gholson, Athens; Clerk, G. M. Ragsdale, Pontotoc; W. H. Brown, Jackson.

Pontotoc.—1st Monday in June and December.

Jackson.—4th Monday in January and June.

Missouri.—Judge, Hon. Robert W. Wells, Jefferson City; Clerk, John Harrison, Jefferson City.

Jefferson City.—1st Monday in March and September.

New Hampshire.—Judge, Hon. Matthew Harvey, Hopkinton; Clerk, Albert R. Hatch, Portsmouth.

Portsmouth.—3d Tuesday in March and September.

Exeter.—3d Tuesday in June and December.

New Jersey.—Judge, Hon. Philemon Dickerson, Paterson; Clerk, Edw. N. Dickerson, Paterson.

Trenton.—3d Tuesday in January, April, June and September.

New York.—Judges, Hon. Samuel R. Betts, New York; Hon. Alfred Conkling, Auburn; Clerks, James W. Metcalf, New York; Aurelian Conkling, Auburn.

New York.—1st Tuesday in every month.

Albany.—3d Tuesday in January. Utica, 2d Tuesday in July. Rochester, 3d Tuesday in May. Auburn, 3d Tuesday in August. Buffalo, 2d Tuesday in November.

North Carolina.—Judge, Hon. Henry Potter, Raleigh; Clerk, John M. Jones, Edenton.

Edenton.—3d Monday in April and October. Neubern, 4th Monday in April and October. Wilmington, 1st Monday after the 4th Monday in April and October.

Ohio.—Judge, Hon. H. H. Leavitt, Steubenville; Clerk, William Miner, Columbus.

Columbus.—3d Monday in July and 2d Monday in November.

Pennsylvania.—Judges, Hon. John K. Kane, Philadelphia; Hon. Thomas Irwin, Pittsburg; Clerks, Thomas L. Kane, Philadelphia; R. B. Roberts, Pittsburg.

Philadelphia.—3d Monday in February, May, August and November.

Pittsburg.—1st Monday in May and October.

Williamsport.—1st Monday in October.

Rhode Island.—Judge, Hon. John Pitman, Providence; Clerk, John T. Pitman, Providence.

Newport.—2d Tuesday in May and 3d in October.

Providence—1st Tuesday in August and February.

S. Carolina.—Judge, Hon. Robert B. Gilchrist, Charleston; Clerk, W. Y. Gray, Charleston.

Charleston.—3d Monday in March and September, 1st Monday in July, and 2d Monday in December.

Tennessee.—Judge, Hon. M. W. Brown, Nashville; Clerk, Jacob Mc Gavock, Nashville; James L. Talbot, Jackson; James W. Campbell, Knoxville.

Nashville.—4th Monday in May and November. Jackson, 2d Monday in October and April.

Knoxville—3d Monday in April and October.

Texas.—Judge, Hon. John C. Watrous, Galveston; Clerk, Thomas Bates, Galveston.

Galveston.—1st Monday in February.

Vermont.—Judge, Hon. Samuel Prentiss, Montpelier; Clerk, Edward H. Prentiss, Montpelier.

Rutland.—6th of October. Windsor, 24th of May.

Virginia.—Judges, Hon. James D. Hallyburton, N. Kent, C. H.; Hon. J. W. Brockenburgh, Lexington; Clerks, A. E. Cowdery, Norfolk; Erasmus Stribling, Staunton.

Richmond.—12th of May and November. Norfolk, 30th May and 1st of November. Staunton, 1st May and October. Wytheville, Wednesday after 3d Monday in April and September. Charleston, Wednesday after 2d Monday in April and September. Clarksburg, last Monday in March and August. Wheeling, Wednesday after 1st Monday in April and September.

UNITED STATES COMMISSIONERS.

(*Vid. ante, page* 189, § 338.)

The convenience of the Bar in having the names of reliable gentlemen in the various states, familiar with taking depositions and other semi-judicial duties, suggested the insertion of the following list—but not till it was too late to extend it farther than the Atlantic states, without delaying the publication of the work.

Connecticut.

Francis Fellamer, Hartford.
Charles R. Ingersoll, New Haven.
John J. Cleveland, New Haven.
James A. Hovey, Norwich.

Georgia.

Joseph Bancroft, Savannah.
Charles S. Henry,   "
Wm. W. Holt, Augusta.
Samuel A. Bailey, Columbus.
Alfred Iverson,   "
James Smith, Macon.

Maine.

Thomas Amory Deblois, Portland.
John Rand,   "
George F. Shepley   "
William Willis,   "
Phillip Eastman, Saco.
Frederick Hobbs, Bangor.
James S. Rowe,   "
Aaron Hayden, Eastport.
Daniel T. Granger, Eastport.

Massachusetts.

Edward G. Loring, Boston.
George T. Curtis,   "
George S. Hillard,   "
Charles Sumner,   "
James M. Bunker, Nantucket.
William W. Story, Boston.
Benj. F. Hallett,   "
Charles Levi Woodbury, Boston.
Oliver Prescott, New Bedford.

Maryland.

John Hannan, Baltimore.
John Carrerl,   "
Levin Gale, Baltimore.
H. D. Evans,   "

New Hampshire.

Samuel Cushman, Portsmouth.
Lory Odell, "
John Kelly, Exeter.
Asa Freeman, Dover.
Asa Fowler, Concord.
Warren Lovell, Meredith,

Luther D. Sawyer, Ossipee.
Samuel D. Bell, Manchester.
Horace Chase, Hopkinton.
L. Chamberlain, Keene.
David Dickey, Newport.
Josiah Quincy, Rumney.

Jared W. Williams, Lancaster.

New York.

Alex. Gardiner, New York.
James W. Metcalf, do.
George W. Morton, do.
Richard E. Stilwell, do.
John W. Nelson, do.
Charles W. Newton, do.
Henry J. Hilton, Albany.

Augustus A. Boyce, Utica.
Joseph F. Sabine, Syracuse.
Aurelian Conkling, Auburn.
Lysander Farran, Rochester.
Henry K. Smith, Buffalo.
Leander Babcock, Oswego.
Wm. H. Shumway, do.

John O. Dickey, Sacketts Harbor.

Pennsylvania.

Thomas L. Kane, Philadelphia.
Jabez Burchard, Philadelphia.

George Plitt, Philadelphia.
Charles F. Heazlitt, Philadelphia.

South Carolina.

H. Y. Gray, Charleston.

George Buist, Charleston.

William Blanding, Charleston.

Vermont.

Norman Williams, Woodstock.
David Robinson, Bennington.
Robert Pierpont, Rutland.
Silas H. Hodges, "
Sam'l Swift, Middlebury.

Wyllys Lyman, Burlington.
George F. Houghton, St. Albans.
Oramel H. Smith, Montepelier.
Edward H. Prentiss, "
Charles Davis, Danville.

Ira H. Allen, Irasburgh.

Virginia.

Peter V. Daniel, jr., Richmond.

William T. Hendren, Norfolk.

INDEX.